P9-CDD-495

Readings in Education

EXPLORATION SERIES IN EDUCATION

Under the Advisory Editorship of
JOHN GUY FOWLKES

READINGS IN EDUCATION

EDITED BY Arthur Foff
SAN FRANCISCO STATE COLLEGE

AND Jean D. Grambs
SUPERVISOR OF ADULT EDUCATION
PRINCE GEORGE'S COUNTY, MARYLAND

HARPER & BROTHERS · PUBLISHERS · NEW YORK

READINGS IN EDUCATION

Printed in the United States of America

For information address Harper & Brothers
49 East 33rd Street, New York 16, N. Y.
M-F

Library of Congress catalog card number: 56–6086

CONTENTS

EDITOR'S INTRODUCTION

There is widespread and strong evidence that throughout the ages many individuals other than those who have specialized in the experiences of teaching and learning have a deep and active interest in how human beings learn and how to teach. During recent years there has been an increasing attempt in the curricula for the preparation of teachers to bring the writings of nonprofessional educators "on education" to the attention of prospective teachers. This is a laudable but difficult matter. It is indeed fortunate that a scholar in the realm of literary arts and a scholar in education have joined in the task of gleaning, compiling, and presenting the sayings on "education" as recorded by educators and "noneducators." *Readings in Education* offers carefully selected contributions in a variety of forms and styles of literary expression. Not only is the material included in the following pages substantial and pertinent to those preparing for teaching but also provocative and therefore interesting.

Readings in Education, by Foff and Grambs, along with *An Introduction to the Study of Education*, by Frasier, provide a scholarly and stimulating body of text material for introducing those who are preparing to be teachers to their profession. Also those who are experienced teachers will find much food for thought in this volume.

John Guy Fowlkes

PREFACE

Editing a book of readings is an unusual educational experience. When the idea was first discussed the editors felt that, while there would be many good items to use, there probably would not be an overabundance of material of the type that was sought. We were surprised, therefore, to discover not only that there were many excellent items, but that making a choice between them was going to be difficult indeed. If we could have used all of our favorites we would have had enough to fill several more volumes of this size. There has been a tendency among educators to deprecate the writings about education and by educators. Our experience has been most heartening in disproving that attitude. There is a wealth of astute, sound, and stimulating writing about schools and students and teachers. It is regrettable that much of it, in the form of journal articles, soon gets lost among the volume of later publications. If nothing else, this book of readings will give a wider audience to some material that otherwise would be seen and pondered by only a few.

The editors have received from the outset the warm and enthusiastic encouragement of George Willard Frasier, and the existence of this volume is in the main due to his help and interest. Both editors also wish to express a particular professional debt to Lucien B. Kinney of Stanford University, who gave both of us, as students, a profound and lasting sense of the importance and value of teacher education.

The editors wish to thank Mr. R. J. Hall for his invaluable assistance in preparing the manuscript. Mrs. Betty Tompson of the San Francisco State College Library staff was most generous in assisting the editors.

ARTHUR FOFF
JEAN D. GRAMBS

November, 1955

PART II

Planning for Teaching

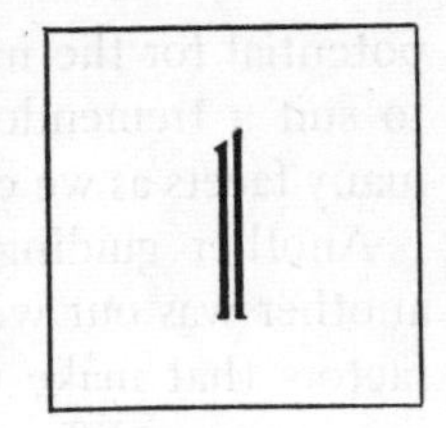

AN INTRODUCTION

If you believe in children, you believe in education.

If you believe in America, you believe in education.

If you want a good life for yourself and your own children, and desire also to make a contribution to the good society, then you can become a teacher.

Reading this book may help to reaffirm your belief in education and make more firm your dedication to teaching.

At this moment in history, the United States faces a critical teacher shortage. Our population is on the upsurge. It is familiar news almost everywhere in the country that more children are coming to school, more children are staying in school longer, but that there are not enough classrooms or teachers to meet the growing need. Not only are more teachers needed, but more teachers who are better trained, better able to teach children and young people in a changing and challenging world.

It has been said many times recently, with ample publicity, that teachers are not paid well enough to attract the kind of talent and ability we need. Perhaps this is so. It may also be true that, in the best interests of the teaching profession, this kind of public display of our concern over low salaries and lack of inducements to persons of talent may work to discourage even further those whom we would most like to attract to the ranks of teaching. It is the belief of the editors of this volume that education is capable of attracting many of our finest young adults: young adults of intelligence, sympathy, and perception who will welcome the chance to work in close proximity to others, who will glow in the deep emotional satisfaction of a rigorous task capably performed, who will willingly devote their lives and energies to intelligence and democracy.

Frankly, then, one significant purpose in creating this volume was to introduce education as a career and vocation to those young people in our colleges who might otherwise not see the full potentialities of this profession. The selections chosen were picked not only because they presented important information or ideas or points of view regarding education and the teaching process, but because they would convey to the reader a sense of the excitement, the variety, the tremendous potential for the individual teacher. Since there are many opportunities in teaching to suit a tremendous range of talents and interests, the readings selected cover as many facets as we could encompass within one volume.

Another guiding purpose that caused us to choose one selection rather than another was our wish to give more than just an objective description of the various factors that make up the educational process. What we were after in our volume was quite a different type of game. We wanted something a bit closer than the usual objective report: we wanted not a map of the battle, but rather the actual heat and light of the campaign itself. We wanted the reader not only to *think* education in its myriad aspects and variety but also to *feel* it. Thus, we decided to use every kind of literature available, provided it was relevant to our purpose, important in its outlook, and high in quality. So it is that the reader will find the scientific humanism of John L. Childs juxtaposed with the neo-scholasticism of Robert M. Hutchins; the sociological vision and humor of a Willard Waller balanced by the psychological orientation of a Roger Barker; the sober, judicious statement of the educational wing of the National Association of Manufacturers thrown into bold relief by the original insights of anthropologists Margaret Mead and Ruth Benedict.

But this was not all. We sought after more than just a series of essays and articles, invigorating and stimulating though these may be. Essays and articles of all manner and method we had to have certainly and we have included them here: the hard-thinking forward-looking prose of Ordway Tead; the wisely rational, warmly democratic defense of Henry Steele Commager; the scholarly disciplined work of sociologist Frederic Terrien and child psychologist Celia Burns Stendler.

Beyond this, there had to be more than one genre of literature; beyond the essay, the critique, the scholar's research, there had to be the pyrotechnic intuition of poets like Walt Whitman and W. H. Auden; the humorous social criticism of Dickens; the compact and poignant portraiture of John Steinbeck; the evocative and disturbing autobiographical fragment by Alfred Kazin; the comic but illuminating piece by James Thurber on his own efforts to get an education. Yes, it is, we trust, all here. Reading for the taking—all the richness of education, its paradoxes and problems, its dilemmas and triumphs, its tragedies and some of its comedies, too.

It may be that our use of prose fiction and poetry requires a word in passing. While ordinary prose, such as exposition, appeals to our intelligence, the more dramatic forms appeal also to our feelings. The former gives us the idea; the latter gives us the *act*. Henry James once remarked that fiction was more real than reality; that is, it presents us with our major problems freed of trivia and shows us the prime patterns of our lives, freed of the cluttering and confusing detail of the quotidian. Selections of this sort permit us to present to the reader the marvelous, terrifying, and exciting variety of experiences and situations and feelings that *really* tell us about education.

A breadth of viewpoint and the widest possible range of subjective portrayals of the educational scene were sought because it is only through exposure to many possibilities that an individual can know what he himself must stand for. Literature, like life, has its alternatives. The sin of our day is not that men shift from position to position without any abiding and meaningful commitment, but that commitments are made without consciousness of their implications, that men will risk everything for one principle without realizing that there are other *principles*, that in a dynamic society flexibility is itself a very genuine morality.

While originally this book was intended for students who were first considering education as a career, the editors feel that its uses could be far wider than this initial starting point. It can be utilized and enjoyed by the experienced teacher as well as the beginner; by the layman who wishes to understand more about the profession and the problems faced in the educational process.

So far as we know, this anthology is the only one of its kind now in existence: a volume which *systematically* explores the main areas of education through both dramatic and professional literature. In seeking materials for it we had, of course, to exclude more than we could include. We faced an embarrassment of riches in many chapters, finding ourselves sometimes with enough really exciting pieces to make a whole book for one area only. It is hoped that, having had this taste of the literature on education to be found in the professional journals, the popular magazines, fiction, and poetry, the reader will continue to read widely in all such realms to continue his education about education.

The organization of the book was deliberate. A book of readings can give the student many new ideas, but the very nature of the volume means that synthesis and critical understanding must either go on inside the reader or be guided by other sources. We felt that the most useful method of organizing the material would be to follow the pattern of an outstanding text in introduction to education. Such a text is that of George W. Frasier, *An Introduction to the Study of Education* (rev. ed., Harper & Brothers, 1956). These two volumes together will provide the student with a consistent and systematic introduction to the field of education. Either volume of course can be used independently, but used together they constitute a unique correlation of sound textbook presentation with rich supplementary readings.

A note on the analysis and discussion introductions to the selections:

As you can gather from having read this far in our introductory statement, the editors of this volume chose selections that would be *stimulating*. This means that you may not agree with some of the selections. The editors do not necessarily agree with them, either. However, each one says something important about education, whether we like it or not. The introductory paragraphs are designed to point out some of the important points made by the author of the selection that are particularly vital for the reader to consider. Not every piece has such an introduction. Some readers may want to read the selection first, then return and consider the points made by the editors regarding that particular item. And certainly any instructor who uses this volume will have ideas to suggest to his class that will add to the reader's understanding.

In summary, the editors would like to say this to the reader: These selections have been chosen because they view the educational process as something that happens to *real people*. Children are not ciphers, teachers are not puppets, schools are not factories. What happens in our educational institutions is something that happens to *people*. As soon as we lose sight of the individual human aspects of education we can forget all our words like *democracy*, and *freedom*, and *frontiers of knowledge*. The items were chosen, too, because each one in some way affirms a basic faith in the educational process. Tired educators abound; they are a menace to children, to society, and to themselves. These are people who have lost the feeling and the faith in education—assuming it ever touched them. The spark of inspiration, which our current sophisticated generation is likely to belittle and to that extent lose some of its own soul, is something education cannot do without. But inspiration cannot be taught. It cannot be found from preachments. It is what makes the difference between education that stifles and education that enriches and frees. We hope you will find that kind of inspiration among the readings in this volume.

2 SUCCESS IN TEACHING

HOW DO YOU KNOW A GOOD TEACHER?[1]

Dorothy McCuskey

It's funny about good teachers. People almost always agree as to who they are, but no one has ever succeeded in writing a prescription, or even a description, functional enough so that we can tell in advance just who is going to make an outstanding teacher. Some good teachers are pretty, but then still more of them never were beautiful even when they were young. Some of them are women and some are men, and no analyst can claim that sex has anything in particular to do with being a good teacher. Good teachers may be fat or lean, young or old; they may teach in kindergartens or in great universities. No outward characteristic, except possibly eager eyes and smiling lines around a mouth, are going to give us much clue as to what makes a good teacher.

Perhaps we have been looking in the wrong place. Perhaps the way to discover what makes a good teacher is not to look at the teacher at all. Perhaps we should rather be looking at the pupils.

Watching pupils come into a classroom will tell you a lot about the teacher. Do they smile as they enter? If they do, we can be fairly sure that the teacher is someone who likes and understands boys and girls. (For "boys and girls," we can perfectly well substitute "young people," or "human beings." It comes out the same in the end.) When teachers understand boys and girls, then many other things follow almost as corollaries. Security—emotional as well as physical—is one of the basic needs of the human being. A smile is more than good manners; it is the symbol that in this classroom a group of children have found a friendly atmosphere in which they are free to grow and to learn.

SIGNIFICANT SIGNS

Other signs are significant, too. Do the children go up to the teacher as they come in? If he is good, there will probably be things they want to tell him or to ask him: "We have a new puppy at our house." "Here is a poem I wrote last night." "I found this moth on the way to school. What kind do you think it is?" "How far can you see land from out at sea?" And so it goes, with each comment noted in the back of a busy mind. For good teachers don't teach classes, they teach individuals. True, the individuals

[1] From *Understanding the Child* (Oct., 1947), Vol. 16, pp. 107–111. Reprinted by permission.

usually are placed in school groups, but no good teacher ever thinks that being in the sixth grade, or in Senior English, makes the pupils all alike. Writing a poem at home may be a regular form of self-expression to one child; to another it may be a miraculous creation, a painful bursting of the bonds of inhibition. The good teacher will know which it is, and he will know what to do. Publish it in the school paper? That would mean triumph to one child, a violation of confidence to another. Good teachers know their pupils.

This regard for individuals will be seen in many aspects of a good teacher's classroom. For one thing, the seats will be various sizes, for pupils do not come in neat sizes like shoes, even though they are all twelve, or all going to Harvard College. A good school environment, which means cleanliness, proper seating and lighting, are very important to health and physical growth. A good teacher recognizes the importance of these factors.

MANY BOOKS

There will be many books in this classroom, too, and they will be on differing levels of reading difficulty. Good teachers, liking good tools, usually have books at hand, even though well-stocked libraries are accessible. There will be more than books here, too. An elementary classroom will have science equipment, homemade, if need be, for good teachers tend to be ingenious. Good teachers usually use a variety of tools, so that there will be signs of radio or musical instruments, charts, visual aids, or constructions. Some people learn one way, some another, and good teachers do not miss any bets.

But we are getting ahead of our story. These pupils are still coming into the room—this clean, attractive room full of interesting possibilities. It is important to note what the children do after they have laid aside their wraps. Do they settle idly in their seats, looking wistfully out the window? Or engage in horseplay with a wary eye to see what they can get away with? In some schools they do, but that behavior is not indicative of good teaching, even though "the bell hasn't rung yet." In a modern classroom of a good teacher, there is much work—physical and mental—to be done. Responsible individuals look after the plants and animals, prepare materials for the day. A group may be conferring on the details of a morning panel discussion, and the chairman of the painting committee for the stage sets may be calculating how many days she and her group will need to finish. One has a story to copy for the school paper, and another helps a third with arithmetic. Work is begun because work is important, to an individual or to a group, or both; work is begun because these children have been taught good work habits. Responsibility is assumed because responsibility has been entrusted.

THE HARD ROAD TO DISCIPLINE

Such a teacher takes the hard road to developing true discipline. Here is not the discipline of folded hands and absolute silences; here is the discipline of busy hands and of reasonable quiet so produced because "that's the way other people work best." Good discipline is self-discipline, discipline that works whether the teacher is in the room or out of it, discipline that works on the playground, in the street, or in the home. If our standards of good teaching have changed as much as our standards of good discipline, then there is no wonder that we have been puzzled at how to identify a good teacher.

It is possible that our standards of good teaching really have changed also. "She really knows her subject matter" has been the sometimes unwilling, half-hearted praise of a teacher. The good teacher does "know his subject matter," but more than that, he has a clear idea of what subject matter is for. Sheer skill in "factoring" is no more functional than solving crossword puzzles, but an ability to use mathematical concepts in buying, in building—in short, in living—is vital indeed. The battles of the Civil War no longer have much significance in themselves, but the effect of the war in making the South a colonial dependency of the East is one dominant factor in present-day economy. It is not facts, or mastery of materials, which characterizes a good teacher. It is mastery plus creativity that makes teaching live.

IS EACH CHILD VALUED?

Our American free public schools exist because they are the essential base on which rest the major premises of democracy. Only a literate people, capable of exercising judgment, may justly claim the privilege of exercising the rights and duties of a democratic citizenship. Democracy is based upon the tenet of the inherent worth of every human being. This is therefore an important touchstone whereby to test the teacher. In this classroom, is each child valued? Is there the same consideration for the dirty urchin with the runny nose as for the pretty girl with curls? Does the Negro child "belong"? Is there provision so that the child who learns slowly may progress at his own rate? And equally important, does the gifted child receive the challenge of learning experiences at his level, or is he allowed to float in a sea of mediocrity?

Regard for the individual is only one of the touchstones of democracy. The democratic citizen is a participating citizen, and he learns as he does. He will hardly learn the techniques of democracy in the classroom of a dictator. If group planning is one of the ways by which adults get streets paved, auditoriums built, and a good candidate to run for office, then pupils must learn to plan for the common good. Good teachers are always alert for opportunities wherein their pupils may learn to make democratic decisions and to abide by those decisions.

While the classroom will reflect the many vital interests of a good teacher, neither he nor his pupils are likely to stay there exclusively. If the teacher is to know pupils as individuals, then he will need to know parents as people too. If his aim is facts *plus*, then he will find much of his *plus* in the community. Libraries, museums, industries, public officials will all become a part of the school program.

It is very significant that more than 33,000 children wrote in to the Quiz Kids radio program to recommend their teacher as the year's best. Did they write only to win prizes for themselves? It is not likely. They wrote because they had experienced that creative something that had made their school year a memorable one of growth. They wrote because in their teachers they had found friends who valued them at their highest level, and had made them believe in themselves. They wrote because under the guidance of these teachers they had felt intellectual stimulation. They wrote because in these classrooms they had had an opportunity to think and to do.

EASIER IN THE ELEMENTARY SCHOOL

Admittedly, it is easier to identify a good teacher on the elementary level than anywhere else. For one thing, there are more of them there than anywhere else. If you look for four-leaf clover where four-leaf clovers are, they aren't hard to find. So with teachers. But even on the secondary and college levels where the fetish of "subjects" and "efficient administration" makes it very difficult to do good teaching, good teachers still find a way. Pupils are shot into a room in groups of thirty to fifty, and forty minutes later they are shot out again.

But in those precious forty minutes some skillful teacher has helped them to understand human nature as it is interpreted in writing, has helped them find beauty in music, words, or form. Some skillful history teacher has perhaps capitalized on the Greek crisis to teach—just ancient history? No, he has likely taught ancient history as it throws light on modern problems of living, or he and his class may have explored a little further what it means to be a citizen of a democracy. "Take the next chapter for tomorrow" is never enough for a good teacher. "Take the great challenges to modern living." "Take the atomic bomb." "Take the fact of one divorce to every three marriages." "Take graft and corruption in public office." "What are the underlying causes of these problems?" "What can people do about them?" Thus, science, history, literature, human relations come to a focus in the living experience of the pupil. Using the methods and tools of science, the experience of history, the vision of literature, a skillful teacher helps a future citizen to solve his problems.

What does it all add up to? In looking at learners, have we discovered anything about teachers? Some general characteristics begin to appear.

To begin with, good teachers seem to be vital people. They have wide interests and they get along well with other people. Teachers as a group tend to center on *people* rather than on *things*. For example, an outstanding printing teacher doubtless gets great satisfaction from a beautiful specimen of the printer's art. But if that were his major interest, he would stick to printing. The clumsy efforts of beginners would drive him crazy. This teacher, however, likes to help people learn. He likes to see ideas develop, likes to see the relationship between people and the products they produce. Every teacher has two skills —those of his speciality and those that enable him to guide learning in people. Mastery of a speciality is common, but skill in human relations distinguishes the outstanding teacher.

It may be said with some assurance that the good teacher is a happy, well-balanced person. He almost has to be. For if bitterness, frustration, or envy intrude into the relationship between teacher and learner, then the basic conditions of effective human growth are destroyed. True, this criterion would exclude many "famous" teachers, but often these teachers were famed for their eccentricities, rather than for the development of their students. No truly great teacher would be excluded by such a definition.

It hardly needs be said that the good teacher is skilled in the theory and practice of his speciality. Many skilled practitioners of the teaching art fail to reach greatness because they don't know why they do what they do. Their skills are adequate for limited situations, but when they need to plan new programs to fit different types of pupils or changing needs of society, they are lost. For example, the recent migrations of war workers brought great numbers of Spanish-speaking pupils into schools where teachers had been accustomed to worrying only about language problems such as "you was" and "ain't." The traditional methods would scarcely serve for these up-rooted, bi-lingual or non-English speaking children unless the methods were firmly rooted in a basic philosophy which gave some clue as to what to do and how to do it.

WIDENING HORIZONS

Further, no good teacher ever believes that he has attained mastery of his subject or of how to teach it. He knows that he must always grow, always widen his horizons. For instance, not only science teachers and science textbooks, but all teachers became "obsolete," in Norman Cousins' phrase, when the atomic bomb was produced. Up to that time, the development of attitudes and techniques of international cooperation had been the speciality of a few. It suddenly became an imperative of human life. Like the home-owner who reaches farther and farther into the weedy lot beside him with each mowing of the lawn, the good teacher penetrates farther and farther into undiscovered territory. Science leads to international relations, English to semantics, semantics to mathematics, homemaking to art, art to history, and so on without end. Whereas research scholars attempt to find out "more and more about less and less," the great teacher will usually be found knocking down the barriers between different aspects of human knowledge.

It is implicit that good teachers recognize their unique function in democratic society. They recognize the loss there is to society if their students do not have an opportunity to develop to their maximum potentiality. They recognize the tremendous gain there is if they do their work well. They know that teaching in a democracy means not only living democratically within the classroom, but that it means participating as a citizen in the life of the community.

Finally, and inescapably, good teachers believe in the fundamental importance of schools and of teaching. No man can reach the highest pinnacle of his art, or of his profession, without believing in its inherent worth. Teachers are optimists. They have to be. There are many failures in their human materials, and many inadequacies in the facilities their communities provide for them. In spite of that, however, teachers know that if we have made progress in our slow climb from barbarism to civilization, if we are struggling toward the practice of democracy, much of the credit is due to the teachers of the world.

I WAS A HOBO KID[1]

Billie Davis

DISCUSSION AND ANALYSIS

This selection poses the problem of the migrant child, who, because of the vocation (or lack of it) of his parents, is often homeless as well as school-less. Moving from one area to another, such a child seldom has a sense of permanence or belonging. If the child feels sufficiently dislocated, he or she may eventually reject the society which he believes has rejected him. On the other hand, as the author shows, the very seriousness of the situation indicates the chance for benign action. The public school, because of its commonality, because it is an institution one finds everywhere, may become a surrogate home. Before this can occur the school must have friendly and understanding teachers and administrators,

[1] From *The Saturday Evening Post*, December 13, 1952. Copyright 1952 by The Curtis Publishing Company. Reprinted by permission of the author.

who realize that their task can be an emotional as well as an educational one.

In a consideration of this selection, several topics are worth thought and discussion. For example, in what ways is the plight of the general transfer student parallel to that of the migrant student? What, if any, characteristics of the good teacher, as laid down in the piece by Dorothy McCuskey, are evidenced by educators in the article by Mrs. Davis? Are the portraits of Miss Williams and Miss Euland convincing, or are they "too good to be true"? How are socio-economic factors involved in the attitudes of the children and teachers in this selection? Do you find that W. H. Burton's "Education and Social Class in the United States" in Chapter 8 throws any light on the schooling of migrant and other similarly underprivileged children?

When I was a small ragged hobo, sitting on the ground beside a campfire, hungrily licking the fishy oil from the lid of a sardine can as I studied my history lesson, I was beginning already to understand the relationship between public education and personal liberty.That is why I am surprised and disturbed at what seems to be a popular lack of appreciation for our schools today. Somehow the prevalent attitude awakens within me a little fighting urge. I want to tell the American people something about our schools—something they must have forgotten. Or it may be that some have never recognized that which I consider to be the greatest value of our system. I want to make certain that they recognize it now, and I can show them plainly by telling them my story.

I, perhaps more than most persons, am a product of the public schools. I was born into that unique clan of American gypsies —gypsies by environment and manner of living rather than by blood. You used to find them camped under the bridge or down at the dump or out by the stockyards near almost any small Southern town. You could see their battered autos along the highways throughout the Middle West. I do not speak of the migrants who fled to California from the dust bowl, but of the vagabond people whose home was the open road. Sometimes they picked cotton or fruit. Sometimes they shucked corn. But mostly they traveled from town to town peddling novelties, trading horses, sharpening scissors or making keys.

Mine was a rustic-furniture family. That is, dad made chairs, tables and novelties from young willows which grew by the river. He liked the word "rustic" and used it proudly to set himself apart from the common "willow workers." I was the star peddler of the household. My earliest recollection is of starting out in the morning to peddle baskets. They were small willow baskets, complete with crepe-paper roses. With my arm through one handle and a basket in each hand, I could carry three. Up one side of the street and down the other I went, praying the next house would have a doorbell, hating old cracked paint which cut my knuckles and screened-in porches through which no one could hear my knock, anxiously watching for dogs and dreading more than anything else to meet another child.

Along the well-kept streets of these middle-class neighborhoods where most of our peddling was done I met many children, and the contrast which I made to them I could not fail to notice. They looked so clean and cared for—so smooth, I used to think. My thick, too-curly hair was a mass of snarls which went for days without a combing. My dress was usually dirty and never ironed. How I wanted to be like the children who played in the pretty yards! *How can I be like them?* I asked myself desperately. *How can I ever be like people who live in houses?* And I ran quickly away from the clean, smooth children, so they could not stare and laugh.

That is why I began to notice school buildings, I think. There were so many children around school buildings. I would hurry by them, sometimes skipping a few houses in my peddling. I could not stand to peddle with the school kids watching. The school kids stared and laughed and threw sticks. They pointed at my high-laced canvas shoes which had cost fifty cents at the dime store. School kids wore regular leather shoes. Nice oxfords or shiny black shoes with straps. They laughed most of all at my shoes.

But somehow I was never angry at them. I could see for myself why they laughed. It seemed to me that school kids had a right to laugh at a dirty camper kid who peddled baskets and wore no stockings with tattered canvas shoes.

School kids. Perhaps I had found the secret. Perhaps school made the difference between rubber bums like us and people who lived in houses. The idea became an obsession, so that by the time I was six years old I had developed a philosophy: You will not be a camper always if you go to school and get real smart. Anybody can be clean and smooth and live in a nice house if he is smart. And school can make you smart.

One day while I was peddling, a man gave me some money and told me that it was for new shoes. My dad whistled when he saw the bills. "There's enough here for you and Eva each a pair of leather shoes," he said. Eva was my little sister.

We went to town, and what pure ecstasy we knew as we tried on leather shoes! Finally we picked out black patent-leather sandals with little red buckles. Of course we wore them out of the store, and proudly to our camping place on the edge of town. I could hardly wait until we got to camp so I could be alone with Eva. I had a marvelous plan.

At last mom and dad seemed to forget us, and I urged Eva to go for a walk with me. She was only five years old, and, already tired from our shopping trip, tried to refuse.

"But we're going to do something real fun," I declared, taking her hand firmly, and practically forcing her to accompany me.

We walked several blocks to a brick school building. It was after school hours and only a few children lingered on the grounds. I was somewhat disappointed at this, but certainly not discouraged in my purpose. Across the school yard I led my little sister, and then on the sidewalk, around and around the building. Finally her patience was spent.

"What are we going to do?" she wailed.

"We're doing it now, dopey," I scolded the bewildered child. "We're pretending we're school kids!"

Schools, I had learned, were free, and every child was supposed to go. "You see, Eva," I explained, "there are real laws about it. The laws are to make all of us go to school so we'll learn how to be clean and pretty and smart. Like people who live in houses. Don't you think that's wonderful?"

The tired little girl was not too impressed at the time, but after that we found a schoolhouse often, and she grinned and squeezed my hand as we shared our secret game.

Of course the idea of school was not so

inviting to dad. It meant staying awhile in one place, and that was not too good for the rustic business. So for two years after I was old enough to begin school I was not allowed to go, and I lived in a state of constant longing and frustration. I would peek into the windows of empty schoolrooms. Sometimes after school hours I would slip furtively inside the building for a fleeting glimpse of a classroom and some books. I would touch a desk wonderingly with my finger tips and stare fascinated at a blackboard.

Then the big day came in that unexpected, unplanned manner which seems to rule the destiny of vagabonds. We were camped this bright September on the grounds of an old fort in Wyoming. It was a most unlikely place for campers to be in the autumn. They should have been heading south. But there was to be a pioneer celebration at the old fort, and some of the campers were carnival people. They persuaded my folks to make paper flowers and rustic novelties for prizes at their booths. Soon several families of campers had organized into quite a layout of concessions, and it looked as though we would be at the fort for several weeks.

"I'm going to send my children into town to the consolidataed school," I heard one of the women tell my mother. "There's a school bus comes by right out here on the highway. Why don't you send your girls?"

"Oh, yes, mother, do, please! Oh, please do!" I interrupted excitedly, clapping my hands and dancing about until I almost upset the kettle of mush on the campfire. "Please let us go to school!"

Somehow like a miracle there were new dresses. There were long red pencils, fat yellow tablets and a little lard pail with nail holes punched through the lid to let air in to the fried-dough-and-side-pork sandwiches. And Eva and I stood with a group of children by the highway, waiting for the school bus, swinging the pail between us, whispering ecstatically to each other, "We're going to school! Like people who live in houses. We're going to be school kids for truly now."

On the bus were several mothers who seemed to be accompanying younger children. We heard one speak to another of getting her child "enrolled."

"Do we have to get enrolled?" Eva asked me, her words and voice expressing the same fear which I was beginning to feel. "What's enrolled? Who'll enroll us?"

"We can enroll ourselves," I told her smugly. "After all, schools are free and there's even a law that we're supposed to go. So I guess they'll let us in all right."

At the school I kept trying to show the same confidence. We stood quietly in a hall watching mothers and pupils and teachers scurry in all directions. Just as I was beginning to feel uncontrollable panic there was a bell, a sudden rush, and then we were alone in the hall. We went through the open door of a classroom and announced to the teacher, "We'd like to go to school here, please."

"Of course, girls," she said in a matter-of-fact tone which put us at ease. "I will take you to the office."

In the office a lady asked a question: "Where do you live?"

"We don't live anywhere," my sister replied.

"Oh, you live somewhere," the lady insisted, looking puzzled, as though trying to decide whether Eva was impertinent or dull. "Now tell me. Where do you live?"

I thought Eva would cry, but she puckered her face resolutely and held back the tears.

"We don't live anywhere," she explained with studied patience; "we just camp."

The lady smiled and was kind. She did not seem to care that we were camper kids.

She said she was glad to have us in the school. And I knew she really was.

Soon I had a room and a teacher. I had some books and crayons. And most wonderful of all, I had a desk. A certain special place which was mine—just like each other desk. When I sat there I was equal to anyone else. I had the same materials and the same opportunities. Outside they could jeer at my clothes and laugh because I lived in a tent. They could follow me with cutting taunts when I peddled on the streets. But when I sat at my desk in school no one could laugh at me. I had found the secret key to equality and achievement. I had found the magic place where money and clothes and houses did not count. So long as I sat at the desk and learned my lessons well I could be free of the sickening inferiority which accepted with morbid understanding the slights and cruelties of others. I could be, yes, even superior. Some of the clean, smooth children did not do so well as I in school. Next time they called me a dirty gypsy it would not hurt me so. Perhaps I could get even a little angry with them, and say to myself, *Who do they think they are? What's so grand about leather shoes anyway? After all, I get better grades in spelling.* And then I would not bleed so much inside.

There were many schools as the years went by. There were proud new consolidated schools of yellow brick. There were sand-scratched wooden cubes along Nebraska lanes, and powdery crumbling red brick cubes in little square towns of Kansas. There were city schools, squeezed in as though they were holding their breath, trying not to take too much room from the hot, paved yards where the swings were. There were flat schools in the Southwest—schools with mud-pie walls and no stairs at all. There were some special schools, too, different from any others, like the one in Denver with tall white mansion columns and the one in California with black marble around the doors.

Every school held for me a mystical secret beauty. Every school was my personal friend. It wanted me. There were laws that said so. It wanted to make me smart and pretty and smooth, like the people who lived in houses. And in each town I strolled serenely up the walk to the school building, almost forgetting that I was a camper. I found a teacher and said again, as I had on that first day, "I would like to go to school here, please."

Without exception, I was greeted with kindness. Of course there were some startled exclamations, some smiles and some slightly irritated mutters. Usually there was a bustling off to an office to talk to a gray-haired lady with a hearing aid or a somber bald man who rubbed his eyes and chewed his glasses. Always there were questions.

"No address?"

"No transfer from previous school?"

"No report card? Have you studied long division?"

"No, sir, but I belong in the fourth grade. Just put me in the class and let me try it. If I can't do the work, you can put me back a grade, can't you?"

I did not mind the questions, for in the end they smiled and showed me to a room and a teacher. Always I would marvel at the fact that there was a desk which seemed to be waiting just for me. I would squeeze its edges and touch my cheek reverently to its marred surface. My desk!

All this talk of poorly trained, underpaid teachers, striving for the privilege of becoming mechanical robots enslaved by some insensitive assembly line for a good union wage per hour, cannot drive from my mind the memory of the teachers who have shaped my life. There was Miss Williams, kind and motherly, who let me stay in at recess and water her plants. She had found me hiding in the fire escape. It was a big round pipe on the outside of the building, through which pupils could slide to the ground in case of fire. Many of the school buildings used to have them. I would crawl up inside them at recess to hide, so the children on the playground could not tease me. Miss Williams saw me through her window and let me climb in over the window sill as though we were playing a game. She did not scold, but rather laughed with me about it. She did not ask a question, but always, after that, she had some work for me to do at recess. I understood her motive, and yet it did not crush my spirit to accept her favor. I felt that she knew I understood and we shared a plot together. The whole situation was simply a temporary inconvenience which a camper kid had to put up with until she could get enough schooling to catch up with the people who lived in houses.

There was Miss Euland, quick and proficient, who told me one day that she had noticed I was squinting, and she wanted me to accompany her next time she had an appointment with her eye doctor. On the day of the appointment she called for me in her car and took me to a fine restaurant for lunch. Then we went up in the elevator and across the soft carpets to sit in the most elegant chairs I had ever seen. I enjoyed every minute of the process which followed—looking through holes, reading signs, watching little lights. By the end of the day Miss Euland had become the fairy godmother of my dreams.

A few days later she handed me a small box. "Here are your new glasses," she said. "The doctor wants you to wear them every day."

"Glasses!" I was astonished. "But I cannot buy glasses!"

"You do not have to buy these glasses, my dear," said Miss Euland. "They were paid for before you were born."

She saw my confusion and led me to the wide seat under the window there in her classroom. "You see," she explained, "when I was a little girl I needed glasses, but my parents could not afford to buy them for me. A kind neighbor of ours took me into town one day, just as I took you. We had lunch together, and then she took me to her eye doctor and ordered glasses for me. I tried to refuse them at first, and then I told her that I would pay for them as soon as I could. She told me that I could pay for them someday, but she would rather I would not pay her. She said that I should find a little girl who needed glasses and make my payment by doing for this other child what had been done for me. So these glasses which I give you today are in reality the payment for a debt I owe."

Then Miss Euland said to me the nicest thing that anyone had ever said. It was the nicest thing because it meant that she knew I would not be a camper all my life. She believed in me, for she said, and I knew she meant it, "Someday you will pay for the glasses of some other little girl."

That was what made me love teachers. They believed in me. They seemed to expect good things from me. The local children shunned me because I was a dirty gypsy. The camper kids called me smarty and stuck-up because I liked school and would not dip snuff or chew on cigarette butts. Even my parents mocked me, ridiculed my "highfalutin ways" and laughed at me for "trying to be like those nasty nice schoolteachers." But the teachers seemed to know me as I was. They could see the spirit flickering dimly within that tattered caricature of childhood. They cared enough to fan the trembling flame.

At last there came that torrid, shimmering afternoon when our old Model A Ford puffed and steamed across the dried sea bottom of a little valley in Southern California. Could we pick dates? Green beans? Carrots? Should we go on inland to Bakersfield and maybe hit some fruit on up the San Joaquin? Or try our luck peddling over the coast way? The conversation was listless. Maybe we should flip a coin.

Then I saw the school building. It was sprawled yellow stucco, surrounded by date palms and back-dropped with a row of dusky hills like the stage setting for an operetta. Somehow in that little valley the heat formed a visible mist which wrapped the scene in a soft, sheer, rosy veil. I caught my breath so sharply that the others noticed.

Dad grinned sardonically, "Billie sees a schoolhouse."

"After all, dad," I defended myself, "it is October, and this is the year I should be in high school."

The events which followed might seem fantastic to the conventional thinker, but to the capricious mind of the rubber bum there was nothing remarkable about the fact that two hours later we were pitching our tent beside a row of tamarack trees in that hot little bowl of a valley. If the spot was wide enough for a tent, and if the sheriff did not interfere, then we belonged here as much as we belonged in any place. Our neighbors were water and trees and grass. Where these were, we could be at home. Neither was it remarkable, in view of my background and experience, for me immediately to claim as "my school" the local consolidated Valley High, and to take it for granted that I would be welcomed there as a student.

The next morning I boarded the school bus and went to the yellow stucco school in the date garden. I walked into the building and approached, with my usual request, the first teacher I saw, "I would like to go to school here, please."

I had thought that this registration would be a bit more difficult than usual, since this was high school, I was starting late in the term and I had no record whatsoever of my previous schooling. But, to my surprise, the teacher acted as though she had been expecting me. "Go right through that second door," she said.

In the room I was handed some forms and a pencil and told to be seated at a long table where several other pupils were filling out forms. There seemed to be a number of new pupils. As I looked about the room I realized that they were the children of migrants who had recently followed to California the hope of better jobs and more money. Evidently the school was used to registering transient pupils, and the process had been planned carefully. It had been planned so well, in fact, that the same course of study was offered to all. As I read my schedule card my heart sank: cooking, general math, clothing, English, hygiene. This was a tragedy! I could not just sit here and let it happen with no protest at all! I held up my hand to attract the attention of a teacher.

"Do we have no choice of subjects?" I asked. "I understood that in high school it would be possible for each pupil to choose a course of study."

I was one of a group of transient pupils, and no doubt I appeared to be rather an insolent one at that. The teacher was busy. Often I have thought how easily she could have brushed me aside. Instead she came and sat by me.

"There are electives," she explained, "but we have arranged this course for you because it is a basic course which we are sure you will find profitable and enjoyable while you are here. It is a little late in the term for you to begin some of the subjects."

"But I can't spend all that time on cooking and sewing," I declared. "I must begin training for my career. Already I am older than most pupils in my grade."

"Would you like to speak to the principal?"

"Yes, please, I would."

Not once did she act irritated or scornful, and when she introduced me to the principal, her voice was the voice of a friend.

"What subjects do you have in mind?" the principal asked, and as he spoke he took from his desk a panoramic schedule which seemed to list all the subjects offered by the school. I looked down at the list and scanned it rapidly.

"History, dramatics, English and Spanish," I said.

"And what is this career you are planning to train for?"

"I want to be either a writer or a radio announcer," I answered without hesitation, "and I want to become qualified to teach journalism and public speaking, so that if I can't make good in either of these fields I can teach them in high school."

The principal puckered his brow, but his eyes grinned, and the teacher choked on a giggle.

"Dramatics is an upper-division elective, and it seems a little late to start a foreign language." The principal looked at the teacher in such a way that the statement became a question.

"Well, if her English grades have been good and she works hard—"

They called in the teacher of Spanish to ask me a few questions. Then two other teachers came to see me, and the final result was that I was enrolled in history, English, Spanish and even the coveted upper-division dramatics class.

Five months we camped under the tamarack trees and I went to the yellow high school. Dad seemed to like the sunny valley, and we could earn a living by all of us picking dates or beans or carrots and making regular trips to surrounding towns to peddle. I continued to take my baskets from door to door, as I had since early childhood. And through five months of continuous living in one spot our lives did not change. We cooked on the campfire and each dipped into the kettle to fill a tin bowl and then squat upon the ground to eat. We slept in a row on one long pallet which covered most of the floor of the tent. At night, after the others had settled on our family bed behind me, I would sit on the ground in the small place left near the front flap of the tent. Before me would be an overturned orange crate, and upon it an ancient kerosene lantern to give light as I did my homework. But somehow in those days I seldom thought of myself as being a dirty little camper. I hated to peddle, of course, and sometimes I wished desperately for close friends. I longed for pretty clothes and a house as much as I ever had. But I did not think of myself as merely a hobo. I was the freshman who had the leading part in a play at Valley High!

We had to leave the little valley before school was out that spring, but the next fall I found another high school in another town, and its spirit was the same. In the classroom, on the debate team, on the school-paper staff, and finally in my cherished blue cap and gown as I spoke at the commencement exercises, I found freedom and equality which gave me faith and inspired me to try to be what it seemed that my school expected me to be.

Rare, even for an aesthetic adolescent, was the sentiment I experienced as I sat on the platform that night of high-school graduation. I thought of the two-room, unpainted shack out on the highway where my family of eight was staying currently. I thought of all the tents and wagons and campgrounds and worn-out autos. I thought of the dirt and lice and canvas shoes. I looked down at the neat blue-and-white pumps which I was wearing at the moment, and thought of the Clothing Order Form No. 80653 from the local relief agency which had made them possible.

Then I looked at the rows of blue gowns. Two hundred and fifty blue gowns.

Young people from wealthy and prominent families in royal-blue gowns like mine. I looked at the blue gown next to me. It was worn by the boy who would give his speech just before I gave mine. His dad was director of the welfare agency where I got the clothing order for my shoes.

Suddenly I knew what was meant by "democracy," "free people," "the American way." It was not sickly, sentimental thinking. It was strong and clear and mature. It was logical. I, an unkempt hobo from nowhere, had, in this high school of considerable size and reputation, become editor of the school paper, and then of the yearbook. I had served on the varsity debate team. I had been president of the scholarship federation and a member of the student council.

This talk I was always hearing around the campfires and in the lines at the relief office—about the rich crushing the poor, and the workingman not having a chance—it did not add up. But why did some people feel crushed? Why did some peoples of other nations fight against our American way? The answer came to me again, just as it had when I had peddled by the schoolhouse long ago. School made the difference. It may have been that some kind fate had led me to the right schools, and the undesirable teachers wise destiny had withheld from my acquaintance. But the fact was indisputable still, that school could make the difference. How unlimited could be the effects of proper education!

I looked at the row of solemn teachers and wondered if they realized the potential power of their influence to shape a life, to change a destiny, to free a world. I wished that I could help them to recognize their power and encourage them to use it with wisdom and purpose. I longed to express my appreciation and pay them some appropriate tribute. I looked down at the notes of my speech: What East High Has Meant to Me. Childish. Inadequate. Someday I would write a real tribute to the teachers and to the public schools of the United States of America.

Many times since that night I have remembered the vow. I have picked up a pen or sat at the typewriter and tried to think of a fitting tribute. But proper words have never come. There is so little that I can say concretely. Except that I am not a camper now. I am a citizen, clean and smooth, equal to other citizens. And I live in a house.

THE TEACHER AS HERO

Arthur Foff

The socio-economic status of teachers today, as always, is extremely low relative to the importance of the services performed. One of the bitterest ironies of American culture is that education is prized whereas teachers are contemned. This situation works to the detriment of pupil, parent, teacher, and community alike. Although Californians in a recent election considered, without much distinction, underpaid scavengers on the one hand, and underpaid teachers on the other, it is nevertheless something of a dilemma that the vocation of the greatest men of all ages—of Buddha, of Socrates, of Aristotle and of Christ—has not yet been accorded the status of a full profession in the United States.

This crow that every teacher must eat (with the possible exception of those university professors who have arisen to such eminence that they can appear on television panel shows) can be explained partly on the basis of historical and economic factors. Such an explanation, however, should not be pushed so far or generalized so highly that it excludes the concrete, human attitudes operating within a given social context. Insofar as these attitudes or opinions are precipitants of behavior, they have a significance that is proportionate to the intensity and pervasiveness with which they are held.

When we talk about these attitudes as configuration rather than conglomerate, we are referring to the stereotype of the teacher. And this stereotype, as Waller, Grambs, Brown, and many other educators and scholars have realized, is one of the prime reasons why the American public school teacher has assumed the stigma of a scapegoat rather than the aura of a hero. Waller wrote: "In analyzing the opinion people have of teachers, it is necessary to reckon with the teacher stereotype which partly reflects and partly determines that opinion." [1] Jacques Barzun has had his tilt at stereotypes, too.

> Try as I may, I cannot think of any of my colleagues who has "retained something of the professor in his features," reptiles though they may be. They look like any other Americans; they are no more round-shouldered than bank presidents, they play golf and tennis and watch football, they marry and beget children, laugh and swear and have appendicitis in a thoroughly normal way. They are far less absent-minded than waiters in restaurants and they do not look a bit more like one another than a comparable number of doctors or mechanics.[2]

But people think they do; the stereotype persists!

What we assume is that the teacher *could* be viewed as a hero instead of a dolt. This might entail the surrender of prejudice plus a host of stock gags on the part of those who control and operate our mass media of communication, but it is within the realm of possibility. Doctors, nurses, lawyers, aviators, football players, cops, newspapermen, composers, stamp collectors, gangsters, frog-men, farmers, even a dog and a mule,[3] all have been glorified in movies, comic books, radio programs, television, and the daily newspapers. But the teacher, victim of a negatively rather than a positively charged stereotype, goes on being a perpetual butt of other people's humor—a kind of Casper Milquetoast with chalk on his trousers and McGuffey in his hand.

If we look for portraits of teachers in our mass media—say, television—we come up with a program like "Our Miss Brooks." Eve Arden, who plays the title role with relish, invests Miss Brooks with singular angularity. This is quite in accord with the stereotype of the woman teacher in the American novel.[4] For teachers in these novels tend, like Miss Brooks, to be thin rather than buxom. If they are pretty, the prettiness is of a slender, boyish type rather than that of a grown woman. Gestures are sharp (how often Miss Brooks cocks a pointed shoulder in cynical despair!) and humor is quick and sarcastic. It is clear, too, that Miss Brooks is using teaching as a stopgap until she can find a suitable (she's getting old enough so that almost *any* male will do) mate. Even her unending pursuit of the frightened and elusive Mr. Boynton has a hungry and predatory quality.

Although we cannot predict what turns

[1] Willard Waller, *The Sociology of Teaching*, New York, John Wiley and Sons, Inc., 1932, p. 58.

[2] Jacques Barzun, *Teacher in America*, Boston, Little, Brown and Co., 1945, p. 25.

[3] Lassie and Francis.

[4] A complete discussion of the stereotype of both the male and female teacher may be found in the author's doctoral dissertation, "Teacher Stereotypes in the American Novel," Stanford University, 1953.

"Our Miss Brooks" will take, we know what happens to her sisters in American prose fiction. They grow older, but not happier, loving but unloved, wanting but unwanted, eternal strangers who devote their lives to the education of other women's children, graying, sharpening, harshening with the years, becoming autocrats in the classroom and recluses in the community, accepting their roles as old maids as they once accepted their roles as young schoolmistresses, dimly seeking some answer to all the pains and frustrations they can neither articulate nor understand.

Mr. Boynton, as his Dickensian tag name implies, is not quite adult; he is *boy*ish. He flees the responsibilities of love and marriage as he would the ire of his principal, Mr. Conklin. His ideal evening consists of a trip to the local soda fountain with Miss Brooks. There everything is Dutch treat, perhaps because he is penurious, but more probably because he is underpaid. The source of his lack of maturity lies, no doubt, in the general misconception that whoever works with children must be childish himself. Luckily for the growth of our population, this notion has not yet been extended to parenthood.

Neither Miss Brooks nor Mr. Boynton is of heroic stature. Certainly, neither could serve as a model for the young in the same sense that Annie Oakley and the Lone Ranger serve. Yet, in real life both are extremely attractive, and, in this respect, they offer more positive portraitures than those found in prose literature. The male schoolteacher in the American novel is usually stooped, gaunt, and gray with weariness. His suit has the shine of shabby gentility and hangs loosely from his undernourished frame. The woman, as we have already indicated, is in her younger years slim and boyish; later on, she will become shrill and witchlike. In short, to succeed as a teacher, one must fail as a man or woman. Little wonder that education is commonly regarded as the refuge of unsalable men and unmarriageable women.

If education is worth while, if helping our children to become productive and democratic citizens is important, then the stereotype of the teacher is harmful not only to the individual and his profession but also to the community. Men and women who have to live narrow, unlovely lives in order to conform to the preconceptions of the public are not likely to prove generous and inspiring guides to that same public's youth. Since it ascribes the role of the teacher, the stereotype also impairs recruitment—a serious difficulty when one considers our alarming teacher shortage.

Agreeing that this situation ought to be remedied is easier than uncovering the remedy. However, certain suggestions can be offered. The first step toward shattering the stereotype will be to sensitize educators to its existence. Once this has been accomplished, once we have ceased to type ourselves, we can turn our energies toward better public relations. Strengthening the profession, in all ways possible, should also do much toward investing its members with greater self-respect and dignity.

Whatever the sovereign cure may be, it will not appear overnight, for the problem is fed by some of the most pervasive cultural disorders of our time. We are an ambivalent people: ambivalent toward education, toward authority, toward our own ideals. But perhaps this is a hopeful sign. If the pendulum swings too far in one direction, we at least possess the capacity to let it swing back in the other. Lincoln, that gaunt, homely man who so closely resembles the portrait of the male teacher in literature, was often called a buffoon before he became President. It may be too much to ask that educators be viewed as heroes, but surely we have the right to protest being treated as scapegoats.

LET'S GROW UP PROFESSIONALLY[1]

Lucien B. Kinney

Is education an art, a science, a craft, or a profession? Each viewpoint has its supporters. Those who classify education as an *art* are impressed with the importance of adapting teaching practices to the special needs of the pupils, to the specific situation, and even to the personal characteristics of the teacher himself. Unless carried to the point where the inference is drawn that "teachers are born, not made," it is useful to emphasize these qualities.

To others, the degree of expertness revealed by the competent teacher or administrator is an outstanding quality. The fact that such expertness can be acquired only through practice in the real situation, preferably under competent guidance, suggests the analogy to *craftsmanship*. Most commonly this classification is by implication, through programs of preparation designed around apprenticeship training.

To those interested in measurement and experimentation, the concept of education as a *science* has a special appeal. Many of the current problems in education require the methods of science for their solution. The prestige of the sciences today lends attractiveness to the thought that education might take its place, along with psychology, sociology, and anthropology, in the family of behavioral sciences. Those with this aspiration continually remind us that exactitude and objectivity in measurement, along with controlled experimentation, are the bases for progress in any science.

WHAT DIFFERENCE?

While each of these classifications highlights an important characteristic of education, none is functionally adequate. Each one tends to emphasize one aspect of the vocation while overlooking others equally important. To take into account the significant characteristics and responsibilities of education as a vocation, those in the field are increasingly tending to assume that education is a *profession*. The growing professional consciousness of educators, including teachers, administrators, and organizational leaders, is truly impressive.

It is important to recognize that the concerns of those who stress the professional status of education are not concerned with the identification of an elite or privileged group of vocations. Professional status has prestige, but what is even more important, it has responsibilities. The same factors that identify professional status, impose on its membership special obligations to society, such as defining and maintaining professional standards, developing and enforcing a code of ethics, and various others. In view of the close relationship between professional services and public welfare, it is a matter of first importance both to society and to the members that the question of professional status in education should be explored, and professional responsibilities be identified.

IS IDENTIFICATION POSSIBLE?

Yet to identify a profession as such is not a simple matter. It is true that, in the public mind, a certain group of vocations have been generally recognized as professions. One of their common characterstics is that the services performed by their members satisfy an important social need. Competence implies legal control. Beyond this, however, is the fact that the behavior

[1] From *California Teachers Association Journal*, February, 1955, pp. 7–9. Reprinted with permission.

of individual members has a certain public quality, yielding priority to the interests of society in accord with a more or less explicit code of ethics.

While these criteria are too vague for precise purposes of classification, they serve to call attention to the fact that the problem is a real and practical one. To define professional status and responsibility in education the questions to be answered are these:

How are the vocations with professional status to be identified? Is education one of these?

What are the general responsibilities of those occupying membership roles in any profession and specifically, in education?

To what degree have these responsibilities been accepted and acted upon in education? What steps are to be taken in order that they may be more effectively fulfilled?

CHART I

Characteristics Common to the Profession

An Occupation Becomes a Profession When:

A. The social need for its services is acknowledged by its members as involving an obligation to society which takes precedence over the personal interests of the members and their clients.
   1. Hence a profession defines explicitly its functions and its ethics.
   2. Adherence to the code of ethics is mandatory for continuance of membership.

B. The required proficiencies are not mechanistic or stereotyped, but are based on competent diagnosis and adjusted to each situation.
   1. Hence a profession is based on well-developed fields of science.
   2. Work procedures are evolved from systematically tested techniques.
   3. A protracted and highly organized program of preparation is required.

C. Control of membership is needed to guarantee competence, ethically and technically.
   1. The general public is very unlikely to be competent to judge the extent to which professional workers fulfill criteria A and B above.
   2. Hence, licensure is required, with standards defined by the profession and legalized by the state.

D. Organizations and corporate activities are required to facilitate and insure the fulfillment of criteria A, B, and C.

CHART II

Membership Responsibilities in a Profession

1. Providing for a high quality of membership.
   - 1.1 Recruitment of persons of high calibre.
   - 1.2 Testing the validity of procedures for selecting members of the profession.
   - 1.3 Developing effective programs of member preparation (pre-professional and professional).
   - 1.4 Encouraging experimental development of effective professional procedures.
   - 1.5 Encouraging in-service growth of professional competence.
2. Accumulating a body of validated professional procedures.
   - 2.1 Drawing upon and interpreting the contributions of the basic sciences.
   - 2.2 Encouraging research on professional problems as well as on scientific problems.
   - 2.3 Systematic testing and validating of professional procedures.
     - 2.31 In the preparing institutions.
     - 2.32 In the field.
       - 2.321 Publicize and evaluate new, original procedures.

2.322 Facilitate exchange of information.
2.323 Organize and compile this information.
2.4 Promoting the experimental attitude toward all professional procedures.
2.41 Every teaching method, for example, viewed as a hypothesis, instead of taken as authoritatively sound or approved dogma.
3. Leadership in formulating and enforcing standards.
3.1 Operational definitions of the performance functions of members.
3.11 See *Measure of a Good Teacher*, CTA, 1953.
Factors in Teaching Competence, NCTEPS, 1954.
3.2 Study and definition of professional goals, jointly with the public.
3.3 Defining minimum requirements for licensure.
3.4 Promoting better accreditation of professional institutions through State-profession cooperation.
3.5 Evolving and enforcing a functional code of ethics.
3.6 Developing techniques for separating incompetent members from the profession.
4. Promoting the organizational life of the profession.
4.1 Seeing that prospective members are adequately prepared for organizational membership.
4.2 Achieving and maintaining appropriate economic conditions for work.
4.3 Achieving and maintaining appropriate social conditions for work (relations with the community).
4.4 Achieving and maintaining appropriate professional conditions for work (relations between professional members).
4.5 Cooperating among the several organizations within the profession in discharging the above responsibilities.

MEMBERSHIP RESPONSIBILITIES

These questions call attention to the criteria of professional status on the one hand, and the responsibilities of the membership on the other. The former are the characteristics to be found in any vocation that is classed as a profession. The latter are the consequences of these characteristics. The degree to which the responsibilities of membership are being accepted and fulfilled at any time is a measure of the professional maturity of the membership.

It would be convenient if the literature provided a clearcut set of criteria for present purposes. However, both colloquially and technically, the usage of the word "profession" is so loose as to make most definitions useless. Thus the dictionary definition has to make allowance for the connotation that differentiates the professional from the amateur athlete. Then census, in its occupational classification, defines the professional worker largely on the basis of length of preparation required. With procedures in the crafts and many other vocations coming more and more to depend on science, the usefulness of this definition as a sole criterion is rapidly disappearing.

There is, however, a considerable body of literature, mainly in the fields of the "senior" professions, dealing with professional criteria and responsibilities from various points of view. It is true that criteria and responsibilities are rarely differentiated, nor is the cause and effect relationship between the two ordinarily recognized. These distinctions, however, become clear upon analysis, and it is possible to find a reasonable consensus on four major criteria of professional status. These are outlined in Chart I.

PROFESSIONAL TASKS

Perhaps the most revealing characteristic of professional status is the fourth criterion, the necessity for organized, corporate action. This arises from the most basic and distinctive of all the professional criteria, namely, that the members of a profession have major responsibilities to society, over and above the duties of the individual members. In non-professional occupations, when the members have fulfilled their individual duties, the occupation as a whole has discharged its responsibility to society. But when the members of a profession have carried out their individual duties as practitioners, the formidable tasks of the profession still remain. These are outlined in Chart II.

While differing in detail and complexity among the professions, these tasks are common to all, by virtue of the factors that identify professional status. Since the responsibility for their performance extends to every member of the profession, a clearly defined basis becomes available for the identification of membership in a given profession: membership includes all who have primary responsibilities for performing one or more of the professional tasks of the profession. In education, this obviously includes the teachers, administrators, and other certified personnel who carry on the school program. Beyond this, however, membership extends to a variety of other groups including organizational leaders, state school officers, and those responsible for the preparation of professional personnel in education. Where a broad and complex field requires many areas of specialization, the development of many vested interests often conceals the common area of responsibility among special groups. In education also, the situation is further confused by the fact that legalized controls of membership have been established for only a portion of the membership. To suppose that membership in the profession is determined by organizational affiliation, or by legal licensure, is to ignore the basic characteristics of professional status and the basic facts of membership responsibility. Professional solidarity and effectiveness are to be achieved only through acceptance of the common responsibility imposed by the professional tasks, which represent the unifying factor in any profession.

AIMS OF ORGANIZATION

The functions of the professional organization become clear if it is regarded as an instrument of the profession for achievement of the professional tasks. Many of these tasks constitute collective responsibilities of the entire membership, such as: definition of professional goals, compiling a code of ethics, maintaining quality of membership, and promoting economic welfare and security of the membership. Effective unified action on these problems requires coordination, education of the public and membership alike, and corporate cooperation with other groups and the lay public which is possible only through an overall professional organization.

Within the membership of most professions one finds groups, formal and informal, identified with special interests and activities, and often specially prepared for important roles within these areas. As these become well defined, specialized organizations tend to appear. It is not surprising in so diversified a profession as education, to find many areas of organized specialization. Whether there are too many, as has been asserted, can be determined not merely by counting, but by clear definition of organizational functions, to reveal whatever duplication exists. What is of more significance is that the centrifugal force of specialized interests must be balanced by an effective overall organization concerned with common professional goals.

Even from this brief survey it is clear that education has, to a high degree, the qualities that identify it as a profession. Its members are, accordingly, endowed with professional responsibilities that need to be taken into account in programs of preparation. In view of the social importance of the professional tasks, this must be recognized as a necessary area of practitioner competence. The preparation of the practitioner is incomplete unless he is prepared, as an effective member of the professional organization, to perform them.

A closer examination of the professional tasks to identify areas of neglected and accepted responsibilities would go beyond the scope of the present review. Such scrutiny might be expected to reveal that while some obligations have been defined and accepted, others have remained unrecognized. Some of the most serious problems in education have their sources in this neglect, and the failure of the practitioner in education to realize that his obligations for effective membership in the professional organization rank with his obligations as an effective member of the school organization. Their solution demands a clear understanding of professional status and its attendant responsibilities, by each individual member.

WE MUST STUDY STATUS

For this reason a systematic study of professional status and responsibility in education deserves top priority among the organized activities of the profession. It is needed to define clearly the role of the professional organizations, to clarify their policies, and to define their lines of action, in building an efficient program of education. Even more important, perhaps, is the development of professional consciousness as it contributes to professional effectiveness. It was noted at the outset that professional status is a practical matter. Yet it would be unwise to overlook the fact that professional prestige has real and practical significance for educators in their relationships with the public.

As members of a profession of recognized importance, and with demonstrated competence to fulfill its responsibilities to society, educators should be in a position to expect partnership participation, cooperation, and support from the public. Probably the most convincing evidences of professional status are the professional attitudes and self-direction of a membership that understands the nature and importance of its responsibilities.

THE SOCIOLOGY OF THE "BORN TEACHER"[1]

Jean D. Grambs

"Now that Miss Jones is just a born teacher."

"He is just a 'natural' in the classroom."

"There is nothing we can do to make a teacher out of Bob."

Such phrases as the above are to be heard wherever educators or lay persons discuss teachers. It seems to make no difference who the observers are; certain individuals stand out in classroom performance as having a kind of natural gift in dealing with the teaching situation. Teacher education institutions are only too keenly aware of the vast gulf that separates these seemingly naturally gifted teachers from the rest of the group, some of whom seemed doomed always to mediocre or even incompetent teaching careers. But the "born teacher" stands out, often, long before he has ever read an education text or had a course in methods.

[1] From *The Journal of Educational Sociology*, May, 1952, pp. 532–541. Reprinted by permission.

It would be a fine thing if, first, we had sensitive enough selection devices to point out these "born teachers" when they first appear for training. We could then give them some additional polish, deepen their instinctive insights, and be confident of their teaching success. Or, second, if we knew enough about what went into the making of these "born teachers" we might better duplicate such experiences (if they are experiential and not basic in "innate" teaching types) in the teacher education courses.

The purpose of this paper is to analyze some of the role attributes of the teaching situation in an attempt to see what kinds of individuals might be most adaptable to the role demands of the job, and then develop the implications of this analysis for teacher education.

The concept of role has seemed a very fruitful one in understanding the individual, his social relationships, and how his behavior, attitudes, and attitudes of others towards him shift and change.[2] Growing up involves one in many role shifts; from child to adult, from non-worker to gainful worker, from non-voter to citizen, from son to father. The growing person is surrounded by individuals representing many role relationships and role behaviors. The culture gives him, in addition, many avenues for learning what is role appropriate patterns of dress, language, manner, and attitudes via the media of movies, television, radio, periodicals, newspapers, as well as word of mouth. Some roles have high status and are sought for, others have low status and are only accepted because of necessity.[3] Job satisfaction is closely related to the socially positive or socially negative role concepts that are identified with a given job. There are several questions that must be raised in looking at the teacher role: 1. How does the culture view the role of the teacher? 2. How adequately does the culture provide opportunity for learning role-appropriate behavior as an aspect of preparation for teaching?

THE TEACHER ROLE IN OUR CULTURE

We will not attempt here to do a complete job of defining the teacher role, but merely give some indicators that throw light on the basic question, namely, what role learning precedes entry into teaching on the part of the beginner. To consider the teacher role, it is useful to see how the teacher appears from the various viewpoints which might most influence the role concepts of future teachers:

1. The students. After the parents, the teacher is typically the adult with greatest impact on the social world of the child. He controls important gateways: grades, promotion, opportunities to learn vital skills. The teacher sets the value system of the world of knowledge, rewarding certain abilities, punishing others. He shares with the parent the task of developing concepts of right and wrong in the young. The socializing role involves the teacher in basic conflicts with youth who, under teacher direction, must give up primitive impulses and immediate gratification for symbolic and remote rewards. The life of the teacher is hidden from the view of the student; what he does or is like outside the classroom is a mystery. The pervasive fear of failure in the classroom induces feelings of great ambivalence towards the teacher in terms of the possible success or failure of the student.
2. The parent. The parent funnels to the child (who in some instances will himself become a teacher) his basic atti-

[2] Ralph Linton, "Concepts of Role and Status," in T. M. Newcomb and Eugene L. Hartley, *Readings in Social Psychology*, New York, Henry Holt and Co., 1947, pp. 367–370.

[3] Bruno Solby, "The Role Concept in Job Adjustment," *Sociometry* (May, 1944), Vol. 7, pp. 222–229.

tudes towards teachers, derived from the parent's past experiences as a student, and present involvement with the teachers of his child. The teacher, to the parent, is sometimes an adult ally in socializing the child; this is when the class goals of parent and teacher coincide. To other parents the teacher is a competitor for the child's affection, and one who may be emphasizing goals and values rejected by the parent. The teacher stands as a gateway in terms of the parent's ambition and hope for his child, and the ambivalent reaction of the child is repeated in his parent's feelings. The inadequacies of the parent are revealed by the behavior of his child which the teacher notes, thus the parent feels exposed in his relations with the teacher, with consequent belittling, belligerence, or retreat into inferiority.

3. The public. The teacher stereotype, widely exhibited via cartoons, shows the teacher as a woman, unattractive and harassed, in some conflict situation with the young, in which the child emerges triumphant. The need to defeat the teacher is clear. There is no parallel attack on other professional groups such as doctors or ministers, though lawyers and politicians get similar treatment.

   Another public views the teacher as slightly less dangerous than the demagogue. Suspecting the actual influence of the teacher, such a view strives to reduce the role of the teacher to a mechanical drill master teaching only the fundamentals.[4]

   Still another public sentimentalizes the teacher, stressing the inspirational influence of the great, "born" teacher. Such inspiring persons are sometimes portrayed as wielding influence due to sympathetic interaction with pupils, sometimes because of their complete disregard for student personality as they pursued truth. Most of these teachers are assigned to university levels; such persons did not *learn* how to teach.[5]

The teacher role in our culture also is a product of many historical factors. At the public school level, early teachers were often tramps or scoundrels, who taught poorly and sometimes viciously. The influx of women into the teaching profession during the last fifty years has lowered the status of the profession to the degree that the public assigns women lower social status than men, thus a profession which enrolls many women is suspect for the man.

The role of the teacher in our culture, then, is one of relatively low professional status. In addition, the teacher is an object of tremendous ambivalent feelings, and wields great power in the life of the individual. These conflicting pressures serve to confuse and distort the eventual acceptance of the teaching role by those who become teachers.

The views of the teaching role described above are notably lacking in empathy or identification with the teacher. Current fiction about teachers reinforces this finding. While actually few books or stories are written about teachers, those that do are of mediocre quality. And in addition, the focus is most often upon the teacher as a person; the teaching function, the classroom feelings of the teacher, are only rarely—and then very briefly—presented.[6]

Everyone knows the teacher, but no one knows what teaching is. No one sees the

[4] Ernest O. Melby, *American Education Under Fire*, Freedom Pamphlet, New York, Anti Defamation League of B'Nai B'Rith, 1951.

[5] Houston Peterson, *Great Teachers Portrayed by Those Who Studied Under Them*, New Brunswick, Rutgers University Press, 1946.

[6] An excellent example of this kind of fiction is the following: Mabel B. Farwell, "Men! Men!" *American Magazine*, September, 1951, pp. 33.

See also, Antoinette Ciolli, "The Teacher in Fiction," a brief bibliography, (mimeo.), New York, Brooklyn College Library, Reference Division, April, 1949.

person as a teacher. The individual in our culture has had numerous contacts with the teacher. The average student, for instance, probably has had a minimum of eight different teachers in the elementary school, as many as 20 different teachers in high school. For those who go to college, they will react to another forty or so professors in their four undergraduate years. There is no lack of knowledge of the teacher, on the part of the person as a student. But it is a well known experience for the student to be completely unable to explain how the teacher helped him learn; what it was in the teaching situation that helped or hurt. Introspection on the part of students about the *teaching process* is very unrewarding; few students are able to get any insight into what the teacher really did.

In summary, then, we can say that the future teacher learns to view the teacher role from a negative cultural viewpoint, and is, typically, prevented from obtaining any genuine insight into the teaching function.

LEARNING THE TEACHER ROLE

Let us now look at what opportunities may be available for the individual to learn to accept the teaching function, since presumably it is those who accept it most easily who are our "born" teachers.

The pathway to teaching lies through successful completion of college work. This implies successful handling of elementary and high school situations. The successful learner becomes the teacher. But the successful learner in the public school system is not necessarily the most successful person in his peer group and other out-of-school relationships. Studies show that girls excel boys in the public schools because of greater verbal facility or greater ability to comply, or both.[7] Boys are more apt to drop out of school than girls.[8] Thus learning becomes more synonymous with feminine values and interests. The boy who succeeds in school is a "sissy." Students in general who succeed are usually suspected of "apple polishing,"—and "teacher's pet" is a fighting epithet. The future teacher has, in all probability, because of greater intellectual ability, been on the periphery of his peer group, if not actually ostracized. He learns, then, either to reject peer values and ally himself with the adult world (an attitude towards children and youth that is a definite handicap in later teaching) or, while perhaps not actively moving out of his peer group, he recognizes that his greatest security comes from the student role, a role in which he is highly successful and attains his greatest rewards. Then, at the professional level in teacher education, we attempt to reconvert them; to pull such students out of this comfortable student position, and put them in the opposing camp. Not recipient, but giver; not rewardee but rewarder.

While the future teacher has most probably been a highly successful student, he cannot escape the general evaluation of learning that pervades the peer group. The complexities of today's world have tended to make in-school learning ever more remote from reality, since reality itself is far too huge, too confusing, too unmanageable.[9] In reaction to the high content of abstraction in the school, the student escapes into his own "real world" of peer groups, a phenomenon that is occurring at ever younger ages. The learner develops a

[7] Dean Lobaugh, "Girls and Grades—a Significant Factor in Evaluation," *Sch. Sci., and Math.*, April, 1947, pp. 763–773.

[8] Ellsworth Tompkins, "Where Are the Boys?" *School and Society* (July 2, 1949), Vol. 70, pp. 1–2.

[9] Kingsley Davis, "Adolescence and the Social Structure," in "Adolescents in Wartime," *The Annals of the American Academy of Political and Social Science*, November, 1944, pp. 13–14.

general tolerance of school, but a mistrust of education since it is so remote from his daily problems and immediate interests. Teachers are then a part of this great pretense; professors in government are a laugh, if not downright dangerous. The anti-intellectuality of the average American, while having many other historical roots, is reinforced by current in-school experiences. The halo of general disorientation to what really matters in life surrounds the person as a teacher. This too is the cultural milieu of the person becoming a teacher.

We find, then, two conflicting forces at work determining the character type of those who enter teaching. On the one hand, being successful students, they tend to overvalue academic achievement; it becomes the difficult task of the educational staff to reintroduce them to people. On the other hand, they too have taken on some of the basic cultural suspicion of the academic, and the nearer they get to teaching the more apt are they to become either over-defensive about the academic world, or unwilling participants in an activity they suspect is of little worth in the eyes of the public. Such influences make it difficult indeed for the average individual to accept the teaching role gracefully. He has had experiences which tend to make him distrust teachers, and other experiences that make him more than happy as a student.

Let us now look at another aspect of the problem. To what extent have teaching situations been available at the informal level, prior to entry into the profession? Presumably, some actual participation in teaching situations, of whatever nature, would serve to make the formal teaching role more easily assimilated. Most future teachers come from upper-lower or middle class families.[10] They are specially motivated to seek professional status, often a status superior to that of their parents. This push for upward mobility comes because of parental ambition, sometimes in spite of it. The small size of today's families precludes any possibility of the future teacher having many opportunities to "teach" younger siblings or relatives. And the play group is one of peers; children are carefully shepherded away from playing with those younger than themselves by parental pressure and school rules. The environment does not offer him a chance to learn to protect—to teach—others.

Thus we see two sets of circumstances that isolate the individual who goes into teaching from any trying out of the teaching role. First because he has been too successful as a student, or the student culture forbids anyone from coming too close to the teacher, and second, because the rearing of children today isolates the individual from contacts with anyone but adults or peers, preventing any possibility of a "teaching" relationship to younger, dependent, children. *There have been no extensive culturally approved situations* in which to learn how to absorb the tremendous challenge of the group towards the teacher-leader. It is this challenge—this attack—that is so difficult for the teacher to understand and accept and channel in productive lines. Acquiring the teacher role, then, becomes a very difficult problem, so difficult in fact that few teachers are able to come up to the level of competence needed for vital education.

In view of the discussion above, we can begin to detect, perhaps, some of the forces that produce the "born teacher." It is my contention that such individuals are those who have escaped or circumvented the above cultural conditioning. They have had a chance to explore the teaching role in childhood and youth. Such experiences

[10] Lloyd Warner, Robert J. Havighurst, and Martin B. Loeb, *Who Shall Be Educated?* New York, Harper & Brothers, 1944.

as the following are, it is suggested, responsible for the difference:

1. Older child who played a mother-substitute role with several younger siblings.
2. Isolated from peer group relations, but access to younger age groups.
3. In school given the chance to assist frequently and successfully as a teacher's helper in the instruction of others—but without the connotation of "teacher's pet."
4. Acquired leadership roles in peer groups as an adolescent; been able to accept the conspicuousness of leadership and the constant public attention to one's behavior, another important facet of the teaching role.

Another factor might be added: The degree of identification of the individual with teachers, with being a teacher, with a parent who was a teacher. The dynamics of this relationship as contributing to future teaching competence are unclear. On the one hand, identification would presumably make it easier later to *be* the teacher with which one identified. But on the other hand, to identify with the teacher presumably means rejecting those who are taught. So that one who had too closely taken on the empathetic relationship to the teacher would be least able, as a teacher himself, to appreciate and like children, and the things of childhood. But this needs further exploration.

In summary, then, since our culture makes it so difficult to learn the teacher role, and instead surrounds this role with ambivalent and negative attitudes, only those few persons who escape this cultural conditioning through informal teaching relationships and leadership positions can move easily into teaching. Only such can withstand and recover from the shock of the teaching situation.

IMPLICATIONS FOR TEACHER EDUCATION

1. Selection. If our hypothesis is true—and further research is needed for verification—then we need to obtain detailed autobiographical materials on prospective teachers to find out what opportunities were available to them for trying out the teaching role in their own personal history. Leadership roles also would be important. Such factors should then be weighted heavily in encouraging individuals to continue into teaching.

2. Teacher education procedures. It seems obvious that in teacher education we must make up for the lacks of the culture. We must provide many informal teaching situations with younger persons, so that the neophyte may gain confidence in meeting the challenge of the group in a more protected, permissive, less hostile climate than in the classroom, in order better to meet the attack adequately in the school. Continual examination of the emotional demands required in such group situations is imperative so that the future teacher can, via intellectual short cuts, make up for the cultural lacks of his own personal history. Role-playing situations should be extensively utilized to get into the "feel" of the teacher-student, teacher-parent, teacher-teacher, and teacher-administrator relationships on an other-than-verbal level.

Verbalization without the base in experience with real people does not and cannot make teachers. We see this abundantly in the public school classroom. And since so few enter teaching who have had such real experiences with children and teaching situations in their own past, it is up to the teacher education institution to fulfill this need—a need that the culture not only neglects, but makes extraordinarily difficult to overcome.

THE TEACHING PROFESSION

3

EDUCATION AND THE CHANGING SELF[1]

Arthur T. Jersild

DISCUSSION AND ANALYSIS

In classic Greek drama the tragedy or agony of the hero is usually followed by a moment of insight in which the hero is graced by an understanding of the personal and environmental causes that necessitated his downfall. The idea that understanding of oneself is of prime importance is also central to much of the world's great philosophy and literature. Jersild obviously shares this belief. In systematically applying it to education he argues that before the teacher can deal with the emotional problems of his students he must have solved many of his own problems and must be at least conscious of those he has not resolved. "Disturbed" teachers are better off teaching straight subject-matter courses in traditional areas by traditional methods.

Critics of such a point of view would be quick to challenge the notion of the teacher as therapist. If personality disorders exist, they are the medical property of the psychiatrist and not the province of the educator. These critics also deplore the emphasis on personality. What they are concerned with is character—the moral structure of the human being—and this, they feel, is best shaped by the content and discipline of the traditional curriculum.

Where do you stand in this dispute? Which type of teacher will you be? Is it possible that there are arguments on both sides of the fence? What suggestions of Jersild's do you find especially illuminating? Do you believe the notion of self-concept can be of practical value?

[1] From Arthur T. Jersild, *In Search of Self*, pp. 100–108. Copyright, 1952, by Teachers College, Columbia University. Reprinted with the permission of the Bureau of Publications.

THE IMPACT OF THE SELF-CONCEPT ON THE WORK OF THE TEACHER

Often when teachers are asked to accept a changed outlook on their work it means that they must add another task to the burdens they already carry. But to adopt the self-concept as a basic concept in education will not add to a teacher's load in the long run, for it will make the job of teaching more meaningful and significant and, therefore, more rewarding. It will help to obviate the feeling of futility which many teachers now have concerning their work. It will free many teachers, especially at the high school and college levels, from the constant need to rationalize or to justify (to themselves or their colleagues) the importance of what they are doing. It will give life to many a task which otherwise requires only a mechanical process of memorization.[2]

In attending to the thousand and one details involved in teaching, it often occurs to the teacher whose heart is in his work to ask himself what difference this or that effort or activity makes in the lives of his students or in his own personal or professional growth. Such questions will often occur to teachers at the college level, if they have the courage to look at what they are doing as they plod through their classes, make assignments, give tests, confer with individual students, try to keep up their scholarly work and their writing, run to seminars, departmental meetings, staff meetings, committee meetings, meetings of professional organizations, world without end. Similar questions must occur frequently to teachers at the high school, elementary, and lower levels, for even though their pupils are younger, they are in the process of more rapid growth and they are, in a broad sense, more educable than the more or less eager college student.

The self-concept offers teachers a principle which integrates the basic features of their task and all the little details that go into it. Without a unifying principle much in education and much that happens in everyday life seems like a series of disconnected fragments. Even some of the most progressive ideas and methods in education can be carried out in a detached, mechanical manner. But when we apply the self-concept we have something challenging. We cannot apply this concept without self-involvement. Teaching then becomes for the teacher a way of expressing, utilizing, and developing the resources of his own nature.

The more a teacher can see his work fitting into a large conception, the easier it will be for him to deal with the details of his job. He need not waste energy in rationalizing his work or justifying himself. He will see that much of what now happens in school is in the interest of conformity, in the interest of carrying out stereotyped notions. The better he understands this, the better he can calculate the minimum of busy work he must do for the sake of conformity and the freer he will be to use his energies for productive purposes. He will have less need for continually making separate and new decisions.

One who has grasped the big thing finds it easier to take care of little details. A poet has said that it is through having a

[2] By way of example, think how the dry bones of history would come to life if the teacher and the class consider the story of Sparta and see the Spartans not as a curious folk, long since dead, but as people whose counterparts are with us today, seeking under the mask of a Spartan approach to life to get away from themselves and to live up to a pathetic, false image. Consider how Banquo's ghost would cease to be a quaint fantasy in a difficult book but a stark reality to all who have known the pangs of conscience. We would not then hear a hollow verdict such as was made by the high school class, of which this writer was a member many years ago, after reading *Silas Marner*, "Too bad old Si lost all his dough."

universal view of things that God is able to keep watch over all His creatures; not even a little sparrow falls to the ground unnoticed by Him.

The larger the teacher's conception of his work and the greater his self-involvement in it, the better able he will be to keep his eye on each individual pupil's struggle to be himself.

PSYCHOLOGICAL CONTENT OF THE GENERAL CURRICULUM

Nearly everything in the curriculum is charged with psychological meaning when viewed from the standpoint of what it might do to help learners find themselves, realize their potentialities, use their resources in productive ways, and enter into relationships which have a bearing on their ideas and attitudes toward themselves.

Most of what comes under the heading of the social studies, for example, might contribute directly or indirectly to a learner's understanding of human problems and motives, including his own. It is an easy step from a consideration of economics to an inquiry into the human values, needs, aspirations, and competitive tendencies involved in economic affairs. It is possible to inquire how learners project their own self-revealing attitudes onto economic issues. In the teaching of history it would require only a modicum of insight into human behavior to show the psychological content in historical events which often transparently reveal the aspirations and frailties of human beings, their courage or lack of it, their tendency to be governed by greed, fear, hostility, and false pride, and their capacity for generosity and devotion. History, like economics, provides a rich opportunity for helping learners to examine some of their own motives as they identify themselves emotionally with this or that hero or cause, or express their fears or inferiority feelings, or vent their hostilities by proxy upon historical characters and events.

The physical education program especially abounds in psychological possibilities. In it children can learn to discover and accept their bodies, to face up against false and prudish attitudes of shame and guilt which some of them have learned to associate with nakedness. Here they can discover, try, and test their capacity for acquiring enjoyable skills; here they can learn to recognize their competitive tendencies and the healthy as well as the morbid features of competition. Here they are introduced to a psychological laboratory in which they see, in raw form, acts of meanness, cruelty, and hostility which are symptomatic of emotional poverty or mental conflict; and they can observe behavior which reflects good sportsmanship, greatness in defeat, ability to "take it," and behavior which reveals a self rich in resources and inner assurance.

The psychological content that might be drawn from courses in literature is well recognized. Biographies and autobiographies offer a mirror in which one can study a reflection of oneself. In poetry one can hear the echo of one's own feelings, and drama and fiction are filled with conflicts such as occur in daily life.

If teachers in the various subjects and specialties within the curriculum draw upon these psychological resources they will not minimize the importance of their special subject matter areas. We are not advocating that one area should be minimized so that psychology may be magnified. The word psychology need never be used. The more each teacher of a special subject draws upon the psychological content of that subject, the more the special area will be maximized. To use physical education as an example, psychological purposes will not detract from physical education but add to its glory.

THE TEACHER'S EMOTIONAL INVOLVEMENT

When an effort is made to promote the concept of self-understanding in the classroom one of the most impressive effects is the emotional impact of such work upon the teacher. In many classes pupils, when given an opening, will reveal a wide range of emotional problems. Sometimes a child or an entire group will release a flood of feeling. In classes with children who have long been "problems" and who have been kicked around in the school system (and probably in the home and the community) for several years, a raw display of emotion—of hostility, anxiety, and despair—can have a staggering effect upon a new teacher and even upon one who has had much experience in working with such children. The anxiety that is displayed may be so intense that it is frightening. The hostility may be so naked that a person who has long schooled himself to conceal hostility even from himself (as most teachers do) recoils from it. The grievances revealed may have a bitterness beyond anything the teacher has faced in the polite society from which he comes.

Such a display of feeling can be very threatening to a teacher. In addition, the teacher may be overwhelmed by the terrific needs that are laid bare: the needs of the children are so great, and the teacher may realize that his ability to help is so limited that it seems hopeless even to try.

The teacher will feel especially threatened if he is one who places so high an expectation upon himself that his reaction to a problem presented by a pupil is that he should be able to find an immediate solution. Such an expectation is unrealistic and is likely to lead to feelings of frustration, guilt, and self-disparagement.

Another source of difficulty is that the problems presented by pupils to the teacher are likely to touch upon his own unresolved problems. Most teachers have such problems, because teachers are people, too.

When, for example, students discuss troubles they have in getting along with their parents, the teacher may have difficulty because (either known or unknown to him) he has not himself resolved his own relationships. He may retain grievances against his own parents which he does not clearly recognize but which still trouble him. He may have a tendency to blame his early upbringing for the difficulties he faces in his present life. He may have irrational feelings of guilt about not having been as dutiful a child as he should have been. And so on.

When pupils raise problems relating to sex the teacher may feel threatened because of his own sexual problems. In a culture such as ours, it is likely that most persons who are old enough to teach will have unrecognized problems pertaining to sex unless they have had psychological counseling of a kind which few teachers in training now receive. It will therefore be difficult for them to sort out the ways in which their own attitudes toward sex are healthy or compulsive, or colored with anxiety, or distorted by irrational feelings of guilt, or imbued with hostility or inferiority or other forms of self-derogation. They may be doubtful whether they have a tendency to overplay the importance of sex (suspecting that they are "too interested") or to minimize or ignore sex (because they are frightened by it), or they may have a disquieting suspicion that through the discussion of sex they are seeking to gratify vicariously their own erotic desires.

These are only a few of the perplexities that the subject of sex might arouse when it is brought into class discussion. Nor will the problem be solved simply by recognizing that practically all teachers have perplexities of one sort or another.

A display of emotion of any kind may be threatening to certain teachers. Some people become embarrassed or frightened when confronted by any expression of strong feeling. Some are especially uncomfortable when inferiority feelings are exposed. Some become flustered by a simple, genuine show of affection.

Baffling emotional problems may arise because the teacher puts severe demands upon himself. He may demand of himself that he be immune to emotional effects, such as those described above—as though anyone could sincerely be concerned with the emotional problems of others without becoming emotionally involved himself. He may demand that he be able to do something, and soon, to solve or alleviate the difficulties presented to him. In dealing with a youngster who has deep-seated emotional conflicts, the teacher may expect that he should be able to "reach" the child and in a short time help him. It might be impossible for even a highly competent psychoanalyst or clinical psychologist to "reach" such a seriously disturbed child until after a long period of treatment. But even if a teacher is told this, he still might not be able to keep from expecting more of himself than is reasonable.

Because of emotional involvement in one form or another, a teacher may feel so disturbed, or so threatened, or so frustrated in his work with young people that he finds it impossible to go on. Some teachers who have tried their hand at courses dealing with psychological problems go back into the straight subject matter field. One teacher who was observed in this study commented that it is restful to go back and teach an academic subject to a dull normal class after having wrestled with emotional problems of a group of troubled children.

Teachers will differ, of course, in the extent to which they become involved beyond their capacity to endure, and in the extent to which they demand more of themselves than is reasonable. For this reason, some teachers will be better suited than others by temperament and disposition to go into work of the kind we here are considering. The process of selection will probably involve considerable trial and error.

But even when the teachers who undertake the work are well suited for it, they will continue to be under emotional pressure. There will be times when the work is taxing and frustrating. There will be times when the most devoted teacher will waver. He may have doubts concerning his ability to accomplish anything worth while. Such wavering and doubt may be brought about by many factors. Even if the teacher is doing a good job, the outcomes may not be obvious. Even if the outcomes are obvious, they may still fall short of what the teacher hopes for. Whether outcomes are obvious or not, the teacher may come in for criticism from other teachers, from parents, and from pupils, who do not understand or appreciate the nature of the work that is being done and who may actively resist it.

It is therefore important to help teachers to get emotional support in maintaining their morale. One great source of help is the moral support teachers can give to one another when they are engaged in this work in the same school or in neighboring schools. Group meetings of such teachers are likely to involve a much greater sharing of feelings than occurs in the usual meeting of a teaching staff.

DIFFICULTIES OF COMMUNICATION BETWEEN EDUCATORS AND PSYCHOLOGISTS: SOME SPECULATIONS[1]

Roger G. Barker

A practical social issue of immediate personal and professional importance to many psychologists is the relationship which exists between them and the personnel of related disciplines. As an instance we may consider some social interrelations between psychologists and educators. This will serve, also, as an example of the more general problem of difficulty of communication within social groups. That this problem is of great theoretical and practical significance, there can be no doubt. Effective intra-group communication is essential to group action, and the break-down of communications is a frequent source of failure of group undertakings. Tragedies such as that which occurred at Pearl Harbor obviously are due in part to faulty communication within government organizations. Less dramatic failures are continually occurring. In the instance to be considered, difficulties of communication between psychologists and educators handicap both, for each depends in an important degree upon the other: psychologists for jobs and socially significant problems; educators for a scientific basis for school practices.

THE CULTURAL BACKGROUND OF TEACHERS

Difficulties in communication occur when the psychologist and potential educator first meet in the college classroom. Anyone who has taught child psychology to teachers and student-teachers has inevitably noted a resistance to certain findings and viewpoints in psychology and a difficulty on the part of some students in comprehending without distortions certain common ideas about the behavior of children. This is not surprising, and it is certainly not peculiar to teachers. We know a great deal about selective awareness, rationalization, compulsive behavior, repression, and other phenomena of motivation wherein it is impossible to comprehend some ideas, and possible to comprehend but not act upon others. However, little has been done in the way of specifying the conditions existing in the teaching situation which give rise to this behavior. Recent social-psychological research suggests where we should look.

The meaning of an observation depends upon its context or frame of reference, and an important source of this context is the culture of the observer. All students bring their private cultures to class with them; they interpret the facts of child behavior, for example, in accordance with their own beliefs, and with those of their families, their churches, their school boards, and their associates. Although teachers do not differ from other students here, there is evidence that teachers tend to be selected from a common cultural background, and hence tend to interpret the findings of child psychology with a common bias. Years ago Coffman (2) showed that teachers as a group come from the lower middle classes of the social structure. This is in line with the recent findings of Warner and his collaborators (3, 9) that schools

[1] From *The Journal of Educational Psychology* (Sept., 1942), Vol. 33, pp. 416–426. Reprinted by permission.

are an important channel of social mobility in our culture, and that teachers are one of the mobile groups in the population. Here is a profession where, without the usual requirements of money and family, it is possible to attain admission to higher social strata. The profession of education attracts large numbers of persons who value social achievement, and it in turn fosters these values. Besides providing immediate social advantages to persons of the lower middle classes, teaching is a well recognized route to higher professional levels. Great numbers of the population can say, "I taught for a while," and many teachers frankly consider the profession a respectable temporary occupation until something better turns up.

For these reasons, in the culture of many teachers the ideology of individual progress, attainment, betterment, and self-improvement, all defined in terms of social status, loom very large. They bring to the study of child psychology a design for living in which the test of value is social achievement. Under these circumstances important facts of child psychology are bound to be resisted. For example, the facts of unconscious motivation and the inheritance of intellectual abilities run counter to fundamental assumptions in the culture of great numbers of teachers. Such facts must, therefore, be denied, reinterpreted, or misunderstood if the pattern of teachers' lives is not to be seriously disturbed. Even the finding that such activities as play, art, literature and science, can give emotional satisfactions and serve as substitutes for thwarted needs has a very special significance in a culture where adjustment, satisfaction, and happiness do not exist apart from social attainment. Insofar as the "escape" and "releasing" effects of these activities contribute to the effectiveness of social achievement, they are considered desirable by these people, just as adequate sleep and recreation are considered desirable. But insofar as such activities contribute to the satisfaction of the individual in his present social position, and remove from him the anxiety that leads to social striving, they are considered undesirable. As a substitute for social mobility such activities are to be deprecated. Many teachers are seriously concerned about the great amount of satisfaction and lack of anxiety they find in their students. A recurring motif in the papers written by many teachers is the expression of a concern for the failure of students to take advantage of their opportunities to better themselves. The anxieties that many teachers feel most keenly come from their failure to arouse in their students the social ambitions of which they consider the students worthy. With such a system of values, it is obviously impossible for teachers to accept and act upon the suggestions of mental hygienists who hold other cultural values, and to adopt procedures that are likely to increase the sort of behavior the teachers strongly deplore.

This is but a single example. There are many other facts about the private worlds of teachers into which they must with difficulty fit the findings of child psychology. For example, the social groups from which teachers largely come tend to have strong religious convictions and standards of morality in terms of which behavior is categorized as right or wrong. One wonders what the many teachers who come from such groups and for whom such beliefs are very central make of such observations as the ego-centricity, the amorality, and sexuality of children. There is, in addition, the whole field of personal motivation, the highly individual needs that bring teachers to work with children: Substitute parenthood, easy domination, security, service, etc., all of which give the facts of child psychology very particular, personal meanings in order that teachers may use children for their own purposes.

If these assumptions are true, it is not difficult to understand why the education of teachers should be less satisfactory than that of physicians and engineers. Physicians and engineers are probably selected from social strata where there is less conflict between accepted mores and the facts with which they must deal. In addition, engineers and physicians have a much longer and more rigorous period of initial training that provides to a considerable extent for an appropriate background of viewpoints and attitudes.

Here is one of the primary facts that those who would improve teachers' knowledge of children must face. It is related to the general problem of acculturation, particularly to the question of the fate of cultural fragments introduced into new cultures. It is for students of culture change to say what, if anything, can be done about such a state of affairs, if it is desirable that something be done. Two elementary facts may be mentioned, however. First, the very short contact most teachers have with the "foreign" ideas of child psychology means that the influence of these ideas must be slight. Until teacher training in psychology is much more thorough, this state of affairs will certainly continue. Secondly, the motivation of most teachers, at least during the period of their training, is such as to insure a minimum of learning. To all but a few the required psychology courses are a necessary nuisance to be endured with a minimum of involvement in order that most attention may be devoted to chosen academic fields.

An additional aspect of the situation that makes the problem even more difficult lies in the fact that many of the aspects of the behavior of teachers with which psychologists are concerned derive from very central needs of the person, whatever the cultural background may be. Parent-child behavior is so deeply embedded in the personality structure the culture enforces from the first day of life that rational argument is relatively ineffective in modifying many aspects of it. This means that the behavior of adults toward children is so firmly built into the personality that it is in some respects compulsive. Furthermore, much of this behavior is closely related to central evaluative convictions of religion, morality and socially acceptable conduct. In our culture few facts of engineering or agriculture, for example, come into conflict with fundamental personality mechanisms, or accepted religious and social practices. Doubtless there is more conflict and resistance in the case of medical knowledge. But one can hardly think of a fact of child behavior, a technique of discipline, or a goal of child education about which most persons do not have strong, emotionally toned convictions. It appears, therefore, that many other applied scientists: engineers, physicians, agriculturalists, etc. are better able emotionally to face the facts with which they must deal than are teachers.

FORCES IN THE TEACHING SITUATION

The teacher of teachers finds that viewpoints and procedures that are fully understood, mastered, and accepted outside the teaching situation are not infrequently ignored in schoolroom practice. This suggests that, in addition to factors in the general culture which prevent teachers from accepting some facts of child psychology, there are conditions in the school situation itself which prevent them from acting upon the knowledge they have intellectually accepted. Reference will not be made here to possible administrative restraints upon particular practices, but to the structure and dynamics of the general teaching situation. This is a complicated matter, of course, but there is one aspect of the situation of teachers that accounts for much. Teachers appear to be placed in conflicting, overlapping, social situations to a greater extent than are most professional people. Teachers must be highly sensitive to the changing demands of many relatively independent groups: their classes, their colleagues, their administrators, their communities. Because of their exposed and dependent position, the behavior of teachers is very sensitive to these simultaneously acting, but independent and often conflicting influences. Consider some concrete determinants of a teacher's behavior in the classroom. First of all, there is the classroom situation: the attitude of the pupils, the requirements of the lesson, and the teacher's intentions and ideals with respect to it. At the same time the teacher's behavior is to some extent determined by the facts of the larger school situation: perhaps an uncertainty as to the attitude of the administration toward his work; a feeling of frustration, failure, and abuse because a colleague has received an "unwarranted" salary increase; or a feeling of futility over the small prospect of professional advancement. There is also the community situation which the teacher cannot escape and to which he is particularly sensitive: limitations upon his personal freedom in some political, social, and economic spheres, and coercion in others.

The fact that not all such overlapping situations enter the focus of attention during the class period does not, of course, mean that they are not operative. Recent work by Lewin and his students (5) in experimental situations and by Roethlisberger and Dickson (7) in factory situations has demonstrated that in overlapping situations where the forces are in conflict, behavior is modified even when one situation completely dominates consciousness. On the basis of such findings one could predict, for example, that a teacher's intended enthusiasm in his classroom when it overlaps with a larger school situation where disappointment and frustration are dominant, and with a community situation where coercion and insecurity are important factors, would be considerably tempered and perhaps become totally ineffective. The extent of the modification would depend upon the relative potencies of the overlapping situations and the constellation of their forces.

The importance of these aspects of the immediate situation for the improvement of educational practice is this: So long as the situations that overlap with the classroom are not taken into consideration and made to support or, at least, made not to conflict with the good intentions of the teacher, his practices will be more or less at variance with his intentions, since conscious intentions constitute only a part, and often a minor part, of the total constellation of forces acting upon him.

The experience of the Western Electric Company in Chicago in dealing with these kinds of problems in the work situation is pertinent in this connection (7). A staff of interviewers, who partly by giving opportunities for emotional expression, partly by promoting cognitive insight, and partly by securing adjustments in the work situations, have been able with remarkable success to resolve the conflicts of the overlapping work, factory, family, and community situations. These aspects of the workers' situation have been found to have a much greater influence upon productivity than the physical conditions of work. Such procedures have very great possibilities in the schools as a means of freeing the teacher to follow his best intentions in the classroom.

THE ACADEMIC STATUS HIERARCHY

Difficulties of communication exist not only between psychologists and student-teachers, but also between psychologists and their colleagues of the education departments within the colleges. The situation in great numbers of institutions is such that there is often not only lack of professional interchange, but in many cases hostility between psychologists and educators. Many education departments offer their own instruction in psychology, often duplicating courses given in the psychology departments. Even within such education departments the channels of communication between psychologists, educators, and training-school teachers are likely to be restricted, with the consequence that there is little integration between psychological principles and teaching practices.

An important source of this state of affairs is undoubtedly the status of education and psychology in the hierarchy of disciplines in the colleges. That a status hierarchy does exist is evident from even a casual acquaintance with college institutions. In general, the long-established, pure sciences and the liberal arts are near the top. Astronomy, physics, chemistry, mathematics, history, are full of prestige, they set the pattern of educational behavior for the other disciplines. Near the bottom of the hierarchy are the applied sciences and vocational subjects. Commerce, agriculture, hygiene, journalism, are in lower classes of the academic world — and amongst the lowest of these is education. There is probably some variation in the stratification from institution to institution, though without doubt a very general agreement exists.

Such hierarchies of status are recognized as characteristic of many social groups; they are in no way peculiar to academic institutions (3, 9). Recent research has revealed something of the significance of such class structuring for the behavior of the persons within the classes (4). The effect of mobility upon behavior is of especial importance in the present connection. Individuals or groups of individuals are mobile when they are in the process of changing their class identification to an upper or to a lower class. While this change of class identification is in process, the individual is in a very insecure, overlapping position. If he is upwardly mobile he is trying to throw off his attachments with the class below him and to strengthen his connections with the one above him. This process has been studied in connection with such diverse hierarchies as color stratification in Negroes (10), race stratification in the Jews (5), social and age stratification in many groups (3). In all of these cases upward mobile individuals exhibit many similarities in behavior. Three of these are of importance here: (1) antagonism toward lower class individuals with whom identification is possible; (2) antagonism toward higher class individuals who will not admit equality of status; (3) emphasis upon the symbols of class, *i.e.*, exaggeration of upper class symbols and suppression of lower class symbols.

As a relative newcomer amongst the sciences the status of psychology in the hierarchy is as yet indefinite. However, it is certainly neither in the lowest nor in the highest brackets (11). That the generality of psychologists are desirous of establishing a high academic status for their science seems inevitable. That they exhibit the same behavior as mobile persons in other class hierarchies seems inevitable also. At least such behavior is easily observed. The antagonism of psychologists to education and educators appears to be essentially the same kind of behavior as the antipathy of the "light" Negro for the dark, of adolescents for younger sibs, of the liberal Jew for the orthodox, of higher class persons for their lower class relatives. Such behavior is, of course, fully rationalized in all of these cases and its existence is frequently vehemently denied. The fact remains that in general psychologists lose academic status by fraternizing on equal professional terms with educators, and in such a case cannot be expected to do so. On the other hand, by emphasizing their ties with such upper class disciplines as mathematics, physics, and physiology, psychologists improve their status, and they cannot be expected to do otherwise. The strength of these forces toward academic acceptability in keeping individuals in low-paying jobs and working on problems of little potential significance is frequently obvious. That they should cause aloofness toward educators is in no way remarkable.

Psychologists have other antagonisms that contrast dramatically with their antagonism toward education. Medicine is undoubtedly above psychology in the professional hierarchy. However, there is much antagonism expressed by clinical psychologists toward psychiatrists. Superficially this is not unlike the criticisms expressed of educators. However, in this case the behavior appears to be on a par with the resentment of the ambitious brown Negro against the high yellow, or the contempt of the aspiring middle class person for the decadent 400. A psychologist's professional status is improved if he is accepted as an equal in a medical group; however, this infrequently happens; usually he is included only as technician or an assistant. To be excluded by those of higher-status professional disciplines is as adequate a reason for resentment as to be excluded from the tables of the best families.

The position of educators in the academic hierarchy is low, but educators are also mobile and react to the aloofness of higher class psychologists in the same way that psychologists react to the coolness of psychiatrists. There is this difference, however: The status of medical people is so secure that contact with lower class psychologists is not dangerous. Defensive reactions are therefore not necessitated. In the case of educators and psychologists, however, the insecurity of both gives rise to mutual defensive reactions that tend progressively to magnify the original schism.

This does not mean that the criticisms of psychologists of educators and *vice versa* are all groundless rationalizations; many are justified. However, professional hierarchical positions may dominate the personal relations of the individuals involved, provide a reason for nursing legitimate grievances, contribute to the failure to compromise disagreements, and, in consequence, operate as a causative factor for the poor communication between psychologists and educators in colleges.

DIFFERENCES IN EMPHASIS

Another reason for the communication difficulties of psychologists and educators may be mentioned. It appears to lie in the fact that educators and academic psychologists are very largely concerned with different phenomena, although they have frequently failed to recognize this.

Behavior is a continuum from birth to death, and to study behavior it is necessary arbitrarily to select particular segments for analysis. These may be as short as reaction times or as long as biographies. The longer segments of behavior contain the shorter, but they cannot be explained in terms of the shorter, or in terms of the concepts that are adequate to explain the shorter segments.

A teacher who catches a glimpse of a pupil on the stairs and asks, "What is that child doing?," might receive several true answers: namely, (1) flexing certain muscles and relaxing others; (2) stepping downward from the fourth to the fifth step; (3) going downstairs; (4) leaving the school building; (5) running away from school. It is obvious that a curve representing the teacher's degree of interest in these replies would rise from answer (1) to answer (5). In other words, the teacher is more interested in actions (achievement of effects) than in actones (mechanisms of achievement), to use the terms employed by Murray (6), or more in molar than in molecular behavior, to use the terms of Tolman (8). On the other hand, a curve representing the interest of the generality of academic psychologists would descend from answer (1) to answer (5). This is probably true in large part because the competence of psychologists is much greater in the field of actone than in that of actions. The triumphs of experimental psychology have been achieved in studies of sensation, perception, reflex action, conditioning, etc. Necessarily, much of the instruction in psychology must be devoted to such molecular behavior. It is true and it is important; but it does not provide a basis for an understanding of the molar behavior with which teachers must be largely concerned. Why this is true is a technical matter that cannot be considered here, but it may be illustrated by an incident from other fields.

A roving reporter in looking for a story had arrived at the railway station as a heavy freight train slowly passed through the yards. He approached a spectator who turned out to be an engineer and asked him to explain briefly and simply why the train was moving; he received this reply: "Because the force of the steam against the pistons is greater than that of the resistance of the opposing forces of gravity and friction; that is why the train is moving along the tracks." The reporter next turned to a spectator who was an economist and propounded the same question. In this case he received this reply: "That train is loaded with wheat; there's a great demand and a good price for wheat in Chicago at the present time, that is why the train is moving down the track." It is obvious that these two true explanations of different segments of the same phenomenon are in no way interchangeable, that the engineer will receive no help from the economist's explanation and *vice versa.* In terms of this analogy, it may be said that in the past psychologists have very largely given educators engineering answers to economic problems. Until this is changed the usefulness of psychology to education will remain limited.

That many psychologists desire to do something about this is evident from the frequent attempts made to integrate psychology with life and with education. One can commend this move without being unaware of the tendency to become merely popular and to present literary psychology in such books and courses. Explanations of molar behavior to be adequate must be just as strictly scientific as explanations of molecular behavior. Until psychologists can deal rigorously with the behavior with which educators must be concerned it is inevitable that educators will refuse to take the suggestions of psychologists as seriously as they should be taken.

There are other less basic reasons for the misunderstandings between academic psychologists and teachers. One of these that may deserve mention here is the confusion of viewpoints and terminologies that abounds in psychology today. It is understandable why the educator who does not have the time to reconcile one viewpoint with another in his own thinking is likely to cast a plague on all the houses of psychology after attending several courses or reading several books. This state of affairs is a product of the rapidly developing state of the science at the present time, and little can be done about it. However, an effort can be made to secure consistency in the brand of psychology taught in any sequence of practical education courses. There are undoubtedly several schools of psychology that have practical usefulness for education if followed consistently. However, the jumble of superficial viewpoints with which teachers are likely to be presented under the banner of eclecticism is likely to be of limited value.

The hypotheses which have been proposed to account for communication difficulties between psychologists and educators are based upon casual observation and are stated in terms particular to the instance considered. This consideration may serve, however, to indicate that here is a fertile field for conceptual clarification and experimentation upon a social problem of great practical and theoretical importance.

BIBLIOGRAPHY

1. Barker, Roger G., Dembo, Tamara, and Lewin, Kurt. *Frustration and Regression*. University of Iowa Studies in Child Welfare, Vol. XVIII, No. 1, 1941.
2. Coffman, Lotus D. *The Social Composition of the Teaching Population*. Teachers College, Columbia University, Contribution to Education, No. 41, 1911.
3. Davis, Allison, Gardner, Burleigh B., and Gardner, Mary B. *Deep South*. Chicago, University of Chicago Press, 1941.
4. Davis, Allison, and Dollard, John. *Children of Bondage*. Washington, American Council on Education, 1940.
5. Lewin, Kurt. "Self-hatred Among the Jews." *Contemporary Jewish Record* (1941), 4:219–232.
6. Murray, Henry A. *Explorations in Personality*. New York, Oxford University Press, 1938.
7. Roethlisberger, F. L., and Dickson, William J. *Management and the Worker*. Cambridge, Harvard University Press, 1939.
8. Tolman, Edward C. *Purposive Behavior in Animals and Man*. New York, Century Co., 1932.
9. Warner, W. Lloyd, and Lunt, Paul S. Yankee City Series, Vol. I: *The Social Life of the Modern Community*. New Haven, Yale University Press, 1941.
10. Warner, W. Lloyd, Junker, Buford H., and Adams, Walter A. *Color and Human Nature*. Washington, American Council on Education, 1941.
11. Winter, John E. "The Status of Experimental Psychology Among the Laboratory Sciences." *Science, New Series* (1942), 94:96–97.

TEACHERS AS A MINORITY GROUP[1]

Jean D. Grambs

Minority group identification carries with it certain behavioral patterns that often impede the process of integration in the total community. Likewise, this kind of self-identification interferes with adequate adjustment to the frustrations of personal and work situations, and inhibits the development of stable reactions to changing social demands. Such generalizations regarding the effect of minority group membership can accurately be applied to typical minority groups such as Negroes, Jews, and ethnic groups in which the process of Americanization has not as yet been completed. It is because minority status produces the kind of behavior that makes social adjustment so difficult that much effort in recent years has been directed toward reducing the crucial aspects of group differences. In the same way, workers in the field of education have been seeking ways and means for making teachers more effective in the larger community, as well as assuring the teacher as an individual of a satisfying and mature personal development. Juxtaposition of the fact that teachers on the whole are not as effective

[1] From *The Journal of Educational Sociology*, February, 1949, pp. 400–405. Reprinted with permission.

persons as the profession needs, and the description given above of the effects of minority group status, produces an interesting relationship; the hypothesis may be advanced that one cause for the lack of professional achievement by teachers as a group may be due to the fact that teachers' behavior in some respects is restricted in the same way as is that of "recognized" minority groups.

There are, obviously, two phases to the problem: one, the status of education as a profession as viewed from the outside, and, second, the reactions of the teacher as an individual to some of the unique aspects of the teaching situation. The professional world, on the whole, places the teacher in the lower brackets in terms of status recognition. Shaw's phrase, "Those who can, do; those who can't, teach," reflects the scorn of other academic disciplines for teachers, and particularly of course for male teachers. The teacher understands this rating, and tends to accept it. Minority groups typically occupy inferior status positions in a hierarchy; while teachers may be superior to others in the social scale, in terms of the professions, teachers are of low status. This is analogous in effect to the Negro who considers himself above the Jew, but feeling superior in this fashion in no way compensates for the rankling of unfair status in the hierarchy which is subjectively considered most significant, the *non*-Jewish white community. Thus the teacher, while superior to the majority of other occupational groups, is not at all happy about the low status of education in the professional hierarchy.

How does the teacher react to this low status valuation? There is constant belittling of the accomplishments of education on the one hand, and inordinate taking on of credit for significant functions on the other. When discussing their jobs with those outside the profession, teachers will make cynical and derogatory remarks about their work, the school system, other teachers, and the important ideas in education, even though they themselves do not necessarily act in terms of this cynicism within the privacy of their classrooms. Some teachers, however, even carry this point of view to the student, discouraging their better students from entering such a socially unrewarding profession. One of the problems in recruiting superior individuals to the profession has been this very factor of the classroom teacher who deliberately (or unconsciously) counsels students against entering the teaching profession. Such attitudes are similar to the anti-Semitism of Jews who will try to identify with the higher status non-Jewish community by being overcritical of other Jews, with whom identification means status loss. The cynical, seemingly embittered teacher who makes derogatory remarks about the profession may be in part motivated by this need to show others that he is not a "real" member of a low status group—rather an unwilling and superior captive—and thus not to be condemned along with those who *really* are teachers!

While teachers complain bitterly about poor financial returns, and accuse society of failure to appreciate their valuable function, it is difficult to get educators to act together as a group to remedy this situation. There are innumerable teachers' organizations, but few are marked by strong feelings of group solidarity. Leadership is usually conciliatory and accommodating. It is not easy to get very many of the members to take an active part in group planning and in carrying out programs. Teachers talk enviously of the strength of the American Medical Association and yearn for some sort of professional organization that could speak with as much power in the realm of education, but the creation of such a professional body has so far not occurred. A feeling of inferiority prevents a number of teachers from allowing themselves to be identified with teachers' organizations. Within the groups themselves, "minority group behavior" often can be seen in the innocuousness of social action recommended, the oft-expressed fear of offending public opinion, and the considerable bickering and vying for status that goes on among the various areas of teaching specialization. Minority status identification results therefore in the lack of organized professional direction, confusion of aims, and an extreme sensitivity to public appraisal.

A further element in the picture that restricts the productive output of the teacher is the frustrations involved in rarely being able to be publicly successful. The successes of the profession are limited; little public acclaim is awarded the teacher who is good, certainly little financial reward is possible. Achieving the status of a teacher—and it is an upward mobility for many individuals in the profession—also means a dead end. There is no higher status that one can acquire. For women teachers in particular, the classroom is frequently the limit of their social recognition. Men can perhaps more readily become principals, superintendents, and athletic coaches. This is similar to the Negro who, no matter how much he succeeds in the fields of sport, art, or letters, still is unable to shake off the stigma of caste. Success, then, is never complete, only partial.

The behavior of teachers as members of a minority group is an outgrowth of other aspects of the role of the teacher in the community. The teacher in the small community is conspicuous. Everyone knows who the teacher is; children are everywhere, and seem to be countless little spies reporting on what the teacher is doing. The typical reaction is that of the young teacher who remarked, "I feel as if I lived in a goldfish bowl." Although neighbors and friends observe each other casually in their daily routines, teachers are subjected to many more such observations, since their range of acquaintances is wider than for most others in the community. All 500 children of a school will eventually know Miss Smith, the fifth-grade teacher; many of the parents will know her. What she wears, what she does, and whom she is seen with are commented on by many people. It is no wonder that Miss Smith feels conspicuous. This sort of conspicuousness is, in some respects, similar to that felt by the Negro; wherever he goes he is immediately "seen." The teacher likewise is always recognized as "teacher." And recognition in the context of the American Puritan tradition also implies judgment. To be known is flattering if one is of high status, otherwise it is hardly to be desired.

Most teachers who enter the profession are unprepared for this kind of public living. To be suddenly the object of general scrutiny is acceptable and may even be pleasant for a few months; thereafter it often becomes a burden, and to many individuals a constant source of irritation and confusion. The insistent demand by teachers that they be allowed to live "normal" private lives stems as much from this feeling of being watched as from actual interferences with teachers' lives. The pressure to behave discreetly, while overt in some communities, is a subjective impression on the part of the teacher as well; he knows he is being watched. It is thus difficult to throw off a feeling of self-consciousness and the pressure of acting "properly"; this in turn frustrates the spontaneous reactions of the teacher as an individual and often may be the cause that turns the teacher into an irritable, defensive, rigid person.

Thus there are two distinct elements that give credence to the idea that teacher behavior derives in some measure from feelings of minority group membership: first, low status in a given hierarchy where high status is desired, and, second, conspicuousness above that of the average person. It is suggested that these two factors interfere with the teacher's ability to respond adequately to the professional and personal situations in which he finds himself.

If the reasoning is sound, what can be done about the problem? Persons who go into the teaching profession are not prepared for the conspicuousness of their position in the community. Living in the public eye comes as a shock, and the individual as a teacher is not ready to deal with this phenomenon positively. In the training of teachers some consideration of this difficulty might be appropriate in order to equip the new teacher with some psychological expectation of what will occur. The selection of individuals stable enough to take continued scrutiny is another factor to be considered. The problem of the young unmarried teacher who, during his first teaching years, is also seeking a marriage partner is an added complication.

The other aspect of this problem, that of the low status of the teaching profession, is part of the larger picture of the academic hostility to education. Both student and faculty opinion militate against the effectiveness of education instruction. To deny the existence of this negative opinion will do no good; to recognize the problem with the students themselves may go a long way toward reducing the hostility of the students. It is just "not the thing" to approve too highly of education classes; students genuinely interested in education become very perturbed by the atmosphere of negative criticism, and often themselves succumb to it. Against this pressure of group opinion, one course of action would again be to recognize the existence of the problem, and within the courses themselves seek to do the most effective possible job of education consistent with the theories expounded. While poor education may go on unnoticed in other academic departments, it is highly undesirable that education classes be vulnerable to the charge of "poor education." To be guilty of such charges is like admitting to the general public that all the statements of inferiority are, in fact, true, and that education instructors must continue to act like inferior beings. Overcompensation, trying to be more academic and "scientific" than the most academic department is unfortunately a symptom of minority status identification.

The preceding analysis of the status and role of teachers from the viewpoint developed by those who have studied minority group behavior should be subject to careful research and study. A better understanding of the social status of the teacher would in time, it is hoped, lead to the development of teachers who can be effective in the profession to the degree that society so urgently needs. Eventually a self-concept for teachers free of minority group identification should evolve.

HOW PROFESSIONAL AM I? [1]

Grace I. Kauffman

A Selftest Designed to Emphasize the Positive

Directions: Indicate your selfappraisal on each item by placing a dot on the line to the right somewhere between "low" and "high." When you have finished, connect the dots with straight lines.

LOW HIGH

I. Teacher-pupil Relationships

Do I—

[1] Individualize pupils in my teaching? ....

[2] Try to find out their capacities and abilities? ....

[3] Refrain from the use of sarcasm? ....

[4] Avoid embarrassing a child before the group? ....

[5] Create an atmosphere of friendliness and helpfulness in the classroom? ....

[6] Provide for democratic participation of pupils? ....

[7] Try to improve my methods? ....

II. Teacher-teacher Relationships

Do I—

[1] Recognize accomplishments of colleagues and tell them so? ....

[2] Refrain from adverse criticism of a colleague's method or work except when requested by a school official for the welfare of the school? ....

[1] From *Journal of the National Education Association,* April, 1950, p. 286. Reprinted with permission.

LOW HIGH

[3] Refrain from blaming the previous teacher for inadequate preparation of pupils? ....

[4] Avoid letting jealousy of a good teacher adversely affect my personality development? ....

[5] Avoid unkind gossip *of* and *among* colleagues? ....

[6] Have a respectful attitude toward the subject-matter and work of other fields? ....

[7] Refrain from interfering between another teacher and pupil unless called upon for advice or assistance? ....

[8] Avoid criticism of an associate before his students and before other teachers? ....

III. Teacher-administrator Relationships

Do I—

[1] Talk things over with the administrator next above me? ....

[2] Support the policies and programs of my principal and superintendent? ....

[3] Avoid criticism of my principal and superintendent in public? ....

	LOW	HIGH

IV. Teacher-board of Education Relationships

Do I—

[1] Support the policies of my board? ....

[2] Have the goodwill of my board as a person of professional integrity? ....

[3] Respect my contract obligations? ....

[4] When contemplating a change of position, make a formal request thru my superintendent to the board of education for release from my contract? ....

[5] Give sufficient notice when asking for release from my contract? ....

[6] Use my local professional organization to convey constructive suggestions and criticisms to the board thru my superintendent? ....

V. Teacher-public Relationships

Do I—

[1] Remember that I am a public servant? ....

[2] Try to exemplify to the public the best qualities of a teacher? ....

[3] Participate in community activities that are not directly connected with my profession? ....

[4] Contribute of my time and/or money to the various community drives? (Community Chest, and the like.) ....

[5] Show by my life that education makes people better citizens and better neighbors? ....

VI. Teacher-profession Relationships

Do I—

[1] Keep myself informed about best practices in my field? ....

[2] Belong willingly to my professional organizations—local, state, national? ....

[3] Contribute of my time and talents to my professional organizations? ....

[4] Accept responsibility in my professional organizations? ....

[5] Help to make possible a democratic approach to school administrative authorities thru teacher organization channels? ....

[6] Speak proudly of the importance of the service of education to society? ....

[7] Maintain my efficiency by reading, study, travel, or other means which keep me informed about my profession and the world in which I live? ....

[8] Dignify my profession? ....

[9] Encourage able and sincere individuals to enter the teaching profession? ....

[10] Avoid using pressure on school officials to secure a position or to obtain favors? ....

[11] Refuse compensation in the selection of text-

	LOW	HIGH
books or other supplies in the choice of which I have some influence?	....	
[12] Refrain from sending for sample copies of texts merely to build up my own library?	....	
[13] Refrain from accepting remuneration for tutoring pupils of my own classes?	....	

Interpretation: If your profile is reasonably straight and close to "high," you are professional and your school and community should be very proud of you! If your profile zigzags and is close to "low," then you probably need remedial exercises in ethical practices to improve your professional outlook. You should: [1] Concentrate on the ethical principles on which you rated yourself the lowest. [2] A few months from now take this test again, using a different color to draw the connecting lines. Check to see whether you have improved.

A BILL OF RIGHTS FOR STUDENT TEACHERS[1]

J. Martin Taylor

Bills of rights have an abiding and profound place in the hearts of men. From King John's capitulation on the banks of the Runnymede in 1215 through the French Rights of Man in 1789 such declarations have been political in nature and have had their origin in the minds of the would-be recipients of such rights. Our American Bill of Rights of the crucial revolutionary era was no exception.

Since World War II a bill of rights has served the "G.I." well, and is rapidly becoming an American institution. But the nature of the term has changed. No longer is it characterized by an origin based on agitation. This is significant, it points up the progress we have made in moving from revolutionary to evolutionary processes. Jones' Bills of Rights for School Administrators and School Board Members are not a result of clamoring by the members of those respected bodies. Schorling's Bill of Rights for Teachers, and Andrews' Bill of Rights for Supervising Teachers are both undoubtedly the result of foresight and educational statesmanship; but has the pendulum swung too far? The change in method is good, the change in origin is probably unwholesome. We find rights being handed down to groups whose membership should have an active and direct role in developing them.

It is certainly significant and school people should be concerned with the fact that throughout an earnest movement to improve schools in general and teacher education in particular, the last bill of rights to appear is that for student teachers—the very people for whom the entire teacher education program exists! It is late enough to suggest a bill of rights for them. The following rights are well rooted in psychological principles and provide implications for the administration of teacher-preparation programs.

1. *The right to be wanted.* Never should a student teacher be assigned to a supervising teacher who is unsympathetic or "lukewarm" to teacher education in general or to student teachers in particular.

2. *The right to choose.* Some degree of choice should be allowed student teachers in the supervising teacher with whom they will work and when practicable, in the lo-

[1] From *Phi Delta Kappan, November,* 1953, p. 120. Reprinted with permission.

cation, size, and type of laboratory situation.

3. *The right to readiness.* Having met the requisite professional courses is not always assurance of readiness to teach. The student teacher has a right to some assurance of success before he is placed in a teaching situation.

4. *The right to adequate and varied experience.* Not only should the classroom experiences be rich and varied but the student teacher is also entitled to an adequate sampling of extra-class and extra-school experiences of the type and nature in which he will be expected to engage as a full-time teacher.

5. *The right to an accounting.* At regular intervals the student teacher should have an evaluation of his teaching. Such appraisals should be frank, businesslike, and constructive.

6. *The right to a reasonable load.* In fairness to himself and to the public-school pupils whom he teaches, a student teacher should have the right so to schedule his work that he has ample time for his laboratory work.

7. *The right to transportation.* When the laboratory is off-campus and commutation is necessary, the student teacher has a right to expect that convenient and comfortable transportation be provided.

8. *The right to professional guidance.* The student teacher has a right to frequent individual conferences with both the supervising teacher and the institutional supervisor for planning work, for discussing observed lessons, and for problems incident to teaching.

9. *The right to professionalized instruction.* In professional and academic preparation the student teacher has a right to instructors whose methods of teaching are exemplary of those he is expected to use.

10. *The right to share in evaluation.* As a culmination of his regular self-evaluations the student teacher has a right to participate in the final evaluation of his laboratory experience.

IS TEACHING A PROFESSION?[1]

R. Roderick Palmer

Student teachers, administrators, and other educators at the University of Maryland recently outlined and studied various factors which focus attention again to the question: Is teaching a profession? Some considerations basic to the investigation of the numerous facets of this question were:

Failure of teachers en masse to affiliate with local and national professional organizations.

Apathy on the part of teachers en masse to becoming highly professionally-minded.

Lack of cohesion, solidarity, and support of the profession by teachers affiliated with professional organizations.

Division of teacher groups on issues involving membership, representation, and acquisition of benefits for the profession as seen in the work of teacher unions and local and state teacher organizations.

The wide divergence between administrator and teacher groups.

Failure of teachers en masse to replenish periodically their educational preparation through additional study and schooling.

The throes and woes teachers exude and experience in "in-service training" and opening of school "pre-planning" despite the special pay or provisions made by various systems.

[1] From *Phi Delta Kappan*, January, 1953, pp. 139–140, 142. Reprinted with permission.

Failure of teachers en masse in subject-matter areas to affiliate with national organizations specifically concerned with those respective areas.

Failure of teachers en masse to subscribe to educational periodicals.

Certain segments of the profession not always considered on level with other segments, i.e., elementary education.

Lack of nation-wide professional esprit de corps among school personnel as exhibited by personality clashes and professional jealousies.

Failure of teachers and administrators alike in establishing and supporting a nation-wide system of interneships for teachers.

Lack of evidence that the teaching profession on the national level is in a state of flux; that is, constant changes, improvements, higher standards, and momentous and pointed cases which indicate the fast pace and growing esteem of a profession.

Use of teaching as a stepping stone to entering other professions.

Failure of the profession to expend its best efforts in recruitment and pre-selection of teachers.

Inasmuch as these indictments offer diversified opportunities for arguments, causes, and answers, it should be said in the outset that the term "profession" carries with it many ramifications. Examine a few definitions of a profession:

A *profession* is an occupation involving relatively long and specialized preparation on the level of higher education and governed by a special code of ethics.[2]

A *code of ethics*, professional: (1) a statement of ideals, principles, and standards of professional (as distinguished from personal) conduct approved by the professional group and voluntarily adhered to by its members as individuals; (2) A set of standard of professional conduct tacitly accepted and followed by members of the profession.[3]

Codes of ethics are important agencies for social control. . . . Hence it is that the ideal of all the professions is public service and not monetary gain. The constructive aim of each of the professions must therefore be the public good. The member of each of the professions has as his means of livelihood the heritage of the ages in his science. His earning power and his opportunity for immortality of influence depend upon the careful work of countless predecessors. The training necessary to a mastery of a professional gives the opportunity, but not the reason for enforcing high standards of conduct throughout the profession.[4]

Western civilization recognizes a profession as a vocation founded upon prolonged and specialized intellectual training which enables a particular service to be rendered.[5]

These statements illumine certain qualifications the teaching profession demands of its members. Other factors that can be read in these definitions are: prolonged education and preparation, secured either at universities or teacher education institutions, during interneship, or in "in-service" training, and following; need for an esprit de corps and a rigid code of ethics for members of the profession; need for cohesion, solidarity, and support of the profession; need for continued raising of standards; and need for highly professionally-minded personnel.

Lack of full-scale affiliation with national and local teacher organizations, the wide divergence between teacher-administrator groups, and the problem of whether to support teacher unions or local teacher organizations raise the question of the effi-

[2] Carter V. Good, *Dictionary of Education*, New York, McGraw-Hill Book Co., 1945, p. 310.

[3] *Ibid.*, p. 80.

[4] *The Annals of the American Academy of Political and Social Sciences* (1922), Vol. 104, p. vii.

[5] *Encyclopedia of Social Sciences*, New York, The Macmillan Co., 1937, p. 476.

cacy of movements geared to reach professional levels and ideals. Professional educational associations were formed in the middle of the 19th century; these did much to co-ordinate methods of education and to improve professional standards of teachers.[6] Today, statistics show the existence of hundreds of such organizations. But the number of employed teaching personnel who are not members of these organizations is appalling. Take a look at the medical, clerical and legal professions. One will find a different story. This assertion is true not only as far as affiliation is concerned but in solidarity, preparation, qualifications for membership, allegiance to ethics and ideals, and evidences of constant effort expended toward advancement and improvement.

The question of the status of the teaching profession is illuminated by this statement of the National Education Association:

Public-school teaching is a profession for which a certificate, or license, is required by state law as a condition of admission. In practically every state the kinds of certificates, the qualifications required for each kind, their issuance, renewal, exchange, revocation are matters of state law or state board of education regulation.

Most states have many kinds of certificates related to the grade level or subject the teacher expects to teach. Different qualifying conditions are required for each type of certificate in addition to the general conditions such as age, proof of good health, oath of allegiance, and evidence of good moral character. A certificate is evidence of professional preparation.

Requirements for admission to the teaching profession need to be standardized so that the qualifications for certification, especially for elementary teachers, are more nearly uniform among the states because the standing of the profession is determined as much by the inadequately prepared teachers as by those who have earned graduate degrees. Teachers who hold emergency certificates should be required to qualify for regular certificates because the prestige of the teaching profession is limited by its admission standards.[7]

Robert H. Morrison, assistant commissioner for higher education in New Jersey, discusses the question of the teaching profession. His conclusions are:

Teaching has attained the following characteristics of a profession: (1) Teachers are motivated primarily by their desire to serve others. (2) The success of teachers is not measured by the amount of salary they receive. (3) Teachers constantly strive to improve their competence. (4) Teachers control the standards for issuing licenses to beginning teachers. (5) Teachers practice a high code of ethics.[8]

This noted educator says further:

Teaching has not yet fully attained professional status in that: (1) Teachers in many communities have not based their professional training on a period of preprofessional education which is both liberal and intellectual in nature. (On the basis of preliminary training teaching has attained professional status in some communities but is seriously deficient in meeting this standard in the nation and particularly in the elementary grades. Nineteen states have laws and certification regulations which require four years of college training of all teachers before initial certification. Nearly all states require college graduation before initial certification for high school teachers. In some states, high school graduates may qualify for certification to teach in elementary grades.)

[6] *Encyclopedia Britannica*, Chicago, University of Chicago (1948), Vol. 7, p. 1007, "Educational Associations."

[7] National Education Association, *Research Bulletin*, "Teachers in the Public Schools," Washington, National Education Association, Dec., 1949, p. 130.

[8] Robert H. Morrison, *NEA Journal*, "The Teaching Profession," March, 1950.

(2) Teachers in large numbers have not accepted the responsibility for interesting the most capable youth in teaching as a profession.[9]

In defense of many of the indictments projected for discussion herein, it may be said that in the United States the Federal government has no authority to require standard courses of study, organization, standards, ethics, teacher training, management, methods or finance as in those countries where education is directed by the central government; yet a United States system has grown up through the zeal of teachers who have disregarded state boundaries to join with their co-workers in conferences and in educational investigation. The result has been that educational methods and standards, materials, processes and attitudes have become nearly uniform.

[9] *Ibid.*, p. 101.

Authorities have pointed out that owing to the great number of persons employed in public school teaching, the wide territory over which they are scattered, the inadequate preparation of many of them, it is difficult to develop and to maintain a thoroughly well-organized professional consciousness, expressing itself in the recognition of a definite series of professional ideals and an explicit code of professional ethics. Though a number of local teachers organizations in the United States have formulated statements of professional ideals and codes of professional ethics there is for American teachers as a whole, nothing similar to the "Principles of Medical Ethics" of the American Medical Association, or the "Principles of Professional Practice and the Canons of Ethics" formulated by the American Institute of Architects.

VARIETIES OF PRESTIGE AND OF DISREPUTE[1]

Willard Waller

DISCUSSION AND ANALYSIS

The late Willard Waller was one of the most original sociologists to take a look at the process of education. His volume *The Sociology of Teaching,* though now out of print, is a classic of its kind. So astute were his insights, so penetrating was his language, so comprehensive were his observations, that his work truly stands alone as a description of the inner workings of the school as an institution.

How pervasive is the problem of status! Here we see it in terms of the prestige of a teacher. Davis and Havighurst look at it later in terms of child growth. We see it again in the career of the Chicago schoolteacher in the article by Becker. Burton analyzes the social class system—a status system—as it affects school programs. And certainly the problem of school sororities as reported by Taves in Chapter 13 arises from the desire of individuals to seem better, to have more prestige, than others. How do you see persons motivated by the need for status and prestige? What incidents can you observe now that substantiate Waller's analysis?

[1] Abridged from Willard Waller, *The Sociology of Teaching,* chap. 16, "Varieties of Prestige and Disrepute," pp. 247–278. Copyright, 1932, by Willard Waller. Reprinted by permission of the publisher, John Wiley and Sons, Inc.

Prestige is what makes the leader different from anybody else. It is not a real quality, but a consequence of the way in which those who are under his sway think about a particular leader.

Prestige is carried by social images to which the leader is assimilated. Flesh-and-blood humans do not conform to these prestige-carrying patterns, but are made over into them by the dream-work of idealization. The leader is always made over in the minds of his followers. What fits the pattern they have decided upon for him is kept. What does not fit is thrown away. So it occurs that every man's leader is a man after his own heart, and no man lives in a universe populated by heroes who exceed him in complexity of mental organization. Prestige is a quality of the whole arising from the way in which the parts of the hero are fitted together.

In unrestricted social life, the varieties of prestige-carrying images are infinite. In the institution they are fewer, because only certain types of images can sift through the institutional network. Within every institution certain typical images are the usual carriers of prestige or its opposite.

We leave aside the questions of the origin of social images, of their relation to the imagined qualities they carry, and of their effect upon the contact human beings have with each other. We turn now to a consideration of certain social images to which school teachers are assimilated. These images are configurations, or patterns, into which the teacher's personality is organized in the child's mind. Some of the images existed before the teacher came into the life of the particular youngster; these were superimposed upon the teacher from the early experience of the child, particularly his experience of his parents, and relevant attitudes were transposed with the images. Other images appear to have been manufactured on the spot from the materials at hand. It is our purpose here to be thoroughly inductive, and to present descriptions of these organizations of ideas and attitudes rather than interpretations of them. That important and unsolved problems of theory are connected with the social image is clear, but we have not here the space, nor do we presume the ability, to make any contributions to them.

Let us consider first those social images whose value to the teacher is a positive one. Some images which carry prestige when the teacher is assimilated to them are: (1) the parent substitute, (2) the image of the cultural or social ideal, (3) the image of the officer and the gentleman, (4) the image of the patriarch, (5) the image of the kindly adult, and (6) the image of the love object. These images are not always clearly distinguishable, but we can roughly classify teachers as deriving prestige from one or more of the images just noted.

When the child assimilates his teacher to one of his parents, attitudes are transferred from teacher to parent. Men and women teachers acquire meaning for the child, in so far as they do acquire meaning, in terms of the parent to whom they are assimilated. The man teacher, as in after life the employer, the doctor, and the priest, among others, is assimilated to the father image. If the father is feared, the teacher is feared with a fear that emanates from no personal experience of him. If the father is hated, the teacher is royally hated, since he may be made to serve as a convenient outlet for a father hatred which the child may not wish to admit to himself. The woman teacher is frequently assimilated to the mother. If the attitude toward the mother is one of unalloyed affection, then the attitude of the child toward his teacher will tend to reproduce the same undivided pattern. If the mother is thought of as a thwarting agent, the child will clearly see the thwarting activities of the teacher and will treat her accordingly. Women teachers, especially in the early grades, find it a very convenient technique to play the part of the mother to their pupils, and apparently there are no very serious objections to it. Women teachers are also occasionally assimilated to the father image.

The discussion of the cultural or social ideal as a prestige-carrying image has been anticipated in the discussion of the social background of the teacher. Social classes exist in all societies, and the admiration of each class for those above is one of the fundamental social facts. A teacher enjoys prestige derived from this source if he manages to categorize as a member of the upper classes. Students may dislike a teacher who manifestly does not belong to their own group, but they hold him none the less in awe. In the rural districts, where learning is not widely diffused, the school teacher is often held in near reverence because he is a learned man, but to be accurate we must remark that this attitude is not wholly a matter of class feeling, being in part produced by the superstitious veneration of the unlettered for one who knows the esoteric lore of books. The native American teacher has great prestige in immigrant districts because he was born in this country, and this seems a purer case of respect for the cultural ideal than the former example. In the slums, also, pupils who have had experience only of slatternly and dirty women will often venerate and well-nigh worship their clean and well-dressed teacher. It may be argued that prestige due to the supposed superiority of one social class over another is not to be had in a democratic society, but this is not true. Because of the great social mobility of American society both parents and teachers set much store by a person who embodies upper-class qualities, and whom they can use as a model of imitation. Lower-class parents and lower-class students tend to see the problems of the upper-class teachers in terms of their own daily dilemmas, and to judge these teachers by their own unreal standards of what ladies and gentlemen ought to be; many amusing situations and some tragic ones arise from this fact, but on the whole the masses judge fairly both the person and his qualities, and appropriate only those qualities, as they respect only those persons, that may be of some use to them.

Some teachers acquire prestige quite like that of the army officer. We may therefore speak of them as conforming to the image of the officer and the gentleman. The prestige of the officer has a long tradition behind it, and it usually assumes a definite form. The officer is a member of the ruling group, as such different from enlisted men and set off from them as the members of self-conscious ruling groups always are set off from those they rule. The officer represents the dominant group; he must cast his personality into that mold whenever he is in the presence of members of the subordinate group. The officer is made of finer clay than men, certainly of different clay. He wears better clothes than the enlisted man, and different clothes. His clothes are different to distinguish him from the men and they are better to help him maintain his prestige. Neatness is required of enlisted men, but the officer must attain in this respect an unbelievable perfection; who is not immaculate is no officer. The officer must live like a gentleman. He must stop in a good hotel. He must eat in the better restaurants. He must smoke expensive cigarettes. He must travel on the Pullman. He carries no packages. He engages in gentlemanly sports and avocations. He does not consort with women to whom privates have access. He can go to the head of a queue but he cannot shine his own shoes. The officer never slops over. Certain ceremonies of respect are due him. All these things serve to mark the officer off from the men. Very important are the things the officer cannot do. It is what one does not do that determines whether he is a gentleman or not. As James puts it, "To ignore, to disdain to consider, to overlook, are the essence of the 'gentleman.'" One who is an officer and a gentleman is distinguished from all others by a certain kind of poise, a characteristic "seeking-avoiding balance," an inhibition of action and reservation of opinion which enables the individual to preserve the integrity of his personality in crisis situations. The person who most lacks this poise is the diffuse and poorly balanced extrovert.

Likewise a teacher who is erect, a little stiff, who dresses with a quiet good taste and is scrupulously neat, who takes the respect paid him as his right, who is always the poised and inhibited member of the ruling class, who uses the technique of command skillfully and always keeps his distance—a teacher of this sort acquires a prestige which is the first cousin of the prestige of the army officer. Because of the almost complete cessation of human intercourse which this prestige requires, it is perhaps unfortunate for the school room, but it is nevertheless important in the schools as they are.

Prestige of a special sort usually attaches to the patriarch in the schools. This is prestige derived from association with the father image, in all probability, but it is prestige which not uncommonly exceeds the prestige of the father image (perhaps because it is less ambivalent than the prestige of the real father). The typical case seems to be that of the elderly man who takes a fatherly interest in all his students, controls by influence only, applauds achievement but does not always insist upon details, and excites the liveliest affection in all his students. It may be that he teaches with unparalleled incompetence, but his students hear him gladly and always insist that they have learned much from him. His very foibles, his very weaknesses, his inability to be severe, his willingness to be sidetracked from the lesson, and his absent-mindedness on examination day are great points in his favor. These elder teachers play a very important rôle in the impressment of mores, and it could easily be argued that they choose the better part, that what they lose in academic efficiency they gain in personal influence. Many a school system contains such a patriarch, but there is rarely room for more than one in any system. Colleges and universities develop a cult about the school patriarch. His sayings, even the bitter ones, his anecdotes, his whimsies, his kind deeds, and the memory of his face and voice are passed down reverently from one generation to the next. It is noteworthy that age alone does not make a patriarch. It is rather certain personal qualities which make one known and remembered as "the old man," and by no means all old men have those qualities. There are naturally many more persons who have certain elements of patriarchal effectiveness than persons who conform to the pure type. The pure type is relatively rare, and is therefore, for our purpose, not very important, but the patriarchal rapport is not rare. Witness the number of teachers of whom students speak, jestingly but not without respect, as "the old man." Even those teachers with a mixed form of the patriarchal rapport are very important to students, for they furnish them an opportunity to express symbolically their emotions toward their own fathers. Even women teachers are sometimes known to embody a mixed form of patriarchal authority.

Another important image sometimes imposed upon the teacher, or formed about his personality, is that of the kindly and understanding adult. The image has certain overtones from either the father or the mother. If the home life of the child is happy, the kindly teacher may derive elements of prestige from both parents. Sometimes, however, especially where the child's relationship with his parents is not fortunate, the kindly teacher becomes very important without such reenforcement. In such a case the teacher becomes emotionally significant simply because we grow into a relationship that is pleasant and satisfying and away from one that is not. Usually the understanding and kindly adult is the praising adult as well. It is part of the technique of a certain kind of social work to find something that the child can do well and then to praise him for it. This involves giving the child the impression that one understands him and appreciates his real qualities. Slightly different is the rapport established by the sympathetic adult. This is the adult who attempts to win the child's confidence, to listen to the story of his troubles, and endeavors to let the child know that he realizes the nature of his difficulties and feels with him in them. This rapport is likely to be very strong on account of the transference mechanism. Because it is so very strong it is a little dangerous for the child, who is then unduly susceptible to any injury which the teacher, as a teacher, might work upon him.

The whole matter of control by praise is puzzling and a bit paradoxical. Where it is wisely carried on, it may result in the most happy relations between students and teachers. Where it is unwisely applied it is absurdly ineffective and ultimately very damaging to the student. Praise must always be merited, and it must alway be discreet, else all standards disappear. Cheap praise both offends and disappoints, and it breaks down the distinction between good and bad performances. Praise must always be measured; it must not resort to superlatives, for superlatives give the comfortable but deadening sense of a goal attained. Such praise as is used must open the way to development and not close it. Praise must always be sincere, for otherwise it is very difficult to make it seem sincere, and if it does not seem sincere it fails to hearten. Praise as a means of control must be adapted to particular students. It is a device to be used frequently but only on a fitting occasion rather than an unvaried policy. Control by a rapport based upon sympathy likewise calls for delicate distinctions. Sympathy, to be of value, must not be the facile emotionalism of a fool, but the measured feeling of somebody who completely understands. One of the uses of understanding is to know when one is being imposed upon.

The category of the love object is one which may have either positive or negative value for the teacher. To make one's self a love object to students is a technique which has its greatest utility in the first few grades of school. Teachers of primary grades may apparently control their students most easily and most pleasantly by making themselves acceptable mother substitutes. This rapport is rapidly replaced, for the majority of students, by the traditional order of dominance and subordination with social distance, but for a few years more the teacher may retain her position as a love object in spite of the interposition of distance, shaping up then as a resplendent goddess to be worshipped from afar off. Even in high school, women teachers sometimes profit by going to some pains to categorize favorably as women; subtle adaptations of dress and manner may allow them to do this without losing their effectiveness in the teaching rôle. They must, of course, surround themselves with sufficient distance to remain far off and mysterious. This rapport is often of great utility in the management of high-school boys, whose idealism and chivalry may be utilized by such a technique when they would rebel at more obvious attempts to exploit them. One of the most important values of prestige as a love object comes from an abnormality of sex life, from the homosexual crushes which high-school girls, particularly, conceive for their women teachers. Women willing to play upon these girls of the Schwarmerei age have no difficulty in obtaining a following in any high school.

The disrepute into which teachers fall, the hatred which they beget, and the contempt which they sometimes arouse, may likewise be thought of as the product of certain personal configurations into which they fit. We turn now to a consideration of the more common of the unfavorable categories.

One of these is the easy mark. There are some teachers who can be put upon; they are easy marks. From the easy mark a student can get a good grade without working for it, or he can commit an offense in his presence and remain unpunished, or he can offer him a personal affront without harm, or get off from an imposed punishment with a flimsy excuse or a half-hearted apology. Sometimes personal qualities of the highest value may make a teacher an easy mark; excessive amiability may make him suffer too many affronts or be too charitable, a highly sympathetic nature may betray him to impostors, or a keen sense of human values may make it difficult for him to administer routine discipline to the children fed into the hopper of the educational system. Or it may be a trait of a different nature that betrays him, a lack of courage which he tries to hide beneath a pose of good nature, a lack of mentality which enables students easily to hoodwink him, or a lack of understanding of juvenile social life which prevents him from knowing what it is all about. Whatever the cause, the results are the same; students do not respect and they quite possibly hate such a teacher. The catastrophe is perhaps not so complete in cases of the first sort as in those of the second, for teachers who fail by reason of their virtues may have other virtues to redeem them, or compensating vices. Perhaps the worst case is that of the person who lacks courage to face the barbarism of young persons in school, for his attempt to mask his fear beneath an amiable exterior never quite succeeds and he is ultimately found out.

To the young teacher, one of the most disillusioning discoveries that he makes about the social realities of school life is that teachers are often made to suffer for their virtues. In a common-sense world, it would seem that amiable and sympathetic teachers, teachers who try to apply the golden rule in the school room, would have a high reputation in the eyes of their students. But they rarely do, and they never do in the orthodox school unless they are able to form some sort of compromise between friendliness and dignity. It is painful to see fellow teachers whom one knows to be persons of unusual qualities in disrepute with students because of those qualities, painful to see them suffer because they are genial and sympathetic, painful to see the evidences of disrespect and hatred which students give them. The young teacher casts about for a reason. It is not easy to find. Part of the answer may be made by reference to the general disrespect which young persons in our culture have for a person who impresses them as "soft," and this explanation has particular weight because of the traditional patterns of social interaction in the school; the teacher's personality must be a little hard if it is to survive the strain of the hard situation in which the teacher is placed. A related principle is that the competence of teachers is judged by reference to other teachers, and a teacher who does not do as others do, or as others would obviously like to do, is judged incompetent. Since most teachers are strict, one who is not strict does not know his business; either he does not know that he ought to be strict or he does not know how to be strict. In either case he is incompetent. He who would be good to students must first "sell them the idea." The definition of the situation is so clear in most classrooms, in terms of dominance and subordination, strictness, mutual antagonism, offences and punishment, that it is not possible for any but a most unusual teacher to adjust his relations with students to any other pattern. For a teacher who shows other traces of incompetence, this is probably a sufficient explanation of his disrepute.

The experienced teacher has a ready explanation for the failure of her good-natured colleague. Miss Jones fails "because she doesn't make those students respect her." Apparently this is a true explanation, but it still leaves some important questions unanswered. Why is it necessary to force students to "respect" the teacher, in the sense that her colleague, who has in mind a definitely institutional sort of respect, means? Why is it ever necessary for a teacher to "make students respect her"? Why do students not respect the pleasant Miss Jones rather than her cross and bad-tempered colleagues? These are puzzling questions, and one can never be quite sure that he has worked out a satisfactory answer to them. Something may be gained by going back on Miss Jones's steps and trying to discover what, by reason of her extreme equability, she did or failed to do that made the difference.

One important fact is that she failed to establish any boundary between teacher rights and pupil rights; she failed to establish a clear definition of the situation. As a result, her students from day to day kept extending the boundaries of their own rights and privileges at the expense of those of Miss Jones. In the absence of a rigid definition of the situation, a definition is worked out by the interaction of human forces; it is natural, then, that students should extend their activities until they come into contact with the real boundaries of the situation. Older persons sometimes learn not to impose upon good nature, for they have internalized the rule; but young persons have rarely attained to this moral delicacy. A further important fact is that there is here a motivation for imposing upon Miss Jones, a hostile motivation which prompts students to see just how far they can push things with her. This is not hostility toward Miss Jones, not personal hostility—not yet. It is the hostility which most students feel for most teachers. Miss Jones is pilloried for the misdeeds of all her students' other teachers. The activities of her students continue to push this good-natured teacher into a corner; they will push her as far as she will go. It is now a process beyond her control and more or less beyond the control of students; they are bound up in the process because they are involved in a rivalry to see who shall go furthest. Ultimately, whatever her good nature, whatever her phlegm, a point is reached where she feels the situation to be unbearable. She makes a stand. If she tries the technique of appeal, her appeals fail because she has no personal standing, and she becomes pitiable and somewhat odious. If she tries to command, she fails and makes herself ridiculous. By this time something has happened to her equanimity, and she has decided to fight. She enforces her commands with punishments. She defends her position desperately. Now the students begin to hate her. They hate her as they do not hate the teachers who have been strict from the first. Her stand has come too late, and the things which she is punishing now have become established as the rights of the students in her classes. Has she not permitted them on previous days? The precedent is against her. She must use more punishments than other teachers in order to enforce her points; her students will feel that it is unjust that they should be made to suffer for her incompetence. Have they not already decided that she is incompetent? She must use stronger punishments than other teachers; she must punish right and left; sometimes she imposes quite unreasonable penalties; she never dares relax. It is thought that she hates students, that her previous good nature was an illusion. Soon students hate her; they hate her so much that no penalties will be sufficient to restore her authority. That is the end.

The above may be regarded as a natural historical account of the life of the good-natured teacher. It is a process observable over and over again in any school system. With different classes, it is often repeated several times over with the same teacher, for the amiable are often slow to learn. The process has many variants, but the same general outline seems to underlie them all. Especially does the above pattern come out sharp and clear in the case of the teacher whose good nature with students is coupled with a considerable regard for their good opinion and some effort to be popular with them, popular as a person rather than as a teacher, for a chasm yawns between these two types of popularity. In some cases the teacher, after a long struggle, or through the use of heroic means, wins his struggle to establish domination. More often some sort of compromise arrangement is reached whereby the relation is enabled to continue, although it never becomes satisfactory to either side. If the teacher repeats the process in his second year, it is not likely to be so extreme. Many cases, however, are so extreme that the teacher, however well trained and skillful in instruction, is without value for the ordinary school system, and has to be dropped in the middle of the year or relieved of many of his duties.

The experienced teacher who has learned "how to make those students respect him" is involved in no such situation as that which centers about the teacher who is too good-natured or the teacher who wants to be popular. He at once sets up a rigid definition of the situation in terms of his own dominance. If he sets it up quickly enough and firmly enough, it is never questioned afterwards. Such minor threats as are made upon his dignity he is able to repel easily. It costs him, to be sure, something in the way of initial unpleasantness. He has to accept the disrepute which goes with being a school teacher, and there may be, early in the year, some pretty definite evidence that his students find him unpleasant and some less definite evidence that some of them dislike him. But if he has established his dominance so that it is not again questioned, the hatred toward him never really becomes personal. And, what is even more to the point, the absence of friction between personalities leaves the way clear for real friendliness to grow up within the known boundaries of the situation. Primary group attitudes spring up which make the situation human and bearable. Often such a strict teacher wins the liking of his students after the initial hate has passed away and his dominance has been softened by habit and acquaintance. Of him the students say, "He is strict and he puts up with no nonsense. But he knows his business and I guess he's not such a bad old fellow after all." In the "after all" is something significant. Earlier impressions are contradicted by later ones, with both the teacher who begins by being popular and the one who begins by being unpopular; the latter is in a better position because it is human nature to react excessively to such contradictions, to be more bitter over a quarrel with a friend than over a quarrel with an indifferent person, and to be more grateful for friendly advances from an enemy than for like advances from a friend. From this fact arises the practical wisdom of superintendents who advise their teachers to "come down on them pretty hard at first, because it is better to relax after a while than to tighten up." All very good if one knows how to "come down on them."

Nor is our explanation of the disrepute of the amiable yet complete. It will never be complete, for we must leave it suspended from certain paradoxical generalizations about human nature, for it is a true fact, and one not easy for the optimist to accept or the scientist to understand, that throughout the whole of human life the qualities of amiable persons are held at a low valuation. It is contrary to common sense, but it is true. Perhaps the reason is that those who fail to make themselves felt are not considered as persons, for which reason their favors, being taken as a matter of course, get no thanks, and they themselves get no love.[2] The meaning of good temper, then, is in bad temper. From a realization of this fact and an attempt to compensate for it, as well as the notion that it is not fair to impose upon good nature, arises the terrible wrath of some good-natured men. Some teachers, indeed, knowing themselves to be afflicted with the vice of laxity, try to establish themselves in the minds of students as persons who are usually quite easy but merciless when aroused. It is not at all a bad arrangement, for it permits them to be aroused rarely.

It is less difficult to account for the ill repute of teachers of the sort next to be described, for they represent a type of human being that has little standing in any group. This is the type of the egregious ass, or the nincompoop. We use these terms with a perfect awareness that they lack that exactness which terms should have which make any pretension to scientific accuracy, but since we are speaking of social types, and looking at them from the outside through the eyes of others, and since this is exactly what we think of such persons as being, the value terms will have to stand. The ass is usually a person of rather low intellectual power, though he need not show any defect of intelligence in the usual sense of the term; his lack is rather on the side of mental flexibility. The ass has little social sense, practically no awareness of the meaning of his activities or those of others in group life, no "sense of proportion." Most of all does he lack a true conception of his own place in the group; his exaggerated idea of his own value distorts all his perception of others. The ass is out of touch, and he makes the most amazing blunders in that subtle interchange of human reactions which makes up our life. His humor is humor relished almost entirely by himself, if it is relished at all. There is a certain laugh, a forced giggle, in the upper register of the voice, given with a rising inflection rather than the usual falling inflection of laughter, often coupled with a shaking of the head or other evidence of enjoyment, evoked by situations which others do not think of as funny, indulged in with a total disregard of what others may be thinking of him—this laugh we think of as asinine, and we know that the man who laughs that way is an ass. Or it may appear merely as an overloud laugh over a joke in which others do not participate. It has a correlate in a fairly well identifiable smile. What effect such a personality has upon students may well be left to the imagination. When the revolt begins, he rarely has personal force

[2] Cf. the following statement from Park and Burgess, *Introduction to the Science of Sociology*, p. 574: "In general, we may say that competition determines the position of the individual in the community; conflict fixes his place in society. Location, position, ecological interdependence—these are the characteristics of the community: Status, subordination and super-ordination, control—these are the distinctive marks of a society."

enough to meet the situation vigorously, and he attempts to meet it with piteous but unmoving appeals. It is difficult to be sympathetic with such a person, however pathetic his plight may be. It is especially difficult for the young.[3]

Another type of teacher who frequently gets into trouble is the one who is known to be incompetent, either in subject matter or in the disciplining of classes. In smaller systems, and occasionally in the larger ones, it commonly occurs that teachers are called upon at the last minute to teach subjects in which they have not adequate preparation, so that sometimes the most well-meaning instructors are put into situations where they are incompetent. There are others, of course, who feel that they can teach any subject by keeping a few minutes ahead of their classes, an opinion which obtains some support from certain alleged authorities on educational method. The situations in which incompetent instructors are put, and the shifts to which they resort in order to maintain their prestige, are sometimes ludicrous. There was the case of the foreign language teacher who was called upon to teach English. His students, suspecting the inadequacy of his grasp of the subject, laid a trap for him. In the day's lesson there occurred an *-ing* form of an English verb. "Professor Smith," came the question, "is this word *going* a gerund or a participle as it is used here?" The professor was completely baffled, but did not desire to admit it. Quickly he thought of a way out. "Well," he said, "there's some question. I would not want to settle that arbitrarily for you. That wouldn't be democratic. Let's take a vote on it. How many say it's a gerund? One, two, three, four, five. Is your hand up or not, Nelson? Now Johnson, if you don't stop making those silly faces I shall have to send you from the room. Now how many say it's a participle? How many say this form of *going* is a participle? Oh, easily the majority. How many? Ten. Yes, easily the majority. Well, it is a participle. Now don't laugh, *I'll stick you every one*. It's a participle." First-year Latin is sometimes taught by teachers commandeered for the purpose without reference to their preparation for the task. One person who struggled through a year of teaching Latin without having studied it previously reported that he had been able to get quite satisfactory results by his "answer-your-own-questions-method." This meant that when a question was asked or a dispute arose the teacher refused to be called into it, but forced the entire class to look through their books until they found something relevant. If there was a dispute, that suited him all the better, for he was the debating coach, and besides it helped to pass the class hour. The discipline of this teacher was not good, but he ascribed his failure in that respect to his policy of "being human" with his students rather than to his incompetence. Either factor, in his case, would have been sufficient to account for difficulty in discipline. A defect in preparation which becomes obvious to students is fatal to a teacher's prestige, although it goes without saying that such a defect must be extreme before students can become aware of it. Further, if a teacher's inability to discipline his classes becomes obvious, he also categorizes as an incompetent.

Another kind of disrepute into which the teacher falls is that of the tyrant. The teacher ideal of the stricter sort of school is probably that of the benevolent despot, as that phrase is used by some school men. But a benevolent despot knows how far to push his domination, and he knows how to relax it. The martinet, put in the same position, knows neither of these things; he

[3] See Somerset Maugham's description of an irresistibly comic, though tragic, character in *The Moon and Sixpence*.

requires too great a perfection, he attempts to maintain too complete a domination, and he uses methods too vigorous for his purpose.

The words of a person who talks much are little considered; those of persons who speak little have a scarcity value which makes them heeded. Especially is this true of teachers and of all persons who must live by ordering others about. Explanations of commands detract from their force, and completeness of personal expression, by filling in all the gaps in the picture of a personality, makes idealization difficult and therefore detracts from prestige. Especially does excessive loquacity operate to a teacher's discredit if he attempts to discipline by a flow of words, or mingles humor and discipline, or talks so much that he becomes ridiculous. There is no more incompetent teacher than the fool who talks too much, and talks rot. . . .

When a command is lost in a flood of words, its force is lost. When the talkativeness of the teacher wells out of an urge for social expression, so that it is self-revelatory talkativeness, the relationship between teacher and student breaks down by reason of a lack of social distance. When the excessive talk comes out of a feeling that it is necessary to explain disciplinary action to a student, it betrays an underlying fear of the loss of the student's good will (a lack of institutional courage), a fear strong enough to blot out utterly the common-sense realization that when a student is punished for a manifest and red-handed dereliction he knows well enough why he is being punished. And when the teacher is worried about the imposition of penalties, his students know that they have really the upper hand. The technique of arguing down objections, and of cajoling refractory boys into good behavior, does not work. Nor does it help to joke about a penalty, for such humor is rarely relished by the person punished; the punishment is a very serious thing to him. It is difficult to reconcile the two aims of humor and of discipline.

Another type of teacher who rarely fails to obtain the disrespect of his classes is the weakling. The weakling may be intelligent, and he is quite possibly well prepared for his job on the intellectual side. He is almost certain to be on the positive side of the moral ledger, and he is frequently a pietist. But he lacks sufficient physical stamina to win the respect of students as a physical object. And there is some subtle lack in his moral make-up which prevents him from standing out against the opinion of the student group and makes it difficult for him to face unpleasant situations with the unpleasantness which can solve them. He lacks the hostility reactions which one needs for success in the ordinary school. He cannot fight. It is worthy of remark that a sadistic strain in the teacher's make-up is a useful aid in securing subordination from students, especially if it is balanced by a certain amount of friendliness and a strong sense of justice and organized into a personality deserving of respect on other grounds. Sometimes this is what the weakling lacks, but it does not seem too cynical to suggest that this element is not so often entirely lacking as inhibited by fear.

The flirtatious teacher also gets into disrepute. Sex, as we have shown elsewhere, is much in evidence throughout the whole of school life, and it is unavoidably present in the attitudes which students and teachers have toward each other. A highly sublimated sort of sex appeal is sometimes made the basis of favorable rapport, but it is a rapport which may, with its emphasis slightly askew, degenerate rapidly. This is the case with the flirtatious teacher. The flirt is the man or woman teacher who is frankly open to the charms of students of opposite sex. Where teachers usually attempt to exclude such matters from their relations with students, these teachers attempt to bring them into play. Sometimes they wish to exploit their students sexually by means of their authority, but more often they merely open themselves to exploitation by students whose charms they appreciate. Sometimes the sexual motivation toward students is conscious and ruthless. In other cases it is never recognized for what it is, or, as in the case of young women teachers, it is merely a by-product of their whole social training up to that point. In any case, an attitude of the teacher which lays him open to frankly sexual interchange with students is one which has damaging effects upon his control of his classes. It makes nepotism unavoidable, and on those grounds it is hotly resented by those in the class who receive no favors. Where there is a marked age difference between students and teacher, any pronounced sex interest on the part of the teacher will seem depraved or ridiculous, although an older person may on occasion disguise a strong sexual interest in a particular student as a fatherly or motherly interest. Where there is only a slight age difference between student and teacher, the worst effect, for the teacher, of establishing a love relation with one of his students is that it involves him in the student world. It is, further, likely to involve him in an unfavorable manner.

Our most important point concerning the love relation in the schools may be stated in quite general terms. The rapport of the love relation is quite incompatible with dominance and subordination as it is established in the schools. Further, the love relation, even in its incipient stages, is incompatible with the maintenance of such social distance as is expected of the teacher. The sexual motivation of the student (or the teacher) prompts him continually to attempt to break down barriers; if the student succeeds in his attempt, the teacher loses standing, and if he does not succeed he becomes troublesome and bitter. It is a failure to reckon with this mechanism which accounts for much of the trouble which women teachers have with girls in the age of crushes. It might be pointed out also that the flirtatious teacher loses standing in the school and the community because of his violation of that principle of morality which holds that those who stand in an authority relation should not exploit that relation for personal reasons. This is a very strong taboo indeed, and has led in some cases to violence or indignity on the part of townsmen toward the teacher who failed to respect it. It is perhaps vaguely realized that the flirtatious teacher violates the special ethics of the image relations, that morality which requires that those who stand in relations which have special force because of their emotional reenforcement from other sources, as teachers, preachers, lawyers, doctors (especially psychiatrists), and priests, should not exploit that rapport for any purpose of their own.

Another type of disrepute into which the teacher falls is that of the caricature. Apparently it is of the nature of the teacher as an occupational type to get out of touch with the community of men in general, and to develop his own special way of life without much thought of the world that is not the school. When this process of specialization has gone on for a long time, the teacher may develop into a caricature of the occupational type. Now the occupational type of the teacher is, as we shall see, usually developed by way of an adaptation to the conditions of teaching, but when the teacher has passed a certain point in the development of occupational traits he becomes so completely out of touch with human beings in general that even his teaching is handicapped. Then he has become a caricature, and the caricature is ridiculous. It is not only ridiculous in itself, but it tends to make all other teachers ridiculous because of their similarity to it in some essential qualities.

A teacher who comes to be much hated is the bully. The bully attempts to keep his students under control by keeping them in a constant state of fear. He badgers students, threatens them, lords it over them, keeps them in fear of sudden displays of anger, and uses the social technique of one who is determined to have his way by unpleasant means if possible. His is the institutional variety of quarrelsomeness. The bully speaks in a badgering or blustery tone of voice, one that suggests that he is already angry and that he is likely if at all irritated to become much more angry, which may convey the idea that this teacher never did care very much about students anyway, and is now at the end of his patience with them. This voice may be shrill and sharp, though it is not so in the typical case; it is more likely to be full and fuzzy, as if a number of ragged edges of emotion adhered to it. The classroom manner of many teachers is built upon this bullying technique as a basis.

The loud voice and dire threats with which the school year begins tend to lose their force unless they are followed by a yet louder voice and more blood-curdling threats in the near future, and there is an easily attained limit to this process. It has the further disadvantage that it puts a nervous strain upon both students and teacher which, though it may be a spur to the dull and a challenge to the idle, is an obstacle to achievement for many students. Further, it is a method which will make a teacher hated, unless it is in the folkways, and even then if the teacher is not able to balance it by some pleasant traits of character.

But it should be stated emphatically that the bully often gets by, and that his students often develop a real affection for him. He gets results from students whom other teachers have given up. And he has at least the psychological advantage of the initiative, he "has the jump on his students." Sometimes it even gets abroad that he is a rough old codger but he has a heart of gold and "would give you the shirt off his back if he thought you needed it." This, it may be said, is often true of teachers whose classroom personality is most definitely given over to bullying, and it helps them to obtain forgiveness. It is said that boys will take any abuse from a man whom they consider just and from a man who, "away down under," likes them. But perhaps the most important point in the bully's favor is that he has color and that he gives his small but discriminating public a good show.

There are some teachers who have ego-gratifying devices which interfere with their teaching efficiency. They find in the classroom an opportunity to cultivate expansive moments, and they manipulate their teaching procedure with a view of squeezing from it as many such moments as possible. The list of ego-swelling poses, of tricks which give the teacher that pleasant feeling of being somehow a very remarkable fellow, of sayings which are thought to make others wonder and admire—this list is literally endless. Pride everywhere betrays men into a fall, and it betrays other men, perhaps, as consistently as teachers, but the teacher is in a position of unusual temptation. He has the attention of a large group, and it is his job to keep that attention constellated upon himself. To expand his personality to include the entire group, and yet to refrain from using the expanded contact as a means of gratifying his private wishes, to include other personalities within the control of one's own and yet to exclude the interior self, in a word, to dominate impersonally, is a truly great achievement, and it is not so amazing that the teacher usually lacks this extraordinary grace as that he ever has it.

The pride-fulfilling devices of teachers do not always affect their student relationships unfavorably, and these devices are, in fact, useful if they do not pass certain bounds or bring the teacher into direct conflict with his students. Self-dramatization is effective if it includes relatively little of self and drives home important elements of subject matter; it is difficult to tell when it becomes a vice. A habit of trying to say things well is a good habit, and students are usually grateful for a teacher who has it. But a teacher who says things well may go out of his way to find things to say well, and once he has started he may range further and further afield in his search for epigrams. In the extreme case, he becomes "one who says smart things smartly," a "wise-cracker." Somewhere he has crossed the invisible line that separates good practice from bad. This is but one example. There are other ego-gratifying mechanisms which injure only the teacher himself; an example of this is a certain brilliant, ultra-sophisticated teacher of English who, in the apt phrase of a colleague, "has so many poses to keep before the public that he never has time for anything else." Many teachers whose rapport with students is excellent are accustomed to nourish their self-feelings at the expense of their colleagues, particularly of underlings, and the devices they employ are uncountable.

We are here concerned with a particular variety of disrepute into which teachers fall if they allow their ego-feelings to obtrude themselves too obviously into their transactions with students. Two different mechanisms are involved in these cases: first, that the individuals involved become ridiculous because they make ridiculous claims upon the students' respect, either by priding themselves upon ridiculous things or by gross exaggeration of their own merits; secondly, that they attempt to gratify their own self-feelings by making an attack upon students, and receive, as a general thing, repayment in kind. Animosity aroused by some direct attack usually supplies the motive for caricature of the sort first mentioned, and if there is no such animosity the inherently ridiculous claims of the teacher may pass unchallenged. It is incredibly difficult for the teacher to ascertain when he crosses the line and becomes ridiculous. The moral obtuseness with which such teachers pursue their egotistic aims is remarkable, the more so since it is so often coupled with neurotic keenness in ferreting out remote implications of status. The psychology of the inferiority complex seems to be the necessary background for the understanding of these cases. The underlying sense of inadequacy is in them, and compensatory behavior and the basic life lie. Such is the egotist.

Ego involvements of the sort under discussion are to be found in other cases which we have mentioned. They are basic in the martinet, the bully, and the overtalkative teacher, but it seemed best to illustrate them by a special selection. It is heartening to reflect that this type has its opposite, that there are many teachers who tread warily among the feelings of students and colleagues. They walk softly, as the saying is, and they go far. They have learned how to disarm, which is a special technique and one requiring much practice —a very long art.

This completes our presentation of the varieties of prestige and disrepute which attach to the teacher. Most of these have been illustrated by cases drawn from actual life and as faithfully portrayed as circumstances would permit. Some readers will object, as they have every right to do, that these cases are not typical. Teachers who represent these behavior mechanisms in such extreme form are in fact rare, and these cases are therefore statistically atypical. But they illustrate common mechanisms and it seems to have served the purposes of exposition to use them. The alert reader will also recall that we are here dealing with social images, which are by definition distortions of impressions of persons; we are dealing quite frankly with illusion, and not with reality. We have therefore filtered most of these cases through the minds of students, and have been less concerned with what these persons really were than with what others thought they were. This is not the place for a discussion of the various kinds of selves, and it should be clear enough that this procedure is justifiable. We have been concerned with one kind of social self, and our studies do not preclude that these same persons, seen from another vantage point than that of students or colleagues, might appear to wear different faces.

Ordinary teachers rarely exemplify any of these types in unmixed form. The successful teacher is usually experienced by his students with overtones of two or three of the prestige-carrying images, and has quite possibly some things in his personality which suggest the images of negative value. The attitudes of students toward the best of teachers are in most instances ambivalent, and the net effect of the teacher's personality depends upon the relative weight of counterpoised attitudes, or upon arrangements which allow both sorts of attitudes to be expressed. It would be misleading, of course, to explain student attitudes toward teachers entirely on the basis of these social images, for there are many other images, and there is always, in addition, something of the uniquely personal which enters into the impression which the teacher makes upon the pupil. But when this that is uniquely personal creeps in, it is because the institution cannot keep it out, and the interaction which then arises no longer pertains to those illusions of prestige and disrepute upon which rests the institutional leadership that teachers practice. Teachers are shapes seen in a fog, and students have fog-bound attitudes toward them; the shapes are human and occasionally personal, and yet the most significant thing is that they are seen in a fog. The analysis of the teacher into personal and institutional elements is a task which cannot fail to challenge the research worker of the future.

PART 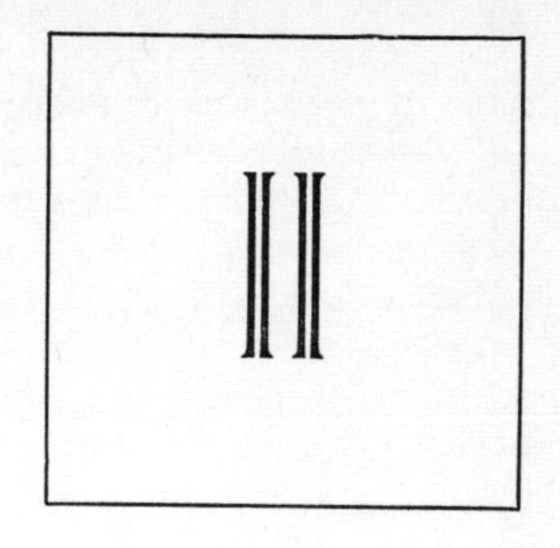

Foundation Fields in Teacher Education

4 HISTORICAL FOUNDATIONS OF EDUCATION

OF STUDIES[1]

Francis Bacon

DISCUSSION AND ANALYSIS

Francis Bacon (1561–1626) was one of the leading luminaries of the Elizabethan period. So extensive was his genius that many have supposed him to be the true author of the works of Shakespeare. While this hypothesis is not tenable in the light of modern scholarship, it is certainly true that Bacon had exceptional talents as a writer. He was, moreover, a philosopher of note and held many important governmental posts, including that of Lord Chancellor. His style is polished, witty, complex, and exceptionally meaty. He remarks that "Some books are to be tasted, others to be swallowed, and some few to be chewed and digested." Bacon himself, like many of the other authors in this volume, can be most fully enjoyed only after thorough chewing.

Even so, one cannot help but note the truth of many of Bacon's observations despite an interval of over three centuries. Bacon is, of course, a classic; as such, we can presume he commands the admiration of a neoclassicist like Robert M. Hutchins (Chapter 5). One might well wonder what Dr. Hutchins would make of a statement such as Bacon's "To spend too much time in studies is sloth; . . . to make judgment wholly by their rules is the humor of the scholar." On the other hand, in suggesting certain studies to remedy various intellectual deficiencies, Bacon subscribes to a faculty psychology that would be well implemented by a rigid subject-matter curriculum. What illumination does the chapter on psychological foundations cast on this theory?

Studies serve for delight, for ornament, and for ability. Their chief use for delight is in privateness and retiring; for ornament, is in discourse; and for ability, is in the judgment and disposition of business. For expert men can execute and perhaps

[1] From *The Essays of Sir Francis Bacon*, 1625.

judge of particulars, one by one; but the general counsels, and the plots and marshalling of affairs, come best from those that are learned. To spend too much time in studies is sloth; to use them too much for ornament is affectation; to make judgment wholly by their rules is the humor of a scholar. They perfect nature, and are perfected by experience; for natural abilities are like natural plants, that need pruning by study; and studies themselves do give forth directions too much at large, except they be bounded in by experience. Crafty men contemn studies; simple men admire them; and wise men use them; for they teach not their own use; but that is a wisdom without them and above them, won by observation. Read not to contradict and confute; nor to believe and take for granted; nor to find talk and discourse; but to weigh and consider. Some books are to be tasted, others to be swallowed, and some few to be chewed and digested: that is, some books are to be read only in parts; others to be read, but not curiously; and some few to be read wholly, and with diligence and attention, Some books also may be read by deputy, and extracts made of them by others; but that would be only in the less important arguments, and the meaner sort of books; else distilled books are like common distilled waters, flashy things. Reading maketh a full man; conference a ready man; and writing an exact man. And therefore, if a man write little he had need have a great memory; if he confer little, he had need have a present wit; and if he read little he had need have much cunning, to seem to know that he doth not. Histories make men wise; poets witty; the mathematics subtile; natural philosophy deep; moral grave; logic and rhetoric able to contend. *Abeunt studia in mores.* Nay, there is no stand or impediment in the wit, but may be wrought out by fit studies; like as diseases of the body may have appropriate exercises. Bowling is good for the stone and reins; shooting for the lungs and breast; gentle walking for the stomach; riding for the head; and the like. So if a man's wit be wandering, let him study the mathematics; for in demonstrations, if his wit be called away never so little, he must begin again; if his wit be not apt to distinguish or find differences, let him study the schoolmen; for they are *cymini sectores*: if he be not apt to beat over matters, and to call one thing to prove and illustrate another, let him study the lawyers' cases: so every defect of the mind may have a special receipt.

THE OLD AND THE NEW SCHOOLMASTER[1]

Charles Lamb

My reading has been lamentably desultory and immethodical. Odd, out-of-the-way, old English plays and treatises, have supplied me with most of my notions and ways of feeling. In everything that relates to *science*, I am a whole Encyclopædia behind the rest of the world. I should have scarcely cut a figure among the franklins, or country gentlemen, in King John's days. I know less geography than a schoolboy of six-weeks' standing. To me a map of old Ortelius is as authentic as Arrowsmith. I do not know whereabout Africa merges into Asia; whether Ethiopia lie in one or other of those great divisions; nor can form the remotest conjecture of the position of New South Wales, or Van Diemen's Land. Yet do I hold a correspondence with a very dear friend in the first-named of these

[1] From *Essays of Elia*, 1823.

two Terrae Incognitae. I have no astronomy. I do not know where to look for the Bear, or Charles's Wain; the place of any star; or the name of any of them at sight. I guess at Venus only by her brightness—and if the sun on some portentous morn were to make his first appearance in the West, I verily believe that, while all the world were gasping in apprehension about me, I alone should stand unterrified, from sheer incuriosity and want of observation. Of history and chronology I possess some vague points, such as one cannot help picking up in the course of miscellaneous study; but I never deliberately sat down to a chronicle, even of my own country. I have most dim apprehensions of the four great monarchies; and sometimes the Assyrian, sometimes the Persian, floats as *first* in my fancy. I make the widest conjectures concerning Egypt and her shepherd kings. My friend *M.*, with great painstaking, got me to think I understood the first proposition in Euclid, but gave me over in despair at the second. I am entirely unacquainted with the modern languages; and, like a better man than myself, have "small Latin and less Greek." I am a stranger to the shapes and texture of the commonest trees, herbs, flowers—not from the circumstance of my being town-born—for I should have brought the same inobservant spirit into the world with me, had I first seen it "on Devon's leafy shores,"—and am no less at a loss among purely town-objects, tools, engines, mechanic processes.—Not that I affect ignorance—but my head has not many mansions, nor spacious; and I have been obliged to fill it with such cabinet curiosities as it can hold without aching. I sometimes wonder, how I have passed my probation with so little discredit in the world, as I have done, upon so meagre a stock. But the fact is, a man may do very well with a very little knowledge, and scarce be found out, in mixed company; everybody is so much more ready to produce his own, than to call for a display of your acquisitions. But in a *tête-à-tête* there is no shuffling. The truth will out. There is nothing which I dread so much, as the being left alone for a quarter of an hour with a sensible, well-informed man that does not know me. I lately got into a dilemma of this sort.

In one of my daily jaunts between Bishopsgate and Shacklewell, the coach stopped to take up a staid-looking gentleman, about the wrong side of thirty, who was giving his parting directions (while the steps were adjusting), in a tone of mild authority, to a tall youth, who seemed to be neither his clerk, his son, nor his servant, but something partaking of all three. The youth was dismissed, and we drove on. As we were the sole passengers, he naturally enough addressed his conversation to me; and we discussed the merits of the fare, the civility and punctuality of the driver; the circumstance of an opposition coach having been lately set up, with the probabilities of its success—to all which I was enabled to return pretty satisfactory answers, having been drilled into this kind of etiquette by some years' daily practice of riding to and fro in the stage aforesaid—when he suddenly alarmed me by a startling question, whether I had seen the show of prize cattle that morning in Smithfield? Now as I had not seen it, and do not greatly care for such sort of exhibitions, I was obliged to return a cold negative. He seemed a little mortified, as well as astonished, at my declaration, as (it appeared) he was just come fresh from the sight, and doubtless had hoped to compare notes on the subject. However he assured me that I had lost a fine treat, as it far exceeded the show of last year. We were now approaching Norton Folgate, when the sight of some shop-goods *ticketed* freshened him up into a dissertation upon the cheapness of cottons this spring. I was now a little in heart, as the nature of my morning avocations had brought me into some sort of familiarity with the raw material; and I was surprised to find how eloquent I was becoming on the state of the India market—when, presently, he dashed my incipient vanity to the earth at once, by inquiring whether I had ever made any calculation as to the value of the rental of all the retail shops in London. Had he asked of me, what song the Sirens sang, or what name Achilles assumed when he hid himself among women, I might, with Sir Thomas Browne, have hazarded a "wide solution." My companion saw my embarrassment, and, the alms-houses beyond Shoreditch just coming in view, with great good-nature and dexterity shifted his conversation to the subject of public charities, which led to the comparative merits of provision for the poor in past and present times, with observations on the old monastic institutions, and charitable orders;—but, finding me rather dimly impressed with some glimmering notions from old poetical associations, than strongly fortified with any speculations reducible to calculation on the subject, he gave the matter up; and, the country beginning to open more and more upon us, as we approached the turnpike at Kingsland (the destined termination of his journey), he put a home-thrust upon me, in the most unfortunate position he could have chosen, by advancing some queries relative to the North Pole Expedition. While I was muttering out something about the Panorama of those strange regions (which I had actually seen), by way of parrying the question, the coach stopping relieved me from any further apprehensions. My companion getting out, left me in the comfortable possession of my ignorance; and I heard him, as he went off, putting questions to an outside passenger, who had alighted with him, regarding an epidemic disorder that had been rife about Dalston, and which, my friend assured him, had gone through five or six schools in that neighborhood. The truth now flashed upon me, that my companion was a schoolmaster; and that the youth, whom he had parted from at our first acquaintance, must have been one of the bigger boys, or the usher.—He was evidently a kind-hearted man, who did not seem so much desirous of provoking discussion by the questions which he put, as of obtaining information at any rate. It did not appear that he took any interest, either, in such kind of inquiries, for their own sake; but that he was in some way bound to seek for knowledge. A greenish-colored coat, which he had on, forbade me to surmise that he was a clergyman. The adventure gave birth to some reflections on the difference between persons of his profession in past and present times.

Rest to the souls of those fine old Pedagogues; the breed, long since extinct, of the Lilys, and Linacres: who believing that all learning was contained in the languages which they taught, and despising every other acquirement as superficial and useless, came to their task as to a sport! Passing from infancy to age, they dreamed away all their days as in a grammar-school. Revolving in a perpetual cycle of declensions, conjugations, syntaxes, and prosodies; renewing constantly the occupations which had charmed their studious childhood; rehearsing continually the part of the past; life must have slipped from them at the last like one day. They were always in their first garden, reaping harvests of their golden time, among their *Flori* and their *Spici-legia;* in Arcadia still, but kings; the ferule of their sway not much harsher, but of like dignity with that mild sceptre attributed to King Basileus; the Greek and Latin, their stately Pamela and their Philoclea; with the occasional duncery of some untoward Tyro, serving for a refreshing interlude of a Mopsa, or a clown Damætas!

With what a savor doth the Preface to Colet's, or (as it is sometimes called)

Paul's Accidence, set forth! "To exhort every man to the learning of grammar, that intendeth to attain the understanding of the tongues, wherein it contained a great treasury of wisdom and knowledge, it would seem but vain and lost labor; for so much as it is known, that nothing can surely be ended, whose beginning is either feeble or faulty; and no building be perfect, whereas the foundation and groundwork is ready to fall, and unable to uphold the burden of the frame." How well doth this stately preamble (comparable to those which Milton commendeth as "having been the usage to prefix to some solemn law, then first promulgated by Solon, or Lycurgus") correspond with and illustrate that pious zeal for conformity, expressed in a succeeding clause, which would fence about grammar-rules with the severity of faith-articles!—"as for the diversity of grammars, it is well profitably taken away by the king majesties wisdom, who foreseeing the inconvenience, and favorably providing the remedie, caused one kind of grammar by sundry learned men to be diligently drawn, and so to be set out, only everywhere to be taught for the use of learners, and for the hurt in changing of schoolmaisters." What a *gusto* in that which follows: "wherein it is profitable that he can orderly decline his noun, and his verb." *His* noun!

The fine dream is fading away fast; and the least concern of a teacher in the present day is to inculcate grammar-rules.

The modern schoolmaster is expected to know a little of everything, because his pupil is required not to be entirely ignorant of anything. He must be superficially, if I may so say, omniscient. He is to know something of pneumatics; of chemistry; of whatever is curious, or proper to excite the attention of the youthful mind; an insight into mechanics is desirable, with a touch of statistics; the quality of soils, etc.; botany; the constitution of his country, *cum multis aliis*. You may get a notion of some part of his expected duties by consulting the famous Tractate on Education addressed to Mr. Hartlib.

All these things—these, or the desire of them—he is expected to instil, not by set lessons from professors, which he may charge in the bill, but at school-intervals, as he walks the streets, or saunters through green fields (those natural instructors) with his pupils. The least part of what is expected from him is to be done in school-hours. He must insinuate knowledge at the *mollia tempora fandi*. He must seize every occasion—the season of the year—the time of the day—a passing cloud—a rainbow—a waggon of hay—a regiment of soldiers going by—to inculcate something useful. He can receive no pleasure from a casual glimpse of nature, but must catch at it as an object of instruction. He must interpret beauty into the picturesque. He cannot relish a beggar-man, or a gipsy, for thinking of the suitable improvement. Nothing comes to him, not spoiled by the sophisticating medium of moral uses. The Universe—that Great Book, as it has been called—is to him indeed, to all intents and purposes, a book, out of which he is doomed to read tedious homilies to distasting schoolboys.—Vacations themselves are none to him, he is only rather worse off than before; for commonly he has some intrusive upper-boy fastened upon him at such times; some cadet of a great family; some neglected lump of nobility, or gentry; that he must drag after him to the play, to the panorama, to Mr. Bartley's Orrery, to the Panopticon, or into the country, to a friend's house, or his favorite watering-place. Wherever he goes, this uneasy shadow attends him. A boy is at his board, and in his path, and in all his movements. He is boy-rid, sick of perpetual boy.

Boys are capital fellows in their own way, among their mates; but they are unwholesome companions for grown people.

The restraint is felt no less on the one side, than on the other.—Even a child, that "plaything for an hour," tires *always*. The noises of children, playing their own fancies—as I now hearken to them by fits, sporting on the green before my window, while I am engaged in these grave speculations at my neat suburban retreat at Shacklewell—by distance made more sweet —inexpressibly take from the labor of my task. It is like writing to music. They seem to modulate my periods. They ought at least to do so—for in the voice of that tender age there is a kind of poetry, far unlike the harsh prose-accents of man's conversation.—I should but spoil their sport, and diminish my own sympathy for them, by mingling in their pastime.

I would not be domesticated all my days with a person of very superior capacity to my own—not, if I know myself at all, from any considerations of jealousy, or self-comparison, for the occasional communion with such minds has constituted the fortune and felicity of my life—but the habit of too constant intercourse with spirits above you, instead of raising you, keeps you down. Too frequent doses of original thinking from others restrain what lesser portion of that faculty you may possess of your own. You get entangled in another man's mind, even as you lose yourself in another man's grounds. You are walking with a tall varlet, whose strides out-pace yours to lassitude. The constant operation of such potent agency would reduce me, I am convinced, to imbecility. You may derive thoughts from others; your way of thinking, the mould in which your thoughts are cast, must be your own. Intellect may be imparted, but not each man's intellectual frame.

As little as I should wish to be always thus dragged upwards, as little (or rather still less) is it desirable to be stunted downwards by your associates. The trumpet does not more stun you by its loudness, than a whisper teases you by its provoking inaudibility.

Why are we never quite at our ease in the presence of a schoolmaster?—because we are conscious that he is not quite at his ease in ours. He is awkward, and out of place, in the society of his equals. He comes like Gulliver from among his little people, and he cannot fit the stature of his understanding to yours. He cannot meet you on the square. He wants a point given him, like an indifferent whist-player. He is so used to teaching, that he wants to be teaching you. One of these professors, upon my complaining that these little sketches of mine were anything but methodical, and that I was unable to make them otherwise, kindly offered to instruct me in the method by which young gentlemen in *his* seminary were taught to compose English themes.—The jests of a schoolmaster are coarse, or thin. They do not *tell* out of school. He is under the restraint of a formal and didactive hypocrisy in company, as a clergyman is under a moral one. He can no more let his intellect loose in society, than the other can his inclinations.—He is forlorn among his coevals; his juniors cannot be his friends.

"I take blame to myself," said a sensible man of this profession, writing to a friend respecting a youth who had quitted his school abruptly, "that your nephew was not more attached to me. But persons in my situation are more to be pitied, than can well be imagined. We are surrounded by young, and, consequently, ardently affectionate hearts, but *we* can never hope to share an atom of their affections. The relation of master and scholar forbids this. *How pleasing this must be to you, how I envy your feelings*, my friends will sometimes say to me, when they see young men, whom I have educated, return after some years' absence from school, their eyes shining with pleasure, while they shake hands with their old master, bringing a present of game to me or a toy to my wife, and thanking me in the warmest terms for my care of their education. A holiday is begged for the boys; the house is a scene of happiness; I, only, am sad at heart.—This fine-spirited and warm-hearted youth, who fancies he repays his master with gratitude for the care of his boyish years—this young man—in the eight long years I watched over him with a parent's anxiety, never could repay me with one look of genuine feeling. He was proud, when I praised; he was submissive, when I reproved him; but he did never *love* me—and what he now mistakes for gratitude and kindness for me is but a pleasant sensation, which all persons feel at revisiting the scene of their boyish hopes and fears; and the seeing on equal terms the man they were accustomed to look up to with reverence. My wife, too," this interesting correspondent goes on to say, "my once darling Anna, is the wife of a schoolmaster.—When I married her—knowing that the wife of a schoolmaster ought to be a busy notable creature, and fearing that my gentle Anna would ill supply the loss of my dear bustling mother, just then dead, who never sat still, was in every part of the house in a moment, and whom I was obliged sometimes to threaten to fasten down in a chair, to save her from fatiguing herself to death—I express my fears, that I was bringing her into a way of life unsuitable to her; and she, who loved me tenderly, promised for my sake to exert herself to perform the duties of her new situation. She promised, and she has kept her word. What wonders will not a woman's love perform?—My house is managed with a propriety and decorum, unknown in other schools; my boys are well-fed, look healthy, and have every proper accommodation; and all this performed with a careful economy, that never descends to meanness. But I have lost my gentle, *helpless* Anna!—When we sit down to enjoy an hour of repose after the fatigue of the day I am compelled to listen to what have been her useful (and they are really useful) employments through the day, and what she proposes for her tomorrow's task. Her heart and her features are changed by the duties of her situation. To the boys, she never appears other than the *master's wife*, and she looks up to me as the *boys' master*; to whom all show of love and affection would be highly improper, and unbecoming the dignity of her situation and mine. Yet *this* my gratitude forbids me to hint to her. For my sake she submitted to be this altered creature, and can I reproach her for it?"—For the communication of this letter, I am indebted to my cousin Bridget.

THE GRADGRIND SYSTEM [1]
Charles Dickens

DISCUSSION AND ANALYSIS

Charles Dickens, an eminent Victorian, is among the world's literary masters. His ability to combine moral satire and caricature is surpassed by no one in the English language unless it be Jonathan Swift. By no means least among his accomplishments is his gallery of pedants, among whom Thomas Gradgrind and Mr. M'Choakumchild are leading

[1] From *Hard Times*, 1854.

examples. The names of the two men—and Dickens was exceedingly fond of such "tag" names—suggest not only their character but also their methods. Have you yourself ever heard of or actually met teachers of this sort?

Those who advocate a curriculum devoted to rote memory and the retention of facts might well ponder Bitzer's definition of a horse. While such a definition may be correct scientifically within a limited scope, it fails to provide us with an image of a horse. (This same problem of the divergence between "science" and experience is posed on a philosophical level in Whitman's poem "When I Heard the Learn'd Astronomer" in Chapter 5.) Moreover, in his narrowness and his belaboring of the obvious, Mr. Gradgrind is decidedly unscientific.

You may find it instructive and amusing to draw a Dickensian portrait of your notion of a totally unsatisfactory instructor. Can you also draw a literary portrait of a successful teacher? Can you project your vision into the future to encompass an image of yourself as an educator ten or fifteen years from now?

"Now, what I want is, Facts. Teach these boys and girls nothing but Facts. Facts alone are wanted in life. Plant nothing else, and root out everything else. You can only form the minds of reasoning animals upon Facts: nothing else will ever be of any service to them. This is the principle on which I bring up my own children, and this is the principle on which I bring up these children. Stick to the Facts, sir!"

The scene was a plain, bare, monotonous vault of a schoolroom, and the speaker's square forefinger emphasised his observations by underscoring every sentence with a line on the schoolmaster's sleeve. The emphasis was helped by the speaker's square wall of a forehead, which had his eyebrows for its base, while his eyes found commodious cellarage in two dark caves, overshadowed by the wall. The emphasis was helped by the speaker's mouth, which was wide, thin, and hard set. The emphasis was helped by the speaker's voice, which was inflexible, dry, and dictatorial. The emphasis was helped by the speaker's hair, which bristled on the skirts of his bald head, a plantation of fire to keep the wind from its shining surface, all covered with knobs, like the crust of a plum pie, as if the head had scarcely warehouse-room for the hard facts stored inside. The speaker's obstinate carriage, square coat, square legs, square shoulders —nay, his very neckcloth, trained to take him by the throat with an unaccommodating grasp, like a stubborn fact, as it was— all helped the emphasis.

"In this life, we want nothing but Facts, sir—nothing but Facts!"

The speaker, and the schoolmaster, and the third grown person present, all backed a little, and swept with their eyes the inclined plane of little vessels then and there arranged in order, ready to have imperial gallons of facts poured into them until they were full to the brim.

* * *

Thomas Gradgrind, sir. A man of realities. A man of facts and calculations. A man who proceeds upon the principle that two and two are four, and nothing over, and who is not to be talked into allowing for anything over. Thomas Gradgrind, sir

—peremptorily Thomas—Thomas Gradgrind. With a rule and a pair of scales, and the multiplication table always in his pocket, sir, ready to weigh and measure any parcel of human nature, and tell you exactly what it comes to. It is a mere question of figures, a case of simple arithmetic. You might hope to get some other nonsensical belief into the head of George Gradgrind, or Augustus Gradgrind, or John Gradgrind or Joseph Gradgrind (all supposititious, non-existent persons), but into the head of Thomas Gradgrind—no, sir!

In such terms Mr. Gradgrind always mentally introduced himself, whether to his private circle of acquaintance, or to the public in general. In such terms, no doubt, substituting the words "boys and girls," for "sir," Thomas Gradgrind now presented Thomas Gradgrind to the little pitchers before him, who were to be filled so full of facts.

Indeed, as he eagerly sparkled at them from the cellarage before mentioned, he seemed a kind of cannon loaded to the muzzle with facts, and prepared to blow them clean out of the regions of childhood at one discharge. He seemed a galvanising apparatus, too, charged with a grim, mechanical substitute for the tender young imaginations that were to be stormed away.

"Girl number twenty," said Mr. Gradgrind, squarely pointing with his square forefinger, "I don't know that girl. Who is that girl?"

"Sissy Jupe, sir," explained number twenty, blushing, standing up and curtsying.

"Sissy is not a name," said Mr. Gradgrind. "Don't call yourself Sissy. Call yourself Cecilia."

"It's father as calls me Sissy, sir," returned the young girl, in a trembling voice, and with another curtsy.

"Then he has no business to do it," said Mr. Gradgrind. "Tell him he mustn't. Cecilia Jupe. Let me see. What is your father?"

"He belongs to the horse-riding, if you please, sir."

Mr. Gradgrind frowned, and waved off the objectionable calling with his hand.

"We don't want to know anything about that here. You mustn't tell us about that here. Your father breaks horses, don't he?"

"If you please, sir, when they can get any to break, they do break horses in the ring, sir."

"You mustn't tell us about the ring here. Very well, then. Describe your father as a horse-breaker. He doctors sick horses, I dare say?"

"Oh, yes, sir."

"Very well, then. He is a veterinary surgeon, a farrier and horse-breaker. Give me your definition of a horse."

(Sissy Jupe thrown into the greatest alarm by this demand.)

"Girl number twenty unable to define a horse!" said Mr. Gradgrind, for the general behoof of all the little pitchers. "Girl number twenty possessed of no facts, in reference to one of the commonest of animals! Some boy's definition of a horse. Bitzer, yours."

The square finger, moving here and there, lighted suddenly on Bitzer, perhaps because he chanced to sit in the same ray of sunlight which, darting in at one of the bare windows of the intensely whitewashed room, irradiated Sissy. For the boys and the girls sat on the face of the inclined plane in two compact bodies, divided up the centre by a narrow interval; and Sissy, being at the corner of a row on the sunny side, came in for the beginning of a sunbeam, of which Bitzer, being at the corner of a row on the other side, a few rows in advance, caught the end. But, whereas the girl was so dark-eyed and dark-haired, that she seemed to receive a deeper and more lustrous color from the sun when it shone upon her, the boy was so light-eyed and light-haired that the selfsame rays appeared to draw out of him what little colour he ever possessed. His cold eyes would hardly have been eyes, but for the short ends of lashes which, by bringing them into immediate contrast with something paler than themselves, expressed their form. His short-cropped hair might have been a mere continuation of the sandy freckles on his forehead and face. His skin was so unwholesomely deficient in the natural tinge, that he looked as though, if he were cut, he would bleed white.

"Bitzer," said Thomas Gradgrind. "Your definition of a horse."

"Quadruped. Graminivorous. Forty teeth, namely twenty-four grinders, four eye-teeth, and twelve incisive. Sheds coat in the spring; in marshy countries, sheds hoofs too. Hoofs hard, but requiring to be shod with iron. Age known by marks in mouth." Thus (and much more) Bitzer.

"Now girl number twenty," said Mr. Gradgrind, "you know what a horse is."

She curtsied again, and would have blushed deeper, if she could have blushed deeper than she had blushed all this time. Bitzer, after rapidly blinking at Thomas Gradgrind with both eyes at once, and so catching the light upon his quivering ends of lashes that they looked like the antennae of busy insects, put his knuckles to his freckled forehead, and sat down again.

The third gentleman now stepped forth. A mighty man at cutting and drying, he was; a government officer; in his way (and in most other people's too) a professed pugilist; always in training, always with a system to force down the general throat like a bolus, always to be heard of at the bar of his little public office, ready to fight all England. To continue in fistic phraseology, he had a genius for coming up to the scratch, wherever and whatever it was, and proving himself an ugly customer. He would go in and damage any subject whatever with his right, follow up with his left, stop, exchange, counter, bore his opponent (he always fought all England) to the ropes, and fall upon him neatly. He was certain to knock the wind out of common sense, and render that unlucky adversary deaf to the call of time. And he had it in charge from high authority to bring about the great public-office millennium, when commissioners should reign upon earth.

"Very well," said this gentleman, briskly smiling, and folding his arms. "That's a horse. Now, let me ask you girls and boys, Would you paper a room with representations of horses?"

After a pause, one half of the children cried in chorus, "Yes, sir!" Upon which the other half, seeing in the gentleman's face that Yes was wrong, cried out in chorus, "No, sir!" as the custom is, in these examinations.

"Of course, No. Why wouldn't you?"

A pause. One corpulent slow boy, with a wheezy manner of breathing, ventured the answer, Because he wouldn't paper a room at all, but would paint it.

"You *must* paper it," said the gentleman, rather warmly.

"You must paper it," said Thomas Gradgrind, "whether you like it or not. Don't tell *us* you wouldn't paper it. What do you mean, boy?"

"I'll explain to you, then," said the gentleman, after another and dismal pause, "why you wouldn't paper a room with representations of horses. Do you ever see horses walking up and down the sides of rooms in reality—in fact? Do you?"

"Yes, sir!" from one half. "No, sir!" from the other.

"Of course no," said the gentleman, with an indignant look at the wrong half. "Why, then, you are not to see anywhere, what you don't see in fact; you are not to have anywhere, what you don't have in fact. What is called Taste, is only another name for Fact."

Thomas Gradgrind nodded his approbation.

"This is a new principle, a discovery, a great discovery," said the gentleman. "Now, I'll try you again. Suppose you were going to carpet a room. Would you use a carpet having a representation of flowers upon it?"

There being a general conviction by this time that "No, sir!" was always the right answer to this gentleman, the chorus of No was very strong. Only a few feeble stragglers said Yes; among them Sissy Jupe.

"Girl number twenty," said the gentleman, smiling in the calm strength of knowledge.

Sissy blushed, and stood up.

"So you would carpet your room—or your husband's room, if you were a grown woman, and had a husband—with representations of flowers, would you," said the gentleman. "Why would you?"

"If you please, sir, I am very fond of flowers," returned the girl.

"And is that why you would put tables and chairs upon them, and have people walking over them with heavy boots?"

"It wouldn't hurt them, sir. They wouldn't crush and wither, if you please, sir. They would be the pictures of what was very pleasant and pretty, and I would fancy—"

"Ay, ay, ay! But you mustn't fancy," cried the gentleman, quite elated by coming so happily to his point. "That's it! You are never to fancy."

"You are not, Cecilia Jupe," Thomas Gradgrind solemnly repeated, "to do anything of that kind."

"Fact, fact, fact!" said the gentleman. And "Fact, fact, fact!" repeated Thomas Gradgrind.

"You are to be in all things regulated and governed," said the gentleman, "by fact. We hope to have, before long, a board of fact, composed of commissioners of fact, who will force the people to be a people of fact, and of nothing but fact. You must discard the word Fancy altogether. You have nothing to do with it. You are not to have, in any object of use or ornament, what would be a contradiction in fact. You don't walk upon flowers in fact; you cannot be allowed to walk upon flowers in carpets. You don't find that foreign birds and butterflies come and perch upon your crockery; you cannot be permitted to paint foreign birds and butterflies upon your crockery. You never meet with quadrupeds going up and down walls; you must not have quadrupeds represented upon walls. You must use," said the gentleman, "for all these purposes, combinations and modifications (in primary colors) of mathematical figures which are susceptible of proof and demonstration. This is the new discovery. This is fact. This is taste."

The girl curtsied, and sat down. She was very young, and she looked as if she were frightened by the matter-of-fact prospect the world afforded.

"Now, if Mr. M'Choakumchild," said the gentleman, "will proceed to give his first lesson here, Mr. Gradgrind, I shall be happy, at your request, to observe his mode of procedure."

Mr. Gradgrind was much obliged. "Mr. M'Choakumchild, we only wait for you."

So Mr. M'Choakumchild began in his best manner. He and some one hundred and forty other schoolmasters had been lately turned at the same time, in the same factory, on the same principles, like so many pianoforte legs. He had been put through an immense variety of paces, and had answered volumes of head-breaking questions. Orthography, etymology, syntax, and prosody, biography, astronomy, geography, and general cosmography, the sciences of compound proportion, algebra, land-surveying and levelling, vocal music, and drawing from models, were all at the ends of his ten chilled fingers. He had worked his stony way into Her Majesty's Most Honorable Privy Council's Schedule B, and had taken the bloom off the higher branches of mathematics and physical science, French, German, Latin, and Greek. He knew all about all the water-sheds of all the world (whatever they are), and all the histories of all the peoples, and all the names of all the rivers and mountains, and all the productions, manners, and customs of all the countries, and all their boundaries and bearings on the two-and-thirty points of the compass. Ah, rather overdone, M'Choakumchild. If he had only learned a little less, how infinitely better he might have taught much more!

He went to work in this preparatory lesson not unlike Morgiana in the Forty Thieves: looking into all the vessels ranged before him, one after another, to see what they contained. Say, good M'Choakumchild: when from thy boiling store thou shalt fill each jar brim full by and by, dost thou think that thou wilt always kill outright the robber Fancy lurking within—or sometimes only maim him and distort him!

MAN'S EDUCATION[1]

Jean Jacques Rousseau

DISCUSSION AND ANALYSIS

Jean Jacques Rousseau (1712–1778) is one of the most important figures in the history of education. Because his own life was far from exemplary his theories have been savagely attacked since their inception. To dismiss ideas because of their maker, however, is as absurd as refusing to use electric lights because one disapproves of Edison. The fact is that many of Rousseau's beliefs have been influential in the formation of our political democracy as well as in the creation of modern education and its methods. Rousseau was among the first figures of the Enlightenment to insist that the true function of a good government is to act as a referee rather than as a policeman. This doctrine he based upon the belief that man is inherently perfectible and good, rather than intrinsically evil. Jefferson, among others, was profoundly influenced by Rousseau's equalitarian theories.

In the field of education Rousseau stressed the importance of childhood as a formative period. The significance of this stress may be ascertained only after one realizes that without it we would probably not have the profound work of men such as Pestalozzi and Freud. Rousseau is also largely responsible for the notion that the best education is "natural." He felt that experience was the most effective type of learning, and that the

[1] From the book *Emile, Or Education* by Jean Jacques Rousseau. Everyman's Library, published by E. P. Dutton & Co., Inc. Reprinted with the permission of the publisher. *Émile, ou De l'Éducation* first appeared in 1762.

good teacher should appeal to the child's natural curiosity rather than superimposing upon him the meaningless facts and rules of the adult world.

In studying the present selection from Rousseau, you will find it worth while to underline key ideas. Then, as you go on through the text, you may profitably observe how often these ideas and their variants occur. One of Rousseau's most frequently quoted statements is that "The only habit the child should be allowed to contact is that of having no habits. . . ." Is such a prescription practical? What application does it have in a rapidly changing technological society?

Which of the following authors do you feel are in agreement with Rousseau's educational philosopy? Which in disagreement? Charles Lamb; Grambs; Hutchins; Childs; Jersild; Tead; Whitman; Steinbeck; Burton; Benedict. Give your reasons for your choices.

Rousseau relates an anecdote of a child who was silenced by being beaten by a nurse. At first, Rousseau mistook the reaction of the child for fear, but shortly afterwards he saw that "the poor wretch was choking with rage." How might such an anecdote be related to the problem of discipline in the classroom?

Are Rousseau's four maxims in accord with the findings of contemporary child psychology? Would you, in any way, supplement or qualify these maxims?

As I said before, man's education begins at birth; before he can speak or understand he is learning. Experience precedes instruction; when he recognises his nurse he has learnt much. The knowledge of the most ignorant man would surprise us if we had followed his course from birth to the present time. If all human knowledge were divided into two parts, one common to all, the other peculiar to the learned, the latter would seem very small compared with the former. But we scarcely heed this general experience, because it is acquired before the age of reason. Moreover, knowledge only attracts attention by its rarity, as in algebraic equations common factors count for nothing. Even animals learn much. They have senses and must learn to use them; they have needs, they must learn to satisfy them; they must learn to eat, walk, or fly. Quadrupeds which can stand on their feet from the first cannot walk for all that; from their first attempts it is clear that they lack confidence. Canaries who escape from their cage are unable to fly, having never used their wings. Living and feeling creatures are always learning. If plants could walk they would need senses and knowledge, else their species would die out. The child's first mental experiences are purely affective, he is only aware of pleasure and pain; it takes him a long time to acquire the definite sensations which show him things outside himself, but before these things present and withdraw themselves, so to speak, from his sight, taking size and shape for him, the recurrence of emotional experiences is beginning to subject the child to the rule of habit. You see his eyes constantly follow the light, and if the light comes from the side the eyes turn towards it, so that one must be careful to turn his head towards the light lest he should squint. He must also be accustomed from the first to the dark, or he will cry if he misses the light. Food and sleep, too, exactly measured, become necessary at regular intervals, and soon desire is no longer the effect of need, but of habit, or rather habit adds a fresh need to those of nature. You must be on your guard against this.

The only habit the child should be allowed to contract is that of having no habits; let him be carried on either arm, let him be accustomed to offer either hand, to use one or other indifferently; let him not want to eat, sleep, or do anything at fixed hours, nor be unable to be left alone by day or night. Prepare the way for his control of his liberty and the use of his strength by leaving his body its natural habit, by making him capable of lasting self-control, of doing all that he wills when his will is formed.

As soon as the child begins to take notice, what is shown him must be carefully chosen. The natural man is interested in all new things. He feels so feeble that he fears the unknown: the habit of seeing fresh things without ill effects destroys this fear. Children brought up in clean houses where there are no spiders are afraid of spiders, and this fear often lasts through life. I never saw peasants, man, woman, or child, afraid of spiders.

Since the mere choice of things shown him may make the child timid or brave, why should not his education begin before he can speak or understand? I would have him accustomed to see fresh things, ugly, repulsive, and strange beasts, but little by little, and far off till he is used to them, and till having seen others handle them he handles them himself. If in childhood he sees toads, snakes, and crayfish, he will not be afraid of any animal when he is grown up. Those who are continually seeing terrible things think nothing of them.

All children are afraid of masks. I begin by showing Émile a mask with a pleasant face, then some one puts this mask before his face; I begin to laugh, they all laugh too, and the child with them. By degrees I accustom him to less pleasing masks, and at last hideous ones. If I have arranged my stages skilfully, far from being afraid of the last mask, he will laugh at it as he did at the first. After that I am not afraid of people frightening him with masks.

When Hector bids farewell to Andromache, the young Astyanax, startled by the nodding plumes on the helmet, does not know his father; he flings himself weeping upon his nurse's bosom and wins from his mother a smile mingled with tears. What must be done to stay this terror? Just what Hector did; put the helmet on the ground and caress the child. In a calmer moment one would do more; one would go up to the helmet, play with the plumes, let the child feel them; at last the nurse would take the helmet and place it laughingly on her own head, if indeed a woman's hand dare touch the armour of Hector.

If Émile must get used to the sound of a gun, I first fire a pistol with a small charge. He is delighted with this sudden flash, this sort of lightning; I repeat the process with more powder; gradually I add a small charge without a wad, then a larger; in the end I accustom him to the sound of a gun, to fireworks, cannon, and the most terrible explosions.

I have observed that children are rarely afraid of thunder unless the peals are really terrible and actually hurt the ear, otherwise this fear only comes to them when they know that thunder sometimes hurts or kills. When reason begins to cause fear, let use reassure them. By slow and careful stages man and child learn to fear nothing.

In the dawn of life, when memory and imagination have not begun to function, the child only attends to what affects its senses. His sense experiences are the raw material of thought; they should, therefore, be presented to him in fitting order, so that memory may at a future time present them in the same order to his understanding; but as he only attends to his sensations it is enough, at first, to show him clearly the connection between these sensations and the things which cause them. He wants to touch and handle everything; do not check these movements which teach him invaluable lessons. Thus he learns to perceive the heat, cold, hardness, softness, weight, or lightness of bodies, to judge their size and shape and all their physical properties, by looking, feeling,[2] listening, and, above, all by comparing sight and touch, by judging with the eye what sensation they would cause to his hand.

It is only by movement that we learn the difference between self and not self; it is only by our own movements that we gain the idea of space. The child has not this idea, so he stretches out his hand to seize the object within his reach or that which is a hundred paces from him. You take this as a sign of tyranny, an attempt to bid the thing draw near, or to bid you bring it. Nothing of the kind, it is merely that the object first seen in his brain, then before his eyes, now seems close to his arms, and he has no idea of space beyond his reach. Be careful, therefore, to take him about, to move him from place to place, and to let him perceive the change in his surroundings, so as to teach him to judge of distances.

When he begins to perceive distances then you must change your plan, and only carry him when you please, not when he pleases; for as soon as he is no longer deceived by his senses, there is another motive for his effort. This change is remarkable and calls for explanations.

The discomfort caused by real needs is shown by signs, when the help of others is required. Hence the cries of children; they often cry; it must be so. Since they are only conscious of feelings, when those feelings are pleasant they enjoy them in silence; when they are painful they say so in their own way and demand relief. Now when they are awake they can scarcely be in a state of indifference; either they are asleep or else they are feeling something.

All our languages are the result of art. It has long been a subject of inquiry whether there ever was a natural language common to all; no doubt there is, and it is the language of children before they begin to speak. This language is inarticulate, but it has tone, stress, and meaning. The use of our own language has led us to neglect it so far as to forget it altogether. Let us study children and we shall soon learn it afresh from them. Nurses can teach us this language; they understand all their nurslings say to them, they answer them, and keep up long conversations with them; and though they use words, these words are quite useless. It is not the hearing of the word, but its accompanying intonation that is understood.

To the language of intonation is added the no less forcible language of gesture. The child uses, not its weak hands, but its face. The amount of expression in these undeveloped faces is extraordinary; their features change from one moment to another with incredible speed. You see smiles, desires, terror, come and go like lightning; every time the face seems different. The muscles of the face are undoubtedly more mobile than our own. On the other hand the eyes are almost expressionless. Such must be the sort of signs they use at an age when their only needs are those of the body. Grimaces are the

[2] Of all the senses that of smell is the latest to develop in children; up to two or three years of age they appear to be insensible of pleasant or unpleasant odours; in this respect they are as indifferent or rather as insensible as many animals.

sign of sensation, the glance expresses sentiment.

As man's first state is one of want and weakness, his first sounds are cries and tears. The child feels his needs and cannot satisfy them, he begs for help by his cries. Is he hungry or thirsty? there are tears; is he too cold or too hot? more tears; he needs movement and is kept quiet, more tears; he wants to sleep and is disturbed, he weeps. The less comfortable he is, the more he demands change. He has only one language because he has, so to say, only one kind of discomfort. In the imperfect state of his sense organs he does not distinguish their several impressions; all ills produce one feeling of sorrow.

These tears, which you think so little worthy of your attention, give rise to the first relation between man and his environment; here is forged the first link in the long chain of social order.

When the child cries he is uneasy, he feels some need which he cannot satisfy; you watch him, seek this need, find it, and satisfy it. If you can neither find it nor satisfy it, the tears continue and become tiresome. The child is petted to quiet him, he is rocked or sung to sleep; if he is obstinate, the nurse becomes impatient and threatens him; cruel nurses sometimes strike him. What strange lessons for him at his first entrance into life!

I shall never forget seeing one of these troublesome crying children thus beaten by his nurse. He was silent at once. I thought he was frightened, and said to myself, "This will be a servile being from whom nothing can be got but by harshness." I was wrong, the poor wretch was choking with rage, he could not breathe, he was black in the face. A moment later there were bitter cries, every sign of the anger, rage, and despair of this age was in his tones. I thought he would die. Had I doubted the innate sense of justice and injustice in man's heart, this one instance would have convinced me. I am sure that a drop of boiling liquid falling by chance on that child's hand would have hurt him less than that blow, slight in itself, but clearly given with the intention of hurting him.

This tendency to anger, vexation, and rage needs great care. Boerhaave thinks that most of the diseases of children are of the nature of convulsions, because the head being larger in proportion and the nervous system more extensive than in adults, they are more liable to nervous irritation. Take the greatest care to remove from them any servants who tease, annoy, or vex them. They are a hundredfold more dangerous and more fatal than fresh air and changing seasons. When children only experience resistance in things and never in the will of man, they do not become rebellious or passionate, and their health is better. This is one reason why the children of the poor, who are freer and more independent, are generally less frail and weakly, more vigorous than those who are supposed to be better brought up by being constantly thwarted; but you must always remember that it is one thing to refrain from thwarting them, but quite another to obey them. The child's first tears are prayers, beware lest they become commands; he begins by asking for aid, he ends by demanding service. Thus from his own weakness, the source of his first consciousness of independence, springs the later idea of rule and tyranny; but as this idea is aroused rather by his needs than by our services, we begin to see moral results whose causes are not in nature; thus we see how important it is, even at the earliest age, to discern the secret meaning of the gesture or cry.

When the child tries to seize something without speaking, he thinks he can reach the object, for he does not rightly judge its distance; when he cries and stretches out his hands he no longer misjudges the distance, he bids the object approach, or orders you to bring it to him. In the first case bring it to him slowly; in the second do not even seem to hear his cries. The more he cries the less you should heed him. He must learn in good time not to give commands to men, for he is not their master, nor to things, for they cannot hear him. Thus when the child wants something you mean to give him, it is better to carry him to it rather than to bring the thing to him. From this he will draw a conclusion suited to his age, and there is no other way of suggesting it to him.

The Abbé Saint-Pierre calls men big children; one might also call children little men. These statements are true, but they require explanation. But when Hobbes calls the wicked a strong child, his statement is contradicted by facts. All wickedness comes from weakness. The child is only naughty because he is weak; make him strong and he will be good; if we could do everything we should never do wrong. Of all the attributes of the Almighty, goodness is that which it would be hardest to dissociate from our conception of Him. All nations who have acknowledged a good and an evil power, have always regarded the evil as inferior to the good; otherwise their opinion would have been absurd. Compare this with the creed of the Savoyard clergyman later on in this book.

Reason alone teaches us to know good and evil. Therefore conscience, which makes us love the one and hate the other, though it is independent of reason, cannot develop without it. Before the age of reason we do good or ill without knowing it, and there is no morality in our actions, although there is sometimes in our feeling with regard to other people's actions in relation to ourselves. A child wants to overturn everything he sees. He breaks and smashes everything he can reach; he seizes a bird as he seizes a stone, and strangles it without knowing what he is about.

Why so? In the first place philosophy will account for this by inbred sin, man's pride, love of power, selfishness, spite; perhaps it will say in addition to this that the child's consciousness of his own weakness makes him eager to use his strength, to convince himself of it. But watch that broken down old man reduced in the downward course of life to the weakness of a child; not only is he quiet and peaceful, he would have all about him quiet and peaceful too; the least change disturbs and troubles him, he would like to see universal calm. How is it possible that similar feebleness and similar passions should produce such different effects in age and in infancy, if the original cause were not different? And where can we find this difference in cause except in the bodily condition of the two? The active principle, common to both, is growing in one case and declining in the other; it is being formed in the one and destroyed in the other; one is moving towards life, the other towards death. The failing activity of the old man is centred in his heart, the child's overflowing activity spreads abroad. He feels, if we may say so, strong enough to give life to all about him. To make or to destroy, it is all one to him; change is what he seeks, and all change involves action. If he seems to enjoy destructive activity it is only that it takes time to make things and very little time to break them, so that the work of destruction accords better with his eagerness.

While the Author of nature has given children this activity, He takes care that it shall do little harm by giving them small power to use it. But as soon as they can think of people as tools to be used, they use them to carry out their wishes and to supplement their own weakness. This is how they become tiresome, masterful, imperious, naughty, and unmanageable; a development which does not spring from a natural love of power, but one which has been taught them, for it does not need much experience to realise how pleasant it is to set others to work and to move the world by a word.

As the child grows it gains strength and becomes less restless and unquiet and more independent. Soul and body become better balanced and nature no longer asks for more movement than is required for self-preservation. But the love of power does not die with the need that aroused it; power arouses and flatters self-love, and habit strengthens it; thus caprice follows upon need, and the first seeds of prejudice and obstinacy are sown.

First Maxim.—Far from being too strong, children are not strong enough for all the claims of nature. Give them full use of such strength as they have; they will not abuse it.

Second Maxim.—Help them and supply the experience and strength they lack whenever the need is of the body.

Third Maxim.—In the help you give them confine yourself to what is really needful, without granting anything to caprice or unreason; for they will not be tormented by caprice if you do not call it into existence, seeing it is no part of nature.

Fourth Maxim.—Study carefully their speech and gestures, so that at an age when they are incapable of deceit you may discriminate between those desires which come from nature and those which spring from perversity.

The spirit of these rules is to give children more real liberty and less power, to let them do more for themselves and demand less of others; so that by teaching them from the first to confine their wishes within the limits of their powers they will scarcely feel the want of whatever is not in their power.

A PRIVATE LESSON FROM A BULLDOG[1]

Edward Eggleston

"Want to be a schoolmaster, do you? You? Well, what would *you* do in Flat Crick deestrick, *I'd* like to know? Why, the boys have driv off the last two, and licked the one afore them like blazes. You might teach a summer school, when nothin' but children come. But I 'low it takes a right smart *man* to be schoolmaster in Flat Crick in the winter. They'd pitch you out of doors, sonny, neck and heels, afore Christmas."

The young man, who had walked ten miles to get the school in this district, and who had been mentally reviewing his learning at every step he took, trembling lest the committee should find that he did not know enough, was not a little taken aback at this greeting from "old Jack Means," who was the first trustee that he lighted on. The impression made by these ominous remarks was emphasized by the glances which he received from Jack Means's two sons. The older one eyed him from the top of his brawny shoulders with that amiable look which a big dog turns on a little one before shaking him. Ralph Hartsook had never thought of being measured by the standard of muscle. This notion of beating education into young savages in spite of themselves dashed his ardor.

[1] From *The Hoosier Schoolmaster* by Edward Eggleston, chap. 1 (excerpt) and chap. 13 (complete). Copyright 1928 by The Macmillan Company. Reprinted with permission of the publisher.

He had walked right to where Jack Means was at work shaving shingles in his own front yard. While Mr. Means was making the speech which we have set down above, and punctuating it with expectorations, a large brindle bulldog had been sniffing at Ralph's heels, and a girl in a new linsey-woolsey dress, standing by the door, had nearly giggled her head off at the delightful prospect of seeing a new school-teacher eaten up by the ferocious brute.

The disheartening words of the old man, the immense muscles of the young man who was to be his rebellious pupil, the jaws of the ugly bulldog, and the heartless giggle of the girl, gave Ralph a delightful sense of having precipitated himself into a den of wild beasts. Faint with weariness and discouragement, and shivering with fear, he sat down on a wheelbarrow.

"You, Bull!" said the old man to the dog, which was showing more and more a disposition to make a meal of the incipient pedagogue, "you, Bull! git aout, you pup!" The dog walked sullenly off, but not until he had given Ralph a look full of promise of what he meant to do when he got a good chance. Ralph wished himself back in the village of Lewisburg, whence he had come.

"You see," continued Mr. Means, spitting in a meditative sort of a way, "you see, we a'n't none of your saft sort in these diggin's. It takes a *man* to boss this deestrick. Howsumdever, ef you think you kin trust your hide in Flat Crick schoolhouse I ha'n't got no 'bjection. But ef you git licked, don't come on us. Flat Crick don't pay no 'nsurance, you bet! Any other trustees? Wal, yes. But as I pay the most taxes, t'others jist let me run the thing. You can begin right off a Monday. They a'n't been no other applications. You see, it takes grit to apply for this school. The last master had a black eye for a month. But, as I wuz sayin', you can jist roll up and wade in. I 'low you've got spunk, maybe, and that goes for a heap sight more'n sinnoo with boys. Walk in, and stay over Sunday with me. You'll hev' to board roun', and I guess you better begin here."

Ralph did not go in, but sat out on the wheelbarrow, watching the old man shave shingles, while the boys split the blocks and chopped wood. Bull smelled of the new-comer again in an ugly way, and got a good kick from the older son for his pains. But out of one of his red eyes the dog warned the young schoolmaster that *he* should yet suffer for all kicks received on his account.

"Ef Bull once takes a holt, heaven and yarth can't make him let go," said the older son to Ralph, by way of comfort.

It was well for Ralph that he began to "board roun'" by stopping at Mr. Means's. Ralph felt that Flat Creek was what he needed. He had lived a bookish life; but here was his lesson in the art of managing people, for he who can manage the untamed and strapping youths of a winter school in Hoopole County has gone far toward learning one of the hardest of lessons. And in Ralph's time, things were worse than they are now.

A STRUGGLE FOR THE MASTERY

The school had closed on Monday evening as usual. The boys had been talking in knots all day. Nothing but the bulldog in the slender, resolute young master had kept down the rising storm. A teacher who has lost moral support at home, can not long govern a school. Ralph had effectually lost his popularity in the district, and the worst of it was that he could not divine from just what quarter the ill wind came, except that he felt sure of Small's agency in it somewhere. Even Hannah had slighted him, when he called at Means's on Monday morning to draw the pittance of pay that was due him.

He had expected a petition for a holiday on Christmas day. Such holidays are deducted from the teacher's time, and it is customary for the boys to "turn out" the teacher who refuses to grant them, by barring him out of the school house on Christmas and New Year's morning. Ralph had intended to grant a holiday if it should be asked, but it was not asked. Hank Banta was the ringleader in the disaffection, and he had managed to draw the surly Bud, who was present this morning, into it. It is but fair to say that Bud was in favor of making a request before resorting to extreme measures, but he was overruled. He gave it as his solemn opinion that the master was mighty peart, and they would be beat anyhow some way, but he would lick the master fer two cents ef he warn't so slim that he'd feel like he was fighting a baby.

And all that day things looked black. Ralph's countenance was cold and hard as stone, and Shocky trembled where he sat. Betsey Short tittered rather more than usual. A riot or a murder would have seemed amusing to her.

School was dismissed, and Ralph, instead of returning to the Squire's, set out for the village of Clifty, a few miles away. No one knew what he went for, and some suggested that he had "sloped."

But Bud said "he warn't that air kind. He was one of them air sort as died in their tracks, was Mr. Hartsook. They'd find him on the ground nex' morning, and he 'lowed the master war made of that air sort of stuff as would burn the dog-on'd ole schoolhouse to ashes, or blow it into splinters, but what he'd beat. Howsumdever he'd said he was a-goin' to help, and help he would; but all the sinno in Golier wouldn't be no account again the cute they was in the head of the master."

But Bud, discouraged as he was with the fear of Ralph's "cute," went like a martyr to the stake and took his place with the rest in the schoolhouse at nine o'clock at night. It may have been Ralph's intention to preoccupy the schoolhouse, for at ten o'clock Hank Banta was set shaking from head to foot at seeing a face that looked like the master's at the window. He waked up Bud and told him about it.

"Well, what are you a-tremblin' about, you coward?" growled Bud. "He won't shoot you; but he'll beat you at this game, I'll bet a hoss, and me, too, and make us both as 'shamed of ourselves as dogs with tin-kittles to their tails. You don't know the master, though he did duck you. But he'll larn you a good lesson this time, and me too, like as not." And Bud soon snored again, but Hank shook with fear every time he looked at the blackness outside the windows. He was sure he heard footfalls. He would have given anything to have been at home.

When morning came, the pupils began to gather early. A few boys who were likely to prove of service in the coming siege were admitted through the window, and then everything was made fast, and a "snack" was eaten.

"How do you 'low he'll get in?" said Hank, trying to hide his fear.

"How do I 'low?" said Bud. "I don't 'low nothin' about it. You might as well ax me where I 'low the nex' shootin' star is a-goin' to drap. Mr. Hartsook's mighty onsartin. But he'll git in, though, and tan your hide fer you, you see ef he don't. *Ef he don't blow up the schoolhouse with gunpowder!*" This last was thrown in by way of alleviating the fears of the cowardly Hank, for whom Bud had a great contempt.

The time for school had almost come. The boys inside were demoralized by waiting. They began to hope that the master had "sloped." They dreaded to see him coming.

"I don't believe he'll come," said Hank, with a cold shiver. "It's past school-time."

"Yes, he will come, too," said Bud. "And he 'lows to come in here mighty quick. I don't know how. But he'll be a-standin' at that air desk when it's nine o'clock. I'll bet a thousand dollars on that. *Ef* he don't take it into his head to blow us up!" Hank was now white.

Some of the parents came along, accidentally of course, and stopped to see the fun, sure that Bud would thrash the master if he tried to break in. Small, on the way to see a patient perhaps, reined up in front of the door. Still no Ralph. It was just five minutes before nine. A rumor now gained currency that he had been seen going to Clifty the evening before, and that he had not come back though in fact Ralph had come back, and had slept at Squire Hawkins's.

"There's the master," cried Betsey Short, who stood out in the road shivering and giggling alternately. For Ralph at that moment emerged from the sugar-camp by the schoolhouse, carrying a board.

"Ho! ho!" laughed Hank, "he thinks he'll smoke us out. I guess he'll find us ready." The boys had let the fire burn down, and there was now nothing but hot hickory coals on the hearth.

"I tell you he'll come in. He didn't go to Clifty fer nothin'," said Bud, who sat still on one of the benches which leaned against the door. "I don't know how, but they's lots of ways of killing a cat besides chokin' her with butter. He'll come in—*ef* he don't blow us all sky-high!"

Ralph's voice was now heard, demanding that the door be opened.

"Let's open her," said Hank, turning livid with fear at the firm, confident tone of the master.

Bud straightened himself up. "Hank, you're a coward. I've got a mind to kick you. You got me into this blamed mess, and now you want to crawfish. You jest tech one of these 'ere fastenin's, and I'll lay you out flat of your back afore you can say Jack Robinson."

The teacher was climbing to the roof with the board in hand.

"That air won't win," laughed Pete Jones outside. He saw that there was no smoke. Even Bud began to hope that Ralph would fail for once. The master was now on the ridge-pole of the schoolhouse. He took a paper from his pocket, and deliberately poured the contents down the chimney.

Mr. Pete Jones shouted "Gunpowder!" and set off down the road to be out of the way of the explosion. Dr. Small remembered, probably, that his patient might die while he sat there, and started on.

But Ralph emptied the paper, and laid the board over the chimney. What a row there was inside! The benches that were braced against the door were thrown down, and Hank Banta rushed out, rubbing his eyes, coughing frantically, and sure that he had been blown up. All the rest followed, Bud bringing up the rear sulkily, but coughing and sneezing for dear life. Such a smell of sulphur as came from that schoolhouse.

Betsey had to lean against the fence to giggle.

As soon as all were out, Ralph threw the board off the chimney, leaped to the ground, entered the schoolhouse, and opened the windows. The school soon followed him, and all was still.

"Would he thrash?" This was the important question in Hank Banta's mind. And the rest looked for a battle with Bud.

"It is just nine o'clock," said Ralph,

consulting his watch, "and I'm glad to see you all here promptly. I should have given you a holiday if you had asked me like gentlemen yesterday. On the whole, I think I shall give you a holiday, anyhow. The school is dismissed."

And Hank felt foolish.

And Bud secretly resolved to thrash Hank or the master, he didn't care which.

And Mirandy looked the love she could not utter.

And Betsey giggled.

ELOQUENCE—AND THE MASTER'S GILDED DOME[1]

Mark Twain

Vacation was approaching. The school-master, always severe, grew severer and more exacting than ever, for he wanted the school to make a good showing on "Examination" day. His rod and his ferule were seldom idle now—at least among the smaller pupils. Only the biggest boys, and young ladies of eighteen and twenty, escaped lashing. Mr. Dobbins's lashings were very vigorous ones, too; for although he carried, under his wig, a perfectly bald and shiny head, he had only reached middle age and there was no sign of feebleness in his muscle. As the great day approached, all the tyranny that was in him came to the surface; he seemed to take a vindictive pleasure in punishing the least shortcomings. The consequence was, that the smaller boys spent their days in terror and suffering and their nights in plotting revenge. They threw away no opportunity to do the master a mischief. But he kept ahead all the time. The retribution that followed every vengeful success was so sweeping and majestic that the boys always retired from the field badly worsted. At last they conspired together and hit upon a plan that promised a dazzling victory. They swore in the sign-painter's boy, told him the scheme, and asked his help. He had his own reasons for being delighted, for the master boarded in his father's family and had given the boy ample cause to hate him. The master's wife would go on a visit to the country in a few days, and there would be nothing to interfere with the plan; the master always prepared himself for great occasions by getting pretty well fuddled, and the sign-painter's boy said that when the dominie had reached the proper condition on Examination Evening he would "manage the thing" while he napped in his chair; then he would have him awakened at the right time and hurried away to school.

In the fullness of time the interesting occasion arrived. At eight in the evening the school-house was brilliantly lighted, and adorned with wreaths and festoons of foliage and flowers. The master sat throned in his great chair upon a raised platform, with his blackboard behind him. He was looking tolerably mellow. Three rows of benches on each side and six rows in front of him were occupied by the dignitaries of the town and by the parents of the pupils. To his left, back of the rows of citizens, was a spacious temporary platform upon which were seated the scholars who were to take part in the exercises of the evening; rows of small boys, washed and dressed to an intolerable state of discomfort; rows of gawky big boys; snowbanks of girls and young ladies clad in lawn and muslin and conspicuously conscious of their bare arms, their grand-

[1] From *The Adventures of Tom Sawyer*, Harper's Modern Classics edition. Originally published in 1876.

mothers' ancient trinkets, their bits of pink and blue ribbon and the flowers in their hair. All the rest of the house was filled with non-participating scholars.

The exercises began. A very little boy stood up and sheepishly recited, "You'd scarce expect one of my age to speak in public on the stage," etc.—accompanying himself with the painfully exact and spasmodic gestures which a machine might have used—supposing the machine to be a trifle out of order. But he got through safely, though cruelly scared, and got a fine round of applause when he made his manufactured bow and retired.

A little shamefaced girl lisped "Mary had a little lamb," etc., performed a compassion-inspiring curtsy, got her meed of applause, and sat down flushed and happy.

Tom Sawyer stepped forward with conceited confidence and soared into the unquenchable and indestructible "Give me liberty or give me death" speech, with fine fury and frantic gesticulation, and broke down in the middle of it. A ghastly stage-fright seized him, his legs quaked under him and he was like to choke. True, he had the manifest sympathy of the house—but he had the house's silence, too, which was even worse than its sympathy. The master frowned, and this completed the disaster. Tom struggled awhile and then retired, utterly defeated. There was a weak attempt at applause, but it died early.

"The Boy Stood on the Burning Deck" followed; also "The Assyrian Came Down," and other declamatory gems. Then there were reading exercises and a spelling-fight. The meager Latin class recited with honor. The prime feature of the evening was in order now—original "compositions" by the young ladies. Each in her turn stepped forward to the edge of the platform, cleared her throat, held up her manuscript (tied with dainty ribbon), and proceeded to read, with labored attention to "expression" and punctuation. The themes were the same that had been illuminated upon similar occasions by their mothers before them, their grandmothers, and doubtless all their ancestors in the female line clear back to the Crusades. "Friendship" was one; "Memories of Other Days"; "Religion in History"; "Dream Land"; "The Advantages of Culture"; "Forms of Political Government Compared and Contrasted"; "Melancholy"; "Filial Love"; "Heart Longings," etc., etc.

A prevalent feature in these compositions was a nursed and petted melancholy; another was a wasteful and opulent gush of "fine language"; another was a tendency to lug in by the ear particularly prized words and phrases until they were worn entirely out; and a peculiarity that conspicuously marked and marred them was the inveterate and intolerable sermon that wagged its crippled tail at the end of each and every one of them. No matter what the subject might be, a brain-racking effort was made to squirm it into some aspect or other that the moral and religious mind could contemplate with edification. The glaring insincerity of these sermons was not sufficient to compass the banishment of the fashion from the schools, and it is not sufficient to-day; it never will be sufficient while the world stands, perhaps. There is no school in all our land where the young ladies do not feel obliged to close their compositions with a sermon; and you will find that the sermon of the most frivolous and the least religious girl in the school is always the longest and the most relentlessly pious. But enough of this. Homely truth is unpalatable.

Let us return to the "Examination." The first composition that was read was one entitled "Is this, then, Life?" Perhaps the reader can endure an extract from it:

In the common walks of life, with what delightful emotions does the youthful mind look forward to some anticipated scene of festivity! Imagination is busy sketching rose-tinted pictures of joy. In fancy, the voluptuous votary of fashion sees herself amid the festive throng, "the observed of all observers." Her graceful form, arrayed in snowy robes, is whirling through the mazes of the joyous dance; her eye is brightest, her step is lightest in the gay assembly.

In such delicious fancies time quickly glides by, and the welcome hour arrives for her entrance into the elysian world, of which she has had such bright dreams. How fairylike does everything appear to her enchanted vision! Each new scene is more charming than the last. But after a while she finds that beneath this goodly exterior, all is vanity: the flattery which once charmed her soul now grates harshly upon her ear; the ballroom has lost its charms; and with wasted health and embittered heart she turns away with the conviction that earthly pleasures cannot satisfy the longings of the soul!

And so forth and so on. There was a buzz of gratification from time to time during the reading, accompanied by whispered ejaculations of "How sweet!" "How eloquent!" "So true!" etc., and after the thing had closed with a peculiarly afflicting sermon the applause was enthusiastic.

Then arose a slim, melancholy girl, whose face had the "interesting" paleness that comes of pills and indigestion, and read a "poem." Two stanzas of it will do:

A Missouri Maiden's Farewell to Alabama

Alabama, good-by! I love thee well!
But yet for a while do I leave thee now!
Sad, yes, sad thoughts of thee my heart doth swell,
And burning recollections throng my brow!
For I have wandered through thy flowery woods;
Have roamed and read near Tallapoosa's stream;
Have listened to Tallassee's warring floods,
And wooed on Coosa's side Aurora's beam.

Yet shame I not to bear an o'er-full heart,
Nor blush to turn behind my tearful eyes;
'Tis from no stranger land I now must part,
'Tis to no strangers left I yield these sighs.
Welcome and home were mine within this State,
Whose vales I leave—whose spires fade fast from me;
And cold must be mine eyes, and heart, and tête,
When, dear Alabama! they turn cold on thee!

There were very few there who knew what "*tête*" meant, but the poem was very saisfactory, nevertheless.

Next appeared a dark-complexioned, black-eyed, black-haired young lady, who paused an impressive moment, assumed a tragic expression, and began to read in a measured, solemn tone.

A Vision

Dark and tempestuous was night. Around the throne on high not a single star quivered; but the deep intonations of the heavy thunder constantly vibrated upon the ear; whilst the terrific lightning revealed in angry mood through the cloudy chambers of heaven, seeming to scorn the power exerted over its terror by the illustrious Franklin! Even the boisterous winds unanimously came forth from their mystic homes, and blustered about as if to enhance by their aid the wildness of the scene.

At such a time, so dark, so dreary, for human sympathy my very spirit sighed; but instead thereof,

"My dearest friend, my counselor, my comforter and guide—
My joy in grief, my second bliss in joy," came to my side.

She moved like one of those bright beings pictured in the sunny walks of fancy's Eden by the romantic and young, a queen of beauty unadorned save by her own transcendent loveliness. So soft was her step, it failed to make even a sound, and but for the magical thrill imparted by her genial touch, as other unobtrusive beauties, she would have glided away unperceived—unsought. A strange sadness rested upon her features, like icy tears upon the robe of December, as she pointed to the contending elements without, and bade me contemplate the two beings presented.

This nightmare occupied some ten pages of manuscript and wound up with a sermon so destructive of all hope to non-Presbyterians that it took the first prize. This composition was considered to be the very finest effort of the evening. The mayor of the village, in delivering the prize to the author of it, made a warm speech in which he said that it was by far the most "eloquent" thing he had ever listened to, and that Daniel Webster himself might well be proud of it.

It may be remarked, in passing, that the number of compositions in which the word "beauteous" was over-fondled, and human experience referred to as "life's page," was up to the usual average.

Now the master, mellow almost to the verge of geniality, put his chair aside, turned his back to the audience, and began to draw a map of America on the blackboard, to exercise the geography class upon. But he made a sad business of it with his unsteady hand, and a smothered titter rippled over the house. He knew what the matter was and set himself to right it. He sponged out lines and remade them; but he only distorted them more than ever, and the tittering was more pronounced. He threw his entire attention upon his work, now, as if determined not to be put down by the mirth. He felt that all eyes were fastened upon him; he imagined he was succeeding, and yet the tittering continued; it even manifestly increased. And well it might. There was a garret above, pierced with a scuttle over his head; and down through this scuttle came a cat, suspended around the haunches by a string; she had a rag tied about her head and jaws to keep her from mewing; as she slowly descended she curved upward and clawed at the string, she swung downward and clawed at the intangible air. The tittering rose higher and higher—the cat was within six inches of the absorbed teacher's head—down, down, a little lower, and she grabbed his wig with her desperate claws, clung to it, and was snatched up into the garret in an instant with her trophy still in her possession! And how the light did blaze abroad from the master's bald pate—for the sign-painter's boy had *gilded* it!

That broke up the meeting. The boys were avenged. Vacation had come.

NOTE.—The pretended "compositions" quoted in this chapter are taken without alteration from a volume entitled "Prose and Poetry, by a Western Lady"—but they are exactly and precisely after the school-girl pattern, and hence are much happier than any mere imitations could be.

CHANGES IN THE ROLE OF THE TEACHER[1]

David Riesman

DISCUSSION AND ANALYSIS

As you have read the descriptions of the teacher given by Lamb, by Dickens, Eggleston and Twain, you have certainly said to yourself, "Thank heavens times have changed!" While the teacher may face different tests today, such as those presented by the students in Evan Hunter's story from the *Blackboard Jungle* in Chapter 13, or "One-World Kids" in the same chapter, assuredly the teacher's situation has changed for the better.

In what ways the teacher's role has changed—and whether we can be glad or sorry—is the subject of this selection from *The Lonely Crowd.*

Riesman speaks, in this comment on the teacher, about inner-directed, other-directed, and tradition-directed. Perhaps a word of explanation of these terms will help the reader see the points that Riesman makes. A person who is inner-directed acts through personal conviction, is not dependent on the approval or commendation of others, but can pursue those ends he deems important without regard for public appraisal. The person who is tradition-directed is guided primarily by his understanding of what has been always thought of as the right thing to do. Possibly the opinion of his ancestors is more significant than opinion of his contemporaries. If convinced that what he is doing is in accord with established patterns, he will not be swayed by mere public opinion. The other-directed person looks to the world around him for validation of his own existence, of his values, of his very soul. If "the crowd" is doing it, he thinks it is probably right, though he is more concerned with what the crowd is doing than with what is right or wrong to do.

The above definitions hardly do justice to the richness of interpretation that will be found in the body of the book from which this excerpt is taken. As you read about teachers in terms of these categories of behavior, you may or may not agree with Riesman's analysis. For instance, he feels that the modern school is dominated by other-directed goals; what was meant to be liberating is now thwarting. He feels, too, that the teacher in an other-directed school now is more concerned with "adjustment" than with intellectual competence. Do you agree? What evidence do you see in classrooms to support or refute the claims of Riesman? What kind of school do you think Riesman would feel more truly served individual needs in a free society?

[1] From *The Lonely Crowd,* by David Riesman with Nathan Glazer and Reuel Denney. Copyright 1950, 1953, by Yale University Press. Reprinted by arrangement with Yale University Press.

You will note that Riesman refers to the doctoral study of Becker on the career of the Chicago schoolteacher, which we have included as a selection in Chapter 12. You may find it instructive to turn now to this article and see in what way Riesman has made use of such source data to build up his case.

Riesman says that instead of seating children arbitrarily, a sociometric form determines who sits next to whom. Do you know what sociometrics is? A sociometric form is a device for finding out who likes or rejects whom; it is called sometimes a "friendship finder." Teachers develop great concern over children who have no friends, as revealed by this device. Do you think all children should always have friends? But on the other hand, what is the person without the group? How can you, as a teacher, find the balance between conformity and individuality that helps to develop mature persons?

Much could be said about the changing configuration of adult authorities, other than the parents, as society moves from dependence on inner-direction to dependence on other-direction. Largely for economic reasons the governess, mammy, or hired tutor, for instance, virtually disappears from middle- and upper middle-class homes. One significant consequence is that children are no longer raised by people who hold up to them the standard of a family or class. Such a standard is good training in inner-direction—in the acquisition of generalized goals; it is at the same time a partial buffer against the indiscriminate influence of the peer-group. But there is another more subtle consequence. The child who has been raised by a governess and educated by a tutor gains a very keen sense for the disparities of power in the home and in the society. When he goes off to boarding school or college he is likely to remain unimpressed by his teachers — like the upper-class mother who told the school headmaster: "I don't see why the masters can't get along with Johnny; all the other servants do." Such a child is not going to be interested in allowing his teachers to counsel him in his peer-group relations or emotional life.

Furthermore, the presence of these adults in the home—somewhat like the extended family in earlier eras—helps reduce the emotional intensity of parent-child relations. Though the child knows who is boss in the home, he can still play these other "officials" off against parental authority. And, indeed, the inner-directed parents, frequently not overeager for warmth from the child, are quite willing to have the child's experience of affection associated with persons of lower status. The inner-directed young man raised under these conditions learns to find emotional release with prostitutes and others of low status. He becomes capable of impersonal relations with people and sometimes incapable of any other kind. This is one of the prices he pays for his relative impermeability to the needs and wishes of his peers, and helps account for his ability, when in pursuit of some end he values, to steel himself against their indifference or hostility.

Grandmothers as authorities are almost as obsolete as governesses. There is no room for them in the modern apartment, nor can they, any more than the children themselves, find a useful economic role.

Nevertheless they endure, concomitant with the increased longevity of the later population phases. The increased personalization of relationships that other-direction brings means that "strangers" in the home are less and less endurable: the in-law problem, a standard joke in many cultures over many centuries, takes on new meaning where sensitive, highly individuated people live without characterological defenses against others.

The elimination of the grandmother from a central role in the home is, moreover, symbolic of the rapidity of the changes we are discussing. She is two generations removed from current practices on the "frontier of consumption." While the parents try to keep up with their children, both as a means of staying young and as a means of staying influential, this is seldom possible for the grandparents. Hence their role in the formation of the other-directed character is negligible. Far from presenting the child with a relatively consistent "family portrait," standing in back of the parents and strengthening them, grandparents stand as emblems of how little one can learn from one's elders about the things that matter.

A parallel development removes another set of parent surrogates who played an important role in earlier periods: the older brothers or sisters who, like sophomores, hazed the younger in subjecting them to the family pattern of discipline. Today the older children—if there are any—are frequently more willing to earn cash as baby sitters than to supervise the training of their own younger brothers and sisters. The lure of a job may get children to work outside their homes; that still makes sense to them. But within their own home they are the privileged guests in a rather second-rate hotel, a hotel whose harassed but smiling managers they put under constant pressure for renovation.

THE TEACHER'S ROLE IN THE STAGE OF INNER-DIRECTION

One important authority, however, remains: a proxy parent whose power has probably increased as a consequence of the shift to other-direction. This is the schoolteacher, and we turn now to a fuller exploration of the change in her role.

In the period when inner-direction insures middle-class conformity, school starts relatively late—there are few nursery schools. The teacher's task is largely to train the children in decorum and in intellectual matters. The decorum may be the minimum of discipline needed to keep order in the classroom or the maximum of polish needed to decorate girls of the upper social strata. As schools become more plentiful and more readily accessible and "democratic," the obligation to train the child in middle-class speech and manners—that he may be aided in his rise above his parents' rank—falls upon the teacher. But the teacher does not work close to the child's emotional level. And the teacher regards her job as a limited one, sharply demarcated from the equally rigorous task of the home.

The physical setting in school reflects this situation. Seating is formal—all face front—and often alphabetical. The walls are decorated with the ruins of Pompeii and the bust of Caesar. For all but the few exceptional children who can transcend the dead forms of their classical education and make the ancient world come alive, these etchings and statues signify the irrelevance of the school to the emotional problems of the child.

The teacher herself has neither understanding of nor time for these emotional problems, and the child's relation to other children enters her purview only in disciplinary cases. Often she has simply no authority: she is a common scold with too large a brood. Or she manages to maintain discipline by strictures and punishments. But these absorb the emotional attention of the children, often uniting them in opposition to authority.

In the recent Swedish movie *Torment* we see this pattern still at work in the near-contemporary scene. Teachers and parents share the task of instilling inner-directed values. The villain is a harsh and overbearing, neurotic prep-school teacher. All the boys hate him; some fear him; no self-respecting boy would dream—despite the teacher's groping efforts—of being his friend. The hero is a boy who rebels, not so much because he wants to but rather because he is forced to by his teacher. He and his friends suffer, but their parents and teachers do not invade their lives, and they have privacy with each other and with girls, so long as no serious breach of decorum is evident. This rebellion itself—its success is not the issue—is part of the process of developing an inner-directed character.

An equally moving portrait is Antonia White's novel of a girl's convent school, *Frost in May*. Though the nuns at the school go quite far in "molding character" and viciously cut down signs of spontaneity and open-mindedness in the gifted heroine, they have back of them only the old-fashioned sanctions of penance and salvation. Their charges break or bend or run away or join the church—they do not open up to the nuns as friends. The very existence of uniforms, as in a military school, symbolizes the walls that separate the authorities from the children.

We may sum all this up by saying that the school of this period is concerned largely with impersonal matters. The sexes are segregated. The focus is on an intellectual content that for most children has little emotional bite. Elocution, like female accomplishment, is impersonal, too; the child is not asked to "be himself"—nor does the school aim to be like "real life." Teachers, whether spinsterly or motherly types, do not know enough, even if they had the time and energy, to take an active hand in the socialization of tastes or of peer-group relations. While parents may permit the teachers to enforce certain rules of morality directly related to school, such as modesty of dress and honesty in examinations, and to inculcate certain rules of manners directly related to social ascent, they hardly allow interference with play groups, even in the interests of enforcing ethnic or economic democracy. The teacher is supposed to see that the children learn a curriculum, not that they enjoy it or learn group cooperation. The present practice of progressive grammar schools which decide whether or not to take a child by putting him in his putative group and seeing how he fits in would hardly have been conceivable.

Nevertheless, despite the social distance between teacher and child, the school's unquestioning emphasis on intellectual ability is profoundly important in shaping the inner-directed character. It affirms to the child that what matters is what he can *accomplish*, not how nice is his smile or how cooperative his attitude. And while the objectivity of the criteria for judging these skills and competences is rightfully called into question today—when we can see very clearly, for instance, the class bias in intelligence tests and written examinations—the inner-directed school is not aware of such biases, and hence its standards can appear unequivocal and unalterable. For this reason these standards can be internalized both by those who succeed and by those who fail. They are felt as real and given, not as somebody's whim. Thus the school reinforces the home in setting for the child goals that are clear to all and that give direction and meaning to life thereafter.

Whatever the security children gain from knowing where they stand—a security they no longer have in the other-directed progressive school—we must not forget how harshly this system bears on those who cannot make the grade: they are often broken; there is little mercy for them on psychological grounds. Brains, status, perhaps also docility, win the teacher, rather than "personality" or "problems." Some of the failures rebel. But these, too, are hammered into shape by the school—bad shape. Occasionally the frontier and other opportunities for mobility provide an exit for the academically outclassed; and, still more occasionally, the rebel returns, like a mythical hero, having lived his troubles down, to alleviate the guilt of other misfits and give them hope for their own future. By and large, however, the very unequivocality of the school's standards that gives the children a certain security also means that the standards will be internalized even by those who fail. They will carry with them the aftereffects of emotional shock whose violence lies beyond criticism—sometimes even beyond recall.

THE TEACHER'S ROLE IN THE STAGE OF OTHER-DIRECTION

Progressive education began as a movement to liberate children from the crushing of talent and breaking of will that was the fate of many, even of those whose inner-direction might have seemed to them and to the observer stable and sound enough. Its aim, and to a very considerable degree, its achievement, was to develop the individuality of the child; and its method was to focus the teacher's attention on more facets of the child than his intellectual abilities. Today, however, progressive education is often no longer progressive; as people have become more other-directed, educational methods that were once liberating may even tend to thwart individuality rather than advance and protect it. The story can be quickly told.

Progressive schools have helped lower the age of school entry; the two- to five-year-old groups learn to associate school not with forbidding adults and dreary subjects but with play and understanding adults. The latter are, increasingly, young college graduates who have been taught to be more concerned with the child's social and psychological adjustment than with his academic progress—indeed, to scan the intellectual performance for signs of social maladjustment. These new teachers are more specialized. They don't claim to "understand children" but to have studied Gesell on the "fives" or the "nines"; and this greater knowledge not only prevents the children from uniting in a wall of distrust or conspiracy against the school but also permits the teacher to take a greater hand in the socialization of spheres—consumption, friendship, fantasy—which the older-type teacher, whatever her personal desires, could not touch. Our wealthier society can afford this amount of individuation and "unnecessary" schooling.

Physical arrangements, too—in seating, age-grading, decoration — symbolize the changes in the teacher's function. The sexes are mixed. Seating is arranged "informally." That is, *alphabetic* forms disappear, often to be replaced by *sociometric* forms that bring together compeers. This often means that where to sit becomes problematical—a clue to one's location on the friendship chart. Gesell grading is as severe as intellectual grading was in the earlier era; whatever their intellectual gifts, children stay with their presumed social peers.[2] The desks change their form, too;

[2] Howard C. Becker ("Role and Career Problems of the Chicago Public School Teacher," unpublished Ph.D. dissertation, University of Chicago, 1951) has been observing the classroom consequences of the decline of the practice both of skipping grades and of holding children back who must repeat the

they are more apt to be movable tables with open shelves than places where one may hide things. The teacher no longer sits on a dais or struts before a blackboard but joins the family circle.

Above all, the walls change their look. The walls of the modern grade school are decorated with the paintings of the children or their montages from the class in social studies. Thus the competitive and contemporary problems of the children look down on them from walls which, like the teacher herself, are no longer impersonal. This looks progressive, looks like a salute to creativeness and individuality; but again we meet paradox. While the school deemphasizes grades and report cards, the displays seem almost to ask the children: "Mirror, mirror on the wall, who is fairest of us all?" [3]

While the children's paintings and montages show considerable imaginative gift in the pre-adolescent period, the school itself is nevertheless still one of the agencies for the destruction of fantasy, as it was in the preceding era. Imagination withers in most of the children by adolescence. What survives is neither artistic craft nor artistic fantasy but the socialization of taste and interest that can already be seen in process in the stylization of perception in the children's paintings and stories. The stories of the later progressive grades are apt to be characterized by "realism." This realism is subtly influenced by the ideals of the progressive movement. Caesar and Pompeii are replaced by visits to stores and dairies, by maps from *Life*, and by *The Weekly Reader*; and fairy tales are replaced by stories about trains, telephones, and grocery stores, and, later, by material on race relations or the United Nations or "our Latin American neighbors."

These changes in arrangement and topic assist the breakdown of walls between teacher and pupil; and this in turn helps to break down walls between student and student, permitting that rapid circulation of tastes which is a prelude to other-directed socialization. Whereas the inner-directed school child might well have hidden his stories and paintings under his bed—like the adult who, as we saw, often kept a diary—the other-directed child

---

grade. The teachers, faced with a group of identical age but vastly different capacities and willingnesses, meet the situation by dividing the class into two or three like-minded groups. Mobility between groups is discouraged, and children are encouraged to imitate their groupmates. The teacher herself, in the public schools, is probably inner-directed, but she is forced by her situation to promote other-direction among her charges.

The following quotation from Mr. Becker's interviews is a poignant example of how a teacher will promote other-direction in her efforts to get the children to have more interesting weekends: "Every class I have I start out the year by making a survey. I have each child get up and tell what he did over the weekend. These last few years I've noticed that more and more children get up and say, 'Saturday I went to the show, Sunday I went to the show' . . . I've been teaching twenty-five years, and it never used to be like that. Children used to do more interesting things, they would go places instead of 'Saturday I went to the show, Sunday I went to the show' . . . What I do is to give a talk on all the interesting things that could be done—like going to museums and things like that. And also things like playing baseball and going on bike rides. By the end of the term a child is ashamed if he has to get up and say, 'Saturday I went to the show, Sunday I went to the show.' All the rest of the children laugh at him. So they really try to do some interesting things."

[3] Still more paradoxically, it often happens that those schools that insist most strongly that the child be original and creative by this very demand make it difficult for him to be so. He dare not imitate an established master nor, in some cases, even imitate his own earlier work. Though the introduction of the arts into the school opens up the whole art world to many children, who would have no time or stimulation outside, other children are forced to socialize performances that would earlier have gone unnoticed by peers and adults.

reads his stories to the group and puts his paintings on the wall. Play, which in the earlier epoch is often an extracurricular and private hobby, shared at most with a small group, now becomes part of the school enterprise itself, serving a "realistic" purpose.

The teacher's role in this situation is often that of opinion leader. She is the one who spreads the messages concerning taste that come from the progressive urban centers. She conveys to the children that what matters is not their industry or learning as such but their adjustment in the group, their cooperation, their (carefully stylized and limited) initiative and leadership.

Especially important is the fact that the cooperation and leadership that are inculcated in and expected of the children are frequently contentless. In nursery school it is not important whether Johnny plays with a truck or in the sandbox, but it matters very much whether he involves himself with Bill—via any object at all. To be sure, there are a few, a very few, truly progressive schools where the children operating on the Dalton plan and similar plans exercise genuine choice of their program, move at their own pace, and use the teacher as a friendly reference library; here cooperation is necessary and meaningful in actual work on serious projects. Far more frequently, however, the teacher continues to hold the reins of authority in her hands, hiding her authority, like her compeer, the other-directed parent, under the cloak of "reasoning" and manipulation. She determines the program and its pace—indeed, often holding the children back because she fails to realize that children, left to themselves, are capable of curiosity about highly abstract matters. She may delay them by making arithmetic "realistic" and languages fun—as well as by substituting social studies for history. In extreme forms of this situation there is nothing on which the children have to cooperate in order to get it done. The teacher will do it for them anyway. Hence when she asks that they be cooperative she is really asking simply that they be nice.

However, though the request seems simple, it is not casually made: the teacher is very tense about it. Deprived of older methods of discipline, she is, if anything, even more helpless than the parents who can always fall back on those methods in a pinch, though guiltily and rather ineffectively. The teacher neither dares to nor cares to; she has been taught that bad behavior on the children's part implies poor management on her part. Moreover, she herself is not interested in the intellectual content of what is taught, nor is this content apt to come up in a staff meeting or PTA discussion. These adult groups are often concerned with teaching tolerance, both ethnic and economic; and the emphasis on social studies that results means that intellectual content and skill become still more attenuated. Consequently, the teacher's emotional energies are channeled into the area of group relations. Her social skills develop; she may be sensitive to cliques based on "mere friendship" and seek to break them up lest any be left out. Correspondingly, her love for certain specific children may be trained out of her. All the more, she needs the general cooperation of all the children to assure herself that she is doing her job. Her surface amiability and friendliness, coupled with this underlying anxiety concerning the children's response, must be very confusing to the children who will probably conclude that to be uncooperative is about the worst thing one can be.

Of course the teacher will see to it that the children practice cooperation in small matters: in deciding whether to study the Peruvians or the Colombians, in nominating class officers for early practice in the great contemporary rituals of electioneering and parliamenteering, and in organizing contributions for the Red Cross or a Tag Day. Thus the children are supposed to learn democracy by underplaying the skills of intellect and overplaying the skills of gregariousness and amiability—skill democracy, in fact, based on respect for ability to do something, tends to survive only in athletics.

There is, therefore, a curious resemblance between the role of the teacher in the small-class modern school—a role that has spread from the progressive private schools to a good number of the public schools—and the role of the industrial relations department in a modern factory. The latter is also increasingly concerned with cooperation between men and men and between men and management, as technical skill becomes less and less of a major concern. In a few of the more advanced plants there is even a pattern of democratic decision on moot matters—occasionally important because it affects piecework rates and seniority rules, but usually as trivial as the similar decisions of grammar-school government. Thus the other-directed child is taught at school to take his place in a society where the concern of the group is less with what it produces than with its internal group relations, its morale.

5

PHILOSOPHICAL FOUNDATIONS OF EDUCATION: Theory Guides Practice

SOCIETY AND EDUCATION[1] and ADJUSTMENT TO THE ENVIRONMENT[2]

DISCUSSION AND ANALYSIS

Aristotle once said, "We all philosophize, whether we will it or no." A little thought can convince one of the truth of this statement. Our overt behavior, our institutions—including our schools—our political and religious systems, all are based on more or less consistent sets of assumptions. Collectively, these assumptions can be termed philosophies. Since education, like everything else, finds its sources in such assumptions, it is most important that we be aware of them. A really satisfactory philosophy should be held with conviction and a high degree of consciousness. It should also, like any hypothesis, be internally self-consistent and externally in accord with the facts.

Up to now we have discussed a variety of topics, such as success in teaching, the nature of a good teacher, and teaching as a profession, without necessarily examining the ideas behind our arguments. To say that "Mrs. Hart is a swell teacher because she helps us to adjust to the world as it is" is, in fact, to make a value judgment wherein it is understood that adjustment should be a prime aim of education. The alert student may also detect the implication that the world is all right as it is and need not be changed to suit the needs or demands of individuals.

[1] From *Education and Morals*, chap. 2, by John L. Childs. Copyright 1950 by Appleton-Century-Crofts, Inc. Reprinted with the permission of the publisher.

[2] From *The Conflict in Education in a Democratic Society* by Robert M. Hutchins, pp. 2–25. Copyright, 1953, by Harper & Brothers. Reprinted with the permission of Harper & Brothers.

The two prose selections in this chapter offer us two quite opposed points of view. By studying the arguments carefully, the student will be aided in bringing his own unconscious assumptions to light. This, in turn, should help him in formulating a coherent and consistent philosophy of education of his own. Once he has started on this road, he should check and test his formulations by reference to concrete situations and readings. He should ask himself, for example, if his ideas of the good teacher are now the same as they were when he first read Chapter 2. How have they changed? Hutchins suggests that a university should be more concerned with criticizing the professions than with training members for them. Are there any selections in Chapter 3 that seem to contradict Hutchins' idea? In reconsidering the readings from Chapter 4 one should try to understand how philosophies of education may be affected by historical developments. Does a knowledge of history "free" one, at least to some extent, from the forces of history?

In comparing Hutchins and Childs, you should note the firmness of both articles. Is it possible to agree with both? To disagree? Do you feel that Childs is more democratic than Hutchins? Or do you think both men are democratic, but merely wish to approach their ideals via different roads? Childs states that "A school best provides for the growth of the child when it maintains living interaction with the community of which he is part." How does Hutchins disagree with this viewpoint? How do you imagine Childs might criticize Hutchins' notion of the university as a "center of independent thought"?

SOCIETY AND EDUCATION

John L. Childs

The purposes and the subject-matters of the school are not developed by a process of adult contemplation carried on in a social vacuum, nor do they arise spontaneously from the interests and activities of school children. They are invariably developed through the evaluative and selective response of adults to the traditions, the conventions, the life practices, and the changing conditions of their society. Thus a school is a very human institution. Its program is never formulated by "nature," by "history," by "the state," by "religion," by "science," or by any impersonal agency or process; it is always constructed by ordinary human beings whose value judgments and educational selections are necessarily influenced by factors of time, place, status, interest, belief, knowledge and custom. Both religious and secular programs of education bear the marks of the particular societies in which they have originated, as well as the definite cultural interests they have been designed to serve.

Search into the materials and the purposes of any school and you will come upon that which extends beyond the school. You will encounter the language, the literature, the practical and fine arts, the science, the institutions, the moral ideals, and the faiths of an historical, human group. You will find these things, however, not in the gross form in which they exist and function in the society that creates the school, but abstracted, sifted, classified, and graded into a curriculum for the nurture of the young. Considerations both of group welfare and of pedagogy play a part in this process by which the affairs of a human society are selected and transformed into a curriculum for the school. But no matter how drastically these life materials may be refined and rearranged in the subject-matters and activities of the school, they are always taken originally by somebody, for some definite purpose, from the totality of the ways of life and thought of a human society. As these group practices, interests, beliefs, and outlooks change, the program of the school also changes. In this basic sense education *is* a social affair. Educational choices are always, in the last analysis, social choices.

HUMAN INTERESTS AND THE PURPOSES OF EDUCATION

The historical and the comparative study of man's educational activities shows that the actual ends for which different societies, and different groups within the same society have chosen to educate have been many and various. . . . Adults tend to make central in their program for the nurture of the young whatever they consider of major importance and value in their ways of life and thought. Even the needs and the possibilities of the young are always defined in terms of the particular mode of life that the adults who organize the school desire and expect the young to lead. It is therefore natural that educational purposes, materials, and methods have differed as widely as have types of human association, systems of value, and patterns of authority and leadership.

Military castes, for example, have resorted to education in order to fashion the young into efficient "bayonets" for their armed forces. Social and political despots have used education for the purpose of breeding devoted and docile "subjects" of their autocratic regimes. Revolutionary communists have organized schools to train the young in the ideology of the class-struggle, and to fashion them into "militant warriors" in the world-struggle to overthrow the existing capitalist system. Supernaturalists have elaborated school rituals and programs in order to nurture "devout believers" in a revealed plan of life and education. Literary humanists have made a curriculum of the "great-books" and have sought to develop the "gentleman of culture"—the cultivated person who is possessed of "the conscience of truths valid for all and the will to undertake duties common to all." Experimental scientists have sought to develop the "man of the laboratory," equipped with the attitudes, faiths, and allegiances implicit in the objective experimental process of discovering and testing truth. Ardent nationalists have demanded a common system of schools devoted to the cultivation of the "patriot"—the obedient citizen whose final authority and supreme object of affection and loyalty is the fatherland. Absolute pacifists have founded schools dedicated to world brotherhood and the religion of humanity, and designed to create the "conscientious objector"—the person who instinctively believes that "all war is sin" and who will have no part in its organized slaughter of fellow human beings. Private enterprisers have propagandized for a school that will make each child into a "rugged individualist," committed beyond recall to the system of private ownership and the principle of "free" and "unregulated" acquisition. Liberals have sought a school system that would cultivate the "informed and critical mind," contending that the "enlightened citizen" is the only secure foundation for a humane mode of existence.

Diverse as the foregoing educational purposes and programs are, they have certain common features. Each of these educational programs defines some historical group's conception of basic life interests and meanings. Each has a conception of the kind of person it wants the school to produce, and its norm or standard for human personality is derived from its interpretation of fundamental group values and relationships. Each of these groups is concerned to construct a definite program through which its preferred and predominant pattern of living will be bred into the dispositions and the habits of the young. It has no thought of letting "the child develop in his own way," whatever that may be held to mean. Each expects that its teachers will be faithful in the work of communicating its chosen values to the young. Although the "ethical" quality of these programs varies enormously, they are all "moral" undertakings in the elemental meaning of the term *moral:* each has its governing principles of evaluation and choice in matters of taste, faith, allegiance, and human conduct.

LIFE IMPERATIVES AND EDUCATIONAL PROGRAMS

Fortunately, the clash in purpose and program is not quite so sharp as the foregoing list of life interests and educational objectives suggests. The history of education shows that the predominant life-alternative, or value, favored by any particular cultural group, or sub-group, has seldom been the sole interest included in its total educational program. Militarists, tyrants, revolutionists, supernaturalists, literary-humanists, scientists, nationalists, pacifists, capitalists, and liberals: all, alike, live under the compulsions of the here and now. This means that each must take account of the stubborn requirements of human existence—collective and personal. In order to provide for these life-imperatives, adults have to do more than train the young in a single cherished and selected aspect of life; their educational programs must also provide some opportunity for the new-born to learn about the varied human arts and institutionalized practices that are essential to the maintenance of their society.

A militarist, for example, may be consumed by his interest in guns and soldiers, but in his total political and educational program he courts disaster if he ignores the need for bread, and that whole structure of economic and social institutions and relationships by which bread is produced and distributed. As a militarist he may have no regard for letters and science as such, but in the modern world an illiterate, and scientifically and technologically untrained army has little chance to survive in the ordeal of total war.

The supernaturalist educator may esteem salvation in the life beyond the grave above all other values, but he cannot afford to be indifferent to the mundane aspects of life. Most parents will not accept discipline in the life eternal as a substitute for competence in reading, writing and arithmetic. They also expect their children to learn geography, science, history and civics as well as the doctrines that comprise the catechism of the church. The curricula of church and public schools therefore have much more in common than one might suspect if he has heard only the strictly theological defense of the religious school. Supernaturalists are also children of their age; they are not wholly immune to the "climate of opinion" in which they live and think. Today, the tendency increases in their ranks to reject asceticism and all forms of withdrawal from society as modes of preparation for the life eternal, and to hold instead that the best preparation for the next world is the most adequate and meaningful living in the present.

So, also, for the literary-humanist: he may believe that the "unkillable classics" constitute the only significant source of human enlightenment, but when he designs his educational program, stubborn realities will demand that he give some attention to our scientific and technological ways of thinking and of making a living. When he builds his school plant, he will probably furnish it with the best of modern equipment. More than he is aware modern influences will also pervade the classrooms of his school—even the imperishable principles of the classics will be taught and studied by those whose minds have been conditioned by the affairs of their own age and society.

The utilitarian-vocationalist may be passionately devoted to narrow technical training in the interest of more efficient and more profitable production, but the imperatives of the life of an organized community—a community without which his whole system of technology and factory production could not survive—will require him to give place to many other life interests and subjects in the curriculum of his vocational school.

The experimentalist may accord the attitudes and methods of scientific inquiry the supreme place in his philosophy of life and education. But when he undertakes to organize a school for the nurture of the young, he will find that the important and distinctive demands of family, economy, vocation, government, religion, and art will compel him to make educational provision for many human interests other than the disinterested pursuit of truth. All of the subject-matters of life can and should be explored by the critical and objective method of experimental science, but the method of science is in no sense a substitute for a direct experience of these varied subject-matters. Important and fundamental as is the interest in knowledge, it is by no means the only human interest, and it would be a very inadequate school that restricted its attention to the method of experimental inquiry.

The shift from an agrarian to an industrial-urban civilization has greatly strengthened this tendency to broaden the perspectives, the interests, the purposes and the subject-matters of the school. For most of human history, the young have learned the arts by which life is sustained, not primarily by instruction given in the school, but by direct and responsible participation in these productive activities under the supervision and direction of the adults engaged in them. In our highly articulated, specialized, and technological civilization, this ancient system of apprenticeship is rapidly disappearing, and with it is going much of the opportunity of the young to learn through direct sharing in the productive affairs of their community. In order to adjust to this transformed social and economic situation, the functions and the responsibilities of the school have been greatly expanded, and the period of schooling has been correspondingly extended.

It is only natural that this rich and diversified curriculum, open to all the children of the community, should have greatly altered the educational situation. One consequence has been a decline in the emphasis on the transmission of doctrines in the education of the young. In a school in which increasing attention must, of necessity, be given to the preparation of the young for the things that they have to do as citizens and as members of particular occupational groups, concern with mundane affairs tends to take much of the time that used to be centered on the study of doctrines and the memorizing of moral maxims. In our complex, technological society the school has been compelled to give major attention to the introduction of the young to those basic life functions upon which the general welfare depends.

THE DEMOCRATIC CONCEPTION AND THE AIMS OF EDUCATION

The development of democracy has also eliminated certain historic types of educational purpose and program. In any society that is really governed by the democratic principle of the worth and dignity of each human personality exploitive systems of education are necessarily precluded. The democratic community negates its own moral foundations whenever it regards the child as a mere potential "bayonet" for its armed forces, as a mere future "hand" in its system of factory production, or as a mere instrument of any kind to be fashioned for the perpetuation of an established institution, or the interests of a special class. A society that is grounded in the conception that governments are instituted among men to promote "life, liberty and the pursuit of happiness," and which holds "that whenever any form of government becomes destructive of these ends, it is the right of the people to alter or to abolish it" cannot consistently support an educational practice that is designed to fashion human beings into the mere instruments of the state. The supreme moral trait of the democratic community is that it has no good other than the good of individual human beings.

Moreover, in a democratic society authority and leadership in education, as in government, are not supposed to be lodged in the hands of any ruling group—hereditary, military, ecclesiastic, or economic. It is the very essence of democratic theory that authority and ultimate control in all public affairs should be transferred from all such limited groups to the people as a whole. In accordance with this principle we have sought to organize a system of public schools in the United States in which the responsibility for the determination of the educational program would rest with the local communities, and with the various state authorities, not with the Federal government—that is, with the parents and their own chosen representatives on local school boards, not primarily with national or church officials. It has been our conviction that a school system thus responsive to the interests and the preferences of parents would tend to make the needs and the welfare of the child its primary concern. We have also assumed that schools which are controlled by the very groups whose children are enrolled in them could not easily be manipulated to serve the special interests of privileged classes. On the whole, events have justified this faith; the American school has been disposed to make the growth, not the exploitation, of the child its controlling objective.

But even in a democratic society the needs of the immature do not define themselves, nor do they remain constant in a world in which change is real. As we have already emphasized, in order to define desirable patterns of growth for the individual child, we must take account of the kind of life that we expect and desire him to lead. This pattern of life is not an isolated and private thing. It involves, to be sure, the individual child with his distinctive native endowment, but it equally involves the community with its public modes of life and thought. The deeper the regard of the educator for the worth and dignity of the child, the deeper his interest in the community should become. Any program of education tends to become abstract, formal, and therefore a mechanical routine whenever its purposes and materials are considered to be the property of a self-sufficient school, for this means that dynamic continuity between the work of the school and the life that goes on outside the school has been disrupted. A school best provides for the growth of the child when it maintains living interaction with the community of which he is a part.

NAMES AND REALITIES IN HUMAN CONDUCT

A theory of morals is of course implicit in the foregoing view of the relation of the program of the school to the ongoing affairs of its society. This moral theory holds, in the first place, that human rights and human responsibilities do not constitute a separate and fixed system, but that they are conditioned by the concrete ways in which a human group makes its living and carries on its whole schedule of interrelated life activities. This theory assumes, in the second place, that as knowledge grows and new means of control and modes of living develop, traditional patterns of human rights and duties may also have to be modified. In other words, this social conception of education is the correlative of a moral theory which holds that morals are related to human interests and evolving conditions of life, and hence are not absolute and transcendental, but empirical, institutional, and historical in nature.

It is easy to deceive ourselves and to conceal this empirical and social character of morals. All that is necessary to make morals appear to be unconditioned and immutable is to concentrate attention on moral terms or names, and to ignore the actual human relationships and behaviors that are denoted by these moral terms. Thus an educator may affirm that even revolutionary social changes are of no concern to him, for he knows that in each and every society a child should be taught to be unselfish, to be honest, to be chaste, to be loyal, and to make his behavior conform to all of the fundamentals of the moral code. There is, to be sure, a measure of truth in this educational affirmation, for in the course of its experience the human race has gained many ethical insights. But this emphasis on continuity and permanence in the moral life of man becomes harmful whenever it is taken to mean that new knowledge and powers of human control, and altered conditions of life, do not make necessary fresh appraisals of the behaviors that are to be considered authentic expressions of these traditional moral principles.

For example, changes in modes of production have in no way eliminated the importance of the distinction between the "selfish" and the "unselfish" in human conduct, but these economic changes are calling for a fundamental review of the rights of both the owner and the worker. Considerations of public welfare in our interdependent world are now demanding that the right of the owner to do as he pleases with that which he owns, and the right of the worker to leave his job when and as he desires, be altered. Now these are not superficial moral changes; they involve fundamentals in human relationships and behaviors in the economic sphere. The meaning of the concepts of "selfishness" and "unselfishness" must be revised to correspond to these new realities in our interdependent ways of making a living. So also in the realm of family relationships. The development of effectual contraceptive measures has aroused deep controversies about what should now be considered "moral" in this aspect of human behavior. The evidence indicates that a new standard is developing in this ancient sphere of the "moral," and already important church groups are strongly supporting on ethical grounds the principle of planned parenthood. Nor does the concept of "loyalty" in the realm of political affairs automatically define itself. World-wide totalitarian political movements have resulted in novel political affiliations and practices which have raised the most difficult kind of questions about the meaning of citizenship and the criteria by which "loyalty" is to be measured in contemporary political, educational and similar public undertakings.

In brief, unless education is to serve outmoded and reactionary ends, it must accept responsibility for defining the kind of behaviors which now should be associated with such traditional and basic moral categories as "honesty," "unselfishness," "chastity," "loyalty," "equality," "responsibility," and "freedom." The present has its deep continuities with the past, but it also has its significant discontinuities. The discontinuities, moreover, are as real as the continuities. Education, during this period of social transition and strain, will not promote democratic interests, if it seeks to make "moral absolutes" out of historic rights and forms of human conduct. To serve democratic purposes, education must play its part in the important task of moral discovery. It can do this only as it is willing to continue to examine and test its educational values by whatever we gain of new knowledge and also by that structure of human relationships and activities which is ever developing in the society outside the school. An unexamined morality is not fit to fashion the educational program of a democracy in this period of social transition. Apart from intelligent study of the changing affairs of its society, the school has no adequate means of determining the worth of its moral foundations. Recognition of the reality of change must be one of the fundamental principles in the philosophy of education of our period.

BASIC MEANINGS IN THE SOCIAL INTERPRETATION OF EDUCATION

Measured by all the crucial scientific criteria, human beings constitute a common *biological* family. All members of this human family share a basic organic inheritance. But *culturally* they are members of many different human societies. These societies, located in various parts of the world, are the products of a long development. They have their common features, but they also have their distinctive traits. Each of these societies, taken as a whole, is unique. The things which differentiate one human group from other territorial and cultural groups are no less real than those elements in its ways of life and thought that it shares with other human societies. It was this perception which led the Commission on the Social Studies of the American Historical Association to declare that:

> Education always has a geographical and cultural location; it is therefore specific, local, and dynamic, not general, universal, and unchanging; it is a function of a particular society at a particular time and place in history; it is rooted in some actual culture and expresses the philosophy and the recognized needs of that culture. . . .
>
> Although the basic biological equipment of man seems to be comparatively invariant and may therefore be expected to give certain common elements to education everywhere and at all times, human civilization has characteristics of neighborhood, region, nation, and more extended cultural areas, which lend unique qualities to every working educational program, however persistent and pervasive may be the universal elements entering into it.[3]

It is significant that the eminent members of this Commission of the American Historical Association decided to emphasize in their concluding Report that deliberate education should be viewed not primarily as a function of humanity in

[3] American Historical Association, *Conclusions and Recommendations*, The Report of the Commission on Social Studies, New York, Charles Scribner's Sons, 1934, pp. 31–32.

general, but rather as a function of particular human societies, each with its own individualized past, its own language and literary heritage, its specialized skills and modes of making a living, its distinctive structure of customs, laws, and institutions, as well as with its own unique beliefs, sentiments, moral outlooks, and conceptions of human excellence and of human destiny. For the historian, accustomed to think in the categories of time and place, societies are many, not one; dynamic, not static; individualized and evolving, not fixed specimens of an immutable human pattern. Individual human beings, in their actual psychological natures, are creatures of these historical cultural groups. They think, evaluate, and respond out of an intellectual and moral consciousness that is saturated and hallowed by the history and the achievements of their people. It is not surprising then that when these culturally conditioned groups of human beings undertook the deliberate nurture of their young, they should have created systems of schools which in their subject-matters and their purposes reflected the societies into which they had been born, and which had shaped the very forms of their own being.

But this argument from history is not decisive. The fact that education down to the present has been an undertaking which has varied with factors of time and place, does not in and of itself warrant the conclusion that education in our shrinking and closely integrated world should continue to be that sort of an enterprise. It is wholly fair to ask those who adopt the social interpretation of education to justify their position in terms not of historical origins, but rather in terms of present human values. Certainly a discussion of education and morals should be willing to meet this demand, for the deepest concern of morals is with what *should be*, not simply with the description of what *has been*, or *now is*. We shall therefore conclude this discussion of society and education by enumerating some of the considerations that make it desirable for us to continue to view education as a human undertaking in which factors of time and place are centrally important.

In the first place, this social theory of education is in harmony with the imperatives of educational practice. In spite of present cultural changes, no advocate of universalism in education has been bold enough to contend that the children of the United States should be nurtured in the Chinese language, or that the children of China should be nurtured in the English language, or that the children of these two countries should be educated in a new world-language. In other words, in the case of such basic interests as language and literature, it is generally recognized that stubborn historical factors make it both necessary and desirable that the program of the school be rooted in the cultural heritages of actual human groups. Even following the total military defeat of Japan and Germany, no one has recommended that the children of these two countries be educated in the language of one of the victorious Powers.

The situation is no less compelling when we come to the subject of history. Men in different parts of the world have had their own and distinctive experiences, and these diversified pasts are not dead; they constitute the very substance of the cultures in which men now live and through which they develop their objects of allegiance and devotion. History, moreover, is the past of the present, and to be significant must be explored from the perspective of some actual present. These perspectives are as many as are present human societies. Hence proposals for "objectivity" in the teaching of history have never assumed that the children of the world should be taught a colorless, universalized human history. These proposals for more impartial historical textbooks have recognized the necessity and the desirability of plural accounts of what human beings, organized in different societies, have done and undergone. The demand for objectivity in the preparation of school history books has therefore been the demand that these various cultural and national accounts strive to be more accurate and fair in their report of other cultures and other national groups, particularly in their interpretations of past transactions and conflicts with these groups. It has been accepted that it would mean impoverishment, not enrichment, were all of these individualized human records to be merged in one common, authoritative history of universal man.

The same considerations obviously hold for vocational education, for education in citizenship, for worthy home membership, and for the creative use of leisure time. Without taking into account the operating institutions and practices of its own society, the school would have no adequate means for the construction of its educational program in these vital dimensions of human experience.

Since the school, in one way or another, must make this reference to the affairs of its society, the adherents of the social interpretation of education hold that this evaluation of the life of a people should be made deliberately with public responsibility for whatever cultural selections and rejections are actually involved in the construction of its program. The ends of objectivity will be better served in education when choices among life-alternatives are recognized and avowed, not concealed or denied.

This social view of education, in the second place, can help us overcome the tendency to *formalism* in the work of deliberate education. The constant temptation of the school is to permit its materials and schedules of activities, once they have been selected, classified, graded, and organized into a curriculum, to become an autonomous program of self-perpetuating interests and subjects. The school begins to die both emotionally and intellectually whenever it thus becomes imprisoned in an inherited curriculum and begins to turn its back on the society that it was organized to serve. To make the communication of meaning a living thing, the teacher must grasp the connection of his "subject" or sphere of human interest and knowledge with that which his people have suffered and enjoyed and with that which they now do and undergo. Education, moreover, is an affair of the young just as literally as it is an affair of the heritage of the group. These young are living as well as learning. They live by participating in the affairs of their family, neighborhood, community, and country. A primary aim of education should be to make this participation more meaningful by placing it in a wider historical and geographical and cultural context, and by helping the young to acquire the knowledge, the skills and the techniques which make this participation more effectual. Growth in meaning and growth in capacity for participation in the life of a human group are not effectually cultivated in a school which makes its own world a rival and a substitute for the world outside the school. An increasing number of educators perceive that both "subjects" and "children" become abstractions whenever they are dealt with as entities independent of the life of the community. They recognize that educators can become wise about the nurture of the immature members of their society only as they continue to grow in their understanding of that world *from* which the young come to school, *in* which they continue to live during the period they study as pupils in the school, and *to* which they must go to work out their own careers when their years at school have been completed.

The social conception of education, in the third place, can help save us from the evil of utopianism in education. By utopianism is meant any projection of social and educational ends which fails to take responsible account of actual cultural conditions, and hence evades responsibility for developing the concrete means by which its ideal ends are to be achieved. Whenever we view moral ideals as absolute and unconditioned things, we are apt to get involved in this kind of romanticism. Our country, for example, is committed by both religious and political ideology to the principle of the dignity and worth of "all men." To the extent that we believe in democracy we are necessarily opposed to all patterns of discrimination and enforced segregation based on factors of religion, race, color, sex, class, or national origin. But notwithstanding our official democratic affirmations, the plain fact is that the ideal of equality in the economic, political and cultural affairs of our country is at present most inadequately realized. Our historic system of property ownership often operates in present-day industrial society so as to favor a privileged few at the expense of the many; our political system in its actual operation in many states now denies Negroes elemental civil rights; and existing American attitudes and practices tend to subject the members of minority religious groups to a variety of discriminations. Education in and for democracy must share in the struggle to get rid of these inequalities. But educators can assist in this important task of democratic, social reconstruction only as they recognize that these discriminations are stubbornly grounded in the past experience of the American people. That experience still lives in characteristic mental habits. The pioneer and agrarian experience of the American people, for example, has disposed many of both farm and city to a firm faith in the system of economic individualism, even though their own interests would now be better served in a regime of coöperative planning. We misconstrue the nature of the present economic problem if we do not appreciate the strength of this faith in individualism, and discern the ways in which it is often manipulated by minority groups that have a vested economic interest in the maintenance of the *status quo*. Experience also demonstrates that racial attitudes and the group mores that underlie our segregated school system have deep roots in the past. It is apparent that education can serve as an agency for social progress only as it takes full account of these group attitudes and the factors in our cultural history which have produced them.

But to take account of existing attitudes and prejudices does not mean that we must weakly surrender to them; it rather means that our proposals for reconstruction should be so formulated that they will strengthen, not weaken, the forces that are striving to dissolve this legacy of discrimination. Democratic advance is undoubtedly a function of human courage as well as of intelligence, but no amount of courage will bring us nearer the goal of equality unless that courage is informed by the kind of understanding which comes from historical and social analysis.

Education frequently fails to enjoy the coöperation of many thoughtful people of genuine democratic interest because of its tendency to make vague moral slogans a substitute for analysis of the conditions with which it has to deal. Actually we know our moral ends only as we know something of the means by which these ends are to be attained. Because the social interpretation of education tends to focus attention on conditions and means it gives promise of developing a morality in education that will be free from the weakness of sentimental utopianism.

Finally, the social interpretation of education can help us discern the defects of traditionalism in education. By traditionalism is meant not sincere regard for the human past, but rather the social and educational view which assumes that we already have a completed system of truth concerning the essentials of human nature, moral values, and the patterns of human civilization, and which also assumes that this completed system contains the answers to whatever problems of human belief, human conduct, and social policy may beset us. On this basis, education becomes merely a process by which the young are indoctrinated with the truths of this closed, authoritarian system. Only those educators who are so immersed in a system of intellectual and moral abstractions that they are immune to the instructions of ordinary human experience, can thus convince themselves that change, and novelty, and moral uncertainty are not real factors in the experience of human beings.

In our period of profound social transformation and transition it is no contribution to the resolution of the problems of mankind to minimize the drastic nature of the adjustments which men must now make if they are to continue to survive. In later chapters we shall explore in some detail the nature of these adjustments and the importance of nurturing the young in a morality that is more consonant with the life imperatives and life possibilities of the new age we are now entering. Every resource in our intellectual and moral heritage will be needed to help us make satisfactory adjustments to these emerging modes of life, but we shall also do well to accept the fact that we are confronted with novel life conditions which call for real moral pioneering if we are to make our new powers of control over the physical environment serve the ends of a good life. Both the nature of our problems and the means for resolving them will be more adequately understood if old and young seek to educate and re-educate themselves in terms of the actual social situations in which they are now involved. A fundamental merit of the social interpretation of education is that it invites educators to view their task as a significant part of the total task of building a civilization that is in harmony with the deep moving forces in the modern world.

ADJUSTMENT TO THE ENVIRONMENT

Robert M. Hutchins

Every ambition, at least every formal, material, institutional ambition, of the reformers, philanthropists, and optimists of the nineteenth century has now been achieved. They wanted to end slavery, lengthen life, raise the standard of living, establish universal free education, and create one world. Science and technology were to be the principal instruments by which happiness and prosperity were to be forged. Science and technology have performed nobly. But the optimism is gone.

Thirty-five years ago we could sing with Shelley:

> The world's great age begins anew,
> The golden years return,
> And earth doth like a snake renew
> Her winter weeds outworn:
> Heaven smiles, and faiths and
> empires gleam,
> Like wrecks of a dissolving dream.

Now we question whether legal slavery is the only slavery there is, whether a longer life is necessarily a good thing if that life is aimless, whether improvement in the material conditions of existence can solve the fundamental problems of existence, whether one bad world may not be worse than many, and whether science and technology can give us the wisdom to use the power they have brought us for the benefit rather than the destruction of mankind. We question particularly whether universal compulsory free education is, as we always supposed it was, a sufficient method of dealing with all the issues raised by freeing the slaves, giving everybody the vote, and developing industrialism.

The Enlightenment based its hopes of progress on the spread of universal education; and one of its children, Edward Gibbon, in his celebrated chapter summarizing the reasons for the fall of the Western Empire, relieves the fears of Europe by saying that there never will be another barbarian conqueror. His reason is simple. War now requires the knowledge of a large number of arts and sciences. Hence to excel in war the barbarian must cease to be barbarous. Since man first discovered how to master the forces of nature all history has been tending toward this goal. Gibbon's final remark is, "We may therefore acquiesce in the pleasing conclusion that every age of the world has increased and still increases the real wealth, the happiness, the knowledge, and perhaps the virtue of the human race."

The conclusion is pleasing, but seems to be false. There is evidence that the rate of increase in real wealth is declining and none that the happiness and virtue of the human race are increasing. And we know now that a conqueror equipped with knowledge can be more barbarous, as well as more dangerous, than any of his unlettered predecessors.

As for those expectations of political equality and justice which were founded on universal education, Aldous Huxley could say not long ago, "But in actual historical fact, the spread of free compulsory education, and, along with it, the cheapening and acceleration of the older methods of printing, have almost everywhere been followed by an increase in the power of ruling oligarchies at the expense of the masses."

This proposition, if true, is certainly one of the most sensational paradoxes in human history. The sensation is in the fact that it was totally unforeseen. For two hundred years proposals to broaden the suffrage have uniformly been accompanied by proposals to broaden education. Those who have wanted political power for the masses and those who have opposed political power for them have always agreed in this, that, if they were to have political power, they must have education. Huxley finds that, as they have got education, their political power has diminished instead of increasing.

Arnold Toynbee discovers the explanation for the failure of universal education in the rise of what are called the media of mass communication. He says, "The bread of universal education is no sooner cast upon the waters of social life than a shoal of sharks rises from the depths and devours the children's bread before the philanthropists' eyes. In the educational history of England, for example, the dates speak for themselves. Universal compulsory gratuitous education was inaugurated in this country in A.D. 1870; the Yellow Press was invented some twenty years later—as soon as the first generation of children from the national schools came into the labor market and acquired some purchasing power—by a stroke of irresponsible genius which had divined that the educational philanthropists' labor of love could be made to yield the newspaper king a royal profit."

Mr. Toynbee even goes so far as to imply that the totalitarian state is a reaction against what he calls "the enormity of the Yellow Press—and of other instruments, like the Cinema, that have since been invented for the same lucrative business of making a profit out of the entertainment of the masses." He naturally finds this remedy worse than the disease. His conclusion is: "Thus in countries where the system of Universal Education has been introduced, the people are in danger of falling under an intellectual tyranny of one kind or another, whether it be exercised by private capitalists or public authorities."

Mr. Toynbee has a remedy to propose. He says that the only course open to us in the fight against intellectual tyranny is "to raise the level of mass cultivation to a degree at which the minds of the children who are put through the educational mill are rendered immune against at least the grosser forms of either private or public propaganda."

Mr. Toynbee's remedy is singularly like that offered by Victor Ratner, once vice-president of the Columbia Broadcasting System, who says, "Radio is made in the image of the American people. To lambaste it is itself un-American. The critics hit at it because they claim to be shocked at what the United States' people are. Radio fits the people. The masses like comic books, Betty Grable, broad comedy, simple drama—it's vulgar, fast, simple, fundamental. Critics of radio often speak about the people's fare; yet they seem to refuse to face the facts about the people's taste. Such criticisms are really criticisms of the American educational system for not raising the cultural level of Americans; for not getting them interested in the better things when they are young. Radio then gets the blame for this failure."

The proposal is to remake the public, to fend off the influences of the media of mass communication, by raising the level of mass cultivation through the system of universal compulsory education.

This leads first to the very large question whether and to what extent the state of mind of the public is or can be the result of its educational system. Universal free compulsory education would seem to be a reflection of what the country wants. One of the most important ideas about education is compressed into the Platonic line: "What is honored in a country will be cultivated there." This is true at the highest levels, in determining the course of research and advanced study. The interest in science and technology in the United States today must result from the honor in which scientists and technologists are held and from the high value that is set upon their work. It is even truer at the level of universal compulsory education, because the object of the system must be to make the children as far as possible what their parents or the ruling group in the community want the next generation to be. This is what will be honored in the country. It does not seem an exaggeration to say that a system of universal free compulsory education, however expensive or prolonged, can do no more than try to give the people what they want already. It cannot make them want something different. If the American people honored wisdom and goodness as they now honor power and success, the system of universal free education would be quite different from what it is today. But how can the system of universal free education, which is busily cultivating what the people now honor, teach them to honor something else?

This would seem to be sufficient answer to Mr. Ratner, and it may even be a sufficient comment on Mr. Toynbee. But there are other answers, too. As the arrangements in other parts of the world show, there is no inherent reason why the American radio should be conducted for profit; and there is no reason why it should be conducted as it is; even if it is conducted for profit. To give all the best time to vaudeville and all the rest to soap opera is a crime for which the fine music that comes occasionally over the air cannot atone. Why should Mr. Ratner demand that the educational system do for him something he could at least in part achieve himself? A man who has a monopoly, and then sells shoddy merchandise, can hardly blame the low taste of the public or the ineffectiveness of its educational system for his prosperity. The public has nowhere to turn. Mr. Ratner has no monopoly; but he and his colleagues in other broadcasting companies are so busy imitating one another that what the listener finds on one station he will find on another; and, if he does not like what he finds, he must turn his radio off altogether.

The final answer to Mr. Toynbee and Mr. Ratner is that from the point of view of time alone they have proposed an undue burden on the schools. As Alfred North Whitehead remarked, "The whole problem of education is controlled by lack of time. If Methuselah was not educated, it was his own fault or that of his teachers." A child is in school for only a small portion of his life, and even when he is of school age he is not protected, after hours, from the terrific storm of propaganda that now beats upon the citizen. The notion that the child can be inoculated against propaganda once and for all in childhood seems naïve. It is hardly possible that this task can be accomplished for life in eight, twelve, or sixteen years.

Nevertheless we must admit that Mr. Toynbee is on the right track, even if his track is not long enough to carry us to our destination. He suggests, in his talk of raising the level of mass cultivation, the reason why universal education has failed to achieve the intellectual, social, and political results expected of it and has, in fact, produced results exactly opposite to those which were confidently hoped for. It cannot be said that the sort of popular education now prevalent in America, and destined, I believe, to spread over the West, has raised the level of mass cultivation, or has been engaged in cultivation of any kind.

How do you get a country to want to raise the level of mass cultivation? This depends on criticism, criticism by individuals, minorities, and centers of independent thought. This is the reason for academic freedom and freedom of speech generally. The best definition of a university that I have been able to think of is that it is a center of independent thought. It may be a good many other things as well; but, if it is not this, it has failed. The principal function of a professional school in a university is not to train men for the profession, but to criticize the profession. Unless criticism of the culture is permitted, the culture cannot be changed; certainly the schools will not be permitted to change it.

How do you get a country to permit criticism? This can only be done if the country recognizes that an uncriticized culture cannot long endure. The hope of the West is that the church and the university are still free. I must add that there is no hope in the university unless it takes seriously its mission as a center of independent thought.

Any opinion that a man holds simply because it has been pumped or pounded into him is no good, because it cannot last. Children should be brought up in good habits; but those habits cannot endure the stress and strain of circumstances unless they have some foundation in the convictions of the person who has them. Durable conviction about the affairs of this world is a matter of reason. It is easy to show by reason that Marxism is a fallacious doctrine. But what if the person with whom you are discussing it has never learned to reason? Since we cannot hope to insulate our young people from access to the false doctrines in the world, the thing to do is to train them so that they can see the falsity in them. This means helping them learn to think for themselves.

Am I saying that the public should not control the educational system? Certainly not. I am saying that the public should understand education. And it would do no harm if teachers and professors understood it, too. Indoctrination and propaganda have no place in it. The private opinions of teachers are not to be pumped or pounded into young people any more than the majority opinion is. But in my observation, which covers a very long period, there is not much danger to our youth from the improprieties of their instructors or the radical views that they may entertain. I am sure that 75 per cent of the professors at the University of Chicago voted for Landon. A far greater danger is that the majority will exert pressure on the educational system for indoctrination in and compulsory adoption of the majority opinion. The rule of the majority without free discussion and criticism is tyranny.

If the public, the teachers, and the professors all understood the educational system, we could develop a tradition in this country that would be far more effective in giving us the kind of education we need than laws, witch-hunts, or regulations that teachers must subscribe to oaths that, as Governor Warren of California has said, any traitor would take with a laugh. On the side of the teachers and professors, the professional tradition would mean that they taught responsibly. On the side of the public the tradition would mean that the public restrained itself in the exercise of its legal control.

Because I am concerned with the development of this tradition I deplore every futile, childish, and irrelevant activity in which the educational system engages. Educators do things that the public wants in order to get the support of the public. They do little to explain to the public why it should not want the things it does. I like intercollegiate football, but I recommended its abolition at Chicago, because the game in its industrial, big-time form has nothing to do with education and yet has the effect of diverting everybody's attention from the educational problems with which universities should be wrestling. So I deplore the multiplication of trivial courses, in cosmetology, fishing, and tapdancing, which swell the catalogues of great American universities and which have no purpose except to help the student wile away four years without using his mind. Think of the most futile, childish, irrelevant subject you can—think of parlor games, think of self-beautification, think of anything you like—I will undertake to find it for you among the courses offered by American institutions of higher learning.

I had no sooner written these words than *Life* magazine came along to prove my point by announcing that at an American university it is possible to get college credit for being a clown, something that even I, after decades of disillusionment, could never have thought of. *Life* concludes its account with words that might well be the epitaph of the higher learning in America: the students, says *Life*, regard this work "as just part of a normal liberal education." I need say no more to show that neither the public nor the educational profession has a clear conception of education. They have no standard by which to judge what belongs in education and what does not.

What belongs in education is what helps the student to learn to think for himself, to form an independent judgment, and to take his part as a responsible citizen. Although I will admit that in the hands of Socrates any subject can be made important, even clowning, because any subject can lead to important questions, there was only one Socrates, and I know of none in any educational system today. We have to frame the course of study of American schools, colleges, and universities in the light of the capacity of ordinary teachers. If the object of the educational system is to help young people learn to think for themselves, it should help them to think about the most important subjects, and these are discussed in the greatest works of the greatest writers of the past and present. To destroy the Western tradition of independent thought it is not necessary to burn the books. All we have to do is to leave them unread for a couple of generations.

In the United States little effort is made to raise the level of mass cultivation through the schools. The leading theories or doctrines of education say nothing on this subject.

The first of these doctrines is the theory of adjustment. Here the object is to fit the student into his physical, social, political, economic, and intellectual environment with a minimum of discomfort to the society. Freud took the view that the object of education was to make young people healthy and efficient, to adapt them to their surroundings, to make them successful in the terms of the society in which they were brought up. His summary is: "I should go so far as to say that revolutionary children are not desirable from any point of view." This caution seems unnecessary; for no society would tolerate a revolutionary educational system.

So T. S. Eliot seems to give his powerful sanction to an educational program that adapts the child to the political organization under which he is to live.

So the chief aim of the program of UNESCO in fundamental education, which is the principal program of the organization, is to enable the peoples of underdeveloped countries "to adjust themselves to their changing environment."

In America the doctrine of adjustment is perhaps the leading theory. Here it results from a misconception of John Dewey. Since he is not a clear writer, his followers may perhaps be excused for their failure to notice that when he talked about adjustment to the environment, he meant that the environment should first be improved. Dewey was essentially a social reformer, and it is tragic that he should have laid the foundation for the proposition that the aim of education is to adjust the young to their environment, good or bad.

The theory of adjustment or adaptation was carried to its logical extreme in a women's college in America, which based its curriculum on a job analysis of the diaries of 323 mature women. The categories of the activities of these women constitute the structure of the curriculum, without regard to whether or not mature women ought to do or are now doing the things that 323 of them were doing when this poll was taken.

Thus it will be seen that the theory of adjustment leads to a curriculum of miscellaneous dead facts. The way to adjust to the environment is to learn the facts about the environment. Since it is impossible to tell what the environment will be, the student can only be informed about the environment that exists while he is in school. But all that is known with certainty about the environment is that it will be different by the time the student has to adjust himself to it.

The doctrine of adjustment or adaptation is not well adapted to America. America is, and always has been, a society in transition. Seventy million Americans live in a different house today from the one they occupied ten years ago. America is the example par excellence of the rapidity of technological change. Vocations employing thousands of men may be wiped out overnight and be replaced by others that were not thought of the day before.

One of the most popular courses in the American schools is stenography. Think of the havoc that will be wrought if the dictating machine becomes the standard method of conducting office correspondence. A great American university has established a school of what is called cosmetology, announcing that what it called the profession of beautician "is the fastest growing in this state." Think what will happen to the graduates of this educational institution if self-beautification for ladies becomes as simple a matter as it is for men.

America is probably the easiest place to earn a living in the world. Yet more emphasis is placed on vocational training in the American schools than in any others. There are many reasons for this; but the one I wish to mention now is an example of the proposition that what is honored in a country will be cultivated there. We must admit that what is honored in America is material success. All you have to do to understand this is to compare the position of intellectuals and artists in America with their position in Europe. The model American is the successful businessman. Artists and intellectuals are regarded in the light of charity patients or excess baggage. Consequently the attention of the American is drawn at an early date to the necessity of adjusting himself to his economic environment in such a way that he will be successful.

I shall attempt in a moment a general critique of the doctrine of adjustment or adaptation. Here I wish to mention one or two consequences of that branch of the doctrine which deals with economic or vocational adjustment. The question it raises is this: assuming that the young must adjust to their environment, including their economic environment, can the educational system manage, supervise, and direct the whole job? In particular, can the educational system give a boy as good a training for a particular task in industry as the industry itself could give him? In America technical institutes of the European type are virtually unknown. Vocational training is given along with all other types of training in the same schools. Because of the relative ease of vocational instruction and because of the immediate interest it excites on the part of the pupil, such instruction has the tendency to force out of the course of study any other kind of instruction. Yet we learned in the war that the airplane companies could produce in a few weeks better airplane mechanics than the schools could produce in years. The pupils in the schools were necessarily trained by obsolescent teachers with obsolescent machinery. Hence the result of the emphasis on vocational training in America is poor mechanics without education.

America is not only the easiest place to earn a living in the world; it is also the place with the most leisure in the world. The average industrial worker in America gets more than fifty dollars for a forty-hour week. He now works twenty hours a week less than he did forty years ago. At the same time that industrial operations have been simplified to the point where little or no training is required for them—they can in fact be performed by twelve-year-old children—unprecedented leisure has opened before the American citizen. Still one of the principal aims of the educational system is to educate the citizen to work for a living. It does not educate him at all in the right use of his leisure.

The new found leisure of the American is therefore spent in relaxation, and that provided by the tavern and the television set is almost equally demoralizing. The prospect that television opens before us in America, with nobody speaking and nobody reading, suggests that a bleak and torpid epoch may lie ahead in which the population will eventually sink, in accordance with the principles of evolution, to the level of the lowest forms of vegetable life.

Scientists of the University of Chicago have lately detected something that looks like moss growing on the planet Mars. Perhaps Mars was once inhabited by beings like ourselves, who had the misfortune, some millions of years ago, to invent television. The twin aims that have animated mankind since the dawn of history, the conquest of nature and relief from drudgery, now almost accomplished in America, have ended in the trivialization of our lives.

There are, of course, many reasons for this; but one of them surely is that our educational system has given us no resources that we can employ to give our leisure time significance. When we are not working, all we can do is to amuse ourselves. The deep and permanent melancholia that underlies the American temperament must be ascribed, in part at least, to the boredom that the perpetual search for amusement at length induces.

The whole doctrine of adjustment to the environment seems to me radically erroneous. As I have said, it leads to a curriculum of miscellaneous dead facts. It leads to vocational training, which the schools are not equipped to give and which misses the most important contribution that the schools can make. But it is far more urgent that we notice that our mission here on earth is to change our environment, not to adjust ourselves to it. If we become maladjusted in the process, so much the worse for the environment. The message that UNESCO should carry to the people of backward countries is not that they should adjust themselves to their changing environment, but that they should change their environment.

If we have to choose between Sancho Panza and Don Quixote, let us by all means choose Don Quixote. Or, to pass from models supplied by fiction to those offered us by real life, let us remember that Socrates and Gandhi did not seek to adapt themselves to society as they found it. They attempted to re-make society, and the fact that they died in the attempt in no way detracts from their glory or from their value as examples to other men. To Freud we may oppose Kant, who said, "Parents usually educate their children merely in such a manner that, however bad the world may be, they may adapt themselves to its present conditions." This may suggest to us that the doctrine of adaptation is not so new as its proponents would have us believe. Kant goes on: "But they ought to give them an education so much better than this, that a better condition of things may thereby be brought about in the future."

The pressure in America, especially intense now in this period of the cold war, is toward a flat conformity of life and thought. University professors are being required in some states to take special oaths attesting that they have never been members of the Communist party, and this in spite of the fact that, unless a recent ambiguous decision of the Supreme Court has changed the law, it is perfectly legal to be a Communist in the United States. The irresponsible fulminations of Senator McCarthy strike terror into the hearts of innocent government employees. Students who exhibit the slightest variation from established fashions of thought and action ask me whether they are neurotic. And, in fact, I attribute the popularity of psychoanalysis in the United States in large part to the prevailing impression that everybody who is not just like everybody else, or, worse still, who does not want to be, must be sick. The only serious doubt that one may have about democracy is whether it is possible to combine the rule of the majority with that independence of character, thought, and conduct which the progress of any society requires.

Against the tendency toward conformity the universities of America have been unable to fight effectively. One of the most interesting questions about university education in America is this: why is it that the boy who on June 15 receives his degree, eager, enthusiastic, outspoken, idealistic, reflective, and independent, is on the following September 15, or even on June 16, dull, uninspired, shifty, cautious, pliable, and attired in that symbol of respectability, worn by the vice-presidents of all banks, a double-breasted blue serge suit? Why are the graduates of the great American universities indistinguishable from the mass of the population who have never had their advantages? Why are the organized alumni of the country dedicated to the affectionate perpetuation of all the wrong things about their universities, such as intercollegiate football and drinking parties?

The answer lies in part where Mr. Toynbee found it, in the relative weakness of higher education compared with the forces that make everybody think and act like everybody else. Those forces beat upon the individual from birth on, almost twenty-four hours a day, and constitute an enormous obstacle to any educational effort. So much is this the case that it is now seriously argued in some quarters in America that, since education cannot compete with the comic book, it should absorb it and substitute elevating and instructive comic books for textbooks.

But the deeper answer is that everybody is supposed to be like everybody else. The doctrine of adaptation has won the day. A university that produced graduates who did not slide unobtrusively into the scenery would be accounted a failure, and perhaps a menace.

At least during a cold war, the doctrine of adaptation leads remorselessly to indoctrination. I will read you a few exemplary passages from a letter addressed to all the teachers in a Middle Western city by the superintendent of schools, who, under the law of the state, has the power to oust any of them from their jobs. The superintendent says, "The threat to American institutions by international communism makes imperative that greater emphasis be given in our schools to the study of the meaning, significance, and the value of American Democracy. Indoctrination has never been in good repute among educators in the United States. . . . It now appears necessary for the schools in the United States to indoctrinate American youth for American Democracy. . . . In our present confused world, it is essential in America that we teach our young people that American Democracy is the best government in the world and that we explain why it is the best. . . . They must understand that American Democracy was founded on private enterprise and that this economic system has brought forth a great and powerful nation which will continue to grow even stronger by perpetuating and protecting private enterprise." And so on.

Although I believe that democracy is the best form of government, that the American democracy is a very good form of democracy, and that the economic system known as private enterprise has made significant contributions to the development of my country, I ask myself whether it is possible for the American democracy to be improved and whether the American system of private enterprise has no defects, and also whether pupils who have been indoctrinated as this superintendent proposes can be expected to take an active part in improving the American government or remedying the defects of the American economic system. I also feel some sympathy for the confusion and disappointment that these pupils will experience when they emerge from the dream world of indoctrination and face the facts of life.

Here we see the doctrine of adaptation reduced to an absurdity; for the passion to adjust the young to the environment has so carried away this superintendent that in the name of adjustment he proposes to adjust the young, not to the environment, but to his conception of the environment, which can only result in maladjusting them to the environment as it actually is.

We hear during the cold war in America that the American way of life is in danger. You would suppose, to listen to the people who say this, that the American way of life consisted in unanimous tribal self-adoration. Yet the history and tradition of our country make it plain that the essence of the American way of life is its hospitality to criticism, protest, unpopular opinions, and independent thought. The great American word has always been freedom, and, in particular, freedom of thought, speech, and assembly. Asserting the dignity of man, and of every man, America has proclaimed and protected the freedom to differ. America has grown strong on criticism. It would be quite as consistent with the American way of life to offer prizes for the most penetrating criticism of our country as it would be to offer prizes to those who have done the best job of advertising it. The heart of democracy is independent criticism; the basic freedom is freedom of thought and expression.

Non-legal methods of persecuting people into conformity are steadily gaining popularity in the West. Such methods are little better than purges and pogroms. The ideas to which the West, and a large part of the East, are most bitterly opposed are the police state, the abolition of freedom of speech, thought, and association, and the notion that the individual exists for the state. Yet in practice there may not be a significant difference between a society in which such compulsions are exerted by the tyrannical power of the state and one in which they come from the tyrannical power of public opinion.

The doctrine of adjustment or adaptation explicitly excludes any consideration of standards. The adjustment must take place, whether the environment is good or bad. An educational system that is based on this theory must, therefore, ultimately become a system without values. I shall hope to show that an educational system without values is a contradiction in terms.

WHEN I HEARD THE LEARN'D ASTRONOMER[1]

Walt Whitman

When I heard the learn'd astronomer,
When the proofs, the figures, were ranged in columns before me,
When I was shown the charts and diagrams, to add, divide, and measure them,
When I sitting heard the astronomer where he lectured with much applause in the lecture-room,
How soon unaccountable I became tired and sick,
Till rising and gliding out I wander'd off by myself,
In the mystical moist night-air, and from time to time,
Look'd up in perfect silence at the stars.

[1] From *Leaves of Grass*, first published in 1855.

PSYCHOLOGICAL FOUNDATIONS OF EDUCATION: Children Learn and Grow

"WHEN I GROW OLDER"[1]

W. Allison Davis and Robert J. Havighurst

DISCUSSION AND ANALYSIS

This provocative selection takes a look at the process of growing up in a refreshing and original way. As you read it, you will surely recall your own feelings of looking longingly up the age ladder to the "big kids" and contemptuously down at the "little squirts" who were, thankfully, younger.

There are many interesting points to be made about this selection. For instance, you may want to read further in the literature of social anthropology, about the rituals of primitive societies when they initiate the adolescent into adulthood. Margaret Mead's studies collected in one volume under the title *From the South Seas* (1939, William Morrow) is a good place to start. Perhaps you can find the opportunity to observe graduation ceremonies in a nursery school, an elementary school, a junior high, and a senior high school. How do these look from the vantage point afforded by the comments of Davis and Havighurst?

The authors make an important point, one which, however, they leave us to develop further. They say that when a child is in a church, a lodge, or a school he is "*in an institution more complex than he can understand.*" How can we interpret the school to the growing child? What does he understand about his education? Perhaps if we can tell youngsters more about the school, how it is run and why, our students will be more willing learners.

[1] From *Father of the Man*, Chapter XVIII, by W. Allison Davis and Robert J. Havighurst. Copyright, 1947, by W. Allison Davis and Robert J. Havighurst. Reprinted by permission of and arrangement with the authors and Houghton Mifflin Company, the authorized publishers.

Full soon thy Soul shall have her earthly
freight,
And custom lie upon thee with a weight,
Heavy as frost, and deep almost as life!
—William Wordsworth

Age is the ladder by which the young child hopes to climb to his Arcadia.

Next to becoming his parents' favorite child, his desire to grow older is the closest to his heart. Very early he discovers that other children, whether in his family or his nursery school, measure his prestige by his age. On the ladder of age, each step will lead him to higher privileges at home and at school, to sweeter triumphs over more and more "small fry," and to more dazzling signs of prestige. To grow older is to pursue a golden series of age-posts, each leading him to a little wayside station of prestige, and each promising him greater pleasure in the future.

Everything good, he is told by his parents, comes with age. More than anything else, therefore, the child yearns to become bigger and older. At first, he counts time in units of social behavior. When he stops soiling his pants, he will be acting like a "big boy," he is told. When the little girl learns to get up at night, instead of wetting the bed, she will be a "big girl," like her older sister, or "like mama."

Soon the child discovers, however, that he will not become older today, nor tomorrow, but only *step by step*. The road of age opens continuously into larger highways, with farther vistas. When he is two or three, he may leave his crib, and have a real bed like brother's or daddy's. When he is older, he may go to nursery school and have books of his own and ride in the school's station wagon. When the girl is older, she may have a china doll, and later she may have ice-skates and a pleated skirt. The coming of good things is continually restrained by the slow process of growing older and larger (and presumably wiser).

When the child is three or four, he may play outside his yard, and go as far as the corner. He attains his first major triumph in self-direction when he wins the right to cross the street by himself. When he grows still older, he may go to school by himself, to the grocery store, and to the movies. The boy may even wear pants with a "fly." At six or seven, he may get away from Eton suits, and wear clothes like a "big boy's"—knickerbockers, and shoes with heel-plates. Some day, he hopes, he may actually carry money to school to *buy* his lunch.

To the young child, therefore, age seems to be the key which unlocks all the forbidden doors of life. It is the magic gift of adults, which brings power, and social acceptance. It lifts the barriers to the most inviting and mysterious roads, opening toward freedom and adventure. Do not his parents have the largest bedroom, stay up latest, sit at the head of the table, and go and come as they please, simply because they are older? As long as he is young, he must be the underdog, he must yield, he must obey. It is not easy for a child to be always inferior, simply because he is younger.

Yet this is what the family really demands of him. The family is a hierarchy, in which status is based upon age and sex. The parents' greater age is their supreme source of authority. Their age prescribes their behavior; they are to act as protectors, teachers, and masters; as the prime and all-powerful source of both the gifts and the punishments of life.

The child, on the other hand, occupies a weak status. He must act dependent, he must accept control and leadership, and at times he must be deferential and knuckle under. In most families, of course, he is allowed a safety-valve, such as minor forms of aggression, and hidden acts of impudence, or sabotage. But these are the compensations usually allowed the *inferiors* in any hierarchy.

As children and as young adults, most people in our society must learn to accept their subordination to older people—in school, on the job, and in the family. Some children learn to accept this age-inferiority without losing their capacity for initiative. They do not become hostile to the older person, simply because he is older. Like most children, they strive to earn greater privileges, but they do so *within the age-framework laid down by their parents.* They run hard, but they run within the lanes.

Other children, however, regard this as an unfair race. At a very early age, they begin to say to themselves, "To the deuce with the lanes. This isn't a fair race, *it's an organized racket.* If you're smarter and faster than the pompous old big-shots, who think they run it, you should spring out of the starting holes quickly. Soon you will be running out by yourself, in the open country, where there are no lanes."

Such children strive, even more vigorously than the usual child, for *the privileges of their older brothers and sisters.* They push hard against these controls of age, which their parents have set up. Lunging and panting, they throw their very bodies against the ramparts of age-privileges. Others, fighting by cunning and by steady, constant infiltration, wear away the will and patience of the parents who are defending the age-barriers—and break through the walls of authority.

These children are out to "beat the game" of age-privileges, and none can say that they are foolish to do so in our competitive society. In fact, many parents encourage their children to grow up faster than is usual; to memorize songs and doggerel at two or three years, to dress older than their years, to skip grades, and so on.

The child who is hostile toward a parent is especially likely to rebel fiercely against these age-restrictions. (Such a child is certain to be a problem during his adolescence; then he wants to become a man, or woman, at once.) Furthermore, children who rebel against age-controls are likely to rebel also against *their family's social status.* Some of these rebels flee "downward" from the social-class position of their family. By "disgracing" their family, by refusing to accept its social-class culture, these children really attack their parents where it hurts most.

Many other rebellious children are ambitious for all kinds of higher status: first in age, later in economic and social position in the world. Some of these "strivers" have become deeply hostile toward a parent in early childhood. Later these children find that, by improving themselves socially (by climbing to a higher social class than that of their parents), they can become *superior* at last to their parents, in spite of their inferiority in age. The ironic twist to such stories is that such children often have been pushed to become "climbers" by the parents, themselves.

On the opposite side are the children who want to remain *little* boys, or *little* girls always. Usually these are overindulged, spoiled children. Their parents have not asked them to meet the normal tasks, to learn the usual social habits expected of children their age. From the first years, they may have been "overprotected" (relieved from even moderate training-demands) by their parents. They probably were not required to stay dry at night, even when they had attained the necessary physical development. They were still permitted to mar or to break furniture and toys, after they were seven or eight years old. Or the mother may have kept such a child in babyish clothes far too long, or have allowed him to sleep with her until he was half grown, or given him no responsibility for the care of his room, or clothes, or person. Children who have been helped by their parents *to escape* the normal tasks of growing older seldom "grow up" in their later personalities. They still want to be indulged, and protected; they need to be sheltered from the demands of school, of work, and of marriage, just as they have been excused from the earlier tasks of childhood.

Age also troubles the *intimidated* or frightened child. Like the spoiled child, he also "grows older" very slowly. He stays "childish" too long because he has been frightened by his parents into thinking that he cannot assume greater responsibility, nor meet harder competition, as he comes to each new age-step. First, the parents may have kept him too long in a baby's status, either through severe discipline, or through emphasizing unduly his physical weakness, or illnesses. Next, they may have kept him subordinated too long as a "little boy" or "little girl"; then as an adolescent. Finally, they have trained a man or woman who is *afraid that he is not old enough*, even at thirty or forty, to meet the normal competition and difficulties of life.

But perhaps the first child has the hardest time of all with the age-barriers. Whereas the younger children in a family compete for the privileges, and imitate the behavior, of the older *children* principally, *the first child must try to imitate the parents themselves*. For a long time, his parents are his principal models; yet to compete with them is impossible, and to imitate them is nearly so. For the *younger* children, the "age-climb" between themselves and the older children is gently sloping. For the *oldest* child, who is trained directly by the parents and who looks directly to them for his models in learning to talk, to use the toilet, and so on, the "age-climb" is tremendously steep.

Frequently, the oldest child is chosen likewise as the banner carrier, the father-or-mother substitute in the family. Thus, he is pressed to act as an adult too early in life. (If his parents are also seeking to *rise in the social scale*, they very likely will push him too fast, and stimulate him toward achievement too early.) It is likely also that he learns more slowly, because his models for imitation (the parents) are too far advanced, and their behavior is too complex. The younger brother or sister often learns more easily and quickly, because he imitates *a simpler model*, namely, the older child.

In brief, the older child probably is more likely to stay immature. First, he may fail to "grow up" because he wants to act like the baby, who replaces him. Second, he may fail because he faces a *higher "age-barrier"* than do his brothers and sisters, namely, that between his parents and himself.

When the young child, leaving the nursery school, receives his awestruck initiation into the "big school," he finds there his Great World. He discovers at once that this whole society is ranked, tier above tier, by age. He meets also an institution which is far larger, far more intricate, and more powerful than his family. At first, the "big school" overwhelms his imagination. It is too complex, too omnipotent for him to understand. He is nothing. The school with its teachers, its principal, its vast numbers of pupils, its endless activities, its tremendous authority, is everything. It is "above him." It is a great society, super-individual and infinitely complex, like the world, itself.

Before he is out of the kindergarten, the child knows that his "place" in this school world is *beneath all the other groups*, because they are all older. The children of each successive grade appear supermen to those below them, because they have unattainable privileges, skills, and signs of status. There is little or no intimate association between even a third-grader and a fourth-grader! Each has his own "place," his own world; each has his own sphere in school, on the playground, and on the way home *after school.* Each stays in his place, most of the time. Each grade looks up longingly and respectfully to the grades above. The child of aggressive spirit, who gets out of his age-place, is punished by ridicule, snubs, or beatings. All the others are kept in their "places" by the psychological force of prestige, of the superior status and culture of the older children, and of custom.

In school, the young child finds also a dazzling series of offices and positions, all held by older pupils. He sees them stretched above him, rank upon rank. He envies them and he worships them. He thirsts to be older, so that he may be a monitor who supervises children in the halls and toilets, or a white-belted patrol boy who guides pupils across the street. As a six-year-old, he looks in awe at the eighth-grade pupil, who, coming straight from the Principal herself, brings the teacher fateful messages to be signed. Infinitely far above him, so high that he does not become aware of them until he reaches the third or fourth grade, are the gods on the highest peak of the "age-climb," the big boys on the track-team, or the baseball team, or the basketball team, the giant athletes of the "75-pound-class" or the "95-pound-class," who have the honor of the school, itself, in their keeping.

If age thwarts him, it also brings him, however, the highest of consolations, a group of *his own.* At five years, he moves out of his nursery-school friendships, or his neighborhood group, which consist of only two or three children having little sense of unity. He becomes a member of a larger, tighter circle of children, who are more cohesive and more conscious of themselves as a group. These are his "own bunch," his "gang," his age-mates, his autonomous part of children's society. They create a social world of his peers.

For the first time, he has the comfortable feeling that he has a group of his own, a group outside of the family. Here he is not under the thumb of his parents. This is his personal circle of intimates, where he "belongs," where he suffers no arbitrary stigmas of inferiority in age, and where he can compete for prestige. From this time on, whether he is in elementary school, high school, college, or adult life, he will find nothing so emotionally rewarding as his "own gang." He "fits in" with these folks. They have nearly the same level of maturity. They "speak the same language," they like similar games, and share the common culture of their age-group. With them he forms his closest friendships; with them he is at ease because he knows how to act; with them he feels that he is accepted, and knows that he has a respected "place."

Later, his heart always will beat faster with these old friends from earlier days. It will be good to find them in the next grade, as he moves up in school; or to meet them after graduation from elementary school, reunited in high school; or in later years, when they have scattered to follow their own individual hopes, to have them return and look him up, for old times' sake. They are still his "own crowd," his own age-and-friendship group. They have shared the same situations, loyalties, way of life. He will never feel so much at ease with any other group. As he grows older, he will learn that early friendships take deep roots, throughout the long impressionable days of youth, and that new ties of equal strength seldom develop after he has become an adult.

He is bound to these friends of his own age, furthermore, by ceremonies which have marked their common progress. These age-rituals, celebrating his success in rising from one age-step to the next, are the most important in his life. For the middleclass child, they begin with his christening and his birthday parties. At much later ages, they include his graduation from high school, college, or professional school; his marriage-ceremony, and even his funeral! In between these are his graduation ceremony at nursery school, his graduation exercises in elementary school, and his confirmation or baptism in the church. These are the public occasions celebrating his growing older. Each ceremony occurs, it is important to recall, before an impressively large audience, composed both of *children and of the parental generation.* He thus receives the attention and approval both of his peers and of his superiors in age.

For the very young child, his birthdays are the high points of his life. He looks forward to them for many months, and insists upon counting half-years, in stating his age. Certainly until he is six, his birthday parties are the most important events in his life. They dramatize *him* alone; he is the center of interest for his parents, for his brothers and sisters, and his friends. At the party, his new age, which brings new privileges and status, is publicly recognized by his peers. They are noticeably impressed by his greater importance.

His graduation from *nursery school* is often celebrated by pageants, recitations, and by other thrilling, or terrifying, performances. They take place before an audience composed of mothers, a few fathers, his teachers, and of both the "little" and the "big" pupils. His paintings and other completed work are on display. Important adults make long speeches. At the most solemn moment of all, he marches in a line before this audience, and receives his certificate of graduation from the Director of the nursery-school staff. The children clearly take these ceremonies very seriously. Few societies or tribes have equally elaborate and significant age-ceremonies for *children who are not more than five years old.*

At graduation from elementary school, at baptism or confirmation, at initiation into a high-school secret society or into the youth-auxiliary of a lodge, and at high-school graduation, both the ceremonies and the audience are far more impressive. Upon each of these occasions, the growing individual faces an audience which is really an embodiment of society, the all powerful. Before this microcosm of the larger world, he is taken into a higher age-rank; he is publicly given a higher status and told (at great length) that he has deeper responsibilities to Society.

On each of these occasions (in the school, lodge, or church) the child is in an institution more complex than he can understand. He is going through a revered ritual passed down through the ages. He is received finally into a larger life, or status, by a great assembly of adults and adolescents.

Some primitive societies have very elaborate ceremonies initiating children or adolescents into a higher age-group. But our own society has two of the most impressive age-ceremonies in the world. One of these is religious, namely, final confirmation or baptism. It usually occurs when the child enters adolescence, and marks his passing out of childhood. In a high Episcopalian church, in a Catholic church, and in those revivalistic churches where the convert must undergo a probationary period and see "true visions" before baptism, these ceremonies are both prolonged and emotionally cathartic. From them, the person who is leaving childhood gains a deep sense of the infinite complexity of the adult society.

In its modern spectacular form, high-school graduation may be even more unforgettable than baptism to the boys and girls who go through it, together. For most of them, it solemnizes the end of an era, of an age. Now they will have to assume many of the responsibilities of adults. In our large cities, the ceremony takes place in a tremendous auditorium, banked with a great display of flowers and plants. From two to five thousand people are present. None of the graduating class has ever appeared before so large an audience; very few will again in life.

During the last two decades, these ceremonies have flowered like a Hollywood pageant. Now there is a symphony orchestra. The graduates wear caps and gowns, as if they were college graduates. There are impressive "speech-choruses," announcing, in tones of doom, various patriotic or moral truisms. There are numerous dialogues and orations by the students, full of allegorical meaning, like a morality play.

Then the adult society has the final say. Through the Superintendent of Schools and the Principal, or some person of even greater authority, the most serious and heavy responsibilities are passed down to the graduates. Finally, each graduating student has his individual moment in the spotlight. Alone, he walks across the stage toward the Superintendent. As he receives his diploma, his *full* name is called out to the vast audience. They applaud his individual achievement of having passed successfully the longest task of adolescence, that of completing high school.

Our wistful five-year-old has become a young man or woman. At last, he has climbed all the steps, age by age, from nursery school to the beginning of adulthood. For the moment, his eyes are dazzled by visions of his own importance, and he believes in truth that he has reached his Arcadia. Then he begins to discover gradually that the ladder of age still stretches high above him, and that he must climb far beyond adolescence and high-school graduation, if he wishes to be "old" and powerful.

THE COURSE OF HEALTHY PERSONALITY DEVELOPMENT[1]
Midcentury White House Conference on Children and Youth

Many attempts have been made to describe the attributes of healthy personality. They have been put succinctly as the ability to love and the ability to work. A recent review of the literature suggests that the individual with a healthy personality is one who actively masters his environment, shows a unity of personality, and is able to perceive the world and himself correctly. Clearly, none of these criteria applies to a child. It seemed to us best, then, to present for the Conference's consideration an outline that has the merit of indicating at one and the same time the main course of personality development and the attributes of a healthy personality.

This developmental outline was worked out by Erik H. Erickson, a psychologist and practicing psychoanalyst who has made anthropological field studies and has had much experience with children. It is an analysis that derives from psychological theory, to which is added knowledge from the fields of child development and cultural anthropology. The whole is infused with the author's insight and personal philosophy.

In each stage of child development, the author says, there is a central problem that has to be solved, temporarily at least, if the child is to proceed with vigor and confidence to the next stage. These problems, these conflicts of feeling and desire, are never solved in entirety. Each shift in experience and environment presents them in a new form. It is held, however, that each type of conflict appears in its purest,

[1] From Midcentury White House Conference on Children and Youth, *A Healthy Personality for Every Child.* Copyright 1951 by Health Publications Institute, Inc., Raleigh, North Carolina. Reprinted by permission of the publisher.

most unequivocal form at a particular stage of child development, and that if the problem is well solved at that time the basis for progress to the next stage is well laid.

In a sense personality development follows biological principles. Biologists have found that everything that grows has a groundplan that is laid out at the start. Out of this groundplan the parts arise, each part having its time of special ascendancy. Together these parts form a functioning whole. If a part does not arise at its appointed time, it will never be able to form fully, since the moment for the rapid outgrowth of some other part will have arrived. Moreover, a part that misses its time of ascendancy or is severely damaged during its formative period is apt to doom, in turn, the whole hierarchy of organs. Proper rate and normal sequence is necessary if functional harmony is to be secured.

Personality represents the most complicated functioning of the human organism and does not consist of parts in the organic sense. Instead of the development of organs, there is the development of locomotor, sensory, and social capacities and the development of individual modes of dealing with experience. Nevertheless, proper rate and proper sequence are as important here as in physical growth, and functional harmony is achived only if development proceeds according to the groundplan.

In all this it is encouraging for parents and others who have children in charge to realize that in the sequence of his most personal experiences, just as in the sequence of organ formation, the child can be trusted to follow inner laws of development, and needs from adults chiefly love, encouragement, and guidance.

The operation of biological laws is seen, also, in the fact that there is constant interplay between organism and environment and that problems of personality functioning are never solved once and for all. Each of the components of the healthy personality to be described below is present in some form from the beginning, and the struggle to maintain it continues throughout life.

For example, a baby may show something like "autonomy" or a will of his own in the way he angrily tries to free his head when he is tightly held. Nevertheless, it is not until the second year of life that he begins to experience the whole conflict between being an autonomous creature and a dependent one. It is not until then that he is ready for a decisive encounter with the people around him, and it is not until then that they feel called upon to train him or otherwise curb his free-questing spirit. The struggle goes on for months and finally, under favorable circumstances, some compromise between dependence and independence is reached that gives the child a sense of well-being.

The sense of autonomy thus achieved is not a permanent possession, however. There will be other challenges to that sense and other solutions more in keeping with later stages of development. Nevertheless, once established at two or three years of age, this early sense of autonomy will be a bulwark against later frustrations and will permit the emergence of the next developmental problem at a time that is most favorable for its solution.

So it is with all the personality components to be described. They appear in miniature early in life. The struggle to secure them against tendencies to act otherwise comes to a climax at a time determined by emergence of the necessary physical and mental abilities. There are, throughout life, other challenges and other responses but they are seldom so serious and seldom so decisive as those of the critical years.

In all this, it must be noted in addition, there is not the strict dichotomy that the analysis given below suggests. With each of the personality components to be described, it is not all or nothing: trust *or* mistrust, autonomy *or* doubt, and so on. Instead, each individual has some of each. His health of personality is determined by the preponderance of the favorable over the unfavorable, as well as by what manner of compensations he develops to cope with his disabilities.

THE SENSE OF TRUST

The component of the healthy personality that is the first to develop is the sense of trust. The crucial time for its emergence is the first year of life. As with the other personality components to be described, the sense of trust is not something that develops independent of other manifestations of growth. It is not that the infant learns how to use his body for purposeful movement, learns to recognize people and objects around him, and also develops a sense of trust. Rather, the concept "sense of trust" is a short-cut expression intended to convey the characteristic flavor of all the child's satisfying experiences at this early age. Or, to say it another way, this psychological formulation serves to condense, summarize, and synthesize the most important underlying changes that give meaning to the infant's concrete and diversified experience.

Trust can exist only in relation to something. Consequently a sense of trust cannot develop until the infant is old enough to be aware of objects and persons and to have some feeling that he is a separate individual. At about three months of age a baby is likely to smile if somebody comes close and talks to him. This shows that he is aware of the approach of the other person, that pleasurable sensations are aroused. If, however, the person moves too quickly or speaks too sharply the baby may look apprehensive or cry. He will not "trust" the unusual situation but will have a feeling of uneasiness, of mistrust, instead.

Experiences connected with feeding are a prime source for the development of trust. At around four months of age a hungry baby will grow quiet and show signs of pleasure at the sound of an approaching footstep, anticipating (trusting) that he will be held and fed. This repeated experience of being hungry, seeing food, receiving food, and feeling relieved and comforted assures the baby that the world is a dependable place.

Later experiences, starting at around five months of age, add another dimension to the sense of trust. Through endless repetitions of attempts to grasp for and hold objects, the baby is finally successful in controlling and adapting his movements in such a way as to reach his goal. Through these and other feats of muscular coordination the baby is gradually able to trust his own body to do his bidding.

The baby's trust-mistrust problem is symbolized in the game of peek-a-boo. In this game, which babies begin to like at about four months of age, an object disappears and then reappears. There is a slightly tense expression on the baby's face when the object goes away; its reappearance is greeted by wriggles and smiles. Only gradually does a baby learn that things continue to exist even though he does not see them, that there is order and stability in his universe. Peek-a-boo proves the point by playful repetition.

Studies of mentally ill individuals and observations of infants who have been grossly deprived of affection suggest that trust is an early-formed and important element in the healthy personality. Psychiatrists find again and again that the most serious illnesses occur in patients who have been sorely neglected or abused or otherwise deprived of love in infancy. Similarly, it is a common finding of psychological and social investiagtors that individuals diagnosed as a "psychopathic personality" were so unloved in infancy that they have no reason to trust the human race and, therefore, no sense of responsibility toward their fellow men.

Observations of infants brought up in emotionally unfavorable institutions or removed to hospitals with inadequate facilities for psychological care support these findings. A recent report says: "Infants under six months of age who have been in an institution for some time present a well-defined picture. The outstanding features are listlessness, emaciation and pallor, relative immobility, quietness, unresponsiveness to stimuli like a smile or a coo, indifferent appetite, failure to gain weight properly despite ingestion of diets which are entirely adequate, frequent stools, poor sleep, an appearance of unhappiness, proneness to febrile episodes, absence of sucking habits." [2]

Another investigation of children separated from their mothers at six to twelve months and not provided with an adequate substitute comes to much the same conclusion: "The emotional tone is one of apprehension and sadness, there is withdrawal from the environment amounting to rejection of it, there is no attempt to contact a stranger and no brightening if a stranger contacts him. Activities are retarded and the child often sits or lies inert in a dazed stupor. Insomnia is common and lack of appetite universal. Weight is lost, and the child becomes prone to current infections." [3]

Most significant for our present point, these reactions are most likely to occur in children who up to the time of separation at six to nine months of age had a happy relation with their mothers, while those whose relations were unhappy are relatively unaffected. It is at about this age that the struggle between trusting and mistrusting the world comes to a climax, for it is then that the child first perceives clearly that he and his environment are things apart. That at this time formerly happy infants should react so badly to separation suggests, indeed, that they had had a faith which now was shattered. Happily, there is usually spectacular change for the better when the maternal presence and love are restored.

It is probably unnecessary to describe the numerous ways in which stimuli from without and from within may cause an infant distress. Birth is believed by some experts to be a painful experience for the baby. Until fairly recently doctors were likely to advise that babies be fed on schedule and that little attention be paid to their cries of hunger at other times. Many infants spent many of the waking hours of the first four months doubled up with colic. All of them had to be bathed and dressed at stated times, whether they liked it or not. Add to these usual discomforts the fact that some infants are handled rather roughly by their parents, that others hear angry words and loud voices, and that a few are really mistreated, and it will not be difficult to understand why some infants may feel the world is a place that cannot be trusted.

In most primitive societies and in some sections of our own society the attention accorded infants is more in line with natural processes. In such societies separation from the mother is less abrupt, in that for some time after birth the baby is kept close to the warmth and comfort of its mother's body and at its least cry the breast is produced. Throughout infancy the baby is surrounded by people who are ready to feed it, fondle it, otherwise comfort it at a moment's notice. Moreover, these ministrations are given spontane-

[2] Harry Bakwin, "Emotional Deprivation in Infants." *Journal of Pediatrics* (Oct., 1949), Vol. 35, pp. 512–529.

[3] John Bowlby, M.D., Summary of Dr. René Spitz's observations, unpublished manuscript.

ously, wholeheartedly, and without that element of nervous concern that may characterize the efforts of young mothers made self-conscious and insecure by our scientific age.

We must not exaggerate, however. Most infants in our society, too, find smiles and the comfort of mother's soft, warm body accompanying their intake of food, whether from breast or bottle. Coldness, wetness, pain, and boredom—for each misfortune there is prompt and comforting relief. As their own bodies come to be more dependable, there is added to the pleasures of increasing sensory response and motor control the pleasure of the mother's encouragement.

Moreover, babies are rather hardy creatures and are not to be discouraged by inexperienced mothers' mistakes. Even a mother cat has to learn, and the kittens endure gracefully her first clumsy efforts to carry them away from danger. Then, too, psychologists tell us that mothers create a sense of trust in their children not by the particular techniques they employ but by the sensitiveness with which they respond to the children's needs and by their over-all attitude.

For most infants, then, a sense of trust is not difficult to come by. It is the most important element in the personality. It emerges at the most vulnerable period of a child's life. Yet it is the least likely to suffer harm, perhaps because both nature and culture work toward making mothers most maternal at that time.

THE SENSE OF AUTONOMY

The sense of trust once firmly established, the struggle for the next component of the healthy personality begins. The child is now twelve to fifteen months old. Much of his energy for the next two years will center around asserting that he is a human being with a mind and will of his own. A list of some of the items discussed by Spock under the heading, "The One Year Old," will serve to remind us of the characteristics of that age and the problems they create for parents. "Feeling his oats." "The passion to explore." "He gets more dependent and more independent at the same time." "Arranging the house for the wandering baby." "Avoiding accidents." "How do you make him leave certain things alone?" "Dropping and throwing things." "Biting humans." "The small child who won't stay in bed at night."

What is at stake throughout the struggle of these years is the child's sense of autonomy, the sense that he is an independent human being and yet one who is able to use the help and guidance of others in important matters. This stage of development becomes decisive for the ratio between love and hate, between cooperation and wilfulness, for freedom of self-expression and its renunciation in the make-up of the individual. The favorable outcome is self-control without loss of self-esteem. The unfavorable outcome is doubt and shame.

Before the sense of autonomy can develop, the sense of trust must be reasonably well established and must continue to pervade the child's feeling about himself and his world. Only so dare he respond with confidence to his new-felt desire to assert himself boldly, to appropriate demandingly, and to hurl away without let or hindrance.

As with the previous stage, there is a physiological basis for this characteristic behavior. This is the period of muscle-system maturation and the consequent ability (and doubly felt inability) to coordinate a number of highly conflicting action patterns, such as those of holding on and letting go, walking, talking, and manipulating objects in ever more complicated ways. With these abilities come pressing needs to use them: to handle, to explore, to seize and to drop, to withhold and to expel. And, with all, there is the dominant will, the insistent "Me do" that defies help and yet is so easily frustrated by the inabilities of the hands and feet.

For a child to develop this sense of self-reliance and adequacy that Erickson calls autonomy, it is necessary that he experience over and over again that he is a person who is permitted to make choices. He has to have the right to choose, for example, whether to sit or whether to stand, whether to approach a visitor or to lean against his mother's knee, whether to accept offered food or whether to reject it, whether to use the toilet or to wet his pants. At the same time he must learn some of the boundaries of self-determination. He inevitably finds that there are walls he cannot climb, that there are objects out of reach, that, above all, there are innumerable commands enforced by powerful adults. His experience is much too small to enable him to know what he can and cannot do with respect to the physical environment, and it will take him years to discover the boundaries that mark off what is approved, what is tolerated, and what is forbidden by his elders whom he finds so hard to understand.

As problems of this period, some psychologists have concentrated particularly on bladder and bowel control. Emphasis is put upon the need for care in both timing and mode of training children in the performance of these functions. If parental control is too rigid or if training is started too early, the child is robbed of his opportunity to develop, by his own free choice, gradual control of the contradictory impulses of retention and elimination.

To others who study child development, this matter of toilet training is but a prototype of all the problems of this age-range. The sphincters are only part of the whole muscle system, with its general ambiguity of rigidity and relaxation, of flexion and extension. To hold and to relinquish refer to much more than the bowels. As the child acquires the ability to stand on his two feet and move around, he delineates his world as me and you. He can be astonishingly pliable once he has decided that he wants to do what he is supposed to do, but there is no reliable formula for assuring that he will relinquish when he wants to hold on.

The matter of mutual regulation between parent and child (for fathers have now entered the picture to an extent that was rare in the earlier stage) now faces its severest test. The task is indeed one to challenge the most resourceful and the most calm adult. Firmness is necessary, for the child must be protected against the potential anarchy of his as yet untrained sense of discrimination. Yet the adult must back him up in his wish to "stand on his own feet," lest he be overcome by shame that he has exposed himself foolishly and by doubt in his self-worth. Perhaps the most constructive rule a parent can follow is to forbid only what "really matters" and, in such forbidding, to be clear and consistent.

Shame and doubt are emotions that many primitive peoples and some of the less sophisticated individuals in our own society utilize in training children. Shaming exploits the child's sense of being small. Used to excess it misses its objective and may result in open shamelessness, or, at least, in the child's secret determination to do as he pleases when not observed. Such defiance is a normal, even healthy response to demands that a child consider himself, his body, his needs, or his wishes evil and dirty and that he regard those who pass judgment as infallible. Young delinquents may be produced by this means, and others who are oblivious to the opinion of society.

Those who would guide the growing child wisely, then, will avoid shaming him and avoid causing him to doubt that he is a person of worth. They will be firm and tolerant with him so that he can rejoice in being a person of independence and can grant independence to others. As to detailed procedures, it is impossible to prescribe, not only because we do not know and because every situation is different but also because the kind and degree of autonomy that parents are able to grant their small children depends on feelings about themselves that they derive from society. Just as the child's sense of trust is a reflection of the mother's sturdy and realistic faith, so the child's sense of autonomy is a reflection of the parents' personal dignity. Such appears to be the teaching of the comparative study of cultures.

Personal autonomy, independence of the individual, is an especially outstanding feature of the American way of life. American parents, accordingly, are in a particularly favorable position to transmit the sense of autonomy to their children. They themselves resent being bossed, being pushed around; they maintain that everybody has the right to express his opinion and to be in control of his affairs. More easily than people who live according to an authoritarian pattern, they can appreciate a little child's vigorous desire to assert his independence and they can give him the leeway he needs in order to grow up into the upstanding, look-you-in-the-eye kind of individual that Americans admire.

It is not only in early childhood, however, that this attitude toward growing children must be maintained. As was said at the outset, these components of the healthy personality cannot be established once and for all. The period of life in which they first come into being is the most crucial, it is true. But threats to their maintenance occur throughout life. Not only parents, then, but everybody who has significant contact with children and young people must respect their desire for self-assertion, help them hold it within bounds, and avoid treating them in ways that arouse shame or doubt.

This attitude toward children, toward all people, must be maintained in institutional arrangements as well. Great differences in educational and economic opportunity and in access to the law, discrimination of all kinds are threats to this ingredient of mental health. So, too, may be the over-mechanization of our society, the depersonalization of human relations that is likely to accompany large-scale endeavor of all kinds.

Parents, as well as children, are affected by these matters. In fact, parents' ability to grant children the kind of autonomy Americans think desirable depends in part on the way they are treated as employees and citizens. Throughout, the relation must be such as affirms personal dignity. Much of the shame and doubt aroused in children result from the indignity and uncertainty that are an expression of parents' frustrations in love and work. Special attention must be paid to all these matters, then, if we are to avoid destroying the autonomy that Americans have always set store by.

THE SENSE OF INITIATIVE

Having become sure, for the time being, that he is a person in his own right and having enjoyed that feeling for a year or so, the child of four or five wants to find out what kind of person he can be. To be any particular kind of person, he sees clearly, involves being able to do particular kinds of things. So he observes with keen attention what all manner of interesting adults do (his parents, the milkman, the truck driver, and so on), tries to imitate their behavior, and yearns for a share in their activities.

This is the period of enterprise and imagination, an ebullient, creative period when phantasy substitutes for literal execution of desires and the meagerest equipment provides material for high imaginings. It is a period of intrusive, vigorous learning, learning that leads away from the child's own limitations into future possibilities. There is intrusion into other people's bodies by physical attack, into other people's ears and minds by loud and aggressive talking. There is intrusion into space by vigorous locomotion and intrusion into the unknown by consuming curiosity.

By this age, too, conscience has developed. The child is no longer guided only by outsiders; there is installed within him a voice that comments on his deeds, and warns and threatens. Close attention to the remarks of any child of this age will confirm this statement. Less obvious, however, are experts' observations that children now begin to feel guilty for mere thoughts, for deeds that have been imagined but never executed. This, they say, is the explanation for the characteristic nightmares of this age period and for the over-reaction to slight punishment.

The problem to be worked out in this stage of development, accordingly, is how to will without too great a sense of guilt. The fortunate outcome of the struggle is a sense of initiative. Failure to win through to that outcome leaves the personality overburdened, and possibly over-restricted, by guilt.

It is easy to see how the child's developing sense of initiative may be discouraged. So many of the projects dreamed up at this age are of a kind which cannot be permitted that the child may come to feel he is faced by a universal "No." In addition he finds that many of the projects are impossible of execution and others, even if not forbidden, fail to win the approval of the adults whom he has come to love. Moreover, since he does not always distinguish clearly between actuality and phantasy, his over-zealous conscience may disapprove of even imaginary deeds.

It is very important, therefore, for healthy personality development that much leeway and encouragement be given to the child's show of enterprise and imagination and that punishment be kept at a minimum. Boys and girls at this stage are extraordinarily appreciative of any convincing promise that someday they will be able to do things as well, or maybe better, than father and mother. They enjoy competition (especially if they can win) and insistence on goal; they get great pleasure from conquest. They need numerous examples of the kinds of roles adults assume, and they need a chance to try them out in play.

The ability that is in the making is that of selecting social goals and persevering in the attempt to reach them.

If enterprise and imagination are too greatly curbed, if severe rebukes accompany the frequently necessary denial of permission to carry out desires, a personality may result that is over-constricted. Such a personality cannot live up to its inner capacities for imagination, feeling, or performance, though it may overcompensate by immense activity and find relaxation impossible.

Constriction of personality is a self-imposed constriction, an act of the child's over-zealous conscience. "If I may not do this, I will not even think it," says conscience, "for even thinking it is dangerous." Resentment and bitterness and a vindictive attitude toward the world that forces the restriction may accompany this decision, however, and become unconscious but functioning parts of the personality. Such, at least, is the warning of psychiatrists who have learned to know the inmost feelings of emotionally handicapped children and adults.

This developmental stage has great assets as well as great dangers. At no time in life is the individual more ready to learn avidly and quickly, to become big in the sense of sharing obligation and performance. If during this pre-school period the child can get some sense of the various roles and functions that he can perform as an adult, he will be ready to progress joyfully to the next stage, in which he will find pleasurable accomplishment in activities less fraught with phantasy and fear.

There is a lesson in this for later periods of personality development as well. As has been said before, these conflicts that come to a head at particular periods of a child's life are not settled once and for all. The sense of initiative, then, is one that must be continually fostered, and great care must be taken that youngsters and young people do not have to feel guilty for having dared to dream.

Just as we Americans prize autonomy, so too do we prize initiative; in fact, we regard it as the cornerstone of our economic system. There is much in the present industrial and political mode of life that may discourage initiative, that may make a young person think he had best pull in his horns. What these tendencies are and what they may do to youngsters and to their parents, who too must feel free if they are to cultivate the sense of initiative in their children, is a subject that warrants much serious discussion.

THE SENSE OF ACCOMPLISHMENT

The three stages so far described probably are the most important for personality development. With a sense of trust, a sense of autonomy, and a sense of initiative achieved, progress through the later stages is pretty well assured. Whether this is because children who have a good environment in their early years are likely to continue to be so favored, or whether it is because they have attained such strength of personality that they can successfully handle later difficulties, research has not yet made clear. We do know that nearly all children who get a good start continue to develop very well, and we know that some of those who start off poorly continue to be handicapped. Observations of this sort seem to support psychological theory in the conclusion that personality is pretty well set by about six years of age. Since, however, some children develop into psychologically healthy adults in spite of a bad start, and since some who start well run into difficulties later, it is clear that much research is needed before this conclusion can be accepted as wholly correct.

To return to the developmental analysis, the fourth stage, which begins somewhere around six years of age and extends over five or six years, has as its achievement what Erickson calls the sense of industry. Perhaps "sense of accomplishment" would make the meaning clearer. At any rate, this is the period in which preoccupation with phantasy subsides, and the child wants to be engaged in real tasks that he can carry through to completion. As with the other developmental stages, there are foreshadowings of this kind of interest long before six years of age. Moreover, in some societies and in some parts of our own society children are trained very early to perform socially useful tasks. The exact age is not the point at issue. What is to be pointed out is that children, after a period characterized by exuberant imagination, want to settle down to learning exactly how to do things and how to do them well.

In contrast to the preceding stages and to the succeeding ones, this stage does not consist of a swing from a violent inner upheaval to a new mastery. Under reasonably favorable circumstances this is a period of calm, steady growth, especially if the problems of the previous stages have been well worked through. Despite its unspectacular character, this is a very important period, for in it is laid a firm basis for responsible citizenship. It is during this period that children acquire not only knowledge and skills that make for good workmanship but also the ability to cooperate and play fair and otherwise follow the rules of the larger social game.

The chief danger of this period is the presence of conditions that may lead to the development of a sense of inadequacy and inferiority. This may be the outcome if the child has not yet achieved a sense of initiative, or if his experiences at home have not prepared him for entering school happily, or if he finds school a place where his previous accomplishments are disregarded or his latent abilities are not challenged. Even with a good start the child may later lapse into discouragement and lack of interest if at home or school his individual needs are overlooked—if too much is expected of him, or if he is made to feel that achievement is beyond his ability.

It is most important for health of personality, therefore, that schools be conducted well, that methods and courses of instruction be such as will give every child the feeling of successful accomplishment. Autobiographies of juvenile delinquents show time and again a boy who hated school—hated the fact that he was marked out as stupid or awkward, as one who was not as good as the rest. Some such boys find in jobs the sense of accomplishment they miss at school and consequently give up their delinquent ways. Others, however, are handicapped in job finding and keeping by the very fact that in school they did not develop the sense of industry; hence they have work failure added to their other insecurities. Nor is delinquency the only or the most likely outcome of lack of success in school. Many children respond in a quieter way, by passive acceptance of their inferiority. Psychologically they are perhaps even more harmed.

Our Puritan tradition maintains that children will not work except under the spur of competition, so we tend to fear the suggestion that all should succeed. To help children develop a sense of accomplishment does not mean, however, merely giving all of them good marks and passing them on to the next grade. Children need and want real achievement. How to help them secure it, despite differences in native capacity and differences in emotional development, is one of the school's most serious challenges.

School, of course, is not the only place in which children at this stage of development can secure the sense of industry. In work at home there are many opportunities for a child to get a feeling of mastery and worthwhile endeavor. Rural youth groups and their urban counterparts cater to this need, and many recreation programs put as much emphasis on work as on play. School, however, is the legally constituted arrangement for giving instruction to the young, so it is upon teachers that the professional responsibility for helping all children achieve a sense of industry and accomplishment rests.

In addition to aiding personality development in this way, teachers have many opportunities for reconfirming their pupils' sense of trust, autonomy, and initiative or for encouraging its growth in children who have been somewhat hampered by previous life experiences. Teachers cannot work alone, of course, either in aiding a child in the development of new capacities or in strengthening old ones. Jointly with parents and others they can do much, not only for children of already healthy personality but also for many whose development has been handicapped.

THE SENSE OF IDENTITY

With the onset of adolescence another period of personality development begins. As is well known, adolescence is a period of storm and stress for many young people, a period in which previous certainties are questioned and previous continuities no longer relied upon. Physiological changes and rapid physical growth provide the somatic base for the turmoil and indecision. It may be that cultural factors also play a part, for it has been observed that adolescence is less upsetting in some societies than in others.

The central problem of the period is the establishment of a sense of identity. The identity the adolescent seeks to clarify is who he is, what his role in society is to be. Is he a child or is he an adult? Does he have it in him to be someday a husband and father? What is he to be as a worker and an earner of money? Can he feel self-confident in spite of the fact that his race or religion or national background makes him a person some people look down upon? Over all, will he be a success or a failure? By reason of these questions adolescents are sometimes morbidly preoccupied with how they appear in the eyes of others as compared with their own conception of themselves, and with how they can make the roles and skills learned earlier jibe with what is currently in style.

In primitive societies adolescents are perhaps spared these doubts and indecisions. Through initiation rites, often seemingly cruel in character, young people are tested out (and test themselves out) and are then welcomed into a socially recognized age category in which rights and duties and mode of living are clearly defined. In our society there are few rituals or ceremonies that mark the change in status from childhood to youth. For those who have religious affiliations, confirmation, joining the church, may serve this purpose in part, since the young people are thereby admitted, in this one segment of their lives at least, to the company of adults. Such ceremonies serve, in addition, to reaffirm to youth that the universe is trustworthy and stable and that a way of life is clearly laid out.

Graduation ceremonies might play a part in marking a new status were it not that, in present-day America, status is so ill defined. What rules of law and custom exist are too diverse to be of much help. For example, legal regulations governing age of "consent," age at which marriage is permitted, age for leaving school, for driving a car, for joining (or being required to join) the Army or Navy mark no logical progressions in rights and duties. As to custom, there is so much variation in what even families who live next door to each other expect or permit that adolescents, eager to be on their way, are practically forced into standardizing themselves in their search for status. In this they are ably abetted by advertisers and entertainers who seek their patronage, as well as by well-meaning magazine writers who describe in great detail the means by which uniformity can be achieved.

In this urge to find comfort through similarity, adolescents are likely to become stereotyped in behavior and ideals. They tend to form cliques for self-protection and fasten on petty similarities of dress and gesture to assure themselves that they are really somebody. In these cliques they may be intolerant and even cruel toward those they label as different. Unfortunate as such behavior is and not to be condoned, intolerance serves the important purpose of giving the group members at least the negative assurance that there is something they are not.

The danger of this developmental period is self-diffusion. As Biff puts it in *The Death of a Salesman*, "I just can't take hold, Mom. I can't take hold of some kind of a life." A boy or girl can scarcely help feeling somewhat diffuse when the body changes in size and shape so rapidly, when genital maturity floods body and imagination with forbidden desires, when adult life lies ahead with such a diversity of conflicting possibilites and choices.

Whether this feeling of self-diffusion is

fairly easily mastered or whether, in extreme, it leads to delinquency, neurosis or outright psychosis, depends to a considerable extent on what has gone before. If the course of personality development has been a healthy one, a feeling of self-esteem has accrued from the numerous experiences of succeeding in a task and sensing its cultural meaning. Along with this, the child has come to the conviction that he is moving toward an understandable future in which he will have a definite role to play. Adolescence may upset this assurance for a time or to a degree but fairly soon a new integration is achieved, and the boy or girl sees again (and with clearer vision) that he belongs and that he is on his way.

The course is not so easy for adolescents who have not had so fortunate a past or for those whose earlier security is broken by a sudden awareness that as members of minority groups their way of life sets them apart. The former, already unsure of themselves, find their earlier doubt and mistrust reactivated by the physiological and social changes that adolescence brings. The latter, once secure, may feel that they must disavow their past and try to develop an "American" personality.

Much has been learned and written about the adolescent problems of the boys and girls whose early personality development has been impaired. How they can be helped, if their disorders are not too severe, is also fairly well known. The full implications of these findings for parents, teachers, and others who would guide youth are still to be worked out but, even so, there is considerable information.

Less well understood are the difficulties and the ways of helping adolescents who grew up in cultures that are not of the usual run. These boys and girls may have been privileged in having had a childhood in which there was little inhibition of sensual pleasures, and in which development proceeded by easy, unselfconscious stages. For them, difficulties arise if their parents lose trust in themselves or if their teachers apply sudden correctives, or if they themselves reject their past and try to act like the others. The new role of middle-class adolescent is often too hard to play. Delinquency or bizarre behavior mark the failure.

How to reach these boys and girls, how to help them attain their desire, is a matter not well understood. It is clear, however, that they should not be typed by pat diagnoses and social judgments, for they are ever ready to become the "bums" that they are called. Those who would guide them must understand both the psychology of adolescence and the cultural realities of the day. There is trust to be restored and doubt and guilt and feelings of inferiority to be overcome. The science of how to do this is still pretty much lacking, though here and there teachers, clergymen, probation officers, and the like are highly successful in the task.

Hard though it be to achieve, the sense of identity is the individual's only safeguard against the lawlessness of his biological drives and the authority of an overweening conscience. Loss of identity, loss of the sense that there is some continuity, sameness, and meaning to life, exposes the individual to his childhood conflicts and leads to emotional upsets. This outcome was observed time and again among men hard pressed by the dangers of war. It is clear, then, that if health of personality is to be preserved much attention must be given to assuring that America makes good on its promises to youth.

THE SENSE OF INTIMACY

After the sense of identity, to a greater or less extent, is achieved it becomes possible for the next component of the healthy personality to develop. This is the sense of intimacy, intimacy with persons of the same sex or of the opposite sex or with one's self. The youth who is not fairly sure of his identity shies away from interpersonal relations and is afraid of close communion with himself. The surer he becomes of himself, the more he seeks intimacy, in the form of friendship, love and inspiration.

In view of the early age at which boy and girl attachments are encouraged today, it may seem strange to put the critical period for the development of the sense of intimacy late in adolescence. The explanation is that, on the one hand, sexual intimacy is only one part of what is involved, and, on the other, boy-girl attachments of earlier age periods are likely to be of a somewhat different order. Regarding the latter point, it has been observed by those who know young people well that high-school age boys and girls often use each other's company for an endless verbal examination of what the other thinks, feels, and wants to do. In other words, these attachments are one means of defining one's identity.

In contrast to this use of friendship and companionship, boys and girls late in adolescence usually have need for a kind of fusion with the essence of other people and for a communion with their own inner resources. If, by reason of inadequacies in previous personality development, this sense of intimacy cannot be achieved, the youth may retire into psychological isolation and keep his relations with people on a formal, stereotyped level that is lacking in spontaneity and warmth or he may keep trying again and again to get close to others, only to meet with repeated failure. Under this compulsion he may even marry, but the role of mate is one he can rarely sustain, for the condition of true two-ness is that each individual must first become himself.

In this area of personality development as in the others, cultural factors play a part in sustaining or in discouraging the individual in his development. American culture is unusually successful in encouraging the development of the feelings of independence, initiative, industry, and identity. It is somewhat less successful in the area of intimacy, for the culture's ideal is the subordination of sexuality and sensuality to a life of work, duty, and worship.

Consequently, American adolescents are likely to be unsupported by their parents and to find little confirmation in story or song for their desire to sense intimately the full flavor of the personality of others. In many of them, then, the sense of intimacy does not develop highly and they have difficulty in finding in close personal relations the outlet for tension that they need.

There is some evidence that a change in conventions and customs in this respect is in the making, however. Too abrupt change in any such cultural matter is not to be urged, but it is to be hoped that gradual, frank discussion can bring about gradual alteration in attitude and overcome the dangers inherent in the traditional rigidity.

THE PARENTAL SENSE

"Parental sense" designates somewhat the same capacity as that implied in the words, creativity or productivity. The individual has normally come to adulthood before this sense can develop fully.

The parental sense is indicated most clearly by interest in producing and caring for children of one's own. It may also be exhibited in relation to other people's children or by a parental kind of responsibility toward the products of creative activity of other sorts. The mere desire for or possession of children does not indicate that this component of the healthy personality has developed. In fact, many parents who bring their children to child guidance clinics are found not to have reached this stage of personality development.

The essential element is the desire to nourish and nurture what has been produced. It is the ability to regard one's children as a trust of the community, rather than as extensions of one's own personality or merely as beings that one happens to live with.

Failure to develop this component of the healthy personality often results in a condition which has not been adequately categorized clinically. Although a true sense of intimacy has not developed, the individual may obsessively seek companionship. There is something of egotism in this as in his other activities, a kind of self-absorption. The individual is inclined to treat himself as a child and to be rivalrous with his children, if he has any. He indulges himself, expects to be indulged, and in general behaves in an infantile or immature manner.

There are both individual and social explanations of the failure to develop an adequate parental sense. Individually, the explanation may be found in the inadequate development of the personality components previously described. In some people this failure goes far back. Because of unfortunate experiences in childhood they did not arrive at a firm sense of trust, autonomy, and the rest. In others it is only inadequacies in later stages, especially in the development of the sense of intimacy, that are at fault.

Socially, as has been suggested throughout this analysis, healthy personality development depends upon the culture's ideals and upon the economic arrangements of the society. In order that most people may develop fully the sense of being a parent, the role of parent, both mother and father, must be a respected one in the society. Giving must rank higher than getting, and loving than being loved. The economy must be such that the future can be depended upon and each person can feel assured that he has a meaningful and respected part to play. Only so can most individuals afford to renounce selfish aims and derive much of their satisfaction from rearing children.

THE SENSE OF INTEGRITY

The final component of the healthy personality is the sense of integrity. In every culture the dominant ideals, honor, courage, faith, purity, grace, fairness, self-discipline, become at this stage the core of the healthy personality's integration. The individual, in Erickson's words, "becomes able to accept his individual life cycle and the people who have become significant to it as meaningful within the segment of history in which he lives."

To continue Erickson's description, "Integrity thus means a new and different love of one's parents, free of the wish that they should have been different, and an acceptance of the fact that one's life is one's own responsibility. It is a sense of comradeship with men and women of distant times and of different pursuits, who have created orders and objects and sayings conveying human dignity and love. Although aware of the relativity of all the various life styles that have given meaning to human striving, the possessor of integrity is ready to defend the dignity of his own life style against all physical and economic threats. For he knows that, for him, all human dignity stands or falls with the one style of integrity of which he partakes."

The adult who lacks integrity in this sense may wish that he could live life again. He feels that if at one time he had made a different decision he could have been a different person and his ventures would have been successful. He fears death and cannot accept his one and only life cycle as the ultimate of life. In the extreme, he experiences disgust and despair.

Despair expresses the feeling that time is too short to try out new roads to integrity. Disgust is a means of hiding the despair, a chronic, contemptuous displeasure with the way life is run. As with the dangers and the solutions of previous periods, doubt and despair are not difficulties that are overcome once and for all, nor is integrity so achieved. Most people fluctuate between the two extremes. Most, also, at no point, either attain to the heights of unalloyed integrity or fall to the depths of complete disgust and despair.

Even in adulthood a reasonably healthy personality is sometimes secured in spite of previous misfortunes in the developmental sequence. New sources of trust may be found. Fortunate events and circumstances may aid the individual in his struggle to feel autonomous. Imagination and initiative may be spurred by new responsibilities, and feelings of inferiority be overcome by successful achievement. Even late in life an individual may arrive at a true sense of who he is and what he has to do and may be able to win through to a feeling of intimacy with others and to joy in producing and giving.

Evidence of such changes is found in the case records of psychiatrists and social workers. Common sense observation attests that similar changes in health of personality are sometimes accomplished without benefit of any form of psychotherapy. Much remains to be learned about this, however, especially about how life itself may serve as therapeusis.

For the healthy personality development of children and youth it is necessary that a large proportion of adults attain a sense of integrity to a considerable degree. Not only parents but all who deal with children have need of this quality if they are to help children maintain the feeling that the universe is dependable and trustworthy. Integrity is relatively easily attained and sustained when the culture itself gives support, when a meaning to life is clearly spelled out in tradition and ceremony, and roles are clearly defined. Our culture, with its rapidly changing technology and its diversity of value standards, leaves much for the individual to work out for himself. In the American dream, however and the Judaeo-Christian tradition on which it is based there are values and ideals aplenty. In the interest of the welfare of children and youth, in order that a generation of happy individuals and responsible citizens be reared, it is highly important that these values and ideals be brought into prominence and that the promise of American life be kept.

THE ORIGIN OF TULARECITO[1]

John Steinbeck

DISCUSSION AND ANALYSIS

In his long career as one of America's leading storytellers, John Steinbeck has maintained an interest in simple or primitive characters. His fondness for such personalities is analogous to his predilection for tales about farms and ranch hands. He seems to be telling us that both types

[1] From *The Pastures of Heaven,* included in *The Portable Steinbeck.* Copyright 1932 by John Steinbeck. Reprinted by permission of The Viking Press, Inc., New York.

of person are significant because they are close to the earth, and therefore close to the mystery of creation.

Tularecito is one of Steinbeck's most memorable primitives. His birth is slyly reminiscent of other miraculous births in the great secular and religious literature of the world, wherein the infant who is to become a hero is discovered abandoned in a bush or thicket. Although Tularecito only attained the mental growth of a six-year-old, he possessed "strange and obscure gifts." It is one of the bitterest ironies of the story that these gifts set in motion a chain of events that culminate with Tularecito's being committed to an asylum. Most students will be quick to realize that this situation is not unique, for all of us have heard many narratives of artists doomed to struggle and poverty because of the very authenticity of their talent. How many of us, however, would recognize a similar problem in the classroom? In illustration, let us take the case of the child who constantly argues with the teacher. To the young teacher, such a pupil may be particularly disturbing. Might not this affinity for argument be channeled, however, so that it was an asset both to its owner and to the class?

Compare the two teachers in the story. Which do you feel best handled the problem of the retarded child? Steinbeck's sympathies appear to lie with Molly Morgan, who "knew all about him [Tularecito], had read books and taken courses about him." Yet, Miss Morgan's understanding backfires. Although she cares far more for the boy than Miss Martin does, her very concern leads to the complete loss of Tularecito's freedom. How do you account for this?

Tularecito is an extreme example of the common problem of the retarded child. Moreover, "the retarded child," as most experienced teachers know, is a convenient but not very accurate label for a multitude of problems and cases. In teaching, one has "bad days" in which even the most brilliant of pupils are slow to comprehend. The emotional problem of communication on such days is much the same kind of problem that Miss Morgan and Miss Martin faced. How will you face it? Do you think that Steinbeck may be saying that the problem of Tularecito was insoluble, not because of the school, but because of the society which refused to recognize and respect his talents? How can a teacher best meet this type of dilemma? How does the psychological maturity of the teacher herself become a crucial factor in the situation?

Comment on the following statement from the story: "No one can make a garden as he can. No one can milk so swiftly nor so gently. He is a good boy. He can break a mad horse without riding it; he can train a dog without whipping it, but the law says he must sit in the first grade repeating 'C-A-T, cat' for seven years."

If schools were fully oriented to the growth and development of their students could such a remark be made?

The origin of Tularecito is cast in obscurity, while his discovery is a myth which the folks of the Pastures of Heaven refuse to believe, just as they refuse to believe in ghosts.

Franklin Gomez had a hired man, a Mexican Indian named Pancho, and nothing else. Once every three months, Pancho took his savings and drove into Monterey to confess his sins, to do his penance, and be shriven and to get drunk, in the order named. If he managed to stay out of jail, Pancho got into his buggy and went to sleep when the saloons closed. The horse pulled him home, arriving just before daylight, and in time for Pancho to have breakfast and go to work. Pancho was always asleep when he arrived; that is why he created so much interest on the ranch when, one morning, he drove into the corral at a gallop, not only awake, but shouting at the top of his voice.

Franklin Gomez put on his clothes and went out to interview his ranch hand. The story, when it was stretched out of its tangle of incoherencies, was this: Pancho had been driving home, very sober as always. Up near the Blake place, he heard a baby crying in the sage brush beside the road. He stopped the horse and went to investigate, for one did not often come upon babies like that. And sure enough he found a tiny child lying in a clear place in the sage. It was about three months old by the size of it, Pancho thought. He picked it up and lighted a match to see just what kind of a thing he had found, when — horror of horrors! — the baby winked maliciously and said in a deep voice, "Look! I have very sharp teeth." Pancho did not look. He flung the thing from him, leaped into his buggy and galloped for home, beating the old horse with the butt end of the whip and howling like a dog.

Franklin Gomez pulled his whiskers a good deal. Pancho's nature, he considered, was not hysterical even under the influence of liquor. The fact that he had awakened at all rather proved there must be something in the brush. In the end, Franklin Gomez had a horse saddled, rode out and brought in the baby. It did not speak again for nearly three years; nor, on inspection, did it have any teeth, but neither of these facts convinced Pancho that it did not make that first ferocious remark.

The baby had short, chubby arms, and long, loose-jointed legs. Its large head sat without interval of neck between deformedly broad shoulders. The baby's flat face, together with its peculiar body, caused it automatically to be named Tularecito, Little Frog, although Franklin Gomez often called it Coyote, "for," he said, "there is in this boy's face that ancient wisdom one finds in the face of a coyote."

"But surely the legs, the arms, the shoulders, Señor," Pancho reminded him. And so Tularecito the name remained. It was never discovered who abandoned the misshapen little creature. Franklin Gomez accepted him into the patriarchate of his ranch, and Pancho took care of him. Pancho, however, could never lose a little fear of the boy. Neither the years nor a rigorous penance eradicated the effect of Tularecito's first utterance.

The boy grew rapidly, but after the fifth year his brain did not grow any more. At six Tularecito could do the work of a grown man. The long fingers of his hands were more dexterous and stronger than most men's fingers. On the ranch, they made use of the fingers of Tularecito. Hard knots could not long defy him. He had planting hands, tender fingers that never injured a young plant nor bruised the surfaces of a grafting limb. His merciless fingers could wring the head from a turkey gobbler without effort. Also Tularecito had an amusing gift. With his thumbnail he could carve remarkably correct animals from sandstone. Franklin Gomez kept many little effigies of coyotes and mountain lions, of chickens and squirrels, about the house. A two-foot image of a hovering hawk hung by wires from the ceiling of the dining room. Pancho, who had never quite considered the boy human, put his gift for carving in a growing category of diabolical traits definitely traceable to his supernatural origin.

While the people of the Pastures of Heaven did not believe in the diabolic origin of Tularecito, nevertheless they were uncomfortable in his presence. His eyes were ancient and dry; there was something troglodytic about his face. The great strength of his body and his strange and obscure gifts set him apart from other children and made men and women uneasy.

Only one thing could provoke anger in Tularecito. If any person, man, woman or child, handled carelessly or broke one of the products of his hands, he became furious. His eyes shone and he attacked the desecrator murderously. On three occasions when this had happened, Franklin Gomez tied his hands and feet and left him alone until his ordinary good nature returned.

Tularecito did not go to school when he was six. For five years thereafter, the county truant officer and the school superintendent sporadically worked on the case. Franklin Gomez agreed that he should go to school and even went so far as to start him off several times, but Tularecito never got there. He was afraid that school might prove unpleasant, so he simply disappeared for a day or so. It was not until the boy was eleven, with the shoulders of a weight lifter and the hands and forearms of a strangler that the concerted forces of the law gathered him in and put him in school.

As Franklin Gomez had known, Tularecito learned nothing at all, but immediately he gave evidence of a new gift. He could draw as well as he could carve in sandstone. When Miss Martin, the teacher, discovered his ability, she gave him a piece of chalk and told him to make a procession of animals around the blackboard. Tularecito worked long after school was dismissed, and the next morning an astounding parade was shown on the walls. All of the animals Tularecito had ever seen were there; all the birds of the hills flew above them. A rattlesnake crawled behind a cow; a coyote, his brush proudly aloft, sniffed at the heels of a pig. There were tomcats and goats, turtles and gophers, every one of them drawn with astonishing detail and veracity.

Miss Martin was overcome with the genius of Tularecito. She praised him before the class and gave a short lecture about each one of the creatures he had drawn. In her own mind she considered the glory that would come to her for discovering and fostering this genius.

"I can make lots more," Tularecito informed her.

Miss Martin patted his broad shoulder. "So you shall," she said. "You shall draw every day. It is a great gift that God has given you." Then she realized the importance of what she had just said. She leaned over and looked searchingly into his hard eyes while she repeated slowly, "It is a *great gift* that God has given you." Miss Martin glanced up at the clock and announced crisply, "Fourth grade arithmetic—at the board."

The fourth grade struggled out, seized erasers and began to remove the animals to make room for their numbers. They had not made two sweeps when Tularecito charged. It was a great day. Miss Martin, aided by the whole school, could not hold him down, for the enraged Tularecito had the strength of a man, and a madman at that. The ensuing battle wrecked the schoolroom, tipped over the desks, spilled rivers of ink, hurled bouquets of Teacher's flowers about the room. Miss Martin's clothes were torn to streamers, and the big boys, on whom the burden of the battle fell, were bruised and battered cruelly. Tularecito fought with hands, feet, teeth and head. He admitted no honorable rules and in the end he won. The whole school, with Miss Martin guarding its rear, fled from the building, leaving the enraged Tularecito in possession. When they were gone, he locked the door, wiped the blood out of his eyes and set to work to repair the animals that had been destroyed.

That night Miss Martin called on Franklin Gomez and demanded that the boy be whipped.

Gomez shrugged. "You really wish me to whip him, Miss Martin?"

The teacher's face was scratched; her mouth was bitter. "I certainly do," she said. "If you had seen what he did today, you wouldn't blame me. I tell you he needs a lesson."

Gomez shrugged again and called Tularecito from the bunk house. He took a heavy quirt down from the wall. Then, while Tularecito smiled blandly at Miss Martin, Franklin Gomez beat him severely across the back. Miss Martin's hand made involuntary motions of beating. When it was done, Tularecito felt himself over with long, exploring fingers, and still smiling, went back to the bunk house.

Miss Martin had watched the end of the punishment with horror. "Why, he's an animal," she cried. "It was just like whipping a dog."

Franklin Gomez permitted a slight trace of his contempt for her to show on his face. "A dog would have cringed," he said. "Now you have seen, Miss Martin. You say he is an animal, but surely he is a good animal. You told him to make pictures and then you destroyed his pictures. Tularecito does not like that—"

Miss Martin tried to break in, but he hurried on.

"This Little Frog should not be going to school. He can work; he can do marvellous things with his hands, but he cannot learn to do the simple little things of the school. He is not crazy; he is one of those whom God has not quite finished.

"I told the Superintendent these things, and he said the law required Tularecito to go to school until he is eighteen years old. That is seven years from now. For seven years my Little Frog will sit in the first grade because the law says he must. It is out of my hands."

"He ought to be locked up," Miss Martin broke in. "This creature is dangerous. You should have seen him today."

"No, Miss Martin, he should be allowed to go free. He is not dangerous. No one can make a garden as he can. No one can milk so swiftly nor so gently. He is a good boy. He can break a mad horse without riding it; he can train a dog without whipping it, but the law says he must sit in the first grade repeating 'C-A-T, cat' for seven years. If he had been dangerous he could easily have killed me when I whipped him."

Miss Martin felt that there were things she did not understand and she hated Franklin Gomez because of them. She felt that she had been mean and he generous. When she got to school the next morning, she found Tularecito before her. Every possible space on the wall was covered with animals.

"You see?" he said, beaming over his shoulder at her. "Lots more. And I have a book with others yet, but there is no room for them on the wall."

Miss Martin did not erase the animals. Class work was done on paper, but at the end of the term she resigned her position, giving ill health as her reason.

Miss Morgan, the new teacher, was very young and very pretty; too young and dangerously pretty, the aged men of the valley thought. Some of the boys in the upper grades were seventeen years old. It was seriously doubted that a teacher so young and so pretty could keep any kind of order in the school.

She brought with her a breathless enthusiasm for her trade. The school was astounded, for it had been used to ageing spinsters whose faces seemed to reflect consistently tired feet. Miss Morgan enjoyed teaching and made school an exciting place where unusual things happened.

From the first Miss Morgan was vastly impressed with Tularecito. She knew all about him, had read books and taken courses about him. Having heard about the fight, she laid off a border around the top of the blackboards for him to fill with animals, and, when he had completed his parade, she bought with her own money a huge drawing pad and a soft pencil. After that he did not bother with spelling. Every day he labored over his drawing board, and every afternoon presented the teacher with a marvelously wrought animal. She pinned his drawings to the schoolroom wall above the blackboards.

The pupils received Miss Morgan's innovations with enthusiasm. Classes became exciting, and even the boys who had made enviable reputations through teacher-baiting, grew less interested in the possible burning of the schoolhouse.

Miss Morgan introduced a practice that made the pupils adore her. Every afternoon she read to them for half an hour. She read by installments, *Ivanhoe* and *The Talisman;* fishing stories by Zane Grey, hunting stories of James Oliver Curwood; *The Sea Wolf, The Call of the Wild*—not baby stories about the little red hen and the fox and geese, but exciting, grown-up stories.

Miss Morgan read well. Even the tougher boys were won over until they never played hooky for fear of missing an installment, until they leaned forward gasping with interest.

But Tularecito continued his careful drawing, only pausing now and then to blink at the teacher and to try to understand how these distant accounts of the actions of strangers could be of interest to anyone. To him they were chronicles of actual events—else why were they written down. The stories were like the lessons. Tularecito did not listen to them.

After a time Miss Morgan felt that she had been humoring the older children too much. She herself liked fairy tales, liked to think of whole populations who believed in fairies and consequently saw them. Within the safe circle of her tried and erudite acquaintance, she often said that "part of America's cultural starvation was due to its boorish and superstitious denial of the existence of fairies." For a time she devoted the afternoon half hour to fairy tales.

Now a change came over Tularecito. Gradually, as Miss Morgan read about elves and brownies, fairies, pixies, and changelings, his interest centered and his busy pencil lay idly in his hand. Then she read about gnomes, and their lives and habits, and he dropped his pencil altogether and leaned toward the teacher to intercept her words.

After school Miss Morgan walked half a mile to the farm where she boarded. She liked to walk the way alone, cutting off thistle heads with a switch, or throwing stones into the brush to make the quail roar up. She thought she should get a bounding, inquisitive dog that could share her excitements, could understand the glamor of holes in the ground, and scattering pawsteps on dry leaves, of strange malancholy bird whistles and the gay smells that came secretly out of the earth.

One afternoon Miss Morgan scrambled high up the side of a chalk cliff to carve her initials on the white plane. On the way up she tore her finger on a thorn, and, instead of initials, she scratched: "Here I have been and left this part of me," and pressed her bloody finger against the absorbent chalk rock.

That night, in a letter, she wrote: "After the bare requisites to living and reproducing, man wants most to leave some record of himself, a proof, perhaps, that he has really existed. He leaves his proof on wood, on stone or on the lives of other people. This deep desire exists in everyone, from the boy who writes dirty words in a public toilet to the Buddha who etches his image in the race mind. Life is so unreal. I think that we seriously doubt that we exist and go about trying to prove that we do." She kept a copy of the letter.

On the afternoon when she had read about the gnomes, as she walked home, the grasses beside the road threshed about for a moment and the ugly head of Tularecito appeared.

"Oh! You frightened me," Miss Morgan cried. "You shouldn't pop up like that."

Tularecito stood up and smiled bashfully while he whipped his hat against his thigh. Suddenly Miss Morgan felt fear rising in her. The road was deserted—she had read stories of half-wits. With difficulty she mastered her trembling voice.

"What—what is it you want?"

Tularecito smiled more broadly and whipped harder with his hat.

"Were you just lying there, or do you want something?"

The boy struggled to speak, and then relapsed into his protective smile.

"Well, if you don't want anything, I'll go on." She was really prepared for flight.

Tularecito struggled again. "About those people—"

"What people?" she demanded shrilly. "About what people?"

"About those people in the book—"

Miss Morgan laughed with relief until she felt that her hair was coming loose on the back of her head. "You mean—you mean—gnomes?"

Tularecito nodded.

"What do you want to know about them?"

"I never saw any," said Tularecito. His voice neither rose nor fell, but continued on one low note.

"Why, few people do see them, I think."

"But I knew about them."

Miss Morgan's eyes squinted with interest. "You did? Who told you about them?"

"Nobody."

"You never saw them, and no one told you? How could you know about them then?"

"I just knew. Heard them, maybe. I knew them in the book all right."

Miss Morgan thought: "Why should I deny gnomes to this queer, unfinished child? Wouldn't his life be richer and happier if he did believe in them? And what harm could it possibly do?"

"Have you ever looked for them?" she asked.

"No, I never looked. I just knew. But I will look now."

Miss Morgan found herself charmed with the situation. Here was paper on which to write, here was a cliff on which to carve. She could carve a lovely story that would be far more real than a book story ever could. "Where will you look?" she asked.

"I'll dig in holes," said Tularecito soberly.

"But the gnomes only come out at night, Tularecito. You must watch for them in the night. And you must come and tell me if you find any. Will you do that?"

"I'll come," he agreed.

She left him staring after her. All the way home she pictured him searching in the night. The picture pleased her. He might even find the gnomes, might live with them and talk to them. With a few suggestive words she had been able to make his life unreal and very wonderful, and separated from the stupid lives about him. She deeply envied him his searching.

In the evening Tularecito put on his coat and took up a shovel. Old Pancho came upon him as he was leaving the tool shed. "Where goest thou, Little Frog?" he asked.

Tularecito shifted his feet restlessly at the delay. "I go out into the dark. Is that a new thing?"

"But why takest thou the shovel? Is there gold, perhaps?"

The boy's face grew hard with the seriousness of his purpose. "I go to dig for the little people who live in the earth."

Now Pancho was filled with horrified excitement. "Do not go, Little Frog! Listen to your old friend, your father in God, and do not go! Out in the sage I found thee and saved thee from the devils, thy relatives. Thou art a little brother of Jesus now. Go not back to thine own people! Listen to an old man, Little Frog!"

Tularecito stared hard at the ground and drilled his old thoughts with this new information. "Thou hast said they are my people," he exclaimed. "I am not like the others at the school or here. I know that. I have loneliness for my own people who live deep in the cool earth. When I pass a squirrel hole, I wish to crawl into it and hide myself. My own people are like me, and they have called me. I must go home to them, Pancho."

Pancho stepped back and held up crossed fingers. "Go back to the devil, thy father, then. I am not good enough to fight this evil. It would take a saint. But see! At least I make the sign against thee and against all thy race." He drew the cross of protection in the air in front of him.

Tularecito smiled sadly, and turning, trudged off into the hills.

The heart of Tularecito gushed with joy at his homecoming. All his life he had been an alien, a lonely outcast, and now he was going home. As always, he heard the voices of the earth—the far-off clang of cow bells, the muttering of disturbed quail, the little whine of a coyote who would not sing this night, the nocturnes of a million insects. But Tularecito was listening for another sound, the movement of two-footed creatures, and the hushed voices of the hidden people.

Once he stopped and called, "My father, I have come home," and he heard no answer. Into squirrel holes he whispered, "Where are you, my people? It is only Tularecito come home." But there was no reply. Worse, he had no feeling that the gnomes were near. He knew that a doe and fawn were feeding near him; he knew a wildcat was stalking a rabbit behind a bush, although he could not see them, but from the gnomes he had no message.

A sugar-moon arose out of the hills.

"Now the animals will come out to feed," Tularecito said in the papery whisper of the half-witless. "Now the people will come out, too."

The brush stopped at the edge of a little valley and an orchard took its place. The trees were thick with leaves, and the land finely cultivated. It was Bert Munroe's orchard. Often, when the land was deserted and ghost-ridden, Tularecito had come here in the night to lie on the ground under the trees and pick the stars with gentle fingers.

The moment he walked into the orchard he knew he was nearing home. He could not hear them, but he knew the gnomes were near. Over and over he called to them, but they did not come.

"Perhaps they do not like the moonlight," he said.

At the foot of a large peach tree he dug his hole—three feet across and very deep. All night he worked on it, stopping to listen awhile and then digging deeper and deeper into the cool earth. Although he heard nothing, he was positive that he was nearing them. Only when the daylight came did he give up and retire into the bushes to sleep.

In midmorning Bert Munroe walked out to look at a coyote trap and found the hole at the foot of the tree. "What the devil!" he said. "Some kids must have been digging a tunnel. That's dangerous! It'll cave in on them, or somebody will fall into it and get hurt." He walked back to the house, got a shovel and filled up the hole.

"Manny," he said to his youngest boy, "you haven't been digging in the orchard, have you?"

"Uh-uh!" said Manny.

"Well, do you know who has?"

"Uh-uh!" said Manny.

"Well, somebody dug a deep hole out there. It's dangerous. You tell the boys not to dig or they'll get caved in."

The dark came and Tularecito walked out of the brush to dig in his hole again. When he found it filled up, he growled savagely, but then his thought changed and he laughed. "The people were here," he said happily. "They didn't know who it was, and they were frightened. They filled up the hole the way a gopher does. This time I'll hide, and when they come to fill the hole, I'll tell them who I am. Then they will love me."

And Tularecito dug out the hole and made it much deeper than before, because much of the dirt was loose. Just before daylight, he retired into the brush at the edge of the orchard and lay down to watch.

Bert Munroe walked out before breakfast to look at his trap again, and again he found the open hole. "The little devils!" he cried. "They're keeping it up, are they? I'll bet Manny *is* in it after all."

He studied the hole for a moment and then began to push dirt into it with the side of his foot. A savage growl spun him around. Tularecito came charging down upon him, leaping like a frog on his long legs, and swinging his shovel like a club.

When Jimmy Munroe came to call his father to breakfast, he found him lying on the pile of dirt. He was bleeding at the mouth and forehead. Shovelfuls of dirt came flying out of the pit.

Jimmy thought someone had killed his father and was getting ready to bury him. He ran home in a frenzy of terror, and by telephone summoned a band of neighbors.

Half a dozen men crept up on the pit. Tularecito struggled like a wounded lion, and held his own until they struck him on the head with his own shovel. Then they tied him up and took him in to jail.

In Salinas a medical board examined the boy. When the doctors asked him questions, he smiled blandly at them and did not answer. Franklin Gomez told the board what he knew and asked the custody of him.

"We really can't do it, Mr. Gomez," the judge said finally. "You say he is a good boy. Just yesterday he tried to kill a man. You must see that we cannot let him go loose. Sooner or later he will succeed in killing someone."

After a short deliberation, he committed Tularecito to the asylum for the criminal insane at Napa.

7

SOCIAL FOUNDATIONS OF EDUCATION: The School and the Community

PSYCHOLOGICAL INTERPRETATIONS OF RURAL LIFE FOR CHILDREN AND ADOLESCENTS[1]

Hugh M. Bell

It is relatively common to speak of "rural" and "urban" differences, and yet it is somewhat difficult to find a rational basis for such differentiations. The commonly accepted distinction is that used by the census in which a rural community is defined as one with less than 2500 people. But when various communities are compared it is apparent that some with less than 2500 people have more in common with large urban communities, so far as cultural advantages are concerned, than others with over 2500 in population. Clarification might result from use of the term "rural" to refer to people who live on the land and derive their income through its cultivation and through the raising of plants and animal stock thereon, and employing the term "urban" for all other persons not thus engaged. While this occupational definition seems more logical than the census distinction, it has not been employed in statistical studies on rural-urban differences. Most of the studies on psychological differences have involved samples from the extremes of the rural-urban continuum and have found marked differences in mental ability and other personality traits.

Studies which have been conducted on mental differences between rural and city children indicate clearly that rural children tend to make lower scores on standardized intelligence tests than city children. A typical study is that by Pressey and Thomas[2] in which they compared intelligence test scores of "city," and "good farm," and "poor farm" children. They found that only 36 per cent of the children on the good farms came up to or exceeded the mean of city children, and only 22 per cent of those on the poor farms reached or exceeded the mean of city children.

In summarizing the studies on rural and

[1] From *California Journal of Elementary Education* (May, 1950), Vol. 18, pp. 240–243. Reprinted with the permission of the author and the Bureau of Textbooks and Publications of the California Department of Education.

[2] S. L. Pressey and J. B. Thomas, "A Study of Country Children in a Good and a Poor Farming District by Means of a Group Scale of Intelligence," *Journal of Applied Psychology* (1919), Vol. 3, pp. 283–286.

city children in so far as mental ability is concerned Anastasi writes:

Surveys have consistently shown the rural school child to be inferior in performance on current tests of general intelligence.[3]

The search for an explanation of these differences reveals two possible answers. One group of authorities contends that the inferiority of the rural child is due to the fact that the more intelligent and energetic are leaving the farm, thus depleting the rural racial stock. It is also pointed out that people with low ability tend to migrate to the farm because the simpler, routine jobs are more in keeping with their capacities. Critics of this hereditary point of view state that the dull as well as the bright tend to migrate to the city. Furthermore, they contend that the intelligence tests used to bring out these differences have been, for the most part, standardized on city children, both the items in the tests and the norms employed reflecting the city rather than the rural environment. They also state that there are as wide variations in groups living in different sections of a city as are found between city and rural areas.

The environmentalists believe that these differences in mental ability are the result of variations in cultural advantages. In an investigation of play activities of city and rural children, Lehman and Witty[4] found that city children had many more opportunities to play, which gave them more experience in vocabulary building and in the development of social understandings. In another study, by Shimberg,[5] the author constructed two information tests, one containing items reflecting the city and one the rural environment. These two tests were both given to rural and city children and it was found that the average city child was inferior to the rural child on the test built around rural life and that the average rural child was inferior to the city child on the test reflecting urban living conditions. One of the most significant studies of the influence of rural environment on mental ability is that by Baldwin, Fillmore, and Hadley[6] in which they found that mental tests of infants revealed no important differences between rural and city children, but as the pupils progressed through elementary school an increasing inferiority among the rural children became evident.

It seems reasonable to conclude from these and similar studies that much of the difference which is found in the mental ability of rural and city children is due to the rural child's lack of opportunity for educational and cultural development, and that if children living in rural areas were provided learning opportunities equal to those of city children they would tend to equal them in ability.

Most of the studies which have been made on rural and urban children have been concerned with differences in mental ability because these differences may be objectively measured at that level. In considering the differences between rural and urban adolescents, one must rely mainly on the clinical method and ordinary observation. Adolescence, for most individuals, regardless of where they live, means an intensification of self-awareness which is due primarily to the suddenness with which

[3] Anne Anastasi, *Differential Psychology*, New York, The Macmillan Co., 1937, p. 558.

[4] Harvey C. Lehman and Paul A. Witty, *The Psychology of Play Activities*, New York, A. S. Barnes & Co., 1927.

[5] M. E. Shimberg, "An Investigation into the Validity of Norms with Special Reference to Urban and Rural Groups," *Archives of Psychology*, 1929, No. 104.

[6] Bird T. Baldwin, Eva Abigail Fillmore, and Lora Hadley, *Farm Children: An Investigation of Rural Child Life in Selected Areas of Iowa*, New York, D. Appleton & Co., 1930.

the child is confronted with the necessity of assuming the role of a young adult. Gardner Murphy points out in a recent book [7] that whenever an individual is engaged in activities in which he is well skilled and confident, the self tends to recede into the background of consciousness, but when the individual engages in activities which are unfamiliar, the self emerges into the foreground of consciousness resulting in embarrassment and feelings of inadequacy. These feelings become strong motivating forces in the youth's search for adequacy and personal effectiveness. The youth wants to be accepted, to feel that he belongs and is not left out of his age group.

Rural youth faces many conditions in his environment which tend to intensify his self-awareness and his feelings of social inadequacy when in contact with his urban associates. They may not belong to groups which are well known to their friends such as Job's Daughters, the Boy Scouts, the high school band or the football team. This is particularly true of the rural youth who lives on the farm where he has farm chores to do as soon as school is out. Living on the farm not only denies him opportunity for social participation, but also robs him of an important source of conversational material. Being able to talk easily to people means having shared experiences with them.

Rural youth may also experience intensified self-awareness because his father's job does not rank high in social prestige in comparison with the fathers of city youth. Such professions as law, medicine, and dentistry are rated high, while farming ranks low in studies of occupational preference among adolescents. Then again the rural youth may be embarrassed because he comes from no place in particular or from some small place that is not well known. In his conversation with other youths he is unable to discuss with them the thing he knows most about, namely, his home and its surroundings, and must content himself to let the urban youth take the lead in conversation. Ignorance of urban social customs and fashions is another source of embarrassment to rural young persons. The latest thing in dress and fashion is often the current topic of conversation among people of his age.

Rural youth lacks opportunity to learn how to bluff and pretend he understands, or to discount the importance of things of which he is ignorant—techniques which city youth uses to keep up a good front. His response to social situations frequently is simple and direct, allowing his feelings to rise easily to the surface without disguise. This presents his more sophisticated urban associates with the opportunity of anticipating his intention and jesting at his lack of social acumen. Such ribbing sometimes causes him to withdraw within himself and to employ timidity and shyness as forms of self-protection, or to become overaggressive, loud, and noisy. The latter type of social compensation often works well during the middle teens, but as the youth approaches his twenties his associates expect a more subtle and socially considerate type of social response.

Differences in mental ability and other personality traits do exist between rural and urban children and youth, and one of the principal determinants of these differences is the educational and cultural environment. What then can be done to enrich the environment of the rural child? In the first place, better reading facilities should be provided for rural homes. Teaching in rural schools should be made more attractive to counteract the well-known tendency for the more capable teachers to gravitate to city schools. Rural youth needs

[7] Gardner Murphy, *Personality, a Biosocial Approach to Origins and Structure*, New York, Harper & Brothers, 1947.

more opportunity for group participation. Passive amusements such as the radio and motion pictures never take the place of active social participation in the development of effective personalities. Rural youth should also have the opportunity to benefit from intelligent vocational counseling based on a knowledge of his capacities and interests and the demands of various occupations.

In this brief article it has been pointed out that differences in mentality and other personality traits between rural and urban children and youth exist; that these differences are due primarily to the lack of educational and social advantages for rural children; that broad generalizations should be avoided in considering a particular locality; and that society should continually work toward enriching the environment of rural children to enable them to attain maximum personality development.

WHO THINKS WHAT ABOUT EDUCATORS?[1]

Frederic W. Terrien

DISCUSSION AND ANALYSIS

It is probable that all professions develop their own myths. Such myths, taking the place of genuine evidence, serve to reinforce what "everyone knows" about some phases of the job to be done, the relationship between practitioners and subjects, and so forth. Education, too, is surrounded by many myths. One of the most prevalent is that children do not like school. Yet research in a number of instances demonstrates that the overwhelming majority of students at any grade level, from first through twelfth, really do like school! There are numerous myths about community restrictions upon teachers' behavior, and yet again inquiry reveals that communities—today—typically expect teachers to act like reasonable and respectable human beings, no more and no less.

One favorite myth that seems to muddy up the educator's perception of the public is that by and large the public looks down on the teaching profession, resists paying a good wage, and cold-heartedly assigns teachers to a kind of sterile second-class citizenship. This selection reports the research by a sociologist testing out some of these myths. To what extent do the findings of Terrien support the view that the public is conservative and unsympathetic when it comes to teachers' needs? Is one justified in speaking about "*the* public" or "publics" when referring to attitudes about teachers?

Research is very helpful in dispelling myths. But research is also likely to reveal things overlooked or not known. What new facts about the attitude of people toward education does Terrien bring out? Another interesting question to consider: If you were to plan a campaign to (1)

[1] Reprinted from *American Journal of Sociology*, September, 1953, pp. 150–158, by permission of The University of Chicago Press. Copyright 1953 by The University of Chicago.

bring in teachers of a minority group, (2) raise teachers' salaries, or (3) support teachers' freedom to strike, to which particular groups in the community would you appeal to gain your strongest support? Which groups would be most opposed to such suggestions?

Cook, Almack and Greenhoe, Counts, Coutu, Deeg and Paterson, Edmiston and Starr, North and Hatt, Waller[2] and others have done much to establish the place of the teacher and his work in the social and occupational hierarchy. Most of the writings, however, have been based on personal—though often brilliant in insight—observation or on polls of one or another special interest group. Few claim to represent general public opinion. Where opinions on which the status of teachers was determined were those of a national cross-section, as in the case of the North and Hatt study, the statements about educators and education were incidental to the placing of occupations in a hierarchy set up by popular evaluation. A typical study, that of the Metropolitan School Study Council's Educational Dynamics Committee of 1946–47, at Columbia Teachers College, summarized a series of interviews with high-school students, teachers, and parents in forty-seven communities. While this study concentrated on the status of educators and education, it was based on the opinions of a limited sample of the general public.

The object of this study was to assess the status of educators and of education, largely at the secondary level, from the opinions of a representative sample of the people of a small American community. The data are from a survey of public opinion conducted by the author and a staff of interviewers during the spring and summer of 1948 in New London, Connecticut. The present paper will treat of the status of educators.

METHODS

The universe for the survey was the 1947 voters list of New London, comprising 12,770 persons. Of a total population of 30,456 (1940 Census), those twenty-one years old or over numbered 20,668. The sample was a random 5 per cent, 639 persons, who were interviewed in their homes or places of business by means of a lengthy schedule.

The schedule contained a series of key questions relating to the status of educators—for example, the professional level of teachers. The summary statement of replies to each question is broken down and analyzed with reference to sex, age group, nativity, parenthood, religion, occupation, education, and income. By such analysis we discover what opinions on educators are significantly related to the selected characteristics of New London's voting population.

To secure direct comparisons to be

[2] L. A. Cook, R. B. Almack, and F. Greenhoe, "The Teacher and Community Relations," *American Sociological Review* (Apr., 1938), Vol. 3, pp. 167–174; George S. Counts, "The Social Status of Occupations: A Problem in Vocational Guidance," *School Review* (Jan., 1925), Vol. 33, pp. 16–27; Walter Coutu, "The Relative Prestige of Twenty Professions as Judged by Three Groups of Professional Students," *Social Forces* (May, 1936), Vol. 14, pp. 522–529; Maethel E. Deeg and Donald G. Paterson, "Changes in Social Status of Occupations," *Occupations* (Jan., 1947), Vol. 25, pp. 205–208; R. W. Edmiston and C. H. Starr, "Youth's Attitude toward Occupations," *Occupations* (Jan., 1948), Vol. 26, pp. 213–220; C. C. North and Paul K. Hatt, "Jobs and Occupations: A Popular Evaluation," in Logan Wilson and William L. Kolb, *Sociological Analysis*, New York, Harcourt, Brace & Co., 1949; and Willard Waller, *The Sociology of Teaching*, New York, John Wiley & Sons, Inc., 1932.

treated by the methods of the chi square and significance of difference, the age groups were reduced to five: 21–29, 30–39, 40–49, 50–59, and 60 plus. Under "Nativity" two groups were set up, native-born and foreign-born. The religious category was split into Protestant, Catholic, and Jewish. Six arbitrary divisions were set up under "Occupation": professionals, proprietors, clerical workers, service workers (including protective service), skilled laborers, and laborers. The Federal Security Agency's *Dictionary of Occupational Titles* was used to classify the occupations of the interviewees. Under "Education" appear grammar school, some high school, high-school graduation, and some college. Finally, under "Income Level," three groups were set aside after scrutiny of the returns: a low group, comprising incomes up to $2,499 per year; a middle group, ranging between $2,500 and $3,499; and a high group, with annual incomes of $3,500 and over.

The differences or comparisons cited are statistically significant, and in all these instances, unless otherwise noted, *P* is at the 1 per cent level of confidence.[3]

For convenience, the questions concerning the status of educators are divided into four generalized groups. The first is heterogeneous, pertaining to a variety of attitudes toward teachers. The second group is broadly related to the community activities of teachers; the third treats of their professional status; and the fourth, of their financial condition.

[3] The author is deeply indebted to Clyde Milton Hill and Maurice Rea Davie, of Yale University, and to Ruby Jo Reeves Kennedy and Mason Record, of Connecticut College, for their advice at the field stages of this project. The interview analysis, scoring, transfer to IBM cards, sorting, and calculating was completed by a small staff subsidized by the Stanford Committee on Supplementary Research Grants. The statistical computations were the work of Richard J. Hill, of the University of Washington.

ATTITUDES TOWARD TEACHERS

The Friends of Teachers

The first question in this group was: "Are there any grade or high-school teachers among your particular group of friends?" The percentage distribution of the replies was as follows: Yes, 45.9 per cent; No, 53.5 per cent; No answer, 0.6 per cent.

Females showed a higher affirmative response than did males—a result which might have been anticipated, since the great majority of American public school teachers are female. Unlike sex, age was not found to be related to the replies. The third factor, nativity, showed a significant difference in the opinions of persons of native and of foreign birth. Parenthood and religion were not significantly related to friendship with teachers. Occupation, however, was related. Persons in the general category of clerks have friends who are teachers significantly more often than do those in the immediately adjacent occupational categories. A test of the significance of the difference between replies of clerks and those of proprietors and of service workers showed, at the 5 per cent level of confidence, that teachers are more likely to be friends of the clerks. The more advanced the individual's education, the more likely he was to have teachers as friends. No significant relationship was found between income level and friendship with teachers.

The next question was closely related to the first: "If there are no teachers among your friends, would you welcome any as members of your group?" Since this question applied properly only to those who replied negatively to the first, no correlations were run. Less than 1 per cent answered that they would *not* welcome teachers as members of their group. The replies of these few persons generally indicated a lack of common bond with teachers: "No, we have nothing in common"; "No, they are probably not my type."

Minority Group Discriminations

The second subgroup of questions under the general heading "Varied Attitudes" contained three items aimed at discovering the degree to which there was discrimination against teachers from minority groups. The first question read, "Should teachers coming from minority groups be employed (in the schools of New London)?" The replies were: Yes, 85.6 per cent; No. 12.4 per cent; No answer, 2.0 per cent. Males, significantly more than females, answered this question in the affirmative, as did Jews significantly more than Protestants and Catholics combined. A negative response was given significantly more often by the native-born than by the foreign-born ($P = 0.02$).

The next two questions, concerning which minority representatives should *not* be hired and why, yielded no further correlations but served to isolate the direction of prejudice. Of the 12.4 per cent who thought that teachers coming from minority groups should *not* be hired, nearly all specified Negroes. One or two persons in each instance voiced sentiments against Orientals, Italians, Catholics, Jews, and Communists. The objection to minority-group members—aside from the usual stereotyped statements of their "inferiority"—was principally rooted in an unwillingness to have their children taught by Negroes.

The Sex of Teachers

The next subgroup of questions concerned opinions on the sex of teachers. The first of two questions read, "Do you prefer men or women teachers at the high-school level?" The answers were distributed thus: Men teachers, 16.1 per cent; Women teachers, 2.2 per cent; No preference, 77.3 per cent; No answer, 4.4 per cent. Men replied in favor of men significantly more often than did women. The foreign-born were more pro-male than the native-born ($P = 0.03$), the Catholics than the Jews, and skilled laborers more than all other occupational groups.

The Conduct Expected of Teachers

Most studies conclude that persons in education feel that the general public expects an especially high standard of conduct from teachers. A pair of questions in this survey checked on the item. The first question was phrased thus: "Should the standards of conduct for teachers differ from those of other good citizens?" The replies were: Yes, 16.3 per cent; No, 83.3 per cent; No answer, 0.4 per cent. The older the interviewee, the more likely he was to feel that the standard of conduct of teachers should differ from that of other good citizens ($P = 0.001$). Foreign-born respondents held this opinion significantly more than did native-born respondents.

The second question asked of those who thought teachers' standards of conduct should differ, the reasons for their belief. The replies were about evenly split between those who thought that teachers should teach good behavior by example and those who thought that they should be "more moral."

OPINIONS CONCERNING THE COMMUNITY ACTIVITIES OF TEACHERS

The second of the major groups of questions covered three topics; community activities, unionization, and political activities.

Community Activities

The first question read, "Do the high-school teachers of New London join in the activities of the community, such as the League of Women Voters, Rotary, Kiwanis, church groups, Red Cross, athletic groups, and the like?" The distribution of the answers was: Yes, 61.2 per cent; No, 8.9 per cent; No answer, 29.9 per cent.

The next query read, "In your opinion, *should* teachers join in community activities?" This was answered thus: Yes, 92.0 per cent; No, 2.2 per cent; No answer, 5.8 per cent.

Finally, the respondents were asked, "If you know any teachers personally, what specific organizations are they in?" The fact that several organizations were named in the first question may have had considerable effect; on the other hand, the named activities may have been an accurate reflection of the popular conception of the interests of teachers. Of the total of 639 interviewees, 106, or 16.5 per cent, named some community activities in which they believed the teachers engaged. Those cited four or more times, with the percentages of times cited by the 106 interviewees are given in Table 1. The large "No answer" category on the first and second questions probably reflects a fact demonstrated by the first question in the survey itself—namely, that a majority of the interviewees did not have friends who were teachers. Hence, for just over half the respondents replies were based on general observation only. No significant correlations were obtainable for these questions.

TABLE 1

	Per Cent
Rotary *	26.4
Red Cross	24.5
Church activities	22.6
League of Women Voters	18.9
Kiwanis *	8.5
"Y" activities	7.5
Elks *	7.5
Masons	6.6
Scouts	5.7
Zanta	5.7
American Association of University Women	3.8
Athletic activities or groups	3.8
Community Chest	3.8
USO	3.8

* The women's auxiliary was included.

UNION ACTIVITIES

The matter of the unionization of teachers is one which generated strong popular feelings during the depression of the 1930's and again during the immediate postwar years. It is one, further, on which teachers themselves are sharply divided. Because of its recurrent importance, the item was taken up on this survey. The first of two questions dealing with it was, "Do you think that teachers are justified in unionizing?" Replies were distributed as follows: Yes, 68.9 per cent; No, 26.4 per cent; No answer, 4.7 per cent.

Males replied significantly more often in the affirmative than did females ($P = 0.05$). Laboring groups, as one would expect, when their combined opinions were contrasted with those of the combined professional and proprietor groups, proved themselves more in support of unionization. The older respondents were less likely than the younger to support teacher unionization, and this "conservative" opinion was shared by childless persons ($P = 0.05$), and by Protestants as opposed to Catholics. The greater the individual's education, the less likely he was to feel that teachers have the right to unionize.

Respondents who commented extensively on the unionization of teachers were chiefly concerned with the possibility that the "right to organize" would mean association with the big labor unions. Apparently a teachers' union for protection and adequate pay found support, but a union as a power-building organization did not. In the ideology of most unions, the strike is the logical ultimate step in the achievement of goals. That this should not apply in the case of teachers' unions, however, seemed to be the opinion of most respondents. To the question "Do you think teachers are justified in striking?" the replies were as follows: Yes, 32.9 per cent; No, 62.4 per cent; No answer, 4.7 per cent. On this second question, males supported their original standing favoring unionization, and again laboring groups, as contrasted to the combined professionals and proprietors, were more convinced of the justice of strikes. Older respondents proved less likely than the younger to feel that the strike, like unionization itself, was justified ($P = 0.001$), and in the same way the upper-income group, as compared with the combined lower-income groups, significantly opposed the use of the strike ($P = 0.05$).

Comments on this aspect of teacher activities were numerous. Many interviewees felt that a strike was unwise and should be resorted to only in extreme cases. Most objectors to striking appeared to regard the strike as, in effect, against the students and, in addition, as actually impossible because of the official nature of the teachers' position. Illogically, a number of interviewees protested that teachers should be paid enough so that they would not *have* to strike. The most notable *non sequitur* was that of one respondent who said, "Well, it all depends on what the child has done."

Political Activities

Like union membership, political activity among teachers has engendered warm debate. To the question "May teachers be active politically if they so desire?" replies were: Yes, 80.1 per cent; No, 17.8 per cent; No answer, 2.1 per cent. Females significantly more than males replied in the affirmative, but no other correlation was found between opinions and the various socio-economic conditions. The comments, while numerous, were confined almost entirely to qualifying the majority position with the stricture that the political activities of the teachers should not cut down the time devoted to their work or their objectivity.

OPINIONS CONCERNING THE PROFESSIONAL STATUS OF TEACHERS

The third group of questions undertook to discover in several ways how the people of the community compared teachers with persons in other occupations.

Professionalism

The first question read, "Do you consider high-school teaching to be one of the professions?" The affirmative replies reached near-unanimity: Yes, 96.7 per cent; No, 2.0 per cent; No answer, 1.3 per cent.

Job Comparisons

The next three questions approached the matter of status by means of comparisons. All questions were designed to be shown to, rather than asked of, the interviewee. They were:

Which of these occupations is about on the same social level as high-school teaching?
1. Factory worker 2. Pharmacist 3. Plumber 4. Executive of large business 5. Policeman 6. Waiter 7. Doctor 8. Shoe clerk 9. Laborer 10. Proprietor of a small business 11. Shop foreman 12. University professor

(number)..................

In the processing of the replies, the occupations were grouped in virtually the same general categories as were the occupations of the interviewees themselves, the exception being the lumping of all "labor" occupations under one heading. A great many of the respondents listed more than one job from the choices, but in such cases most of these clustered in one general category or another; the predominating category, therefore, was selected as characterizing the response of the interviewee. So processed, the replies in Table 2 appear in

TABLE 2

	Per Cent
Choices predominantly in:	
Professional category	44.3
Proprietor category	21.9
Clerical category	0
Service category	3.6
Labor category	5.0
Disparate choices without pattern	5.6
Choices predominantly in both professional and proprietor categories	9.9
No answer	9.7

terms of that percentage of the interviewees who marked one or another general category of occupations as being on the same level as high-school teaching. When the first five items in the table were analyzed, it was found that the older the respondent was, the more likely he was to compare teachers with professionals ($P = 0.05$). Foreign-born persons significantly supported the stand that teachers are "professional" ($P = 0.05$), while native-born interviewees tended to select jobs from the list which were in the proprietor category ($P = 0.02$). More childless persons than those with children made up that small percentage of persons who held that jobs in the labor category were comparable to teaching. Almost all who refused to comment explained that they held that all people and all occupations are on the same social level.

Further enlightenment on the comparative position of teaching was sought by asking the interviewees, "In the matter of *salary*, where do you think the high-school teacher *should* stand on this list (about equal to what number)?" The replies, when processed in the same manner as were those for the preceding question, showed considerable variance therefrom (Table 3). In the surprisingly large percentage of respondents who felt that teachers' salaries should be comparable with those of persons in the labor category, males were significantly better represented than were females ($P = 0.02$). Reflecting their replies on the preceding query, foreign-born persons were more convinced that the salaries of teachers should be comparable with those of persons in the professional category, while native-born interviewees felt that they should be comparable with the proprietor category ($P = 0.05$). When the replies were analyzed according to occupation and education, it was found that the higher the interviewee's occupation fell on the census gradient or the more his years of schooling, the more likely he was to believe that teachers' salaries should approximate those in both the professional and the proprietor categories, as contrasted with those prevailing in other categories (by occupation, $P = 0.01$; by education, $P = 0.05$).

TABLE 3

	Per Cent
Choices predominantly in:	
Professional category	32.1
Proprietor category	21.8
Clerical category	0.8
Service category	7.5
Labor category	11.3
Disparate choices without pattern	4.7
Choices predominantly in both professional and proprietor categories	3.3
No answer	18.5

Finally, a clarification of teacher status in terms of other occupations was sought in a question phrased thus: "In the matter of *importance to the community* where do you put high-school teachers on this list (about equal to that of what number)?" Once again, a marked shift of emphasis may be noted in the replies (Table 4). Females, significantly more than males, believed that teaching was comparable in importance to professional occupations, while in that small percentage of persons who compared the importance of teaching to that of jobs in the labor category, males predominated. Again, the native-born, more than the foreign-born, compared the importance of teaching with that of positions in the proprietor category. In the sizable percentage of interviewees who equated teaching to the service and labor categories, professionals and proprietors were significantly less represented than were persons in the laboring groups ($P = 0.02$). The job most often selected by the latter for comparison was that of

TABLE 4

	Per Cent
Choices predominantly in:	
Professional category	51.6
Proprietor category	12.8
Clerical category	0
Service category	11.4
Labor category	3.6
Disparate choices without pattern	5.6
Choices predominantly in both professional and proprietor categories	2.8
No answer	12.2

"policeman." Most of the comments attested to a widespread public belief in the importance of teachers—a number placing them above any other occupational group.

THE FINANCIAL STATUS OF TEACHERS

The fourth and last group of questions concerning educators was on their financial status. The questions were divided into two groups: the first was made up of four queries on salaries, and the second was a single question whereon the respondent was asked to comment generally.

TEACHERS' SALARIES

It should be remembered that the field work for this report was completed in the early summer of 1948. The first question was, "What is your estimate of the average yearly salary of teachers in the high schools of New London?" The replies were distributed as in Table 5. The correlations between responses to this question and various socio-economic factors proved particularly interesting. It was discovered, first, that the "higher" the occupational level of the respondent, the higher was his estimate of teachers' salaries ($P = 0.05$). Next, it was found that the greater the in-

TABLE 5

	Per Cent
$1,799 and less	3.9
1,800–1,999	3.0
2,000–2,249	12.4
2,250–2,399	2.8
2,400	4.4
2,401–2,749	17.4
2,750–2,999	5.9
3,000–3,249	14.4
3,250–3,499	1.6
3,500 and up	5.9
No answer	28.3

dividual's education, the higher was his estimate of the teachers' salaries, and, finally, that the higher the respondent's income level, the higher was his estimate of these salaries ($P = 0.001$).

The interviewees were next asked: "Do you feel that the teachers are, in general, underpaid, overpaid, or fairly well paid?" The replies fell as follows: Underpaid, 60.6 per cent; Overpaid, 0.9 per cent; Fairly well paid, 32.4 per cent; No answer, 6.1 per cent. The first correlation which proved significant was that Jews, more than Catholics and Protestants, believed that the teachers were underpaid. Reflecting the results of the previous question, it was found that the greater the respondent's education ($P = 0.05$) and the higher his income ($P = 0.02$), the more likely he was to believe that the teachers were underpaid.

The next question was: "What would you consider a good starting salary for a high-school teacher?" The replies, distributed on the same scale as the previous question, ranged as shown in Table 6. The single significant correlation paralleled one found on the previous questions: the higher the respondent's income, the higher his estimate of the proper starting salary for teachers.

The final question in this group read, "what would you consider a good top salary to be paid, say, after fifteen years' teaching?" The replies for this question quite naturally required a different scaling than did those for the preceding salary items. They were distributed as in Table 7. Once again, occupation, education, and income proved to be significant. The higher the interviewee was placed in the occupational continuum, the greater his education, and the higher his income ($P = 0.05$), the higher was the top salary which he believed suitable for teachers.

TABLE 6

	Per Cent
$1,799 and less	3.8
1,800–1,999	4.5
2,000–2,249	13.9
2,250–2,399	5.0
2,400	6.7
2,401–2,749	19.6
2,750–2,999	3.4
3,000–3,249	16.3
3,250–3,499	0.6
3,500 and up	9.7
No answer	16.5

TABLE 7

	Per Cent
$3,499 and less	22.2
3,500–3,999	15.0
4,000	11.4
4,001–4,499	2.5
4,500–4,999	8.5
5,000–5,499	12.4
5,500 and up	6.6
No answer	21.4

GENERAL STATEMENTS

In order to elicit the respondents' general opinions concerning teachers and their status, an open question was included: "How do you account for the present difficulties of primary and high-school teachers in the United States?"

The replies were first grouped by the predominant reason (Table 8). Whether or not the interviewees reached in this survey had an accurate appreciation of the historical background of teaching in this country, they evidenced a fair knowledge of prevailing conditions. The following comments are necessarily selected, and hence unrepresentative from a statistical standpoint; they demonstrate, however, the more perceptive range of opinion tapped by the survey.

"About 350,000 teachers," said one interviewee, "have left the profession since 1941. Financially they are at a low level, and they have low prestige. The competition with other more lucrative positions and those with more prestige pull people away from teaching. There is a poor attitude in the community toward a teacher. Many girls take it up as a stop-gap until they get married." Said another: "The teachers are underpaid; possibly it is because they are not regarded with as much consideration as they should be in the community, whether personally or politically." A third said: "The community looks upon teachers as outsiders and won't give them a chance to become active in the community. It regards them as a class apart." Others stated: "Youngsters have lost respect for their teachers within the last few decades, since much of the discipline has been taken out of the schools and out of the hands of the teachers"; "The world is upside down"; "Heartaches go along with teaching; the teachers can get better jobs." One respondent was particularly explicit: "I attribute their difficulties to three things: first, the unwillingness of the average person to pay for the cost of good education; second, the lack of public recognition of the importance of education; and, third, control of education by political groups." Another remarked: "Teachers are underpaid because they haven't given enough effort to fighting for themselves, for adequate compensation." Others said: "Teachers are afraid to take part in controversies; they are at the mercy of school boards"; "This is a time of lowered morale—a lag between material and spiritual achievements."

SUMMARIES BY SOCIO-ECONOMIC FACTORS

It remains to reassemble the material according to the characteristics of the people holding the opinions. This section of the report summarizes opinions of teacher status in eight categories. Statistically significant correlations were found in all categories.

Table 8

	Per Cent
Teachers are underpaid	51.2
General economic conditions in the country are accountable	5.5
The public is uninterested in education	2.5
Teachers lack prestige	2.3
Administrative policies in education are faulty	1.9
There are too few teachers	1.4
No answer	35.2

Sex

Males interviewed in this study differed from females, in that they were more likely

1. To favor the employment of teachers from minority groups
2. To favor the hiring of men teachers
3. To feel that teachers are justified in unionizing and in striking
4. To be among those who felt that the teachers were comparable to persons in the occupational category of laborer, with reference to the pay they should receive and their importance to the community

The males differed from the females, in that they were less likely

5. To have teachers as friends
6. To feel that teachers should be free to be active politically
7. To compare teachers to professionals as to their importance to the community

Age Group

The older the respondents, the more likely they were

1. To feel that the standards of conduct for teachers should differ from those of other good citizens
2. To compare teachers to professionals in social level

and the less likely they were

3. To feel that teachers are justified in unionizing and in striking

Nativity

The native-born differed from the foreign-born in that they were more likely

1. To have teachers as friends
2. To oppose the hiring of teachers from minority groups
3. To believe that teachers were comparable to proprietors in social level, salary, and importance to the community

The foreign-born were more likely

4. To believe that the standards of conduct for teachers should differ
5. To prefer men to women for teaching positions
6. To feel that teachers were comparable to professionals with reference to social level and salary

Possession of Children

Childless interviewees differed from those who had children, in that they were more likely

1. To feel that teachers are not justified in unionizing
2. To be among the few who felt that teachers were comparable to laborers in social level

RELIGION

Protestant interviewees differed from Catholic interviewees, in that they were more likely

1. To feel that teachers are not justified in unionizing
2. To believe that teachers should be comparable to professionals with reference to salaries

Catholics differed from Jews, in that they were more likely

3. To prefer men as teachers

Jews differed from Protestants, in that they were more likely

4. To believe that teachers should be comparable to proprietors with reference to salaries

Jews differed from Protestants and Catholics, in that they were more likely

5. To believe that teachers from minority groups should be employed
6. To believe that teachers were underpaid

OCCUPATION

It was discovered that the higher the place of the respondent in the occupational hierarchy,

1. The higher was likely to be his estimate of the teachers' current salaries and of suitable top salaries to be paid after fifteen years of experience
2. The more likely he was to believe that teachers' salaries should be comparable to those of both professionals and proprietors

Respondents in the two laboring groups differed from those in the professional and proprietor groups, in that they were more likely

3. To feel that teachers are justified in unionizing and in striking
4. To feel that teachers were comparable to laborers and service workers with reference to their importance to the community

EDUCATION

The greater the education of the interviewee, the more likely he was

1. To have friends who were teachers
2. To believe that teachers' salaries should be comparable to those of both professionals and proprietors
3. To believe that the teachers were underpaid

The greater the education of the interviewee,

4. The higher was his estimate of the teachers' current salaries, and also of suitable top salaries

and the less likely he was to

5. Feel that teachers are justified in unionizing

INCOME LEVEL

The higher the income level of the interviewee,

1. The higher was likely to be his estimate of the current salaries, of a good starting salary, and also of a suitable top salary for the teachers
2. The more likely he was to feel that the teachers were underpaid

The upper-income group, as contrasted to the two lower-income groups, was

3. More likely to feel that teachers are not justified in striking

THE SCHOOL IN AMERICAN CULTURE[1]

Margaret Mead

DISCUSSION AND ANALYSIS

Because she is not only an incisive commentator on education, but also one of the world's leading anthropologists, Margaret Mead brings to the present discussion a wideness of understanding and broadness of background that few possess. We feel that she sees the problem of the school in American culture in terms of a deep historical and geographical context. Such an outlook not only gives us perspective but sharpens the focus of our investigation as well. The student will gain a greater appreciation of this piece if he underlines those sections of the selection which, either directly or indirectly, draw upon Dr. Mead's knowledge as an anthropologist.

Among innumerable seminal ideas is Dr. Mead's comment that the image of the private academy reflects "all of America's ambivalence about . . . tradition, about class." Do any of the other selections in this chapter touch upon this ambivalence? Again, Dr. Mead's statement regarding "the conflict between the school oriented toward the past and the school oriented toward the future" casts light on current attacks on "progressive education." What is the nature of this light? Does it illuminate any of the historical selections—for instance, the piece by Mark Twain? How?

Dr. Mead offers us several types or models of teachers. To which do you believe you will most nearly conform when you are a teacher? Will you blend the qualities from several models? After studying this piece, you may want to examine your own background to find where and how you may best fit into the educational system. Is such an examination helpful? If it is more disturbing than helpful what should you do? Forget the problem? Examine it more thoroughly? Seek advice from a competent counselor?

In any discussion of American schools, of "the American school system," of "the public school," if you listen carefully, you can see these images come and go, the loved and longed-for image of the little red schoolhouse, the deprecated and worried-over image of the city school, and the image of the private academy, which contains all of America's ambivalence about England, about tradition, about class. The affectionate note with which the little red schoolhouse is invoked is a statement of our sense of conflict between the academy that perpetuates the past—which in Amer-

[1] Reprinted by permission of the publishers from Margaret Mead, *The School in American Culture* (pp. 11–30). Cambridge, Mass.: Harvard University Press. Copyright, 1951, by The President and Fellows of Harvard College.

ican terms means limiting the future, tying us to the old world and its caste lines and age-old solutions—and the city school which belongs only to the future, which turns out pupils who, because they cannot look back, have, in a sense, no perspective at all, but only the dreadful urgency of moving on, moving away from, knowing only that what was once theirs by birthright is bad and un-American, that what is NOT that, what is new and up to the minute, must therefore be American and good.

All three of these themes have become interwoven in our contemporary American culture so that a tenth-generation American, educated in private schools, will have difficulty persuading his child, who has learned to speak Spanish from an upper-class but foreign mother, that it is not something shameful and disgraceful to be heard speaking a foreign tongue on the street. And the contrast between the mischief of the country boy and the delinquency of the immigrant slum boy has vanished too, so that the select suburb in which tenth-generation Americans and successful third-generation Americans live side by side has its juvenile delinquents also. It has its quarrels among the parent taxpayers as to whether foreign languages are to be taught in the schools, its conflicts as to whether the teacher is to be treated as an equal, as the emissary of a strange outside world, or as the poorly paid custodian of the gateway to "culture."

If we turn from images to look formally at the history of American education, of its theory and its practice, the conflict between the school oriented toward the past and the school oriented toward the future, with the seldom obtainable dream of a school which would hold the world steady, will be found to be a prevailing theme. This theme is expressed in many forms: in the struggle between the classics and modern languages; in the struggle between "at least one foreign language" and none at all; in the struggle between academic studies and vocational preparation; in the arguments about required courses versus electives, in which shared conformity to a common past is opposed to selectivity which is a preparation for an unshared future.

Before I go on to discuss the part which this threefold picture of the school has played and is playing in American educational theory and practice, I should like to turn for a moment to the contrasts and comparisons provided by primitive societies on the relationships between the generations. Primitive societies are our models for slowly changing homogenous societies in which the children's lives faithfully repeat, gesture for gesture, and experience by experience, the lives of their parents and grandparents. Through the investigation of such slowly changing societies, we can form a picture of type relationships between the old generation and the new, against which such relationships, when they occur in an age of rapid change like our own, take on additional meaning. In these slowly changing primitive societies we find great variation as to which age group inducts the young child into his society; the baby may spend most of its time with its mother or father, or in the arms of an older sister or brother, or by the side of a grandmother or grandfather. Each is a possible way to learn the intricate, beautifully patterned way of perceiving the world and acting within that set of perceptions which a culture offers each child born within it.

But if we examine in detail some of the implications of the parent-child, sibling-child, and grandparent-child rearing situations, we find certain systematic differences. Those societies in which young children are reared by grandparents—of which certain North American Plains Indian tribes are typical—have an enormous degree of conservatism. The culture survives, even as the buffalo disappear; the land is taken away by the advancing white peoples, and the tepee is displaced by the shack. Still the language, the way of thought, of the past endures. Sometimes we find only one or two survivors of a whole language group, two toothless, half-deaf old women, who will, however, have clung to their language and their memories, and are still able to dictate long texts to the patient ethnographer. This conservatism, this cherishing clinging to the old, can be related to the role which the grandparent played in the lives of Indian children, to the way in which the child, even as it struggled and wriggled in an ecstasy of beginning movement, apprehended in the tonus of the grandparental arms the sort of pact which its lively little body would someday make with death. As old hands and old voices, speaking with the gentleness and resignation of a people who saw human lives as like grass which grew up in the morning and at night was mown down, informed the child of the way that men and animals, the sun and the moon and the stars, seeking and power, vision and practicality, life and death were to be viewed, so the child was able to incorporate in early childhood all that his culture had to offer him. In such a rounded understanding, nothing was left unexplained, uncontemplated, which later would challenge or threaten. And the Indian has remained as one of our chief examples of the tenacity of a people who, robbed of every condition of their lives, still clung to the form, to the pattern, meeting night after night to gamble for buffalo nickels where once the stake was a war horse.

At the opposite extreme, we find the cultures in which it is the child nurse—the elder sister or less frequently the elder brother—who carries the younger child about on a hip almost too slight to bear the burden. Instead of the tremor of old age, there is the tenseness of the hands which can hardly lift, the hands which are almost unable to readjust the carrying sling, or shift the baby from one hip to another. These child nurses, far from having learned the nature of the whole life cycle from their old grandmothers, are just out of babyhood themselves, and were reared by other children. The child on the hip is not something infinitely young and remote, waiting at the end of memory, but the child whom one was yesterday, with all the fears and urgencies which have just been partially mastered in the self. These are the cultures in which the growing child is kept close to infancy, sometimes only by way of keeping a great awareness of the rhythms of its own body, so that later dancing and love-making will be equally easy and graceful, as in Samoa. Sometimes also the child is kept close to the images of infancy, so that the ritual resolutions of its early terrors are expressed in the theater by conflicts between witch and dragon, who reënact on a stage the conflicts which the child experiences in its relationships to father and mother, as in Bali. Or the child nurse may help the child retain its passivity, in a world where every adult is egging it on to continuous unremitting displays of energy and anger, as among the Iatmul. Among this head-hunting tribe of the Sepik River, where adult relationships are violent and assertive, the theater is a series of tableaux in which all movement is frozen and static, in contrast to the theater of Bali where a people whose daily life is ordered and gentle are able to express the most violent emotions. In the spontaneous drawings and in the play of the children of the child-nurse age we can find the links which permit their child charges to retain the feeling that makes the adult theatrical presentation both possible and meaningful, as the Balinese child keeps alive the capacity for plastic expression of feeling and the Iatmul child, who in his adult life must be stormy and noisy, keeps his capacity for stillness.

The child nurse may be seen not as the guardian and ally of any particular aspect of early childhood, but rather as a way in which the child's response within its culture is kept intact in spite of the pressures which will later fall upon the adolescent and the adult. From the child nurse there passes to the native child a kind of license to be itself, from one who has not yet departed far enough from that closeness to the experience of early childhood to be able to withdraw the license. And so we have a second model, the society in which the resources of early childhood, whether in directness of bodily expression or richness of phantastic elaboration or denial of the adult structuring of the world, are preserved for children, and therefore for adults also, because the child learns not from someone who has traversed the whole round of life, but from someone still very close to its beginning.

The two models of child and grandparent upbringing are brought together again when we consider the aristocratic society in which the upper-class child has a nurse drawn from the peasantry and in which the child of the peasant class is cared for by its grandmother, while the mother works in the fields. Here, the peasant child, like the Plains Indian child, is exposed to the whole of the culture which will be its for life, caught tightly in a mesh that it cannot break, born a peasant to die a peasant. In the same society the same type of peasant woman, not always so old, is performing quite a different function for the child of the aristocrat, keeping alive in it impulses and dreams which its more educated, differently controlled parents would, if they were its mentors, disallow. So the peasant nurse keeps alive in the aristocratic child his sense of his own body and himself, which can then tolerate the rigors of court etiquette, rigid demands for posture and gesture, for honor and conformity to the demands of caste; while, as a peasant she communicates to her own grandchild a way of life in which body and self play a different part, upon a simpler stage.

The third model, the model which echoes the little red schoolhouse image, is that in which children are reared not by grandparents who represent the whole traditional definition of life, or by children whose own eager little mouths have hardly left the breast, or by nurses whose own peasant standards of eating and drinking perpetuate the pleasures of the breast with a frank enjoyment which is banished from ballroom and audience chamber, but by parents, by people of early maturity, the present possessors and inheritors of the adult world. This is the typical middle-class position: a family economically well enough off so that the mother is not burdened down with field or farm duties—or overwhelmed with more children than she can feed and care for, in which the father is making his way, actively, in a world of change and commerce, a world of entrepreneurship and profit. In such a rapidly changing world, grandparents are likely to be out of date, behind the times, also to a degree rejected, as it was they who reared the present parents, and reared them purposefully and determinedly to become responsible, time-bound, goal-oriented adults. In such a world also elder siblings are busy themselves learning to outstrip their parents. They have too much to do to be efficient baby tenders; they must learn the skills and arts which will be necessary for success. Furthermore, the middle-class parent will distrust the child nurse, as also the servant girl is distrusted. The child who is to be inducted into a world where life is real and life is earnest must be exposed from the beginning to the model parent, who must herself, and himself, punish and reward the growing child. This middle-class picture is not only true of our own American middle-class life, but also can be found in primitive societies like that of the Manus of the Admiralties, a tribe of stone-age fishermen. The Manus are efficient, profit-seeking, earnest, moral people, concerned to rear their children to follow the same pattern—not so much of life, as of goal seeking. And among the Manus the older children practice in play the arts of adult life, and the parents care for the children, who learn to think of adults as persons who are completely masters of their environment.

The child who is reared according to this third model—reared by parents who are at the height of their careers, far from childhood, and facing an old age about which they know little and expect little—grows up, far from its infant awareness of its body, far from the memory of the childhood fantasies which fed eagerly and hungrily on the very meagre set of symbols which such a culture possesses, but alert and ready to face a relatively new and uncharted world, in a thoroughly learned and thoroughly charted way. Close contact with the grandparent leaves little room for welcoming change or sailing strange seas. Close contact with child nurse or peasant nurse keeps the child so *en rapport* with its body and the arts and rituals whose meanings it is able to retain that it also will be, on the whole, uninterested in change and conquest. But parent-rearing produces a child who faces toward a partial future, who can conceive life as an unwritten chapter of a book that is unfinished.

But these three models which I have been discussing are models drawn from slowly changing homogeneous societies; I have been able to speak of a life in which those who rear were similarly reared, in which all the lullabies one sings to children are the lullabies one heard as a child. If such models are to be of any use in considering the problem of the teacher in the American school today, we must add to them from the actual situation in our own society, the condition of rapid change. We must add to them both the reflection in all adults, whether of the parent or of the grandparent generation, the changes through which they have passed, the fact that they were reared by parents whose hands were already fumbling before unfamiliar doors, or with hands which lay flaccid with despair in a world they had not dreamed of and could not cope with. We must picture the adult who has been reared in a dozen tones of voice, reprimanded, rewarded, cajoled, and teased and appeased according to half a hundred systems, who has learned to move about somehow, in a series of rooms in which the very arrangement of the furniture either diagrams the lack of harmony in the tastes which gradually assembled it or in its perfection of harmony will give him a pattern which he is not likely to repeat. And to this picture of an adult who in personality is the expression of the great heterogeneity and rapid changes in our current society, we must add the picture of children who differ from the children who came ten years before them, and differ also from the children who will follow them, as children reared on schedules are followed by children rocked to sleep, to be in turn succeeded by children reared according to some new one of the prescriptions through which a newly self-conscious society is attempting to meet newly realized needs. The condition in our society today is dramatized by the late-born child, whose mother finds that nothing that she learned ten years ago about how to treat children or of what to expect from them, can be applied to this newcomer, who seems even to have learned to cry with a new note in its voice, who will have to have different clothes, will display different tastes, and will weep for quite different reasons. Where, in slowly changing societies, the adults are confronted by children whom they know—for were they not such children themselves, just such children with the same fears, the same joys, the same bits of mischief and rebellion—the adults in the modern world face children who are not only unlike their own past childhood, but who are actually unlike any children who have ever been in the world before.

How then does the teacher—the teacher who may stand at the door of the academy, or its successor the academic high school, ready to induct these unknown children into the tradition of the past, and the teacher who stands at the door of the crowded slum school, ready to prepare her pupils to enter the future by leaving their past—how does this teacher fit into the changing world in which she is called upon to play so sensitive and significant a role?

We may consider for a moment the way in which the teacher can approximate to each of the three generation positions: the grandparent who has seen the whole of life, the parent who is living it day by day, and the child or nurse who is the custodian not of the child's future so much as of the child's immediate past.

The type teacher who comes closest to the grandparental role is the teacher of the classics, or the teacher who treats mathematics and science as if they were classics, fixed and immutable, as unchanged and unchanging as the figures on Keats' Grecian urn. The gifted teacher of the classics conveys to the child a sense of the roundedness and relatedness of life, of the way in which each period repeats in its own way an old story that has already been written in a more gracious and finished way in the past. Any budding desire to explore the new, to make new conquests, can be gently, benignly reduced to the expected, by a reference to Diogenes or to Alexander. As man has been, man will be; one can learn to write different but not better sonnets in a world which has dignity and form. The teacher in the academy was typically such a teacher laying the groundwork for an orderly acceptance of a world which, however different today's version seemed, was mercifully never new.

The teacher in the overcrowded city school—where there were too few seats and too few books in a room filled with strange smells from foreign eating habits and foreign sleeping habits—is closest to the parent model, as she struggles to get her pupils to face away from the past and toward the future. She teaches her pupils to acquire habits of hygiene and of industry, to apply themselves diligently to prepare to succeed, and to make the sacrifices necessary to success, to turn a deaf ear to the immediate impulse, to shatter any tradition which seems to block the path to the goal, but to shatter it in a way and with the sanctions of the entrepreneur. This teacher is closest to the model in which the parents rear the child to a kind of behavior rather than to fit within a tradition. When she imitates the teacher of the academy and teaches her pupils to learn memory gems, she will find she faces confusion, because she is teaching them the past of older Americans in order to give them a future, and this contains contradictions. How will these children born in hospitals, treated at clinics, who celebrate a holiday in the biggest movie theater, use such memory gems as "I remember, I remember the house where I was born," or "over the river and through the wood to grandfather's house we go; the horse knows the way to carry the sleigh through the white and drifting snow"? She will be happiest when she teaches modern history, with the next pages still to be written, in a "current events" class; or when she teaches science as a way of looking at life which is constantly changing, constantly discarding what has been the best hypothesis for a better one. She—like the middle-class parent—faces forward into a future that is only partially charted, and so she must furnish her children with a kind of behavior, a method of exploration, rather than with the parchment map, with its lines drawn in lovely fading colors, that is available to the teacher in the academy classroom.

The third model, the child nurse or the peasant nurse, the teacher whose task is to stay close to the young child's bodily impulses and exuberant imaginative attempts to take in the world around him, is a new type of teacher. She has come into being as one gifted thinker after another—Froebel, Montessori, Anna Freud—rebelled against the price which modern, urbanized, industrialized Europeans and Americans were paying for their new kind of civilization. From Germany, from Italy, from Vienna, from England, and from the United States there came a demand for some form of education which would fit the little child—a chair and table to fit his body, materials with which he could work out his groping attempts to relate inner and outer world, and teachers who would kneel beside him, give him a shoulder to cry on or a body which could be turned into a steed, who would be allies of his infancy, rather than surrogates either of the finished world of tradition or of the fluid world-in-the-making of the entrepreneur. First in the kindergarten, and later and much more articulately in the nursery school, we have developed an educational pattern which contains some of the values of the child nurse, or the peasant nurse, in which sensitive teachers, who must almost always be young because of the strenuous physical demands of working with little children who are permitted to move about freely, are taught how to ally themselves with the immediacies of the world of the little child.

But in all three parallels which I have drawn, parallels which, like all figures of speech, impose an extra degree of order and so distort the reality—for in the teeming schoolrooms of America we find all three types of teacher and every possible blend, in every sort of situation—I have still ignored the changing children and have spoken as if the children who face these different kinds of teaching were themselves all of the same stuff as the teachers from whom they learn. If the children to be taught were of the same stuff as the teachers, we would still have a problem in initially training teachers for any one or any combination of the roles which I have outlined. The teacher who is adequately to represent the order of the past, the dignity and beauty of tradition, must, in the course of her training come to terms with her own past. The Latin lines she wrote so unwillingly, the theorems in geometry which were resented, the parents and teachers who were responsible for making her learn her lessons, must all be reëxamined, the rebellion exorcised or transformed, so that she can become the whole-hearted and resigned exponent of traditional learning.

The teacher who is to help a generation go away from and beyond their parents, who is to be forever exhorting her pupils to be up and doing, has a different task; she must relive her childhood and exchange the specificity of the demands which her parents and teacher made upon her for a new set of demands, which she will make, in the same tone of voice, upon her pupils. Where the teacher who represents the past and tradition must accept directly and finally both what she herself has been taught and those who stood for the past, the teacher who must urge her pupils to desert or surpass their parents has to abandon the matter but, in a way, keep the manner. She comes to terms during her training, if that training is to succeed, not with her own parents as they themselves were with all their weaknesses and strengths, but with the demands which parents and teachers in the abstract have a right and a duty to make on children. She must give up any overfaithful clinging to the particulars of her own past, if she is to face a roomful of children for whom it is her duty to wish a future very different from that which their own parents' lives offer them.

Congruently, the type teacher of our city and town schools today is a girl who is—in the words of the contemporary class analysis—mobile upward, moving from lower class to lower middle class, or from lower middle class to a better middle-class position. She is someone who must transcend her own past and so in a sense is the better prepared to help her pupils repudiate theirs and become mobile also. The type teacher of the academy or the academic subjects in a modern high school is, on the other hand, mobile downwards, clinging to a past she is in danger of losing, as a family that has fallen on hard days clings to the family portrait and the grandfather's clock.

The type nursery-school teacher is the girl from an upper middle-class background, who finds herself desperately out of sympathy with the verbal facility and concern with things rather than with people that seems to her a predominant characteristic of her world. Very often inarticulate and academically "slow," better able to communicate with a touch of the hand or the slant of a painted line than with words, she can become a nursery-school teacher only if she can come to sufficient terms with her own rebelliousness against adult standards—against, indeed, the whole adult world—so that while she acts as the little child's ally, she does not hold the child back. Very often the nursery-school teacher, and also the child therapist, is not a special kind of adult who has kept a closeness to his or her own childhood, which however is completely reorganized and made anew, but rather a young adult who is continuing to live out an unrealized childhood, and who, after a few years, wearies of the repetitive game and becomes a supervisor, or teaches teachers, or decides it is more rewarding to deal with adults than with children. The teacher who within the school fulfills one of these roles which have a formal relationship to the child-rearing practice of the grandparent, parent, or child-nurse patterns seems to be the more successful the less she is acting out some unresolved and overdetermined past, and the more she has reassimilated and revised her past to fit into the teaching role which she has chosen.

CURRICULA—SELECTIVE PATHWAYS TO SUCCESS[1]

W. Lloyd Warner, Robert J. Havighurst, and Martin B. Loeb

CLASS AND CURRICULA

In what ways does the school contribute to the American status system? How does the school function in this status system? Those are the problems we are here investigating. First, let us look at what is taught in school against the background of the American status system. In the technical language of school personnel, "what is taught" in school is described as "the curriculum." In many high schools throughout the country there are different curricula or courses leading to different kinds of

[1] Reprinted from *Who Shall Be Educated?* (Chapter V) by W. Lloyd Warner, Robert J. Havighurst and Martin B. Loeb, by permission of the publisher. Copyright, 1944, by Harper & Brothers.

diplomas and to different walks of life. In some large communities we find that there are different schools for these different courses, such as manual training school, vocational school, commercial school, technical school, trade school, and so on. Not all communities can afford such elaborate programs, but we find variations from the extremes of many courses and schools to schools with one generalized curriculum.

Who takes what curriculum in high school? How is the choice made? Such are the questions we must ask and answer. We might first look at a high school where there are no formal differences of curriculum but where elective courses differentiate the college preparatory from other students. The school superintendent of Old City, in talking about the school's role in the choice of courses, says:

> I try not to encourage them all to go to college but neither do I try to discourage them. I do feel that it is much better that those who will not make good college material do not go to college and I try to impress on them that there is no magic in college and that those who make good there would probably make good anyway. I also must keep in mind the fact that if our students go to college and make a poor record it reflects on us and hurts our standing and for that reason I try to discourage the poorer students from going to college. Another thing that must be kept in mind is that the students who go to college seldom return here and the students who are going to make good citizens and taxpayers ten years from now are those who are not of exceptional ability and are not college material.

He states further at another time:

> I have noticed that although a student must have at least medium ability to enter college, the way the courses are given he may go through and get a degree and all he will have will be an assortment of courses such as impractical psychology, sociology, economics, and things like that which I admit are good things but with the average student don't prepare him for actual life. The result is that a boy who might have made a good brick-mason comes out with a smattering of useless knowledge and a feeling that brick work is beneath him and he just struggles along with some work he is not fitted for. You know, when I was a boy, the professors and teachers used to tell us that we should be ambitious and that if we were and worked hard each of us might get to be president. As a result we had these big ideas and struggled for something that we might have known we couldn't get. I don't believe in that and so I try to tell them that it is better to be a farmer and have a comfortable and happy life than try to be something you are not fitted for.

We see what actually happens if we consider the 191 students who were graduates of the Old City High School over a five-year period. This number includes all the white high-school graduates except those who attended private schools. The accompanying table shows what happened to these people after graduation and what the social make-up of the group was.

The group called "middle" is made up of those about whom not enough is known to stratify exactly so that it consists of both upper-middle and lower-middle class people. The group called "lower" is made up of all upper-lower and lower-lower class people. The group marked "unknown" were those about whom there was insufficient information for classification, but for the most part these came from the rural areas or from a near-by orphanage.

We must note that most of the upper-class students attend college but that they form only 7 per cent of the total graduating class. The upper-middle class students make up 28 per cent of the graduating class and 69 per cent of them go on to college, whereas the lower-middle class makes up 23 per cent of the graduating

College Attendance of High-School Graduates in Old City

Class	Number	% of Total by Class	Number Attending College	% of Each Social Class Attending College	% by Social Class of All Who Attend College
Upper	14	7	10	72	14
Upper middle	54	28	37	69	51
Middle	31	16	18	58	25
Lower middle	43	23	7	16	10
Lower	19	10	0	0	0
Unknown	30	16	0	0	0
Total	191	100	72	—	100

class and only 16 per cent of them go on to college. Stated another way, of all those who go on to college, the upper-class students constitute 14 per cent, and there are no lower-class students during this period who go on to college.

One boy, the son of an immigrant truck farmer of lower-middle class status, won a national essay contest and will go to college on a scholarship and probably will rise in status. Another lower-middle class boy who did not have much scholastic ability but who was an excellent football player went on to college and one can predict upward mobility for him because he also has an affable personality. Two lower-middle class sisters who are talented musicians continued their musical training after high school and at the time of the study had already begun to participate freely, albeit as artists, with upper-middle and upper-class people.

There are four curricula in the Yankee City high school. The Latin course, including modern and classical languages as well as history and mathematics, is designed to prepare students for college. The scientific course emphasizes physics and chemistry and prepares the student for college study, but it does not equip him to get a job in an applied science. The commercial course, with such subjects as typewriting, shorthand, and commercial English, is supposed to train the pupil so that he can get a job when he leaves high school. The general course provides a high-school pupil with an adequate education for immediate adjustment to life. To reiterate, the first two courses provide preparation for college and the last two for immediate acceptance of adult status. A "D" mark is not passing in Latin or scientific curricula but it is passing in general or commercial. This is indication of the scholastic difference between the Latin and scientific and the general and commercial curricula.

All the pupils from the upper-upper class went to private schools which prepared for college. All the lower-upper pupils in the public high school were in the scientific or the Latin course. Eighty-eight per cent of the upper-middle class, 45 per cent of the lower-middle class, only 28 per cent of the upper-lower, and 26 per cent of the lower-lower took college-preparatory work. As the social class declines, there is a progressive drop in the percentage of the pupils who take courses to prepare them for college, and there is a progressive increase in the percentage of pupils who take the commercial and the general courses. Only 12 per cent of the upper-middle class pupils took the commercial and the general courses, compared with 55 per cent of the lower-middle class, 72 per cent of the upper-lower, and 74 per cent of the lower-lower.

The evidence is clear that the class system of Yankee City definitely exercises a control over the pupils' choices of curricula. Supplementary interviewing of teachers and principals abundantly demonstrated this point. The children of the two upper and the upper-middle classes, in overwhelming percentages, were learning and being taught a way of life which would fit them into higher statuses. On the other hand, the lower-middle and the lower-class children, in their studies in the high school, were learning a way of life which would help adjust them to the rank in which they were born.

In the elementary school all the children from all the classes are given the same formal training. In high school social differentiation begins. The formal education of the high school itself clearly contributes to the social differences which begin to appear in the personalities of the children. Nevertheless, a certain percentage of the lower-class children in high school do take the preparatory course for college. Those who do are usually socially mobile and are using the high school to equip themselves for climbing to a higher rung on the social ladder. They are said by their teachers to be "more ambitious" than the others.

The class differences in choice of high-school course show up in other interesting ways. The principal, for instance, says that the standard of teaching lowers as one goes from Latin to general course. He says:

In the past the teaching was different in the Latin group from the scientific group, but now they are both to be the same. There was a recognizable difference in the quality of teaching formerly so that you weren't able to shift one pupil from the scientific to the Latin curriculum, although you could shift him from the Latin to the scientific. Next year there will more than ever be a difference in the college and non-college group. It is like having two schools within one building. This difference exists in English as a subject, but also in the other studies. For example, take the General Science Course III and the Chemistry course given in the scientific curriculum. The latter is more difficult and includes more material and is better taught than the former.

This teaching difference is not particularly perceptible to the students. According to one bright boy from the upper-lower class:

The Latin curriculum only means that Latin is inserted in that curriculum. Even if you don't go to college the Latin curriculum does you some good. I wish that I had taken the commercial course because now I expect to study advertising in some school in Boston. When I entered high school, I thought I might go on to college, but I can't now. I wish though we didn't have to study French. If I flunk French, I might have to graduate in the general curriculum. That would be too bad.

Even though this boy does not believe there is much difference in the courses he knows the social value of graduating in the Latin curriculum. In discussing school activities, this same boy says:

On the school magazine staff there are more from the Latin division than from any of the others, that is, three Latin students, two general, two commercial and two scientific.

Three Latin division students are active editors on the yearbook, all, that is, except for the business manager, who is from the scientific division.

We find further that the people in these various curricula stick together and vie for social recognition. For instance, we hear a boy discussing the school leaders.

Kathleen Regan is vice-president of the Student Council, and is very popular with her classmates. She belongs to the Tri-Hi Club, is on the magazine staff, was a class officer in a previous year, and had a leading part in the cast of the senior play. Whenever there is any party, Tri-Hi dances, etc., around, John Burton usually takes Kathleen. She is a darn good kid; she has been in my class four years now, in the Latin division. You know the friendships one makes in school last for a long time.

Then there is Ruth Larkin, president of the English Club, in the Latin division, and on the Student Council as a result of being president of the English Club.

And William Carlyle, auditor of his year, business manager of the yearbook, member of Hi-Y, editor-in-chief of the magazine, has held class offices, doesn't go around with any special kids, and in school doesn't hang around with anybody in particular. He wouldn't be getting the recognition that he is if it wasn't for his friends in the scientific division, who elected him to his office. This is common in the case of quiet kids. He is an honor student.

The intellectual talent of these children is being trained and prepared for upward mobility. They are now feeling the effect of this combination of curriculum and talent in their increase in status.

Social class shows its influence more directly in these school activities. About Mike Ryan, an upper-lower class boy, we are told that he is

a popular little Riverbrooker. He was elected president of the sophomore class by a margin of three or four votes. The election was between him and Edwin Hatley from up the Hill. The election was really between the Riverbrookers and the Hill, and it took three or four ballots to reach the decision. Finally, Ryan won by six votes. Both these kids are very friendly with each other. The kids were voting for the one that came from their section of the city.

In athletics, however, this accent on social background and future plans (college) are not important or may be in fact reversed.

Peter, our rugged football star, comes from the tough section of the city, where they think a lot of the football players that come from there. He chums around with Eddy. They are both to be captains of the football team next year. Their parents work in shoe factories. Eddy's father died suddenly last year. Had a heart attack before the football season. The family is struggling along. They have always been poor. An older brother, Sydney, probably is the only means of support now. The mother naturally stays at home because they have small children.

Gordon Warren is a redheaded football player called the "carrot-topped demon." The fellows are always laughing when he is around. He does a lot of dancing and has a swagger all his own on the dance floor. The girls all like him as he has a very likeable character; he is a jolly kid, has freckles, red hair, and has a glass eye. He comes from the South End.

In discussing another boy from the lower-lower class, our informant shows how differentiation is present and how by being good enough in schoolwork and doing the right thing one can get in with the "higher-ups" and if "the friendship is lasting" one can "really get ahead."

Now, there is Mike, an active member of the Student Council, treasurer of the senior class, and treasurer of the Student Council. He comes from the poorer section of the city. He is in the Latin course and will probably win a scholarship. He is very well liked by those that know him in the school. He plays football, baseball, and doesn't go around with any girl, doesn't show any inclination for stepping out. When the Hi-Y club puts on a party or social, Mike doesn't seem to have any trouble getting a girl, so I guess he's all right. His parents are pretty poor, I imagine, but that doesn't hold against him. I think just as much of him as I do of the kids up the Hill. In fact, more. The kids from the Hill are from a richer class. You don't have to come from the Hill to be in that group, but they usually stick together

—they usually have a clique of their own. I don't know whether they think they're better than other kids, although maybe the poorer kids think they are snobs. My class is pretty free from that. Those that stick together are usually well liked. Most of these kids are very well liked by kids from the other division.

HOW THE STUDENTS MAKE THEIR SELECTION OF CURRICULA

As we have seen, the social class status of a pupil and his family has considerable influence in the choice of high-school curriculum so that lower-upper, upper-middle, and lower-middle class children go in strongly for the college preparatory course and the others tend to choose the more vocational courses. This tendency of social class standards to overrule ability leads to a good deal of reshuffling or attempted reshuffling by the high-school teachers. That is, they have to try to change some of the good students from the vocational courses to the college preparatory courses and, by giving failing marks, they change students from Latin or science to the general course.

If the pupil is intent on getting ahead and does not have the characteristics which the teacher thinks are necessary, he is dissuaded from pinning his hopes too high. If the student, on the other hand, is not confident enough in his ability to get ahead but the teacher recognizes this ability, it is the teacher's responsibility to start him on the right path.

A woman teacher in the high school says:

Children in the grammar school make very silly decisions. Two of the four girls who are highest in the senior class this year elected commercial or general their freshman year, and shifted to Latin at the end of the freshman year; but neither one can graduate in Latin because they haven't had the first year of Latin. If they had been guided to make the correct decision earlier they would have been able to graduate in the Latin curriculum.

The high-school principal generalizes about the changes from the college preparatory courses:

The changes made by the pupils from a Latin or scientific curriculum to the commercial or general were usually forced, that is, a pupil should never have been there. Such things as failure to do the work properly force a pupil to change in order to be able to graduate. It is a tragedy, the large number who are taking Latin or scientific curricula who shouldn't really be there. They come to high school with some idea that they ought to prepare for college whether they have the ability or not.

Note the idea of place, that is, a pupil in the Latin or scientific is "there," he isn't just taking a special course.

The condition of the high-school equipment and building is an example of the influence of the social class system on the schools. No upper-uppers and a small portion of the lower-uppers send their children to the local school. These people, by controlling the banks and large industries, control the financing of the city; and, although the school has been inadequate on all scores for thirty years, no money has been allotted to build a new school.

A new school was important for the upper-middle class who based their hopes for "getting ahead" on education. It was the City Council that controlled the funds, however, and they knew who controlled the town. The City Council frustrated the efforts of the upper-middle class Board of Education to get a new school. A high-school boy says:

I showed the school board all through the school building the other day, and showed them all the sore spots. The school board is all for having a new building. A City Council committee, including the mayor, also visited the school and this committee thought that only the laboratory was inadequate and thought that it was foolish to have such a little room way up on the top floor for a laboratory.

The history of educational institutions in Yankee City goes a long way back into the eighteenth century. Since the beginning, Yankee City set up grammar schools in which the three R's were taught. In 1831 a high school was begun for boys. In 1843 a high school for girls was begun, and in 1844 a free school for boys and girls was opened. All those schools were privately endowed, and they were the basis of the Yankee City high school, which was started in 1868 as an amalgamation of the other three schools. The purpose of the three schools was to prepare the boys for college and the professions and the girls for teaching, as well as to give them subjects which were "solid and useful." Only "the better class" of young person went on to secondary education. As the demand for educated people grew in the United States and high schools expanded, the Yankee City High School was adapted to the changing situation. This was done by adding vocational and commercial courses to the Latin and scientific courses. The school board, however, steadfastly refused to increase the building accommodation, so that in 1932 the high school, planned to seat 350 students, was squeezing in 800.

WHO PREPARES FOR COLLEGE IN HOMETOWN

The Hometown school has a fine building and an undifferentiated curriculum so that the same high-school education is available to all the children, whether they have college ambitions or not. In Hometown, 80 per cent of the boys and girls of high-school age attend high school. Why do they go? What do they and their parents expect from a high-school education?

First of all, no upper-upper class family has children in high school. The lower-uppers and upper-middles account for about the same proportions of pupils as one would expect from their proportions in the total population. The lower-middles contribute less than one would expect and the upper-lower and lower-lower contribute more, probably because the lower-class people have larger families and, therefore, more prospective pupils.

Of all high-school students classified as lower-upper or upper-middle, 88 per cent will go on to college while only 12 per cent of those in the three bottom classes expect to go to college. Of the total high-school pupils, 20 per cent are preparing to go to college and 80 per cent were definitely not going to college.

College Expectations and Social Position
Proportion of High-School Students Expecting to Go to College

Class	Hometown	Yankee City
	Per Cent	Per Cent
Upper upper		
Lower upper	100	100
Upper middle	80	88
Lower middle	22	45
Upper lower	9	28
Lower lower	0	26

In the accompanying table we can see how the college expectations of high-school students compare with their social class positions. College expectations in Hometown were determined largely on the basis of the high-school principal's judgment concerning the probability of college attendance for each individual student. Combined with this was a consideration of the emphasis placed on strictly academic work and the stated expectations of the students about going on to college. It is important to notice that the greater proportion or all the upper-middle and lower-upper classes will go on to college while only a small proportion or none at all of the three lower groups expect to go to college. When we look at college expectations of Yankee City youth, we see a somewhat similar picture. Proportionately more lower-middle and lower-class students in Yankee City are thinking in terms of college, but this derives from the fact that in Yankee City there is a fund which helps boys to go through college and also from the fact that a smaller proportion of lower-class students are in high school. College expectation of Yankee City students is derived from figures on curriculum choice.

Very few Hometown boys and girls have gone away to private preparatory schools. People of the higher strata were unanimous in saying, "It's not done in Hometown."

Mr. Peabody sends his son, Kenneth, to one of the famous New England "prep" schools. He says, "I can see a difference," and such invidious comparisons annoy some people in Hometown. In Yankee City almost all upper-upper children and many lower-upper and some upper-middle children are sent to private schools.

In Hometown, adults of any given class seem to vary considerably with respect to the education they have had, and this seems to be the more true in the higher strata. There are men in the higher strata who are not high-school graduates and some who are graduates of professional schools having considerable prestige; and there have been college men on WPA along with adults who have attended less than seven grades of grammar school.

As a rule, the adults in any given class expect their children to receive the "same" or "better" education than they themselves received, and their primary evaluation of "education" is in terms of quantity; they think in terms of "how many grades" or "how many years" of high school or college. When they evaluate the "quality" of education, they use either or both of two kinds of rough measures: first, the measures of pupil performance (marking system, graduation honors, etc.) and, second, the social prestige of the school involved.

How does the high school fulfill the expectations of the people of Hometown? The curriculum is to a large extent built around requirements for college entrance, and for the 20 per cent of the students who continue their education in institutions of higher learning the preparation is adequate, if judged by the subsequent academic achievement of Hometown students at colleges. This college preparatory group is preponderantly upper-middle and lower-middle class, with a few lower-uppers and upper-lowers.

Other students in the high school take mostly courses in the college preparatory curriculum with some vocational subjects instead of Latin, modern languages, and mathematics. There are agricultural courses, business and secretarial courses, and an apprenticeship program by which students are trained as clerks in the stores or as workmen in the factories.

For the children of high-status families "life begins in college," for the high school no longer provides the class training people of these positions have so long expected of it. "Life begins in high school" for the lower-middle and lower classes. Hometown people feel that they are very "democratic" and do not like to be at all reminded of their stratified status system. It is up to Mr. Mercer, the school principal, to provide a high-school curriculum and learning system that fulfills the requirements of all without too noticeable differentiation. Also, he has to do this in a way that will not offend his school board, which consists of three upper-middle class men and two lower-uppers. Here is what Mr. Mercer says:

> What I'm interested in is the curriculum in the wider sense—that includes the school orchestra, dances for young people, and things like that. Curriculum in the narrow sense is the traditional thing; par-

ents want their kids to have the same things they did. You can't change this, you can't change the curriculum in the narrow sense—I know you can change these other things [the extracurricular activities] but you can't change the traditional curriculum.

So Andrew Mercer steers his way between the extremes of an education suited, on the one hand, to the majority and, on the other hand, to the most powerful. His success is shown in that he has come up from a lowly position—country boy "with no poise"—to be an accepted member of the upper-middle class. Even Judge Scott, one of the town's most successful social arbiters, finds him a fine fellow—"got what it takes," he says.

The attitude of "getting ahead" pervades the whole of Hometown and there is "democratic" social atmosphere reminiscent of the late nineteenth century. The bulk of the population (91 per cent) is lower-middle and lower class; and there still seems to be room "at the top." We see examples of this attitude in action in the Rotary Club program to Americanize the lower-class ethnic population. At a Rotary dinner for the Polish boys' baseball team the team captain said that all the boys hoped to grow up to belong to Rotary (a middle-class organization). The school fits into and adds to this attitude toward upward mobility. This is best exemplified in the reaction against a differentiated curriculum in the high school. The democratic way seems to be to give everyone the same educational opportunities—the same as required for those at the top, namely, college preparatory courses.

The school system of Hometown, especially the high school, reflects the democratic belief that everyone has a chance to "get to the top." In other words, the democratic ideal of "opportunity for all" is a guiding principle and the school is the main instrument of opportunity. It performs this function, as the schools did more generally a generation or two ago in America, by offering an undifferentiated general academic education; he can take this opportunity who will.

It is clear now that Kenneth Peabody and Tom Brown will go to college, like nearly everyone else at their status level. They will have social pressure applied to them to push ahead. Joe Sienkowitz and his brother come from a class where few go on to college, but Joe with his musical ability and his brother with athletic talent will rise in the status system because they will translate the power given them by their talent into social recognition. Bob Jones and his kind are destined to populate the lower levels of our social system.

SOME HIGH SCHOOLS PROVIDE A SINGLE PROGRAM FOR YOUTH OF ALL STATUSES

In certain large cities, the undifferentiated high school, which we have seen in Hometown, is in general favor, even though the schools are large enough to permit differentiation.

One of the more significant social experiments of our time is being carried on in a number of city high schools in the Middle West and West. In Denver, Tulsa, Des Moines, Phoenix, Los Angeles, Oakland, and other cities like them, the high schools are nearly all of the "comprehensive" type. All students are in a single curriculum, with many individual electives, but without hard and fast divisions into college preparatory, commercial, vocational, etc. Thus there are no divisions on the basis of which claims to social status can be made. All kinds of students are in the same English, mathematics, and history courses, regardless of their college-going intentions. Some students elect commercial or other "vocational" subjects in preference to "college preparatory" subjects, but they are not set off as a separate group of students with a separate curriculum. This situation holds also for most of the small cities like Hometown where the enrollment is too small to permit much differentiation of curricula.

The schools in these cities are criticized by many upper-middle class people because they do not have "high standards" and do not "prepare well for college." Yet a comprehensive and careful study of the college records of students from several of these schools shows that in college they do as well as or better than do the graduates from traditional college-preparatory curricula and traditional high schools with a college-preparatory emphasis.

It is probable that the criticisms coming from upper-middle class people come in part from uneasiness over the threatened disintegration of social-status lines in the high school with the disappearance of clearly marked differences among curricula. On the other hand, these schools are praised by many educators for the contributions they make to democratic citizenship and to helping boys and girls achieve the task of growing up in a complex society. It may be suspected that these high schools draw a good deal of their popular support from lower-middle and lower-class parents who want their children to have "all the advantages of education," and do not like the discrimination implied by differentiation of curricula.

A FEW HIGH SCHOOLS SERVE YOUTH OF A SINGLE STATUS

In sharp contrast to the cosmopolitan high school serving youth of all statuses is the high school of certain metropolitan suburbs, which draws students from a narrow segment of society. In such suburbs as Bronxville and Manhasset (New York City), Winnetka and Lake Forest (Chicago), Grosse Pointe (Detroit), and Shaker Heights (Cleveland), the population is preponderantly upper-middle class, and the high school is remarkably homogeneous as to social status. Of course, there are many gradations of status in a suburb of this type, but these are mainly subdivisions of a national upper-middle class. While the teachers in these communities point with pride to their one or two Negro or Chinese students and to the children of chauffeurs, cooks, and grocerymen, the fact is that youngsters like these, who make up the backbone of the public-school population of the ordinary town, are a conspicuous minority in the upper-middle class suburb. Thus, in such a community, the school is largely a one-status institution.

COLLEGES ALSO FIT THE STATUS SYSTEM

At the college level there is a variety of institutions corresponding roughly to social differences in college students as well as to their differences in vocational goals.

Teachers' colleges and normal schools draw their students largely from lower-middle and upper-lower class families. Tom Brown's teacher, Virginia Crane, attended normal school and graduated from a teachers' college.

Junior colleges are so varied in type that no single generalization can be made concerning them. The municipal junior colleges, such as the Chicago City Junior Colleges, tend to draw students from lower-middle and lower classes. Some private junior colleges, especially those for girls, draw largely from the upper-middle class, giving their students a training closely adapted to the social and vocational life of that class. Stephens College is an example of this group.

The state and municipal universities come nearest to getting a cross section of young people. However, the bulk of their students are from upper-middle and lower-middle class families. For example, the University of California at Berkeley draws heavily from middle-class families in the

San Francisco Bay region, while many boys and girls from upper-class families go to Stanford.

The church-related college and the independent liberal arts college of the South, Middle West, and West also draw from upper-middle and lower-middle class families, though with significant differences due to the predominance of liberal arts or of religious emphasis in their programs. Oberlin, Carleton, Beloit, Knox, Ohio Wesleyan, DePauw, Pomona, Whitman, Davidson, and Mercer are citadels of the middle class.

The old-established eastern colleges and universities draw from the upper-middle and upper classes, with a sprinkling of mobile lower-middle class youth. These are the "Ivy League" institutions—Yale, Harvard, Princeton, Dartmouth, Amherst, Williams, Hamilton, Haverford, etc. Like them are a few colleges and universities west of the Alleghenies, of which Stanford is the outstanding example.

The generalization that different curricula and types of institutions are adapted to different statuses is illustrated by Goetsch's study. She found that the hierarchy of family income was reflected in a hierarchy of courses pursued by students in higher institutions, as shown in the accompanying table.

Parental Income and College Courses

Curriculum	Median Parental Income
Law	$2,118
Medicine and Dentistry	2,112
Liberal Arts	2,068
Journalism	1,907
Engineering	1,884
Teaching	1,570
Commercial	1,543
Nursing	1,368
Industrial Trades	1,104

In each of these groups of institutions we see that the program is adapted to boys and girls from a certain portion of the social range. But equally significant is the fact that in nearly all these schools and colleges there is a substantial minority from lower positions in the social heap who are achieving social mobility through their education.

THE ORGANIZATION OF CITIZENS COMMITTEES[1]

Mary P. Endres

DISCUSSION AND ANALYSIS

In recent years, as you have no doubt observed, schools have become page-one stories. What is happening in the schools and to the schools is of intense public concern. While the public has always been interested and closely involved in our public-school system, there seems to be a new burgeoning of interest reaching many more laymen in many more areas of the country. Some of the interest has been highly vocal and highly critical. Educators have become alarmed over the type and quality of the attacks on the schools in some areas, attacks which seem motivated less by interest in promoting better education for young people than by the intention of promoting the power of certain individuals or foisting a

[1] From *The School Executive*, January, 1952, pp. 56–57. Reprinted by permission.

particular philosophy of education or social organization upon school personnel. The results of this kind of attack have been viewed with considerable perturbation. Some prophets of doom predict a retreat from the precious vantage point afforded by the tradition of academic freedom. You will hear this problem discussed many times in your professional life, and many solutions will be offered.

Among the most promising solution to the problem of disruptive attacks, and one which provides a means of channeling public interest in constructive and coöperative work with the schools, is the development of citizens committees for the public schools. How these committees can work is described in the following article.

Citizens committees are whole-heartedly supported and encouraged by some educational leaders. Others feel that they exert undue influence on lay opinion in areas that are essentially for professional decisions. With which group would you agree? Endres states, and we have also suggested this point above, that the citizens committee is a good way to head off vicious criticism. What other valid reasons would you give for suggesting that school leadership encourage the formation of citizen groups? Furthermore, what role should school personnel take in organizing and working with such committees? Should a teacher or school administrator be an officer of a *citizens* committee?

There is a growing body of material on such committees and the kinds of community and organizational problems they have met. You will be able to obtain much help from the National Citizens Commission for the Public Schools, 2 West 45th Street, New York 36, New York. Another very important source for materials is the National Commission for the Defense of Democracy Through Education, National Education Association, 1201 16th Street, N.W., Washington 6, D.C. From the latter agency you can obtain fascinating case studies of communities and their schools.

"*We reaffirm our faith in cooperative planning by school and community groups in order to serve better the needs of youth and society. All such cooperative activities must be carried on in close relationship with the board of education, the body legally constituted to operate the schools.*"

This resolution adopted at Atlantic City in 1951 by the American Association of School Administrators represents a basic belief that if schools are to be good it involves sharing and planning all of the way by citizens and professional people working together. Because public schools are public business, earnest participation on as broad a basis as possible is solicited and desirable.

With the many organized attacks today designed to destroy or harm public education, it becomes more important than ever that we distinguish between honest criticism and effort and vicious criticism and effort. Communities should not wait until their public schools have been attacked before citizens committees are formed. It is much more democratic and constructive to channel the energies and efforts of interested citizens into something positive that will improve public schools rather than to confine efforts to meeting vicious organized attacks. This does not mean, however, that one should not examine the arguments of groups with differing opinions.

A felt need on the part of community members to improve local public schools should be the motivating factor in the formation of any citizens school committee.

It is recognized by all that the board of education is the legal instrument through which people operate their schools. It is paramount, therefore, that at the outset there be complete understanding between board of education and citizens committee. It is advisable that authorization for the formation of the citizens group come from the board of education. Joint meetings to define the areas of operation and responsibility of the two groups would be profitable at the outset.

ADVICE TO THE ADVISERS

To whom is the committee advisory? Is it the board of education? the PTA? the teaching staff? Will the citizens group ever do anything more than advise? Are there some action programs where the enlistment of citizens groups would be beneficial? Channels of communication between the board of education and the citizens group should be two-way. Each group must be assured of a sympathetic interpretation of its program by the other.

The press, radio, and printed brochures offer means of publicizing the reasons for establishing citizens groups and the nature of their work. Whether or not the individual citizen feels free to participate through a citizens group depends upon the open-door policy of the committee. In fact, the committee may well become the contact between the patrons of a school community and a board of education. It is desirable that this contact constitute actual participation rather than spectacular meetings and lip service to high-sounding goals.

WHO SHALL BELONG?

Shall representatives be elected by the people? Shall they represent organizations? Should there be a limit as to number? How can we be sure that the various geographic, political, social, economic, racial and religious groups are represented?

Each community must decide these issues for itself. Certainly in some areas, the very need for a citizens group grows out of the fact that there are many groups of people within a community and that all should have representation on a planning council. Every group should have a balance between parents and non-parents, urban and rural residents, veterans and non-veterans, old and new residents, lower and upper economic groups.

The needs of a particular situation must be kept well in mind when determining the number of people who should work together. Undoubtedly, a small committee can be more efficient than a large committee in formulating a recommendation. But for discussion purposes, one should tap all the facets of a community in order to get a cross section of ideas and suggestions.

After committees are set up, a provision for term of office of committee members should be made. Terms should not all expire at the same time, but a retirement plan should be developed in order that new members are introduced to the work of the group in cooperation with some holdover members.

HOW SHOULD IT OPERATE?

It is apparent that there is a need for some rules or bylaws under which citizens committees should operate. They should define the officials needed for the organization; where, when, and how often the meetings should be held; whether there is to be an operating budget; and whether there should be a prepared agenda. The committee will have to decide also whether it needs consultant services, whether they will employ staff workers, or whether they may wish to have small subcommittees. It may be necessary to decide how to avoid becoming a tool of special interest groups with ulterior motives.

Capable and responsible leaders will undoubtedly logically step into positions of leadership. Much of the success of the venture will depend on them. It will require time, patience, and great understanding to harmonize the many viewpoints and differing attitudes of all involved.

A PRESCHOOL WORK CONFERENCE

From the kitchens and the farms, from the offices and the factories, 65 members of one small rural community in the Midwest came to school last August to participate with the teaching staff and members of the board of education in a preschool work conference which had as its theme, *How Can We Improve Our Schools for Boys and Girls?* Small discussion groups of not more than ten participants were set up for the purpose of defining problems and issues facing education, with particular emphasis on those affecting the local community. The groups had been encouraged to list all apparent problems, specific or general, small or large.

Identified as major issues were such questions as: "How are spiritual values brought into the school program?" "How can we draw interest in the school from the entire community?" "Is the guidance program continuous from kindergarten through secondary school?" "How can we do a better job of guiding children in social development, still maintaining individuality?"

There were also specific problems that trouble any school: "Can we make a school policy regarding birthdays?" "What about smoking in school buildings?" "Can we solve the problem of lunch money collection?" "Where may upper grade girls keep the blue jeans that they use for physical education?"

A two-day work conference session followed, in which lay citizens met with board of education and professional staff members to discuss the questions and to set up plans for solving problems. The general group then met together and pooled the recommendations and findings of the small study groups.

These were some of the ideas thrown into the hopper:

"Since we believe that the old method —adults laying down all the rules and regulations—stilted a child's freedom to develop socially, we recommend that parents and teachers allow children to discover that responsibilities are necessary and let them share those responsibilities with one another, that adults teach children to realize that all privileges which we expect to enjoy carry with them responsibilities to be shared, and that we teach children to know the real meaning of freedom."

"Since it is true that mere tolerance of an individual may harm and not help, and that really to belong an individual must know he is accepted, fits in and is loved, we recommend that we teach racial tolerance by bringing out the fact that every race has its great men and has made worthwhile contributions, and that we stress the fact that it is not what one is but what he does that counts."

"All food or other expense from homes will be eliminated on birthdays. Teachers will decide with children in each room how they will observe a child's birthday."

Some of the recommendations included provision for permanent citizens committees in various areas. The preschool work conference provided the framework through which citizens could find opportunities to express themselves in relation to the school program. "When men work together a school can be built, a child can grow and a world can be shaped to a better purpose."

OUR SCHOOLS HAVE KEPT US FREE[1]

Henry Steele Commager

No other people ever demanded so much of education as have the American. None other was ever served so well by its schools and educators.

From the beginning education has had very special, and very heavy, tasks to perform. Democracy could not work without an enlightened electorate. The various states and regions could not achieve unity without a sentiment of nationalism. The nation could not absorb tens of millions of immigrants from all parts of the globe without rapid and effective Americanization. Economic and social distinctions and privileges, severe enough to corrode democracy itself, had to be fought. To our schools went the momentous responsibility of inspiring a people to pledge and hold allegiance to these historic principles of democracy, nationalism, Americanism and egalitarianism.

Because we are a "new" nation we sometimes forget how very old are some of our institutions and practices. The U.S.—today the oldest democracy in the world and the oldest republic—also has the oldest public school system in the world. The famous Ould Deluder Satan law of 1647 which set up a system of community-supported schools in Massachusetts Bay Colony was, in its day, something new under the sun. "As a fact," wrote Horace Mann, himself one of its later products, "it had no precedent in world history, and as a theory it could have been refuted and silenced by a . . . formidable array of argument and experience. . . ."

What compels our interest, however, is not only the daring of that law, but the accuracy with which it reflected our national character and foreshadowed our history.

How did it happen that this little frontier colony of some 15 or 20,000 souls, clinging precariously to the wilderness shelf, should within a few years have established a Latin School, Harvard College and a system of public education? Why this instant and persistent concern for education—so great that education became the American religion? For it is in education that we have put our faith; it is our schools and colleges that are the peculiar objects of public largess and private benefaction. Even in architecture we have proclaimed our devotion, building schools like cathedrals.

None of this reflects any peculiar respect for learning or for scholarship. There has never been much of that, and there is probably less of it today than at any previous time in our history. Only in the U.S. could the term "brain trust" be one of opprobrium; only here is the college professor a stereotype of absent-mindedness and general woolliness.

Yet the paradox in all this is more apparent than real. It is not because education advances scholarship that it has been so prized in America—but rather because it promised to bring to real life the American dream of the good society. So declared the great Northwest Ordinance of 1787: "Religion, morality, and knowledge, being necessary to good government and the happiness of mankind, schools and the means of education shall forever be encouraged." And the generation that fought the Revolution had energy enough left to create a dozen new colleges, establish state universities and provide for common schools by

[1]From *Life*, October 16, 1950. Copyright, Time Inc., 1950. Reprinted by permission.

munificent land grants. Even the Encyclopaedia Britannica could observe sourly of this generation that "notwithstanding their addiction to those occupations of which lucre is the sole object, Americans were duly attentive to cultivate the field of learning, and they have ever since their first foundation been particularly careful to provide for the education of the rising progeny." And, in our generation today, when the critical pedant of the Old World disparages American academic traditions, we are prone—and with much reason—to answer tartly: it has never been the Americans who succumbed to the evil and meretricious appeals of Fascism, Nazism or Communism.

Let us look at the specific tasks which our triumphant faith in education imposed on our schools. The first and greatest task was to provide an enlightened citizenry in order that self-government might work. Though the earliest settlers in New England used the word democracy only as a rebuke, they had in fact embarked upon an experiment in democracy. With independence the problem of self-government became urgent. It is important to remember that self-government had not been tried before on such a scale. The founding fathers confidently believed they had found the key. "To be long-lived," as Benjamin Rush observed, "republics must invest in education."

Has our investment succeeded? None can doubt that it has. Americans have, in short, made democracy work. They established a nation, held it together, and expanded the original 13 to 48 states—while steadily pursuing the grand objectives of the framers of the Constitution: their "more perfect union" *did* establish justice and domestic tranquillity, and secure the blessings of liberty. Through all their history they elected some mediocre presidents but never a wicked or a dangerous one; they never yielded to a military dictator; they avoided revolutions; they settled all problems by compromise except the greatest one, slavery, and perhaps that could not be settled by compromise; they revealed in every crisis an ability to select able leaders. Only a people taught self-government could record these achievements.

The second great task imposed upon education and on the schools—the creation of national unity—was equally difficult.

In 1789 no one took for granted the blessing of the "more perfect union"—for what, after all, was the basis for an American nation? Its geographical basis was so large as to defeat itself, for how hold together an area of continental dimensions thinly inhabited by some four million people? The historical basis was almost nonexistent: differences that separated South Carolinians from Connecticut Yankees seemed to be greater than the bonds that united them.

Yet we created unity out of diversity, nationalism out of particularism. Powerful material forces—the westward movement, canals and railroads, a liberal land policy—sped this achievement.

But just as important were intellectual and emotional factors—what Lincoln called those "mystic chords of memory, stretching from every battlefield and patriot grave to every living heart and hearthstone." These were the contribution of poets and novelists, editors and naturalists, historians and jurists, orators and painters—and the medium through which they worked was the school. Through the whole 19th Century, novelists like Cooper and Sims and Hawthorne, poets like Bryant and Longfellow and Whittier, painters like Trumbull and Stuart and Peale, historians like Jared Sparks and George Bancroft, schoolmen like Noah Webster with his Spellers and the McGuffeys with their Readers—all these and scores of others created and popularized that common group of heroes and villains, that common store of poems and stories, of images and values of which national spirit is born. These men gave to Americans, old and new alike, a people's common language with which to voice a people's common heritage:

God sifted a whole nation that he might send choice grain over into this wilderness; As for me, give me liberty or give me death; If they mean to have a war, let it begin here; One if by land, and two if by sea; These are the times that try men's souls; I only regret that I have but one life to lose for my country; I have just begun to fight; Millions for defense, but not one cent for tribute; Don't give up the ship; We have met the enemy and they are ours; Liberty and union, now and forever, one and inseparable; I propose to fight it out on this line if it takes all summer; Damn the torpedoes; Government of the people, by the people, for the people; With malice toward none, with charity for all.

And then there were the songs and the pictures, too. In school and lyceum, children came to learn and remember at least snatches of the "Concord Hymn" or "Old Ironsides" or the "Midnight Ride of Paul Revere." From famed paintings they learned to recognize Wolfe dying on the Plains of Abraham, Penn making a treaty with the Indians, Washington crossing the Delaware, Boone pushing his way through the Cumberland Gap. Through its young eyes the young people came to see itself as one nation.

The third task imposed on education, and particularly on the public schools, was that which we call Americanism. Each decade after 1840 saw from two to eight million immigrants pour into America. No other people had ever absorbed such large or varied racial stocks so rapidly. In this, America could proclaim both its pride and its welcome in the inscription in the base of the Statue of Liberty:

Give me your tired, your poor,
Your huddled masses yearning to breathe free.
The wretched refuse of your teeming shore.
Send these, the homeless, tempest-tost to me;
I lift my lamp beside the golden door.

How, after all, were these millions of newcomers to be "Americans"—in language, in ways of life and thought, in citizenship? The nation's first and main answer was the public school. Most of the new millions, eager though they were to be Americanized, were too old for school, but their children went to the public schools, adapting themselves with children's speed to American ways, and taking home with them the idiom, the habits, the very thoughts and standards they picked up in the schoolroom and on the playground. Mary Antin tells us, in her moving *Promised Land*, what school meant to the new masses: "Education was free. . . . It was the one thing that [my father] was able to promise us when he sent for us; surer, safer than bread and shelter.

"On our second day I was thrilled with the realization of what this freedom of education meant. A little girl from across the alley came and offered to conduct us to school. My father was out, but we five between us had a few words of English by this time. We knew the word school. We understood. This child who had never seen us until yesterday, who could not pronounce our names, who was not much better dressed than we, was able to offer us the freedom of the schools of Boston! No application made, no questions asked, no examinations, rulings, exclusions; no machinations, no fees. The doors stood open for every one of us."

That magic open door imposed upon American schools such a responsibility as the schools of no other country have ever had to meet. Doubtless the necessity of teaching immigrant children even the most elementary subjects slowed up the processes of formal education in many schools. Yet those schools have done the astounding job asked of them: they have literally made millions of Americans.

There is a fourth and final service the schools have rendered the cause of American democracy. This most heterogeneous of modern societies—profoundly varied in racial background, religious faith, social and economic interest—has ever seemed the most easy prey to forces of riotous privilege and ruinous division. These forces have not prevailed; they have been routed, above all, in the schoolrooms and on the playgrounds of America. In the classroom, the nation's children have lived and learned equality—all subject to the same educational processes and the same disciplines. On the playground and the athletic field, the same code has ruled—with the reward of honor and applause heartfully given to achievements to which all could aspire equally. The roster of "foreign" names on our high school and college football teams has seemed worth a feeble joke to many an unwitty radio comedian. Who can seriously doubt that the cause of democracy is served when it is a Murphy, a Schwartz, a Groglio or a Levitsky that the cheering stands applaud? If, through the 19th and well into the 20th Century, American schools performed such magnificent service, the question remains: do they still serve the nation well? And is education still the American religion?

The evidence is conflicting. Americans in many ways still confess their faith in education, still impose upon it tasks performed elsewhere by home, church or industry. More young people are going to college and university today than went to high school only 30 years ago. Public appropriations have mounted to $5 billion annually. While the federal government has accepted a larger share of responsibility for education than ever before, private philanthropy continues unabated and we still build colleges with the fervor that other ages gave only to their cathedrals.

Yet there is other evidence of a more sobering nature. The proportion of our national income devoted to education has declined in the last decades, and $5 billion for public education compares rather poorly with the $8 billion spent on liquor or the $19 billion on automobiles each year. Most school-teachers are underpaid, many buildings are antiquated, most colleges and universities are in desperate financial plight. And—even graver than the material picture—the decade that has witnessed the greatest rush to American universities has also witnessed savage attacks upon their intellectual integrity and independence.

The American mind today seems deeply worried about its school system as it never has been before. In the vast literature on education there is more discontent than complacency, more blame than praise. There is an uneasy feeling that the schools have somehow failed to do their job.

Yet no one seems very positive as to what the job of the schools is today. It is oddly ironic—to say the kindest—to hear people who rear their children on comics complain that the schools fail to instill a love of literature.

It is shocking—to say the truth—to hear the very people who support teachers' oaths and textbook censorship contend that the schools are failing to encourage greater intellectual independence.

We need to get our standards straight and clear. Many of the old purposes and criteria have disappeared, and the people have not defined new ones to take their place. The 19th Century school, for example, had an enormous job in "Americanization"—but it was a clearly defined job, universally willed by the people. Today's school faces a nice problem in deciding whether its education should reinforce nationalism—or inspire internationalism.

Two developments have further blurred the picture inherited from the 19th Century. First: schools no longer have anything like the monopoly in education they then exercised. Today they share responsibility with the movies, the radio and television and, to a far larger extent than before, with the newspapers and the magazines: for millions of Americans *Life* and the *Reader's Digest* have supplanted the McGuffey Readers.

Second: with the phenomenal growth of higher education, the new demands of industry and the professions, the government and the military, the function of elementary and secondary education has become more narrowly educational than ever before. In a day of specialization schools are called on more and more to prepare not so much for life, citizenship or democracy as for particular tasks and competences.

This means that we have placed our schools in a crossfire of conflicting demands. While we still want them to perform broad social functions, we impose upon them narrower educational functions.

The old expectation persists that schools be training grounds for democracy and nationalism. The new demands are implacable—that schools not only prepare young people for college, but somehow manage to teach domestic economy, driving, machine shop, current events, world history and typewriting at the same time.

There is a further difficulty—the one that most of us are reluctant to recognize. Schools reflect the society they serve. Many of the failures we ascribe to contemporary education are in fact failures of our society as a whole. A society that is indifferent to its own heritage cannot expect schools to make good the indifference. A society that slurs over fundamental principles and takes refuge in the superficial and the ephemeral cannot demand that its schools instruct in abiding moral values. A society proudly preoccupied with its own material accomplishments and well-being cannot fairly expect its schools to teach that the snug warmth of security is less meaningful than the bracing venture of freedom. In all this, to reform our schools is first to reform ourselves.

For a century and a half American schools have served and strengthened the commonwealth. They provided a citizenry as enlightened as any on earth. They justified and vindicated democracy's promise. If society clearly defines the new duties it wishes our schools to fulfill and if it steadfastly supports them not only with money but also with faith, they will surely justify that faith in the future as they have in the past.

THIS WE BELIEVE ABOUT EDUCATION[1]

National Association of Manufacturers, Educational Advisory Committee and Council

DISCUSSION AND ANALYSIS

This document is a very interesting one. Education, as you are now probably aware, is big business. Just glance at the advertising in such magazines as *Nation's Schools*, or *The School Board Journal*, or the

[1] The Summary, which follows the Introduction, is based on several illuminating sections. Because of space limitations, the editors have been forced to exclude these

Journal of the National Education Association, and you can see also that business has a big stake in education. We not only must provide teachers for millions of school children, but each of these must be equipped with pencil, paper, books, desks. There must be pencil sharpeners and cafeteria trays, light fixtures and bleachers, typewriters and motion-picture screens. The modern school is a costly building to erect, and costly to maintain.

Let's look even further. Without an educated populace, business could not operate. Secretaries are needed who can read and spell as well as operate machines; men are required who can measure and read directions, who can prepare reports and repair motors. The work of a technological world requires an educated worker. Thus business is directly dependent upon mass education to provide the millions of workers who are needed. Industry and business also carry on the training in specific skills; but without a basic foundation in the schools, neither business nor industry could afford to operate.

What, then, does business think about education? What do you think the average businessman thinks about the schools? Does he like what the schools are doing? Does he feel the schools are doing a good job?

The statement that follows interests us because it goes deeper than just the selfish concern of business with either selling equipment to the schools or obtaining skilled workers. It tells us what business representatives and educators do agree are some of the basic guide lines that should help determine policies in the public schools of a democracy. The conclusions that are presented contrast a liberal position with a somewhat more conservative one. As you read these paragraphs, you may want to check which of the contrasting statements most reflects your own opinion, and which reflects what you think to be the opinion of the general public. Then go out and test your idea of what the general public thinks!

---

sections: The Purposes of Education in America; The Support of Education; The Responsibilities of Educators; The Responsibilities of Industry to Education; The Ultimate Responsibility for Education. For the complete statement, interested students should read the entire text of *This We Believe About Education*, New York, National Association of Manufacturers, 1954. The selection which follows has been reprinted by permission of the Education Department of the National Association of Manufacturers.

About This Statement

The Special Education Subcommittee of the Educational Advisory Committee and the Educational Advisory Council of the National Association of Manufacturers was appointed for one purpose—to focus attention on areas of agreement between educators and industrialists which would serve as a basis for better understanding and more effective cooperation between these two groups. This Statement contains a brief outline of the premises and the reasoning that led to specific areas of agreement, and a final recapitulation of the Subcommittee's conclusions.

The Educational Advisory Committee and the Educational Advisory Council of the NAM, in a joint meeting on October 27, 1953, approved the Statement of the Special Education Subcommittee which is presented here. It is hoped that this effort will be received by both industrialists and educators in the spirit of tolerant good will in which it was conceived and in which it was conscientiously prepared. If the Statement makes a contribution to further discussions which will result in better understanding and closer relationships between Education and Industry, it will have served its major purpose. . . .

—ROBERT H. W. WELCH, JR., CHAIRMAN

INTRODUCTION

The National Association of Manufacturers, throughout its history, has consistently supported Education in America. Strong statements have been issued periodically, setting forth the beliefs and positions of Industry. Yet the mutual confidence which so obviously should exist between Industry and Education has suffered many shocks over the years.

At a meeting of the NAM Educational Advisory Committee held in January, 1952, several leading educators were invited guests. They, too, it developed, were concerned over an apparent deterioration in relationships. Some of the causes seemed inadvertent and isolated, but there were also evidences of deliberate intent.

It was recognized that a great majority of American businessmen and American educators have little or no criticism to make of each other, but over the past several years attacks by some businessmen on the philosophy or practices of some educators have been widely publicized. Similarly, there has been articulate criticism of business and industry by some educators. Resentment has resulted on both sides.

Anxiety was expressed at the January meeting lest the friction and misunderstanding increase. It was suggested that a Subcommittee could well be established to study the situation and to propose constructive counteraction. Thus the Special Education Subcommittee was conceived and appointed. It comprised six industrialists from the NAM Educational Advisory Committee and six educators from the NAM Educational Advisory Council.

At the outset, the Subcommittee agreed that misunderstanding and suspicion between Education and Industry should be reduced to a minimum and eliminated if possible, and that there should be established widespread and general understanding, confidence, and cooperation between these two vital groups in America.

Scrutiny of misunderstandings led the Subcommittee far afield. Among causes for disagreement they found such factors as the proper boundaries of academic freedom, objective teaching versus subjective indoctrination, responsibility for teachers' actions and activities, and the distinction between justifiable, constructive criticism and malicious attacks. Ultimately the Subcommittee found itself considering the place of Education in American life—its purposes and practices, its direction and support, and the real measure of Education's contribution to the happiness and welfare of the American people.

As the Subcommittee went beyond the limits at first contemplated for the study, two questions arose. The first was why representatives of these two segments of American society should be combining to make a joint appraisal of one of them. In other words, if Industry and Education were to study Education, why should they not also take a look at Industry? It was agreed that there was no reason why they should not, but such a study was not this Subcommittee's assignment. The second question was whether the Subcommittee was duplicating the work of other organized groups, such as the Commission on Financing Higher Education, and the Educational Policies Commission of the National Education Association. Such was not the intent, but it did seem that a brief survey of certain fundamentals regarding Education was necessary to provide background and a clearly understood basis for the study.

Short summarizations of the most significant assumptions regarding fundamental aspects of Education are included in this Statement in order to show the lines of thought that led to the final conclusions.

The Subcommittee has endeavored to be fair and tolerant of conflicting opinions. It sought to establish principles, or areas of agreement, broad enough to be accepted by men of good will. It endeavored to clarify causes or areas of disagreement. It tried to be practical, and to present a Statement that will be a useful guide in determining future attitudes of individuals and organizations, in both Industry and Education.

The conclusions reached are presented in a series of connected and contrasting paragraphs in the final section of this Statement. Generally speaking, the first paragraph under each point expresses the more liberal viewpoint. The second paragraph records the more conservative opinion. It should be emphasized that educators are not speaking in one paragraph and industrialists in the other. The division of opinion was *within* these groups and not *between* them. . . .

SUMMARY: THIS WE BELIEVE ABOUT EDUCATION

1. That the purposes of education are many and varied in America, where a high degree of freedom has prevailed in the growth of both private and public education. Wide variation in accepted educational purposes, while decried by some, is to be expected and should be accented as a natural development in a society which encourages great diversity in its search for truth. There probably is no one single purpose of education acceptable to all, but some rather widely accepted purposes without reference to their order of importance may be generalized as follows: (a) To prepare the individual to make a living and to make progress in his vocation, or to help in that process; (b) To prepare the individual for mature and complete living—personal and family, social and civic—in today's world, and to help develop the moral, ethical, and spiritual values which benefit both the individual and society; and (c) To increase man's understanding of the arts, sciences, and humanities, and his appreciation of his cultural heritage.

1a. But that acceptance of purposes should be related to the size, grade level, and nature of the educational institutions and to the learners who are to attend those institutions. The purposes of education should be determined by the needs of the learners, and in this nation there should be available ample variety in learning opportunities. The relative emphasis to be placed on the different purposes of education should be determined with wide latitude and consideration for all concerned. In all education due regard for excellence of educational programs and quality of teaching should be given. This is an important requirement for the preservation of a society of free individuals.

2. That all established relationships between individuals, and between the individual and society as a whole, are subject to change, and that any effort on the part of Education or of particular educators to keep the American social organization static instead of dynamic, or to prevent or to ignore change, would be contrary to the proper spirit and purpose of American Education.

2a. But that acceptance and evaluation of change should proceed from a fundamental and firm belief in the American form of government, in the free, private, competitive enterprise system, and in the maximum freedom for the individual that the essential functions of government in a complex modern civilization will permit.

3. That every teacher in America should

have the unquestioned right to impart knowledge objectively concerning all matters related to the subject he teaches. Teachers of economics or of government or of any of the social sciences should discuss without hesitation the theories, practices, and histories of all systems of government including the government of collectivist states, to the extent required for the properly balanced organization of a particular course. When subject matter does deal with governments and ideologies, teachers should take into consideration the maturity and grade level of the learners. The younger the pupil and the more elementary the instruction, the less excuse there is for deviation from objective teaching. Completely objective teaching, however, especially of the social studies, while a desirable goal, can scarcely be expected or achieved in actual practice by teachers who are also thinking human beings; reasonable deviation from this absolute standard should not expose any teacher to attack, intimidation, or insecurity of his position.

3a. But that neither freedom of speech nor freedom of academic inquiry and instruction gives a teacher the right to a captive audience of impressionable young people, as a target for propaganda on behalf of theories or practices that are disapproved by the community which has put that audience in his charge for other purposes. Within limitations dictated by the circumstances of his semi-official position, a teacher should be free to express his personal opinions and to take direct and active interest in community problems. The teacher should assume his responsibility as a citizen in the community, but he has no right to the classroom as his private pulpit. Nor should a proper regard for the prejudices of individual human beings and tolerance for differing opinions extend to the point of giving a teacher the right to intolerance of beliefs with which *he* does not agree, nor to the conversion of his teaching into exclusive indoctrination of any social or political philosophy.

4. That no attack on any teacher or on his teaching, because of his individual ideological convictions (short of advocacy of the overthrow of the government), should be supported or condoned.

4a. But that bona fide attempts, based on reasonable evidence, to show that a particular teacher is taking advantage of his position to preach a social philosophy opposed by his local community or by the group his institution primarily serves, rather than to teach about it objectively, are to be considered judicially and not construed or distorted as attacks, either on academic freedom or on the whole American educational system.

5. That complaints of subversive activities or collectivist indoctrination of students by individual teachers should be weighed and given consideration by the legally constituted school authorities in preference to any such action by any outside agency, governmental or otherwise. This procedure should be followed whether the complaints are initiated by resident members of the local community, by members of the group served by the particular institution employing the teacher, or by some other source.

5a. But that it is perfectly proper for American citizens, as individuals, or in groups, or through organizations, to make and publish objective studies of any and all aspects of the educational system, and to obtain as wide distribution of the findings of such studies as they can. A study of the declared methods and stated purposes of education, as taught in the various colleges or by individuals in these colleges; a study of the textbooks being used or offered for use in educational institutions; a study of the articles, essays, speeches and books put forth by influential educators as guides to other members of the teaching profession—all these are quite properly within the province of observation and scrutiny. Few educators would wish to single out the educational system as the one area of American public life which should not be subjected to constant study and criticism. Those few who would must not be allowed to do so.

6. That businessmen, the public, and educators should view with proper and customary caution sweeping charges made by any group which studies the educational system and publishes adverse findings as to its methods, purposes, or practices, or as to the ideological loyalties of some of its leaders.

6a. But that smearing the groups or the individuals responsible for such criticisms is not satisfactory refutation of their evidence or of their arguments. Charges which cannot be substantiated should be refuted.

7. That while in the choice of textbooks, determination of curricula, and formulation of teaching methods, interested individuals or lay committees may make a healthy and valuable contribution, final decisions should be left with educational administrators, teachers, or committees of teachers, subject to the general authority of boards of education or of college trustees.

7a. But that the people who provide and maintain these institutions for the education of their children should have the right of final approval or disapproval of decisions of teachers, committees, and educational administrators, and even boards of education and college trustees. In the case of public elementary and secondary schools, this final decision is exercised through the ballot box in the election of members of boards of education. In the case of institutions of higher learning it is exercised through the action of state legislators, the protests of alumni, or by withholding of grants for financial support. Fortunately, this final decision is frequently cumbersome and slow; this constitutes a safeguard against the rash use of such authority in making decisions. But this right of final authority should always be available if necessary, as a last resort.

8. That constitutionally public education is a function of the several states, and that statewide legislation establishing minimum standards of attendance, minimum educational standards, requirements for facilities, and the pattern of local administration within certain limits of authority and responsibility, is necessary and proper.

8a. But that community responsibility, community administration, and community determination of matters concerning local school systems should not be weakened by centralization of either facilities or control beyond actual requirements for the most efficient and economical educational service in a given area. A thousand errors of policy or practice, however gross some of these errors may be, all tend to cancel each other out in time; and America has gained tremendously by this right of small groups to make progress in all fields of social effort by separate methods of trial and error.

9. That teaching should be regarded as one of the great professions; that teachers themselves should act, and should be regarded by the community, as members of such a profession; that this regard should be shown by paying teachers salaries commensurate with the service rendered by a great profession; and that businessmen, who carry a large part of the tax load, should take the lead in creating everywhere public opinion in favor of a salary standard for teachers which will help to attract the ablest young people and to hold them in the profession.

9a. But that educators should earn and retain this esteem through continuous professional development, and by a careful regard for personal associations, affiliations, and reputations. Teachers should refrain from joining or supporting organizations which lower the stature of their profession in the eyes of the community.

10. That the schools today are expected to assume a wider range of responsibilities, as to preparation of children for adult life, than were expected of schools a generation ago. Hence the educational system should have considerable latitude in familiarizing students with new scientific, technical, and cultural developments; in providing new experiences and outlooks, ideas and knowledge and contemporary concepts which parents—as an older generation—may not be in a position to impart.

10a. But that the schools are still only one of the agencies concerned with the upbringing of youth. The home, Sunday schools and churches, Boy and Girl Scout organizations (simply by way of illustration) are others with varying degrees of influence. The schools should neither try, be expected, nor be permitted to assume exclusive or near-exclusive responsibility. The ultimate final responsibility for the education and upbringing of every child still remains, and should remain, in the family of which that child is a part. The schools must be regarded as agents of, and auxiliary to, parents in the schools' assumption of a part of that responsibility.

11. That educational programs and standards should be as broad and inclusive as practical considerations will permit; that the measureless value of diversity in educational theories and practices, manifesting itself in many ways beyond the few examples cited here, should be fully recognized by both the profession and the public; that this heterogeneity is a chief source of the strength and progress of American Education; and that in Education as in all other divisions of its cultural activities, America should be and remain a melting pot of professional experimentation, and of ideas, purposes, and traditions that merge to make the nation great.

11a. But that too radical or idiosyncratic deviations in educational theory or practice, from the broad standards determined and accepted by preponderant public opinion and professional experience, should not be supported in so universal a nation-wide service as Education.

8

FOUNDATIONS OF EDUCATIONAL ADMINISTRATION: The Organization and Administration of the School

THE SCHOOL[1]

Midcentury White House Conference on Children and Youth

DISCUSSION AND ANALYSIS

You have already read one selection from this report, "The Course of Healthy Personality Development" in Chapter 6. You may be interested in the background of the Midcentury White House Conference. This report comes from the fifth such conference on children. The first two were primarily concerned with children who were socially disadvantaged. The next two gave primary attention to some of the social and economic aspects of children and youth in America. The fifth White House conference, taking place at midcentury, as the title indicates, concerned itself with the psychological situation of American children. That is, how does personality grow and develop in our culture? What things help children grow to adequate maturity? What things hinder such growth? What, furthermore, is a good prescription for healthy personality development? Such questions were discussed in many communities prior to the Washington, D.C., meetings. Then, in a series of conference sessions, participants listened to the expression of many viewpoints. Significant research findings were presented. Scholars and practitioners from every field that had anything to do with the welfare of children were in attendance. Out of these discussions came this report, and several other thoughtful and important documents.

As you read this section on the school, you may well ask yourself, "How

[1] From Midcentury White House Conference on Children and Youth, *A Healthy Personality for Every Child*. Copyright 1951 by Health Publications Institute, Inc., Raleigh, North Carolina. Reprinted by permission of the publisher.

do we achieve the kind of institution described here?" In the section of this report on the selection and training of teachers, how well do you feel present teacher education programs actually train teachers and select them according to the suggestions given here? What bases for selection does this report claim will raise the status of the teaching profession? Do you agree?

The schools of the United States have been concerned with the healthy development of the whole person in more ways and for more years than those not intimately acquainted with their recent history may know. Thinking about the obligations of the school to the whole child, its responsibilities in connection with his wholesome growth as a functioning personality, has been moving ahead steadily and with wide strides. Practice has followed—experimentally, feeling its way, faster in some places than in others, hampered not only by some of the traditional forms of schooling, but also, and perhaps more importantly, by the stringent difficulty of translating novel ideas and fresh dedications into corresponding lines of action.

A NEW VIEW IN A NEW CENTURY

At the turn of the century, the schools were already concerned with the functioning of the individual as a citizen, as a worker and member of society, as a moral character in all his doings and dealings, but all of these objectives were sought chiefly through the imparting of certain specified knowledges and skills. During the first quarter of the new century, education began to conceive of the human being, child and man, more clearly as a social being, the product of interchange between himself and his environment.

By the new line of thinking, what the man becomes, given his native endowment, is not dependent upon what befalls him merely but also upon what he does. An experience is an interchange between a person and a situation, in the course of which both he and the situation undergo change. The very young child learns to seek his ends, the fulfillment of his desires, in the outer world, through doing things in it and to it, manipulating it in ways that he discovers to be appropriate, in ways that work to bring him satisfaction. He is not merely active at random. His activity has meaning. It is directed toward ends. He has purpose.

What he seeks in the outer world is also to a high degree learned. His very desires take on their shape and content through his interaction with this outer world, which thus becomes an integral part of himself. The Hopi child and the child of the prevalent American culture not only seek their ends in different ways; they actually seek different things. At the period when the latter wants to become a cowboy or a locomotive engineer, the former may be making deliberate arrangements to maintain the good and happy thoughts which are part of the Hopi ideal. In the course of seeking and doing, succeeding and failing, enjoying and suffering the results of doing, both American child and Hopi child—all children—acquire a set of meanings.

But the child's experience is in part determined by his purposes. Following his purposes, he builds meanings into his life, and these meanings become a selective influence shaping his further purposes and the new meanings he acquires in the course of his further experience. If his purposes are of a certain order, he is likely to seek out scientific explanations of a thunderstorm, for example, and the persons who can give them to him, and to make weather charts and rainfall estimates, and eventually to propose to become a scientist. If his inclinations are more in the direction of artistic expression, both his human associations and his activities and plans are likely to be guided by these.

If, however, his purposes are thwarted—and very early in life he learned that his human environment could be frustrating and infuriating as well as comforting, supporting, and satisfying—the results are different. He does not stop experiencing, learning, acquiring new meanings and new ways of reacting to situations because of the new meanings, but what he learns, the meanings he acquires, are quite different. And they are likely to be very different, too, from what the person who thwarts him thinks they should be, or intends.

Suppose, for example, when he is quite young, it is his impulse and purpose to run outdoors and prance and yell and outshout the storm. This purpose may lead one day to the development of more and more aesthetic meanings, and to artistic creativity in dance or music. Or possibly one day this child may start to seek other means to dominate the storm and make it serve his purposes, and so acquire an eventual set of meanings that would be called primarily scientific, though empowered still and imbued by his rich early aesthetic-emotional reactions.

But suppose that while he is still at the stage of running and jumping and yelling, or running out to build streams and dikes and waterways, some importunate grown person comes to him and says, "No, that is not what you are to do when there is a thunderstorm. You must learn science. You must read this book about the watershed. You must make a graph of precipitation. You must take this Leyden jar in the laboratory and do as the book says and watch what happens and write it down as I tell you in a notebook. Because you must learn about science. Science is essential for modern man; it is important that you understand about it."

What happens? In all likelihood, the child's intent and purpose are thwarted, and he is angry. He learns that this grown person is not his helpmeet and friend, but his opponent who must be given in to. This adult, all adults, perhaps all persons, become to him hostile and unmanageable, rather than friendly and cooperative. "Human being" becomes a phrase with a pattern of emotional meanings that are not good. He reacts to those meanings, and becomes himself less cooperative, more hostile, in his further dealings with men.

Nor will he even learn that which would make it possible for it to be said of him that he knows science, and is equipped to live in a scientific age. He may hate science, and attempt to wangle his way out of any possible further contact with it. Hating and shunning science, he is not likely to learn very much about it. More important, unless he finds it elsewhere, he will have lost all opportunity for learning the very essence of the scientific age, and of science as it is now understood: the freely inquiring mind, purposefully delving for knowledge—prediction and control. He will not have acquired equipment for the scientific age, but more likely for an age in which all learning inhered in books, was handed down by authority, and used in verbal situations only.

The view of the child and of education that developed after the turn of the century said, in effect, that one must work in accordance with the child's intent and purpose, and not against them. Furthermore, this conception of learning led directly away from treating the child as a diminutive man, without right to respect as a child, because it made clear that, with his lesser experience, he was different from the adult. As a result of his accruing experience—his doing and undergoing—his responses, meanings, purposes change. As today shapes him for tomorrow, tomorrow again shapes him for all future tomorrows. As he lives richly today, and acquires manifold meanings, he lives more richly tomorrow. So it began to be seen that each day must be treated as an end in itself, and the child respected as a child.

Experience was the great teacher after all, and experience could not be confined to the book. The child as a whole lived in a whole environment, and responded to everything that was in it. Along with this recognition came a number of inferences for the practices of education that agree strikingly with the principles derived from another line of thought altogether—a line concerned with the health of the emotions. For education, however, they stemmed instead from concern with the individual as a social being and a social participant, and they may be summarized, at least in part as follows:

That the child is not a small man, but different in his responses and capacities from the man, and different at different levels of his development.

That one should not thwart, crush, disregard the child and his purposes, but must instead treat them with respect, go along with them, cherish and honor them, for each day of life has its own value, and it is out of the fulfillment of childish purposes in always larger terms that he will conceive and ultimately achieve ever greater purposes.

That learning is complex and not simple, that purposes, feelings, attitudes, ways of life, and personal dedications are learned as well as arithmetic, geography, history, and spelling, and that these latter are not and cannot be learned without learning some of the former simultaneously.

That all learnings are social in nature, and are to be valued only in as far as they help make a kind of person who contributes richly, at best creatively, in his social milieu, and finds his basic satisfactions—and so happiness—in so doing.

A DEEPER PERSPECTIVE ON MOTIVE

As such conceptions as these were being studied, clarified, evaluated, carefully translated into more and more aspects of the total school program, and gaining ever wider acceptance, educational thinking was stimulated from another source to delve still further into conditions conducive to the development of healthy and happy personalities. This new thought stream derived from the study and treatment of the emotionally or mentally ill, and can be roughly designated as "the mental hygiene approach." It began to filter into books for teachers in a thin trickle about 1930, has been slowly but steadily gaining force ever since, and has by now become in some quarters a serious educational preoccupation. At first individuals made modest tentative proposals; by now a major movement may be underway.

In many ways the "mental hygiene approach" enlarged and deepened understandings of what had already been laid down in the advance that preceded; in no basic way has it yet proved contradictory. Both educator and mental hygienist hold that behavior is based on purposes, and can be explained in terms of purposes, but yet it is precisely in the concept of motivation that the two lines of thought in a sense diverge. It is not so much that they view purpose differently, or have different conceptions of it, but that it is seen in different perspective and context by each.

In the view of the education that derived from social philosophy, all motivation was subsumed under conscious purpose and intent: an identifiable and reportable wish, desire, goal, resolve. A person finds himself alone and lonesome, wants company, formulates a plan to get it, achieves his purpose, and is satisfied. Or a young man wants to be a doctor, and pursues his goal through studies that last through seven or eight years. Or a poor man to make a lot of money, or a rich one to make still more money. This is purpose as it is ordinarily known: of each and all of these it can be said that at least in some measure "they knew what they wanted."

To the mental hygienist's eye, behavior that is far less readily understandable is also purposive, satisfying some inner need: the person who suddenly feels lonely in the midst of company, the novelist who one day finds he can write no more, the person who always spends more than he makes, the depressed, the accident-prone. The behavior of all these, the mental hygienist says, is purposive.

There is much clinical evidence to the effect that an uneasy life of motive and purposiveness, of drive and yearning, is acted out, so to speak, without formulation in words or conscious intent. And this uneasy life accounts for the behavior of people who are needlessly tense, fearful, gloomy, out of tune wherever they go, unhappy and ineffective. There is some yearning they are trying to satisfy, some wish they want fulfilled, of which they are not aware. Their behavior speaks for them; they are unable to speak for themselves, for they know not what it is they are lacking, what they seek by conduct that is odd, repetitive, not nicely adjusted either to bring them satisfaction or to cope with what confronts them.

To describe and encompass the kind of purpose which is conscious, intentional, properly gauged, and adaptive to the changing circumstances through which it must be achieved, the mental hygienists posit a part of the personality—and just a part—which they call the *ego*, which has been defined as "the organization of individual experience." To the extent that favorable conditions have made it strong, this ego exercises control over experience.

But by this theory, the personality includes more than the ego. It includes also the tumultuous demands of the unsocialized organism and the incorporated prohibitions of the parents in the early years of life. If all goes well with development, the organic energies and impulses, whether of seeking or of avoiding, of love or of hate, find constructive outlet in socialized activity—in what the person does, thinks, imagines, creates. The prohibitions of the parents are formulated into a conscience that checks on the moral quality of acts and events—with feeling but not without responsible personal judgment. The ego is in control. Experience is organized fruitfully. Learning proceeds unimpeded. There is emotional health.

When all does not go well, organic energies and impulses find no sufficient channel into socialized activity. They are embattled with overweening feelings of the forbidden that impede the process by which they would under more propitious conditions find acceptable expression in the outer world of people, things, events. But since they are—or are by this theory assumed to be—true energies, they cannot be denied. They must and do find outlet, not in socially phrased and personally meaningful behavior, but in unusual manifestations, from tics to "temperaments"—and occasionally in serious emotional disturbances and mental disorders.

Now, it is strange, or perhaps not strange at all, that the definition of the ego used in this line of thought coincides with definitions of the self explicit or implicit throughout the most influential educational writing of this century. Which means only that educators in general have concerned themselves exclusively with the aspects of the total behavior of man that are accessible to ready identification and report, the ones in which socialization has progressed fairly and well, so that all is available for direct observation and examination. The odd, the inexplicable, the obscure they passed over—whether as irrelevant or as mystic it is impossible to say, but certainly as not important in describing the social nature of man or in studying its development. Now that means have been found for bringing the previously obscure to light, it becomes apparent that many of the factors back of unusual behavior are not only amenable to control but also furnish clues that are important in understanding all human behavior.

But what then, does this deeper perspective on motive, this view that there are purposes of which the organized self can give no account—what does it have to offer? In what ways does it enrich the educational thinking that preceded?

For those who have come to recognize that one must not crush the child and thwart his purposes, it offers an alternative view of what these purposes are, a more useful interpretation of developmental levels, and a more comprehensive conception of the child's readiness for any kind of learning.

The earlier educational way of thinking saw man as by nature active and purposeful, but took it that all purposes were specific and learned in the course of social experience. The corresponding assumption underlying the work of the mental hygienists is that the human organism is endowed with two basic motives or drives—the drive to secure affection, and the drive to achieve a sense of competence and assurance.

In order to lead eventually into fully socialized behavior these drives must, by this way of thinking, find certain relatively specific forms of expression and gratification at different stages—in infancy, babyhood, early childhood, later childhood, and so on. The stages identified by the mental hygienists can be roughly equated with the periods of growth described by the students of child development who worked at first without the mental hygiene point of view. But to descriptive accounts of characteristic behavior mental hygienists added a rationale concerning the orderly development of the basic drives.

The students of child development told how the child reacts at various stages of growth; the mental hygiene approach attempts an account of why he so reacts, and this provides at least a tentative basis for more insightful and intelligent adaptation of the environment: more sympathetic feeling toward child behavior, more complete understanding of it, greater direct helpfulness, and more astute ability to correct what may already have taken a wrong turn. For one is purblind if one sees, and so takes into account, only what the child now characteristically does. It is essential also to understand from this what he now characteristically seeks.

On careful consideration of this conception of drives and developmental stages, it becomes clear that the mental hygiene approach also adds a new proportion to the concept of readiness. Educators have accepted the idea that one does not impose reading, say, upon a child until he exhibits a certain readiness to read, or to begin to learn to read. To do so would be to thwart his purposes, and so to court evil consequences. But now there are also to be taken into account the child's strivings for trust and autonomy, and, by this age, for a sense of initiative (getting things started on his own) and for a sense of industry (sharing with others in bringing defined undertakings to completion). What role may learning to read play in relation to these?

Quite clearly the capacity to "read for himself" can fortify such sense of autonomy as he has already established, adding the amazing ability to gather meaning from the written word to the other things he can now manage on his own. In similar fashion, it can buttress his sense of initiative, since it unlocks the doors to so much new (though vicarious) experience that he can select and get under way in terms of "individual enterprise," so to speak. And bringing the task of learning to read to completion can contribute mightily to his sense of industry.

The child is not only ready to read, but straining at the leash to make progress in these other ways as well—in ways that refer to his feelings toward himself as a person and in relation to other persons. When this is borne in mind, the process of learning to read can be phrased to serve all these purposes, and so contribute largely to his sense of worth in life and to his sound growth as a personality.

A perhaps more crucial question arises where he fails to exhibit the readiness that might be anticipated of him. What does this indicate about the course of his progress in the definable steps on the way to maturity, and what can be done to help him? Its meaning may be little or much, but without understanding of its relatedness to the rest of what he does, and of what his basic strivings at this period of his life are likely to be, there is no way of telling.

For those who have recognized that learning is complex, that attitudes and ways of life are learned along with knowledge and skills, the mental hygiene approach has provided a firmer grasp on the wholeness of the person—physical, emotional, social, intellectual, spiritual—and a new conception of the integration of the personality.

The "whole person" has seldom been conceived as a true whole. Far more frequently he has been conceived as the sum of a number of parts or aspects: the physical, plus the emotional, plus the social, plus the intellectual, plus the spiritual. Sometimes intellectual status has been seen as a resultant of the forces exerted by other "parts" of the personality: it was observed that the child's capacity to learn was crippled if he was physically under par, emotionally disturbed, short on the kind of social experience that would provide intellectual stimulation. The parts remained, though to a degree mutually interdependent.

But the mental hygienists have found that the baby that is not properly loved fails to respond socially, does not develop intellectually, and is appallingly subject to all the ills that baby flesh is heir to. They have also found that how and when a baby is suckled can mean something akin to supporting love or its lack to him, so that he suffers many of the consequences of insufficient love if this part of what would ordinarily be called his "physical" care is infelicitous. And it would seem that with the young child it can also happen that if the intellectual environment is not stimulating in terms of his strivings, he becomes physically and socially apathetic.

These are intimations only of the organic wholeness of the personality, and they offer more on the effects of the "physical," the "social," and the "emotional" upon the "intellectual" than on the integral functioning of the "intellectual" in the whole. A beginning, if only a small one, has been made at analyzing the relations between physical and emotional states. There is evidence, if only clinical, on how interests and intellectual preoccupations change with physical and emotional conditions or appropriateness of social relations. But the bearing of intellectual nurture on sound total development beyond the stage of babyhood has still to be carefully investigated.

This is one aspect of wholeness in which the mental hygienists are beginning to provide a firmer grasp. But by the notion of the ego and other parts of the personality they provide still another facet to the concept of integration. Everyone is acquainted with the person who knows something is "all right," but cannot do it, or the one who judges it a moral obligation to take some action which he either knows at once he cannot take, or keeps postponing until the time for action has passed, or he finds himself involved in yet another dilemma. Clearly there is lack of integration here. The mind sees, the heart falters, and the hand fails.

Educators have attributed this to faulty integration in past learning situations. The person has learned to judge without having opportunity to carry through into action and to gain the accruing satisfactions. Mental hygienists offer another explanation. When a person sees what is right and wise and just to do, but cannot do it, they assume that the ego—organized individual experience—is not yet strong enough to carry the day against a sense of the forbidden; somewhere in the personality there dwells an overweening "thou shalt not" over which judgment, born of having tried this and tried that, having found success and failure, cannot prevail. Or the impulse life remains so comparatively strong that the lid must always be kept on tight.

As in the case of educators, the difficulty is assumed to be in past experience, but the effective factors in this experience are somewhat differently identified. It is not merely a matter of providing opportunities for judging on one's own, coming to one's own conclusions, carrying these conclusions out, estimating the results, and reformulating judgment and action in accordance. This process is involved surely, but only to the extent that the ego is adequate to it. Otherwise the submerged "thou shalt not's" of the early years give rise to a sense of guilt when independent judgment is exercised; and action fails to follow. Or, if it follows, there is too little basic satisfaction in it, too little exhilarating sense of adventure in accepting consequences and dealing with them, too much feeling of fear and doubt, no matter how "irrational." And the same holds when basic drives and impulses have not found adequate expression through socially acceptable channels.

For the baby or very young child in the home this means careful handling of necessary prohibitions, making them as far as possible reinforcements of his own dawning sense of self-governance as a socially responsible person. And it means also consistent and continuing efforts to help him find acceptable ways to give outward expression to the drives and impulses that may at first seem to him frighteningly ungovernable and "wrong." For the child in school it means at a minimum teacher understanding of the forces that bring about confusion and conflict, make good intellectual judgment unavailing, and either paralyze action or make it apparently capricious.

Should the difficulty be too great, past experiences having been too destructive to the developing ego, special therapeutic help may be required. But should the difficulty be not so great, it may be possible to reinforce the child's ego by standing behind him in his judgment; helping him to deal with the consequences; lending him assurance that consequences can be remade; letting him voice his feelings of incapacity and guilt until they, too, become elements that he can deal with; giving him confidence that his wayward, impulsive desires derive from his sound nature as a human being and can find their way into action and eventual fulfillment.

The proposal that the integration of the personality is ultimately dependent upon relationships with people who may either support the developing ego or undermine it leads to another enlargement that mental hygienists may have to make to the established thinking of educators. *For those who have come to recognize that all learnings are social in nature, it stresses the effects of social experience on the emotional life:* not only ideas, concepts, knowledges, and skills derive from social experience, nor even just the insights and outlooks, attitudes and ideals, that are related to these, but the very stuff of all feeling toward self, others, situations, and events. *In addition, it emphasizes the predominance of feelings towards persons in the child's experience, and the extent to which these feelings pervade his response to all new situations, whether primarily social in nature or not.* And it holds, furthermore, that the feeling life is prior and basic, playing such a fundamental role in experience that all other learnings are acquired in its terms.

The elements of propitiousness in healthy development need no recapitulation here, but it is to be carefully noted that they do not consist exclusively, or even primarily, of what the child responds to "intellectually," but rather in his relationships to other human beings—mother to begin with, and then mother and father, the rest of the immediate family, and gradually a widening circle for whom these first are for a long time (and in some instances forever) the prototypes.

When the fact that all aspects of experience are colored by feelings toward persons is taken seriously into account, the educator's now basic principle that one "learns to do by doing," taken baldly, requires modification. That one does not learn to do by reading about, or memorizing about, or reciting about, still stands, and that one cannot learn to do without doing. But it would yet appear that, in certain circumstances, one may do and still not learn to do, or not learn with full effectiveness, and that this may, more frequently than one might think, be due to the color of feelings for and against persons that tend to permeate all things, events, and undertakings.

This has, in certain large ways, already been recognized. It has been noted, for example, that one may learn to read by reading, and still have no great love of reading, and read as little as possible. The child's purpose in regard to reading, as well as in regard to other things, may be far more closely related to persons strategic in his emotional life than to any more intellectual intent. He may love and want the love of a parent, and so find the parent's interests and ennuis, the things he says and does and does not do, in all ways wonderful and to be emulated. Reading takes on emotional tone and meaning accordingly. Or his purpose may be to buttress an independence of which he does not feel too sure; he may want to "tell off" a parent who to him looms too large and dominant. Then he may seek opportunity to do precisely as the parent does not do, and reading either avidly or indifferently may offer him a means to distinguish himself from this parent, sometimes in no uncertain terms.

As clearly as basic concerns in the two fields of education and mental hygiene converge, however, and much as it can be demonstrated that mutual enrichment is to be derived from joint thinking and endeavor, resulting advances in the schools, though sure, have to date been largely sporadic, and more in the nature of adding one idea to another, or superimposing one upon another, than truly integrative.

But on due consideration, there need be no great surprise that advances should have been in general only tentative and fractional. The mental hygiene approach gives rise only to a new perspective, and calls for no radical departure from previous concerns and dedications; yet a new perspective is exceedingly difficult to perceive, and, without long practice, almost impossible to keep constantly in focus. In addition, mental hygienists and educators tend to speak in different tongues, and so find fruitful communication difficult and sometimes even painful to come by.

THE SCHOOL'S ROLE

In 1948, there were 27,134,126 children in the elementary and secondary schools, 24,036,505 of them in public schools, 309,984 in private schools, 2,787,637 in parochial schools. What are the school's potentialities for furthering the healthy personality development of all these children, and what its limitations? What is its role in relation to other influences in the life of the child? What is its special function?

If it were true, for example, that the personality is set in the very early years of life, the school would be powerless in relation to it. But whereas there is much evidence to the effect that the very early years are of major importance, there is also evidence that crucial phases of development occur during the years that follow.

At about the beginning of his school life the child either develops a sense of competence to bring defined tasks to completion or falls into a prevailing mood of incompetence and inferiority in relation to what confronts him. Later, he either identifies himself as a person, a prospective husband or wife, a worker in one or another line of endeavor, or remains always uncertain as to his place in the scheme of things and confused as to his role. In the latter years of his schooling he is at an age when he learns to give and share love in a characteristically adult way, or else remains an isolate, in a world unpopulated by other warm human beings.

In this developmental sequence the school surely has opportunity to influence personality in vastly significant ways, and there are many who believe that in contemporary society these steps in growth can be successfully negotiated only through propitious school experience. It is perhaps needless to point out that school experience can also either enhance or undermine whatever basic sense of trust, of independence, and of initiative the child brings with him from his earlier life at home.

Moreover, if the school's major function, in contradistinction to that of other institutions, is taken to be that of enabling the young to understand their world and to come creatively to grips with it, then the school has a role which is not only strategic but indispensable in the development of the healthy personality. For without some such capacity, growing appropriately through the years, both child and man are the butts of whatever befalls them rather than always more surely the masters of their experience. Without sound personality, mere intellectual understanding is of small avail, but when increasing understanding and skill are part and parcel of well-rounded growth they contribute mightily to robust feelings about self, others, and the manageability of oncoming events.

All this does not mean that the school operates either without limitations in relation to healthy personality development or in a vacuum. By the time the child comes to school he may already be so emotionally crippled that, without special therapeutic help, he is unable to grow through even the best-contrived of educational experience. Moreover, along with other institutions and agencies striving to contribute ever more effectively to the child's healthy, happy, and responsible living, the school is hampered by still inadequate information about the processes of human development. The field is new, and much remains to be fathomed. Theories of learning so far laid down are difficult to bring into harmony with emerging theories of dynamic psychology.

But it is not only other agencies with consonant aims in relation to healthy personality development that influence the growing child; school, other agencies, and child function in a society and a culture that profoundly affect them all in haphazard ways. For example, much attention has been called to the conflict between the democratic tradition to which the school is dedicated and certain anti-democratic practices and attitudes to which it is often prone, like authoritarianism in human relations, competitiveness rather than cooperation in the classroom and on the playground, racial segregation, and other less tangible forms of intergroup discrimination. This last includes an apparently widespread rejection, so taken for granted as to have been overlooked until recently highlighted, of children of low socio-economic status, and an almost wholesale oblivion to what the school may mean to them and to what they may require of it.

In all this the school only reflects contradictions in the culture. Whether or not such contradictions, purely in and of themselves, are deleterious to healthy personality development is difficult to say, in view of the fact that apparently all cultures are similarly confused and conflicted. There is some evidence that such damage as there may be to the personality varies with the age at which the conflict is encountered and the circumstances of the encounter.

Far more certain is the fact that the anti-democratic end of each conflict is harmful to personality; in this culture, democracy and healthy personality development go hand in hand, democracy providing by definition the most favorable conditions for wholesome living, and in turn requiring well-developed personalities for its proper functioning. In as far as the school can select and choose among the cultural influences it brings to bear upon the child, it therefore filters out, as far as possible, those contradictory to the democratic tradition, just as it attempts to filter out all other influences deleterious to health and wholesomeness.

SOME PERTINENT CURRICULUM CONSIDERATIONS

Traditionally the curriculum has been identified with the "course of study," and has consisted of an enumeration of the topics to be covered in the various conventional subject matter fields. More recently, it has come to be conceived as the sum total of the pupil's experience in the school. This change has resulted from increasing concern with the whole personality and from a new view of learning, by which purposes, feelings, attitudes, ways of life, and personal dedications are seen to be learned as well as subject matter, and by which it is recognized that subject matter is not and cannot be learned without at the same time learning attitudes and ways of life.

Wise selection of experiences appropriate to developing personalities is seemingly less difficult at the early childhood level than in the succeeding years of schooling. The younger child reveals himself more readily, the range of his abilities is narrower, it is comparatively easy to set a stage richly for his growth. By the time he reaches the intermediate grades he retreats from ready self-revelation to adults, and from this time till the end of his schooling the whole world of experience and knowledge, almost infinitely varied, is in some form accessible to him. How to select, arrange, and contrive successive experiences of optimum educational value remains a problem widely studied but still unsolved.

Concern with the pupil's purposes and interests was at one time interpreted to mean a kind of *laissez-faire* of pupil inclination, with a minimum of adult direction. As the idea took hold that desires and inclinations are also learned in response to social situations, adult responsibility for shaping learning experiences came again to the fore, and curriculum makers looked to social demands upon the individual as a source from which to draw curriculum content. More recently there have been repeated attempts to see pupil responsiveness and social demands bifocally, as it were, since in the deepest view human inclination and its social organization cannot be so totally disparate.

From the standpoint of healthy personality development, the question of who selects and regulates the child's experience—the child himself or the controlling adult—is phrased in terms of requirements for freedom and self-regulation, on the one hand, and for outwardly imposed limits on the other. On closer scrutiny, it would appear that the educators' approach to this question and the mental hygienists' refer to different aspects of the same thing, for the culture always poses limits and provides molds through which inchoate primitive inclination must express itself. Nevertheless, the teacher concerned with healthy development is not likely to fare well on the sociological phrasing alone. His impact in his relationships with his pupils is psychological in nature, and his shrewd estimate of required freedoms and limits in each particular situation would seem to be indispensable.

Practically speaking, experimental curriculum work is now based on pupil-teacher planning, the teacher keeping his eye on the so-called "functional areas of living" and on phrasing experiences in terms of the characteristic strivings of pupils at their various stages of development. These "functional areas" have been variously defined, but ordinarily include family living and other personal relationships, civic responsibility, vocational participation, leisure-time activities, maintenance of health—and a philosophy of life pertinent to all of these.

In part because the "functional areas" are indeed life areas and so not reducible to facile schematization, and in part because curriculum planning outside the conventional grooves beyond the elementary grades is still problematical, there remain many unresolved issues in each of these areas. As things now stand, these are not usually stated in terms of alternative effects on personality development, but this does not mean that such considerations are not inherent in them, or are not being increasingly taken into account.

To this there is perhaps one major exception: in the area of family living and personal relationships (sometimes extended to include intergroup relations and even all human relations), recent innovations propose the inclusion of material on the dynamics of behavior in curriculum content—the amount, nature, and relationship to other curricular experiences varying from one experimental situation to another. Such innovations pose a peculiar dilemma to educators concerned with sound social and emotional growth. On the one hand, the schools are dedicated to progressive intellectualization of all facets of pupils' experience, and surely emotions and relationships with people loom large among these. On the other, there is profound and probably well-based skepticism about the degree to which intellectual understanding about emotions leads to better emotional adjustment, and considerable concern that here a little learning may prove indeed a dangerous thing. The answer is thought by some to lie in how closely "learning about" is related to "living through," and in the deftness and insightfulness of teachers.

Before turning from curriculum content to methods of evaluating curricular experience, the role of the expressive arts in education and healthy personality development is perhaps worthy of some special consideration. This is because the expressive arts have been heavily leaned upon in some places to provide outlet for emotions quite rigidly controlled in all other parts of school life. But even in those places where it is recognized that emotions can at no time be strained out of on-going experience, the arts are used for the expression, objectification, and clarification of emotions, sometimes angry and destructive, that can find no other ready and socially acceptable outlet, and which, left unexpressed, are known to lead to some greater or less degree of emotional ill health. They are used also for the intensification and deepening of the whole emotional life. Sometimes art products serve the insightful as a means of learning about pupils' otherwise unrevealed feelings and even about the progress of their development.

But whereas it is generally recognized that drawing, painting, rhythms, and the like are a spontaneous and fruitful part of all healthy young children's activity, occasionally educators are now asking whether some older children, in accordance with their individual differences, may not find better media for artistry and creative expression in scientific experimentation, or in cooking, or in relationships with people than in any of the more conventional art forms. This leads directly to another line of thought which holds that all growth-producing learning is creative in nature, and this to still another, to the effect that true adult creativity in all spheres of life can derive only from having negotiated successfully all the several developmental stages.

Many of the moot questions in curriculum construction would long since have been resolved were available methods of evaluation equal to determining outcomes in the total personality. Then it would have been possible to put any given proposal for achieving favorable goals in child development to the test. But the growth process is not easily amenable to statistical measurement, because it is inherently irreducible to discrete units. Even the observation of isolated behaviors has its limitations because, in the sense of dynamic psychology, it is impossible to interpret any given bit of behavior except in the context of the whole.

In recognition of such difficulties, new methods of appraisal—like anecdotal records and behavior journals, a wide variety of projective techniques, and some sociometric devices—are finding increasing favor. Here the objection has often been raised that the subjective factor is so great as to render such methods no better than clinical observation in evaluating the relative success or failure of any given educational means for effecting change in feeling or in orientation toward self and others. Countering this, there is widespread opinion to the effect that to scorn the clinical is to reject the one appropriate methodology of appraisal now available in this area.

Recently a question has been raised concerning the effects upon children of constant and intensive use of evaluation in relation to all phases and aspects of school experience. Whereas the intention is to evaluate what is done in the school, the outcomes appraised lie in the behavior of the pupil. According to this point of view, he is therefore likely to feel himself under constant scrutiny, which to him may seem more unrelenting and critical than enlightening and helpful. Even when, as is ever more usual, he participates in the appraisal, he asks himself how he is doing, so to say, more frequently and persistently than is perhaps healthy. In addition, his teacher may sometimes come to feel more threatened than guided, with inevitable repercussions on his pupils. This may all be particularly bad for the child who comes from a home where parents are preoccupied with the significance of his every move.

HUMAN RELATIONS IN THE SCHOOL

In school, as at home and elsewhere, the quality of human relations is preponderant among all factors in furthering healthy personality development, and this quality is directly related to emotional stability and warm feelings toward others. Without stability and warmth on the part of teachers, supervisors, and administrators, knowledge about and machinery for improving human relations rest on a shaky foundation.

While emphasizing the importance of warmth, outgoingness, and spontaneity in the teacher's relationship with his pupils, it is perhaps pertinent to call attention to what, from the mental hygiene point of view, is conceived to be his essential role. His is not primarily the role of mothering the child in an intimate dependent relationship that gives large play to immediate gratification of impulse. Rather, he strengthens the child in his efforts to meet the social demands properly made upon him, and helps him find socially acceptable outlets for his feelings. Important among these demands and outlets are his relationships with other children and adults. The teacher properly helps him to cope with others, their feelings toward him, and his toward them. Among the teacher's chief means toward this end are his own basic acceptance of the child and the help he extends to him in attaining status in his group.

Sociometric techniques are a recently developed device intended to reveal the position of each child in a group in terms of the individuals he either seeks out or expresses a desire to be with, and the individuals who either tacitly or explicitly seek him. The teacher uses this information to surround each pupil as far as possible with others who accept him. There are those who doubt that such contrived experience of acceptance does in fact build basic confidence, or that status so acquired is felt in succeeding group situations. Evidence is still being sought. Still others question the advisability of so manipulating group situations, or even the necessity for it, when the group is small enough and fluid enough for the child to find his own way to status within it.

Concern with the contribution of group life to personality has also given rise to a movement for the study of group dynamics. Thus far this movement has contributed a variety of techniques designed to provide greater opportunity for the play of each individual's personality in the group situation. In addition, it has focused attention on an important area of investigation in social psychology closely relevant to the school's concerns.

The pupil's opportunity to find and feel status is perhaps most profoundly affected by the size of his class, the basis on which he has been assigned to it, and the number and intensity of invidious group distinctions reflected in the school. Classes are often so large that pupils can seldom even be perceived as individuals, still less helped to achieve a sense of self-worth in their midst. In addition, overlarge classes tempt to mass methods and much ordering about. Homogeneous grouping, originally designed to protect children from unfair competition, has created at least as many problems as it has solved, largely by giving rise to a kind of invidious distinction. The sense of discouragement, failure, and unworthiness which so frequently befalls children who find themselves in groups designated "opportunity," who are counseled to take vocational rather than academic courses, or who discover that they are in the "slow" reading group in first grade has been well established. Invidious distinctions that haunt the child outside of school as well as within—discrimination on the basis of color, religious affiliation, national background, socio-economic status — are probably even more destructive, and all too frequently the one kind of "setting aside" reenforces the other.

In effect, the whole of school organization is involved in providing the kind of atmosphere in which good human relations flourish. Teachers subject to the indignities of authoritarian administration, the harassments of unrealistic levels of attainment to which every child must be pushed, inadequacy of materials and equipment, too many petty clerical details, and the like are scarcely in an appropriate frame of mind for sensitive responsiveness. In such circumstances as these, pupils inevitably suffer from mounting irritabilities. Fortunately, more and more administrators over the country are devoting their best thought and the largest part of their energies to making their schools happy places in which to live.

GUIDANCE

The preceding discussion of the curriculum and of human relations in the school should make clear how deeply and widely the notion of guidance pervades all aspects of planning in the school concerned with providing optimum conditions for healthy personality development.

But if the younger child ordinarily finds with his teacher the individual relationship he requires, the older child, confronted with an increasing number of adults, a widening world of experience, and more and more important decisions to make, normally seeks and finds some grown person with whom he establishes a relationship of special confidence. At adolescence, too, the boy and girl turn more to people beyond the family for affection, sympathetic interests, and models of what they would like to become.

Partly in response to this, partly because so many schools cannot provide individual attention in the midst of their regular activities, and partly because the conduct of individual relationships with some youngsters on some of their problems requires special training and equipment, expert guidance workers with varying specialties are being added to the staffs of more and more schools.

The vocational counselor has at his fingertips the information required for making a vocational choice, is expert in the use of vocational interest and aptitude tests, knows about the role of work and work experience in developing healthy personality, and about where in the community such experience can be gained. The educational counselor is also expert in tests and measures, usually of the kind designed to identify academic capacities and talents, and is equipped to help youngsters plan and find the schooling that will be most productive for them. The school social worker brings special insights into human relations to bear on many kinds of problems, and is, in addition, well informed on community resources.

From the standpoint of healthy personality development, the prime requisites for every guidance worker are that he be adept at using individual relationships with youngsters in ways that free rather than bind, that he be sufficiently perspicacious about the dynamics of personality to identify the problems brought to him in their fullness, and that he be equipped to help youngsters deal with their individual problems with maximum effectiveness.

But neither guidance workers themselves nor the requirements for healthy personality development would have what has come to be known as "the guidance point of view" confined to individual relationships in some sequestered corner of the school. Case conferences in which guidance counselor, social worker, doctor, nurse, and all those who know a pupil pool their insight with his teachers have been one device by which the insights of each have been shared with all, and children have come to be known not only as individual personalities but as functioning wholes.

SCHOOL-COMMUNITY RELATIONS

The school is sometimes seen as the best place for rendering services known to be needed by all children for the simple and expedient reason that all the children are there. When services are introduced for this reason alone, without effort to integrate the service with the on-going educational program, it is somewhat as though the pupils were seen as a kind of "captive audience" and the school as a mere building to enclose them. Fortunately, however, always greater efforts are now characteristic of both schools and the personnel of special services to make the whole of the child's life in school an integrated experience.

School health examinations, for example, are less and less often isolated experiences, sometimes a little frightening, without relationship to anything that comes before or after in the school milieu. More often they are incidents in the whole functional area of health education, to which not only many subject matters but the whole design of school living contributes. The school doctor or nurse, if only part time, and no matter by whom employed, functions as a regular member of the school staff, participating in case conferences and contributing the insights derived from his or her particular training. In circumstances like these, the advantages of having health services as an integral part of the school are clear.

There are those who point out, however, that in their view, at least, it is fallacious to interpret the conception of the school community to mean that at best the school reproduces in miniature all the services and activities of the community outside. The community of the school has its own function. Through it, pupils learn to use all social institutions effectively and to participate in them creatively. And, in fact, this is what most schools attempt to do in the case of most social institutions and community agencies. The practice of introducing pupils to the community as a regular part of school work is increasing—its economic life; its health, welfare, and cultural institutions; the groups, religious, social, and cultural, that make it up.

By later adolescence, young people feel that they can move toward adult status only if they are taken seriously in the community and are allowed after some fashion to participate responsibly in its affairs. The educational problem then becomes to find real opportunities for this group to do real community work where their services will be regarded neither with condescension nor sentimentality and they may grow in the spirit of community service. Youth of low socio-economic status are thrust into adulthood by the necessity to work, but usually find themselves in the kind of job that offers little or no life enrichment and so confront school and community with another kind of problem.

All this would seem to call for strengthening the means by which school and other community agencies—such as museums, libraries, churches, health and welfare services—interested in children and youth now plan together and learn from one another, and for some special attention focusing on how the pattern of community services provides for healthy personality development.

SCHOOL-HOME RELATIONS

Since the young child looks both to parent and to teacher for help in coping with the problems of expressing himself and relating himself to others characteristic of his particular stage of development, it is clear that communication between home and school should be frequent, easy, and gauged to assure a certain consistency in the demands made upon him. As the child grows older, no longer needs so much consistency in his experience, and begins to take satisfaction in managing his own affairs independently, some schools have found it advisable to discontinue taking his parents in on what he does at school.

To the kind of communication between

home and school required for healthy personality development there are a number of obstacles, perhaps chief among which is lack of understanding of the fact that parents and teachers properly play different roles in the lives of children, both of them essential. This leads to occasional usurping of roles, and may even contribute to certain mutual jealousies and hostilities that all too frequently grow up in any case.

There are many open questions as to how this communication should take place and exactly what it should be about. Group conferences, individual parent-teacher interviews, home visits, letters, and various new-form report cards all are being used; obviously some of these must be supplemented by others for two-way communication. The content of communication for the purposes here proposed is never confined to a report of progress in the acquisition of knowledges and skills, and at its best varies with the parent, the teacher, and the prevailing relationship between them.

The home visit and individual parent-teacher conference also provide means by which the school may learn about the child's family and its cultural patterns. This knowledge may save the school from making a number of mistakes, both in interpreting the child's behavior and in guiding him.

In as far as home-school communication proves helpful to the parent in understanding his child and his own parental relationships, there is a certain amount of parent education implicit in it, whether called by this name or not. Because the fully trained teacher has a certain professional understanding of child development and human relations, there seems every reason for him to share with other professional people similarly equipped in helping the parents who turn to them. It has been found, however, that not every good teacher is good at parent education, and that frequently some special training for such work is advisable.

WHEN SCHOOLING BEGINS AND ENDS

Most children enter school at the conventional age of six, which approximates the time at which most of them are ready to gain a sense of competence in bringing shared tasks to completion and to assume some responsibility for their behavior. Considerably before this, however, the exuberant imagination and bursting curiosity of many youngsters have exhausted the resources their homes offer them for manipulation of the physical environment and exploration of relationships with people. In many of these instances, depending on home and family conditions, nursery school or kindergarten seem to be indicated as soon as the child is able to communicate his wishes and has developed a sufficiently deep sense of security and individuality. This means as early as about three years for some and later than five for others. All this points the necessity for making nursery schools and kindergartens far more widely available, as well as for considerable flexibility in policies on age of admission.

The fact that the school contributes richly to the healthy personality development of younger children is widely accepted; there is every reason to believe that it can make a similar contribution at least throughout adolescence. Gradually the statutory school-leaving age has been rising from fourteen to sixteen, and in some States it is now eighteen. Yet 50 percent of the students who enter high school drop out before graduation.

Many reasons and causes have been identified. Fewer than one might anticipate leave school because their earnings are urgently needed, but for many families the costs of even free public education are high—additional clothing, transportation, books, fees for student activities, and the like. The impossibility of going to college and the unlikelihood, in some communities, of finding a better job on the basis of longer schooling lessen incentive; moreover, 60 percent of the jobs in the United States do not require either college education or long vocational training. The reasons most frequently given by the dropouts themselves reflect school failure and school misery, and seem to point in the main to the fact that the school does not provide experience of value to them.

From other sources comes evidence to indicate that, as one student of the problem has put it, the term "squeeze-outs" is more apt. A large percentage come from backgrounds which leave them without the experience in abstract thought required for good showing on intelligence tests; they are not academically minded; their speech, clothing, and habits deviate from those of the middle income groups conventionally accepted as standard by the school. Early in their school careers they are segregated in large numbers into "opportunity groups," they fail, they "don't fit," and they feel it.

In as far as causes are sheerly economic, various ways out are being sought and some are being found. From the viewpoint of the school's responsibility there is also clearly much need for seeking—of ways by which children of one background may be equally valued with those of another; of curricular experiences designed less for college or vocation and more to give adolescents like these a sense of worthwhile activity, interest, and achievement; of far more individual attention than has been the lot of those many who have dropped out entirely without consultation and advice. Ways are being sought, too, to provide overlapping of school and job. Supervised work experience as a part of the school program, periods of work alternating with periods of schooling, and continuation school for fully employed young workers are some of the directions in which various school programs are experimenting.

SELECTION AND TRAINING OF TEACHERS

The school can contribute fully to the healthy personality development of its pupils only if teachers genuinely like and accept children, like the teaching relationship, and are equipped to guide and support the young as they grow and learn. All this calls for many new facets in the conventional forms of teacher selection and training.

For too long the achievement of certain academic standards has been the main if not the sole criterion for admission to most teacher training institutions, with little or no assessment of the candidate's reasons for wanting to teach, emotional orientations toward children, or general stability of personality. "Character," another common criterion for admission, referred in general to dependability, freedom from "bad habits," and good repute among certain members of the community, rather than to any more specific qualifications for teaching.

But already there is some experimentation looking toward emphasis upon the special qualities and characteristics of personality that bode well for future pupils. The means by which the likely are sorted from the unlikely are still in the experimental stage; sometimes they consist of a series of interviews skillfully conducted, sometimes interviews are based on a biography or personal case history, sometimes a variety of projective techniques are used. Occasionally a candidate is admitted on condition of securing some therapeutic help in the course of training.

Training itself is again still largely experimental, with much effort devoted to finding ways by which knowledge of child development, the processes of learning and growing, dynamic psychology, and the factors that influence personality development may become something far more vital than intellectual understandings alone. Participation in nursery schools and in work with older children and young people, keeping behavior journals, making case histories, participation in interdisciplinary case conferences are on a par with courses and study, complementing rather than supplementing them.

In some places it is also thought advisable to help students cultivate adult interests beyond those they have in children, growth, learning, and, for secondary teachers, a particular "subject matter area"—this for the sake of the linkages that are thought to develop between children's interests and the heartfelt pursuits of adults around them, the student himself, and his own further growth as a person. Generally speaking, work in the creative arts is highly esteemed for these purposes.

In some quarters it is thought that such selection and training will contribute to the solution of the problem of recruitment of teachers for the elementary grades. Poor salaries, limited community status, work under difficult conditions and often rigid supervision are among the major factors usually identified. But the argument runs that if teachers are selected because of their feeling for children and the teaching relationship, and are so educated as to become interesting people in their own right as well as more fully expert in guiding the growth and learning of children, their status will begin to rise, and a break will have been made in an erstwhile vicious circle.

INADEQUACY OF SUPPORT AND INEQUALITY OF OPPORTUNITY

No report on the schools at this time can fail to call attention, however briefly, to the inadequacy with which they are supported and the inequality in educational opportunity in different parts of the country. Larger numbers of children than ever to be schooled, lag in school building programs, higher salaries, and rising costs combine with a degree of public indifference to make money short everywhere for what the schools might do for children.

But while the average per-pupil expenditure is over $200 in fifteen states, it is less than $100 in four. One reason for this is the disproportionately large number of children to be schooled in some States—States which tend to have less than average per capita income. The results of inequality of educational opportunity show up in such statistics as those on the percentage of drop-outs and the number of young men classified as educationally deficient when called up for military duty.

From the point of view of what the schools can contribute to soundness of personality, personal happiness, and responsible citizenship, the number of other ways in which inadequate support and inadequate opportunity show up in the lives of individuals and the life of the Nation must be numerous and pervasive, though incalculable. Every consideration points in the direction of providing not only adequate but equal educational opportunity for all children of school age.

EDUCATION AND SOCIAL CLASS IN THE UNITED STATES[1]

W. H. Burton

DISCUSSION AND ANALYSIS

Dr. Burton, in his analysis of the two challenges presented to the United States by the goals of democratic education, demonstrates the essential unity of the various educational areas covered by this text. Despite the fact that we divide education into such fields as growth and development and educational sociology, we should realize that this is merely for convenience: basically, it is an organic whole. Before plunging into the problem, Dr. Burton must first touch on its historical backgrounds. He is further constrained by the demands of his subject to delve briefly into tests and measurement. What other related fields does his inquiry impinge on?

Dr. Burton believes that the elementary school has had greater success in meeting the first challenge—that of developing minimum literacy and basic citizenship—than the secondary school has enjoyed in meeting its tasks. Do you agree? Support your position with concrete data.

The second challenge to education in our times, says the author, is "to develop cultural unity within a diverse society simultaneously with development of individual talent." In what ways does social-class structure create and complicate this problem? What solutions are suggested? Dr. Burton deprecates "an education based on words." Yet he approves a number of books and also urges educators to study the communication arts. Is this an inconsistency?

"All the children of all the people." Education for all the children of all the people without let or hindrance, without invidious distinctions of any kind has been an aspiration and goal of life in our country from the beginning. The dream and the goal has already presented one challenge which we have partially met. A second and more fateful challenge may be emerging.

[1] From *The Harvard Educational Review*, Fall, 1953, pp. 243–256. Reprinted by permission. The author is indebted to Mrs. Marjorie W. McWhorter of Birmingham Southern College for surveying the literature in connection with preparation of this article.

BRIEF HISTORICAL BACKGROUND

The first Americans lost very little time in setting up schools. The Laws of 1642 and 1647 in Massachusetts Bay Colony requiring that free schools be provided in every village became the basis of our tax-supported schools. The early leaders, however, made no provision to compel parents to take advantage of the schools. We might speculate as to the causes. Was learning so respected that no one dreamed of failure to take advantage of schooling freely offered? Doubtless this was a factor along with other circumstances.

The first law requiring children to go to school was not passed until 1852, almost exactly two centuries after the first laws providing for schools. The last state to pass such a law did so in 1918 although practically all states had such laws by 1900. A process of lengthening the compulsory period and of sharply tightening these laws has gone on since approximately 1900 and particularly since 1915. We need not go into the causes for this, since our purpose for the moment is directed to the effects.

THE EFFECT OF COMPULSORY ATTENDANCE

The eventual effect was that from 1915 onward our democratic dream of education for all the children of all the people became, on the elementary level, an actuality. Therein lay our first and serious challenge.

The school of the United States, despite our aspirations, was until the present century an aristocratic or class school. It catered largely to the so-called "better" classes. Oversimplifying we may characterize the early school as one organized:

a. for children who wished to attend or whose families wished them to attend.
b. for children with the interest and (generally) the ability to get along in the abstract and verbal schooling then offered.
c. for children who were probably going beyond the first levels and whose families supported the ambition for more schooling.

Now then, what happened? Into the school so organized came hordes of children who:

a. did not wish to attend and whose families often did not value education.
b. had no interest and little ability (generally) for the type of education offered.
c. were not going to school beyond the compulsory limit and whose families (generally) supported the exodus into some gainful occupation.

In addition to all the normal children came the lame, the halt, and the blind, the tubercular, the undernourished, the mentally deficient, the already delinquent.

Part I. The First Challenge to Our Schools: To Develop a Minimum Literacy and Simple Fundamentals of Citizenship

For the first time in all history a nation and its schools were called upon to educate all the children of all the people—and do it in the school so far designed for the selected few. We accepted the challenge, but not at first.

The first reaction of the school was to maintain the historic and traditional materials and methods. This was education and had been for some centuries. The "best people" had long approved it. If the "new people" now coming to school could not master it, could not learn, they merely represented proof of the ancient belief that the common people were unfit for education. A sad and tragic era ensued. Elimination from school was shockingly great. The army and census figures showed that in 1914 less than fifty per cent of adult Americans had finished the sixth grade. The harsh and unsympathetic treatment caused the elimination and must have been a factor also in much delinquency and bad citizenship.

One of the great glories of our democracy and of our educational leadership is that we eventually accepted the challenge to meet this unprecedented situation—to educate all the children of all the people.

The turn of the century saw the development of the first so-called intelligence tests and the first subject matter achievement tests. Faulty as the early instruments were, they opened great new vistas. The huge range and nature of individual differences, commonplace now, gave new purposes and directions to the school. Eventually great amounts of information became available showing that the intellectual ability to handle abstractions was not the only kind of intelligence. Other important mental, social, and motor abilities came in for consideration. The range and complexity of special abilities and of special disabilities was increasingly understood. Diagnostic methods and the increasing knowledge of causes of disabilities encouraged the development of so-called remedial measures.

A great body of new knowledge was also being developed in psychology generally, in learning theory and process particularly. Factors far outside the school room were now known to affect achievement in class. Research supplied more new material on personality development, and eventually on causes of personal maladjustment. Controls of behavior such as behavior patterns, constellations of understandings, attitudes, abilities and skills came to be recognized as highly desirable products of education and of learning, along with the typical subject matter outcomes of the traditional school.

The dynamic nature of our democracy, together with far better understanding of democracy, not merely as a political process but as a social theory and way of life, increasingly affected our educational belief and practice.

The educational system of the United States, aided by the great resources in new knowledge met the challenge, namely, to develop an education to serve the wide range of individual differences brought to the school by the influx of all the children of all the people. The most extensive revolution in curriculum content and in methods of instruction ever seen eventually emerged. An important fact, which becomes more important as we consider later the second challenge, is that the answer to the first challenge was aimed at the personal goal of minimum literacy with introduction to citizenship as the only social goal considered. Individual differences between and among persons was the key. This was simple business compared to the new challenge now emerging.

SUCCESS HAS BEEN FAR GREATER ON THE ELEMENTARY LEVEL THAN ON THE SECONDARY

The educational revolution to date is confined largely to the elementary school. The elementary level, both leadership and rank and file, is committed in theory and well on the way in practice to real adjustment to the range of individual differences. Hopelessly unfit curriculums and instructional methods persist but the main battle has been won.

The challenge did not confront the secondary school until the 1930's and stemmed from a set of circumstances different from those which confronted the elementary school. The compulsory attendance laws did affect the secondary schools somewhat, but the huge increase in enrollment followed the depression and the fundamental change in the labor market. The application of the principles of democracy is having some effect but so far chiefly on theory.

The secondary school with approximately seventy per cent or more of eligible students enrolled is now challenged as was the elementary school a third of a century earlier. The leadership in American secondary education is keenly aware of the facts and of the situations created. Individual secondary school staffs here and there are making magnificent efforts to meet the challenge. The secondary school generally, however, is relatively untouched by the developments of the first half of the twentieth century. Again we can not digress into causes; we are concerned for the moment with the facts and possible effects. Conditions within the huge majority of secondary schools are similar to those in the elementary schools before the revolutionary changes. Curriculums and methods are still formal, abstract, verbal, and unrealistic. Students are not introduced in any sensible way to the century in which they live, to its truly great strengths and achievements, to its dangerous tensions, to its imminent and fateful decisions. Certainly they are given no guidance for the second half of the century in which they will live and participate in decisions. So far nothing much has happened beyond tinkering with curriculums and methods. Excellent theoretical proposals are available, but resistance on the practical level is unbelievably stubborn.

The second challenge, discussed below, affects chiefly the secondary school, as the first did the elementary school though both are vitally involved. Failure to meet this challenge may result in (a) the relegation of the present type of secondary school to the status of an extra-curricular activity with a new institution rising to meet the challenge, or (b) in a serious blow to the advancement of democracy in the United States. The first challenge was reasonably well met when all types and conditions of children were given the opportunity to achieve literacy and an introduction to our democratic citizenship. The second challenge is far more complex, aiming at that degree of cultural literacy, moral responsibility, creativity, necessary for the constant upgrading of democracy.

Part II. The Second Challenge Emerges: to Develop Cultural Unity Within a Diverse Society Simultaneously with Development of Individual Talent

The scientific research and philosophic inquiries of the first quarter of the century made us aware of individual differences among learners, of the importance of personality development, and of the principles of democracy as applied to individuals. The second quarter of the century saw the development of another great body of new knowledge, this time in group dynamics, the democratic implications of group discussion and decision, in human relations and particularly in social and cultural anthropology. The anthropologists have demonstrated the social class structure of our society. The implications of these findings raise certain serious questions and present a basic challenge to our society and particularly to the schools.

The people of the United States have been committed from earliest times to a theory of society in which there are no classes, or at least no absolutely insuperable class barriers. Any man, we assert, is free to improve his status, that is, to move upward in the social structure. Education is one of the means, if not the chief means through which the individual may improve himself and his social status. All our far-flung structure of free schools flows from this, plus our insistence enacted into law that all must be exposed to education for a stated number of years.

As we shall see, a number of grave questions arise when we examine theory and practice both in social process and in educational practice. Before proceeding to these questions, let us examine some of the immediate facts, practices, and implications.

THE IMMEDIATE IMPLICATIONS FOR EDUCATION OF THE SOCIAL CLASS STRUCTURE

The culture in general and the particular segment of the culture within which the individual grows up influence learning and behavior in a fundamental manner. Teacher education, until recently, has neglected this vital factor affecting education.

Cultures impose upon their participants a basic set of values and social habits for controlling everyday life activities. Certain general roles are expected of all children as they grow up: a sex role, an age role, and in developed cultures a social class role. A caste role based on race, color, or creed may sometimes be present.

Each child brings to school a collection of values, beliefs, and attitudes, plus behavior patterns through which the values and meanings are expressed. Cultural factors over which he has no control play an important part in making him what he is. These factors are, of course, affected by and affect the biological processes of growth or maturation, the range of individual differences, the interests, purposes, and needs which the individual develops. The constellation of influences playing upon the child is complex; the effects of single components are difficult to trace. Influence is often subtle and hidden from casual observation. Anyone who rears or teaches children must, however, possess such facts as we have at this time. Equally one must be cautious in drawing generalizations, in attributing certain results to one or another factor without reference to the total picture. There is no such thing as "the child." Each one is "a child" with his unique collection of beliefs and behaviors.

The social classes differ materially in approving or stigmatizing certain beliefs, values, and behaviors and in their regard for education. Middle and upper classes particularly stigmatize, in the lower classes, what the upper classes call laziness, shiftlessness, irresponsibility, ignorance, immorality. Within the lower classes, however, some of these are accepted ways of behavior, possessing background and rationale. The lower classes are likely to resent in the upper classes what lower class individuals call "snootiness" or snobbery, good manners, proper language, lack of aggressiveness, or unwillingness to fight.

The middle and the upper-lower classes also believe in and impress on the children the value of "getting ahead" or of "bettering one's self" in life. Children in the middle class largely resist strongly the class values and habits imposed upon them, preferring the less controlled behaviors of the lower classes. Children in the lower classes quite generally accept the values and behaviors of their class. Significantly the latter group is often unaware that its language, manners, and standards are quite unacceptable within other groups.

The efforts of parents and teachers to socialize children precipitates constant conflict between the psychological drives of children and the pressures of the culture. The child's need for physical activity, for sensory enjoyment, for self-direction, and for prestige with age mates fights hard against restraints, controls, and demands for conformance.

Many of the conflicts between parents and children or teachers and children result from grave lack of insight into the nature and effects of constant pressure, open or subtle, to conform to social values and roles. Parents and teachers regard the procedures they use in socializing children as natural and desirable. The *adults* are not even aware that there is any pressure. The *children* are keenly aware of it. The emotional cost to both may be very high. Parents and teachers become irritated and angry. Children become destructive, antagonistic, or sullen, or retreat into periods of negativism. These are not manifestations of "original sin" or of an evil disposition; they are but defenses against the constant "cultural bombardment." The more social the requirements, the more arbitrary and unjust they seem to the "natural" child.

Certain further facts may be summarized briefly as follows:

First, it is important to know that the children in our schools are drawn from the social classes in approximately these percentages: three per cent from the upper class, thirty-eight from the middle class, and fifty-eight from the lower class.

Second, the teaching body, in contrast,

is drawn largely from the middle class. Many teachers simply cannot communicate with lower class children and have no idea of the beliefs and motives of these children. The children in turn trying to communicate are abashed at criticism of their language and behavior which is quite acceptable within their own social group.

Third, the school has generally been geared to the aims, ambitions, moral or ethical standards of the white, prosperous middle class, Protestant, Anglo-Saxon population.

Fourth, the school is not organized to capitalize upon the non-verbal types of intelligence often found among children who have not had access to or constant contacts with books. The school often does not recognize the emergence of high intelligence and creative behavior in forms other than the abstract verbal type long fostered by the school.

The school generally attempts to impose middle class values upon huge numbers of lower class children. Problems, assignments, projects set by the school are, therefore, not at all the same problems when tackled simultaneously by upper and lower class children. The motivations are not at all alike. Many lower class children simply do not value the objectives and processes of the school, hence do not try. The school immediately dubs these children "unintelligent," "uncooperative," or "stubborn." The old class clichés may enter; the children are lazy, shiftless, irresponsible. The facts are that the school often simply does not meet their needs or ambitions, does not operate within their framework of values and motivations. The very tests of intelligence (so-called) and of achievement are now known to be heavily weighted toward middle class experience, knowledge, values, and beliefs. The lower class child, to use his own expression, "Can't win." The school does not give its typical rewards generally to lower class children.

Fifth, the school achievements and the degree of understanding and loyalty to our society and culture are thus definitely affected by the class origins of the children.

The middle class regime simply does not socialize the lower class children. They are neither believers nor participants in the cultural heritage of middle class society. The method of cultural training used by the school has basic effects upon children's *inward acceptance* of cultural objectives, as differentiated from outward conformance. The effects upon morality, delinquency, mental hygiene, and personality development generally are often not what the school thinks they are. We know now that learning situations wherein the child can identify himself with the total social group including adults are far more effective than methods of imposition and pressure.

Sixth, we should note, though this is not strictly a class structure matter, that the gifted child in our schools is often as sadly neglected and unstimulated as is the lower class child.

The school is challenged under the American faith to develop integration and unity within our diverse society; to develop persons possessing, in terms of their capacities, cultural insight, standards, taste, and above all moral responsibility; persons committed to the democratic process in our national life and in the world.

The eight-point discussion which follows is based upon acceptance of the historic American beliefs about society, the individual, and education. Certain very serious questions about the acceptance of these beliefs and the effect of changing beliefs upon education are reserved for the very end of this article.

Detailed development of this challenge would fill a volume. A series of statements with brief supporting discussion must suffice here.

1. All levels of educational workers should be familiar with the structure of

our society; particularly with the summaries of the characteristics of the several social classes making up our society.

The processes of education, of learning, and of teaching can be based only upon the experiential background, the goals and motivations of the learner. This is a commonplace. Any extension of experience, improvement of goals and motivations can be achieved only by methods which do not ignore or insult the learner's origins and present value system, thus preserving his security while challenging to growth and improvement.

2. All levels of educational workers should be familiar with the structure of human personality and the conditions of its growth.

3. All levels of educational workers should be sensitive to efforts to state the over-all goal for our society and for education within that society; should constantly engage in critical analysis designed to keep these goals abreast of new knowledge about society and persons.

The desired goals in any dynamic society are in constant need of critical analysis, reassessment, and restatement. A common cultural background making for common aims, beliefs, and loyalties, together with provision for free development of individuality and creativity are essential to any society.

The values and beliefs of any one social class cannot be imposed upon the society. Several writers have pointed out that certain values and processes of the lower class, usually ignored, may well possess social value. The characteristics of a desirable personality, of desirable social process, desirable social institutions need to be restated constantly as new knowledge and insight appear. The implications of the general aim for the more immediate cultural and personal objectives need to be stated in far greater detail than heretofore and far more clearly. We will doubtless always have social classes but equally important is the preservation of upward mobility and the development of necessary cultural integration and unity.

4. All educational workers should be constantly engaged in the reorganization of curriculum materials and instructional processes with special reference to our new knowledge concerning the nature of our society.

The curriculum movement has been under way for some time in our society and will continue under the impetus of new knowledge, which in fact has been the case always.

Several pages could be filled, at this point, with illustrations. Details of curriculum content and instructional procedures could be listed, all showing the almost complete neglect of the facts concerning the structure, problems, tensions, and maladjustments growing out of this special situation.

Books used in beginning reading practically never base content upon the experience known to the whole range of children using the books. The experience of the huge majority is, in fact, usually ignored. The very books designed to teach children to read actually cannot be read by some of the children. Not a single series of readers includes the experience of lower class children. Certain authors of individual books for free reading by children have boldly broken with tradition and are presenting the lives of many different types within our society. Books such as *Steppin' and Family* by Hope Newell, and *Tobe* by Stella Gentry Sharpe tell of the Negro without caricaturing him. *New Broome Experiment* by Adam Allen portrays the stupidity of anti-Semitism, while John R. Tunis, in *The Keystone Kids* aims at breaking down prejudice against any minority. *Blue Willow* by Doris Gate is the story of a family of sharecroppers, while Caroline R. Stone's *Inga of Porcupine*

Mine tells of miners' families in Michigan. Eleanor Estes is the author of books dealing with people who are not especially prosperous. These are but promises of what must appear in all subject areas.

History and geography are often presented with no bridge from the backgrounds of meaning possessed by the children. The lack of background necessary to understand is usually ignored. Verbal presentations of places the children will never see are unrelieved by any aids toward reality. Equally, no attention is paid to the possible use and value of these materials in the lives of the particular children being taught.

Details, as stated, could be multiplied indefinitely. The result is an education consisting too largely of verbalisms about the nature and problems of our society, instead of experience with social organization and decision making. The outcomes are glib repetition of the verbalisms with no understanding and certainly no appropriate patterns of behavior.

A sweeping and fundamental revision in curriculum materials and instructional processes is needed. The important curriculum movement already present in our schools needs redirection. The attention given to individual differences in ability, in types of interest and endeavor, in achievement should now be supplemented with attention to the facts concerning differences between and among discernible groups.

The basic revision of the nature and distribution of the rewards of the school, marks, prizes, special recognition of any type, the methods of reporting and using evaluations is a part of this curricular development.

5. All educational workers should study the field and processes of the communication arts, with special reference to communication between and among groups of differing backgrounds, goals, and values.

6. All educational workers should be able practitioners of the group process, and of leadership therein.

7. All educational workers should work for increased school-community interaction.

This has always been important and is doubly so in light of the knowledge about the social structure of the community. Only through genuine interaction can educational workers understand the community (from local to international level), and the community understand classroom procedures and the purposes of education.

8. Education is challenged above all to be real.

An education based on words and gained through words has always been a poor preparation for a world of things and persons. Now it is doubly incompetent. Talking about the tensions and maladjustments of our society, of the effect on our society of differing class values and ambitions is not the same as participating in these problems. The strength and achievements of our society can be learned and will beget loyalty only through participation.

TEACHER EDUCATION AND THE NEW CHALLENGE

The sharpest focus in all this is on teacher education. A number of bold, creative efforts are appearing. New patterns of provocative and promising nature are under trial. In general, however, many engaged in teacher education are incredibly unaware of the nature of the society in which they live, incredibly unaware of the problems of many types of persons trying to live in our changing, insecure, and frightening world. The practice in the field is far too often a soggy mediocrity.

The public does not pay for the teacher or the teaching we need—and thereby may hang a disastrous story in the future. This should not prevent our stating goals and working for them.

The teacher should be an educated person, loyal to his own society but a part of the world society also. A teacher who is to inspire respect for the basic values of the society in which the learner is to live must know and believe in the long cultural history of that society. A teacher who is to aid learners to face courageously our changing, often insecure and frightening world, must know why society is in revolution currently; must know how human beings live and grow, must know their motivations and frustrations, their cultural likenesses and differences. A teacher fundamentally ignorant of the structure of his society, and equally ignorant concerning the growth of human personality, cannot aid individuals to become citizens of their world.

A teacher must not only know the moral and ethical values, the persistent truths of his society but must have actively developed a code of values for himself. A teacher fundamentally ignorant of moral values, who has never developed any values or appreciations of his own cannot possibly contribute to the growth of moral character. Giving devices for the development of "citizenship" to a teacher ignorant of the structure and process of democratic society is absurd.

We seem to be in a world-wide period of what may be called "unmorality." This characterizes many aspects of life from day to day, from person to person relationships to international relations. The struggle within and between groups intensifies all this. Understanding, tolerance, recognition of worth between and among all groups within our society and between societies must be achieved. "Civilization is (in truth) a race between education and disaster."

The most important factor in cultural unity and stability may be moral responsibility. It may even be the crucial factor in the integration or disintegration of a mobile, dynamic society. The teacher needs above all to know the place in life of a philosophy or a religion and to have developed one of his own. Achieving cultural unity within a diverse society is not impossible, but it will not come of itself. The challenge to education and to all agencies of enlightenment is unmistakable and not to be escaped or denied.

The problem is intensified by the worldwide "revolt of the masses." Individuals and groups now sit in places and control operations heretofore controlled by very different persons and groups. The new group brings its values and procedures with it. Condemnation of either group by the other is useless. The development of common values designed to achieve improvement of life for all groups should be our concern.

THE MORE REMOTE AND FATEFUL ASPECTS OF THE CHALLENGE

Education is a part of the social process, the school a part of the social structure. Education and the school cannot ever be free from the influences already at work in society, nor from trends which appear. The school reflects the society and culture within which it operates, and must participate in, and influence, any changes which occur.

The class structure within any society contains a number of factors quite apart from education which also affect mobility upward within society—or downward for that matter. Evidence exists, as stated earlier, that education as administered may actually interfere with social mobility and curtail opportunity—a direct reversal of the original faith and practice.

Educational leaders, both theoretical and practical, must be well informed concerning the life of their society, the factors and trends within it which bear upon the thing education was originally designed to do.

Question. Is education at the mercy of the structure of society? Should we direct education openly toward acceptance of and integration with existing structure? Or, can education do something to influence trends within our society?

The actual situation within society becomes, in the light of these questions, a crucial matter. School leaders, practical and theoretical, are remarkably ill-informed concerning the *actual* philosophy and process of their society.

Question. Should education accept and continue to operate on the basis of the typically accepted American tradition that any and all should aspire to life work within what are usually called the more favorable areas: the professions, skilled technologies, independent enterprise in business, or at least to top level directorial positions in industry and commerce?

Some of these areas are desperately overcrowded. Experience in European countries raises serious questions about the social utility of this procedure. A serious question, stated next, emerges at this point.

Question. Do we as Americans *really* believe in our ancient faith—a relatively classless society, or one at least with relatively easy upward mobility for anyone, and surely with no artificial barriers to individual improvement?

Have we in fact deserted our traditional faith in democracy and in the uniqueness of the individual and accepted uncritically the class structure and the placement of given persons in given classes without opportunity (or possibility) of movement from class to class?

Certain people become furiously angry upon hearing the question. Others cynically regard the question as foolish if to them the obvious answer is that we do not believe in or practice our original philosophy. The reaction of serious and loyal Americans is to look the facts in the face seriously and then to try to develop some answers.

We state *explicitly* in many places and on many occasions that we firmly uphold the faith, but the actual operation of social process and of education within the school gives cause to suspect *implicit* acceptance of a far different social and educational theory.

No one knows the answer but our practices raise serious questions and dilemmas. Educational practices briefly mentioned in earlier pages are illustrations. The differentiation of curriculums which is a prominent characteristic of our secondary schools is ostensibly based on "differences in ability." The ability considered is always but one of the important abilities; namely, that required for abstract, verbal, academic work. Others are ignored. Worse than that, the differentiated curriculums are closely related to class differences within the population. The statement is made openly or by implication that certain individuals are destined for certain levels within society. If this is because of their class origins and not because of their "abilities," then we have a serious interference with democratic process. The cosmopolitan high school with a wide range of courses under one roof is often referred to as a "democratic" school. It is in fact not democratic at all. The basis is a design fundamentally different from democracy as American tradition has upheld it.

The developments in the secondary school have been generally produced by the "practical" schoolman, so-called. The operations of the "practical" man are usually based upon expediency, lack of information, and naïve lack of critical insight. The theoretical leaders have also a professional error, namely, the promulgation of doctrinaire solutions due to ignorance of, or failure to recognize, the harsh limitations of reality. *Present unfavorable practices may, therefore, result not from any failure of our faith but from lack of ability and failure to pay attention to such facts as we have.* A number of current proposals by competent theorists and a number of practices developed by competent practical leaders may point the way to a better reassessment of both the extent of our faith and our ability to develop practices in accord with that faith.

Question. Should we not overcome our traditional antagonism to intellectual differences; outgrow our refusal to face the facts of intellectual differences? That is, should we not accept and operate upon knowledge that there are differences in intellectual ability?

Should we not recognize that (a) there are other abilities than the intellectual, with differences here also between persons, and (b) that the other abilities than the intellectual are necessary for the common life?

Granted these facts, we may then attack the two major problems (a) providing general education for all simultaneously with (b) provision for special or differentiated education in terms of individual talents within all of the abilities. One difficulty is to provide general education, common purposes and values thus avoiding artificial divisions within society, and at the same time to maintain a level of quality in the general materials. The other difficulty is to select the various abilities and talents for special training without at the same time unwittingly introducing undesirable group distinctions.

All societies are differentiated except pioneer societies and even there, recognition is given to different contributing groups to the safety and development of the group. We propose here a recognition of differences in capacity on which a democratic system can be built.

Question. Have we the courage and the ability to develop curriculums based not on supposed differences in "ability" but on the hypothesis that we can provide experiences enabling all types and degrees of ability to achieve common cultural understandings, common values, and common understandings of the work of the world?

Have we the courage and the ability to develop curriculums for specialized training and to work for elimination of invidious distinctions between curriculums and their aims?

The answer to those questions turns upon the question that is probably basic to the whole discussion. It is:

Question. Should the leaders of our common life, together with the school workers, stand for a theory of society which would respect and honor any and all types of human endeavor; would regard any contribution to the common life as worthy, regardless of level of difficulty, skill, intangible or material rewards?

The implication is probably nearer to our ancient democratic faith than are most of the current statements and practices. Acceptance of the hypothesis would entail grave responsibility upon all who participate in any capacity in our social process. Particular responsibility rests upon all who are concerned with processes of enlightenment of any type. A long, slow, tedious process of developing and greatly expanding insights within the body politic is indicated, not to mention the tremendous task within the technical processes of schooling in particular and popular enlightenment in general.

A number of alternative conclusions seem to be apparent. We are now actually operating an educational system based on assertions and assumptions of democracy within society, opportunity for individual advancement, but actually showing practices which deny this. Do we wish to continue this or to substitute something else? The answer will depend upon a far more careful analysis of (1) the actual values and beliefs of our society, (2) the assumptions of our educational system, of the practices of that system, and more important, the relation between assumptions and practices.

1. Do we wish to continue a system based on one set of assumptions, but denying these in practice, at least in part? (The cosmopolitan high school with differentiated courses actually operates on acceptance of the class stratification of society, in large part. The very small high school operates as if there were but one class in society, the others being blithely ignored.)

2. Do we wish boldly and aggressively to reaffirm our original faith in a democratic society, with opportunity and mobility, and then stand up and fight for an educational practice in line with the faith? (This means the rejection of expediency and of the retreat into verbalism, and of the retreat from action. This calls for acceptance of a moral imperative, the avoidance of which will entail severe setbacks to education, and could conceivably contribute ultimately to a social disaster of considerable magnitude.)

3. Do we wish with equal boldness to accept stratification in society with its full and ultimate implications and go boldly about the business of education for it?

The latter would probably be universally condemned by our society—without awareness that we could fall into that very practice for lack of clarifying our assumptions and practices. The only legislative proposal for dual schools ever to emerge in our country aroused such a storm of opposition that it has never seriously appeared again. The practice, however, might easily slip up on us unawares.

Our choices depend upon answers to the several questions propounded. Facts relating to some of the questions do not exist. They will be secured in some instances with great difficulty. The writer does not know the answers. He does believe, however, that answers must be developed. Securing the answers must precede the answering of the great current challenge which is emerging. The rising generation of social and educational leaders will not join the ranks of the unemployed for some time.

SEGREGATION IN THE PUBLIC SCHOOLS

Excerpt from the United States Supreme Court Decision, May 17, 1954[1]

DISCUSSION AND ANALYSIS

No more significant and far-reaching change has come about in the public schools in this half-century than will result from the implementing of this decision. Proponents and opponents are going to be arguing the merits of the case long after the Court's final pronouncement is made. How do you feel about this issue? In what ways have your own past educational experiences colored your view of this problem?

As you read these brief remarks with which the Supreme Court explained the basis for its decision, do you recall some of the comments on healthy personality development in the Midcentury White House

[1] Mr. Chief Justice Warren delivered the opinion of the Court.

Conference Report that have a familiar ring? Some people have called this decision a sociological rather than a legal document. Why do you think this is so? Does this invalidate the Court's decision in your mind? Why or why not?

The courts have had a great deal to say about what goes on in education, surprising as that often seems to those who are newly acquainted with the field of education. You may be interested in reading some of the actual cases and decisions which affect in an important way what you do or do not teach. You will find an excellent presentation and summary in Peter Bachrach, *Readings in Freedom,* Stackpole Press, 1953.

. . . We must consider public education in the light of its full development and its present place in American life throughout the Nation. Only in this way can it be determined if segregation in public schools deprives these plaintiffs of the equal protection of the laws.

Today, education is perhaps the most important function of state and local governments. Compulsory school attendance laws and the great expenditures for education both demonstrate our recognition of the importance of education to our democratic society. It is required in the performance of our most basic public responsibilities, even service in the armed forces. It is the very foundation of good citizenship. Today it is a principal instrument in awakening the child to cultural values, in preparing him for later professional training, and in helping him to adjust normally to his environment. In these days, it is doubtful that any child may reasonably be expected to succeed in life if he is denied the opportunity of an education. Such an opportunity, where the state has undertaken to provide it, is a right which must be made available to all on equal terms.

We come then to the question presented: Does segregation of children in public schools solely on the basis of race, even though the physical facilities and other "tangible" factors may be equal, deprive the children of the minority group of equal educational opportunities? We believe that it does. . . .

To separate them from others of similar age and qualifications solely because of their race generates a feeling of inferiority as to their status in the community that may affect their hearts and minds in a way unlikely ever to be undone. The effect of this separation on their educational opportunities was well stated by a finding in the Kansas case by a court which nevertheless felt compelled to rule against the Negro plaintiffs:

Segregation of white and colored children in public schools has a detrimenta effect upon the colored children. The impact is greater when it has the sanction of the law; for the policy of separating the races is usually interpreted as denoting the inferiority of the Negro group. A sense of inferiority affects the motivation of a child to learn. Segregation with the sanction of law, therefore, has a tendency to retard the educational and mental development of Negro children and to deprive them of some of the benefits they would receive in a racially integrated school system.

. . . We conclude that in the field of public education the doctrine of "separate but equal" has no place. Separate educational facilities are inherently unequal. Therefore, we hold that the plaintiffs and others similarly situated for whom the actions have been brought are, by reason of the segregation complained of, deprived of the equal protection of the laws guaranteed by the Fourteenth Amendment. . . .

SOME STUMBLING BLOCKS TO SCHOOL BOARD EFFECTIVENESS[1]

Edward M. Tuttle

Let it be said at the start that, by and large, the American public is ably represented and has reason to be proud of the service rendered by its 70,000 or so local boards of education. The control of public schools at the local level through a local agency authorized by the state is a peculiarly American institution. It is the closest thing we have to home rule in this country, and the fact that most board members serve voluntarily and without material reward, is added evidence of the high regard in which public education is generally held, and the honor felt by our ablest citizens in being asked to give such service to their communities.

Notwithstanding the truth of these general observations, it is also true that many boards—too many—are not as effective as they could be and should be. My contacts in nearly every state of the Union have led me to believe that certain school boards fail to reach their possible effectiveness for one or another of six or seven major reasons. I should like to list these reasons, with a brief comment about each one. I realize that there will be differences of opinion regarding some of the things which seem to me to be stumbling blocks to progress, and that there are all degrees of application. But I believe that a frank consideration of them will be wholesome, and perhaps in some cases further discussion in these columns may result.

These points are none of them new. They have all been discussed in educational literature time and again from many different angles. I simply suggest that we set them down in one list and take a good look at them.

1. *Individual board members are sometimes dominated by partisan instead of by public loyalties.* Whatever these partisan loyalties may be, they cause those who entertain them to lose sight of the main objective of school board service, namely, the highest welfare of the community's children and youth. They also prevent the board member from truly representing the community as a whole, and they inevitably result in a lack of unity on the board which is fatal to effective action.

2. *A lack of written down school board policies, kept up to date.* Recent studies indicate that probably not over 20 per cent of school boards have reduced their policies to writing. The net result is that board action is more often based on expediency than on consistency. This is a frequent reason for confusion and misunderstanding between the board and the administration, between the board and the public, and between the administration and the public. Recently a growing wave of interest in written policies is evident among school boards and their associations, and this particular stumbling block to effective action is one of the easiest to overcome.

3. *Too exclusive attention to the housekeeping problems of the schools.* This is a common weakness of many boards which meet simply to pass upon a budget, pay bills, purchase sites, approve architects' plans and contractors' bids, arrange for insurance, and take care of business affairs. The result of such practice is a failure on the part of the board to understand the values and purposes of public education, and an inability to interpret, defend, and

[1] From *The American School Board Journal*, February, 1953, pp. 5, 8. Reprinted by permission.

support constructive educational programs when the need arises. The housekeeping side of school board operation is only part, and the lesser part in my judgment, of a school board's responsibilities. The board which really fulfills its proper function of policy making devotes fully as much time to building its own background regarding educational programs and practices as it does to taking care of school business. There are various ways in which this can be done.

4. *Abuse of the use of closed, or executive, sessions of the board.* One result of such practice is to create an atmosphere of secrecy and intrigue which is not compatible with a public service. It also results in a failure to keep the public fully informed on school matters at all times. Theoretically, every board meeting should be an open meeting, and actually, legal action can only be taken under such conditions. The only excuses for private discussion by a board are in connection with items like personality problems or the contemplated purchase of building sites. Even in such cases, the wise board which has established good press relations, enables press representatives to benefit by the background discussions, *off the record,* so that later on when the subject breaks, a correct story will result based on all the facts.

5. *The use of standing committees.* This is a point on which there will be some differences of opinion. Some boards still operate on the committee system, but the trend is strongly toward operation as a committee of the whole at all times, except in the case of some special committee temporarily organized for a particular purpose. The biggest objection to standing committees is that in practice they inevitably result in several boards instead of one, both from the standpoint of the administrator and his staff and from the standpoint of the public—one small group of board members is identified with finance, another with buildings, another with personnel, another with curriculum, and so on. When fractions of the board specialize, so to speak, in particular areas of school operation, they soon tend to look upon themselves as authorities and to infringe upon the administrative functions of the superintendent and his staff instead of confining their activities to the making of policy. Finally, such a system gives board members a very uneven understanding of school affairs (intensive as regards their own committee, nebulous as regards the concerns of other committees) and thereby reduces the effectiveness of total board operation. On the other hand, with agenda well planned in advance and with efficient board procedure, there is no reason why all school matters cannot be considered by all members of the board acting together, and this is the manner in which the great majority of school boards operate. The resulting effect on the schools and on the community is much more salutary than under divided responsibilities.

6. *The fiscal dependence of a board of education upon the review, revision, or approval by some noneducational governmental agency or commission is likely to be a major stumbling block to educational progress.* Advocates of both fiscal dependence and independence for school boards advance strong arguments to prove their respective cases. Good examples and bad examples of operation under either system can be cited. It is doubtful that the issue can be settled on the basis of factual evidence. It involves our conception of the relative importance of different social values. The idea that a direct, democratic determination of educational policy is of greater social value than a centralized fiscal management seems to be steadily gaining ground. In the past few years, for example, New York State by legislative action has given complete fiscal independence to practically all of the school boards in that state

on the theory that public education is a continuous, constructive, nonpartisan service to all the people in which they should have a direct voice not complicated by any other consideration than the greatest possible good to children and youth.

7. A *dual administration which divides responsibility for educational affairs and for business affairs within a school system is a fertile source of school board ineffectiveness.* Here again there will be differences of opinion because occasionally, where personal co-operation is of the highest order, the dual system has been made to work. But in most places it has not proved satisfactory to separate financial planning from educational planning. Experience has shown that a school system should have just one executive directly responsible to the board, and that he should be given such assistants, including a business manager, as are needed to carry out the board's policies in all aspects of school operation. The best systems have first determined what the schools should be doing for the community and then have considered the cost. When fiscal planning is put ahead of, or separated from, educational planning, the result is too often disastrous for the educational program.

We have listed above, and briefly considered, seven practices which appear to be stumbling blocks to effective school board action: (1) partisanship; (2) lack of written policies; (3) overemphasis on housekeeping; (4) executive sessions; (5) standing committees; (6) fiscal dependence; and (7) dual control. There may be others which, in greater or less degree, frustrate harmonious and constructive accomplishment. But at least these seven have revealed their handicapping tendencies in a majority of cases. Boards which are operating under any one or more of these conditions would be well advised to study their operation with open minds to determine whether some modification more closely related to widespread trends might not yield as rewarding results for them as for others.

HEALTH FOUNDATIONS OF EDUCATION

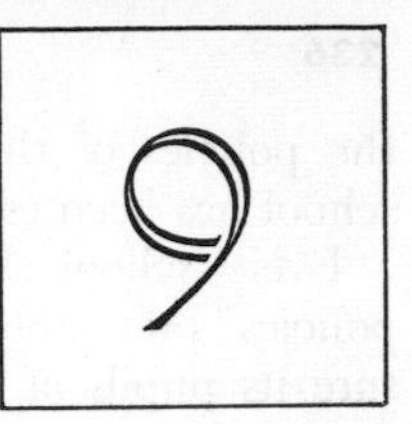

SCHOOL HEALTH POLICIES[1]

National Conference for Cooperation in Health Education

GENERAL HEALTH POLICIES

Health is a primary objective of modern education. Health was named as the first of the seven cardinal objectives of education in the 1918 report of the Commission on the Reorganization of Secondary Education. More recently the Educational Policies Commission has stated: "An educated person knows the basic facts concerning health and disease . . . works to improve his own health and that of his dependents . . . and works to improve community health."

Every school has tremendous opportunities to promote the health of its pupils and of its community. From early childhood to early manhood and womanhood, most children are enrolled in schools and are under the supervision of school staffs for a substantial part of the day for approximately half the days of the year. The conditions under which they live in school, the help which they are given in solving their health problems, the ideals of individual and community health which they are taught to envisage and the information and understanding that they acquire of themselves as living organisms are factors which operate to develop attitudes and behavior conducive to healthy, happy and successful living. In all of its efforts the school must consider the total personality of each student and the mutual interdependence of physical, mental and emotional health.

THE NEED FOR POLICIES

If a school is to make the greatest possible contribution to the continuing health and welfare of its pupils throughout their whole lifetime, it should formulate and apply health policies consonant with the best thought and practice in this field.

Such policies recognize that the total health of the total child in his total life situation is the paramount objective of any school health program. Such policies evolve from increasingly accurate and certain understanding of the needs of children. Such policies are free from fad and prejudice, are subservient neither to unproved speculation nor heavy-handed tradition. Such policies grow out of successful experience, are guided by expert judgment and conform with as well as help give direction to

[1] From *Suggested School Health Policies*, 2nd ed., revised by the National Committee on School Health Policies of the National Conference for Cooperation in Health Education, New York and Minneapolis, Health Education Council, 1946, pp. 7–14. Reprinted by permission of Health Education Council.

the policies of the community which the school has been established to serve.

Every school should establish workable policies, preferably in written form, to assure its pupils of (1) healthful school living conditions, (2) appropriate health and safety instruction, (3) adequate or superior services for health protection and improvement, (4) healthful physical education, and especially (5) teachers and other school personnel with up-to-date preparation so that they are well qualified for their special health responsibilities. Sound policies for the education and care of handicapped children are equally essential.

The Help of Many Is Needed

Schools alone however cannot enable children to attain all the desirable goals of individual and community health. Considering the magnitude and multitude of the diverse and continuing efforts that must be made to satisfy the health needs of children, it is fortunate that many people and groups, in addition to schools, are also greatly interested in promoting health.

Parents have the primary responsibility for the health of their children.

Physicians, dentists, nurses, health officers, social and welfare workers and their official organizations, such as medical, dental and nursing societies; health departments; voluntary health agencies; and social agencies are all rightfully concerned with health activities in their communities.

Cooperation is the keynote essential to the coordination of the efforts of all concerned with child health. Only in this way can schools and communities develop balanced programs of health education and health care. Only thus can a school avoid false emphasis on one phase of its health program with corresponding neglect of other equally vital areas. School health policies must be formulated to achieve the maximum cooperation and coordination both within each school and each school system and between each school and the community.

Health Councils Promote Cooperation

Every school should establish its own School Health Council or Health Committee. Organized on democratic and representative principles, under the authority of the principal school administrator, the School Health Council provides a simple, orderly, and convenient administrative mechanism for determining and implementing wise school health policies in the light of local and immediate needs. Experience in many schools where such councils are now quietly and successfully functioning has already demonstrated their usefulness to the school administrator as well as their value to the children and the community. In the School Health Council should be vested the responsibility for planning the total health program of the school. Cooperation is its keynote too.

The School Health Council should be as comprehensive and representative as possible. Details of organization and operation of each council—its membership, frequency of meetings, scope of authority, program and the like—need follow no preordained pattern and can be best determined by each council for itself.

Initiative for the establishment of the School Health Council is the first requisite. In a one-room rural school, the School Health Council might consist only of the teacher, one interested parent and one representative of the health professions, a local physician or a county health nurse.

In a large metropolitan high school a School Health Council might properly include:

The principal.

A physician, usually the school medical advisor.

A dentist.

A nurse, usually the school nurse.

The health educator, health counselor, or health coordinator.

Teachers—

Of physical education,

Of biology or other science,

Of home economics,

Of handicapped children,

Representing all classroom teachers,

With special interest in health problems.

A psychologist.

A member of the guidance staff.

A nutritionist, usually the school food service director.

A dental hygienist.

The head janitor.

Students, representing the student council or student body.

Parents, representing the Parent-Teachers Association.

Liaison representatives from official or voluntary community health organizations and from the school system health council.

Every school system, under whatever jurisdiction it operates, should have a Central Health Council or Committee with appropriate representation from all schools and from all groups interested in school health. The relationship of the Central Health Council to each of the individual School Health Councils must be determined by experience in each community. In general it is best if the central council guides and gives leadership but leaves each School Health Council with considerable autonomy. At the level of the Central Health Council, where, for example, the city or county superintendent of schools and the city or county health officer meet, the fruitfully cooperative relationships between the school system and the health department can best be worked out.

Schools should work with Community Health Councils wherever they are established and if necessary should take leadership in their organization and direction. Experience in communities that have taken steps toward increasingly effective organization for health education points toward the development of a permanent Community Health Council (City or County Health Council), which carries on cooperative studies and gives impetus to the entire community health program. The schools have a responsibility for sharing in community health planning and should participate wholeheartedly in it.

No child should be handicapped because he fails to receive needed health education and care. Through the cooperative efforts of the many professional and civic groups represented in a Community Health Council, ways can and should be found to provide for the specific health needs of all children.

PROVISIONS FOR HEALTHFUL SCHOOL LIVING

Pupils should be able to live healthfully while at school. This requires attention to standards for school safety and sanitation; to teacher-pupil relationships as they influence mental and emotional health; and to the health of school personnel. In many schools it requires that a wholesome, nutritious lunch be available.

Standards for Safety and Sanitation

Every school has a responsibility for providing a healthful environment: physical, social and emotional. The authority which requires pupils to attend school implies the responsibility to provide an environment as evocative as possible of growth, learning and health. Location of the school should be chosen with a view to ample space for buildings and grounds; to safety from accident hazards, especially traffic hazards; to freedom from noise; to cleanliness; and to the provision of as good drainage as possible. The school should not be at the bottom of the valley nor at the top of an exceptionally high hill. There should be appropriate sunshine and shade and, if necessary, shelter from severe winds. The location should be easily accessible, particularly for small children. Attractiveness of surroundings should not be overlooked.

Construction and maintenance of the school building should be in accordance with, or superior to, standards established by law and by official building and health regulations. Important considerations are adequate size; appropriate ventilation, heating, lighting, and acoustics; adjustable seats with regard for postural considerations; attractive decorations; wide halls; stairways of fireproof construction; doors opening outward on automatic safety latches. Lavatories and handwashing facilities should be adequate and accessible and of appropriate size for the children who use them. There should be an ample number of drinking fountains of approved sanitary design, and these should always be kept in good working order.

Indoor and outdoor gymnasiums, and outdoor play areas with necessary dressing, locker and shower rooms, and—ideally—swimming-pool facilities, should be available. School recreational facilities should be accessible for community use and arranged so that they may be used separately from the rest of the school. Outdoor athletic grounds must have suitable surfaces to avoid lacerating injuries. There should be adequately planned and equipped health service rooms, and separate isolation and rest rooms for boys, girls, and teachers. Assemblies, libraries and other group activity rooms should preferably be located on the ground floor.

Standards for school sanitary facilities are frequently found in building codes of state departments of education and sanitary regulations of state departments of health. They are also available in textbooks on sanitation and on school health.

These standards must be arrived at in cooperation and consultation with health departments, architects and other experts in lighting, sound, ventilation and other special phases of modern school building construction and maintenance. Up-to-date standards must be followed.

Housekeeping procedures and the maintenance of safety and sanitary facilities in the building and school grounds should be under constant supervision. In addition, a complete, detailed survey of sanitary conditions and facilities should be made at least once each year. Written reports, listing recommendations for improvements, should be filed with the principal, superintendent of schools and the health officer and be made available to the public. The individual responsible for sanitary inspections may be the school medical adviser, school nurse, health officer or sanitary inspector, principal or superintendent. In large cities the superintendent of school buildings and grounds will probably have a part in the inspections. In rural schools the teacher or school superintendent or the public health nurse or health officer may perform this function.

Promoting Mental and Emotional Health

A healthful environment requires constant consideration of pupils' emotional and social environment.

Perhaps the most important mental health factor in the school environment is the personality of the teacher. The teacher or principal who is kind but firm, sympathetic but exacting, and friendly but reserved exerts a beneficial influence on emotional health. The nagging, scolding, sarcastic, domineering or emotionally unstable teacher or principal can seriously injure pupils. The same considerations apply to all other school personnel.

The mental health of pupils requires that teaching methods give ample opportunity for experiencing success without exposing the pupil to excessive fatigue, undue worry or other unfavorable emotional stimulation. Disciplinary measures should consider pupil personality of greater importance than the rigid application of arbitrary rules. Types of examinations and methods of promotion should stimulate each pupil to do the best he can rather than discourage or degrade him. Any system of awards should put emphasis on group cooperation rather than on undue competition among individuals.

The Health of School Personnel

A healthful environment requires attention not only to the arrangement of the program within the school day and to student-teacher relationships within the classroom but also to the physical and mental health of all school personnel. Children should not be in contact with sick adults (principals, teachers, supervisors, doctors, nurses, clerks, custodians, secretaries, bus drivers, food handlers). The school staff should be subject to adequate health supervision and guidance. Principals should be given responsibility for sending from school a teacher or other employee whose health condition may be detrimental to pupils or fellow employees.

All school employees should be required to have health examinations including a chest x-ray previous to employment and periodically thereafter. The extent of examinations and their frequency should be determined through cooperative planning by teachers, school administrators, and school medical advisors. Measures for preventing the spread of communicable diseases should include encouraging school employees to stay at home when sick and excluding those who may endanger the health of others.

Since the health of teachers, custodians and other school personnel vitally affects the health of children, teaching and working conditions must be sanitary and safe, teaching and working loads reasonable. Provision for sick leave is needed. Peace of mind is encouraged by provisions for tenure and retirement.

School Food Service

For many pupils, eating lunch at school is a part of healthful school living. Food service at school should be established primarily on the basis of need in each school situation. Good nutrition should be the objective; profit-making should be discouraged; outside financial aid may be needed. The school lunch program should be adequately supervised and fully utilize all educational opportunities, in the direction both of developing good eating habits among all of the children and of improving the appreciation of the normal social ceremony which is "the sauce to meat." This should be done in close correlation with classroom instruction.

The school lunch program affords a commonly neglected "laboratory" for the development of good eating habits. The circumstances surrounding the service of food in themselves create social situations of the utmost influence on the individual. There is social significance in the school food service program.

Eating places in schools should be pleasant rooms, ample in size and seating capacity to permit the leisurely eating of a noon meal by all pupils and teachers who are in the room at the same time. The dining room itself must be bulwarked by adequate kitchen facilities, including proper refrigerating and cooking equipment, storage space, and waste disposal systems. Washrooms for teachers and pupils should of course be provided.

Sanitary regulations of the highest order should be enforced in school eating establishments, including all health department regulations concerning food establishments and food handlers. Workers with respiratory or skin infections, or disease carriers, must not handle other people's food. Regulations relating to sanitation and to the health of food handlers should be put in effect by the school medical advisor in co-operation with the director of food services. Volunteer students or part-time workers, who meet the requirements, may be valuable when full-time trained personnel is not available.

The responsibility for adequate food service, including menus which provide nutritious, wholesome and attractive lunches or other feedings, rests finally with the principal school administrator. This responsibility is properly delegated to a competent director of food service, preferably one trained in the science of nutrition as well as skilled in practical management. Where no such person is available within the system, competent advice should be sought from outside. The recommendations of qualified nutritionists as to menus and management must receive administrative support.

Children need a good breakfast; this is a primary responsibility of the home. Those who do not receive such a breakfast at home, or who are compelled to breakfast unusually early, may need supplementary food at or soon after the opening of school. The so-called mid-morning lunch, if served, should be of a character quickly assimilated and not likely to impair appetite for the noon meal.

ADOLESCENT CONCERNS WITH PHYSIQUE[1]

Alexander Frazier and Lorenzo K. Lisonbee

DISCUSSION AND ANALYSIS

The authors of this study are concerned not with physical development—indeed, they readily admit that there is considerable knowledge of adolescent physical changes—but with how adolescents feel about their changing bodies. Do you consider this an important area of inquiry? The authors also point out that their sample is small. If the sample were enlarged, would you anticipate that the findings would be altered? How? Do you think that the inquiry has limitations other than those mentioned by the authors? Are sexual factors given sufficient emphasis?

Assuming that the study presents us with a true picture of the responses of adolescents to physique, how can these data be of use to the junior-high or high-school teacher?

Do you believe that children in other age groups are equally concerned with physique? What differences, if any, are there between the 8-year-old who wants to be like Superman and the 15-year-old who would like to resemble Tab Hunter or Rock Hudson? Can any harm arise from having models who are near or beyond perfection? If your answer is yes, what sort of intellectual models do you feel ought to be offered to students?

[1] Reprinted from *School Review* (Oct. 1950), Vol. 58, pp. 397–405, by permission of The University of Chicago Press. Copyright 1950 by The University of Chicago.

A major task of adolescence is to adjust to the dramatic physical changes which mark the development of the child into the adult.[2] In addition, the adolescent has, somewhere along the line, the problem of accepting his emerging shape and size as the physique with which he will have to proceed through life. Knowledge of the nature of adolescent physical changes is considerable; however, knowledge about the feelings of the adolescent seems less well documented. In searching for such evidence, the present writers were struck by the frequency with which the small, but intensively analyzed, sample represented in a California study is cited.[3] In order to prepare materials for helping adolescents toward adjustment, it was felt desirable to collect local evidence that might be somewhat broader in its possible implications.

THE PRESENT STUDY

A Questionnaire

The present report covers the responses of all tenth-graders at North Phoenix High School for the year 1949–50. These 580 students, 309 girls and 271 boys, were enrolled in the required biology course. A questionnaire was drawn up to discover how these children saw themselves physically and how they felt about their conceptions of themselves. The major sections of the questionnaire dealt with weight, height and proportions, rate of development, facial appearance, and desire for self-improvement. All students answered anonymously.

For the first three sections, self-description was based on five choices. For example, in the section on height these choices were (1) short, (2) rather short, (3) about average, (4) rather tall, and (5) tall. In Section 4, facial appearance, the student was simply to check those of 59 items that he felt applied to him; items were grouped under "nose," "mouth," "skin," etc. Section 5, dealing with self-improvement, was designed to elicit a free written response. After each item of self-description in Sections 1 through 4, there followed a five-point scale for expression of worry or concern: (1) "Never think about it," (2) "Think about it now and then," (3) "Worry about it a little," (4) "Worry a good deal," and (5) "Worry a lot." To simplify reporting, the responses on this scale from 3 through 5 are combined and considered to represent what we will call *concern.*

Limitations of the Study

In reporting the findings of this survey, the writers acknowledge that whatever generalizations may be drawn must be regarded as highly tentative. The sample is not large. It represents only tenth-graders. The school population is largely middle-class. The attempt to measure concern is undoubtedly ambitious. Yet the need for studies of this kind is so great that the writers wish to offer their results to other persons who are working to collect evidence on the same problem.

Section 1: Weight

How do these tenth-grade boys and girls see themselves in terms of weight? If they think of themselves as heavy or thin, how do they feel about it? Students were asked to rate themselves both for their entire body and for various sections on a five-point scale: (1) too thin, (2) rather thin, (3) about right, (4) rather heavy, and (5) too heavy. They were also to indicate their

[2] This task, along with others, is well defined in the following publication: Robert J. Havighurst, *Developmental Tasks and Education*, Chicago, University of Chicago Press, 1948.

[3] Herbert R. Stolz and Lois Meek Stolz, "Adolescent Problems Related to Somatic Variations," *Adolescence*, pp. 81–99. Forty-third Yearbook of the National Society for the Study of Education, Part I, Chicago, Distributed by the University of Chicago Press, 1944.

degree of concern on the scale described above.

As shown in Table 1, almost a third of the girls see themselves as heavy (combining "rather heavy" and "too heavy"), with more than half of them expressing some degree of concern. Only 13 per cent of the boys describe themselves in this manner, and little concern is expressed by them. Two-thirds of the boys describe themselves as "about right" compared to 54 per cent of the girls. Boys are more inclined than girls to rate themselves thin, although the girls express more concern over thinness. However, boys show more than seven times as much concern about being thin as about being heavy. Throughout this study, boys are found less expressive of concern than girls.

Boys and girls were also asked to describe themselves in terms of weight of body sections (face, neck, shoulders, chest, abdominal section, hips, upper arm, forearm, upper leg, lower leg, and ankles). When the two positions for heaviness and thinness at either end of the scale were combined, items checked as heavy or thin by as many as 25 per cent of the boys or girls served to reinforce the picture given above. Nearly half the girls (46 per cent) think they have heavy hips. Heavy abdominal sections (43 per cent) and upper legs (38 per cent) rank next. The forearm is the only section marked thin by any sizable number of girls (28 per cent). Supposed heaviness of these parts of the body greatly concerns the girls, just as it does in reference to the entire body. Of the girls who consider their hips heavy, 64 per cent express concern. Heavy upper legs bother half the girls so describing themselves; heavy mid-regions, a third.

Thinness of body sections is self-assigned by a considerable per cent of the boys, bearing out the inclination noted in the description of the entire body. One-third of the boys consider their upper arms thin; 30 per cent mark themselves as having thin forearms; 27 per cent, thin chests. One section, the mid-region, is marked heavy by a sizable number (28 per cent). Here again, concern is less pronounced for boys than for girls. Heaviness of abdominal sections concerns one-third of the boys so describing themselves; thinness of upper arm, 27 per cent; thinness of chest, 21 per cent; and thinness of forearm, 20 per cent.

The tenth-grade girls in this study tend to think of themselves as heavy, particularly in certain sections of the body. Girls express a high degree of concern about their weight. Boys tend to think they are "about right," with some inclination toward thinness, particularly in upper arms, forearms, and chests. Boys are less expressive of concern about weight than are girls.

Section 2: Height and Proportions

How do these students see themselves in terms of height and proportions, and how do they feel about their self-conceptions? The questionnaire asked the tenth-graders to describe themselves in terms of a five-point scale for height, width of hips and shoulders, and length of arms, legs, trunk, and feet. The "worry" scale was the same for this section as for the others.

Most of the boys and girls saw themselves as "about average" in height. However as shown in Table 1, girls were a little more inclined to think of themselves as short, boys as tall. As far as concern was expressed, it centered rather dramatically in tallness for girls (49 per cent of the girls who thought of themselves as tall expressed concern) and in shortness for boys (39 per cent concern). Tall boys felt little concern, not much more than did heavy boys.

The items which attempted to get at possible concerns over proportions revealed little, except that a rather large number of girls (37 per cent) consider themselves to have wide hips and express a high degree

TABLE 1. PER CENTS OF 580 TENTH-GRADE BOYS AND GIRLS GIVING CERTAIN DESCRIPTIONS OF THEIR PHYSIQUES AND PER CENTS EXPRESSING CONCERN ABOUT THE CHARACTERISTICS DESCRIBED *

Description	Per Cent So Describing Themselves		Per Cent Expressing Concern	
	Boys	Girls	Boys	Girls
Thin	21	16	22	48
Heavy	13	30	3	55
Short	26	27	39	22
Tall	28	22	4	49
Development early	19	24	6	15
Development slow	17	13	40	36

* The table is read as follows: 21 per cent of the boys and 16 per cent of the girls described themselves as thin; 22 per cent of the boys and 48 per cent of the girls so describing themselves expressed concern about this characteristic.

of concern (60 per cent) about it. Such a self-conception and concern with width of hips is undoubtedly related to their consciousness of heaviness in that region, as revealed under weight. Large feet are accepted as their lot by 28 per cent of the girls, with an expressed concern of 37 per cent. Although 35 per cent of the boys think their feet are large, only 10 per cent of these express concern.

Half the tall girls among these tenth-graders are concerned about their height. Nearly 40 per cent of the short boys express concern. These findings are the most significant in this section of the questionnaire.

SECTION 3: RATE OF DEVELOPMENT

How many of these boys and girls think of themselves as slow or fast in development? How concerned are they? Both sexes were asked to describe themselves in terms of total growth. Boys were also asked to rate themselves as to growth of beard, muscular development, and voice change.

Most of these tenth-graders consider themselves average, as will be seen from the percentages for early and slow development given in Table 1. A larger percentage of girls than of boys think their rate early; more boys than girls see themselves as slow-developing. Concern over early development is not too large with either boys or girls, although more than twice as much for girls.

The most significant fact emerging from this section of the study is that 40 per cent of the boys who consider themselves slow-maturing express concern. This is the highest amount of concern expressed by boys, except that over blackheads and pimples. While the slow-developing girls express 36 per cent concern, the fact that boys of this group are even more expressive is highly indicative of the insecurity that faces slow-developing boys, even at the tenth-grade level. In actual per cents of total boys and girls, those who express concern over what they consider their slow rate of development is only 6 per cent. The number is not large, but the concern is great, particularly for boys.

SECTION 4: FACIAL APPEARANCE

How do these boys and girls describe themselves in terms of facial appearance, and how much concerned are they? For each of the 59 items that might be checked, students were asked to mark also the usual five-point scale of concern.

As shown in Table 2, only 17 of the items were marked by as many as 10 per cent of the girls; 18 items by 10 per cent of the boys. In addition to the nine items common to both sexes (blackheads or pimples; heavy eyebrows; freckles; oily skin; scars, birthmarks, moles; glasses; irregular teeth; too long nose; and receding chin), the girls included high forehead, too round face, too homely, dry skin, thin lips, low

TABLE 2. ITEMS OF SELF-DESCRIPTION CHECKED BY 10 PER CENT OR MORE OF 580 TENTH-GRADE BOYS AND GIRLS, WITH AMOUNT OF EXPRESSED CONCERN

Boys			Girls		
Item of Description	Per Cent Checking	Per Cent of Concern	Item of Description	Per Cent Checking	Per Cent of Concern
Blackheads or pimples	57	51	Blackheads or pimples	57	82
Lack of beard	34	2	Heavy eyebrows	24	11
Heavy eyebrows	27	1	Freckles	23	24
Scars, birthmarks, moles	20	13	Oily skin	22	52
Irregular teeth	17	39	Scars, birthmarks, moles	22	30
Heavy lips	14	5	Glasses	21	31
Protruding chin	13	6	High forehead	19	8
Ears stick out	13	6	Too round face	19	21
Oily skin	12	27	Too homely	18	42
Freckles	12	...	Dry skin	16	43
Heavy beard	11	13	Irregular teeth	16	42
Glasses	11	23	Thin lips	15	13
Dark skin	10	4	Low forehead	13	3
Receding chin	10	4	Too long nose	11	23
Gaps in teeth	10	26	Too big nose	11	44
Too long nose	10	8	Receding chin	10	13
Too thin face	10	15	Odd-shaped nose	10	23
Too large ears	10	8			

forehead, too big nose, and odd-shaped nose. The boys listed lack of beard, heavy lips, protruding chin, ears stick out, heavy beard, dark skin, gaps in teeth, too thin face, and too large ears.

That 57 per cent of both sexes testify to having blackheads and pimples and that both boys and girls are more concerned about the problem than about any other item in the entire questionnaire is the outstanding fact revealed by this section. Both boys and girls express considerable concern also about oily skin, irregular teeth, and glasses. Concern is heavy for girls who think they have a nose that is too big, skin that is too dry, or that they are just too homely.

A few other facts are of interest. We note that nearly twice as many girls as boys wear glasses. Boys express no concern about freckles; girls, 24 per cent. Lack of beard, which a third of the boys acknowledge, causes little "worry," reinforcing what we had found on this item under rate of development.

Apparently, complexion problems form the chief physical worry of these tenth-grade boys and girls. Nothing else, in either this or other sections, looms as large in affecting so many and in "worrying" a majority of both boys and girls who are affected.

SECTION 5: DESIRE FOR SELF-IMPROVEMENT

The fifth part of the questionnaire was designed to find out what tenth-grade boys and girls thought of the desirability of changing themselves. This question was asked: "Would you change your physical self in some way if you could?" As shown in Table 3, two-thirds of this group said they would.

What kinds of changes are desired? In a second question, students were asked, if they desired change, to specify in what

TABLE 3. NUMBER AND PER CENTS OF 580 TENTH-GRADE BOYS AND GIRLS DESIRING SOME CHANGE IN PHYSICAL SELVES

Sex	Yes		No		No Answer		Total	
	No.	Per Cent	No.	Per Cent	No.	Per Cent	No.	Per Cent
Boys	164	61	92	34	15	5	271	100
Girls	222	72	60	19	27	9	309	100
Both	386	67	152	26	42	7	580	100

ways. As shown in Table 4, the responses have been broken down and classified for both boys and girls by areas, number of items for each area, percentages, and rank order. However, before examining the total picture, it may be of interest to look at the desires of each sex separately.

THE CHANGES GIRLS WANT

Girls are highly specific about the ways in which they would like to change themselves, as the following samples indicate:

My hips and legs are too large and fat. If I could have smaller hips and legs, I'd have a much better figure. I'd also like to be a *little* more developed above the waist than I am, but I am not flat. I wish I didn't have so many pimples or had to wear glasses.

(1) I would make myself thinner. (2) I would make my ears lie back. (3) I would make my forehead lower. (4) I would take away my pimples and make my complexion clear and soft. (5) I would make my eyes just a little bigger. (6) I would make my feet smaller.

I would first of all change my nose, as it is huge. I think someday I will go to a plastic surgeon and get my nose changed. I would not be so tall. I would like a wider jaw. I thought when I got my teeth straightened my jaw would be wider, but it is still sharp and pointed. I would like a clear, unscarred complexion. I have blackheads and pimples. I may go to a dermatologist. My eyes are small with short lashes. I have many moles, which I saw a doctor about, but they cannot be removed without scars or pits.

I'd have cute legs, a cute figure, and a shorter forehead. I'd also be three inches shorter and have smaller feet. I'd have blue eyes and blond hair fixed in page-boy. I would weigh 101 pounds.

I would rather not wear glasses. I would lose ten pounds. I would like a complexion that stays nice all the time.

When these responses had been itemized and classified, it was plain that the desires of the girls to change were distributed through most of the categories. Since lack of space prohibits the listing of all the items grouped under each category, only the largest clusters can be mentioned.

Under the category Proportions in Table 4, with 122 items, these clusters were slimmer hips (31), smaller feet (24), smaller waist (17), and good shape (16). The major clusters under the category Complexion (109 items) were clear complexion (42), no pimples (21), and no freckles (16). The category Weight (74 items) lent itself to simple subdivision, more slender (50) and fatter (24). Most of the items under the category Hair (62) were contributed by girls, who wanted to have hair that was dark (15), blond (12), longer (12), or naturally curly (10). Under the category Height (59 items), the girls were chiefly desirous of being shorter (38), although some wished to be taller (17). The chief desire under the category Features (55 items) was to have a nice nose (16) or a pretty face (13). The desires under the category Eyes (52 items) centered in no glasses and better vision (21) and blue eyes (12).

THE CHANGES BOYS WANT

The questionnaire results consistently revealed that the boys were less expressive than the girls. The boys responded with

TABLE 4. AREAS IN WHICH 222 GIRLS AND 164 BOYS IN GRADE X SPECIFY DESIRE FOR SELF-IMPROVEMENT

Category	Girls			Boys		
	Number of Items	Per Cent of Items	Rank Order	Number of Items	Per Cent of Items	Rank Order
Proportions	122	20.6	1	81	24.4	1
Complexion	109	18.4	2	38	11.4	5
Weight	74	12.5	3	50	15.1	3
Hair	62	10.5	4	14	4.2	7
Height	59	10.0	5	55	16.6	2
Features	55	9.3	6	16	4.8	6
Eyes	52	8.8	7	10	3.0	9
Teeth	21	3.6	8	11	3.3	8
Daintiness	13	2.2	9	...	...	...
Strength	...	...	...	46	13.9	4
Personal qualities	9	1.5	10	3	0.9	11
Freedom from disease or deformity	1	0.2	11	5	1.5	10
Unclassified	15	2.5	...	3	0.9	
Total	592	100.1	...	332	100.0	...

answers that were analyzed into 332 items, as compared with the 592 of the girls. A few of these statements in their entirety follow:

I would make my chest bigger than it is now and also my shoulders. I would like to weigh a little bit more, say about twenty to twenty-five pounds more than I do now.

Be bigger and have more muscular development. Be taller and get rid of skin blemishes.

I would make myself look handsomer and not fat. I would have wavy black hair. I would change my whole physical appearance so that I would be handsome, with a good build.

Well, I would start off by putting on some meat, next would be to get rid of my pimples, then to get some muscles, then to get rid of my glasses.

I would build up my upper arm, forearm, chest, shoulder, and abdomen muscles.

I would be taller, more muscular, slimmer, have better posture, lighter and more slowly-growing head of hair, big, broad shoulders, and heavier calves.

Categories of major importance for boys are shown in Table 4 as being Proportions, Height, Weight, Strength, and Complexion. The clusters of items under each of these reveal the chief concerns. Under Proportions (81 items), the chief clusters are better build (17), broader shoulders (17), and larger chest (11). The category Height (55 items) is singularly centered in becoming taller (51). The items under the category Weight (50) are chiefly for heavier (36). The category Strength (46 items), perhaps poorly balanced by what we have termed "Daintiness" for girls, has two chief clusters, better muscular development (28) and stronger (10). For the boys, only one cluster emerges under the category Complexion (38 items), and that is no pimples (16).

These tenth-graders of both sexes are most conscious of a desire to conform to their conceptions of the ideal physical appearance in the areas of proportions, weight, height, and complexion, with a somewhat different rank order for each sex, chiefly notable for a switch in emphasis on complexion and height. Girls are more aware of complexion problems, boys of stature. In addition, a major category, which is plainly sex-determined, appears for both girls and boys among the top five categories. These categories are hair for girls; strength for boys.

Agreement in categories is not borne out, of course, in the clusters of items under weight and height. Girls desire to be thinner, boys heavier; girls want to be shorter, boys taller. In part, these differences may reflect the fact that girls of this age will be more mature than boys. Probably, the differences are largely differences in the ideal physique held in mind by each sex. An interesting check upon another section of the questionnaire is provided by the fact that proportions here rank first, whereas we had failed to elicit much response from the students for that aspect of Section 2. Our items there were apparently not the right ones.

SUMMARY

In order to collect more information about how adolescents think of themselves physically and how concerned they are over their self-conceptions, the writers questioned one tenth-grade group of 580 students in terms of weight, height and proportions, rate of development, facial appearance, and desire for change. As reported here, the findings seem to justify the following generalizations:

1. The girls in this study are inclined to think of themselves as heavy and to express a high amount of concern about their supposed heaviness. Boys think of themselves as about right in weight but incline toward describing themselves as thin, with considerable concern about thinness in the upper arms and chest.

2. Height concerns chiefly the girls who think of themselves as tall, the boys who consider themselves short. Short boys express what is, for their sex, a high degree of concern.

3. Fewer of these boys and girls consider themselves slow in maturing than think themselves early. Most of them see themselves as average in this respect. However, among both boys and girls, the slow-maturing children express high concern. This is particularly outstanding among the boys in comparison with other expressions of male concern.

4. Blackheads and pimples are self-ascribed by a majority of the group. The concern of both sexes is higher for this item than for any other item in the entire questionnaire.

5. Two-thirds of these tenth-graders express a desire for some change in themselves physically, with items relating to proportions leading the categories for both sexes. Weight, height, and complexion are the other top areas in which desired change is common to both boys and girls.

IMPLICATIONS

As an aid toward more effective teaching and counseling, these chief generalizations and some of the other findings seem to suggest a number of guidelines to the writers and to other persons working in biology, health, guidance, and over-all curriculum development in this particular high school. Perhaps some of these tentative proposals for action will interest other educational workers.

1. What is being taught about the normality of weight and height range should be reviewed to find out whether it is sufficiently helpful. Attention needs to be given particularly to nutrition instruction for girls in this age group, who may be attempting to do something on their own about their supposed overweight.

2. Present instruction in the process of maturation needs to be reviewed to see

whether it begins early enough to give fullest guidance and continues long enough to deal with the fears of slow-maturing children, particularly boys.

3. More attention needs to be given in Grade X to complexion disorders—their causes and treatment. This problem looms as a major concern of this age group. Ways in which to help need to be studied broadly by the school.

4. Tenth-graders may profit from help in looking at the ways in which they have gained their conceptions of the ideal physique—as revealed by their statements of changes that they would like to make in themselves. Advertising, as well as movies and novels, may come under discussion.

5. Autobiographical documents, in which younger and older adults report methods they have used to adjust to concerns about physique, are being collected in evening classes of adults by Mrs. Lillian Whitney, director of the psychology department of Phoenix College. These documents promise to provide a rich resource for helping tenth-graders gain perspective.

6. The possibility of devising from this study an instrument for self-assessment of the physique should be explored. Perhaps the health-counseling of biology teachers would be better directed if each student were provided with a form on which he could describe himself physically and tell how he feels about what he thinks he is.

TEACHERS' PROBLEMS[1]

Fritz Redl and William M. Wattenberg

In our modern world, every occupation and every way of life involves some special psychological problems and special advantages. The farmer cultivating a field in comparative solitude, the salesman being jolly no matter how he feels inside, the factory operative staying on good terms with the other girls in her department, the housewife dusting mournfully while listening to a soap opera, the live-wire advertising executive nursing ulcers—all have unique satisfactions and yet all wrestle with more or less troublesome difficulties pertaining to their past—and their present. In all cases, deep in the individual's feelings, there are reasons that led to the choice of life pattern. These may help to make the working part of life a source of deep pleasure. There are dissatisfactions which may also be part of that pattern as it works out. There are relationships with other people which contain elements of both enjoyment and tension.

Over and beyond the normal range of problems, there are those problems arising in certain occupations and professions where the individual's main working tool is his own personality. Just as a carpenter uses a hammer and nails to build the frame of a house, so the physician uses his manner of behavior to create confidence and to secure the sense of urgency that will make a patient follow his advice. The professional man or woman consciously modifies his personality to obtain results for the good of his client. In this sense, then, teaching is a profession and carries with it the special mental hygiene problems and opportunities of all such occupations.

Among the millions of teachers in the world, a large number discover that their occupation makes life more interesting and more worth living. But even though the good points outweigh the bad, the unfortunate aspects are still annoying. Very

[1] From *Mental Hygiene in Teaching* by Fritz Redl and William M. Wattenberg, Chap. 16, pp. 385–409. Copyright, 1951, by Harcourt, Brace and Company, Inc.

much as a man or woman complains of having constant headaches, although the pain endures but an hour or two in a week, the dissatisfactions of teachers are more likely to be talked about and thought about than the moments of comfort and pleasure. For this reason, because they are so important, we shall deal in this chapter very largely with troublesome phases of teachers' professional lives.

FRUSTRATIONS IN TEACHING

In the interest of maintaining a desired classroom atmosphere, most teachers find themselves at times either concealing their true feelings or simulating attitudes they do not really have. They may act cheerful or confident when they are really worried or frightened. They may feign interest in materials with which they are bored. They may work up enthusiasm for youthful productions they regard as ludicrous. In short, they assume in the classroom a personality which is bound to be somewhat artificial, put on consciously because it helps with the job. By the same token, impulses which could be allowed freedom elsewhere must be blocked in the classroom.

Some Typical Conflicts

Teachers who have true professional spirit recognize that the needs of the children should have priority over their own personal wants. This is bound to produce some conflict. At times the contradictions are obvious and dramatic, as they are when a kindergarten teacher with a headache longs for quiet but leads the children in exuberant play because she knows they need plenty of activity. Holding her irritability in check is quite a strain, and we would not be surprised if once in a while she lost a battle with herself. Sometimes the conflict is not quite so obvious; a teacher, angered at some piece of juvenile nastiness, may force himself to inhibit his urge to hand out punishment, and instead deliberately ignore an incident or with forced calm divert the offender to other activity.

For reasons often hard to determine, some child may tempt a teacher to be unfair. Possibly a girl belongs to a nationality, race, or religion against which the teacher cannot help but harbor prejudice. Possibly a face or mannerism awakens echoes of some unpleasant event in his past. Perhaps the child's life symbolizes a pattern of pleasure which was denied to the teacher. The opposite may also be true; a teacher may find his heart going out to a youngster he finds especially appealing. Yet along with such feelings runs the conscious realization that it is bad to be unfair or to have pets, that this could create problems for both the child and the class. The teacher, then, is left struggling with the dilemma of how to handle his feelings and still live up to ideals of fair play and justice.

In schools where teachers come in contact with children very different from themselves in upbringing, there are the additional problems of accepting the differences without surrendering the teachers' own values. For instance, an ardent prohibitionist may have to meet without repugnance parents who she knows drink heavily, must see them as partners working sincerely for the benefit of their children, and still hold true to her feelings about the use of alcohol. Differences in moral codes, different standards of cleanliness, and different social customs may be troublesome to many fine people.

Another problem requiring restraint occurs in a school where the staff is divided into warring factions or where one or more members of the staff are disliked. Most teachers would agree that such divisions should not be aired before children. Yet it is only facing facts to state that when one adult is angered at another he will want to vent that anger and is likely to find relief in making either open complaints or sly digs. We might agree such a tendency ought not to exist, but it does. Holding it in check is necessary, but that very action means bottling up emotional pressure.

Thwarted Expectations

In their daydreams many teachers have seen themselves doing wonders in raising levels of skill and knowledge. Scores on objective tests or examinations are considered the simplest measures of such success. Often, the principal or the community will judge a teacher by those standards. Unfortunately, all children do not oblige by learning easily. Some have low learning ability; others are not interested; still others suffer from emotional upsets. For those teachers who keep their eyes fixed on set subject-matter standards, the children seem to stand in the way. They take on the psychological aspect of being obstacles, obstinate barriers to success. Not only are the teachers frustrated, but the children are the source of their frustrations. The emotional toll for teacher and students alike can be very high.

Even when a teacher's aims are in terms of personality development for the children failure may be unmistakable at times. His ambitions for the children in his room may outrun his power to accomplish what he hopes. For instance, Alma was a bright girl who, her teacher thought, could become a bright and socially alert secretary if only she had a little ambition. Despite several heart-to-heart talks, the girl blithely left school on her seventeenth birthday to become an unskilled domestic servant. Every such incident, and they are frequent, means dissatisfaction for a teacher. Stubborn reality makes this type of frustration an inevitable part of education.

It is very difficult to judge success in helping children to develop and grow. There are no clear criteria to tell us what has been accomplished. Many a day some teachers have gone home wondering what really happened, whether some incident was helpful or harmful. Truly, success can be invisible, and that is small satisfaction.

Objective conditions may raise obstacles. Too many teachers have too many children in their classes. Too often there is too little equipment. When a teacher knows what can be done under good conditions, the poor results achieved in unfavorable conditions are irksome. Equally disturbing is to be forced to use procedures which are second-rate. The new teacher in a stand-pat system who has to do things he knows are ineffective, or worse than ineffective, finds teaching a moral trial. When community pressures or expectations force a staff to ignore their own professional understanding the result is a new set of frustrations. Yet across the country there are thousands of educators itching to make improvements and to try out new ideas who have to hold themselves back in the face of subtle pressures or stern edicts.

What Part of Yourself Can You Be?

An age-old barrier to happiness for teachers has been the tradition that they must set an example to youth, and therefore, must accept stringent limitations on their personal lives. In large cities, such demands rarely operate away from the school, but they are still strict in many smaller communities. However, even if boards of education were to grant complete freedom, many teachers would still feel constrained. They would recognize that some children would choose them as objects of identification and, consequently, would want to exemplify especially high standards of conduct.

This condition has a deep psychological meaning. Teachers put themselves under pressure to exhibit that part of themselves which they feel is in accord with community ideals and to deny other parts from which they feel they could gain satisfaction. The internal pressure is itself a source of dissatisfaction. This accounts for some rather strange behavior from teachers on vacation away from the school's environment. At such times many will deny that they are teachers or, if "trapped" into an admission, will feel very ill at ease. Oddly, in view of all this, vacationing teachers are a rather well-behaved lot. Some go so far as to be disappointed with themselves because, free of restrictions, what escapades they do manage are often pretty tame and decorous.

Amount of Frustration

The amount of personal frustration varies from individual to individual and from situation to situation. Some school systems are so full of blocks and barriers that teachers leave them as soon as possible. There are schools which experience almost a complete turnover of teaching staff every year. Others, by contrast, are such happy places to work that vacancies are rare.

The mere fact that teaching involves some frustrations does not mean it is likely to produce mental illness in teachers. Every occupation has its share of difficulties. Rather, we must recognize that the existence of frustration implies mechanisms for dealing with any conflict to which it could give rise. Overcoming handicaps and learning to live with necessary frustrations can give added spice to the business of teaching. The significant factor for each individual is the way in which the frustrations are met. Knowing they exist may enable us to use our intelligence better in dealing with them.

REASONS FOR CHOICE OF TEACHING

A person's choice of occupation frequently has a good deal of high ardor behind it. The reasons for the selection are deeply planted in the personality structure. They may have much to do with the satisfaction he gets out of adult living. Certainly, they profoundly influence the way he works. Therefore, it is a good idea for us to look at some of the reasons which lead some people to go into teaching. In reading the list below, realize that no person becomes a teacher for one or all of the reasons named. Most made their choice out of a combination of reasons. The list is not a complete one nor is it in order of frequency or importance; undoubtedly there are teachers whose choice could not be accounted for by any of them. However, all are reasonably frequent.

Status

Teaching for many people is a symbol of middle-class status. It is a respectable job, and in every survey of public opinion ranks well toward the top of respected occupations. Many teachers sought the field because it meant they would have a secure standing among their acquaintances.

Family Pressure

Linked with the above is the fact that the status of teaching was valued by the family, and having a son or daughter become a teacher was a family ambition. For many, then, going into teaching was a way of retaining the affection of their parents. Some accepted the goal as their own, and wholeheartedly entered the field. Others were divided in their preference, but as a final demonstration that they were good boys and good girls, did as they were told.

Love for Subject Field

In school, especially high school or college, a number of youngsters develop real affection for some field of study. It may have been a field in which they did particularly well or it may have had some special appeal. Teaching is often the most likely way in which to make a living while continuing with the beloved subject. This is clearly true in such fields as English literature, history, mathematics, and athletics.

Identification with a Former Teacher

Interest in a subject is often a product of having identified with a teacher of that subject. In any event, many young people have admired some teacher, often a relative or friend of the family, frequently one in whose class they were. Admiration gave way to the wish to be like that person. Entering the same profession can be a step in that direction.

Love of Children

A significant number of men and women enjoy being with young people. They may find they are skillful at working with children, and that they enjoy the experience. Perhaps an opportunity to teach a Sunday School class, act as counselor at a camp, or lead a youth group was for them a self-revealing experience. Many girls like to care for babies; caring for children may symbolize a more complete womanhood. Being a teacher is a way of having children to love.

Fun in Teaching

There are many occasions inside and outside school when young people instruct each other. In high school groups, there is always a certain amount of informal tutoring. Young people teach each other how to play games, and in long "bull sessions" work out the meaning of ideas. Some discover that they enjoy intellectual leadership. Just as a girl "fooling around" in a kitchen may gain a joy of craftsmanship in cooking, so others come to relish success in helping people to learn, and turn to the teaching profession as a life work.

Helping to Build a Better World

One of youth's most precious qualities is the idealism which makes them want to fight evil and reform the world. That wish lives on for many people. Some continue to feel it as the most important thing in life. The fact that each generation of children becomes the next generation of parents and citizens invests teaching with practical significance as a way of improving the world. Although the reformist aspect of education seems to have receded from the peak of enthusiasm of the 1930's, careful reading of educational literature shows reform has been a marked concern of teachers from ancient times.

Self-Immolation

For some, the desire to make the world better is coupled with a need to devote themselves to an ideal or a way of life. They feel that they must renounce some of the worldly pleasures. Consequently, some willingly accept popular beliefs that teachers are poorly paid or unlikely to marry, and enter teaching in a spirit of self-sacrifice. We cannot forget that huge systems of parochial schools, notably those maintained by Roman Catholics, are staffed with members of teaching orders, men and women who are expressing their religious fervor by embracing ascetic ways and devoting themselves to the instruction of youth.

Correcting the Shortcomings of One's Own Past

During the years of development, quite a few people encountered unsatisfactory environments or poor relationships with grownups. These dissatisfactions left a mark upon them. They feel a need to go back and rewrite that chapter in their history. Teaching may be a way to do just that. For example, one encounters teachers who were hurt by poor methods used when they went to school. Some act as though their main reason for teaching is to show their former instructors how the job should be done. Another illustration is offered by the men or women still tortured by guilt over past quarrels with brothers or sisters. They now use teaching as a way of being nice to other young people and thus making up for what they feel they did.

Reliving Childhood Patterns

It may be pleasant to be an adult, but in a number of lives some period of early development may have yielded more satisfactions or been marked by fewer conflicts than any subsequent phase. A chance to relive that earlier period seems inviting. Without surrendering dangerously to regression, a teacher has that opportunity. This is often the reason why a teacher has a marked preference for one age group. Thus, for instance, a high school coach can live over and over again the glories of his own triumphs on the basketball court. The same thing applies to all grade levels. As pointed out earlier, the ability of a teacher to feel at one with youngsters may be a highly valuable quality.

Desire for Affection

A large number of adults are starved for affection. They enjoy the feeling that someone likes them. A teacher has contact with many children and knows that they are likely to return good feeling. This possibility makes the educational profession especially attractive.

Need for Security

As recent studies of college students have revealed, an increasing number of educated men and women are showing preoccupation with mankind's old search for security. Teaching offers steady employment and, in many districts, the possibility of a pension. Furthermore, tenure regulations provide extra protection. Such safety is highly valued.

Halfway House to Other Ambition

Because of the security and the steady income, we find that teaching attracts a number of people who have other ambitions but want to be assured of a livelihood. Moreover, in some localities, the closest or least expensive institution of higher learning is a teachers' college or normal school. A number of young people work out life plans in which the first step is to become a teacher; the next step, to go to some other field. Such plans frequently work well, as shown by the fact that every recent Congress of the United States has included at least ten former teachers. More typical, perhaps, is the young lady who was intent on becoming a great writer, but went into teaching so she would be "able to eat." A number of such people enjoy teaching and remain in the field; others fail to reach their original goal and make the best of the situation; still others leave the teaching field.

Need for Power

Many people feel complete only when they can exercise influence, when they can see other people affected by what they do. Although teaching would never satisfy a Napoleon, it does promise many chances for leadership. Furthermore, the youthfulness of a school's clientele makes the establishment of power a certainty. Even though there are some teachers who do hate children and get satisfaction from making their lives miserable, the exercise of power in schools is usually felt as being for the good of the children. It does not entail the direct destructiveness and ruthless competition which makes the winning of domination a source of moral conflict in some other occupations.

Guaranteed Superiority

To a rather large group, another attraction is that in the classroom the teacher is clearly the most well-informed, the most mature, and the most skillful person. The man or woman who has inferiority feelings, who doubts his own worth-whileness can be reassured day after day during school hours. It is a guarantee that there will be one area in life where he is the best.

SIGNIFICANCE OF THE REASONS

A similar analysis could be made for any and every profession. A study of why psychologists became psychologists might yield even more fascinating or rueful discoveries. Our purpose, however, is not that of comparing professions or of debunking claims of virtue. What led a person to enter a profession is significant only to the extent that it helps us understand his present actions and feelings.

Modification of One's Reasons for Teaching

Every single one of the reasons we have listed for joining the educational profession may serve as a start for a happy and useful professional life. What matters is the way the reason is applied. In some instances the reason for choosing the profession blends into a sublimation, which we have already shown to be a way of turning possibly harmful impulses into praiseworthy life patterns. Or a teacher may integrate his principal reason for entering the profession into a larger and more complex structure of goals and ideals. The end product can be a well-rounded life in and out of school.

When Frances Davis was a little girl, for instance, even her mother thought she was bossy. In play groups, it was she who decided what games her playmates would play. She was either the mother, the nurse, or the teacher in games of make-believe. Throughout her school career, she almost always took the lead in activities. Once in a while there were quarrels and she would be left alone. From these she learned to watch the way she gave directions and to be careful to build up the self-esteem of her friends. She became not less dominating but more adroit. To everyone it seemed natural for her to go into teaching. At first she repeated her old mistake of being too bossy, but again learned quickly from the way children reacted. Today if you were to see her walk into a classroom you would know that she knows exactly what she wants to do. She is clearly happy on her "home grounds." She has learned to enjoy being responsible for a group which is working happily and which she is adroitly helping to overcome obstacles. Among the faculty she has the reputation of being an excellent and considerate chairman of committees. Everyone agrees that when she is involved in any project things move smoothly. Each year as the summer vacation draws to an end, she looks forward to the opening of school.

When the Reasons Are Assets

Like Frances Davis, many teachers gain satisfaction from teaching while giving priority to the growth needs of young learners. In their lives they have a balanced feeling of well-being. For such people, the inevitable conflicts and frustrations of the job represent a price they are willing and able to pay for having a happy time at work. Indeed, for some, paying the price may enhance the personal significance of their life patterns. It is only through such explanations that we can account for such apparent anomalies as teachers who turn down more remunerative administrative posts, those who seek out the unusually difficult groups of problem children, and those who fight to postpone retirement on well-earned pensions.

When the Reasons Are Liabilities

At times, of course, the reasons by which a given teacher was attracted to teaching make for trouble. In some instances, the reasons create personal pressures which make it impossible to give priority to the needs of children or which lead to hostile interference with children's growth patterns. Thus, a teacher who seeks affection and goes out of her way to be nice to children may feel bitter when their preoccupation with each other makes them seem ungrateful toward her. The bitterness may lead to an inclination to punish them by increasing the number or severity of restrictions.

For others, the job itself is quite likely to prove unsatisfying. For example, the person who wanted to influence or improve children may be irked by the fact that youngsters with low IQ's seemingly refuse to learn. In such instances, disappointment is inevitable; the sad ending of the story sees a soured man or woman either quitting the profession or, worse yet, dragging along wearily and cynically through the years venting spite on hapless youngsters and colleagues.

For yet other people, the reason for becoming a teacher proves a handicap. The wish to be popular may make them into "softies" who cannot bring themselves to risk resentment by placing needed limits on undesired behavior. The unfortunate victim cannot overcome the frustrations inherent to the work, or else establishes a one-sided relationship to children which invites chaos and poor learning. For all these people teaching may threaten to poison the individual's life.

THE CHANGES TIME BRINGS

The psychological forces that once made a teacher choose that vocation do not remain fixed. They continue to change and develop. The psychological meaning the job has also shifts as one becomes immersed in the day-to-day work. For a great many individuals, becoming a teacher was a goal; once that goal was reached, they had to find something else at which to aim. Perhaps, in their daydreams, the moment they were to face a class was the point where they ended the story with the fairy-tale tag-line, "They lived happily ever after." In this section we want to look at a few of the changes time brings.

Of these changes, the most obvious is that teaching involves much more than many people think it does. There are reports to write, obdurate parents to interview, lunchrooms to supervise, and possibly standards to meet. Lesson plans go to pieces against the hard rocks of psychological reality. When the bubble breaks, the victim moans, "Why didn't someone tell me it would be like this?" Then comes the hard work of rearranging ideas and ideals to fit the professional world as it is.

For a number of teachers, the reality of working with children is far from being a shock. Rather, they find their first years full of excitement. As they meet challenges to their intellectual or emotional mastery, they glow with pride. As new discoveries follow each other they literally eat, drink, dream, and talk teaching. Unfortunately, this does not always last. Gradually they get used to children and work out stock techniques for problems which daily become more familiar. The fine excitement ebbs, and in its place there can come the boredom of dreary routine.

The processes of psychological growth continue to work throughout an individual's life. As we grow older, our needs change. Accordingly, the satisfactions which we once craved and which led us into teaching may become less important as new needs clamor to be satisfied. Possibly, the same old need may grow in a way which cannot be satisfied in the classroom. For example, the desire to have power over people, which once made managing a class look like fun, now demands a wider field for conquest.

Then again, the need we once thought to satisfy by teaching may be met in other ways. Teaching loses its emotional significance as it becomes a side issue. Thus, for instance, the young man or woman who once was starved for affection and counted on getting it from children may develop a circle of companions whose close friendship is more warming than the affection of children. Now the ties of a juvenile group seem pallid, unworthy of effort.

The meaning which children may have in an adult's personal life may also change. An example, which has been overemphasized, is that of a young woman who saw in her pupils the foreshadows of sons or daughters she expected to have. Gradually she may come to see in them bitter reminders that life denied her hopes for romance. Much more commonplace is the almost universal situation, previously described, of children taking on the qualities of obstacles standing in the way of professional success.

Administrative changes take their toll. A teacher who once found satisfaction in working with one age group or in a particular assignment may fall victim to professional opinions which attribute greater prestige to another age group or a different type of teaching. Then, either on his own volition or on the initiative of an administrator, he leaves the type of teaching in which he was happy and moves into a post where satisfaction is lost. The actual situation may not be recognized; instead the discouragement is directed against teaching as an occupation.

Other community pressures may also force teachers into roles they do not want. The basketball coach who revels in working with a team may make his own life miserable trying to be a witty luncheon-club speaker. The gay, enthusiastic new teacher may hate herself as she has to become a stern disciplinarian. The tender-hearted counselor may feel a deep dishonesty in assuming case-hardened cynicism toward children of a minority group which he begins to accept because it is displayed by "everyone who really matters."

In all these ways, the romance many once attached to teaching rubs off. Intimacy with teachers and teaching destroys illusions and misapprehensions. This is not always a bad thing, but it does make problems for a number of people. Naturally, if they can work out a good adjustment to their changed and more realistic concept, they may gain an even deeper satisfaction.

Although in every school system there are some teachers whose lives center around their work, others discover that there is much more to living. Instead of finding their spare time filled with thoughts of teaching, they find that problems from outside school intrude into the classroom hours. If there was ever an expectation that teaching would meet most of life's needs, it evaporates.

Of course, there are some fortunate teachers for whom life's changes bring increasing satisfactions. For them, the reality is richer than their first hopes, excitement increases with knowledge and skill, and they see more in children than they had dreamed. To such lucky individuals, teaching may be an ever better balance wheel for mental health. For the many others, teaching may be a source of difficulty.

Illustrative of the hazards of change is the story of Calvin Muir, a once-proud music teacher. When he first came to Blainesburg, his popularity and his joy grew by leaps and bounds. He liked adolescents, he basked in the praise of the superintendent, and he expanded at the sound of his first bands playing well. For a few years, that was all he wanted. Whether it was the urging of his wife or his own self-intoxication at being hailed by his fellow citizens no one knew for sure, but when he was in his early thirties he began to hunger for bigger worlds to conquer. Money bulked larger in his talk. He became jealous of the athletic coach, he insisted on entering state music competitions, and he began giving music lessons in his spare time. To forestall interference from the superintendent he organized a group of friends and parents to back him in battles within the school board. He became a wily, ruthless fighter who was the storm center of several nasty fights. Two superintendents who fought against him had to resign. Yet, his satisfaction faded as he lost friends in the faculty. Bitterest blow of all, no band of his ever won a first prize. To bolster his self-importance he began to circulate fictions of triumphs elsewhere. He now spends his summers playing in orchestras in summer resorts, and frantically tries to develop schemes which will develop into lucrative work or fame in show business.

WHAT CAN WE DO ABOUT IT?

No one can expect to get from a book the solution to a very deep dissatisfaction. Each individual being very different from every other, there can be no pat solution that will work for everyone. For this reason a trained psychologist snorts at books which purport to solve all personal problems. These books will help a few people, but will leave others untouched or even worse off than before. There are, however, some general strategies which, with intelligent variations, have aided quite a few adults in facing dissatisfactions.

Develop Self-Awareness

The better a person understands himself, the less likely he is to be tossed about by events over which he has no control. This does not mean every adult should psychoanalyze himself. In fact, complete self-understanding is not possible. However, a greater degree of self-awareness can usually be obtained. This is often basic to any attempt to deal intelligently with problems of living. For instance, the teacher who is disgusted with children because they so often fail to learn as she wished, can well examine the source of her discontent. Once she realizes it is due to unrealistic ambitions for the children, she can better meet her own yearning to prove her personal competence by setting herself goals where there is a greater chance of success.

Seek Satisfactions Elsewhere

Very much a part of any self-awareness is knowledge of some of the satisfactions one hopes to attain through teaching. If these expectations run counter to school realities or if they would produce conflict with professional ethics, then there is a chance to remedy the trouble by seeking those satisfactions elsewhere in living. In this manner one can drain off some of the pressures causing difficulty. Thus, a man who yearned for friendly participation in young adolescents' groups, a participation which was denied because of the roles in which a community's young people cast their junior high school teachers, might be able to find what he wanted by acting as a Scoutmaster.

Deliberate Exposure to New Experiences

When life becomes drab and unsatisfactory, a new experience can have a tonic effect. More important, many of us are prone to fall into routines which once were satisfactory and in which we find security. Deliberately broadening one's range of activity may introduce a new and valuable element into the life pattern. It is for this reason that many school systems wisely provide opportunities for exchange teaching and for sabbatical leaves devoted to study or travel.

Re-Evaluate Total Load

In any case, it is a good idea once in a while to get away from daily pressures and then go over one's total life pattern. Some people have problems because they are giving themselves too little to do; others are busy at those things which yield less satisfaction than other activities that have been crowded out; still others have spread themselves so thin that they give themselves no chance to gain satisfaction from anything. A re-evaluation of such patterns may provide the clue to happier living. To cite a very simple illustration: now and then a teacher falls into a pattern of teaching which requires classes to produce so many papers and tests that almost all the time is spent grading papers. Once this is recognized as a source of trouble, a shift to other methods may release time to be spent on more interesting professional reading, visiting with friends, or playgoing.

Study Someone with More Difficult Problems

Some restlessness is caused by failure to live up to the standards one has built in daydreams. It helps, therefore, to compare oneself not only with those who seem to be better off, but also with those facing more difficult problems. The purpose is not so much to develop a Pollyanna attitude as to get perspective. Also, the techniques which are working for someone with a heavier burden may be suggestive.

Evaluate Dissatisfaction

Dissatisfaction itself is worth examining. How widespread is it? How serious? How much of a problem? Obviously, to be irked at one minor aspect of living is quite a different matter from feeling a distaste at everything that happens all day long. A mild irritation has a meaning which cannot be compared with a profound loathing of an entire life pattern. It is one thing to look forward to a chance to complain to one's friend; something quite different to wish one were dead. The degree and extent of one's dissatisfactions must be faced. Not to be overlooked is the possibility that the real object for discontent is not teaching itself, but some condition or relationship elsewhere. The cause of dissatisfaction may be in the private life of the teacher and be displaced to the professional situation.

Look for Help on Specific Questions

Often, a good part of a person's troubles seem to stem from a single problem he cannot solve. Not infrequently, a teacher's life is made miserable, for example, by inability to work with a particular child or to handle one aspect of teaching. If such is true, it would seem wise to get help on that specific point.

Elaine Cotton, for instance, was bothered by her inability to get any spontaneous art work from Miss Hawkins' fifth graders. Each time she was scheduled to be in the room she planned to stimulate a free discussion out of which projects would be developed. Each time she found herself delivering a monologue and then assigning formal exercises. The children seemed scared or stiff or just plain uninterested. Her failure with this one group made her feel like pretending sickness on days she was to come to Miss Hawkins' class. Finally, in desperation, she mentioned the problem to Mrs. Johnson, the principal.

Mrs. Johnson smiled and said, "For goodness' sakes, don't let that get you down. Miss Hawkins believes in running her room so that the children are scared to peep. Don't expect to get any discussion there. You just go in with some interesting things for them to do and start right off by telling them what to do. After they are all at work talk to them one at a time. But I doubt if you will get very far. It is too bad, but she has only a year to go."

Miss Cotton already felt better. She did try Mrs. Johnson's suggestion. Gradually, she broke through the children's wall of fear. They would, rather pathetically, come up to her in the hall or after class, and ask permission to try out their own ideas. She took real pleasure in these little measures of success.

Talk It Over with Friends

So much of any person's life is bound up with other people that it is often impossible to work out a problem by one's self. Just talking about a problem with friends often clarifies the problem. Sometimes, of course, the friends can give active help, but even when this is not the case, talking may provide relief. In addition, it can lead to insight and self-awareness.

Where the nature or the intensity of the difficulties is beyond the point where friends can assist, it may be the height of wisdom to seek professional help. Depending upon the situation, one can utilize the resources of qualified counseling services, social agencies, mental hygiene clinics, or psychiatrists.

Stimulate Group Discussion

As one would suspect, the problems of all teachers are rather similar. Therefore, the pooling of ideas and experiences may help all concerned. The "gripe sessions" in a teachers' cafeteria can have a salutary influence from the point of view of mental hygiene. Even more valuable is systematic and organized consideration of problems, making use of qualified leaders.

Develop Supplementary Areas

At times, the solution to boredom or frustration may involve the planned development of new areas of life. Group action may enable several people to provide each other with the needed activities. Teachers, because of their training in group processes, often do play a large role in such community enterprises. Professional organizations have done yeoman's service, both by directly tackling causes of dissatisfaction and by enabling members to meet some of their own needs through committee work, social gatherings, operation of cooperatives, and other satisfying experiences.

Social action performs another valuable function by helping individual teachers to separate issues. Thus, a campaign for tenure may help some to see that their dissatisfaction with teaching is a result of anxiety derived from staff relationships, rather than a product of classroom relationships.

Recognize New Possibilities in Teaching

When dissatisfaction seems to grow out of a low level of living outside school, many teachers have repaired the situation by looking for and discovering new possibilities in teaching. This is one of the happy results of many curriculum workshops and experimental programs. Child study groups in school systems can be quite effective in this way. Unfortunately, some old-timers, by hostility to such programs, will unknowingly deprive themselves of finding new sources of stimulation in their own classrooms.

SIGNIFICANCE OF STAFF RELATIONS

We must not make the mistake of supposing that all teachers' mental hygiene problems center on the children. Actually, for many there is more personal significance in relationships with other staff members. Many transfers are motivated by desire to join a more congenial group. For quite a few teachers, the decision to stay in the profession or leave it hinges upon the satisfactions they get out of their faculty associations.

What Other Teachers Mean to Us

One aspect of such relations is how the teachers see each other. Just as children cast their teachers in various psychological roles, and teachers similarly see children as filling certain needs, so each teacher may endow the others with various characteristics. For instance, one teacher may see others as rivals, contestants in a competition. Again, one member of a faculty may seek to find someone to protect her, to help her, and upon whom to lean. An experienced teacher may try to cast newcomers in the role of worshiping apprentices or as novices who are bound to make fools of themselves. A new teacher may tremble before the old-timers on the supposition that they are fault-finders. Some of these expectations have deep roots in a person's make-up. The pattern of these expectations may often be analyzed with profit.

Group Spirit

The ways in which the relations we have been describing finally work out depend upon the general tone or group spirit of the faculty. In some schools, bickering and fault-finding are traditions. In others, especially in some big systems, there is no group life worth mentioning. In still others, there is an atmosphere of warm companionship. In some buildings one can almost feel the tension; in others, there is easygoing relaxation. Obviously, a bad psychological climate imperils the mental and emotional health of the staff. It is not something to be shrugged off. Rather, it is a serious problem to be tackled with all the resources that can be mustered.

Finding One's Place in the Group

One of the big tasks of many teachers is to find their places in the faculty group. For some this involves the problem of retaining their own personalities and ideals. On the one hand, they like to be liked by the others. On the other hand, they want to be distinct personalities. The extent to which a group enforces uniformity and the way it reacts to differences are matters which have great weight for individual members. A teacher having difficulties may want to think out his personal strategy in this respect.

Feelings About Role Expectations

A group is quite likely to "type" its members, as we pointed out in our discussion of children's groups. The same thing happens in a school staff. Whether or not what is expected of any individual is based on reality or on legend, the several expectations make for either adjustment or friction. For instance, how would you like to be the teacher everyone assumed would ask laughably silly questions at staff meetings? . . . Such pressures and tensions may be reduced by giving careful consideration to the different viewpoints.

SOME THINGS PRINCIPALS CAN DO

As in all group processes, the development of inter-staff relations often reflects the personality and the methods of the leader. However, a principal has to deal with some forces which are rarely given adequate weight. For instance, the many frustrations inevitably involved in teaching are bound to create some aggressive feelings. These feelings are quite likely to be displaced against the school administration. A principal who understands mental hygiene principles will recognize what is happening and will see a useful role in playing the target, rather than in getting angry and cracking down on his staff. A thoroughgoing mental hygiene for school administrators remains to be written. At this point we shall comment—all too briefly—on a few steps a principal can take to aid teachers.

Keep Routines to a Minimum

Unnecessary restrictions which have to be enforced increase the number of conflicts between teachers and their classes, and raise the probability of tension.

Listen

Much talk helps relieve the speaker's feelings. The principal who can listen instead of arguing or trying to squelch complaints helps relieve tension.

Use Democratic Processes

As shown in the Lippitt experiments on group atmospheres, democratic, as opposed to dictatorial, procedures reduce the harmful outcropping of aggression.

Respect Established Hierarchies

Where there are established channels of dealing with problems or of supplying supervisory suggestion, the principal should respect them. Many adults find it nerve-wracking to try to serve two masters or to please two different people.

Back Up Teachers

Nothing destroys morale faster than for a principal to fail the teachers when they expect his support. Low morale is an outgrowth of their insecurity.

Minimize the Evils of Cliques

When cliques form, the principal should recognize the probability of rivalry. It is as bad for a teacher or a group of friends to be the principal's pet as for a child to be teacher's pet. The unfavored group will naturally feel dissatisfaction with the situation.

Show Equanimity When Mistakes Are Made

The less upset the principal acts when a teacher makes a mistake, the less anxiety will teachers feel. Although many will never be able to get over being tense at the possibility of error, a relaxed atmosphere will reduce the severity of this type of reaction.

Establish Friendly Relations with the Community

By building good rapport with community leaders, a principal can reduce some of the pressures upon teachers. This will ease one source of dissatisfaction and divided feelings.

Keep Detail in Its Place

There is enough normal conflict for a teacher in the relationships with children without adding to it by overemphasizing details. It is hard enough for a teacher truly to give priority to the needs of children. If the school office insists that priority instead be given to records or other routine matters, pressures can approach the intolerable.

Be Flexible

When new problems are met effectively in new ways instead of being forced into old, ill-fitting procedures, teachers feel more sure of themselves.

Give Criticisms in Private

The task of correcting ill-advised procedures and of influencing teachers' conduct involves all the elements discussed in connection with the techniques teachers use to influence their classes. In addition, a teacher's prestige with colleagues and students is very important. Accordingly, when criticism is necessary, it should be delivered in private conferences.

Appreciate Own Role as Example-Setter

In contacts with children and parents, the principal sets an example. To the extent that he is respected and liked the teachers will identify with him. Hence, if his emotional management of daily situations is wise, the wisdom will spread. If he keeps cheerful under attack, happy when confronting problems, unafraid of admitting mistakes, and capable of dealing with juvenile misconduct without paling with alarm or throwing a tantrum, the same qualities are bolstered in the staff. The practice-what-you-preach strategy is of paramount importance.

SUMMARY

Like all professions, teaching carries with it a number of conflicts. To cope with these effectively requires that all concerned apply scientific methods and skills to the study, not only of the children, but also of teachers and the administrative staff.

The key role in the mental hygiene of teachers is played by the school board and the superintendent. There is an emotional chain reaction in every school system which carries feelings and patterns of action from the central office to the individual classrooms. Where the top administrator acts in accordance with good mental hygiene practices, they are more likely to pervade all aspects of the school system. Conversely, if "headquarters" is a place of high tension, teachers will have to shoulder an extra burden in applying psychological knowledge to their dealings with children and parents.

ADDITIONAL READINGS

Barker, M. Elizabeth, *Personality Adjustments of Teachers Related to Efficiency in Teaching*, New York, Bureau of Publications, Teachers College, Columbia University, 1946.

Donovan, Frances R., *The Schoolma'am*, New York, Frederick A. Stokes, 1938.

Heaton, Kenneth L., Camp, William G., and Diederich, Paul B., *Professional Education for Experienced Teachers*, Chicago, University of Chicago Press, 1940.

Prall, Charles E., and Cushman, C. Leslie, *Teacher Education in Service*, Washington, American Council on Education, 1944.

Roethlisberger, F. J., and Dickson, William, *Management and the Worker*, Cambridge, Harvard University Press, 1939.

PART 

Teaching—How and at What Level

THE TEACHING PROCESS

THE HIGH HILL[1]
Mary Deasy

DISCUSSION AND ANALYSIS

In this deftly done and touching story, we, the readers, are presented with a series of contrasts. Miss Farrell's redheaded prettiness is counterpointed by the plainness of Miss Janiek; Elvy Morgum with her thin face and shabby black coat accentuates the expensive, doll-like quality of Sisley Ross; and the apparent selfishness of Margot is balanced by the sensitivity of the narrator. Organizing these contrasts is the symbol of the "high hill in the sunlight, above the hidden valley of childhood." This, of course, is metaphorical language and, as such, suggests more than it says. The student may wish to test his understanding of the story by trying to explain or paraphrase this central image. Would it have been equally effective if the author had said "beyond the confusions of childhood lies maturity"? Why not?

As we have suggested, the two teachers present an interesting study in contrasts, both in appearance and in teaching methods. Although our obvious sympathies lie with Miss Farrell, we should remember that Miss Janiek was also an effective teacher, who brought to her students an "aura of maternal warmth." Yet Miss Janiek often speaks crossly to her pupils, and refers to them as "little savages." How does the author explain this apparent discrepancy? Do you feel that there are teachers like Miss Janiek? What the author seems to be saying is that the way a teacher feels toward her students is more important that what she says to them. Do you agree with such a thesis? What is the real source of Miss Janiek's bitterness?

Such a story presents an arresting analysis of the growth and motives of children. From one coign of vantage it might be termed "child

[1] Copyright, 1948, by Harper & Brothers. Reprinted from *Harper's Magazine* by permission.

psychology in action." That is, as the story ripens toward its end, we can observe a few of the girls in the actual process of maturation; they are the ones who have begun to learn the meaning of words like *mercy* and *love* and *loyalty* and *understanding*. Which of the girls are these? Has the character of anyone else been changed or secured?

Twenty years ago, when I was six years old and went to school for the first time, the new theories of child education hadn't made much impression yet on the public school system, and we still sat all day in one varnished, blackboarded, chalk-smelling room, fighting our way through the thorny prickles of the alphabet, and laying the first staggering foundations of the art of writing. Miss Farrell, our teacher, was red-haired and young and Irish, and she threw herself into the labor of instruction with an earnestness that left her sometimes, I suppose, full of the tears of a sense of desperate inadequacy behind the flushed cheeks, the curling hair, the dark-blue eyes with the Celtic shadows beneath them, that were all that we, with our pride in the possession of a young, pretty teacher, could see.

No doubt she had her moments of self-searching and frightened emptiness, when it must have seemed to her that she was failing both in the task for which the school board had hired her, that of making literate citizens out of us, and in the task which she had imposed on herself, of leading us into the paths of the passionate conviction of human brotherhood that was the mixed legacy of her Irish blood and her American birth. I can remember her eager voice sounding the words that came to us, secure in the closed hidden valley in which children live, with a meaning still too evanescent for us to grasp—words that said *love* and *mercy* and *tolerance*, ripe round syllables that broke and vanished in the thin harsh air of our simpler world.

Miss Janiek, from the third-grade room across the hall, talked to her about it after school, sitting in Miss Farrell's big varnished chair behind the desk, while Miss Farrell, standing beside her, gave her half her attention, the other half being directed at those of us who had stayed behind to erase the blackboards and gather the chalk neatly into white dusty boxes.

"They're little savages," Miss Janiek said. "The whole lot of them." We felt her gaze wandering over us with the darkness, the tenderness, the pungent vitality in it that we sensed without understanding. "Sitting there and watching a person with those blank clear eyes of theirs," she said. And then: "School-teaching! The women who bore those children don't understand them, and yet they expect us to take a good three dozen of them and get inside their minds somehow, put knowledge and skill and morality there—And you're lucky if after three years you've taught them to hold a pen, and add two pairs of figures, and squeeze out the meaning of a row of letters set end to end, that spell out a sentence nobody from the beginning of time was ever interested in reading: *The cat runs, the dog jumps*—"

"No," Miss Farrell said. "There's more than that." She said the words again: *mercy*, and *loyalty*, and *understanding*. "We learned," she said. "Somebody taught us. We weren't born knowing, any more than they were. Now it's our turn to teach—"

"We're going now, Miss Farrell," Sisley Ross said.

We may forget the others, the anonymous outgrown faces, the long-ago names of earliest schoolfellows; but none of us will forget Sisley Ross, because she was the girl with the spun-sugar curls and the cornflower-blue eyes and the pink-and-white dresses, the doll-heroine of our earnest dreams, as perfect and as unattainable as if, fashioned of wax or bisque, she had sat serenely staring from a shop-window, with a price tag, on which there appeared a figure beyond the most fantastic imagined limits of our parents' generosity, dangling quietly from one wrist. She stood in the doorway now; Margot Berry was beside her, waiting to walk home with her, daring any of us, with the imperious, watchful glance of her light-blue eyes, to dispute her prerogative.

"C-a-t, cat," Miss Janiek said. Her eyes brooded over us fiercely. "Teach them that, if you've got to earn your salary. Teach them the immutable rule of two plus two."

"Good night, Miss Farrell," Sisley said. "Good night, Miss Janiek."

"Good night, children," Miss Farrell said. And to Miss Janiek: "There's more than that. You know it, too."

Miss Janiek wore on the third finger of her left hand a gold ring with a diamond held in it by tiny prongs of gold. It was an engagement ring, but she was not engaged any more, because the man who had given her the ring had been a flier in the war (having given up teaching the French language safely and quietly in a city high school to fly the French skies, where there was no need for any language but the stuttering burst of a machine gun), and he had been killed, so that she was left with nothing but the ring, and a photograph, and a memory that seemed queerer company each year for the dark heavy face and the invariable shapeless brown dresses that she wore. There was something about her that reminded us vaguely of our own mothers, as if, without in the least resembling them, she brought to us the same aura of maternal warmth; we knew this instinctively, reading behind manner and speech to the warmth inside, while the other teachers wondered audibly at the attraction she had for us, she who rarely said a word to us that was not spoken in a tone of fierce and desperate exasperation.

I remember the day she brought Elvy Morgum into our room. It was in the morning, and we had just sat down in our places when the door banged open and she came in, thrusting before her a girl of our own age—a small girl, hatless, her features narrow, with a curiously granitelike sharpness about them, beneath a harsh tangle of hair, above an old black cut-down coat of worn velveteen.

"Here's another one for you," she shouted to Miss Farrell, in her clear loud voice. "Elvy, or Elvira, Morgum; it doesn't seem to make much difference; there are Morgums all over the place this morning, and none of them, not even the oldest, seems to know. They tell me there are four more, younger than this one, still at home, so it looks as if you'll have them in permanent supply, as long as they stay in the neighborhood."

With her hand still on Elvy Morgum's shoulder, she gave her a slight thrust forward toward Miss Farrell's desk. We watched as Elvy moved reluctantly across the front of the room, seeing the hitch and drag of one foot as she walked. She stopped beside Miss Farrell's desk, and Miss Farrell said clearly, stretching out one hand to her: "Elvy Morgum. What a pretty name."

"Pretty or not, it's what she'll have to do with till the Lord or a man releases her," Miss Janiek said. "The one I've got is Theophilus, as near as I can make it out. The whole herd of them came wandering in here this morning without parent or guardian, so there's a little confusion about some of the biographical data."

Miss Farrell shook her head; she was smiling, looking over at Miss Janiek.

"I'm one of nine myself," she said. "It's an active life—especially for the mother." She looked back at Elvy Morgum. "I have six brothers and two sisters, Elvy," she said to her. "Would you like to tell me how many you have?"

Elvy stood there at the front of the room without speaking. She looked at Miss Farrell with a dark, wary look, taking her all in, the white soft blouse and the blue skirt and the eyes that were smiling at her, waiting for her to speak.

"The whole set of them are like that," Miss Janiek said. "Silent. Wild. You'd think there wasn't a tongue in the lot of them. You'll have to take time."

"I will," Miss Farrell said.

She took Elvy's hand, and brought her down the aisle, and let her sit at a desk behind Sisley Ross's. Sisley turned round to look at her, not smiling, only staring at her curiously, with her sweet blue-eyed doll's stare.

"This is Sisley Ross, Elvy," Miss Farrell said. "Sisley, would you like to show Elvy where to put her coat?"

"Yes, Miss Farrell," Sisley said.

Even her voice was a doll's prompt obedient pipe at the proper pressure of a button. We watched her go down the aisle, plump and firm in her pink dress and ruffles, with Elvy Morgum toiling slowly behind, hitch and drag, hitch and drag, her figure witchlike in profile above the bunchy black coat.

That was sometime late in January. By mid-February Miss Farrell must have hidden even more often than before the tears of her sense of desperate inadequacy behind the flushed cheeks and the blue Celtic eyes that she showed to us; for she had watched us now every day, for almost a month, sitting before her in an unredeemed and unembarrassed thwarting of every one of the bright words that she had said to us so often. She saw us, no doubt, looking at her with the clear stare of childhood, equally without malice and without mercy, while, behind Sisley Ross, Elvy Morgum crouched in taciturn isolation, the misfit, the unwanted, who wandered alone on the fringe of our games at recess, and trailed home alone after school was out.

For, in spite of Miss Farrell, she had no friends, and when the fourteenth of February arrived, and we were given permission, during the last half-hour of our schooltime, to exchange the Valentines we had bought for each other, scrawling the names that we could scarcely write on the backs of the double heart-shaped bits of paper with the printed verses inside that we could scarcely read, none was left on her desk by little Jasper Corrin, who had been appointed, because he was the best reader in the class, to be our postman.

On Sisley's desk the bright heart-shaped folders fluttered in heaps. None of us had forgotten to send her our tributes, and half-a-dozen of the boys, with spending-money burning in their pockets and admiration burning in their hearts, had lumped the whole sum of money and adoration in one extravagant lacy token, all gilt and froth, that lay on her desk now with its sender's name or a bashful—*Guess Who?*—staggering earnestly across beneath the pierced hearts and the chaste pink-ribboned cupids. We watched as Jasper, walking up and down the aisles with his big box, paused again beside Sisley's desk and laid on it a huge red heart frilled round with stiff white paper. She turned it over without excitement, though it was the handsomest of the lot, and we watched her index finger tracing slowly the letters of the name.

"It's from Elvy Morgum," she announced presently, a little astonishment creeping into her voice.

We looked into Elvy's dark, taciturn face, lit now with a kind of radiant terror of shyness as Sisley turned round to her, all of us wondering by what magical process a Morgum, to whom two-for-a-penny was always half-a-penny too dear, had come into possession of the most magnificent Valentine we had seen that day. But at the same moment there was a cry, sharp and clear, one almost of triumph, and we turned to see Margot Berry standing in her place across the aisle, pointing a steady finger at the great red heart on Sisley's desk.

"It's mine," she said. "*I* gave it to Sisley. *I* bought it for her with my own money."

She came over and picked up the Valentine and showed us the eraser marks over which Elvy had written her name. If we looked closely we could see the *Margot* too, violently erased but still printing the paper with the neat heavy marks of Margot's signature, beneath the narrow scrawl that said *Elvy Morgum*.

"She stole it," Margot said. "She stole it out of the box at noontime and put her name on it instead of mine. I can prove it's mine. Miss Farrell—"

We watched Miss Farrell come down the aisle and pick up the red heart and look at it, and all the while Margot's voice went clamoring on, and Miss Farrell did not even look at her, or tell her to stop. After a while she said to Elvy, in a voice that did not sound angry to us, but full only of an amazed and tremulous desperation: "Did you take the Valentine, Elvy?"

We looked at Elvy again. She was sitting at her desk with her hands shut tight together in her lap and her head thrust forward a little, so that her dark hair fell and hid her face. She didn't say anything, and Miss Farrell asked again: "Did you take because you wanted a pretty Valentine to give to Sisley? Is that it, Elvy?"

"She stole it," Margot said again. "It was mine; I paid for it with my own money."

"Hush," Miss Farrell said.

She looked at the three of them: at Sisley, suspended in polite waiting amazement, at Margot's red clamorous face, at Elvy's bunched stubborn figure crouched in her seat.

"It was very wrong of you to take Margot's Valentine, Elvy," she said (she was doing what the school board expected of her, I learned to understand later, standing there for morality, and the legal statutes of the state of Indiana, and the Ten Commandments themselves, all at one time; but there was something more she wanted to stand there for too, something that said *love* and said *mercy* and said *understanding,* something that rose like a high hill in the sunlight, above the hidden valley of childhood in which we lived). "If you'd come to me," she said to Elvy, "I'd have helped you make Sisley a Valentine, one even prettier than this. We could have made it together, and then it would have been yours to give to her." She turned to us suddenly, her face pink and shining with her earnestness. "You *do* understand, all of you," she said, "that Elvy only took the Valentine because she wanted something nice to give to Sisley? She didn't take it for herself. You *do* understand that, don't you?"

"She stole it," Margot said. "She did too steal it. I'm going to tell my father."

She looked round in clear unbending triumph at our closed and sober and approving faces.

Then it was the day that Miss Janiek lost her ring. Or it wasn't that she had lost it, she said, because she knew exactly where she had put it, on the ledge of the window in the washroom when she had washed her hands; only when she had gone back for it, it was gone, and not even a ring that had been worn as long as that one had been, she said, could have learned how to walk out of a room alone.

"One of those little savages took it," she said, sitting in the big chair behind Miss Farrell's desk on that cold March afternoon after school, her dark eyes brooding over our inadequacies as we industriously pounded erasers together out the window. "Yours, or mine, or poor little Collins' down the hall," she said. "What they'll do with it, heaven only knows. They haven't any more idea of its value—which I must say isn't large, the salaries of high-school teachers in 1917 being what they were—than a tribe of Choctaw Indians in the year 1491."

Miss Farrell said, "Don't. Don't say that. You know you don't mean—"

She was standing behind us, looking out the window at the street below, quiet now after the long rush and chatter of the lines of children streaming from the school, lying straight and deserted except for a single figure toiling slowly along in an old black velveteen coat. Without looking around, we knew what sort of expression there would be in Miss Farrell's eyes as she stood there watching Elvy Morgum disappear down the street, because as much to her as to us the tale of the lost ring must have come as a sudden whisper of sinister conjecture leading deviously to the little figure in the old black coat. I don't know how it was that we *knew*, as soon as we heard the tale of the ring, as certainly as if we had been there watching the sharp profile, the pure eyes, bent over the glittering bauble on the window-ledge, looking at it for a long moment, in terrific indecision, before the grubby fingers, darting forth suddenly, snatched up the round of gold broken by the winking diamond-blaze, and concealed it swiftly in a faded gingham pocket, along with perhaps a half-sucked lemon drop, a rusty penpoint, and a bit of blue glass that she had picked up off the street. But we *knew*, and the knowledge was like something hidden and wicked inside us, as if we, by our absolute yet wholly groundless assurance, were somehow sharing in the darkness of Elvy's crime.

The next day, at recess time, Miss Farrell kept Elvy back in the classroom while the rest of us trooped outside to the sunlit schoolyard. We stood in tight clusters under the bare limbs of the two big oak trees in the north corner of the yard, our games abandoned, standing where we could watch the windows of the classroom, as if we thought that what was happening there was something lurid and violent, that would flash out its meaning to us through the blank long panes. But all that did happen was that after a little while we saw the side door of the school open and Elvy come out. She came across the yard, pausing at a few feet's distance from us, not joining us, but staying on the fringe of things, as she had done ever since she had first come among us. After a while it was Margot who spoke.

"What did she say to you?" she asked.

There was excitement, almost a kind of respect, in the silence with which we waited for her answer. We watched her standing there before us, her eyes going from one to the other of us as if they could not quite believe what they saw: the excitement, the respect, the fearful admiration. She took a step toward us, hesitating on the drag of her lame foot.

"She didn't say anything. I wasn't afraid of her," she said.

Her voice was hoarse, not loud, as if she didn't use it often and it was a little out of practice. We remembered then that we had hardly ever heard it; even when Miss Farrell asked her a question in school, usually she only got up and stood there, silent, her head thrust forward a little, poised stubbornly like the head of a small granite idol.

"Miss Janiek lost her ring," Margot said in a loud voice, as if it were something she was a little afraid to say. "She left it in the washroom; she told Miss Farrell she left it there. Maybe if she doesn't get it back she'll go tell the principal."

Elvy stood there looking at us without moving; her eyes were watching Sisley Ross, seeing the way the pink had come up in her cheeks from the excitement.

"I wouldn't be afraid," Elvy said.

Her voice was still hoarse, but more excited and strained, the way the boys' voices sounded when they were boasting to each other about the things they could do.

"Not even if you were the one that took it?" Margot said daringly.

"Nobody ever said I took it," Elvy said. She was answering Margot, but she seemed to be talking to Sisley all along. "I wouldn't be afraid, even if they did say I took it," she said. We heard her breath coming fast between the words, as if she had been running hard. "I wouldn't be afraid," she said. "Even if I did take it—"

Watching her, we could see the pocket of her dress bulging slightly, fancying the secret hoard inside, the half-sucked lemon drop, the rusty pen-point, and, at the bottom, hard and dangerous and bright, the round of gold and the winking diamond. Something like a sigh escaped us, a long exhalation of fearful admiration. A girl in blue held out a handful of jacks suddenly.

"We're going to play jacks," she said to Elvy. "Do you want to play too? You can have first turn."

She smiled at Elvy, questioningly, almost timidly, but Elvy kept on looking at Sisley Ross.

"Are you going to play?' she said to her, in that same hoarse, unbelieving voice.

Sisley shook her head. "No," she said. "I don't think I want to play. I think I just want to walk around the yard." She waited a minute, watching Elvy, her pink-and-white face serene yet asking. "Do you think you'd like to come, too?" she said.

We saw them go off together across the yard, side by side in the March sunlight, walking slowly, so that Elvy could keep up. They were still walking together when the bell rang and it was time for us to go back into the school again.

It is hard to explain what happened to us after that. Such things—the sudden mob-shift, the peculiar fascination of the deed too dark for our own doing—are always difficult to analyze, though no one who has ever thrilled to the adventures of Jesse James or Robin Hood, or has lived to see, less innocently, the pathological submission of whole peoples to the mere smell and rattle of a lawless violence, is without the knowledge of what they are like.

For our own part, from the moment when, seized with the conviction that Elvy Morgum had dared things beyond the farthest range of our audacity, we watched her walk away with Sisley Ross under our very eyes, we could only fall deeper into the pit of the submission which our wicked knowledge had dug for us. I remember that Elvy was wary at first, half-suspicious, it seemed, that we might suddenly take back again this strange gift of supremacy that we had thrust on her; but as the days passed and we did nothing, her confidence grew, and she began to queen it over us with a kind of frightened taciturnity. She had grasped the fact that her ascendancy over us rested on her ability to represent to us a more violent nature than any of us owned, and she was doing her best, in her small inarticulate way, to keep up to the pitch of the character that we expected of her.

Not, I suppose, that it made a great deal of difference to her whether we bowed to her or not, as long as Sisley Ross remained impressed. We used to watch the two of them, Elvy and Sisley, walking home together, arm in arm, after school; and there were times when Miss Farrell and Miss Janiek watched them too, standing—as on the day that Margot and I heard them talking together—before the windows in our empty classroom, where they could look out over the street below.

That afternoon Margot and I were pasting on the end window the Easter lilies we had cut from stiff white paper (they were the best in the class, chosen after heated competition), and no doubt Miss Farrell and Miss Janiek believed that we could not hear them, for they were keeping their voices low, standing close together at the other end of the room. Miss Janiek said: "Well, she's in the middle of it now. I thought that was what you wanted. Wasn't it?"—and we heard Miss Farrell answer her, her voice sounding quick and unhappy, different from the way it did when she spoke to us: "But not like that. I wanted them to be her friends—"

"Why not like that?" Miss Janiek said. "Why isn't it as good a way as any? It's their world; they've made the laws; and they're satisfied—"

"No," said Miss Farrell. "It isn't the right way. It can never be the right way."

We could see her face in profile—the short, earnest, slightly tiptilted nose, the round chin, the curve of the forehead beneath the bright curling hair, and, behind it, the turn of Miss Janiek's dark head on its powerful neck, the two of them together like the picture of Day and Night in our readers.

"Why isn't it the right way?" Miss Janiek said. "Isn't it the way we do things ourselves in our world, only for the thin breath of fine words that we grudge even the few moments it takes us to say? Are you trying to make them better than we are ourselves?"

"Yes," Miss Farrell said.

Margot and I looked at each other, not understanding, each looking at the other to see if she understood. Then we heard Miss Janiek saying, in a low harsh voice that sounded somehow as if she had just been crying, or was just going to cry: "I don't care; I don't care about any of it. I've got my own thirty-six, and next year they'll be Collins' thirty-six, and the next year someone else's; and by the time they're fifteen years old, if they remember me at all, they'll remember me only as a kind of ogress who kept them in sometimes after school, and made them recite tables and learn the difference between Christopher Columbus and George Washington, when all they wanted was to be outside in the sun—"

Miss Farrell slipped her hand inside Miss Janiek's arm.

"No," she said. "They'll remember you. And not like that, not just the Christopher Columbus and the George Washington part—"

Miss Janiek shook her head.

"I know better," she said. "You're young; you're not used to losing things yet." Then she sounded as if she were trying to laugh. "Lord," she said, "I've even lost my ring, my little round of golden faith, with a diamond in it to remind me that even I was once thought prized and rare."

They did not say that it was Elvy Morgum who had taken the ring, but we stayed secure in our wicked knowledge and our dark, resenting admiration till another afternoon, this time a dripping day late in April, when half a dozen of us, Elvy Morgum and Sisley Ross among us, had stayed behind to help decorate the classroom for May Day. We had finished the decorations, and had on rain capes and overshoes already, when someone came marching in at the open door of the classroom. It was Miss Janiek, and she was holding her left hand stretched out in front of her, looking at it as if she did not quite believe what she saw there—the gleaming golden circle, the bright flash of the diamond.

"In a pawn shop," she cried out, in her strong voice, to Miss Farrell. "A pawn shop, of all places in the world! Along with the little cheap fur jackets, the loving cups, the lost treasured junk of a hundred lives—"

Miss Farrell exclaimed: "But who—?"

She stood before Miss Janiek at the front of the room, her hands tightening on the paste-smeared chain of blue paper rings that she held. Then we all listened while Miss Janiek told the story of the ring. She told it fast, so that we did not have time to translate its meaning into the actualities of our own world as she went along; all that we grasped was a set of wildly colored pictures, like a sequence out of one of the adventure strips in the comic papers, with a gum-chewing janitress, a detective, and a pawn-shop operator who was also a receiver of stolen goods, all pinwheeling together in a terrific welter of cunning and crime. I remember how we stood there, quietly, in our rain capes and hoods, while Miss Janiek brought her story to a close, and then, half-laughing, though there were almost tears in her eyes: "And think of my ring in the middle of all that," she said; "the poor old thing that's gone sedately up and down with me for ten years in my lone spinster existence, after its one romantic moment when Ralph set it on my finger, and I swore I'd wear it forever; because how was I to imagine then that it was going to make more of an actuality of a frizz-haired janitress' dream of owning an imitation seal jacket than of my own dream of marriage and a home?"

She talked to Miss Farrell, and we kept standing there gravely, understanding and yet not understanding what was being said, with our child's ability to take only what was comprehensible and interesting to us out of the words, letting the rest flow by as if we had never heard it. Then it was Margot Berry who turned first and looked at Elvy Morgum, staring at her with her face reddening slowly with the triumph of accusation, and pointing a finger, and saying at last, clearly, as if she were damning her forever with the words: "*You* didn't take it. You never. You never dared."

We could hear Miss Farrell and Miss Janiek still talking, over near the desk, but we were not listening to them any more, because we were watching Elvy standing there in front of us, with her eyes going back and forth under the harsh tangle of her hair. She didn't have on a rain cape; she had on the old black velveteen coat she always wore, and all at once, seeing her standing there in the old black coat, we wanted to make loud, boastful, cruel laughter in the quiet room—the ancient instinct to mock and trample the fallen leader rising in us as simply and as innocently as if we had been the children of the earliest man, before there were any words that said *love* and said *understanding* and said *brotherhood.* I remember Elvy's small rusty pleading voice replying to Margot—"I never said I did. I never said I took it"—the words dying away as her eyes went quickly from one to the other of our faces, seeing the clear unforgiving stare repeated in each. After that she didn't say anything; she only stood there, poised on her sound leg, with her head thrust a little forward in her old attitude of unasking and unhopeful waiting.

"I'm going to walk home with Sisley," Margot said suddenly. She looked round at us, challenging us, challenging Elvy Morgum, to dispute her right. "You can all come along, if you want. Everybody can come but Elvy Morgum."

Then I remember how she moved toward the door, grasping Sisley's hand tightly in her own. I can see us all as if for a moment time had stopped and we were suspended in the moment of decision—Sisley and Margot by the door, Elvy standing alone, her desperate gaze lost in the tangle of her falling hair, the rest of us just poised to move, herdlike, out the door behind Margot. I can see Miss Farrell's startled face, the sudden leap into it of an awareness of the crisis, and Miss Janiek's dark gaze brooding over us. And then, breaking into the silence, Sisley's voice, not so prompt, not so clear, a little desperate itself, but determined with no doll-determination, with no graceful doll-surrender to the pressed button of others' opinion.

"No," she said. "I'm going to walk home with Elvy Morgum."

She pulled her hand out of Margot's and started back into the room toward Elvy. I heard Miss Janiek say something, and I turned around, and there was Miss Farrell standing beside the desk with a look on her face that I did not understand till many years later, because I thought then that she was going to cry, and it took me that long to find out that that is the way people look when they have wanted something for a long time (the bright words, the high hill), and at last someone gives it to them ungrudgingly and beautifully.

"Would you like to walk home with me, Elvy?" Sisley said.

"Well, will you look at that!" Miss Janiek said.

"I'm looking," Miss Farrell said. "I'm looking."

MANY METHODS AND MATERIALS[1]

Charlotte Huck and Doris Young

"Indeed we are teaching that important R—reading," said the principal of Sunnyside School as she welcomed the new member of the Board of Education. "You'll find our teachers using many methods and a variety of materials. As we visit the rooms I think you will see the children are learning to read skillfully and with lasting interest."

The visitor walked down the hall with Miss Bennett who said, "Let's start with a kindergarten, Mr. Thomas."

A quiet group of kindergarten children was listening to a story. Miss Gould came over to greet Miss Bennett and Mr. Thomas. Miss Gould explained that the reader, a second-grade youngster, had prepared her story with her teacher. She was reading *Millions of Cats* with enthusiasm and ease. The second-grade teacher helped each child who came to read choose appropriate stories and prepare them carefully. This still allowed Miss Gould time to tell the old favorites.

As it was time for outdoor play Miss Gould quietly called all those children whose names began with the same sound as duck. Next came the group whose names began like jump, and on until all had gone. Miss Bennett explained, "This game helps the children learn to discriminate sounds. As beginning readers next year, they will need this skill in hearing differences between such words as duck and luck."

"Perhaps we'll find the sixes in this room sharing stories," whispered Miss Bennett as they entered a sunny room. A little girl in pigtails was telling about her baby brother as the teacher wrote her story on the chalk board. Although it was Sharon's story, the other children gave suggestions for better ways of expressing ideas. When her story was completed the children took turns reading it. A freckled Sandy said, "Sharon's story reminds me of our box movie."

Miss Cherry agreed, "It is like the story of 'Our New Pet.' The children in that story decided that a baby brother was the best pet, didn't they? Since your group made it, Sandy, would you like to show it to us again?"

Sandy brought the movie which had been made by drawing pictures on a strip of shelf paper. This simple "film," attached to cardboard rollers, was pulled

[1] From Association for Childhood Education International Bulletin No. 26, *Grouping, Problems and Satisfactions*, pp. 24–31. Reprinted by permission.

through slits cut in opposite sides of a suit-box. The children read the captions under the pictures as Sandy and Helen rolled the film.

Miss Bennett told Mr. Thomas how the stories helped children solve some family adjustment problems.

EXPERIENCES GIVE MEANING

In the next room the teacher was just finishing writing their news of the morning on the board. There seemed to be an air of excitement in the room, and no wonder! Their news told why:

Today is our Big Day!

We are going to the farm.

Tomorrow will be Princess Elizabeth's big day.

She will be crowned Queen.

But today we are going to the farm. The children took turns reading their news: some reading the sentence which told what was going to happen to Princess Elizabeth, others finding the two sentences that were nearly alike, and others finding the number of times the word *day* was used. Before the bus arrived, each child had had an opportunity to read part of the exciting news.

The preparation which had been made for this farm trip was obvious. Pictures of farm animals and buildings were labeled and attractively displayed. Small boxes on the science table contained oats, seed corn, corn on the cob, straw, and hay. Some oats had been planted and were just showing green. Experience charts told of making butter and cottage cheese. Many books containing farm stories were on the library table. Miss Bennett and Mr. Thomas looked at a large spiral-bound drawing tablet. One reading group had made its own story about a Holstein calf. The teacher had printed the story at their dictation and they had illustrated it. This had been placed with the other farm "reference books."

With the arrival of the bus, each child lined up clutching a piece of paper containing a list of animals, plants, machinery, or buildings found on a farm. Miss Bennett asked one of the "young farmers" what he was going to do with his list.

Bill explained, "You see, Miss Bennett, there are so many things to see on a farm that each one of us is going to look for certain things."

Miss Bennett helped Mr. Thomas see the benefits derived from such a trip. "Children get meaning from words as they build meanings from firsthand experiencing. Their lists will help them associate the words with the real objects."

As they passed Mrs. Wieland's room, Miss Bennett realized that the children must be down in the gym having rhythms. "Mrs. Wieland is particularly successful in interpreting our reading program to parents. Do come in and see her fine materials."

They entered a gaily decorated room, literally filled with charts, labels, books, signs, and children's pictures. Mrs. Wieland showed them one of the newest film strips which accompanied one of the readers, supplementing and enriching the content of the stories. They looked at a chart which she had made at the beginning of the year. It told about a red, yellow, and blue balloon and had three bouncing balloons attached to it.

"The children insisted on keeping it in the room and brought new balloons for it frequently," Mrs. Wieland explained. "It's fun to see how ingenious one can be in attracting children's interests. I have found that six- and seven-year-olds are intrigued by reading stories about their own favorite toys and dolls, particularly if these objects are small enough to be attached to a chart or book." She showed them a chart story with a small sail boat tied on it. They saw a booklet containing stories of a Raggedy Ann Doll, and Raggedy Ann herself was attached to the cardboard cover. An experience story about Linda's new dress contained a swatch of the material.

A large riddle book was on the reading table. Each page contained a simple story such as:

I have two wheels.
You can ride on me.
What am I?

On the opposite page there was a large sheet of colored paper with the suggestion "Look and See" written on it. Under the colored paper was a picture of a bicycle and the word *bicycle*. Mrs. Wieland showed them this book and remarked, "If you know what six- and seven-year-olds like, you know how to make learning interesting for them."

Mr. Thomas asked Mrs. Wieland about the books the children use in the first-grade reading program. She showed him several sets of attractive readers and explained their careful construction: their controlled vocabulary, limited number of new words per page, repetition of new words, interesting stories, format and illustrations. She explained the gradation of the books from preprimers to third-grade readers. From her Parents Bookshelf, where she kept books on teaching of reading, child development, and parent-child relations, she drew two readers, published thirty years ago. They compared the old, unattractive, moralistic readers with the modern, attractive ones of today. Mrs. Wieland laughingly said, "These two readers are my best answer for anyone who wants the 'Good old days in education.' "

READING IN DRAMATIC PLAY

In the second grade across the hall, they saw a large streamline train constructed of orange crates and covered with wrapping paper painted a bright yellow. The children were busily engaged in many activities. Miss Melin, the teacher, spoke to the visitors, "This is our 'free choice' time. During our planning period, the children chose the activities they would like. We have to take turns playing in the train.

"The group in this corner is making characters for a story they liked in one of the readers. Miss Nash, our student teacher, told the group the story of *Nothing At All* using a felt board. The children asked to make one of their own. A large board is covered with felt. They are drawing their characters on Manila paper. Strips of flannel pasted on the back will make them adhere to the felt board as the children relate their story.

"Perhaps you would like to watch the group playing in the train. You'll see the game they are playing in the diner involves reading. Joan is waiting for me to hear the story she has prepared to read to the kindergarten tomorrow."

Three children were working in the mail car sorting letters which the group had written previously. Two girls peacefully pretended to be sleeping in their lower and upper berths made of tables securely fastened. The children in the diner were ordering their food from menus they had carefully made. The waiter wrote their orders and gave them to the chef. He, in turn, read the order and filled it by using cutout pictures of food. The waiter then had to remember what each customer had ordered and serve him.

The visitors noticed that the children who were not playing in the train were happily engaged in other activities. A group of four children was playing a word lotto game. Several were painting at the easels. One had painted a picture of a large spotted snake with a beautiful blue bow about its neck! She was illustrating the story of *Amanda* which Miss Melin was reading to the group. Two enthusiastic little girls were matching words and pictures. Each had cards showing three words and three pictures. Brightly colored shoestrings were attached beside the words. By putting the strings in the correct holes they matched word and picture. One boy was working by himself arranging pictures of a story in logical sequence along the chalk rail of the blackboard.

Miss Bennett said, "This is such an interesting room that it is difficult to leave, but I do want you to visit the second and third grade combination."

TEACHING OR HEARING?

"Mrs. Anderson's room is having their reading period now. Let's join one of their groups." Four boys and a girl were discussing one of the stories.

"Have you ever felt lazy in the morning like Jane did? When?" asked Mrs. Anderson. The children told of their experiences.

"Let's read and find out what William was doing all the time Jane was in bed," the teacher suggested. Different children read the page aloud. Mrs. Anderson quietly supplied a word when it was needed. Several times she suggested that a child skip over a troublesome word and finish the sentence. Frequently, the child could then go back and supply the word from the context of the story. At no time were the continuity and the fun of the story interrupted. The children read the next page silently to find out what finally happened to William. They discussed the page and Tom read what William had to say as he descended from the top of the tree. The children did not reread this page, but read on to the end of the story. Before returning to their desks, Mrs. Anderson listed some of the words which had bothered them. The words which she had written on the board were read, discussed, and located again in the story. Mrs. Anderson gave each a piece of drawing paper which they folded into four sections. They decided to draw two funny things which Jane had done and two funny things William had done on that day when the two had agreed to exchange places. They would write a sentence under each picture to describe it, using their books to help them with spelling.

Taking a moment to talk with her visitors, Mrs. Anderson was enthusiastic about the progress this group was making. "I started them last Fall in preprimers and with their own experience stories. They still need much guidance with easy reading materials at their own levels of confidence. They will continue to need help. There is a difference between hearing children read and teaching children to read."

PERFORMING A SERVICE

As they entered one of the third grades, Miss Bennett pointed out its unique contribution to the school. This group served as a communication center for most of the school's bulletins. A movie was scheduled for tomorrow for the primary grades. Two boys and a girl were carefully printing large announcements which could be read by each primary grade. A primary typewriter was used by the children for quick notices. The school secretary came in each morning to consult with the bulletin committee. The one requirement was that it be written simply enough for primary children to read.

This group had also decided to make signs for the various rooms. As Ralph pointed out, when they made the signs large enough for all to see and read, "Then the sevens will learn where the library is, and the word that stands for the library."

And Mary thought that if she passed the sign every day, it would help her learn to spell *library!*

These projects had developed from the interest in their own class bulletin board. Several children were grouped around this board reading the invitation from one of the intermediate grades to a puppet show. Under the S's there was a birthday card for Ellen Shaw from her teacher. Mary, Jim, and Don were reminded of speech lessons. A note of congratulation had been written to Robbie and Peter for the excellent care they had given the doves last week. There were notes from other children, invitations to come and play, children's jokes. Joan came over to show Miss Bennett the note she had found for her mother. Miss Bennett smilingly showed it to Mr. Thomas:

Dear Mrs. Kendall,

I thought you would like to know what a fine job Joan did of sharing her trip experiences with us today. We all enjoyed hearing her read her story of New Salem. Joan's reading is improving daily!

Sincerely,

Catherine Baker

"We encourage the teachers to send frequent, informal reports on children's progress to the parents," Miss Bennett remarked as they left the busy room.

Upstairs they found a group of eight-year-olds sharing the experience of a short, but interesting trip. Their teacher had copied one of the children's stories on a large sheet of oak tag. The children were reading it together.

Our Trip

Lee took us on a tour of the basement of our school. We saw the furnaces and learned how they operate. It cost $46 to heat and light the Big Auditorium. We traced a pipe to our room, and the pipe was in the south bike room. We went to see the panel where Lee controls the heating in different parts of the building. We saw Lee turn on the heating units and we heard the air. There are three furnaces to heat the school. Lee opened the furnace and we saw inside. The flames were real hot when Lee opened the furnace.

Discussion followed with many interesting questions: How much does it cost to heat the building? How many light bulbs are replaced each year? What does one of our third readers cost? These and other questions were recorded and sent by messenger to the school secretary.

Outside the door Miss Bennett hesitated and smiled. "Number work, or reading?" she asked. "It's hard to tell, isn't it?"

WHAT DOES THE LIBRARIAN DO?

"The librarian is helping a group of eight- and nine-year-olds with library skills." They stepped into a comfortable, attractive room where Miss Holmes was explaining shelving of books according to the Dewey system. Large cards with title, author, and number, represented books from the science section. The children arranged these cards in the proper order on the bulletin board.

Next, the librarian referred to the chart which listed the questions the children had asked about insects. She explained the use of the card catalog in locating books they would need. While Miss Holmes helped some of the children use the card catalog, the room teacher, Mr. Haines, worked with others in using encyclopedias. Some of the children sought information in magazines.

As she closed the door, Miss Bennett said, "This group has a keen interest in insects. We'll see their collection later. They plan to prepare an annotated bibliography for the use of other intermediate groups."

SPECIFIC SKILLS ARE NEEDED

"One of the boys told me they expected the silkworms to begin spinning cocoons today," the principal remarked. "Let's stop here in Mr. Haines' room." Two boys were watching silkworms greedily munch mulberry leaves. One boy asked the visitors to see the ants at work in the "anterrarium" his committee had made. Three boys were bringing in the books which the group had checked out of the library earlier in the morning. Another group was selecting pictures for a bulletin board labeled "Helpful and Harmful Insects." "We're going to make a chart showing insect damage to crops," said Mary. "This *Agricultural Yearbook* is just what we need!"

Mr. Haines asked the children to go to their seats. "We have brought the books from the library," he said. "I think you'll find many of the answers to your questions about insects. What part of these books will help you locate information quickly?"

"I think the table of contents helps," remarked Bill. "You can see whether the book has what you need."

"Not always," said George. "Sometimes you find a topic in the index when it isn't listed in the contents."

"That's true. We can use both," said Mr. Haines. "Let's use the index as a guide now. While Kent distributes the books I'll give each of you one of these sample sheets of a make-believe index." Using the sample he called their attention to main topics and sub-topics. "Will this imaginary book tell about trap door spiders? On what page does the longest discussion of bees begin?" After asking similar questions he suggested they examine the index of the book Kent had placed on each desk. "Raise your hand if you think you will find information to answer the first question about insects which is on our chart." He walked about, helping some children with cross references as they looked up various topics. The group continued this reading lesson as Mr. Thomas and Miss Bennett left.

"Science and reading merge, you can see," commented the principal as they walked down the hall. "These science interests and activities provide excellent opportunities to develop skill in critical reading. In one group recently an argument arose as to the speed of airplanes. It was soon apparent that copyright dates had to be carefully checked. Children are learning to distinguish fact and theory, and to watch for such statements as 'scientists believe,' and 'according to present theory.' "

They went into a fourth grade but the children were in the music room. "It takes skill to read pictures, too," said Miss Bennett. "Mrs. Glenn has displayed these pictures about the sugar beet industry at the children's eye level. Notice the questions on this placard at the beginning of the series. These questions under the pictures direct the children to note details, to make comparisons, and to relate the pictures to other reading. Here is a large chart showing the process of making sugar. In this pocket on the bulletin board are slips of paper with each step of the process stated briefly. When a child finishes reading the chart he may test himself by tacking the slips of paper in order on the bulletin board. Then he can check his work by referring to the chart."

AFRAID OF BOOK REPORTS?

"Sharing favorite stories stimulates reading," the principal remarked as she guided the visitor into Miss Davis' room where the nines and tens were chuckling as the teacher read an amusing incident.

The teacher concluded, "And—you'll have to read it for yourself!" Hands waved for the privilege of reading the new book and a waiting list was started. "Who is ready to tell about a book today?" Miss Davis asked. Five hands went up. Each child gave a brief description of his book. "Who would like to hear more about *The Green Ginger Jar?*" "Who would like to hear Bill tell about *Homer Price?*" In this way five groups were formed and the children found places in various parts of the room where interested listeners could hear these "book reports."

HELP FOR SLOW READERS

"Mr. Wallace plans with his ten-year-olds for a daily reading time in which the children select library books or continue reading materials related to current science or social studies interests. Also, I think you will be interested in his work with children who are having difficulty with reading."

They sat near a desk where the teacher was discussing a book with one of the boys. "In what ways was Lee a coward? Was he afraid of everything?" The boy answered thoughtfully. Then Mr. Wallace suggested he begin reading aloud at the place he was reading before they stopped to discuss the characters and plot. Before the teacher moved on to the next desk he made a few notes on a card to indicate Tom's progress.

At the next desk he helped one child check a simple workbook lesson. Then the boy, who was evidently a "slow reader," brought out a scrapbook containing pictures of sports equipment and activities. As Ronnie and Mr. Wallace discussed the pictures the teacher wrote captions on slips of paper. Then the captions and pictures were matched. As Ronnie started to copy the captions in his book the teacher moved on to help another boy who had been testing himself with a set of word cards. Mr. Wallace praised him and helped with the words in the "don't know pile." Then they worked on Mike's report. The book he had selected was obviously too difficult, but Mike was anxious to use it. Mr. Wallace read several paragraphs aloud and helped him interpret the pictures. They moved to the back of the room where a typewriter was available for the use of all. As Mike summarized the important things he wanted to tell, Mr. Wallace typed the report which Mike could now read easily and happily.

WHAT IS CRITICAL READING?

"I think Miss Lane's group is out, too," Miss Bennett remarked. It was obvious that the fifth and sixth graders in this classroom were producing the school newspaper. "The weekly newsmap is very important to this group. Reading and geography are combined as the children read about news over the world. These children also have ordered newspapers from various cities and compare the reports of current affairs. This interest developed with the election last Fall. Miss Lane has been encouraging critical reading in this way."

Next door, sixth graders were beginning to read their weekly newspapers when the visitors entered. "During the first week of school, Miss Watts placed sample copies of various weekly papers for differing ability levels on the reading table. Each child was to select the one he could read easily and the one he felt would be best for him," explained the principal.

Miss Watts invited all the children who were reading about the coronation to come to the discussion center. "Let's see how well we can skim to get facts," she said. "When you find the answer to the question I ask, turn your paper over. Now read quickly to find out when the coronation will take place." This was followed by a series of questions which the children answered readily.

Then she met with another group who had finished reading the first news article in their paper. "What were the most important points in this story?" she asked. Suggestions were made and evaluated. "When you return to your desk, write four important points about jet airplanes in this next article. This will help in reporting to the whole group."

When a majority of the children had finished reading their papers, Miss Watts asked one child to serve as group leader. Sharing news from several papers enriched the discussion for all.

MANY METHODS, MANY MATERIALS

"These teachers certainly have to be acquainted with more books and materials than I realized," Mr. Thomas remarked as they returned to Miss Bennett's office. "Now I understand why so much time is needed to prepare for the school day."

"Yes, a good teacher is constantly looking for new books and materials," answered Miss Bennett. "I have tried to show you today that our teachers are using many methods of teaching reading, and I know you were aware of the wide variety of published materials, teacher-made materials, and children's materials for reading. You've seen ability grouping, interest grouping, and individual procedures. In this developmental reading program the teachers adapt methods and materials to meet the needs and abilities of each child."

GOOD STOCKS AND LESSER BREEDS[1]

Edward N. Saveth

DISCUSSION AND ANALYSIS

The textbook is one of the teacher's best friends. But just because of that, the teacher must be wary that this friend and helpmate does not take over the teaching function. If the textbook is used as a helper, a source for ideas, an organized approach to subject matter, then it undergirds the teaching program. It is when the textbook is used as a crutch for a tired teacher, when it is used uncritically and routinely, when every child goes forward through the pages at the same deadly pace directed to recall the same details, that it is a menace to true education. Have you, as a student, recalled stimulating as well as deadening relationships with a textbook? What would you look for in a textbook for the grade or course you are planning to teach?

In this selection some aspects of textbook content are discussed. This of course is only one study of textbooks, from a rather particular—though very important—point of view. Saveth points out, and other research supports his contention, that some textbooks have, all unwittingly, given students some false lessons about the people in our country. Test yourself: how do you judge "the pioneers" as against "the immigrants"? Where do you think you developed this difference in attitude?

After reading this selection you may find it useful to go to the shelves of the textbook collection in your college and pull down a few of the current volumes. What do the stories or the descriptions say about people? What lessons in human relations will children learn from studying these books? You might find it very useful to look up an additional reference: Irvin L. Child et al., "Children's Textbooks and Personality Development: An Exploration in the Social Psychology of Education," *Psychological Monographs* (1946), Vol. 60, No. 3. This research report explores still another facet of the human-relations implications of textbook content.

[1] From *Commentary*, May, 1949. Reprinted by permission of the author and publisher.

It is scarcely in the nature of an exposé to point out that American legislation on immigration in the past quarter-century, up to and including the recent displaced-persons act, has pandered to the myth of "Nordic superiority." The wellsprings of mind and spirit which feed this myth we know to be as deep as they are dubious—economic competition, social exclusiveness, anti-Semitism, suspicion of the stranger, brute selfishness—and it is difficult to measure accurately the role of any single factor in fixing the myth in the public and legislative mind. Yet complex events may be the result of the coming together of simple forces. A textbook, for instance, of the kind used in an elementary or high school—what could be more simple.

Textbooks have recently been attracting a remarkable share of national and international attention. At the Unesco General Conference in Paris in 1946, a program was adopted for the improvement of textbooks as aids in overcoming international misunderstanding. Last year, the United States National Commission for Unesco sponsored a study by I. James Quillen which reviewed the history of textbook analysis and its influence on the evolution of the curriculum in American schools, and which set forth a plan for an international revision of textbooks. On March 15, the American Council on Education published *Intergroup Relations in Teaching Materials*, a report of a special committee under the chairmanship of Dr. Howard E. Wilson, which scrutinized 266 textbooks used in American schools (but, alas, refrained from mentioning titles and authors), in addition to other teaching materials, for their attitudes toward minority groups.

Immigration comes up for classroom discussion in the teaching of American history, economics, and civics. This is a large subject, with much ground to cover; the classes are overcrowded; the teacher is busy. More often than educators care to admit, both teacher and student become, without resistance, prisoners of the textbook. And these textbooks, in the great majority, proclaim the innate superiority of the "racial stocks" of Northwest Europe. Racism may be forbidden doctrine in our large newspapers and magazines, on the radio and in the movies. But in the public school—prime mover of the nation's mind—it is still rather comfortably at home.

In 1930, Bessie L. Pierce published a study of textbooks "most frequently found in the schools," called *Civic Attitudes in American School Textbooks*. She discovered that the prevailing attitudes toward immigrants were, to put it politely, uncivic, uncivil, and untrue.

Waddy Thompson's *The First Book in United States History* (1923) asserts: "Immigrants that came from the Northern countries of Europe are of a class that make good citizens, and as long as most of the immigrants were of that class all went well. But since the War of Secession most of the immigrants coming to this country have been from the lower classes of Eastern and Southeastern Europe, and they give much trouble. They are for the most part very ignorant, and, having been downtrodden in their homes, they have no respect for law or government. In fact, many of them would like to see the government of the United States destroyed." Many textbooks, in a dizzy flight into political propaganda, even took it upon themselves to urge the restriction of immigration from Southern and Eastern Europe.

This rough handling of the "new" immigrants was in sharp contrast to the gentle treatment of those from the North and West of Europe who came to the United States mainly before the Civil War. Miss Pierce finds the Puritans variously described as "a God-fearing and industrious people," gentle, kind, possessed of good will toward all men, "even toward the cruel king from whom they had fled, and toward the savages of the forests. They valued so highly the freedom to worship God in their own way that they would not refuse the same freedom to others." The French Huguenots were "a particularly desirable class of settlers," and added "a very great contribution to the making of our country." The Dutch are noted for their "usual firmness," enterprise, and industry, and the Scotch-Irish are characterized by the author of one popular textbook as "the sterling, hardy race of men," the best of pioneers, who gave us "some of the most distinguished names in our history." The industry of the early German settlers is also emphasized.

The Irish, who came to American shores in large numbers only in the 40's and 50's of the 19th century, fared not at all well at the hands of textbook writers. Susan P. Lee, in her *Advanced School History of the United States* (1896), found them "wicked and worthless immigrants" who "often sought a hiding place in the large cities where they swelled the ranks of idleness and vice. . . . Their ignorance of all things American, their inability to distinguish between one state and another, and their want of interest or sympathy for the traditions of the past made them undesirable neighbors to men who loved their own states with a passionate devotion." But after the end of the 19th century, textbook writers ceased to accord the Irish special treatment in order to consider immigrants more simply under two headings: "old immigrants" and "new immigrants."

Cornish and Hughes, in their *History of the United States* (1929), characterize the early immigrants as "Good types of immigrants" but found it necessary to head one section: "The new type of immigrant creates alarm." Burch and Patterson, in *American Social Problems* (1929), instruct their readers that Northern Europe is, with the exception of France and Ireland, "Protestant and, generally speaking, accustomed to freedom," while "the southern area is Catholic in religion, and, as yet, not altogether accustomed to free institutions."

Blough and McClure, in *Fundamentals of Citizenship* (1939), decided that a clear-cut tabular presentation would be the most pedagogically efficient manner in which to establish the relative virtues of the two waves of immigration. See their accompanying table.

Immigrants	Early or "Old"	Later or "New"
Birthplace	Northern and Northwestern Europe.	Southern and Southeastern Europe.
Education	Mostly well educated, intelligent.	Not well educated; frequently unable to read and write.
Occupation	Merchants, farmers, skilled workmen, professional men.	Unskilled laborers, few merchants.
Location in which they settled	Rural communities and small towns.	Cities in slum areas.
Purpose in coming	To establish a permanent home; to escape religious persecution or harsh government control.	To gather wealth; to escape training in the army; to return later to Europe.
Kinds of groups	Entire families.	Unmarried individuals; few families at first.
Number becoming citizens	Nearly all.	Small part.

A final ironical accusation: discussing the new immigration from the South and East of Europe after 1880, Morehouse and Graham in their *American Problems* (1923) complain that one of its most deplorable aspects was the way in which it foisted race prejudice on the beautifully innocent native-born: "The races have brought over race antagonisms with them that introduce new discord into our national life."

Immigrants from the South and East of Europe do not lack for company as they run the gauntlet through the textbooks. A study of *The Treatment of the Negro in American History School Textbooks* by Marie E. Carpenter (1941) reveals attitudes toward the Negro, in books for Northern children, not markedly different from those L. D. Reddick[2] had found in Southern textbooks. The average history textbook of 1939 contends that the Negroes were generally well-satisfied as slaves, despite all the careful research which has revealed tremendous dissatisfaction on the part of the enslaved Negro population and a great number of slave revolts; they omit all mention of the half-million free Negroes in the United States before the Civil War; and, despite the mountain of research into the history of the Reconstruction period that proves the contrary, they continue to blame Reconstruction corruption upon the Negro's ignorance, unfitness to vote, and credulousness.

The Chinese, according to Timothy T. Lew ("China in American School Text-Books," *Special Supplement to Chinese Social and Political Science Review*, VI-VII, July 1923), are also treated as a "problem." "The Chinese were *willing* to live in cheap houses and amid poor surroundings," stated the late and venerable Charles A. Beard and co-author W. C. Bagley in *History of the American People* (1923). "This competition by workers who were *willing* to accept a lower standard of living was resented by American laborers." [My italics.]

This last statement by one of our foremost historians is a concession to that logic by which the evils of a young, expanding industrial capitalism are laid at the door of those who suffer from them. The immigrant, it would seem, came to America with the single-minded purpose of acquiring low wages, slums, poverty, corrupt urban political machines, class conflicts, and other embellishments of the "promised land." The Greeks and Syrians were reported to have very strong and morbid predispositions in this direction: M. K. Berry and S. B. Howe, in *Actual Democracy* (1923), told how, upon their arrival in America, "they go at once to the quarters of their fellow countrymen where congestion, disease, and poverty abound."

Thomas Nixon Carver and G. M. Adams, in *Our Economic Life* (1932), thought it obvious that the immigrant "does not require many of the comforts of life." Muzzey's popular *History of the American People* (1929), writes of the new immigrants as "content to work long hours for low wages, debasing the standards of the *American* laborer." The new immigrants, assert Beard and Bagley in *The History of the American People* (1928), "were willing to endure slums, long hours, and other conditions bad for their own health and morals and full of danger to the Americans about them." And if they were not willing to endure them?

To find out where these strange notions come from, and their ultimate effect upon pupils reading these texts, would be an ambitious and long-term (and worthwhile) enterprise, in which a perceptive student might come up with some startling findings. But even a cursory glance at the *Zeitgeist* reveals some of the impelling factors at work.

It was during the 1920's and early 1930's that pseudo-learned books on the "race peril" by Madison Grant and Lothrop Stoddard, extolling the virtues of the "Nordic immigrants" from the North and West of Europe and assailing the "Alpines" and "Mediterraneans" from Cen-

[2] "Racial Attitudes in American History Textbooks of the South," *Journal of Negro History* (July, 1934), Vol. 19, pp. 225–265.

tral, Eastern, and Southern Europe, as inherently inferior, had their vogue. At this same time, it will be remembered, powerful pressure groups such as the American Legion and the Ku Klux Klan were pushing their own ideas as to how American history should be written and as to the relative worth of the constituent ethnic groups of the American population. C. F. Horne, author of *The Story of Our American People,* published in 1926 and sponsored by the American Legion and thirty-three other patriotic societies, including the Daughters of the American Revolution, wrote of the new immigrants as learning "little of their debt to our government" and finding "little cause to love it." He continued: "We thought we were Americanizing the anarchists who came here; we began to realize that they continued hating us."

While the Ku Klux Klan never actually sponsored a textbook (that at least was spared us), it had explicit and strong views on how American history should be taught: "When America became rich through commercial and industrial life . . ." we read in the "Educational Study for the Junior Citizen's Club of the Ku Klux Klan" (*Kourier Magazine,* January 1927), "it very naturally attracted to our shores a flood of immigration from the lands where poverty, tyranny, and ecclesiastical despotism hold sway. . . . This land of Liberty was to them a land of license. They were given the ballot almost before they got rid of the vermin they brought over in their steerage passage."

The role of sheer human ignorance, stupidity, and lethargy in promoting ethnic bias can hardly be overestimated. Textbook authors themselves are generally not scholars and are frequently unaware of the latest scholarly findings. It was as far back as 1909 that John Bates Clark, in his cogent introduction to the *Documentary History of American Industrial Society,* stated: "Americanizing goes on effectively when the economic conditions of this country are such as to ensure it. Conditions take precedence of racial qualities because the change in prevailing conditions is far greater than the changes of race. . . . It is an error to attribute the origin of the difficulty to the races represented by the immigrants or the conditions that prevail in the countries from which they come."

But many of the textbook writers of the following decades paid little or no attention to Clark, or to scholars of similar stature.

One can understand, then, how bias came to be "respectable" in America in the 1920's, and we know that its influence was spurred by depression and Hitler in the 30's. But in the 40's, after the war in which racist doctrines played such a crucial and disastrous role, one would expect a shift, especially in view of the striking change in broad public sentiment manifested among all classes of Americans in the postwar period. And one would certainly expect that in the larger metropolitan centers, like New York and Chicago, where a sizable part of the population is made up of later immigrants and their children, some concession might be made to their sensibilities—and to the truth.

By this time, too, such scholars in the field of immigration as Marcus L. Hansen, Carl Wittke, T. C. Blegen, Oscar Handlin, and G. M. Stephenson had demonstrated at length how primitive and uninformed the textbook writers were. The concept of the new immigrant as a purely "economic man" in contrast to the "idealism" of the older immigrants from the North and West of Europe was shattered by their findings, which pointed out that the economic factor has always been dominant in immigration, that the ebb and flow of the immigrant tide has always been considerably influenced by the trend of the American business cycle, that the Irish and German immigrants of the early 19th century were in their time also accused of being paupers, radicals, slum-dwellers, and of being difficult to Americanize, that the great mass of immigrants were not radical but conservative in outlook.

In order to obtain some idea of what the situation is today, this writer read through textbooks that have been approved for use in 1947 by the Board of Education of New York City for the day and evening high schools and vocational and trade schools of New York.

On the whole it must be said that the textbooks now in use in the New York schools are not quite so objectionable as those used country-wide a decade ago. Also these books devote less space to the subject of immigration in general than did the books published a decade or more ago—reflecting the fact that immigration, except in the past year or two, has not been a subject of vital public concern. However, the difference is of degree rather than of kind; by and large, this means only that the sharp edge of some of the more biting remarks has been removed. As far as the basic attitudes are concerned, there is no remarkable deviation from older patterns.

For example, James Truslow Adams and Charles G. Vannest, in *Record of America*, published in 1935 and used in schools in Brooklyn and the Bronx, reward immigrants from the North and West of Europe with the caption: "Our early immigrants come to find homes," while another caption goes on to say: "Our later immigrants come to find work." An unsuspecting outsider might be led to the belief that the "homes" first referred to were prefabricated.

Vannest and Adams believe that there are important "racial" differences between the people who came to the United States from the North and West of Europe and those who came from the South and East of Europe. Is it only a quibble to demand today that textbooks use the term "race" correctly and in keeping with modern anthropological findings? No competent anthropologist would grant for a moment what the authors of this book would have high school students learn: that "in Europe the population of each nation is largely of one race." There is further confusion in the matter of race in Ralph Volney Harlow's *Story of America* (1943), where the author refers to the Italians, Hungarians, and Poles as "racial groups."

Louis Ray Wells's *Industrial History of the United States*, though published in 1922, is still on the list of books approved for classroom use by New York's Board of Education. It justifies the movement towards the restriction of immigration in the following terms: "We have now ceased to measure greatness by mere numbers, and have begun to examine into the qualifications of those who would seek our hospitality. There has dawned upon many a tardy recognition of the necessity of conserving our human resources with a view to the founding of a better and abler type of man." Not a superman, surely. . . .

Canfield and Wilder's *The United States in the Making* portrays the new immigrants as "willing to work long hours for low wages," and makes the further assertion that immigrants "who settle in cities tended to concentrate in wretched tenements and shanties, thus creating new slum areas." Finally, they quote Chauncey M. Depew as saying: "The ranks of anarchy and riot number no Americans. The [immigrant] leaders boldly claim they came here not to enjoy the blessings of liberty, but to destroy our government and cut our throats, and divide our property." Technically, of course, they are merely quoting "a point of view." One might expect, however, that they give some indication that the "point of view" is a rather warped one.

It is easy to point an indignant finger at a board of education and a board of superintendents for permitting use of these texts. There is also the publisher's responsibility for the subject matter of the text, and the factor of the climate of opinion (or state of apathy) in the general community. But beyond this, however, there is the simple fact that well-meaning authors of textbooks (to give them the benefit of the doubt) seem to shed their professional competence when dealing with immigration. The writings of Turner on the frontier and Beard on the economic interpretation of history are, for some reason, more familiar to the man who writes a textbook than the no less significant findings of Marcus L. Hansen in the field of immigration. While this situation remains, the textbook writer will inevitably tend to substitute easy prejudice for the sober truth.

The social psychologist Otto Klineberg has written that to change group prejudices in children, "the only hope is to reach them early, and to give [them] habits of favourable reactions to other races which will stay with them through life." Our schools even today, by tolerating the kind of history and social science textbooks they do, seem to be doing just the opposite. It is less important to fix the blame for this situation than to work out ways of improving it. Certainly there is no excuse for complacency about this "mis-education by insult," whereby American children are systematically exposed to a racist evaluation of—in so many cases—their own parents and grandparents.

HELPING PUPILS DEVELOP SELF-DIRECTION [1]

Association for Supervision and Curriculum Development

DISCUSSION AND ANALYSIS

"I'll never forget that trip to the circus that our class made in fifth grade."

"There was just something about the way that teacher talked to us about class elections that made us choose, not just the most popular or the prettiest or the handsomest—but the *best*."

"I remember one teacher who always kept on saying to us, 'Now what do *you* think makes this a good or poor report?' That was the hardest question we ever had to answer."

Can you recall some incidents like the above? What do they tell you about teaching? In this selection you will read about many many such incidents, taken from actual classrooms, that no doubt will be recalled in

[1] Reprinted, with permission, from *Toward Better Teaching*, 1949 Yearbook of the Association for Supervision and Curriculum Development, chap. 4, "Helping Pupils Develop Self-Direction," pp. 86–118. Copyright, 1949, by ASCD. The chapter included represents only one of the seven "characteristics of better teaching." The others are "Fostering Security and Satisfaction," "Promoting Cooperative Learning," "Fostering Creativity," "Helping Pupils Develop Values," "Providing Opportunities for Social Action," and "Helping Pupils Evaluate Learnings." The entire book, including the above-mentioned chapters, may be purchased from The Association for Supervision and Curriculum Development, 1201 Sixteenth St., N.W., Washington 6, D.C.

much the same terms as those above by the students who participated. That is good teaching!

As you read these descriptions you may become overwhelmed with the variety of approaches that teachers take. You will undoubtedly feel a stirring of envy of teachers who can do these things so easily—seemingly—with children. Which ones of the techniques described do you feel you could actually carry out? Which ones do not seem suitable to your way of going about things? Do you know why certain approaches to teaching and subject matter appeal to you and others seem very strange and even silly?

Each of us goes about the job of teaching differently. A technique that works wonders with one teacher will fall flat when another teacher tries it. Some ways of working appeal to one age group and are confusing and meaningless at another age level. Thus teaching is a matter of finding those tools and techniques that you, the teacher, find comfortable, and then fitting these to the changing needs and interests of different student groups.

Self-realization is a prerequisite if the individual is to participate successfully in a democratic society. He must be willing and able to analyze himself and the situations in which he finds himself; he must be able to make intelligent decisions; and he must be willing to assume the responsibility of carrying out his decisions.

PUPIL SELF-DIRECTION AN AIM OF BETTER TEACHING

Perhaps the greatest single change in the individual from infancy to maturity is that of growing from dependence to independence. An adult is a person who is, among other things, independent and self-directing; who has developed confidence, courage, and a willingness to face his problems; who has developed standards and values of his own by which to judge his behavior; who is capable of intelligent planning.

The process of growing up, of becoming self-directing, is a long, gradual one. It requires years of growing and experimentation. It is through assuming of responsibility and facing the consequences of his actions that the individual's values and standards grow. For the five-year-old, self-direction consists mostly of assuming responsibility, under guidance, for one's immediate physical and social needs and for developing the capacity for making choices concerned with immediate problems. As the child grows older and gains experience the situations that challenge him are more complex. He becomes concerned with long-range planning and activities that are sustained for longer periods of time. The extent to which the young adult is able to evaluate his potential and plan effectively is the measure of his development of self-direction.

Better teaching recognizes the importance of all experiences which provide for self-analysis and choice-making and the whole series of related experiences leading to self-direction through the method of problem-solving—identification of problem or need, planning to solve the problem, gathering information, considering alternatives, acting upon best judgment, and evaluating outcomes.

A major aim of better teaching is to develop within the individual the ability to become a responsible and self-directive citizen. Not only should the individual have an appreciation of how the responsible citizen should act, but he should be motivated so to act.

The promotion of self-direction calls for a school where there is (a) a decreasing amount of teacher direction as children become more mature, (b) significant undertakings or activities with ample opportunity for planning, sharing, discussing, and evaluating activities, and (c) increasing pupil responsibility for the control of behavior. These conditions are discussed in this chapter and, where possible, examples are presented which illustrate the principles cited.

DECREASING AMOUNT OF TEACHER DIRECTION

Each year in school should find the student less dependent upon the teacher. By the time graduation from high school occurs the student should be so independent that he can pursue studies and solve problems without teacher assistance.

When education is examined from this viewpoint, the role of the teacher becomes clear. His function is to serve as a guide and a resource person. The guidance consists of the gradual withdrawal of teacher direction in terms of the pupil's ability to make decisions. Always there is enough direction to give the pupil a sense of security but not enough to discourage initiative.

The teacher's actions must be based upon a thorough knowledge and understanding of the abilities, interests, backgrounds, attitudes, values, and problems of his pupils. More important, however, the teacher must have faith in the pupil's ability to think and plan. He must believe in pupil participation in planning as the way of growth. He must recognize that guidance and teaching mean helping pupils become increasingly able to analyze themselves and the situations in which they find themselves, to formulate courses of action in terms of the values the pupils hold, and to assume responsibility for carrying out decisions.

Inviting Evaluation of Teacher Leadership

Teachers restrict self-direction in many unintentional ways. Through the organization of the classroom, the types of behavior a teacher praises, the factors given recognition in reports to parents, self-direction is often limited by the teacher. The restrictions may be deliberate or they may be unconscious ones. If the teacher's actions are planned, they can be tools used for the promotion of self-direction. If the teacher is not aware of the effect of his actions, he may find his pupils becoming less independent even though he may believe he is working for pupil self-direction.

When teacher restriction of pupil self-direction appears to be necessary for a time, the teacher may have pupils help analyze the classroom situation. Cordelia McCants found that this sort of discussion was effective with her fifth-grade children: [2]

The lack of cooperation of my boys and girls under the guidance of a substitute during my absence brought about a change in my teaching technic. I had not thought of a suitable plan of attack for the problem that had arisen during my absence, so at this point the method of dictation was the easiest. "What suggestions do you have to offer for this lesson?" or "What shall we do now?" was changed to "We *will* do this." After several weeks of a tense atmosphere for both children and teacher, two pupils in conversation gave me a lead:

MARY: Mrs. McCants, are you going to take us to see *Treasure Island?*

TEACHER: No, Mary. We cannot go to the theater or do any of the things we usu-

[2] Alexander Wilson School, Philadelphia, Pennsylvania.

ally do until we learn to think for ourselves.

RONALD: Mrs. McCants, we have not had to think for the last two weeks. You have been thinking for us.

TEACHER: Why?

RONALD: We didn't think when you were away.

Here was a ready-made opportunity for my class to discuss the best ways to carry on under given circumstances. The following statement was placed on the board and the pupils were asked to finish it in any way they wished:

"If I could choose my classroom I would choose one in which—"

The class completed the statement in many and varied ways. The next day we read, discussed, and tabulated the papers under headings that seemed to describe the type of classroom chosen.

Class Summary

Type of Classroom	*Number*	*Type of Classroom*	*Number*
happy	21	good-mannered	6
quiet	18	self-controlled	7
respectful	16	cooperative	4
nice	15	truthful	4
well-behaved	14	clean	8
neat	12	safe	5
good	10	with privileges	
obedient	10	with class officers,	
working	10	etc.	

No paper mentioned a classroom where children were made to do what was right.

We discussed the terms and found many had used different words, but meant the same thing i.e., "a nice classroom" meant "a happy classroom" or "a good class" meant "an obedient class." I asked for a word under which we might have included most of the words. "Democratic," said Donald.

TEACHER: Do we have a democratic classroom now?

THOMAS: Not since you have been back.

TEACHER: Was it democratic before I went away?

CHILDREN: Yes.

TEACHER: Why?

CHILD: Because you allowed us to decide things and carry on lessons.

TEACHER: Was it democratic while I was away?

ALL: No.

TEACHER: Why?

NELLIE: We didn't have the kind of classroom we put on our paper or the kind we had before you went away.

TEACHER: What kind do you have now?

The children agreed they did not like a forced classroom but Claudia said we had to have it because we could not carry on. One child suggested he felt it had always been forced as I settled all disputes and arguments.

At this point I asked the question, "How might you have carried on while I was away?" Replies that came were:

1. The same as we do when you are here.
2. The way we know is right.
3. Follow after others.

TEACHER: Which way do you think best?

CHILDREN: The one where you think about it.

This account ends without reporting any sequel but it offers an illustration of the kind of thinking children do in the process of learning to be self-directive.

Leslie Bishop used similar procedure in securing guidance from his high school students.[3] At the same time the students were clarifying their ideas of teacher leadership. Mr. Bishop reports the discussion that took place when he asked his students to evaluate his teaching:

VIRGINIA: I like the fact that you have a sense of humor and can take a joke. You have attended all our parties and trips and we appreciate the fact that you will take time to be with us and have fun outside the classroom. We all know you can be serious too.

[3] The New School, Evanston Township High School, Evanston, Illinois.

JUNE: It seemed kinda' funny at first for you to sit in the regular seats instead of behind your desk, but now I like it and we don't think of you so much as a teacher but more as a fellow-student.

MARY: I think the kids appreciate the fact that you will take time with us, maybe working on a report or even talking about dates and stuff. You know what I mean.

AUDREY: I think we ought to have more formal grammar. Sure, we get lots of practice in our speaking and our book reports, themes and journals, and everything you correct, but we have to take Latin and other subjects where we need to know the ins and outs of grammar. I think we should do lots more in class than we do. I like the reading program we've worked out; it's helped a lot.

GEORGE: How many points are you going to score in the faculty-intramural game?

CAROLYN: That's off the subject, George. You tell us that whoever is in front of the class is in charge, but sometimes we get restless and a little noisy. I think you should step in more often and tell us to be quiet. We are usually more quiet when you tell us than when some of our fellow students do.

JIM: Your reports have been good, and that's a kind of model for the rest of us to follow, even if we can't do as well. 'Course we expect you to know everything.

ROSE: This goes back to what Carolyn said. I disagree with her. If you stepped in and put your foot down every time then we'd never learn how to keep quiet by ourselves. We'd always do it because of what you would say. We have to learn self-discipline, that's one reason we're here. If the report or business is important and interesting the students won't want to do anything but listen. Besides we surely are old enough to begin learning how to take care of ourselves by now. If we don't know how, it's time we learned!

It is obvious that the teachers being evaluated by their students in the manner illustrated in the two preceding examples have rapport with their pupils. It has come into being because the teachers have been honest with their groups, have not reacted negatively to criticism, and have let the students know they wanted assistance in the direction of the group work.

The atmosphere in which self-direction can best be fostered is one in which pupils feel secure, free to try new ideas, free to fail, free to be honest. . . .

USING TYPICAL CLASS ACTIVITIES

When teachers want children to be self-directing, it is not difficult to find ways for pupils to gain experience along this line. Not all the situations will be planned. As the following cases illustrate, almost any type of activity may be used by the teacher. The worth of the experience in promoting self-direction is affected primarily by the way the teacher conceives his role. If he is constantly seeking to determine whether he can withdraw and let the pupils solve their problems, the promotion of self-direction will occur many times daily.

In a kindergarten a dispute was a starting point: [4]

JAMES: I made a house with my blocks and while I was gone Billy took some of my blocks to make a train.

BILLY: I thought he was thru playing with them because he walked away and started to play with the clay. I needed some more blocks for my train.

TEACHER: James, I happened to notice that you left your house and joined the other children in clay work. Do you think it is fair just to leave your house standing when other children need blocks?

JAMES: No, I'll tell you what I'll do. I'll make a smaller house and let Billy use half the blocks.

TEACHER: That is a very good idea, James. Now, Billy, don't you think it would

[4] From the professional diary of a student in a college class.

have been a better idea to ask James if he had finished with the house before you took his blocks?

BILLY: Yes, Miss G. I will do that next time.

The two boys walked away together in a friendly spirit. Several minutes later I noticed they were much elated over an idea they had captured to make a long train together. They had apparently forgotten their differences.

Although leading questions were used by the teacher, the questions did not tell the boys what to do. The children had an opportunity to express their opinion and they were allowed to work out the solution to their quarrel.

An illustration of the gradual development of self-direction in a first-grade group is found in the work of Clara Maye Wade:[5]

As one means of developing self-direction in first-grade children a "morning service" was established very early in the year. This period occupied the beginning of the day and varied in length of time.

The teacher acted as chairman during the beginning weeks of the year, being very careful to keep within the understanding of beginners in first grade. Later, little by little as the children matured sufficiently, more and more of the responsibility was shifted to them, even the reading of simple verses or passages from the Bible, care being taken that each child shared in his phase of development to the extent of his maturity.

The same procedure was followed with current events, sharing of interesting ideas, and class planning. In this class the guidance by example was withdrawn gradually as the class members demonstrated increasing skill in self-direction.

As pupils become concerned about worthwhile projects teacher control may be decreased and pupil self-direction proportionately increased. A group of seven-year-olds in Irene Fox's class planned and carried out their own project.[6] The teacher reports:

The children use a work-play room so most of their projects arise from their activities there. They are never suggested or dictated by the teacher.

One day Louise suggested a post office. She gathered her cronies about her in the back of the room to begin their planning. When they had formulated some plans, they included any child who was interested in the planning and play. Not until they were ready for construction did they come to me for advice. Up to that time they had depended on books and their own thinking and planning.

As they built the post office they read in several books concerning its operation. I checked with them one day to be sure they knew the work of the various postal employees and the procedure in the post office. It was most interesting to note how they verified their information to be sure that the post office would operate smoothly. One day it was the number and kind of windows, another it was how to cancel a stamp or the information on a postmark. This project continued the rest of the year because of the interest in it.

Under the full drive of pupil purpose, the teacher became a resource person to whom pupils came for advice when they needed it.

In the same class one pupil was behind the group in his desire to read. The teacher reports how the problem was handled:

Jimmie showed no interest in reading during the first semester of second grade. Since child development was the most important consideration, there was no pressure put on him to begin to read. As the weeks went by his emotional tensions less-

[5] Creston Hills School, Oklahoma City, Oklahoma.

[6] Laboratory School, Kansas State Teachers College, Emporia, Kansas.

ened and his interest in books became more noticeable. After Christmas he looked around for small books he could read. Soon he was reading material of a late first-grade level—if one must use these terms!

During the next weeks, Jimmie's interest in books continued. He often just looked at some. But for increasingly longer periods he read in them. About this time his mother gave him "Bobby Spends a Nickel." Although there were many words in the book which he did not know, he read it over and over again, memorizing phrases which were unfamiliar. Then he brought it to the group to read.

This is only one of a number of incidents which indicate that Jimmie is beginning to take responsibility for his own living and learning.

The absence of pressure to conform to adult-imposed standards led the pupil to establish his own goals. Recognizing that children develop at varying rates, the teacher can make a major contribution to growth in self-direction by allowing the child to work at his own level.

PROMOTING SKILL IN ANALYSIS

To develop self-direction the teacher must constantly extend to pupils the opportunity to participate in the direction of the class. But it does not stop here. Certain skills must be developed by the process. For example, the individual must have skill in analysis, analysis of self and of the environment. On an individual basis this means being able to recognize, accept, and use personal strengths and weaknesses; on a group basis it means being able to determine the factors that promote or handicap group progress.

In both types of analysis, objectivity—the ability to remove personal bias from a judgment—is a necessity. Objectivity is obtained only through recognition of its desirability and through opportunities to practice it.

Encouraging Individual Self-Analysis

A high degree of objectivity is found in an evaluation that a twelfth-grade boy at the Ohio State University made of his work: [7]

> I think that the plaque is fairly done, being as it's my first experience in ceramics. A good many mistakes were made but I think I profited from them all. If I had it to do over again I think I would not have done a plaque but a figure. I was pressed for ideas and I did not take an artistic idea. I learned much about glazes and slips, the chemicals and combinations for making different colored slips. I spent a little too much time on it for the value of it. I enjoyed the experience and at first it seemed as if nothing would turn out. I liked working with my hands altho I'm not very steady. I think I could have conserved time and thought it out more.

Many experiences in the evaluation of his own work lie back of this boy's statements. Ability to evaluate one's work objectively is one of the elements of self-direction.

One of the steps in helping pupils develop the ability to analyze their work is to give them access to information. The following plan was found to be effective in raising accomplishments in scholarship and citizenship in a junior high school: [8]

> Some of us at Randall have felt that our children were not working up to capacity and that they were unaware of how much better work they were capable of doing. Therefore, we directed our efforts toward providing activities which we felt would make them more aware of the levels at which they were working and would encourage higher standards of achievement.
>
> Beginning with the permanent record, the present average of each pupil in schol-

[7] Submitted by John Ramseyer, director of the University School, Ohio State University, Columbus, Ohio.

[8] Reported by Hazel B. Johnston and Mary G. Turner, Randall Junior High School, Washington, D.C.

arship and citizenship was found. Each child was made aware of his average and plotted it on graph paper. This was kept up to date by pupils.

The teachers reporting might have gone one step further in their plan by having pupils figure their own averages. The students might also have considered whether the means of evaluation used by the school were fair and adequate.

Class discussions of the work and actions of students help pupils to see themselves as others see them. They change the situation from one in which students strive to please or displease the teacher to one where class members have access to the unprejudiced reactions of peers. How classmates gave eight-year-old Judy their reactions is reported by Mary McCune: [9]

Judy is argumentative. Barbara, Judy's neighbor, complained one day that Judy snatched her book away from her while she was reading, then kept it and looked at the pictures. Judy scowled while Barbara told her side of the story. Next, as was our agreement, Judy, still looking disagreeable but sure of herself, came before the group to tell her side. She said she had had the book first and that Barbara had taken it from her desk before she was finished with it. She took the chance to grab it back when Barbara asked her to read a funny part. Barbara began to look sheepish now and the following conversation ensued:

JEAN: Judy is right. She did have the book first.

SALLY: Judy went to get the milk and Barbara took the book then.

JOHN: Barbara told me to take the book for her when Judy left the room.

COREEN: I saw Judy grab back the book. She wasn't finished with it. I think Judy was right.

TEACHER: I think Judy was right in wanting the book back, Coreen, but I didn't like the way she took it back. How could Judy have gotten the book back without making Barbara angry?

SANDRA: Barbara should have asked Judy politely.

WALTER: That's what Barbara brought up the problem for because Judy grabbed the book from her, too.

HARRY: You shouldn't take things from inside or on top of people's desks without permission.

RICHARD: At home we can have some things if we ask first.

FLINT: It makes you sore if you come back and your pencil or anything you were using has disappeared.

ROBERT: But Judy didn't have to grab it from Barbara.

TEACHER: Robert, that's a good point. How do you feel when anyone pulls something out of your hands?

FLINT: I'd feel like punching back.

HARRY: It makes you feel mad inside.

TEACHER: When do you feel like handing someone something politely?

LINDA: When they ask politely.

TEACHER: Should we make that agreement between ourselves now?

SANDRA: Ask people for things in a polite way with a smile.

GRETA: Hand things to people in this group this year.

TEACHER: Could we help Judy to settle a problem in any other way next time?

GRAY: She could say to you, "We need your help up here."

TEACHER: That's really the best suggestion, Gray. We promise to stop and help you, Judy. Now, who would you say began the difficulty? (Group thought Barbara did.)

TEACHER: Who did you think needed help most when Barbara told her side?

WALTER: I thought Judy did until she told her side.

TEACHER: Why is it fair to wait to hear all sides before we decide who needs help?

SALLY: Sometimes you could get mad at the wrong boy or girl. It wouldn't be his fault.

DALE: Judy wasn't looking mad when she

[9] Havemeyer School, Greenwich, Connecticut.

told her side and we know Barbara started the trouble.

GRETA: Barbara's going to give the book back, too.

TEACHER: How do you think we could make people want to listen to friendly boys and girls and to help them? How could we get things we want without arguing?

DALE: Ask politely.

GRAY: Smile when you ask.

GRETA: Use a low voice.

BOBBY J.: Always ask permission.

ROBERT B: Say, "We need your help" if it's a hard problem.

As pupils keep records of their work, establish criteria by which they feel they should be judged, and apply these criteria in the evaluation of their work and products, they grow in objectivity and in skill in analyzing themselves.

HELPING GROUPS ANALYZE THEMSELVES

Groups need to analyze their work as the basis for determining effectiveness, accomplishment, or future action. Intelligent self-direction for the individual is fostered by thoughtful participation in group self-analysis.

Such analysis may be made in different ways. A citizenship club sponsored by Addie Lea Head, seventh-grade teacher, evaluated a semester's work in a discussion period: [10]

TEACHER: We are reaching the close of our first semester's work. Will you think with me along these lines? What have we, as a group working together, accomplished? Can you name at least one thing that we have gained by working together this year in the club, something which is not a part of your regular school lessons?

JOHN: I feel the most important thing we have learned has been accepting more responsibility for things.

[10] Clinton P. Russell School, Dallas, Texas.

TEACHER: Will you tell us what you mean? Can you give some example?

JOHN: I remember that you explained to us that the responsibility of keeping our class orderly is really ours. When you arc out of the room, we have learned to keep right on with what we are doing, just the same as we do when you are in here. Nobody seems to want to misbehave, at least not very much.

FRANCIS (the club president): Another important thing we have done this year is to help look after the little children in the halls. I noticed that all of us seem to feel responsible. Sylvia, Jackie, and Yvonne found a little first-grade boy crying because he could not find his coat and cap. They found them for him and sent him home. They did not even call the teacher.

DON: On the playground, I've seen Joe Bob break up two or three fights. He always helps the little boys get their troubles straightened out. One little boy got his foot hurt, and Joe Bob went to see about him and took him to the teacher.

PATRICIA: I noticed how friendly the club members were when I came here. I have changed schools from several different states, and I think this is the most friendly school I have seen. The boys and girls told me about the club and helped me to get acquainted.

BETTY: I came here from another state, too. There the pupils laughed at me and teased me because I am so small for my age. Here I never think about it.

PAUL: I was very timid when I came here. I still am, but the boys in the club have helped me a lot.

JOE BOB: I think Buddy has done a lot of good. Every week he checks and grades our lockers. Four of us have to use one locker, and he always sees that we keep them neat and clean. It gives our front hall a better appearance when people come to see us.

SHIRLEY: Since we've had our club and made so many oral talks, I feel that I can talk so much better when I go anywhere. I think the club work has helped more in that way than any other.

ANNA: I heard some teachers talking about me. It made me "mad" and I decided to show them what I could do.

DELLA JO: I think we all try to take better care of our library books. Last week Jerry brought in a book that someone left lying outside.

MELVA JO: I do not think of anything *special*, but I notice how we all seem to have grown up more, and I don't think we misbehave nearly so much. Of course, sometimes we do.

The interlocking nature of individual and group analysis is clearly demonstrated in the preceding illustrations.

An analysis of an unsatisfactory experience was made through role-playing or socio-drama by John McGill's sixth-grade class.[11]

The teacher reports that at first role-playing had been treated by the group as a novelty but now that the children had become used to it, it was a serious enterprise:

On one occasion two mothers were in the room. The children were at work, most of them at their tables, but a few were moving about the room. Suddenly a fight flared up between a boy and a girl. From their stories and the reports of others, we learned that Tom had been passing by Joan's desk and each time he passed he either budged the table or bumped her arm until finally Joan up and slapped him. Tom, taken by surprise, was resentful and slapped back.

We cleared the corner of the room, and with the very scene of the incident as our stage, two children volunteered to re-enact the situation so we could all see it and discuss it. They did a good job. All the children and mothers had some comments. We located the cause of the trouble, realized how the fight started, and decided on some ways we could act to avoid such difficulties. One of the most important suggestions for remedying such a situation came from a boy who said that we should move the groups of tables farther apart so that people could get by easier.

About this time the mothers left and we talked about their comments. I asked the class to pretend they were mothers and fathers who had seen such a thing. "What would you say then," I asked. Again we had some interesting remarks. Finally we replayed the scene. This time the players were to show how the fight could have been avoided or the misunderstanding settled in a friendly way. This scene in contrast to the first one made the lesson we were learning obvious and meaningful.

Time was running out when one girl suggested that Tom and Joan should do it so that they would feel better. They could "patch things up" this way. So Tom and Joan ran through the scene and came up smiling.

A more mature analysis was made through use of role-playing by a tenth-grade class:[12]

It was necessary for the instructor to be absent from school two days because of illness. One of the Basic Living classes openly rebelled against the substitute teacher on the second day; whereupon she called in the Dean of Boys to discipline the class.

Upon the instructor's return he was informed by a few members of the class that all had not gone well during his absence. After many disconnected comments and explanations, the class was asked if they would like to dramatize the situation so that all of them together could analyze the various elements of the incident. This they readily agreed to do and did forthwith in a very realistic manner. As the socio-drama unfolded, a few questions were interjected to get the group thinking about the causes for the occurrence.

In the discussion after the socio-drama the following conclusions were reached:

[11] Public Schools, Elmont, New York. Mr. McGill is now in the Laboratory School State Teachers College, Potsdam, New York.

[12] Melvin J. Hetland, Battle Creek High School, Battle Creek, Michigan.

1. The substitute teacher entered the room with a chip on her shoulder because of past experiences with some members of the group and immediately assumed a dictatorial attitude, as if expecting trouble.
2. The students immediately became so resentful that they refused to do anything she told them.
3. The Dean of Boys did the only thing he could do, back up the substitute teacher. (This was a student contribution, agreed to by a majority.)
4. The instructor was at fault in not preparing the substitute with adequate information concerning the class and its work at the time.
5. The entire situation was very unfortunate and could have been avoided if the substitute had entered the class with a friendly attitude or at least a neutral one.
6. Emotions are very powerful and seem to constitute a chain reaction that leaves reason far behind.
7. Prejudice against individuals does not decrease of and by itself.

DEVELOPING ABILITY TO MAKE INTELLIGENT CHOICES

Increase in ability to make intelligent choices is effected by giving pupils opportunities to make decisions and helping them formulate courses of action.

Providing Situations Where Pupils Make Decisions

It is important that the daily program be planned with enough time allowed for sharing, discussing, planning, and judging. The following report from Katahryn Renfroe illustrates how provision is made in her first grade for developing self-direction: [13]

In our room we have a sharing period each morning after our opening exercises. During this time the children take charge. One child is chosen to be the leader or chairman. He calls on the members of the class who have something of interest to show or tell to the group. Sometimes, if the teacher is called out of the room, she asks each child to tell and then choose the one to tell next. In this way the children learn to direct their own discussion groups.

After the "Show and Tell Time" is over, the teacher and children discuss their plans for the day. As each decision is made, the teacher writes it on the blackboard, under the date. When all the plans have been completed, the children read the plans from the board over again so that each child understands the words and can refer to the chart throughout the day. In this way each child learns to find out for himself what he should do next, and he can gain much satisfaction from his ability to check his own work and decide when he is ready to make other choices.

Our children learn what they can choose to do during the "quiet time" when they have finished their regular work. They learn how to stir the paints and clean up after they have painted a picture. They learn to get out and use and put away the clay, puzzles, games, letters, slates, Tinker Toys, and other things without disturbing others. As long as they can take care of themselves without bothering those around them, they have the privilege of directing their own activities.

Each morning we ask one child from each row to pass out the crayons. The children always know whose turn comes next and there is never any confusion in this respect. We also appoint housekeepers each week. These children take care of the books and supplies and take the responsibility of straightening our schoolroom before they leave.

All these activities help the children to become more independent in thought and action. Since each child's actions are observed by the whole group, each child learns better self-direction through the approval or disapproval of the group. The children learn to go on with their work whether the teacher is in the room or not.

[13] Brock Park School, Oklahoma City, Oklahoma.

Mary McCune has three periods a day when pupils get together to evaluate and plan together.[14] Says this teacher:

We always meet, as a group, at nine o'clock in the circle. Here we make our plans for the day and since all children understand what the plans are, they can fit them into their day without disturbing me when I'm with individuals or small groups. This meeting in a circle also provides a time for anyone to get help with any problem, and it gives a feeling of "group togetherness and solidarity."

We meet again after lunch to check on how well we have accomplished our individual, self-directed academic work which we call our "Musts." We give help on how to accomplish the "Musts" before closing time. Each day presents new needs. We discuss "Musts" of the day before, hear someone who has greatly improved his flash cards, or analyze spelling errors. We emphasize the good quality of someone's work, teach sounds or review them as required, come to new agreements, discard old ones if we've outgrown them, give attention to just any problem that needs it to improve the quality of the living in the room.

We get together just before we go home, too, to collect our thoughts and speak about a few points that will start us on our way next morning without teacher help. Sometimes a poem is read or even dramatized to send us home in a relaxed, pleasant frame of mind.

Large blocks of time with a class enable a teacher to give pupils more of a part in making decisions. The possibilities are seen in Mildred Rickard's fourth grade: [15]

The children were taken out of a platoon setting and placed under one teacher's guidance for the entire day with all subjects taught in one room by one teacher. Just what the reaction would be was doubtful. Could the program be so enriched that it would hold their interest for the entire day without the able assistance of the so-called "special teacher"?

We began with the organization of the class on a democratic basis with a chairman and various committee heads. Meetings were held, committees were formed, decisions reached and before long things were really happening with the children all having a part. Each child had a goal to attain, a purpose to see successfully carried out.

Our first unit of study had its origin in a discussion period on vacations. This gradually grew into the larger experience unit called "The Family Takes a Trip." Committees took over various vacation areas. Almost at once the teacher found herself in a maze of questions, "Where do we find out about national parks?" "Where do we look to find out about California, about Canada, about transportation, about this, that, and the other thing?"

As is often the case in such a unit of study we dropped everything and brought the problems before the group. It was decided since only a few had been to many of these places and since every committee had the responsibility of working on its own contribution to bring before the group, each would have to "find out" for himself and solve his own problems to the best of his ability. This was the beginning of real self-direction in the group. After seven months planning together, working together, living together, this fifth-grade class has truly developed into one that initiates and plans procedures, is resourceful and self-reliant, and studies a situation before making decisions.

Creating Opportunities for Self-Direction in Class Work

Finding time for self-directed activity has proved more difficult in secondary schools which in many cases have restricted pupil planning and deciding to homeroom and activity periods. However, when teachers believe it important to promote self-

[14] Havemeyer School, Greenwich, Connecticut.

[15] Hawthorne School, Oklahoma City, Oklahoma.

direction, they can do a great deal of it in regular class periods.

A free reading program was the way Nancy Wilson started: [16]

Many of our pupils leave high school and seldom read a book again. The required reading lists and the book reports that are often part of our English courses have many times given pupils a distaste for reading.

With these ideas in mind, I set about organizing a free reading program in my senior high school English classes. One day a week was set aside for free reading. Each student was allowed to choose any book from the main library or the class collection. If he found the book uninteresting or too difficult, he was encouraged to choose another book. Books were often discussed, but no formal reports were required. Each child kept a record of the books read. He indicated whether or not he read the entire book. A brief comment as to difficulty and interest was made. These comments helped me in recommending books to other pupils.

Since the library was inadequate the pupils agreed that it would be wise to pool the money which they would usually spend for textbooks. With this money supplementary texts, reference materials, and books for recreational reading (fiction, biography, short stories, plays, books on aviation) were bought. The pupils themselves helped to make the selection. Reading tests were given at the beginning of the term. Since there were quite a few retarded readers in the class, books as low as the seventh-grade level were chosen.

Helen Merritt reorganized her class in problems of democracy to provide more self-directed activity: [17]

With the removal of war-time transportation difficulties, adequate library facilities were again available to the pupils of our school. The time seemed ripe to make a transition to what may be called a more progressive approach to the teaching of the classes in problems of democracy. Although pupils had shown reasonable enthusiasm for their work and were given some choice in the selection of the problems to be studied, I believed that much might be gained in motivation and in character development if each pupil could come to feel that a problem was really his own. An identity with the adult world might be established were the pupil to grapple with some problem about which he knew adults were concerned.

By way of orientation, two class periods were spent in the library where the pupils were introduced to the general setup of libraries as well as to the tools and materials which would prove helpful to their investigation. This was followed by two periods spent in laying the groundwork for what I termed an experiment on which we would embark together. Considerable effort was used to catch the interest and imagination of each pupil. The burden of making the class an interesting one was to be theirs. The basis for judging the quality of the work was to be how much each contributed to class activity and how much proof each could offer that he had mastered his problem.

The procedure from this point on was as follows: Class discussion of possible subjects which led to the choice of such problems as displaced persons, T.V.A., aid to Europe, the Hughes-Meyers controversy, rehabilitation of veterans, cartels, conservation, and tariff; a summary of class suggestions with additional ones from the teacher of what was to be looked for and what was to be included in the final report. These suggestions, which were to be indicative rather than mandatory, included a brief background of the problem, present status, proposals for solutions, pertinent legislation, agreements or programs suggested or adopted, and personalities connected with the problem. Finally, conclusions based upon the material were to be arrived at. Emphasis was placed upon the tentative nature of these conclusions and their dependence upon fact and not upon opinion.

[16] St. Clair County High School, Odenville, Alabama.

[17] Darien High School, Darien, Connecticut.

Classroom time was devoted to discussion of difficulties encountered, suggestions for resolution, stalemates in the choice of a problem, location of source materials, reports of progress and content. Particular stress was placed upon current aspects of the problem from which heated discussion occasionally arose. For example, the problem of displaced persons disclosed considerable difference of opinion. Short papers on the values received from the work were written at the end of ten weeks. This was purposely placed previous to the time of final grades so that no confusion might arise between values derived in the progress and grades received.

Toward the end of the semester, an opportunity was given for pupils to criticize procedures and technics used in order that the next class might receive the benefit of the criticisms.

Core courses which have been introduced in some secondary schools offer even more opportunity for self-direction on the part of students. Viola O'Bryant reports satisfaction with a core program organized on the following basis: [18]

The core program utilizes a two-period block of time in the senior high school daily schedule. During these two periods the students are under the guidance of one faculty member. It is the function of the core teacher to guide the students in planning in terms of the immediate and long-range problems of study. Within this framework, however, provision is made for individual differences and for the development of skills and fundamentals.

The problem approach is utilized in developing the problems of study. This procedure provides for student experiences in planning, in assuming responsibility, in critical thinking, in self-direction, in creativeness, in taking social action, and in evaluating.

The study of controversial issues on which not all members of the community hold the same opinion has proved to be a fertile opportunity developing skill in problem-solving. The following is an account of how one group attacked an issue which was causing much discussion and which had become controversial because of the local politics involved: [19]

A local issue concerning a change in the form of city government was of much interest to some members of a ninth-grade core group. The issue was of town interest and the movement caused much discussion among the lay people. The question was brought up by a student during an informal discussion period. Ideas and opinions were given by individuals.

The teacher guided the group into doing research on the subject before making decisions. This led to a study of forms of city government. Intensive work was done by small groups for a short period. Students who had lived or visited in towns where different forms were in operation made contributions.

Activities planned, executed, and evaluated by pupil-teacher participation included panel and group discussions; short talks; town meetings showing the different forms in operation; and zone maps, charts, and posters made and explained.

Individual activities included experiences in learning to interpret charts showing structure of forms; to select and organize materials; and to preside over meetings, lead discussions, and serve as moderator of panel groups.

Thruout the study students grew to realize that it is a citizen's duty to understand all factors involved in an issue in order to vote wisely, to discuss intelligently, and to participate effectively in community affairs.

Helping Pupils Formulate and Test Courses of Action

An important skill in self-direction is formulating and testing a course of action. After the situation has been studied, pos-

[18] Lexington High School, Lexington, Alabama.

[19] Reported by Mary Lamb, Troy High School, Troy, Alabama.

sible solutions must be considered and a decision reached as to which one to try.

The process of formulating a course of action involves abstract testing. Will it accomplish what we want? Can we do it in the time we have? Is it better than the other solutions we are considering? Such questions are raised concerning each course of action suggested. Dallas Conklin's seventh-grade students were confronted with a choice: [20]

"They *made* you do your work where I used to live back East," said John in a sullen tone. John was suffering from remorse. He had not completed his arithmetic assignment. His grade was very low. There were drawings of airplanes on his paper.

His teacher looked inquiringly at the faces of the others in the class. It was apparent from their expressions that they expected her to do something about a remark of that sort. Was this a challenge to put her on the defensive? Never. This was the perfect introductory remark. This was a hoped for opportunity to face the class with an issue which might be called "teacher authority versus pupil self-responsibility."

It was a new class. Pupils were just beginning to become adjusted to one another and to a strange teacher. She suggested that they put aside their work for a little while in order to discuss this issue.

"Suppose we list the ways by which a teacher can *make* a pupil finish his arithmetic," she suggested in a tone which implied that there was certainly nothing wrong in such methods. From the pupils came the well-known, time-tried, and worn ways: keep him after school; send for his parents; give him a low grade on his report card; make him do his work at home; punish him by not allowing him to go to assemblies; send him to the office; fail him.

As these threats became more dire, the teacher interrupted her writing at the blackboard to present a challenge to the pupils.

"You have set up a very dismal routine for yourselves," she said. "You want me to be a tyrant standing over you with an imaginary club; you want me to spend my teaching ability thinking up punishments; you want me to become annoyed and unpleasant to live with; you want me to stay after school to punish pupils so that I will have less time to refresh my mind and body with healthy out-of-school activities. And worst of all, you make your school work sound like some horrible drudgery. Is this really the kind of class that would make you feel successful and happy?"

The children responded with a despairing, "No!"

Taking a constructive lead at this time, the teacher said, "Let's work out a different kind of plan. I'll write these items on the board. You can discuss them and then vote as to whether you approve."

Each time we take up a new arithmetic process we will decide in just what way it fits your needs; in other words, how you can apply it.

I will do my best to teach you how to do the work. I will use several different "slants" because different people get the idea in different ways.

We will plan our class period so that there will be a quiet work time. Also, we may divide the class into groups according to the way people work.

We will check and grade every bit of work you do so that you will never feel that your time is being spent just "doing" it.

You will keep a folder in which you will file all of your corrected papers.

You will have a record sheet on which you will record the date, page, and grade of each assignment.

We will have a period each week for filing papers and bringing records up to date.

I will also keep your grades in my record book.

Your progress will be important primarily to *you* and secondarily to me.

[20] Jefferson Junior High School, Long Beach, California.

Miss Conklin reports that the group accepted her proposals and that they held an "accounting" period each Friday. During the year they seemed to forget their desire for teacher authority as they grew into greater responsibility for their own progress.

At the high school level Robert Blake's chemistry club was asked to prepare an assembly program suitable for sophomores.[21] This invitation gave the students large opportunity to formulate and test a course of action:

Several meetings were called to collect ideas. At this point in their classroom work they had seen the action of indicators, solutions, gels, ionization, crystals, and many other chemical phenomena dealing with the most common of chemicals, water. They decided that the subject, "water," had the most possibilities for an interesting group of demonstrations. They further decided that, while parts of the program ought to be instructive, the sophomore class would be particularly interested in seeing an amusing and mystifying program. (The wisdom these seniors showed in discussing the interests and reactions of underclassmen was amazing.) With these decisions in mind, each student combed reference books, texts, and laboratory manuals for demonstrations involving water or chemicals that looked like water. Each demonstration was tried and the directions including specific amounts of chemicals and notes as to the best procedure were written on an index card until about thirty-six demonstrations were listed.

At this point about eight of the most interested students began meeting together grouping the demonstrations into related groups and developing characters and dialog which would present the material in a logical and interesting manner.

The scene revolved around the professor who was teaching a class the properties and uses of water. Among his guest lecturers were an artist who painted with "water colors" getting colored precipitates from colorless solutions: a fireman, who in the process of explaining the use of fire extinguishers started several spontaneous fires and explosions by pouring "water" on combustible material; a prospector, who nearly went mad from thirst when drinking "water" which changed into six different colors; a research man who made "water" run uphill or freeze to "ice" on command; and finally, the scrub woman who could wash out iodine stains in a second, wash colored cloth so that it turned to a different brighter color, and burn cloth without even scorching it.

The success of the project might be measured by several specific incidents. Much of the rehearsal of dialog was done during vacation and evenings without the presence of the adult adviser; in fact several parts of the final performance were new to him. During the performance several demonstrations went unexpectedly, but the participants carried on in such a manner that no one but themselves knew it. Furthermore, interest in self-directed experimentation did not end with the presentation of the program. Within a week after the performance three of the students who took part had started on individual projects developing from their own interests and intellectual curiosity.

The students' behavior during the actual performance was an indication that the formulation and verbal testing had been good.

Students may help each other to formulate and test plans of action. In the following story, Muriel C. Hampton recounts the events which occurred in her fourth-grade class. When a new boy entered, the children had the experience of reviewing their accomplishments to orient him to their situation and also of helping him evaluate his plans for a contribution to the class project: [22]

[21] Stratford High School, Stratford, Connecticut.

[22] Arroyo Seco Elementary School, Pasadena, California.

Jim had enrolled in the fourth grade at a time when most of the shipmodels being built for the classroom harbor were nearly completed. The children welcomed another builder and listed for Jim the equipment and craft which they felt were still needed: (a) new lighthouse, (b) more wharves, (c) marine crane, (d) cargo, (e) another tugboat, (f) drawbridge, and (g) lighthouse tender.

The new boy decided to make a tugboat. After he had pored over the books and pictures in the research file he was ready to present his written construction plans to the group.

"The name of my tugboat is *The Golden Prince*. It will be 12 inches long," Jim read from his "blueprint." "The beam will be 3 inches, the pilot house 2½ inches high, the cabin about 3 inches wide, and the funnel 3 inches high."

Hands shot up all over the room, but Charles couldn't wait to be recognized by Jim. "Twelve inches is 'way too long for a tugboat," he said excitedly. "It would be too big for our harbor."

"Why, that's as long as David's Coast Guard cutter," cried Mary.

"What kind of tug are you making?" Peter asked. "Is it a seagoing tug? They are bigger."

"Yes, but even for a seagoing tug 12 inches is too long. *The Little Giant* is a seagoing tug, and it's only 10 inches long. Isn't it, John?" Raymond turned to John for confirmation.

Jim looked at his ruler and at the models being held up for his inspection. "Well, mine's a harbor tug," he said thoughtfully. "I could make it shorter. Maybe 9½ inches."

"Oh, no! Eight inches would be much better," said Molly with emphasis. "Look. *The Cormoll* is 20 inches long and tugs should look little alongside of a cargo ship."

Larry interrupted her. "I think 9 inches would be OK. That's an inch shorter than *The Little Giant*."

Cries of "Nine inches!" and "Eight inches!" came from several children.

"Let's vote!" Bob called, offering the favorite solution for all difficulties. "How many think that the new tug should be 9 inches long? . . . How many think 8 inches? . . . It's a tie," he announced, turning to the teacher.

"Isn't either length suitable for our harbor?" asked the teacher.

"Yes," agreed the children.

"Then," said the teacher, "why not let Jim make the decision himself?"

Jim twinkled. "Eight and a half inches," he said, and pencilled the correction on his paper.

"I think that the rest of your plan is good," said Molly. Several others nodded their approval, but not everyone was satisfied as yet.

"How wide did you say your cabin would be?" came unexpectedly from Jack, who had been toying with his ruler, apparently not following the discussion too closely.

Jim consulted his drawing. "Oh, about 3 inches."

"Well, the beam of your tug is 3 inches. If you make a 2-inch cabin you could have ½-inch deck on each side," announced Jack.

"How long is the cabin?" asked Larry and Joseph together.

Jim looked at his figures. "I don't know. I didn't plan that."

"You've got to leave room for the stern bitt," warned Susie.

The teacher spoke. "Shall we let Jim think about the measurements of the cabin and ask him tomorrow?"

"Yes."

"Show your paper pattern for the hull," requested Margaret. Jim complied.

There were murmurs of approval. "That's good."

"The bow should be more pointed," said someone from the back of the group.

"No, it's all right," said several at once. "It's just right for a tug's bow."

"I think that Jim could start making the hull today. He's ready," said Allan.

"Those who agree with Allan please raise your hands," said the teacher.

Jim took in the unanimous vote at a glance and started happily toward the lumber rack.

The teacher increased group and individual self-direction by remaining in the background and leaving the presentation of all considerations and the final decision to the class.

Geneva Hood's third grade took an additional step by establishing criteria by which they evaluated their action: [23]

One morning, when the third-grade children were in the circle, planning their work and making plans for evaluating their work, one child spoke up and said, "Why can't we make our own report cards and check ourselves every day?"

I found out that the children didn't like their report cards because they couldn't tell anything about them. But, if they were to make their own and grade themselves, then not only they but their parents would know what they were doing. They made suggestions about what they thought were important things to consider, all agreeing that the "behavior" was the first thing to consider. After much discussion they decided the most important things were:

Have good manners Be a good listener
Be a good sport Be a good example

For their work the important things were:

Finish work
Carry out directions
Work well with others
Be accurate

Each made his own chart, for one month, having a place to check every day.

After trying it out, the children decided it was inadequate, that they would like to add some more. To the "behavior" they added:

Be honest with myself Watch myself

and to "work" they added:

Be neat Extra work

They have never lost interest in keeping the chart and are very conscientious about checking themselves. No one ever sees the chart until the parent comes for a personal conference. Then the child explains it to us. I feel that it has taken care of almost all of our discipline problems and has certainly helped in forming good work habits.

As values are developed, the individual and the group have a set of standards by which to judge their action. The combination of a pattern of values and skill in evaluative procedures is basic to self-direction.

INCREASING RESPONSIBILITY FOR BEHAVIOR

The third aspect of self-direction is self-discipline. Teachers who want pupils to be self-directive gradually allow pupils to assume control over their own actions. If this relaxation of teacher control is accompanied by help in analyzing self and situations and by appropriate guidance in formulating and testing courses of action, no risk of inefficient education is courted. On the contrary, only then is education truly effective.

Self-discipline involves forcing oneself to live up to commitments, to the demands of the situation, and to restrictions imposed by a consideration of others. How far this goes beyond the usual concept of discipline in the school! Ability to fight off the distractions of the environment and carry out responsibilities, a plan, or a commitment is learned through experience.

Assuming Responsibility for Surroundings

Giving pupils responsibility for keeping the schoolroom environment orderly is one device Mary McCune used in developing pupil self-control.[24] She describes one incident in this connection:

MARY D: I take care of desks and Harry's is very messed up.

[23] Nichols Hills School, Oklahoma City, Oklahoma.

[24] Havemeyer School, Greenwich, Connecticut.

GRETA: Last month I had desks and it was untidy then, too.

TEACHER: Who can help Harry?

FRANCES: You could fold all your yellow papers together, Harry.

BOBBY J: Here's an elastic to put around your flash cards, Harry.

BARBARA H: You should take the magazines you shared with us home tonight.

SANDRA (looking inside): Want me to put those specimens in the science corner, Harry?

TEACHER: The children have given you real help, Harry. We're going to games now. Come along when you've finished. (Harry begins folding the papers mentioned.)

GRAY: I'd be glad to stay and help Harry finish so he won't lose so much game time.

BARBARA H: I'll stay too, Gray.

TEACHER (to Mary): I'm glad you discussed Harry's problem with us. No one can keep his desk clean if he doesn't realize it's untidy. I was pleased to see how happy Barbara H. and Gray were to stay and help Harry even during "Game Time." We'll save the best game 'til you three come down because we want to help, too. We appreciate willing helpers.

MARY: Harry took our help with a smile.

CHARLES: He's hurrying to obey, too.

Teacher encouragement and assistance in living up to responsibilities are an important aspect of the learning situation.

LIVING UP TO GROUP STANDARDS

Failure to live up to group-imposed standards of responsibility and conduct was used by Emma Carey as the basis for a class-learning situation.[25]

Jack, a seven-year-old boy, came from a most unhappy home, a home which resorted to corporal punishment when on the slightest provocation the boy's behavior displeased the parents. On at least one occasion Jack had come to school having been seriously punished at night and in the morning having gone without breakfast. On such an occasion Jack became somewhat noisy and unruly when his class visited the library. On returning to his classroom he was asked what book he had selected from the library. He lost complete control of himself; hurled books, scissors, paste; and screamed. Following is the verbatim report of the teacher concerning what transpired between Jack and the group after he became quieted.

TEACHER: Children, Jack and I need your help. Let us go to the circle and talk things over. (Teacher took him by the hand and held him near her.)

CHILD: What made you so mad, Jack?

CHILD: I didn't tattle, Jack, but you did make lots of noise in the corridor.

CHILD: Yes, and you made noise in the library, too.

CHILD: The sixth graders were very quiet so we could use the library.

CHILD: Everyone else was quiet except Jack—and Jean tried to make him keep still.

CHILD: Jean wasn't very nice to Jack.

CHILD: How about it, Jean, did you try to be nice?

JEAN: Well, he wouldn't be quiet. I asked him nicely at first.

JANE: I told Jack he shouldn't make a noise.

TEACHER: Maybe Jack didn't know why he should be quiet.

JACK: Oh, Mrs. Carey, you know I know.

TEACHER: Jack, don't you want to sit on a chair?
(Jack shook his head.)

TEACHER: We are just talking about what happened. We want to talk about helping one another.

CHILD: I did try to help when I asked him to be quiet.

CHILD: Jack doesn't like to be bossed.

TEACHER: What is the difference between helping and bossing?

CHILD: You like people who help you.

CHILD: Helpers are friendly; bosses are mean.

[25] Lillian Rice School, Chula Vista, California.

TEACHER: Well, then it's hard to learn how to be a real helper, isn't it?

CHILD: We can learn how to make them like it.

TEACHER: How do you suppose we can do that?

CHILD: Everyone has more fun when we don't act mean.

CHILD: We can remember it's nicer when people are happy.

CHILD: We can think if what we are doing bothers other people.

TEACHER: Jack, would you like a chair now?

JACK: Can I sit right here?

(Several children offered their chairs, and Jack put his next to the teacher.)

TEACHER: There are so many ways we can be helpful to people. Shall we see if we can make a list of ways to be helpful? Jack, you can see the board better if you put your chair in the circle.

Jack moved into the group very willingly as children moved to make room for him.

CHILD: We should be quiet in the corridors.

TEACHER: Just in the corridors?

CHILDREN: Oh, no.

TEACHER: All the time?

CHILD: Just at quiet work time or when others would be bothered.

TEACHER: How can we tell?

CHILD: Think what others are doing.

CHILD: We should not get angry when people are trying to be helpful.

TEACHER: Jack, do you have any suggestions?

JACK: I don't think we need any more.

CHILD: Oh, look what time it is!

TEACHER: It is time for our recess. Let's get ready.

Immediately all of the children, including Jack, straightened a very upset room and all went happily out to recess. (Incident closed.)

After several weeks Jack has been a happy member of the group. The home conditions have been improved and the children receive warm lunches at noon. Jack is helpful in the room and has brought more things for our "Grocery Store" than any other child. He was given the "big brother" assignment to a boy entering our class, and in spite of the fact that the boy was unexpectedly unruly, Jack handled the situation very nicely. The new boy is another challenge to us.

PROMOTING SELF-CONTROL THROUGH PUPIL ORGANIZATION

One of the most common ways secondary schools have been providing opportunities for self-control has been in student activities. John A. Johnson reports that children and youth assume responsibility for many phases of the intramural programs in Des Moines, Iowa: [26]

The student council (for junior high schools) elects or appoints an athletic committee. This committee has the general supervision of the intramural program. The committee, in consultation with the physical-education instructors, determines the type of tournament to be held in a specific sport. The committee makes the drawings, the time schedules, and the field assignments. These students also help determine general policies and supervise the making of awards.

Each homeroom elects a boy and a girl to act as sport chairmen. These chairmen see that the members of the homeroom are informed as to schedule, check on parents' consent cards and other details. The physical-education instructors appoint the members of the officials' or leaders' club. The members of this club meet regularly with the physical-education instructors and receive instructions in rules, organization, and procedures. When qualified, the members of this club act as officials for the games. The officials' club also selects students to act as score keepers, record keepers, and equipment managers. They also appoint certain members to see that the information pertaining to intramural activities is put in the school bulletin and on the proper bulletin board.

[26] Supervisor of Physical Education, Public Schools, Des Moines, Iowa.

A greater sense of responsibility is shown when pupils become concerned for the welfare of others and take steps to meet the requirements of the situation as they see them. Eula Lee Kilpatrick describes the way an elementary-school council went beyond the local school: [27]

The council is composed of two representatives from each of the eighteen homerooms in the school. These representatives were elected by the student body. They met each Wednesday to discuss problems of safety and safety precautions in and around the school building, pedestrian safety, fire hazards, and safety in the home. The work of the representative group carries its findings and recommendations to the entire student body through classroom safety programs and discussions, or assembly programs.

The school organization has grown with the formation of several neighborhood clubs for the purpose of promoting the interest of the parents, pre-school-age children, and neighbors in safety problems.

Practically every street in the school district now has one of these Neighborhood Safety Clubs which was organized by a school child. These groups meet once a week after school or on Saturday. One child reported:

There are about twenty-one children on my street. We elected officers and talked about home safety. Here are some of the rules:

1. You should not leave glass in your yard and the reason is somebody might step on it without shoes.
2. Keep matches away from small children.
3. Do not leave toys lying around. The reason is somebody might fall and break an arm or leg.
4. Do not stand up in a rocking chair.
5. Do not sit on a window sill with the window open.
6. Do not play around hot water.

[27] Sequoyah School, Oklahoma City, Oklahoma.

Encouraging Groups to Help Individual Members

The class group may assume responsibility for helping one of its members as Vera Darson's eighth grade did: [28]

Last year a new boy joined our group. He was a nice looking boy, muscular, and well-built. School work was easy for him. He read well, spelled well, worked arithmetic with ease, had a flair for art, sang beautifully, and was an outstanding athlete.

When his records arrived the teacher found no mention of any of his fine abilities. The permanent record card contained only references to his being a discipline problem, and to the fact that he had been taken before the Juvenile Court. . . . Out on the school grounds or in the hall he was constantly involved in fighting, at which he fancied himself to be quite an expert. . . . One day, the boy got into some rather serious difficulty at noon and was sent by the officers on duty to the principal. The teacher took this opportunity to bring up the problem with the class.

The children in the class had been very loyal to the newcomer. Not one had ever complained, or tattled on him. Nevertheless, the teacher knew that they were disturbed. She began by telling them that she felt that the problem was as much theirs as hers. The problem was discussed in a very serious manner, without bitterness or anger. Some expressed the feeling that the boy was trying to be smart and cute when he acted as he did. Some thought he should not be allowed to take part in sports until he learned to behave in a more acceptable manner. But eventually, the more mature members of the class expressed the feeling that the boy was frightened and unsure of himself and that he would just dislike us all much more if we took away from him the only things he was really happy doing. They decided that they must all be especially patient with him, and that they must all ignore many

[28] Rigler School, Portland, Oregon.

of the annoying things he said and did. They also decided that it would help him if they showed confidence in him by giving him some important office in the room organization. Best of all, some of the boys who were outstanding leaders in the class pledged themselves to the task of winning his friendship.

The very next day, a situation arose, in which the class proved that they were serious about helping the boy. They had taken a test after lunch, and were in need of fresh air and relaxation. The sergeant-at-arms took charge of the class and they went out to play ball. The teacher was called to the office to answer the telephone. When she finished she looked out on the playground, but her class was not there. Perplexed, she returned to her classroom, where she found them sitting quietly. One member said, "We had to come in because of Harry." Nothing more was said at the time. At the close of the day, one of the boys remained after school and confided that Harry had disagreed with the decision of the umpire and had insisted on fighting it out before the game could proceed. Instead of arguing or fighting, the other twenty-nine turned quietly and came into the building. Harry begged them to come back, promising to be a good sport, but they continued on their way. He followed them dejectedly.

From that day on, a constant improvement was noted in Harry's behavior.

The mature type of self-discipline is that in which the individual faces his problems and makes his decisions in the light of their effect upon others. One group was able to come to agreements about "timing" behavior when they considered the effect of noise and confusion on the individual members of the group: [29]

The fifth graders found that the things which caused them trouble were not really bad behavior but untimely behavior—mixing up the kinds of behavior that are appropriate for play period with those that are appropriate for some other kind of activity. They recognized that it is easy to become careless about these changes in purposes and suitable kinds of action when twenty-five people are living together in the same classroom and using it for a variety of activities. "Cabin fever" can set in even a modern classroom.

For example it was agreed that during work period some talking, even socializing, might not interfere with the accomplishment of the jobs to be done; that moving about is important for some kinds of jobs. The purposefulness of the talking and moving is easily recognized. By experimenting it was found, too, that it is possible to talk under noise instead of trying to talk louder than the noise of power machinery and other tools. Many children were rather surprised to find that they could control several different kinds of voices.

When work period is over and it is time for group planning a distinctly different situation is at hand. The children agreed that any talking not directed to the entire group is disturbing and untimely in terms of what the group is trying to accomplish. Here is an occasion for using a voice loud enough for everyone to be able to hear comfortably. Listening to and thinking about what is said is important so that each is prepared to help further the discussion, complete the plans, and be ready to follow through appropriate action with real understanding of what is to be accomplished.

When it is time to begin individual study it was agreed that getting materials ready quickly, taking off on their own jobs with the idea of getting them done in the allotted time, and allowing those around them to do likewise made quite a different kind of situation. They expect "to feel the quiet" and not have unnecessary or inappropriate interests pulling at their attention. Reminders for those who violate the quiet are also part of the agreement.

Eating lunch in the same classroom makes necessary the getting ready for a still different situation. For this group it means a lunch committee of three setting tables and serving the lunch while the rest of the

[29] Mary Jane Loomis, the University School, Ohio State University, Columbus, Ohio.

children move to chairs away from the tables for a free reading time. Most people never have enough time for free reading so it is a welcome period in the day. The lunch committee can carry on their work with fewer hazards if it is understood that they are the only people in circulation about the room. Conversation at table is an important and enjoyable part of the day. The agreements about it are that conversation not interfere with eating and that it be confined to the table at which they are eating rather than roomwide, for obvious reasons. The observation coming from the children gives it greater importance, however.

Common to all situations is the necessity for being considerate at all times of the other people involved in any situation and for growing in the ability "to size up" a situation and to follow through with appropriate action. Needless to say, there are offenders. But the fact that the situations are recognized as the compelling factors in behavior instead of the teacher establishing the demands from time to time shifts the emphasis from teacher domination to teacher guidance, guidance in recalling the agreements that make for effective, businesslike living in various group situations. When limitations are a matter of group recognition and agreement, they take on much greater importance.

Illustrations have been given of ways teachers promote self-direction by: having pupils analyze their work; allowing classes to solve problems of group living; bringing pupils into the planning of activities; guiding pupils in their self-government; making pupils responsible for the care of their physical environment.

Basic to teaching self-direction is knowing each pupil's strengths and needs. A type of experience that will help one student grow in self-direction may be restrictive to a more advanced pupil. Teaching for self-direction has little chance for success unless teacher loads permit knowing each pupil well.

Finally, it must be recognized that the human being has periods when he does not want to assume responsibility for his own direction, times when he wants to revert to dependence. On such occasions the teacher who is working for pupil self-direction will need to give security and reassurance until the desire for self-direction returns.

THE NURSERY SCHOOL AND KINDERGARTEN

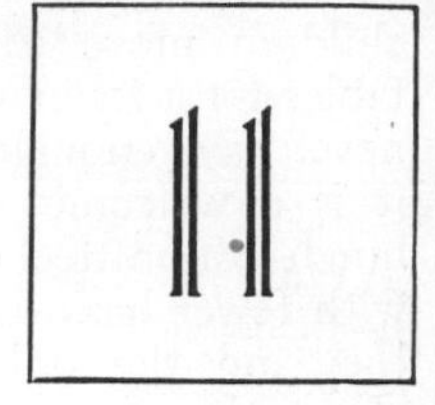

NURSERY SCHOOLS IN RELATION TO AMERICAN CULTURE PATTERN; WHAT ARE WE EDUCATING FOR?[1]

Ruth Benedict

DISCUSSION AND ANALYSIS

One of the fascinating things about our American society is the way in which new institutions arise to meet new needs. Among the recent developments of particular concern to educators is the growth of the nursery school. You may say to yourself, "But I am planning on teaching in the high school. How will what happens in nursery school make any difference to my teaching?" A good question. Can you think of any ways in which experiences the child had in nursery school might make him a more willing or more reluctant scholar in eleventh or twelfth grade? Certainly you will find some answers in this selection by the late Ruth Benedict. What happens in nursery school *will* influence later schooling. How and why and what you do about it is worth exploring.

Davis and Havighurst in their selection "When I Grow Older" (Chapter 6) have some pertinent things to say about the meaning of age to young children. How do they agree with Benedict's comments here? Do you think they are viewing the child from the same or different perspectives?

Many of you who read this volume will yourself be parents—and perhaps in the not too distant future. Before reading this statement consider how you feel about nursery school for your potential offspring. Is it something you would think wise, to send a 2- or 3- or 4-year-old to a nursery school, whether or not there was a mother home to care for him? Or what if mother wanted to work, what then? Now read Benedict's

[1] From *Bulletin of the National Association for Nursery Education* (1948), Vol. 3, No. 2. Reprinted by permission of the National Association for Nursery Education and Dr. Margaret Mead, Literary Executor of Dr. Ruth Benedict.

article. Does this change your feeling about this kind of educational experience? Why? Furthermore, as you read the next selection, by a nursery-school expert, what changes in your point of view have occurred?

You have asked me to speak today as an anthropologist. Anthropologists, whether they talk about the secret societies of the Duk-duks of Melanesia or the food habits of Kentucky or the nursery schools of the United States in 1947, are always the product of a certain kind of training, and they have drawn certain conclusions from their experiences. They have studied tribes and natives in strange corners of the globe, and they have a vivid conviction of how many varieties of a "good life" the human race has been able to invent for itself. From little hamlets of pre-literate pagans to great nations of the modern world, human communities have differed greatly in what they require and value. And whatever their standards are, men's bodies and minds have been habituated to them, and their personalities have taken color from them.

We Americans are no exception. Our characteristic ways of buying and selling, our judgments of success and failure, our habits of voting and church-going, are all ways of arranging life which we share either with the rest of Western Civilization or with the population of the United States or with some small group with which we are identified. They are part of special man-made inventions; the culture of modern civilization or of the United States of America or of Local 7 of the Teamsters' Union.

I shall speak of nursery schools, therefore, not as something every child needs when he gets to be two or three or four years old, but as something which performs certain particular functions in our American society of 1947. I have heard people try to establish a nursery school by arguing that "the" child at three ought not to be exposed to such close and constant companionship with his mother, or that the State had a moral duty to give its future citizens in these formative years an education for which parents are inadequate just because they were parents. I shall not argue on such grounds. As an anthropologist I know that the closest kind of contact with the mother and the most satisfactory education by biological parents has been socially valuable in many societies.

The questions I want to raise are about how our nursery school practices and policies can make their best possible contributions to a particular way of living—in the United States at this moment and in the immediate future.

The nursery school is an especially good example of a growing movement designed to meet a special need in our modern life. Many of the needs the nursery school is designed to fill were created by developments far removed from mother-child relationship. Some of these are due to modern conditions in industry. During the war the argument for nursery schools was quite properly based on the necessity of using the mother's labor in the war effort, and between the two World Wars creches and nursery schools were established to take charge of children of working mothers. As people in any society become more dependent on wages earned in industry, the necessity devolves on the school system for keeping the children of working mothers from loneliness or bad company.

The great urbanization of the United States has also erected a need for nursery schools. Even before the housing shortage, tenements and apartments were too small for growing children. The constant barrage of "don't touch"; "don't be so noisy"; "Don't, Don't, Don't" which a child gets in American apartments is no part of a parental policy of repression but a consequence of the way a modern American home is furnished, the fact that there are co-tenants on the floor below, and the standards of neatness of the American housewife. Therefore there arises the need for nursery schools where big-muscle equipment can be housed and where there is space enough to play with it; there arises the need for a playroom which is furnished for the child himself and not primarily for adults, where he can himself assume the responsibility of getting and taking care of and putting away the things he wants to play with.

The need for nursery schools in the United States today is not altogether based on such changes in the conditions of the objective world. It is also based on special ways in which Americans regard children. This aspect of the need for nursery schools is much less often recognized than the ones which are based on increasing industrialization and increasing urbanization. No society is very verbal and explicit about the special ways in which children are brought up by their parents. Methods of child rearing are not therefore any the less important. Every society has its accepted ways of bringing up its rising generation in ways that will fit them to carry on in adulthood the customs and values of their particular culture. These methods are sometimes extremely authoritarian; sometimes they are so permissive that the child seems to outsiders to have grown up without knowing what discipline is. Sometimes they are warm and yet erratic; sometimes they are cold and yet predictable.

Many societies treat their children as if there were no qualitative differences between them and adults. They recognize, of course, certain quantitative differences in strength, in knowledge, in experience of the world. But children, they think, are just less strong, less experienced adults. Parents therefore need plan to arrange nothing for children which they would not arrange for grown-ups. Children neither eat special foods nor have a special world of "play." This need not mean that in such societies the children are expected to be drudges; it means only that the adult's world, too, makes place for relaxation and pleasurable occasions, and the child shares with his elders. He is not thought to be a creature who plays, and therefore the opposite of his parents, creatures who work.

In such societies, too, if they admire independence and aggressiveness, the little child is admired for naughtiness. If he hits his father publicly, his father will boast of what a strong man his son will be. He believes that a child who controlled his anger and was submissive would naturally grow up to be a submissive man, and this should be avoided by all means. Such peoples often show exactly the same respect for a child's little possessions which they show for any adult's; if the child sells his beaded moccasions for a penny candy, the parents accept the fact that he is perfectly within his rights and he is not scolded. But he has to do without his pretty moccasins. His rights to his possessions are just what any adult's would be. The sanctions for any good behavior are treated as alike at all ages, for children are regarded, like adults, as wanting to do things correctly, and there is therefore no reason for insisting on obedience to parents' commands if adults need not obey commands.

In the United States children are regarded as qualitatively unlike adults. Children play; adults work. Children must eat what is good for them; adults may have their own preferences and show their maturity by indulgences like tobacco and alcohol. Children are asexual, mature adults must manage heterosexual experiences. Practically the only things we insist on consistently from the age of five or six months till death is three meals a day, regular elimination, and fixed hours of sleeping. These three things are all of them acts which most cultures of the world consider to be impossible because of the quantitative difference in the child's size. "How can a year-old baby with such a tiny stomach take enough food if he has only three meals a day?" they ask. More cultures are likely to wait several years before insisting on these regimes for children.

In the United States, however, it is precisely in this physiological field where we train a child to act just as he will when he grows up. In moral and emotional matters we do not grant that he is like an adult. We judge him in great detail as he compares with other three-year olds, other ten-year olds; every year of life has special characteristics and needs special handling. We emphasize one facet of the truth, and societies which emphasize the essential identity of human nature at all ages are emphasizing another. The question is not "Which is better?" One method does not of itself lead to the good life and the other to disaster. The point which needs to be stressed is that in the United States the process of growing-up is discontinuous. One is first a child; later one is grown-up. The two are contrasted with each other, instead of being two phases of the same thing.

Therefore the periods of transition from babyhood to childhood, from childhood to adolescence, from adolescence to maturity are fraught with special problems in the United States. Children are not formally put through an initiation which marks these periods as they are in so many primitive cultures; they are left to find their way alone from one status to another. Often the timing of the transition is physiologically quite unrealistic. The child may be physically and psychologically prepared for a new status much earlier than society allows honorable expression of his new capacities. This is especially true of sexual maturation, but in American culture it is also true of the child's entry into school.

Six years of age is, in many European and Middle Eastern nations, not too old for the child to leave the home nest and venture out into the world. From the point of view of the American student of child development, children in most of the Old World are commonly passive and submissive as compared to those with which they are more familiar. The amount of independence and self-assertion which is allowed an American child of three and four makes the conventional age of six undesirably late for entering school. He has been cramped in his home quarters for some years and those years could have been better spent in nursery school. It is a direct consequence of our methods of child-rearing.

The nursery school is therefore an American solution for the difficult transition period between his years in the isolated family home and in the large school room. As our elementary schools are set up, the usual transition is terribly abrupt, as abrupt as anything we expect any adult to take. It is a great deal to ask of children of six. We need to think of nursery schools, not just as an institution by themselves, but as a way of handling this transition to grade schools so that the child can benefit fully by his later schooling. Perhaps it will be necessary for nursery school teachers to play a role in modifying the routine of our public elementary schools in order to make the nursery school fulfill this function; perhaps it will prove necessary to revise some nursery school procedures. In any case, children's education must be thought of as something which goes on year after year, and each part must be increasingly adjusted to the years that are to follow.

The nursery school has often taken an extreme position against using authority in the classroom. Many articles are written as if the authors supposed that American child-rearing was based on the kind of qualitative identification of children and adults which I described for some American Indian and South Sea tribes. Such articles argue that because the democratic ideal for adults forbids authoritarianism, therefore no command should be given to a child. One should say "This is the way we do things here," not "Put your toys away." In the American way of life, this fear of giving a formal command to children seems to me unrealistic. Both at home and in the grade school obedience is exacted in many matters. We regard it as our moral duty to make the child do right and avoid doing wrong; commands and punishments are a normal part of this process. When some nursery school teachers describe how certain of their children "go to pieces" when they are allowed self-direction may it not be that their particular nursery school practices are too extreme for children brought up in American ways.

Respect for a child's individuality is not incompatible with rules and direct prohibitions; they have been bracketed together in many cultures. The child looks to the adult for help, and sometimes a teacher's too great concern about keeping hands off may be harder for the child than a direct command. The nursery school could well be judged by the standard of the children's cooperation, and not by its avoidance of direct precept.

Strong emphases on never using authority do their special harm in making teachers guilty about the authority they do use. Authority, when there is no guilt in it, has been socially valuable in many cultures. If the teacher feels guilty, the children suffer. In our American culture, there is thus constant danger if we taboo direct commands; "this is the way we do it here" may easily become merely a round-about and embarrassed substitute for a direct command. Given American patterns of child-rearing, it is probably inevitable that this should be so; and what is therefore to be avoided is any set of professional standards which tend to make teachers guilty in such a situation.

There will without doubt be a great expansion of nursery schools in the United States. We are meeting here this year especially to consider this program. From the point of view of the student of culture, any such expansion involves both the elementary school as an institution, and the home—especially the child's mother. There are two ways in which nursery schools can be set up in the thousands of American communities where they are still non-existent. One is as an integral part of the public school system, and the other is as the mothers' cooperative nursery school. Both of these must be thought through in relation to existing cultural patterns of elementary schools, state and federal duplication of funds, and the relation of mothers to nursery school teachers.

Believing as I do in the desirability of rapid establishment of nursery schools, I regard mothers' cooperatives as one of the important possibilities of expansion. I know very well how they failed during the war and yet I believe that they cannot be written off as impossible if we are truly concerned about educational programs for children. Those who believe in nursery schools would do well, I believe, to pay particular attention to the cultural reasons for their wartime failure and to take steps to correct the difficulties.

The difficulty about mothers' cooperative nursery schools goes back to the great American conflict between experts and laymen, between professionals and volunteers. Every welfare society, every community organization testifies to this stress and strain. Professional status is desirable in the United States in and of itself. We have sloughed off the common earlier idea that it was better and more prestigeful to contribute one's services without pay and without training. We do not admire Lady Bountiful today; we give prestige instead to the person who "has a job." So in the mothers' cooperatives, the nursery school teacher is plunged into this great American situation of experts and laymen. But it is a situation where the stresses are raised to the nth power. The mothers have fed their children, disciplined them, know all about them. And they are brought together with an "expert." No wonder the wartime cooperative nurseries failed.

In our American culture, however, there is one way in which it would be possible to meet this situation. We know very well that a professional can be trained to take the responsibility for success in the most difficult sort of job. His whole self-respect becomes involved in solving the problems which his job presents. We could, therefore, train a new sort of nursery school teachers whose stake in their profession would be that they could be successful with *mothers*. At present we tend to write off mothers as failures, and we train for success with *children*.

As long as our nursery school training is oriented in this way, mothers' cooperative schools will fail as they did during the war. But professionals could be trained who would care as much for developing their techniques with mothers as professional nursery school teachers now feel for their methods with children. They would undoubtedly have to respect mothers more, and they would have to create their own professional standards. It would be a new departure, but if the nursery school programs are going to expand as they might, such a new sort of professional training is a "must" for all of us who are interested in the education of the American child.

I have been stressing consequences in nursery school training of my proposition that every educational program must be thought through in relation to American culture patterns. I have been saying that in nursery schools we are educating Americans for full participation in our way of life. Such a position as this is easily misread as an acceptance of status quo, but this is exactly what it does not mean. Culture patterns in the most stable primitive societies nevertheless change, and in Western Civilization change is rapid and inevitable. We must prepare for change. But in such preparation it is necessary to face the problem of what assets and liabilities are available to us in our traditional customs. Change will inevitably occur; we need to be realistic in our planning if we are to be effective in our changing world.

BUILDING FEELINGS OF CONFIDENCE AND ADEQUACY[1]

Katherine H. Read

DISCUSSION AND ANALYSIS

This is one of the most fully developed and most explicit selections in the text, and consequently requires minimal interpretation by the editors or the instructor. A few comments, however, may prove helpful in stimulating further thought. The essay by Dr. Ruth Benedict, for example, may be read as a general comment on the *kind* of task Katherine

[1] From *The Nursery School,* by Katherine H. Read, chap. 7, pp. 125–149. Copyright, 1950, by W. B. Saunders Company. Reprinted by permission of the author and publisher.

Read believes the nursery school ought to perform. We may also profitably consider whether the image of the nursery-school teacher presented by Margaret Mead is consonant with the difficulty of the tasks indicated. Katherine Read is obviously of the opinion that children should not be "nudged" from one developmental stage to another. If the student sees the wisdom of this opinion, he will similarly see an additional reason why a thorough grounding in the psychological foundations of education is necessary to the teacher who would be expert. Finally, Katherine Read realizes that there is always the possibility that parents are not perfect. Do you feel, however, that the proper task of the nursery or any other school is to make up the deficiencies of parents? What type of parents do you imagine the children had in "The High Hill" in Chapter 10? When children reach high-school age (for example, the students in Evan Hunter's "Break the Wall" in Chapter 13), is there anything the teacher can do to remedy the traumas of the first six years?

Feelings of Confidence and Adequacy Are Important for All of Us

"Look here, teacher, I'm bigger than you think. I'm going to have a birthday soon. Let me do this by myself," said Katherine to a well-meaning adult who was trying to help her.

Her words remind us how often adults handicap children by acting as though children were unable to meet situations. A child has a difficult time developing confidence when he is surrounded by people who "help" him all the time. Children are often bigger than we think! Katherine was able to express her confidence in herself as a person able to do things. Few children can do this because they lack not only the verbal ability but the feeling itself.

As adults most of us probably wish that we had more self-confidence. We realize that we are likely to do a thing better when we feel confident than when we are afraid of failing. We realize, too, that we get more pleasure out of doing something when we feel adequate and are free from anxiety. For all of us, feelings of insecurity and inadequacy are handicapping. They do not arise entirely from lack of skill, for the person who has confidence in himself may enjoy undertaking something new in which he lacks skill. But most people are not free enough of doubts about themselves to feel challenged by the unfamiliar.

One of the important ways in which we will use the nursery school as a laboratory will be in trying to understand better how people grow secure and confident as well as how security and confidence are sometimes destroyed. As we observe people in nursery school, we will look for the meaning of their behavior in terms of the degree of security revealed by it. As we work with the children, we will seek for ways of strengthening their feelings of confidence and security. We will ask ourselves at least three questions. First, where do feelings of security and adequacy come from and what helps or hinders their development? Second, how can we identify these feelings in people? Third, what can we do in the nursery school to increase these feelings?

DEFINITIONS

Before we consider these questions we must in some way define the terms, "security" and "adequacy." Let us say that security refers to the feelings that come with having had many experiences of being accepted rather than rejected, of feeling safe rather than threatened. It refers to a person's relationships with people and develops from the way these relationships have been experienced by the individual. Adequacy refers to the feelings which an individual has about himself, his concept of the kind of person he is. This concept, too, grows out of the responses other people make to him. Security and adequacy are closely related. It will be easier to consider them together in our discussion for, as we help the child with one feeling, we are likely to help him with the other.

FOUNDATIONS FOR FEELING ADEQUATE AND CONFIDENT

First, where do feelings of security and adequacy come from?

We have already suggested some of the important areas. They arise out of the way the child's basic needs are met, his experiences with feeding and later with toileting, the kinds of responses he gets from other people, the satisfaction he finds in exploring the world. The attitudes and feelings of his parents are among the most important factors because he depends largely on his parents for the satisfaction of his basic needs.

If the child's first experiences have made him feel adequate and confident because he has been able to get his wants satisfied, to obtain response from people, to have satisfying sensory experiences, he has laid a firm foundation for confidence and security. If he was fed when he was hungry and had attention when he felt the need for it, the world seems a safe place to him and he can face it with the assurance that he will be able to meet the problems it presents. If, on the other hand, his wants have been unsatisfied, if he has failed to get response when he needed it, he has already experienced inscurity and felt inadequate. If he constantly heard the words, "no," and "don't," when he reached for experience, he has already grown to distrust his own impulses. The world does not seem to him a place where he can feel safe, and he builds a picture of himself as a person who is not very adequate to meet the problems it presents. He thinks of himself as a person who is likely to do the wrong thing.

As Will said dejectedly when he looked down at his muddy boots one day in nursery school, "It's sure hard to please anybody when you get right in the mud." He had been having fun in the mud but he knew from past experience that what he did in mud somehow made him unpopular.

INFLUENCE OF ADULTS

Children Are Influenced in Their Feelings by the Attitudes of Adults

Children tend to behave as they feel they are expected to behave, or according to the concept of self they have built up out of the responses of other people to them. Charles, for example, thinks of himself as a boy who gets into trouble. As he and his father came into nursery school one morning, his father remarked, "See how nice and quiet this place is until you get here!" What is a boy like who hears words like these? He is a boy who is noisy and defiant and "difficult." He lives up to the picture his father paints.

When Jim's mother brought him to nursery school, she explained to the teacher as Jim stood beside her, "Perhaps he'll learn to ride a tricycle here. He doesn't know how yet. He doesn't like to learn things. He just tries for a minute and then gives right up." It was not surprising that Jim lacked confidence and was unfriendly with both children and teachers.

Ella was timid, too. She didn't join other children in play, but she did like to paint. She was at the easel painting carefully around the edges of the paper when her mother came for her one day. Her mother saw the picture and she said half scornfully, "Nobody paints like that!" How can one have much confidence if one is considered a "nobody"? Ella didn't expect to be liked!

After Ella had been in nursery school some time and had gained confidence through feeling more acceptance and approval, after she felt more of a "somebody," her behavior changed in an interesting way. She quietly but persistently tried to put herself in as important a place in every situation as she could. For example, she and another child were pretending that their block structure was a truck. "I'll be the driver," said Ella. "No," insisted her companion, "I'm the driver." After a moment's hesitation Ella said, "Then I'll be the man who owns the truck and hires the driver."

Ella's solution was very different from that of Mary who had always felt sure that she was loved. "Can I play with you?" she asked Dick. "No," shouted Dick, and Mary answered calmly, "I could be the maid and sweep and then two people could play together." In the same kind of situation, she was only interested in finding a playmate and did not need to depend on having an important place.

Leighton and Kluckhohn in *Children of the People* make an interesting comment on the attitudes which appear in another culture than our own. They describe the way the Navaho people treat young children in these words, ". . . the Navaho toddler is given self-confidence by being made to feel that he is constantly loved and valued."[2] Would Ella and Jim have behaved differently if they had lived under conditions where they were "constantly loved and valued"? There are many children in our culture who are "constantly loved and valued," but there are many others who are treated as "nobodies" like Ella and Jim even though there is no conscious intent on the part of parents to treat them this way.

The frequency with which the word "big" appears in children's conversation, as "We're big truck drivers," and "Mine's the biggest car," or "I have the most," is perhaps a reflection of the many occasions when we have made the child feel that he is "too little." They are words which are in part a defense against the inadequate feelings which result from being "too little" on many occasions in a world that favors those who are big and have the most.

We live in such a highly competitive society that it is often hard for us to recognize the values that may exist outside of achievement. Parents feel the pressure for accomplishment. They want children who will learn to ride tricycles or who paint good pictures. They push their children, even their toddlers. They do not value them as they are.

We Tend to "Nudge" Children. Dr. James Plant described this tendency of parents to push their children as quickly as possible from one stage to the next as "nudging" the child in his growth. We are likely to "nudge" children on rather than allow them to take time to satisfy their needs in each stage. We do this even though it has been demonstrated that growth proceeds in certain sequences, one stage following another, and that the soundest growth occurs when the child is given time in each stage, "living it out completely" before going on to the next. Dependency, for example, precedes independence and the child who is most independent in the end will be the one whose dependency needs have been most completely met, not the one who was pushed the soonest into being independent. "Nudging" a child from one stage to the next serves to make him feel less secure and more defensive. Children who

[2] Dorothea Leighton and Clyde Kluckhohn, *Children of the People: The Navaho Individual and His Development*, Cambridge, Harvard University Press, 1947, p. 33.

have been pushed through a stage frequently have to go back and experience it again before they are free enough to go on, before they are secure enough to develop further.

We Are Afraid of "Spoiling" Children. Sometimes people are afraid to accept children as they are and to meet their needs because they are afraid of "spoiling" them if they do. They deny and interfere with them needlessly out of ignorance of the growth process. They make it hard for the child to think of himself as an adequate person. "Spoiled" children are in fact those who get attention *when the adult wants to give it* rather than when the child himself needs it. They are those children who are subject to inconsistent interferences rather than given the support of consistent limits by parents who are willing to take responsibility for limits. A "permissive" type of handling which allows the child to live on his own level tends to build secure feeling in the young child rather than to "spoil" him. It reduces to the minimum the denials and interferences which are likely to shake a child's confidence in himself. It accepts him as he is. It helps him feel adequate.

Parents Need to Be Secure People. Accepting the child as he is and meeting his needs freely are easier for people who are themselves secure. A secure person is relaxed, comfortable, permissive and giving. He or she does not feel as much need to make demands on others. Secure people are likely to create the kind of environment in which it is easy for the child to think of himself as an adequate person.

Insecure people are defensive and often demanding. They are likely to set standards which the child can meet with difficulty, if at all. If they are to accept children, parents need to be secure people; yet there are many reasons why parents have a hard time feeling secure today. They are not helped by the economic insecurities and the conflicts in the world or by the kind of homes and communities in which they live or by their education which offers little guidance in understanding the parent-child relationships. Charles' father who spoke in such a belittling way to his son is typical of many parents. He wants to be a successful parent but he is without experience or preparation for his role. Like most people he values success highly and is striving for it in a professional field. His concept of a successful parent is one whose child behaves like an adult. He feels his failure to achieve this goal with Charles. His love for the child is hidden under his constant criticism. He is not a secure parent. He makes Charles an insecure child.

A Child May Be Offered Many Different Kinds of Experiences by Adults

By the time the child reaches the nursery school he will have had many experiences which will determine how secure and adequate he feels. He may have come from a home where he has been accepted by parents secure enough to be permissive and giving. He may have come from a home where there has been little permissiveness, and his parents are too insecure themselves to be able to accept his immaturities. The experiences that he will have in nursery school will add to the foundation he has laid. The acceptance he finds in the teachers, the care with which experiences are adapted to his readiness to meet them, beginning with the experience of entering the school itself, will bring growth in the direction of being more secure and adequate or will handicap this growth. We will consider further the significance of his nursery school experiences as we discuss ways of strengthening his positive feelings.

RECOGNIZING THE CHILD'S FEELINGS

We will raise the question here of how we may recognize a child's feeling. How do we identify feelings so that we may be of help to a child?

Children reveal their feelings through behavior. Sometimes they do it openly and directly. They act as they feel. Sometimes their feelings come out in ways that are harder to identify. We must learn to understand; then we can recognize how plainly they speak to us through behavior.

Observe Behavior First

Perhaps the first step in understanding the meaning of behavior is to be able to look at the way a child behaves without feeling a necessity to change his behavior. We must learn to look at behavior as it is rather than in terms of what we want it to be. We are likely to confuse the meaning of a child's behavior with our own feelings if we try to judge it, if we decide that the child should or should not be behaving as he is.

We learn by observing. We are interested, at first, in learning to understand what feelings are being expressed through each bit of behavior. It may be dangerous to strive for change before we fully understand the forces with which we are dealing. Damage has been done many times when people have acted without sufficient knowledge. Men cut down trees and cleared land only to discover that the soil washed away and that water supplies were endangered because of what they had done. Too much of our energy is spent trying to repair the consequences of hasty action. In the field of behavior as in all fields, we need to observe and learn before we can evaluate a course of action.

There Are Clues to a Child's Feeling in Behavior. We have already pointed out how children differ in the kinds of adjustments that they make in new situations. These differences have meaning. The person who wishes to understand a child will observe carefully how he responds in a new situation. He will not decide how the child should respond and try to force this pattern of response on him. If he does, he may be burying a clue to understanding. He may damage the child and his development.

Children reveal characteristic attitudes in everyday, familiar situations, too. These may be seen in such things as in the way the child walks, runs, holds his hands, in his posture, etc. Posture is, of course, influenced by constitutional and environmental factors, but over and above these, reflections of the child's emotional patterns can be seen in his muscle tensions. One child's hands are relaxed and another's are tense and constantly moving. One child clutches our finger tightly as we walk along with him, a sign of his need for support and the intensity of his feeling. Another lets his hand lie limply in ours, suggesting perhaps the nongiving quality of his relationship with others, in contrast to the warm, responsive grip of still another child who welcomes closeness without clinging to it. These are all clues to help us understand the child's feeling.

Sometimes a conflict the child is feeling is expressed in the movements of his hands, as in the case of the child who is attracted to finger paints yet cannot use them because of the inhibitions he has built up against getting dirty. He may stand at a distance, wiping his clean hands on his suit or wringing them together, showing us the conflict he feels between the desire for sensory experience and the force of the restriction he has known against satisfying this desire.

Clues in Speech

Voice quality and speech offer clues to feelings. The quality of a child's voice may be strained and tight, or relaxed and easy. It may be loud and harsh, or soft and faint, or it may be confident and well-modulated. Even the amount of speech may give some indication of the extent of the child's assurance or of his hesitation. One child talks very little; another chatters almost constantly. These extremes may be a reaction to strains and pressures which are making him feel less confident and less secure than he should feel. Many insistent, needless questions are sometimes a symptom of insecurity, a seeking for reassurance more than for any specific answer. Too often these questions meet an impatient rebuff, not calculated to satisfy the need they express.

Spontaneous singing usually indicates confidence and contentment. The child who sings at play is probably comfortable, and it is worth noting the times and places when singing occurs spontaneously. We can learn from this in what areas or on what occasions a child feels secure. We can provide more of these kinds of experience. We have an important clue here.

For further clues as to how secure and adequate a child feels, we need to listen closely for the meaning which lies behind the words he speaks. An anxious little boy, new at school, talked to the teacher as he lay on his bed, resting. He kept telling her, "I live in Corvallis," and then asked her if she had a car. When she answered, "Yes," he said, "You could take me home." His words clearly indicated the insecurity he was feeling and the way he was trying to reassure himself by clinging to the idea of where he lived and by working out a plan for getting himself safely there. The teacher understood, and reassured him about how his daddy would come for him as he had the day before and how she would stay with him until his daddy came. She did stay near him and helped him find satisfactions in his present environment.

Martha cried one day and wanted her mother to stay at school with her. Her mother consented, somewhat reluctantly. Later she said to the teacher, "You know, I was pretty cross with Martha this morning. Do you suppose that has anything to do with her wanting me to stay with her?" They both agreed that this was probably the explanation of Martha's behavior that day. She was seeking reassurance from her mother. An increase in dependency often means the child is seeking more reassurance that he is loved!

The child who asks the teacher, "Do you want to go outdoors with me?" may really be saying, "I'm afraid to go out by myself. It would help if you wanted to go with me." The teacher needs to understand the meaning back of what he actually says.

The child who says happily, "Isn't this going to be a good gate? I'm building it all myself," is telling us something about what comfortable feelings he has about being an adequate person. This same boy's father once remarked about him, "I think he's one of those fortunate people who like themselves." The child liked himself—and everybody else, and was one of the most likeable children one could meet. He had been "loved and valued" in his family like the Navaho toddler in his.

There is a real consciousness of an emerging self in these words of Katherine —the same Katherine who is "bigger than you think"—when she says, "I'm different from all the other people. When other people laugh, I don't, even if it's silly." Katherine feels secure enough to be different.

Patterns of Behavior Give Clues to Feelings of Security and Adequacy

Defensive behavior is usually a sign of insecurity. Only too often children express their insecure feelings in a defensively aggressive way. They try to conceal the uncertainty they feel by being aggressive. They hit without much provocation. They reject the approaches of other children. One can get valuable clues by observing the way a child reacts to the approaches of another child as well as the way he himself approaches others. The secure child is not on the defensive. He does not feel threatened when another child approaches, but finds it easy to be friendly. The insecure child is likely to be hostile and unfriendly at any approach even before he finds out what kind of an approach it is. While the secure child can share easily when he is ready for group experience, the insecure child cannot afford to share because he fears any loss. His problem is not one of unfriendliness or selfishness but one of degree of security. This is the real problem which needs to be handled, not the symptom.

When someone knocks over Ralph's blocks, for example, he bursts into tears or he may hit at the offender frantically. He exhibits behavior characteristic of the insecure child. It is worth noting that Ralph does not behave this way every time something happens. There are a few children in the group with whom he feels sufficiently comfortable, sufficiently sure of himself, to be able to accept interference without being overwhelmed with feelings of helplessness.

It is important for us to note the people and the areas in which a child shows us by his behavior that he feels secure, if we are to help him. Steven and Sheila behave in a way that characterizes children who feel secure. Steven was pushing a block train along the floor when Sheila, who was riding a tricycle, happened to run into it and knock it over. "Excuse me, Steven," she said. "That's all right," he replied and he hooked the cars together and continued playing.

The child who is very insecure will often be unable to accept even a suggestion by the adult that he (the child) has made a mistake. Jane, for example, had known very little safety and security in any of her relationships with people. She was passive and inhibited, risking very little action. She had been in nursery school several weeks when this incident occurred: During rest, one of the children sat up and began playing. The teacher glanced in his direction, indicating that he needed to be quiet. Just then Jane sat up and the teacher indicated that she, too, needed to be quiet. Jane instantly burst into a storm of weeping, unable to face what seemed to her to be failure. She needed more time to grow secure before she could accept limitation without feeling threatened by it.

Margaret was another extremely insecure, defensive child who acted as though she did not expect friendliness from anyone. After a long period of holding herself back from any contacts in nursery school, she began to play with individual children. She had her first spontaneous, friendly play one morning with Betty. The two of them sat together in the sun playing with clay. It was growing hot so the teacher suggested that they stop playing long enough to take off their sweaters. Betty protested; then she acquiesced, for she was a secure, friendly child. Margaret's reaction was entirely different. She put her head down on the table and began sobbing. All the feelings from which she had momentarily escaped seemed to return. She may have interpreted the request as a threat to deprive her of this rare moment of companionship. Contacts with adults still represented a hostile limitation which she felt helpless to combat. She was the defensive, resentful little girl again. It was a long, slow process, lasting many months, to help this child grow in confidence to the point where she came to trust adults and accept their requests, or protest them without fear. During these months the adults made almost no demands on Margaret and accepted the resistance and defiance she increasingly began to show. Gradually, as she came to trust adults, she was able to accept and conform to requests or limitations from them without being overwhelmed by feelings of helplessness. She showed herself a responsive, warmly affectionate little girl with a real strength of purpose and a capacity to defend the self that she now knew that others would respect.

Thumbsucking May be a Symptom of Insecurity. When we are in nursery school, we are likely to see a child sucking his or her thumb at rest time or when the group is listening to a story or even during a play period. Like all behavior, thumbsucking is a symptom and may indicate a need in the child for more reassurance and greater security than he has found in his experience. He may seek the comfort associated with the earliest satisfactions in nursing because his world seems too difficult to face. It may be a difficult world for him because he is expected to be more grown-up than he is ready to be. He may be expected to be quiet, to inhibit his impulses for touching things, to take over adult ways of behaving at the table or in social situations, to comprehend and maintain the rules for property rights, etc. The strain of living up to all these demands, or of failing to live up to them, may be so great that the child seeks an infantile source of comfort. He turns to his thumb as a refuge. In some cases the world may be a difficult one for the child because he has to respond to many different adults and the attention that they give him and expect from him in return. "Show her how you do this," or "Come give me a kiss," and then "Don't bother me now," all put a strain on a child and confuse him. By sucking his thumb he is retreating into a situation which is not so demanding. The world may be difficult for a child because it is always changing. There may be moves from one house to another, from one town to another. The adults in the home may shift. The coming of another child may change the pattern of relationships. The child who is faced with too many adjustments is likely to retreat to his thumb and depend on it for comfort and assurance.

Whatever the reason in individual cases we can be sure that the child who persists in sucking his thumb after he has become a toddler is finding his world difficult, with more strain and tension in it than he can handle comfortably. He is telling us something through his thumbsucking, and we need to understand. We should not increase his strain by taking away the avenue of comfort that he has found, but we should try to make his life simpler and more comfortable. We should try to reduce the tensions he is under and offer him a greater chance for feeling secure and adequate, so that he may seek other kinds of satisfactions.

Mary Lou Took Her Own Thumb out of Her Mouth. Mary Lou was a round little girl of three who sucked her thumb most of the time at nursery school. She was timid and often held onto the teacher's skirt with her free hand. She didn't venture into activity with other children or even play alone actively.

Mary Lou was the oldest of three children and had always been a "good" girl according to her mother. She had been easy to care for and could even be depended on to watch out for her little sister while her mother was busy with the baby. She seemed content with little to do and never disturbed the babies! It was not hard to imagine that Mary Lou had had very little chance to have the satisfactions that usually come with being a baby. She had had to grow up very quickly, and had had to seek approval by behaving in unchildlike ways. It would have been an empty world for her without her thumb! She remained dependent on the teacher at nursery school for many months, but her interest in the children was plain as she watched a group having fun together. Sitting close to the teacher she sometimes became part of a group at the piano or at the clay table. She had a real capacity for enjoying experiences and a sense of humor which was evident as she felt freer to act. She thoroughly enjoyed the sensory experiences at the clay table, in the sandbox and later in the mud hole in the nursery school yard. She often played alone in the doll corner after she felt more at home.

Some months later she ventured into more active play. She still stood around with her thumb in her mouth part of the time but she was busy in the sandbox or riding the tricycles more of the time. The most marked change came in her behavior after she gained enough courage to use the slide. Sliding was a popular activity and Mary Lou would often stand watching, but resisted any suggestion that she join the group at the slide. At last on a day when no one else was at the slide, she tried it, with her favorite teacher near to hold her hand. It was an effort but she succeeded and went down again and again. She waved gaily to her mother when her mother came that day and showed off her newly acquired skill. From then on she participated more freely in every group. Mastering the slide seemed to give her a great deal of confidence. She even did a little pushing to hold her place in line there and began to stand up for herself in other ways. She was busy and happy. She hardly ever had time for her thumb. By the end of a year some of the adults had even forgotten that she used to suck her thumb! The fact that she no longer needed her thumb told a great deal about the change in Mary Lou and what nursery school had meant to her.

All Nervous Habits Are Symptoms

Other children may express the tensions they are feeling by biting their nails, twisting on their clothes, or sucking other objects. Masturbation is another means of finding satisfaction and a defense against strain. We may do a great deal of harm by attacking the symptom directly and denying the child an avenue of expression while he is still feeling tension and seeking relief and satisfaction. We need to look on all of these so-called "nervous habits" as symptoms whose cause must be sought and treated before the symptom itself can be expected to disappear. Treating the symptom only will tend to make some other form of expression necessary for the child and increase the strain he feels. The thumbsucking child may become a nailbiting child or a masturbating child, for example, if the symptom and not the cause is attacked. We must keep in mind the fact that all kinds of behavior have meanings which we cannot afford to ignore.

Speech Reveals Adjustments

Through his manner of speech a child tells us something about himself, too. In the nursery school we are likely to hear children whose words tumble out in broken rhythm or with many repetitions. Preschool children are just learning to talk and they often cannot form or recall the words as fast as they wish to get their ideas across. In some children this blocking is marked and begins to resemble stuttering.

Because children's speech is in its formative stage, it is especially important for us to handle its development with understanding. The repetition and broken rhythm which sounds like what we call stuttering or stammering is in itself a sign of strain and tension in the child. These strains may be temporary ones such as the piling up of unusual experiences which have fatigued the child or too much excitement just at the point in his growth when he is making rapid progress in learning to talk. Speech may be the most vulnerable spot at the moment and breaks down under the strains. Or the strains may be of long standing such as conflicts over relationships in the family or the piling up of hostilities which are allowed no avenue for expression.

If the emphasis is put on the symptom —the imperfect speech—the result may be a serious and lasting speech disorder. Some speech specialists feel that stuttering does not become true stuttering until the child recognizes and grows afraid that he will stutter. If this is true, it is essential that we exercise care to avoid calling the child's attention in any way to his speech. It is important to avoid asking him to "stop and say it more slowly" as many people will do. It is important for us to accept his speech and attack the conditions which are causing it. We can make it a point to stop and give the child our full attention when he is speaking, so that he will not feel the need to hurry. We can speak slowly ourselves when we speak, so that we will set a pattern in speech that will be easier for him to adopt successfully. But most of all we need to accept the fact that speech like this is a sign that pressures and demands made on this child must be reduced if his speech patterns are to change. Demands for staying dry, demands for standards in manners at the table, demands for staying clean, must be reduced or better yet eliminated if we are interested in helping him with his speech problem. All of the things which we will say later about emotional development can be applied here, but at this point we will only remind ourselves that we must be careful to avoid creating a problem for the child in the way we react to defects in his speech.

Infantile mispronunciations are common and reflect patterns of feeling as well as of speech. The independent experience of going to a nursery school will itself be of help to the child. We can treat the symptom which is established by making sure that the child hears correct speech. Rather than asking him to repeat the word or sound which is not spoken correctly, we can ourselves repeat it so that he has a chance to hear it correctly. If he is interested in books, we can read a great deal to the child whose speech has defective sounds in it, and we can read slowly and enunciate carefully as an aid to him.

It is of interest that types of speech defects vary in different culture patterns. This observation suggests that different ways of bringing up children may have different effects. Among certain Eskimo and Indian tribes, for example, no case of stuttering has ever been recorded. In our culture stuttering is much more common among boys than girls, while there are cultures where the reverse is true. Speech seems to be a sensitive index or response to the pressures which an individual feels. We need to try to understand more than just the words which are spoken.

ACCEPTING THE CHILD'S FEELINGS

We Must Face and Accept Feelings if We Are to Offer Help

Through all these ways a child shows us how he feels. After we have learned to recognize the child's feelings, we must find ways of adding to his feelings of security and adequacy and reducing his feelings of insecurity and inadequacy.

What are some of the ways in which we can do this in the nursery school?

The most important step is to make sure that we really accept the child's feelings—that we do not condemn or blame him for feeling as he does. Perhaps he feels afraid or angry or unfriendly. These may be feelings of which we do not approve, but approval and acceptance are different things. Acceptance means recognizing without blaming. We may not approve but we must accept the feelings that the child has if we are going to help him with them. Our very acceptance will reduce the feeling and make the child less defensive about his fear or his anger or his hostility. Instead of hiding his feelings he can bring them out where he—and we—can do more about them.

We usually find it most difficult to be accepting about feelings which we have had to deny in ourselves. When we were children, we often felt jealous or resentful or hostile, but we may not have been permitted to express these feelings. They were not accepted by the adults around us. We had to act as though we loved a little sister, for example, and were willing to share our dolls with her, or we had to let the neighbor boy ride in our wagon because the adults insisted that children must be generous. Resentment piled up inside us as well as guilt for the feelings that we knew existed in us. We had to carry this burden alone. Now, as adults, we find it hard to be accepting of the child who refuses to share her doll or who pushes another out of the wagon. We project onto her some of the resentment which is associated with this kind of situation for us because of the experiences in our past. We identify ourselves with the adult role now, and feel like punishing the little girl who doesn't want to share her doll or her wagon today. This helps us deny that we were ever like this little girl. But in handling our feelings by denying them, we cannot offer help to children who face problems with their feelings.

The story of what goes on unconsciously is over-simplified by the description we have given, of course, but we can be sure that whenever we feel strongly rejecting of a bit of behavior, there are strong emotional reasons lying in our past experience for such a rejection. For some of us there will be more of these emotionally toned areas than for others and our feelings will be stronger. Few of us will have escaped without some areas of behavior about which we find it hard to be accepting.

If, on the other hand, we were helped to accept our real feelings when we were children, we will now find it easier to be accepting of children as they show their feelings. If the adults with us when we were children said, "It's easy to get mad with someone who takes your things, I know" instead of saying "She's your sister and you must love her and share with her"; then we would have felt understood and could have faced our feelings with this kind of support. Because the adult could accept our feelings, we would not have been as likely to feel afraid or guilty about them. It would have seemed easier to feel and act more generously. This is the kind of help that we want to offer the children we are now caring for.

It is important if we are to help children in this way that we free ourselves of our old defenses. As adults we can now take the step of accepting the reality of any feeling that exists. We have less need to fear the knowledge that we are not always loving and generous. We know that we all found sharing and loving hard at times when we were children and that we felt like hitting. Some jealousy is in fact almost inevitable as children adjust to changing patterns in the family or at school, especially in children who are not too secure. It is not necessary to deny the existence of feeling. Hostile, aggressive feelings exist in all of us. They must be accepted if we are to relieve ourselves, as well as the child, of guilty feelings about them.

Acceptance Helps the Child. The child who refuses to share a toy isn't helped by disapproval and sharing. Neither is the child who is afraid. All these children need to be accepted as they are if they are to feel secure. There is always a reason for their behavior. As we work with the little girl who refuses to share her doll or who pushes her companion out of the wagon, we will accept her feelings and use her behavior as a clue to understanding. We will not ask her to cover up her feelings. We will not be satisfied merely with changing her behavior. We will try to make it possible for her to develop different feelings which will be expressed through different kinds of behavior. We will ask ourselves some questions. What kind of little girl is it who is trying to keep the doll? What unmet needs are driving the child to behave this way? Is she craving affection and substituting the doll for the love she seeks? Does she depend on possessing things to give herself a feeling of security? How can we help her?

We Can Voice Our Acceptance of Feeling. In the first place, we can express our acceptance in words, "I know how you feel. It makes you cross because it's Timmy's turn on the swing and you want it to be yours," or, "It makes you feel cross to have your blocks tumble over, I know," or, "You're pretty mad with me right now because I can't let you play outdoors." Words like these help if they express a real acceptance of the feelings which exist. They are very different from words like, "You didn't mean to hit Bobby, did you?" which are untrue, as the child's reply, "I did, too," tells us. We must be honest and state what is true.

We Can See That Feelings Are Expressed

Next comes the question of what one can do about a feeling that exists after it has been accepted. It's important that feelings be put into action, that they be drained off in ways that are not destructive. If all of us would *do* something, when we *felt* something, we'd be much healthier emotionally. We wouldn't be carrying around hidden feelings that are apt to come out when we are off guard in ways that make us unhappy. We should encourage expression of feelings at the time that they arise. We can be much clearer then as to what the feelings are. We will feel more secure because we will be more likely to handle them in ways that are appropriate.

In Words. There are all kinds of ways to express feeling. Words are one good way. As adults, we tell a friend how we feel and then feel much better! Children are likely to talk things out directly on the spot. They call names, shout lively descriptive insults, and put themselves in a better frame of mind! When they use speech like this, they may be using as good a means of handling feeling as they have at their disposal. It may not be a mature way, but they are not mature people. They cannot write poetry or denounce with eloquence some measure or some person or some oppressor. The language in which they express their rage is limited but it is adequate for them. It expresses their feeling directly instead of hiding it. If they can use language now to drain off feelings, their later responses may be more reasonable. In many cases we are wise to accept their words as expressions of the way they feel. Words like this do no damage to us if we are mature people ourselves, and if we understand what they really mean in a child's development. Listening to an insult or a swear word may not be too high a price to pay in helping a child drain off negative feeling. We can well afford it.

In Crying. Crying is another good way to express feeling, yet many times we hear people say to a crying child, "That didn't hurt. You're too big to cry." The crying may come because there have been too many failures or too much deprivation or frustration. Whatever the reason, the feeling of wanting to cry is there and needs to be accepted, not denied. No one can handle with wisdom feelings he isn't supposed to have. Words like "I know how you feel," when they are said by a person who really accepts the feeling help a good deal more than words like, "You're too big to cry."

In Movements. Motor forms of expression of feeling are common forms for expression. Expressing feeling through movements or muscle activity is a common way for young children to express feeling. A young child may kick or hit or throw. Our job is to help him use motor outlets in a way which will not be damaging to others. He may even need to be put by himself so that he can act in these ways without hurting anyone. If he is older, he may be able to take a suggestion about using a punching bag to advantage. Vigorous physical activity like pounding, or throwing a ball hard against something, will serve as an outlet for feeling. If there is a warm, understanding relationship between child and adult, the child can accept many types of suggestion for draining off negative feelings. The teacher may be successful when she says, "You feel just like hitting someone, I know. Let's run as hard as we can over to that corner. That may make you feel better," and the child may be able to handle his feelings after sharing a run with an understanding, accepting teacher. Our job is to limit him so that he does not use destructive outlets. It is also our job to direct him to outlets that are possible and acceptable.

Through Creative Media. Materials which offer possibilities for creative expression can be used to drain off feelings and make them more manageable. Finger painting, painting at the easel, working with clay, playing in water, even the sandbox or a good old mud hole, will help a child relax as he expresses feelings through these media. Music offers still another possibility and is often used this way by children. Creative materials should be freely available to children because of the value they have as avenues for the expression of feeling. Adults use these same outlets. The child who has found he can turn his feelings into such creative channels has discovered an outlet which will serve him all his life. A child is more secure if he has many avenues of expression open to him. He grows as he can express himself and his feelings through art media. When he is denied self-expression in art media because patterns are set for him, he loses a valuable avenue for the relief of feeling which might help to safeguard him all his life.

CONFIDENCE THROUGH EXPRESSION

Expression of feeling is essential if we are to feel secure and adequate. The child who says, "I'm afraid," already is less troubled by this feeling of fear. The child who says to the stranger, "Go away. I don't like you," will learn to handle his feeling more quickly than the child who says nothing and then bursts into tears when the stranger presses an acquaintanceship on him. Acting in some positive way gives us all confidence. When we do something about the way we feel, we are more confident. Psychiatrists tell us that the child who has been aggressive in his early years and whose behavior has been met with understanding has a better chance to make a good adjustment in adolescence than the submissive child, because the aggressive child has done something about his feelings and learned how to manage them.

THE TIMID CHILD MAY BE REASSURED BY FINDING EVEN "BAD" BEHAVIOR ACCEPTED

We will often see a timid, inhibited child swing over into unduly aggressive behavior as he begins to gain confidence in himself. This may be the first step in gaining confidence. He must first express his feelings and find acceptance for them. Then he can proceed to modify them. The child who has been inhibited may express his feelings in clumsy and inappropriate ways in the beginning. His first expression of feeling may seem exaggerated. It may seem to belong at a much younger level than his present chronological age level. But if his timidity developed in an earlier period because he was afraid of his feelings and the way people would react to them so that he was not able to express feeling, he will need to go back and act as he wanted to act earlier. With understanding guidance he will come through this stage quickly but he must "live out," for however brief a time, a period of expression at the less mature level.

Richard was an inhibited boy who found new experiences difficult to face, who for a long time could not use the toilet at nursery school and who clung to cutting with scissors as his only activity at first. He went through a short period of being very uninhibited before he built up some controls of his own. From being a timid child, dependent on the teacher, he became a child who tried out many forms of behavior which he felt were unacceptable. When he developed more confidence, he began to defy the teachers. For one trying week (for the teachers!) he kept standing on the table at mealtime and throwing food. Because he had previously been afraid to express himself in any way, the teacher accepted his behavior. She sat with him apart from the others and permitted any behavior as long as it did not interfere with mealtime for the other children. When she did restrict him, she did it without blaming or reproving him, and tried to point out what he might do that would serve the same purpose. It was about a week before he no longer seemed afraid of being "bad," before he was reassured that he would be accepted no matter what he did. Then his behavior changed. He began to act like the other children. He was able to accept the limitations ordinarily imposed in the situation without feeling helpless and inadequate. He had less need to act in unacceptable ways and in the end he became a welcomed and respected member of the group. It is worth noting, too, that Richard was probably helped by the safety he felt in knowing that the adult could and would stop him before he did anything serious as well as by the acceptance he felt for his "badness." Johnny, on the other hand, . . . never gained enough confidence to dare to be "bad." Badness fascinated him in others but he remained "good." The guilt which his repressed desire caused him was probably a factor in making him timid and nervous. With far more to handicap him, he could not seem to free himself as Richard did. He never participated spontaneously in group activities.

Children who are already sure of themselves and their acceptance by adults do not need such permissive handling as was given Richard. Confident children might even feel less sure of themselves if they found adults unwilling to limit them when they knew limits were needed. In each case handling must be based on understanding of the needs of the particular child at a particular stage.

A Child Feels More Secure When He Is Having Satisfying Experiences

The child whose needs are being met is more likely to be confident than the one whose needs are not met. This applies to his experience in the nursery school as well as at home. If the school is providing satisfying, stimulating experiences, it makes it easier for the child to be happy and secure. The whole program of the school as well as the equipment provided will contribute to the child's growth in feeling more secure and more adequate. Experiences adapted to the child's level of development, equipment which fits him and makes it easy for him to solve problems, support from adults who understand what his needs are, all make it easier for a child to gain the feeling of security and adequacy that he needs.

Most important of all, in the nursery school the child is thrown with people who are about on the same level of development. He can have fun doing things with other children. Among this group of equals he does not need to feel inadequate for he *can* keep up with them. He can do things as well as many of the others. He gains strength from the feeling that he is like others, from being able to identify himself with people who are at his stage of growth. Belonging to a group of equals constitutes one of the best forms of insurance against feeling little and helpless. We will discuss this point at greater length later, but we mention it here because of the important contribution it makes to feelings of adequacy in a child.

The child needs to find teachers in the school who will accept his positive feelings, too. As teachers, we must be ready to return his smile, to take his hand when he slips it into ours, to take him into our arms when he seems to feel the need of such closeness. We must respond to his warm, friendly feelings. If it is his need and not ours that we are meeting in doing this, we can be sure that he is helped to be more independent by what we do. He will gain confidence as he feels sure of having a warm response from us when he wants it.

Good Teaching Contributes to Development of Adequate Feelings

By the technics we use as teachers we will also help the child grow more secure and adequate. Let us take the situation of a child climbing on the jungle gym as one example, and see what it may mean.

Two-year-old Joan, just learning to climb, cautiously and awkwardly manages to get half-way up in the jungle gym and then calls for help, "Help me. I want down." An adult comes to her rescue and answers the cry by lifting her down. Joan is on the ground, safe, but with all feeling of achievement lost! On another occasion a different adult comes to the rescue. She stands beside the child and says reassuringly, "I'll help you, Joan. Hang on to this bar and put your foot here," thus guiding Joan's climbing back to the ground. Safe on the ground, Joan is elated. She starts right up again and this time is successful in reaching the top. When her mother comes, she can scarcely wait to show her this new achievement.

If, when Joan starts to climb the jungle gym, her mother says in a disgusted voice, "Come on, Joan, you've had all morning to play. I'm in a hurry. You can show me tomorrow," Joan may again lose the feeling that she is a person who can achieve. But if her mother is eager to share the experience and watches her, exclaiming, "That's fine, Joan, you've learned to climb way up high," Joan takes another step in growing confident.

As teachers, we contribute to the child's feeling of security and adequacy if we tell him what he can do rather than what he can't do, if we point out what is desirable or acceptable behavior rather than what is undesirable, and if we direct his expression of feeling into channels which are not destructive and will not cause him to feel guilty. We must not hesitate to stop him when we feel that he needs to be stopped in something that he is doing, but we will be careful to do this in a way that does not make him feel ashamed. We will try to make our suggestions to him before his feeling spills over into undesirable behavior. Whenever possible, we will forestall destructive expressions of feeling although we will encourage expression. By the use of these teaching skills we will help the child develop confidence in the kind of person he is.

SUMMARY

Let us summarize briefly some of the things that we can do in the nursery school to increase a child's feeling of security and adequacy.

1. We can *accept* him as he is, his feelings and his behavior, knowing that there are reasons for the way he feels and acts. We will recognize that hitting and other forms of motor expression of feeling are normal for the young child. We will not blame or shame him for feeling as he does. If we do this, we lessen his confidence in himself as a person.

2. We can help him find acceptable *outlets* for his feelings. It is our responsibility to help him direct his expression of

feeling into some channel that bears a relation to the situation but does no harm. We must be sure that feelings are expressed, however. The really destructive feelings are those that have no recognized outlets.

3. We can try to *meet the child's needs* as he indicates what his needs are, and we can leave him free to develop in accordance with his own growth patterns at his own rate. Thus we will give him confidence and the feeling that he is an adequate person. We will refrain from "nudging" him. Instead, we will try to understand him.

4. We can *acquire skills in handling him* which will increase his confidence, making our suggestions to him in a positive way, reducing the difficulties of the situations he faces, adjusting our demands to fit his capacities, forestalling trouble when we can.

We may add to our understanding of the meaning of security and adequacy as we follow the experiences of a child whose problems arose because she had not felt "loved and valued" enough to be able to meet the demands made on her.

Peggy, Who Had Not Felt Valued Until She Found Friends. Peggy found it possible to grow more secure in the group situation through finding a friend. She was a thin, tense, withdrawn child with an unhappy look on her face. She expressed her resistances passively at first. Her parents had faced difficult personal problems and much unhappiness. They had tried to recognize the needs of their little daughter but had necessarily had little time left for her. She had almost invariably had a secondary place in the family situation, and could hardly have felt herself a very "valued" person. She responded to the teacher's smile at nursery school and stood close beside her. She made no protest when her mother left. She did not express her feelings. She did not participate in many activities. She watched the children and gradually the expression on her face showed her growing interest. Inside she often sat on the piano stool by the teacher, and outdoors enjoyed swinging and singing.

As she was one of the older children in the group, she was taken on walks frequently with one or two other children where she could have attention from the teacher and the variety of experiences she seemed to enjoy. In time, she began to play in the doll corner, wheeling the buggy around the playground with the dolls well covered up. This activity brought her into contact with Alice who loved dolls, too. Alice was round and placid and moved slowly. She was cheerful and outgoing in contrast to Peggy and nearly a year younger. Peggy seemed to feel that here was someone who liked her and wanted her. The teacher helped by placing them together at the table at lunch time. They became friends.

Alice enjoyed Peggy's advanced ideas in a calm way, but for Peggy it was like the opening of a new world to find this friend. She grew more spontaneous and creative, initiating play activities. The two girls would set up housekeeping each day in different spots on the playground. They took walks together and Peggy became more animated and talkative. She smiled and even ran. Her mother reported that she now wanted someone to come up and talk with her about nursery school every night before she went to sleep!

Peggy had always lacked an appetite and her mother reported that for months she had refused milk at home; now she began to eat better, sitting beside Alice. She even began to try to get Alice to follow her in resisting eating.

One day she said, "We don't like broccoli. We're not going to eat it. We're all through." Alice turned to the teacher and repeated Peggy's words half questioningly. Alice always ate everything. The teacher felt that the most important value to preserve in this situation was Peggy's feeling that she could count on Alice, could even lead her. She tried to give an answer that would make it possible for Alice to follow Peggy without losing sight of the standards she had always accepted; so she replied, "If you think you don't like it, I suppose you'll take just a tiny bite to find out."

Alice felt better. She took a tiny bite and said, "No," and both girls decided they were "through." Peggy did seem to gain confidence from having Alice accept her lead in this situation. It didn't interfere with Alice's eating either for only two days later when Peggy said, "We don't like milk. We aren't going to drink it," Alice answered, "Yes, we do. I'm going to drink it." Alice really loved milk.

Peggy said, "Let's just pretend to drink," but Alice answered, "No, let's really," and she poured some and drank it. Peggy poured some and drank it, too. After that she usually drank her milk at school. She had taken a big step forward. It is interesting to speculate whether she could have followed Alice's lead in accepting milk if she had not been successful in getting Alice to follow her lead previously in refusing broccoli and if the teacher had not been able to maintain a neutral position which left both girls free.

As usually happens when a child begins to gain confidence, she began to assert herself more. Some of this asserting took the form of defiance. When it was time to come in she would climb to the top of the jungle gym and announce, "I'm not going in." The teacher appreciated this sign of confidence and helped her by saying, "No, I can see you aren't—not until you are ready."

The teacher usually managed to stay outside with her, picking up equipment so that Peggy would not feel deserted and thus forced to give up her defiance. It was not based as much on hostility as a need to feel herself a person who could control and be important. Soon she had more constructive ways of being a person and did not depend long on escaping to the jungle gym as a different child might have done. She began to play with other children more nearly her age. In a few short months she was acting as though she belonged in the group.

In her home it had been difficult for her to feel adequate and secure. In the group she had found herself to be an adequate person. She had friends. She was happier and much more secure.

One of the most important functions of the nursery school is to increase the child's confidence in himself and his own adequacy and sense of being valued by others. All children should like themselves better after they had lived at nursery school. They should feel more sure of themselves.

THE ELEMENTARY SCHOOL

THE BEGINNING OF FORMAL SCHOOL EXPERIENCE[1]

Celia Burns Stendler and Norman Young

SETTING AND PURPOSE OF THE STUDY

Each year over two million six-year-olds enter first grade in our public schools. This is a unique experience for them; for many it may represent the initial protracted experience with a socializing agent outside the home; for many it may be their first large group contact; for most, even for those who have had preschool, it undoubtedly brings pressures and demands hitherto not felt. It was our thesis in conducting this study that the experience of beginning first grade plays an important part in the socialization of the child; it was our purpose to tentatively explore certain aspects of this experience through interviews with mothers.

We began with descriptions of "sixness" found in the literature. Gesell and Ilg have reported that this is "a trying age" for many a parent. The child is described as difficult, aggressive, explosive, demanding; his behavior is fresh, nasty, insulting, impudent, bratty, rude and argumentative. This is in sharp contrast to his behavior at five when he was "in focus," cooperative, friendly, sympathetic, affectionate, helpful. Following are the affective attitudes listed for six years (7, p. 289–290):

6 Years—Highly emotional. Marked disequilibrium between child and others.
Expansive and undifferentiated. Good or bad; sweet or horrid; adoring or cruel.
He knows "everything"; boasts, brags.
Likes praise and approval; resents correction and is easily hurt by a cross word.
Loves or hates mother.
Rapidly explosive with crying, strikes out physically or verbally, or has temper tantrums.
Quarrelsome, argumentative, explosive, rebellious, rude, "fresh," stubborn, brash.
Noisy, boisterous and easily excitable.
Silly, giggling, grimacing, showing off.
Resents direction, but is also over-conforming.
Domineers, blames and criticizes others, alibis.
Glowers and glows; has fire or a twinkle in his eye.
At times angelic, generous, companionable.
Jealous of possessions of other children.
May not be too responsive to *humor* at this age.
Uses language aggressively: calls names, threatens, contradicts, argues, uses mild profanity.

[1] From *Child Development* (1950), Vol. 21, pp. 241–255. Reprinted by permission of Dr. Stendler and the publisher, Child Development Publications.

But while these writers are willing at this point to accept the picture of sixness as Gesell and Ilg present it, they do question the assumption of the Yale school that the kind of behavior observed at this age level is developmental as they have defined the term. Gesell and Ilg state that the changing patterns of behavior seen in the young child "are not the product of the contemporary environment; they are primarily the expressions of the ancient processes of evolution. . . . In some condensed way the child must retroverse these immense ages. . . . In the vast complexities of his nervous system he matches the vastness of his ancestral past" (7). The writers question this theory which implies a universality and inevitability of developmental stages, a theory which is not substantiated by evidence from other cultures. It is the writers' thesis that six may indeed be a difficult stage but that this is due to the fact that the socialization process is being changed in important ways by the experience of beginning first grade. Some of these possible changes are described below.

1. It was postulated that entrance to first grade is highly significant in the minds of sixes and may bring about certain changes in the child's conception of himself. In order to understand the nature of these changes in self-concept, it is necessary to look at socialization during the child's first six years. Freudian psychology has given us a picture of an infant who brings with him into the world

> an unorganized chaotic mentality called the id, the sole aim of which is the gratification of all needs, the alleviation of hunger, self-preservation, and love, the preservation of the Species. However, as the child grows older, that part of the id which comes in contact with the environment through the senses learns to know the inexorable reality of the outer world and becomes modified into . . . the ego. This ego, possessing awareness of the environment, henceforth strives to curb the lawless id tendencies whenever they attempt to assert themselves incompatibly [3].

While there are many aspects of ego-development which might be considered, the aspect which seems appropriate for this study involves the development of the concept of self. This concept of what is self and what is not-self gradually emerges as the child learns to differentiate himself from his mother. However, because he has been living in an environment which centers around him, his early perceptions of self take the form of "infantile omnipotence" and he sees other individuals only as servants to self. But when he begins walking and talking and becomes part of total society, his actions are curbed. There are more and more prohibitions upon his behavior, so that he may lose some of his feelings of omnipotence and come to a more realistic concept of self.

The experience of beginning first grade, however, may serve as a shot in the arm to bolster the deflated ego. This experience is one that is dramatized considerably in our culture. By the way in which adults discuss school entrance with the child ("So you're going to FIRST GRADE in the Fall"), from remarks of adults and their children concerning future school activities, even from his new haircut and new clothes for the event, the young child gets a feeling of participating in a great and important adventure in which older children whom he recognizes as having age-status, are already participating. Furthermore, it is an adventure in which all sixes share; our culture says at six one leaves home and goes to formal school. To the young child entrance to first grade may seem a major step in the process of growing up, as important as certain initiation ceremonies at puberty in primitive tribes. It is a step away from babyhood and home into the world of peers and older children. It may bring with it feelings of increased self-importance, self-esteem and of ego-identity.

Erikson has described similar effects upon the ego of another important growth experience:

> In turning from the consideration of groups to that of individuals, let me postulate that the growing child must derive a vitalizing sense of reality from the awareness that his individual way of mastering experience (his ego synthesis) is a successful variant of a group identity and is in accord with its space-time and life plan.
>
> A child who has just found himself able to walk seems not only driven to repeat and to perfect the act of walking by libidinal pleasure in the sense of Freud's locomotor eroticism; or by the need for mastery in the sense of Ives Hendrick's work principle; he also becomes aware of the new status and stature of "he who can walk," with whatever connotation this happens to have in the coordinates of his culture's life plan—be it "he who will go far," or "he who will be upright," or "he who might go too far." To be "one who can walk" becomes one of the many steps in child development which through the coincidence of physical mastery and cultural meaning, of functional pleasure and social recognition, contribute to a more realistic self-esteem. By no means only a narcissistic corroboration of infantile omnipotence (that can be had more cheaply), this self-esteem grows to be a conviction that the ego is learning effective steps toward a tangible collective future, that it is developing into a defined ego within a social reality. This sense I wish to call ego-identity [4].

But there are other ways, conflicting ones, in which the child's concept of self may be changed. In first grade the child also sees himself in comparison with other children. He comes to a new and realistic conception of self as he learns that others surpass him in certain skills or that he surpasses them. The feelings of self-importance, of independence which accompany entrance to school, may give way to self-reality and self-deflation as time goes on. As the child tries to assimilate these conflicting self-ideas into the ego, he may show signs of the conflict in the erratic and "unsocialized" behavior described by Gesell and Ilg.

This is not to assume that all children will behave alike with regard to ego-development at six. Ausubel has analyzed the reorganization of ego-structure that takes place during the initial devaluation period at three years of age. According to his analysis, either satellization or incorporation occurs. In the process of satellization,

> the child identifies as a subordinate figure in relation to the dominant role of the parents. By virtue of his complete acceptance of this dependent position, he becomes automatically assured of intrinsic feelings of security and adequacy,—providing, of course, that he is emotionally accepted and valued for his own sake. The rejected child obviously cannot satellize, and is hence compelled to cling to his former untenable ego structure. The extrinsically-valued child—unassured of appreciation for his own sake—is placed in the same position: To remain adequate in his own eyes he feels obliged to fulfill the grandiose pretensions of his infantile ego which his ambitious parents do nothing to deflate. However, in the latter case, the retention of the infantile structure is quite compatible with the adulation with which he is surrounded; whereas in the face of a hostile environment, the rejected child must harbor his omnipotent fancies within [1].

If Ausubel's analysis is correct, it might follow that the satellizing child would differ from the incorporating child in his adjustment to first grade, not only in the way in which he is able to assimilate ambivalent feelings of importance and nonimportance, but also in his acceptance or nonacceptance of dependency relations with the teacher. But, while we admit differences in the effects of school entrance upon children, we see our first job as the more gross one of discovering what, if any, changes in self-concept occur with first-grade entrance.

2. It was further postulated that the changes in behavior described by Gesell and Ilg as occurring at six might be due to the fact that a new socializing agent in the form of the teacher has been introduced. For most first-graders, this is their first experience with a socializing agent outside the home. Even for those who have attended preschool, the concept may be one that is only imperfectly learned at six years of age. Some evidence for the statement that the child recognizes the teacher as a socializing agent may be found in the play life of the young child as he dramatizes the role of the teacher. It is common knowledge that the young child loves to play school. In his play, he typically portrays the teacher as a stern, strict disciplinarian, even though she may be nothing of the sort. By the very intensity with which he plays this exaggerated role, he may be revealing that he sees the teacher as a socializing agent.

And where the child has established satisfactory relations with his mother, the mother-surrogate may present no difficulties, *provided* he sees her as the same kind of socializer as his mother. But where there have been maternal conflicts in preschool years, or where the teacher makes demands that are too different for the child, we may expect behavior difficulties. This, however, is getting ahead of our story. What we were interested in finding out in this study was whether mothers reported changes for the worse, as described by Gesell and Ilg, occurring with first-grade entrance, and the introduction of a new socializing agent. With this knowledge in our possession we could then set up hypotheses to explain differences in adjustment to school, to be tested by more rigorous experimental procedures.

Another aspect of the school experience which may influence the socialization process is that the child now has extended group contacts, and that the peer group may introduce important new learnings. The child learns many things from his peers and many of these learnings come the hard way. He learns from them to take frustration. He learns not to cry on the playground and not to be outstandingly different. But some children may also learn as early as Grade I that one can more easily risk losing an adult's acceptance if one has the support of his peer group. The authority of adults may become weakened as the child grows to appreciate that one can't win with adults by oneself, but one can put up a pretty good battle with one's peers behind one. The process may be analogous to that described by Arnold Green in his report on Polish lower-class family life as seen in a New England community. Green comments on the fact that in large families it is possible for a boy or girl to oppose his parents because he knows he will have the support of one or more of his siblings; his personal security is not threatened by his bid for moral autonomy as is the security of the only child who stands alone in his defiance of parental authority (9). In other words, in the process of growing up, it is necessary to say "no" to one's parents; it is necessary to disobey them. It is easier to risk the possible loss of affection when one has the support of siblings. The same thing may be true in school. The child may have the courage to oppose the authority of the teacher because he knows his peers are behind him, and this knowledge may give tremendous impetus to his growth in independence.

Furthermore, his peers may have standards different from his parents. Margaret Mead in a discussion of cultural surrogates has emphasized the importance of our dependence upon age-mate surrogates in our culture. She says,

> Now it is a recognized feature of our society that children soon after starting school begin to substitute the standards of other children for the standards set by their parents. . . . The surrogates who carry the cultural standards have changed. They are no longer the parents, omnipotent and belonging to another order of being, but one's everyday companions, with the same strengths and weaknesses as oneself. . . . The rejection of parental standards in favor of late-recognized and antagonistic age-grade standards results, therefore, in an attenuation of self-respect and a weakening of the internalized standards [11].

Again, this is not to say that many children at the first-grade level will take even very tentative steps in the direction of substituting age-mate standards for parental standards. Instead of finding identity with the groups, many will see themselves in a mother-surrogate-sibling relationship in school, as the high evidence of tattling to the teacher and battles with peers at six might indicate. If we accept Ausubel's analysis, it may be that the incorporator more quickly adopts age-mate standards, while the satellizer transfers his dependency attitudes from mother to teacher if the circumstances are right. But again, this is getting ahead of our story. Our purpose in presenting this point of view is merely to explain why it was conceivable for us to expect that some mothers would report the child as "sassy," "impudent," "brash," since beginning school, as Gesell and Ilg have described.

3. There was still another hunch to be explored in this study of the impact of public school entrance on socialization and that was in the area of social class differences. However this area will be discussed in a subsequent publication.

This, then, was our theoretical framework. With it in mind we constructed the two schedules to be used in interviewing mothers. The two main theses we attempted to explore were: (1) Entrance to first grade is highly significant in the minds of sixes and may bring about certain changes in the child's concept of self. This is because of cultural expectations, dramatization of the event, and because the child sees it as his initiation into the outside world. (2) Difficulties in adjustment at six may be due to the fact that the socialization process is disturbed by the effects of first-grade entrance with its accompanying pressures for new adjustments.

PROCEDURES

Two interviews were conducted with mothers of first-grade children, one interview just prior to the child's entrance to first grade, the second after he had been in school for approximately two months and had received his first report card. The interviews were carried out in a Midwestern community by ten different interviewers. A sample of public schools was taken, then a sample of 250 parents whose children were to enter first grade in the fall. Two interviews were completed with 212 of this group.

Median age of the group was 6.3 years as of September 1, just prior to entering school.

Using the technique worked out by Warner and Eells (14) the parents were typed as to social class. Occupation, house type, dwelling area and source of income were used in class typing. Five social classes were defined with distribution as follows:

Social Class	*Per Cent*
Upper	4
Upper-Middle	24
Lower-Middle	29
Upper-Lower	36
Lower-Lower	7

RESULTS

In reading the following section, it should be kept in mind that the information presented here is what mothers have chosen to tell.

1. Entrance to first grade is highly significant in the minds of sixes and may bring about certain changes in the child's concept of self. This is because of cultural expectations, dramatization of the event, and because the child sees it as his initiation into the outside world.

In our first interview we asked certain questions with regard to expectation of and preparation for first grade. From mothers' reports of the child's expectations it would seem that he does regard first-grade entrance as a landmark in the growing up process. In the first interview 197 mothers reported that the child was looking forward to school, as compared with 15 mothers where the child was not. Furthermore, parents' answers indicated a high degree of eagerness to enter school as well as the important place in the child's mind school entrance held. "He's raring to go," "He can hardly wait," "It's all he talks about," were typical responses to the question. Where children were negative, mothers told us they had had unfortunate preschool experiences, or were closely tied to home and mother.

All of our beginners, according to mothers, had been exposed to certain kinds of information regarding school. Brothers, sisters, neighbor children had plied him with ideas, some of which were quite favorable and which built up in the child a picture of school as a pleasant place where one did agreeable duties and had a nice teacher. But 17 of our mothers reported that their child had been exposed to adverse criticism of the school. Children were told "Wait till you get to first grade, boy, you'll have to work," "It's not play, boy, you'll have homework and everything. You can't color all day like in kindergarten," "You'd better be good or you get sent to the principal"—or the hall, or spanked or what have you. But regardless of what he was told, according to most of our mothers the first-grader was still "raring to go." Rather than discouraging him, it would seem that such tales only emphasized the fact that he was leaving his babyhood behind and getting ready to enter the new world of the "big kids."

The six-year-old goes to school to learn to read, to write, and to figure, according to our parents. One hundred seventeen responses indicated that as the parents saw it, their child was expecting to work and to learn certain specific skills. The six-year-old expects to have books of his own in his own desk, and to work rather than play in school. Here are the anticipated learnings as reported by mothers. It should be noted that anticipated learnings total more than 100 per cent because some mothers mention more than one learning.

Learnings	*Per Cent of Children Anticipating* (according to mothers)
Reading	56
Writing	30
Creative Activities	25
Social Activities	16
Number	14
Discipline	5
Miscellaneous Responses	25

The high incidence of reading and writing learnings might be explained by the fact that these are the learnings which the parents want most for their children and that in telling us what children expect to learn in school, mothers are really telling us what *they* expect the children to learn. Yet when we asked what would parents like most for their children to get out of school during the first year, the picture is different in certain respects. Here are the learnings mothers want for their children:

Learnings	*Per Cent of Mothers Desiring*
Reading	54
Writing	22
Creative	8
Social Adjustment	31
Number	14
Discipline	28
Special Problems	8
Miscellaneous	25

A comparison of the two tabulations shows that mothers' desires and their reports of what children expect from school are much alike with regard to the 3 R's, but mothers do not emphasize creative activities as much as do the children, and mothers want more in the way of social adjustment, discipline and attention to special problems. Either parents do not communicate their hopes that the school will improve a child's speech defect or help him get over his shyness, or they do not think children perceive such hopes.

Mothers reported a variety of answers to the questions, "What have his parents told him about school?" and "What has he been taught?" While many parents do not tell the child much about the school program (partly because they realize schools have changed and partly because the schools have asked them not to) they do try to prepare the child in other ways. In general, the six-year-old knows the alphabet, some nursery rhymes, can write his name, count, sing, and in some cases, can read. . . .

More important from the standpoint of our problem, the school has been presented as a socializing agency. The child has been told that he must behave himself in school, must mind the teacher, must be quiet, must not interrupt, that the teacher takes the place of his mother and is the boss. In some cases, the teacher has been held over his head as a kind of veiled threat, "You'll have to change your ways when you start first grade." "You won't be able to get away with that stuff in the first grade." "Wait till the teacher sees you acting like that. You won't do it long." Most parents, however, try to present the teacher as a kind and benign socializing agent, "Be nice in school and everyone will be nice to you." "Like the teacher and she'll like you" is the gist of what some children are told.

To supply quantitative data on expectation-preparation for school a plus one was given for each answer indicating positive expectation-preparation, a zero for indefinite or indeterminate response, and a minus one for each answer indicating negative or no expectation-preparation. These were added together and expressed as a sum. Results are shown in the accompanying table. Here we see that most of the parents are reporting positive expectation preparation, with a median score of +3.

Additional information on how dramatic an event first-grade entrance is to the young child came from parents' answers to the questions in the second interview. "Does your child feel that going to Grade I is more important than preschool? How does he show this?" Almost all of our parents answered in the affirmative. Their answers included such comments as, "He acts inflated now. Comes home and says, 'Boy, we sure had some hard work today!' "; "Considers kindergarten children quite babyish. He acts big at home and is proud of his reading. He never showed pride before"; "She thinks going to first grade and

EXPECTATION-PREPARATION FOR FIRST GRADE AS REPORTED BY MOTHERS ON SIX ITEMS

Score:	+6	+5	+4	+3	+2	+1	0	−1	−2	−3	−4	−5	−6
Frequency:	11	48	37	28	33	21	12	5	1	2	3	0	0

learning her letters is the best thing that has ever happened to her"; "Feels she isn't playing any more. Feels important because she brings home so many papers." Out of 202 mothers answering this question, 81 per cent answered positively that the child gave indications of feeling more important, 11 per cent indicated no preschool experience and 8 per cent felt that there had been no change in the child's feeling about himself.

Reports on the child's going off to school the first day corroborated the other evidence that this is a big event and a happy one. Sixty-one per cent of our mothers reported the child went off happily. It is apparent that he is apprehensive; he is reported as not sleeping well the night before, or waking up at 5 A.M. and asking, "Is it time yet?" However, on the whole the reaction as reported by mothers was favorable. They also report that new clothes, the opportunity to walk with pals, or taking the child helped on this first day. Nineteen parents reported difficulty in getting the child off to school. Parents attribute this to unfavorable expectations of school built up in the child's mind by other children, or to immaturity.

What mothers tell us about their child's expectation of, and reaction to, first-grade entrance, then, would seem to substantiate our thesis that this is a very important event for six-year-olds, and one that seems to bring with it observable changes in the self-concept.

2. Difficulties in adjustment at six may be due to the fact that the socialization process is disturbed by the effects of first-grade entrance with its accompanying pressures for new adjustments.

The reader will remember that in the introduction to this paper this particular hypothesis was proposed to explain the kind of behavior Gesell and Ilg reported as typical of the six-year-old.

To see whether the kinds of behavior reported above came with entrance to first grade, four questions in Section 3 concerning changes in behavior were asked of the parents in the second interview, which took place ten or twelve weeks after school had begun. A fifth question had to do with possible changes in attitude toward the mother following school entrance. The five different items in this particular section will be discussed separately first.

a. Does the child act any differently now than before he started to school?

Of the 198 mothers answering this question, 86 per cent reported change in behavior and 14 per cent no change in the child. On the positive side they reported such changes as acting older, taking more responsibility, helping more at home, being less irritable, more self-controlled, having better work habits and the like. On the negative side, such behavior as acting smart-alecky, whining, increased aggressiveness with siblings, more irritability was reported. Of the 170 parents who reported change, 78 per cent mentioned ways in which the child was changing for the better; 22 per cent mentioned change for the worse.

b. Is he more independent? In what ways?

Here again our first-grader tended to get a clean bill of health from the mothers who were interviewed. Almost three-fourths responded positively to the question regarding increased independence. They reported more independence in dressing self, beginning work, entertaining friends, going on errands, shopping for groceries, staying alone at home, bathing, and helping around the house. While it is recognized that growth in independence might represent an unwelcome challenge to some mothers, the items reported by our mothers indicate growth in independence which they regarded as positive.

c. Does he resent being told what to

do? Does he want to do things his own way? More so than before school?

d. Does he blow up more easily now than before he started to school?

Unfortunately, because we assumed the Gesell-Ilg description of sixness would fit our sample, these two questions were worded in such a way that parents reported either that there was no change in the child's tendency to be resentful or to blow up, or that he had changed for the worse. Had we also asked a question regarding change in a positive direction, our result might have indicated more positive change. As it was, with regard to whether the child resented directions more than at the pre-first-grade level, 60 per cent of our parents reported no change, 12 per cent that the child was less resentful and 27 per cent more resentful. In answer to the question about blowing up more easily, 57 per cent of our mothers indicated no change, 20 per cent that the child was improved in this respect, and 23 per cent that he was worse. In other words with regard to the difficult, explosive kind of behavior we had expected to find, most of our mothers reported either no change or change for the better.

Additional information with regard to items c and d came from comments offered by the mothers in responding to these two questions. Mothers who said the child was improved with respect to resenting being told what to do and with respect to blowing up indicated that he was more cooperative, easier to talk to, more reasonable in seeing another's viewpoint. Where no change was reported, many mothers indicated by their remarks that this particular aspect of behavior was not considered a problem. Their comments, "He's always been that way, but I guess most of us don't want to be told what to do most of the time," "He's about the same as he's always been—I guess most kids have some temper when they're growing up," indicate a kind of philosophic acceptance on the part of some mothers of some negative response to direction. We also had mothers who reported no change, because they had never tolerated any such behavior on the part of the child. "I expect obedience from my child; if he doesn't like what I tell him to do and doesn't want to do it, I whip him until he does" was one mother's way of expressing her feeling in this respect. Where negative change was reported, some mothers blamed school pressures. "He has to sit and take it all day, so of course he blows up when he gets home." "It's having to be quiet so long in school—he's full of pent-up energy and explodes at the least little thing around the house" were some of the expressions of this feeling.

e. Does he ever imply that teacher knows more than mother? Hold teacher up as higher authority? Act as if parent doesn't know much? Is condescending in relating school events? Becomes impatient if mother doesn't understand? More so than in preschool years?

These questions were an attempt to get at possible changes in the child's attitude toward his mother as the result of a new socializer in the form of the teacher. We were interested in any evidence parents could give us to support or disprove our hunch that this new socializer would have the effect of weakening the omnipotent position the mother has had, and that this might show up in the child's comparisons of mother with teacher. Fifty-eight per cent of our mothers reported no change in the child's behavior, and 42 per cent indicated change. Explanatory remarks by parents gave us additional information. In general, their remarks might be grouped as follows:

1. Remarks indicating no change in attitude toward parent.
2. Remarks indicating no change observed by parent with explanations of why

there was no change: "I always taught him obedience so none of these questions apply. I taught him respect for his parents."

3. Remarks indicating the reverse—parent held up as higher authority than the teacher: "She always holds *me* up to the teacher. I tell her, 'Well, honey, you have to do it the way the teacher tells you—She's boss there.'"
4. Remarks indicating a change in attitude toward the parent in the direction of lessened omnipotence: "He definitely implies that the teacher is a higher authority from the way he does his schoolwork to the way he puts his coat on." "He thinks the teacher is perfect and that I don't know anything; he corrects me all the time and refers to how perfect the teacher is." "She condescends toward me and is definitely and markedly more impatient when I don't understand."
5. Remarks indicating a change in attitude toward the parent in the direction of lessened omnipotence, with the parent expressing an ambivalent attitude toward it: "Yes, she always aligns herself with the school and teacher, especially when we're having arguments." The interviewer continues with the comment, "The mother seems to admire this trait in her daughter, but this does not prevent the mother from 'doing battle,' so to speak, and letting Lucy know how she (the mother) feels about it. This mother is a 'griper.' She spent about ten minutes telling me of the battles she had had with the teacher, the school nurse, etc., etc. She blows off steam in front of Lucy, and lets her know exactly how she feels."

It seemed to us that these different categories of remarks raise some very interesting questions regarding implications of the differences we found. For some children, it would seem that dependency relations with the mother are so strong that the school does not change them; that for others there is a marked difference, and that the attitude of the mother toward change in the child is a factor to be considered. Reasons for these differences obviously lie in preschool socializing experiences which need further exploration.

In summary, then, on the question of what mothers report regarding their child's behavior, for the particular items in our questionnaire we found most mothers reporting change in the child's behavior, with most mothers noting improvement in some areas and no change or improvement in areas dealing with the child's explosiveness and reaction to authority. No change was also reported by more mothers on the question of teacher-mother status in the child's eyes, but here the difference between no change and change was not so great.

In addition to information concerning mothers' observation of changes in child behavior since first-grade entrance, we also asked questions about the child's liking or dislike for school, since conceivably there might be a relationship between this factor and child behavior. We asked the direct question, "Is the child liking school? his teacher?" but also asked, "Does he ever say anything critical about school? About his teacher?" and, "Has he ever said he didn't want to go back to school? Hesitated to leave in the morning?"

To the first question regarding liking for school and teacher, 92 per cent of the mothers answered in the affirmative, with only 8 per cent being neutral or negative. Many of the answers indicated a high degree of enthusiasm. "Crazy about it—wants to go Saturdays and Sundays." "Cries when he can't go because of a cold." "Loves his teacher—thinks she's a wonderful person" were some of the replies. However, although over-all liking for school was high, 42 per cent of the mothers mentioned criticisms of the school made by the child, and 39 per cent reported there had been days when the child did not want to return to school. Criticisms of the school by the child included criticism of the actions of other children (too noisy, too rough, too naughty), of school rules and regulations (lining up to go to the bathroom, keeping quiet, punishing whole class for one child's naughtiness), of school program (too much work, too much coloring, too little play), of the substitute teacher. To a related question concerning difficulties with other children, 137 mothers reported trouble. Two kinds of difficulties were frequently mentioned, the first of which involved aggressiveness on the part of other children ("Older boys pick on him," "Older girls pick on her," "One child shoves him around"). There were 79 of these complaints where other children were the aggressors. Some mothers reported their own children as being at fault. The other kind of difficulty most frequently mentioned involved situations where a child was excluded from a group ("She cried because they wouldn't let her play with them," "The other girls don't let her jump rope").

SUMMARY AND DISCUSSION

An exploratory study of the possible effects of beginning first grade upon socialization was conducted by means of interviews with mothers. Two interviews were completed with 212 mothers, one prior to first grade entrance, and one after two months of school. Results indicate:

1. In general, children look forward to beginning first grade with a high degree of favorable anticipation. According to what mothers tell us, they look upon the experience as a very important stage in the process of growing up. They have picked up a considerable body of information and misinformation regarding first grade activities and are expecting to work, and to learn certain specific skills in school. The school has also been presented to them as a socializing agency and one which will expect certain standards of conduct from them.

2. In general, beginning first-graders show evidences of change in self-concept in the direction of feelings of bigness and importance, according to what mothers tell us. This was true even for children who had attended nursery school or kindergarten. Preschool apparently does not represent as dramatic a shift away from home, nor does it have the prestige value for children that first grade does.

3. In general, children's behavior improves with respect to such traits as responsibility, helpfulness, good humor, independence and the like following school entrance, according to what mothers tell us. With regard to response to directions and to self-control, either no change or change for the better was reported by most mothers.

4. With regard to attitude toward the mother's authority and importance as compared with the teacher's, most mothers report no change following school entrance. However, a sizable minority report change in status of the mother.

5. In general, first-grade children like school very much. Their greatest task of adjustment is in the area of social relationships. They find it hard to take the aggressiveness of other children, especially when directed against themselves, and to understand the behavior of children when it differs from their standards of goodness and badness.

Our results have led us to abandon the notion that sixes are "out-of-focus." Indeed, the theory that children are inevitably in-or-out-of-focus at a particular age would not jibe with our results. Rather it would seem that if sixes or any other age group show improvement or deterioration we had better look, not to innate causes, but to experiences which they are having in common. Differences between our findings with respect to six-year-old behavior, and those of Gesell and Ilg are no doubt attributable to the difference in the sample.

On the whole, the experience of entering first grade would seem to have favorable effects upon behavior. It would also seem that the experience of beginning school is a highly important one for the six-year-old, and an ego-bolstering one. Whether this is a temporary state of affairs and whether disillusionment will set in later on during the first year in school remains to be seen. We also need to investigate further the hypothesis that ego-enhancement at six and improved behavior are connected. While our data indicate that these two phenomena exist in the parent's mind, it may be that parents think behavior has improved, whereas, actually, because the children are away for a larger part of the day, there are fewer opportunities for behavior difficulties to occur. Further work with children to find out the meaning of this experience for them is necessary.

But we also need to remember that there were different patterns of adjustment reported by mothers following school entrance. Some mothers whose children had been "problem" children before school reported tremendous improvement, but some "problem" children did not improve. One of the next steps in our project will be a study of these varying patterns of adjustment after school entrance with particular reference to earlier socializing experiences.

BIBLIOGRAPHY

1. Ausubel, David P. "Ego-development and the Learning Process." *Child Develpm.* (1949), 20:173–188.
2. Bettleheim, Bruno, and Sylvester, Emmy. "Physical Symptoms in Emotionally Disturbed Children." *Psychoanal. Stud. Child* (1946), 2:353–390.
3. Brill, A. A. (ed.). *Basic Writings of Sigmund Freud.* Introduction, p. 12. New York, Modern Library, 1938.
4. Erikson, Erik Homburger. "Ego Development and Historical Change." *Psychoanal. Stud. Child* (1946), 2: 362.
5. Friedlander, Kate. "Neurosis and Home Background, a Preliminary Study." *Psychoanal. Stud. Child* (1946), 2:425–438.
6. Fries, Margaret E. "The Child's Ego Development and the Training of Adults in His Environment." *Psychoanal. Stud. Child* (1946), 2:85–112.
7. Gesell, Arnold, and Ilg, Frances L. *The Child from Five to Ten.* New York, Harper, 1946.
8. Gesell, Arnold, and Ilg, Frances L. *Infant and Child in the Culture of Today.* New York, Harper, 1943.
9. Green, Arnold W. "The Middle-class Male Child and Neurosis." *Amer. Sociol. Rev.* 1946), *11*:31–41.
10. Klein, Melanie. *Contributions to Psychoanalysis, 1921–1945.* London, Hogarth Press, 1948.
11. Mead, Margaret. "Social Change and Cultural Surrogates." In Clyde Kluckhohn and Henry A. Murray (eds.), *Personality in Nature, Society, and Culture.* New York, Knopf, 1948, 485–511.
12. Mowrer, Orval Hobart, and Kluckhohn, Clyde. "Dynamic Theory of Personality." In Joseph McV. Hunt (ed.), *Personality and the Behavior Disorders.* I. New York, Ronald Press Co., 1944, 69–136.
13. Peller, Lili E. "Incentives to Development and Means of Early Education." *Psychoanal. Stud. Child* (1946), 2: 397–417.
14. Warner, William Lloyd, Meeker, Marchia, and Eells, Kenneth. *Social Class in America.* Chicago, Science Research Associates, 1946.

THE "GOOD LIFE" IN THE ELEMENTARY SCHOOL[1]

Bascom H. Story

DISCUSSION AND ANALYSIS

In this selection, Story lists eight needs of children that have been suggested by Dr. Raths. Compare this list with the developmental stages given in the Midcentury White House Conference report in Chapter 6. Are these two lists really different? Story goes on to list more needs than the eight he quotes. What emphasis do you think he is giving to developmental needs that differs from that of the White House Conference? Erik H. Erikson, a child psychoanalyst, was primarily responsible for the White House Conference statement. Story is an educator. Do you think they approach children from a basically different or essentially similar point of view?

Story discusses rather briefly one of the clichés of modern education, namely, that we educate the "whole child." He goes on to state that we often treat him as though he did come in a variety of unrelated pieces. What aspects of teaching that you remember or have observed support Story's contention? What does a teacher *do* who treats a child as a "whole child"? What does a teacher *do* who ignores this concept?

Story makes an interesting point when he says that, in working with parents, we have too often tried to "sell" a program. What attitude ought we to take toward parents in helping them understand what the school is doing? What do you think the difference in practice would be between a teacher who was trying to "sell" his method of reading as against a teacher who wanted to show parents that he was competent to teach reading? You might want to check Dr. Gray's article on reading that appears later in this chapter for some ammunition on this question.

Good living in the elementary school is a condition characterized by teachers and children working and living together in an atmosphere which is satisfying, and under conditions that make possible the achievement of purposes for which the school is established. This means that the elementary school which is providing for good living will have well-defined purposes, agreed upon by classroom teachers, parents, and children: it will be staffed by personnel who know how to work toward the achievement of those purposes, and who are also willing and able to redefine the purposes in terms of changing conditions and changing needs. This school will have facilities that are developed to enhance, rather than limit, the program of activities to be carried on. The school program will be an evolutionary one—one that is

[1] From *Bases for Effective Learning*, pp. 18–22, Thirty-First Yearbook of The Department of Elementary School Principals of the National Education Association. Copyright, 1952, by the National Education Association. Reprinted by permission.

planned cooperatively by teachers, children, and parents; one that changes in relation to identified needs and in relation to a changing concept of purpose. Its relationship to the community it serves will be both natural and realistic.

CLASSROOM TEACHERS MUST BE HAPPY

The "good life" in the elementary school demands conditions that are conducive to happiness for those who live in it. But sometimes even professional educators fail to realize that to make children happy, teachers themselves must be happy and well adjusted. They must have the ability to recognize and meet their own needs, if they are to understand and be able to meet the needs of children. They must know a great deal about children, about how they learn, and about how to develop a school program that will best serve them.

PROGRESS IN THINKING

Much progress has been made in educational thought concerning child growth and development. Today teachers know more about how children learn and about how to develop effective school programs. Generally accepted ideas which reflect this progress may be stated rather simply and briefly.

In regard to children, we know that they are dynamic by nature—curious and eager to learn. They differ greatly in their abilities and interests; however, they all react as total organisms to their environment and to stimulations arising from their internal nature.

In regard to learning, we have recognized that it is a creative process. As children grow in understanding, attitudes, and appreciation, they seek self-expression through a variety of activities. Learning is also a continuous process and is the result of interaction between individuals and their environment. Learning is satisfying, and is always more efficient and effective when the learner has purpose.

A school program, which reflects what we know about children and how they learn, is flexible, and is continuously adjusted to satisfy the needs of the particular children who are in school. The program provides opportunities for each child to grow and develop along lines suited to his particular abilities. The program must have purpose. It must point toward, and be consistent with, the concept of living in a democratic society.

NEEDS OF CHILDREN

To be happy in a complex society, whether it is a school society or world society, individuals must learn self-direction. They must learn responsibility and precision. They must learn the technics of problem-solving. There must be developed within them the personal security which results from "needs well met." Some of these important needs have been generalized by Raths:

1. The need for belonging
2. The need for achievement and recognition
3. The need for economic security
4. The need to be relatively free from fear
5. The need for love and affection
6. The need to be relatively free from intense feelings of guilt
7. The need for self-respect and sharing in the values that direct one's life
8. The need for driving purposes and understanding the world in which one lives.[2]

Successful participation in American society suggests certain other needs. Children need to develop skill in the use of the tools of learning and communication. They need to learn the fundamentals of good

[2] Louis E. Raths, "Teacher Training and Emotional Needs," *Journal of Educational Sociology* (March, 1951), Vol. 24, pp. 375–376.

health. They need to learn a system of values that will give direction to their day-to-day behavior. They need to be creative. They need to learn the technics of effective group living. They need understandings of the relationships that must exist between the school, the home, and the community, and they must be able to interpret these understandings in relation to national and worldwide concepts of social living.

THE "WHOLE" CHILD COMES TO SCHOOL

Although professional educators are in general agreement that the "whole" child comes to school, there is some evidence that this fact is disregarded, that we continue to treat children as if they arrive at school in a wide variety of unrelated pieces. Too often when we do consider him as a "whole" being, we think of him as "fixed" and not as a dynamic individual. We sometimes are prone to forget that he is a product of society which stimulates as well as impedes certain natural reactions. For children to be happy in school, the basic function of the school program must be to make provision for the total emotional, social, physical, and intellectual growth and development of the child; and to make certain that the aim of this growth and development is the creation of a better society for him and his contemporaries.

LEADERSHIP

An elementary school can meet these needs, can achieve these aims and purposes, and can serve to create a better society, only if the school itself is a dynamic institution. To be dynamic, an elementary school must have leadership with the ability to marshal all the intelligence of the teachers, parents, and children to deal with the solution of common problems. That an elementary school "is no better than its principal" is too often true in a literal sense. Leadership that frees and stimulates, rather than limits and controls, the intelligence of others is certainly a prerequisite to a good school program. The elementary-school principal, who can discover and develop the leadership ability of classroom teachers, parents, and children, is well on the way to creating a school situation where good living is a certainty.

In the same sense, teachers must be good leaders with their children and with the parents of these children. Good teachers cannot be recognized for what they know. They must be recognized in terms of what happens to their students. Technics of teaching have significance only when their application will result in a desirable change in the children to whom these technics are applied. This means that teachers must know and respect children. They must be willing to sacrifice "pet" teaching methods, personal preferences, and professional pride to the more important motive of helping children, individually and collectively, to grow and become better individuals than they now are. As children recognize these qualities in teachers, they can become happy individuals—eager and excited about learning.

UNDERSTANDING PARENTS

Parents have a deep concern for the happiness of their children which is especially evident at the elementary-school level. They also have a unique contribution to make to the effectiveness of the school program. It seems, however, to be characteristic of most of us that we are suspicious of, and antagonistic toward, that which we do not understand. For too long, we have tried to "sell" parents the school program. We must find better ways of securing understanding. The elementary school which provides for good living for children and teachers will inevitably have this understanding. Experience teaches that people are interested in, understand,

and appreciate those activities to which they contribute. The elementary-school program which demands a contribution from parents is most likely to have the interest, understanding, and appreciation of parents. This contribution should be reflected in the planning, in the execution, and in the evaluation of the school program. When school personnel can work with parents in all three of these important steps, many problems that stand in the way of the "good life" for students and teachers will be solved.

CHARACTERISTICS OF GOOD LIVING

The characteristics, then, of an elementary school which provides for the "good life" may be defined specifically as follows:

1. A school program with clearly stated purposes, defined cooperatively by teachers, parents, and children, and subject to change as conditions and needs may indicate.

2. A school staff with the ability to plan, execute, and evaluate educational activities in terms of purposes; individuals who believe in the coordinated intelligence of the group, and who understand and use the method of intelligence in the solution of problems.

3. A school principal who can lead classroom teachers, pupils, and parents to exercise their best efforts toward the achievement of agreed-upon goals; one who is a leader by virtue of ability rather than position.

4. A community whose citizens participate actively in the school program; whose participation is sought and utilized by school personnel in all phases of the school life.

5. A student body that has the respect and understanding of teachers; where the worth of each individual child is appreciated, and where each individual is provided opportunities for growth.

6. A physical plant which allows for a changing program of activities; where facilities are provided to assist teachers and children in the learning-growing process.

7. A program of activities for children developed in relation to the achievement of the purposes of the school; activities that reflect teacher understanding of student needs, abilities, and interests; activities, which in their scope and sequence, indicate a knowledge of and sensitiveness to the total development of the whole child.

A STUDY OF THE REACTIONS OF FORTY MEN TO TEACHING IN THE ELEMENTARY SCHOOL[1]

Dorothy Rogers

DISCUSSION AND ANALYSIS

This research report will make you mad. If it doesn't, you may want to reëxamine your own purposes and goals in seeking a teaching career. Strong words? Yes, indeed. Because this report, through the medium of a check list and a number of open-end questions, elicited some male reactions to elementary-school teaching that ought to be the concern of every educator. As you read this report you will probably be checking mentally the truth or lack of it in the assertions made by the respondents to the questionnaire. The question is, however, not whether what the

[1] From *The Journal of Educational Sociology* (Sept., 1953), Vol. 27, pp. 24–35. Reprinted by permission.

men said was true or not, but the true fact that these statements are their beliefs, and as such *do* motivate behavior and determine goals and aspirations.

An interesting issue is raised by this article, aside from the many that are contained in the data themselves, and that concerns the desirability of having male elementary teachers. What do you believe on this issue? Do you feel it important to recruit men to the field of elementary education? Does your answer depend on your own sex, and therefore reflect your own experience or feelings toward members of the other sex when you were a student? Do you agree with the claims presented by the respondents as to the value of having male teachers in the elementary school?

There are numerous comments in the article regarding attitudes of men toward working with or being subordinate to women teachers and principals. How do you feel about the problem? What evidence do you have that it is easier (or harder) to work with a female administrator? This article refers to men elementary teachers as a "minority group." Do their reactions bear out some of the generalizations about teachers as a minority group contained in the Grambs article in Chapter 3?

We must remember that this article sampled only forty men teachers. You may find it valuable to do some interviewing yourself to see if, in your locality, men teachers agree or disagree with this group. Perhaps if the sample is increased some of the problems described here may not appear so significant; perhaps others will appear.

PURPOSE OF STUDY

In the fall of 1952, questionnaires were submitted to male graduates of the State University Teachers College, Oswego, New York, in order to determine masculine reaction to teaching in the elementary field. These questionnaires included a check sheet of objective questions as well as a number of open-end questions to permit freer expression of individual opinion. In addition, the investigator talked with most of the men, and hence obtained better perspective in interpretation of replies. The present paper will comprise an analysis of forty of the questionnaires which were completely filled out and returned in time for compilation.

The study grew out of an attempt to unearth research concerning men teachers in the elementary school—an effort which brought to light only one other study devoted exclusively to this topic.[2] Nevertheless, the fact that there is a considerable minority of men in the elementary field—and as many administrators are attempting to attract men to this area, the question would appear worthy of investigation.

VITAL STATISTICS

Replies may be interpreted more intelligently against a background of familiarity with certain information concerning the personnel of the group studied. Four of the forty were "veterans" of ten or more

[2] Louis Kaplan, "The Status and Function of Men Teachers in Urban Elementary Schools," Doctor's thesis, Los Angeles, University of Southern California, 1947.

years experience in the elementary classroom; none of the others had taught more than five years—and the median term of service was three years. The age of the men ranged from 23 to 49 years, the median age being 26. Of the 25 men who were married, four had two children, ten one child, and the other 11 none. The small number of children, of course, is partially a reflection of the youth of the men included in the study. As to grade level, one man does some of his teaching in the third grade, all the others in grades three through eight.

INSTRUMENTS USED

The first half of the questionnaire was a check-sheet, from which results were obtained as summarized in the table.

REACTIONS OF FORTY MALE ELEMENTARY CLASSROOM TEACHERS
STATEMENTS OF OPINION (N-40)

	Yes	No	Undecided
I am proud of being an elementary school teacher	90.0%	5.0%	5.0%
If I had it to do again, I would again become an elementary school teacher	70.0	10.0	20.0
I intend to remain as a teacher in elementary school	52.5	30.0	17.5
More men are needed in elementary school	97.5	2.5	0.0
Adolescent boys need a man teacher	72.5	10.0	17.5
Adolescent girls need a woman teacher	27.5	35.0	37.5
Male elementary school teachers are probably better teachers than are female elementary teachers	18.5	55.5	26.0
I feel that the work I am doing is very important and worthy of me as a man	97.5	0.0	2.5
I would dislike having a woman principal	22.5	52.5	25.0
Male teachers feel somewhat isolated among so many female elementary teachers	42.5	47.5	10.0
People look on the male elementary school teacher as a little peculiar	27.5	60.0	12.5
People tend to think of teaching as a sissy job for a man	27.5	60.0	12.5
The male elementary teacher tends to hold a position that is socially inferior in the community	15.0	70.0	15.0
Male elementary teachers should be paid more than female elementary teachers	45.0	47.5	7.5

All data in the ensuing discussion which are not to be found in the table were obtained from an analysis of the second part of the questionnaire, which consisted of 14 open-end questions, as follows:

Would you advise a young man against going into elementary school teaching? Why, or why not?

Do you feel that there is any special reason for concern about the elementary male teacher? Does he have a more difficult time than any other teacher?

What are the most important contributions of male teachers to the elementary school? What do you find to be the sources of greatest satisfaction in your teaching?

What do you find to be the most annoying features about the position of the male teacher in the elementary school?

What are the most common gripes you hear from other men in the elementary classroom teaching field?

Do you object to women principals? Do you feel it is unwholesome to have men work under the direction of women principals? Explain.

Do you feel that you teach in too feminine an environment—among so many females on the same staff with you? How do you feel about it?

In what specific ways are the needs of the male elementary school teacher neglected—for example, as to restroom facilities, places for smoking, etc.?

How do other men feel toward elementary school teachers of their own sex?

Do you feel that teaching in elementary school is having any effect on your personality? Specifically, how?

What recommendations would you make to improve the lot of the male elementary school teacher? This question is very important.

Now let us proceed to an analysis of questions relating to the welfare of the male teacher on the basis of data obtained from the questions just described.

DOES THE MALE ELEMENTARY TEACHER PRESENT SPECIAL PROBLEMS?

It should be determined, of course, whether the male teacher presents any special problems or his difficulties are merely those of elementary teachers in general. Five per cent of the men believed the problem one of special concern; 35 per cent of some concern; 55 per cent of no real importance and 5 per cent did not reply. Complaints centered about conditions in the elementary field that would affect all teachers rather than any special problems relating specifically to males. Nevertheless, it is interesting that such widely divergent views on this question exist:

I don't think there should be any special concern for the male teacher except this —a woman can use punishment on a child with no complaint from parents, that the man teacher would be severely criticized for using. (married; age 30)

He has trouble when male teachers haven't been employed in the school system, but after he proves himself, he is all set. Gradually our presence seems to be accepted more and more. (single; age 23)

It is a very important question. If you wish to retain men, something must be done to change their situation; otherwise, your best people will leave. More attractive employment elsewhere, where the respect and financial compensation of administration, will draw away most of the men. The few "men" left may be in dire need of some self-respect and confidence in their own abilities. (single; age 27)

Additional evidence as to whether a problem exists may be found in answer to this question: Would you advise a young man against going into elementary school teaching? Four men definitely would not, two did not reply, while the other 34 would recommend it, but often with certain reservations. Again, individual opinion extends over a wide range:

I would discourage him. Elementary education from a man's approach is too disappointing. It lacks respect; the salary is poor; your time is never your own. Teachers are meek, spineless individuals who build dreams from professional ethics, and who cannot or won't fight back. (single; age 27)

I personally have enjoyed my work but I am not even, financially, in the upper poor class. How could I recommend teaching to a man when I do not believe it is possible to educate children on a teacher's salary? (single; age 28)

Certainly, I would advise a man to go into elementary teaching. As such, he becomes a spoke in the wheel of world progress and understanding; despite all setbacks, discouragements and slow rewards. (married; age 28)

Yes—but with a big IF—if he likes hard work; if he does not mind taking his job home with him; if he is fond of children in groups; if he feels a definite call to teach, and if he is gifted in everything—music, art, physical education, etc.

In short, all evidence points to the conclusion that most men in the elementary field would recommend their profession to other men, provided they can adjust to certain undesirable features surrounding the profession.

SPECIAL FUNCTIONS OF MALE TEACHERS

If children are as well off without men teachers, perhaps there is no special reason for attempting to make the lot of the male elementary teacher an especially attractive one. Nevertheless, men possess a strong conviction as to their special function in the elementary school. Thirty-nine in forty said that the work they are doing is very important and worthy of them as men; the lone dissenter was undecided. Of 81 items listed as the male's most important contribution, 35 related to the need for masculine influence on children, 35 to the male's ability to perform certain duties better than women and the other 11 were scattered.

It is argued that men teachers are needed especially since male influence on children is inadequate at home as well as at school. Some fathers are divorced or absent for long periods in the service; others work long hours and have little time for their children. The male influence is also limited by the American tradition that caring for young children and taking an interest in them is "sissy." Nevertheless, boys need in their immediate environment an adequate prototype of the well-adjusted male adult with whom to identify and to afford suitable guidance. Girls need such guidance, too, to assist them in their adjustment to a heterosexual world.

The pre-school and primary school child has been influenced (predominantly) by female behavior. More male association should contribute to a more wholesome child. (married; age 26)

In our situation we have to play the role of foster father. The boys come to us with many problems that they wouldn't discuss with women teachers. (married; age 42)

The playground becomes so much more meaningful to the boys with a man to guide and direct them in their games. (single; age 28)

Men believe they also serve to make education more "real." Men have usually had a broader work experience and hence bring to the educational situation a broader base of information.

I feel that men bring a greater sense of reality into a child's life. Many women lose touch with the world because they stay in their own circle. (married; age 27)

I think they create a more realistic, life-like situation in the classroom. (married; age 29)

The staff should profit, too, since the addition of men would provide a more natural social environment for teachers. Furthermore, school policy would be strengthened by representing a masculine as well as feminine point of view.

They offer a sense of security to others in the building. (married; age 24) . . . Give some stability to decisions at faculty meetings. (married; age 30)

Whether or not the claims that men make as to their special function are justified—and they sound valid enough—merely the fact that the men believe in their own worth has significance. It would seem logical that the teacher who believes strongly in the value of his services will discharge them more effectively. In addition, it is mentally healthy to believe in the worth of one's work and should, in turn, reflect favorably on the adjustment of children.

SOURCES OF GREATEST SATISFACTION

The large majority of the men testified that they found classroom teaching deeply satisfying, especially in the area of the teacher-pupil relationship. This finding agrees with a Fortune Poll which reported that only 1 per cent of men teachers said that they seldom enjoy teaching as compared with 7.2 per cent of men in general who said that their work was dull and boring.[3]

The following statements include reasons typical of those men gave for enjoying their work:

Just being with children and learning with them. It allows for individuality and challenge! (married; age 26)

The satisfaction of the boys and girls after a job done well by them. The feeling that I'm doing some good for those kids. (married; age 27)

It is especially significant for the children that their teachers should enjoy their work. It is unlikely that men would report such great satisfaction if they were not doing a reasonably adequate job. Furthermore, it is especially gratifying that men experience such pleasure in the teacher-pupil relationship. This fact tokens well for their function in masculine guidance.

SOURCES OF CHIEF DISSATISFACTION

When asked to name major dissatisfactions, three major sources were revealed —inadequate salary, extra jobs without corresponding compensation, and factors relating to the disproportionate number of women on the teaching staff. A poor fourth was the status of male elementary teachers in the community. Of 73 items of dissatisfaction mentioned, only three could be assumed to indicate a condemnation of teaching itself. These related to "regimentation of routines" and "danger of thinking on the child's level." In general, men were somewhat dissatisfied with conditions surrounding teaching, but otherwise found little to complain of in their work. For clearer understanding, the factors of chief dissatisfaction will be discussed separately.

The Salary Question

Forty-one per cent of the complaints related to salary and to the belief that greater responsibility should be compensated by more pay. Strong opinions were expressed on this question:

The man as a breadwinner in many cases draws the same low salary as a woman. A man thirty years old draws the same salary as girls of twenty-three. (married; age 30)

The inadequate financial position causes the sole provider of the family to obtain secondary employment thus forcing him to divide his time and interests. (married; age 26)

Complicating the problem is the lack of opportunity for promotion within the field of classroom teaching. True, there are automatic increments, but these increases are not sufficient to take care of the demands of a growing family. In consequence, many men either leave the teaching field entirely or go into administration. The higher status of the administrator constitutes an additional temptation to forsake the classroom. Men are almost equally divided among those who feel uncomfortable on a staff predominantly feminine (42.5%) and those who do not find this factor disturbing (47.5%). Ten per cent offer no opinion on this subject. Fifteen per cent of those who offer no objection say that they actually enjoy their largely feminine environment. Note the diversity of views:

At first I felt out of place, but working with women is something one gets used to. In college I attended classes that had both sexes—it does not bother me now any more than it did then. (single; age 25)

Women teachers are easy to work with and

[3] "The Quarter's Polls," *Public Opinion Quarterly* (1943), Vol. 170, p. 488.

place the man in a position of importance. (married; age 30)

Our views—those of two other men and myself, run counter to those of the female teachers in administrative practices, educational beliefs and social attitudes. (single; age 27)

There are too many females around me. At times I am lost as to what to say because we don't have the liberty to say some things, with the exception of talking about some of the pupils and their behavior. (married; age 30)

The way of life of the sexes is so different that most individuals experience a more comfortable "in-group feeling" from the presence of other members of their sex. Discomfort is enhanced in the case of individuals who have had more difficulty in their own psychosexual adjustment.

Comfort and Welfare

One annoyance contingent on the small per cent of males is the absence of adequate restroom and smoking room facilities in many schools—although recent improvements have been reported. While no one listed this factor as a source of major dissatisfaction, almost half (45%) testified that facilities of this type were inadequate in their schools. Perhaps a major reason that these comforts should be provided is merely that men would feel that they are being shown some real consideration as men.

Status in Community

While the majority of men find their status in the community satisfactory, a considerable minority have some doubts on this score. Over half—60 per cent of the men—believe that the community does not adjudge their work to be sissy for a man; the remainder either believe so or are undecided. In the same ratio, men are divided as to whether the community finds the male elementary teacher a little peculiar. Furthermore, while 70 per cent of the men feel that their position in the community is not socially inferior, the other 30 per cent believe so or are undecided. Again, one finds widely diverse views:

People outside the school give the impression that eventually the elementary teacher should want to teach at the secondary level or become a principal. (single; age 34)

During the past summers I worked in a factory with men who knew I was a teacher. They seemed to envy my position. They joked with me about school teaching, but they never ridiculed me for it. However, I feel that many people expect too much from a teacher. They have a "He shouldn't make a mistake" idea. (single; age 25)

People think it is not the kind of a job a male should have. They term us as lazy men who do not want to work. (married; age 30)

I have found little or no antagonism, but rather a feeling of acceptance and community favor. (married; age 24)

The community is sympathetic, understanding and cooperative. Most of the people feel that the child needs more male influence than is now received. (married; age 26)

It is possible that a degree of doubt as to the status of the male elementary teacher stems partially from the inferior position that teaching itself holds among the professions and partially from the association of lower grade teaching with women. As woman's position in the workaday world is traditionally lower than men's in pay and in status; therefore a profession dominated by females may lack status.

Probably men in this field will cease to be worried about appearing "feminine" or "peculiar" when a greater number of males enter elementary classroom teaching. The status of all teachers, men included, will only be raised when persons of outstanding ability are attracted in greater numbers to the profession. While lowering the standard may serve as a stop-gap measure during a teacher shortage, the long-range effect is to make the field appear less desirable—hence, create a continuing shortage.

MALE TEACHERS VERSUS FEMALE PRINCIPAL

About one man in four (22.5%) expressed some objection to having a woman principal while a similar number (25%) are undecided. The remaining 52.5 per cent have no objection to a woman principal although some of them would qualify their replies. One may summarize by saying that while a minority of men prefer male principals, to the overwhelming majority the sex of the administrator appears to be an incidental, or minor factor. Contrasting views follow:

As a generalization I object to women principals. They are so much afraid that a teacher may know more than they do. I have never worked for a woman principal but I would imagine that a man would get along fine with one while the girls would lead a very trying existence. (single; age 28)

I believe it is a better situation for male teachers when they work under a male principal. He feels much more respect for a male principal and will not mind his orders. (single; age 23)

I do not object. If she has what it takes, more power to her. It wouldn't be unwholesome if she's a good teacher. (married; age 26)

While I would prefer men, I would not object if the woman is well balanced and not too picky. (married; age 49)

Some men may object to women principals because of the cultural tradition that women should work for men, instead of the reverse. The question might be raised as to whether it is actually harder to work for most women administrators. Perhaps the woman, feeling a greater pressure to "make good," projects some of this pressure onto those who work under her direction. The only ultimate solution to such problems is the long-range one of effecting greater harmony between the sexes in order to diminish the sometimes unconscious rivalry and hostility that now exist. Mutual respect would remove the pressure on the woman to do the "perfect job" and enable her to perform her duties in a more relaxed fashion.

EFFECT OF ELEMENTARY TEACHING ON MALE PERSONALITY

The large majority of the men (73%) testified that teaching had affected their personality, but not to any great extent. Eighteen per cent thought there had been no effect; the remaining 8 per cent did not reply. Such change as was thought to occur was generally believed to be in a favorable direction. Only one trait, either positive or negative, was mentioned with any significant frequency—that is, the development of patience and understanding. Of eleven men who indicated unfavorable effects, four found that teaching had narrowed their outlook; four feared development of a teacher-type personality; and six thought teaching made them tense, nervous or grim. Examples of good and bad effects are testified to in the following:

Perhaps I am a bit too bossy outside school. (single; age 34)

I feel a lack of adult contacts. I have a feeling of being restricted, also that people generally feel that a man is a little peculiar to become a school teacher. (married; age 30)

I do not seem to have as much patience, but I am teaching under extremely adverse conditions. (married; age 27)

Greater understanding of children and of adults—development of patience, etc. (married; age 28)

I hope my patience is increasing. What effects there are, I feel are beneficial. (married; age 25)

Probably the most significant factor here is that the majority of men believe that changes that take place are generally desirable. This finding would appear to refute the view sometimes expressed that teaching has a detrimental effect on personality.

RECOMMENDATIONS FOR BOOSTING MORALE

Accounting for 28 of 74 suggestions offered for improving men's lot in the elementary teaching profession was that of raising salaries. A second major recommendation was that men not be given extra duties without additional compensation (6 mentions).

One important group of recommendations related to problems growing out of the unbalanced ratio of men and women teachers. Advice on this subject may be summarized as follows—the numbers in parentheses indicating times mentioned: Males should be given the same quality of consideration and respect shown females (7); and equally good restroom facilities (4). The man should be permitted to remain a man, however, and permitted to preserve his masculine individuality in his teaching (4). The best insurance for equal treatment and for not feeling too lonely is to increase the number of male teachers (6). Other recommendations were scattered.

A sampling of these recommendations follows below:

Treat him with honest and sincere respect. Improve the financial standing of the married male—he should at least be able to have a home and clothing equal to those of his neighbor who drives a truck or works in a factory. If you want professional attitudes, then wake up and consider the need of these men—yes, it is money, that dirty, unprofessional stuff that every other profession obtains. Be honest with men entering this profession; don't make false impressions just to meet the huge demand for teachers. (single; age 27)

The N.E.A. might try to put across the idea that a man is not lowering himself by teaching young children. Put across the idea that men can find secure, interesting, and challenging work in the elementary school. (married; age 25)

The male teacher should be accepted not as a male, but as a teacher who can or cannot do his job. If that is done, it will create an atmosphere not of rivalry, but of working together. In this way the children will benefit to greater degree. (single; age 26)

Considering all phases of the elementary school a man gives more, works harder and should be rewarded accordingly, financially and professionally. (married; age 29)

Make sure the teacher can apply himself on the lower level and have a deep understanding of the children in their activities of the day. Have special courses to develop the male's attitude in these respects. He should have some training practical and theoretical, along the lines of teaching younger children. (single; age 23)

Make the salary adequate. Provide good facilities. If it is necessary for him to take over extra duties, compensate him. Have the school administration help to raise his status in the community. (married; age 30)

PERSPECTIVE ON RECOMMENDATIONS

Since only one elementary teacher in 16 is a man, it is a responsibility of the profession as a whole to take recognition of the needs of this minority group. The adoption or implementation of any recommendations must be in terms of changing conditions as more men enter the field and in accord with demands of local situations. At the same time, consideration must be taken of the way that anything done for men might react on women. For example, men might be slightly better satisfied if all principals were males, but probably more would be lost than gained in terms of detriment to general teacher morale. Capable women would suffer especially through having closed to them this avenue of advancement.

PRESENT STATUS OF SITUATION

Although the small number of men in the study would necessarily preclude drawing definite conclusion, certain generalizations might be tentatively drawn, subject to further investigation and adequate confirmation. First, it is heartening that while men dislike frustrations surrounding their work, they are almost unanimous in their enjoyment of teaching. Since men's needs on the whole appear to be those of all persons in the elementary teaching profession, men may unite with women in the cause of obtaining better conditions for teachers as a group. Nevertheless, it is important that this overall generalization not obscure the need for whatever consideration men need as men.

In general, the findings of this study derive additional significance from the fact that they agree closely with the findings of the Kaplan study mentioned earlier. Nevertheless, conclusive answers and recommendations must await the compilation of further data. Future research should include a study of the male teacher from the standpoint of parents, other teachers, and pupils. Meanwhile, it should become a part of the continuing research program in education to continuously appraise and make suitable provision for the mental health of male elementary teachers.

THE CAREER OF THE CHICAGO PUBLIC SCHOOLTEACHER[1]

Howard S. Becker

DISCUSSION AND ANALYSIS

Perhaps in the title above the editors should have underlined the word "Chicago." As you all know, Chicago is like no other city in the world! So we must be somewhat cautious in generalizing from what happens to a teacher in Chicago, to what may happen to you. This is a very important consideration to keep in mind. As you read this article, you may find it disheartening; it will also make you impatient with teachers who develop the kinds of attitudes and feelings described here. "Never," you may say to yourself, "will such things happen to me, nor will I ever feel about teaching as some of these teachers seem to feel." We applaud this reaction. In fact, it is to gain this kind of insight that we chose this article for inclusion. It describes reality; reality is not always the garden of delight that theory may lead us to imagine.

As you read this article you will learn some important truths about education. You will want to compare the ideas on status and prestige with those in the Warner, Havighurst, and Loeb article in Chapter 7. Why is

[1] Reprinted from *American Journal of Sociology*, March, 1952, pp. 470–477, by permission of The University of Chicago Press. Copyright 1952 by the University of Chicago.

it that teachers feel that some kinds of children are "right" and others are "wrong"? Where do such feelings come from? How can the teacher do an adequate job of education if he feels this way? Remember the report of the hobo kid in Chapter 2; this was a child who knew how it felt to be the wrong kind.

You may ask if the problem of the teacher in Chicago is true also of that in other large cities. Furthermore, what aspects of prestige and status affect teachers in small towns, in suburbs, in one-room schoolhouses? What are your career goals? How do they compare with the goals sought by Chicago teachers?

Perhaps the editors owe the reader a word of explanation for selecting this article, as well as the preceding one by Rogers. These are somewhat negative, are they not? Agreed. Some readers may say that, if our purpose is to intrigue the talented and alert student into teaching as a career, we certainly are not going to do it by showing him the seamy side of the ledger. We do not agree. It is our belief, from having instructed many hundreds of future teachers, that it is just this kind of reality that arouses the true zeal of the real educator. Education most desperately needs those who know the real problems we face daily in school and classroom and are determined to use every ounce of energy and intelligence at their command to find more rewarding and more positive solutions. We feel this is the *real* challenge of education. Perhaps we are saying that we need a new kind of missionary, one whose concern is derived from a long hard look at the world and is determined to do his best to *serve*. Such a person will find education tremendously exciting, will find ample scope for his talents, and above all will gain the priceless reward of knowing that he has made something truly worth while of his life.

Abstract

The careers of Chicago teachers exhibit "horizontal" movement among positions at one level of the school-work hierarchy in terms of the configuration of the occupation's basic problems presented by each rather than vertical movement between several such levels. One major career pattern consists in moving from the lower-class school in which careers usually begin; another consists in adjusting, over a period of years, to the problems of such schools. Having settled in a school, the teacher may be upset by changes in neighborhood structure or in the administrative personnel with whom she deals.

The concept of *career* has proved of great use in understanding and analyzing the dynamics of work organizations and the movement and fate of individuals within them. The term refers, to paraphrase Hall, to the patterned series of adjustments made by the individual to the "network of institutions, formal organizations, and informal relationships" [2] in which the work of the occupation is performed. This series of adjustments is typically considered in terms of movement up or down between positions differentiated by their rank in some formal or informal

[2] Oswald Hall, "The Stages of a Medical Career," *American Journal of Sociology* (Mar., 1948), Vol. 53, p. 327.

hierarchy of prestige, influence, and income. The literature in the field has devoted itself primarily to an analysis of the types, stages, and contingencies of careers, so conceived, in various occupations.[3] We may refer to such mobility through a hierarchy of ranked positions, if a spatial metaphor be allowed, as the *vertical* aspect of the career.

By focusing our attention on this aspect of career movement, we may tend to overlook what might, in contrast, be called the *horizontal* aspect of the career: movement among the positions available at one level of such a hierarchy. It need not be assumed that occupational position which share some characteristics because of their similar rank in a formal structure are identical in all respects. They may, in fact, differ widely in the configuration of the occupation's basic problems which they present. That is, all positions at one level of a work hierarchy, while theoretically identical, may not be equally easy or rewarding places in which to work. Given this fact, people tend to move in patterned ways among the possible positions, seeking that situation which affords the most desirable setting in which to meet and grapple with the basic problems of their work. In some occupations more than others, and for some individuals more than others, this kind of career movement assumes greater importance than the vertical variety, sometimes to such an extent that the entire career line consists of movement entirely at one level of a work hierarchy.

The teachers of the Chicago public schools are a group whose careers typically tend toward this latter extreme. Although it is possible for any educationally qualified teacher to take the examination for the position of principal and attempt ascent through the school system's administrative hierarchy, few make the effort. Most see their careers purely in teaching, in terms of movement among the various schools in the Chicago system.[4] Even those attempting this kind of vertical mobility anticipate a stay of some years in the teacher category and, during that time, see that segment of their career in much the same way. This paper will analyze the nature of this area of career movement among teachers and will describe the types of careers found in this group. These, of course, are not the only patterns which we may expect to find in this horizontal plane of career movement. It remains for further research in other occupations to discern other career varieties and the conditions under which each type occurs.

The analysis is based on interviews with sixty teachers in the Chicago system. The interviewing was unstructured to a large extent and varied somewhat with each interviewee, according to the difficulty encountered in overcoming teachers' distrust and fear of speaking to outsiders. Despite this resistance, based on anxiety regarding the consequences of being interviewed, material of sufficient validity for the analysis undertaken here was secured through insisting that all general statements of attitude be backed up with concrete descriptions of actual experience. This procedure, it is felt, forced the interviewees to disclose more than they otherwise might have by requiring them to give enough factual ma-

[3] See Everett C. Hughes, "Institutional Office and the Person," *American Journal of Sociology* (Nov., 1937), Vol. 43, pp. 404–413; Oswald Hall, *op. cit.*, and "Types of Medical Careers," *American Journal of Sociology* (Nov., 1949), Vol. 55, pp. 243–253; and Melville Dalton, "Informal Factors in Career Achievement," *American Journal of Sociology* (Mar., 1951), Vol. 56, pp. 407–415.

[4] The Chicago system has a high enough salary schedule and sufficient security safeguards to be safe as a system in which a person can make his entire career, thus differing from smaller school systems in which the teacher does not expect to spend her whole working life.

terial to make their general statements plausible and coherent.

I

The positions open to a particular teacher in the system at a given time appear, in general, quite similar, all having about the same prestige, income, and power attached to them. This is not to deny the existence of variations in income created by the operation of seniority rules or of differences in informal power and prestige based on length of service and length of stay in a given school. The fact remains that, for an individual with a given amount of seniority who is about to begin in a school new to her, all teaching positions in the Chicago system are the same with regard to prestige, influence, and income.

Though the available teaching positions in the city schools are similar in formal characteristics, they differ widely in terms of the configuration of the occupation's basic work problems which they present. The teacher's career consists of movement among these various schools in search of the most satisfactory position in which to work, that being the position in which these problems are least aggravated and most susceptible of solution. Work problems arise in the teacher's relations with the important categories of people in the structure of the school: children, parents, principal, and other teachers. Her most difficult problems arise in her interaction with her pupils. Teachers feel that the form and degree of the latter problems vary considerably with the social-class background of the students.

Without going into any detailed analysis of these problems,[5] I will simply summarize the teacher's view of them and of their relation to the various social-class groups which might furnish her with students. The interviewees typically distinguished three class groups: (1) a bottom stratum, probably equivalent to the lower-lower and parts of the upper-lower class,[6] and including, for the teacher, all Negroes; (2) an upper stratum, probably equivalent to the upper-middle class; and (3) a middle stratum, probably equivalent to the lower-middle and parts of the upper-lower class. Three major kinds of problems were described as arising in dealings with pupils: (1) the problem of *teaching*, producing some change in the child's skills and knowledge which can be attributed to one's own efforts; (2) the problem of *discipline*, maintaining order and control over the children's activity; and (3) the problem of what may be termed *moral acceptability*, bringing one's self to bear some traits of the children which one considers immoral and revolting. The teacher feels that the lowest group, "slum" children, is difficult to teach, uncontrollable and violent in the sphere of discipline, and morally unacceptable on all scores, from physical cleanliness to the spheres of sex and "ambition to get ahead." Children of the upper group, from the "better neighborhoods," were felt to be quick learners and easy to teach but somewhat "spoiled" and difficult to control and lacking in the important moral traits of politeness and respect for elders. The middle group was considered to be hard-working but slow to learn, extremely easy to control, and most acceptable on the moral level.

Other important problems arise in interaction with parents, principal, and colleagues and revolve primarily around the issue of authority. Parents of the highest status groups and certain kinds of princi-

[5] Later papers will provide detailed analysis and documentation of the statements made in this and the following paragraph.

[6] The class categories used in this estimate are those used by W. Lloyd Warner and Paul Lunt in *The Social Life of a Modern Community*, New Haven, Yale University Press, 1941.

pals are extremely threatening to the authority the teacher feels basic to the maintenance of her role; in certain situations colleagues, too, may act in such a way as to diminish her authority.

Thus, positions at the teaching level may be very satisfactory or highly undesirable, depending on the presence or absence of the "right" kind of pupils, parents, principal, and colleagues. Where any of these positions are filled by the "wrong" kind of person, the teacher feels that she is in an unfavorable situation in which to deal with the important problems of her work. Teachers in schools of this kind are dissatisfied and wish to move to schools where "working conditions" will be more satisfactory.

Career movement for the Chicago teacher is, in essence, movement from one school to another, some schools being more and others less satisfactory places in which to work. Such movement is accomplished under the Board of Education's rules governing transfer, which allow a teacher, after serving in a position for more than a year, to request transfer to one of as many as ten other positions. Movement to one of these positions is possible when an opening occurs for which there is no applicant whose request is of longer standing, and transfer takes place upon approval by the principal of the new school.

The career patterns which are to be found in this social matrix are not expected to be typical of all career movements of this horizontal type. It is likely that their presence will be limited to occupational organizations which, like the Chicago school system, are impersonal and bureaucratic and in which mobility is accomplished primarily through the manipulation of formal procedures.

II

The greatest problems of work are found in lower-class schools and, consequently, most movement in the system is a result of dissatisfaction with the social-class composition of these school populations. Movement in the system, then, tends to be out from the "slums" to the "better" neighborhoods, primarily in terms of the characteristics of the pupils. Since there are few or no requests for transfer to "slum" schools, the need for teachers is filled by the assignment to such schools of teachers beginning careers in the Chicago system. Thus, the new teacher typically begins her career in the least desirable kind of school.[7] From this beginning two major types of careers were found to develop.

The first variety of career is characterized by an immediate attempt to move to a "better" school in a "better" neighborhood. The majority of interviewees reporting first assignment to a "slum" school had already made or were in the process of making such a transfer. The attitude is well put in this quotation:

> When you first get assigned you almost naturally get assigned to one of those poorer schools, because those naturally are among the first to have openings because people are always transferring out of them to other schools. Then you go and request to be transferred to other schools nearer your home or in some nicer neighborhood. Naturally the vacancies don't come as quickly in those schools because people want to stay there once they get there. I think that every teacher strives to get into a nicer neighborhood.

Making a successful move of this kind is contingent on several factors. First, one must have fairly precise knowledge as to which schools are "good" and which are not, so that one may make requests wisely.

[7] Further documentation of this point may be found in Miriam Wagenschein, "Reality Shock," unpublished M.A. thesis, Department of Sociology, University of Chicago, 1951, and in John Winget's Ph.D. thesis, "Ecological and Socio-Cultural Factors in Teacher Inter-School Mobility."

Without such knowledge, which is acquired through access to the "grapevine," what appears to be a desirable move may prove to be nothing more than a jump from the frying pan into the fire, as the following teacher's experience indicates:

When I put my name down for the ten schools I put my name down for one school out around —— ["nice" neighborhood]. I didn't know anything about it, what the principal was like or anything, but it had a short list. Well, I heard later from several people that I had really made a mistake. They had a principal there that was really a terror. She just made it miserable for everyone. . . .

But I was telling you about what happened to me. Or almost did. After I had heard about this principal, I heard that she was down one day to observe me. Well, I was really frightened. If she had taken me I would have been out of luck, I would have had to stay there a year. But she never showed up in my room. . . . But, whatever it was, I was certainly happy that I didn't have to go there. It just shows that you have to be careful about what school you pick.

Second, one must not be of an ethnic type or have a personal reputation which will cause the principal to use this power of informal rejection. Though a transferee may be rejected through formal bureaucratic procedure, the principal finds it easier and less embarrassing to get the same result through this method, described by a Negro teacher:

All he's got to do is say, "I don't think you'll be very happy at our school." You take the hint. Because if the principal decides you're going to be unhappy, you will be, don't worry. No question about that. He can fix it so that you have every discipline problem in the grade you're teaching right in your room. That's enough to do it right there. So it really doesn't pay to go if you're not wanted. You can fight it if you want, but I'm too old for that kind of thing now.

This has the effect of destroying the attractive qualities of the school to which transfer was desired and of turning choice in a new direction.

Finally, one must be patient enough to wait for the transfer to the "right" school to be consummated, not succumbing to the temptation to transfer to a less desirable but more accessible school:

When I got assigned to —— [Negro school], for instance, I went right downtown and signed on ten lists in this vicinity. I've lived out here for twenty-five years and I expect to stay here, so I signed for those schools and decided I'd wait ten years if necessary, till I found a vacancy in the vicinity.

The majority of teachers have careers of this type, in which an initial stay in an undesirable "slum" school is followed by manipulation of the transfer system in such a way as to achieve assignment to a more desirable kind of school.

Thirteen of the interviewees, however, had careers of a different type, characterized by a permanent adjustment to the "slum" school situation. These careers were the product of a process of adjustment to the particular work situation, which, while operating in all schools, is seen most clearly where it has such a radical effect on the further development of the career, tying the teacher to a school which would otherwise be considered undesirable. The process begins when the teacher, for any of a number of possible reasons, remains in the undesirable school for a number of years. During this stay changes take place in the teacher and in the character of her relations with other members of the school's social structure which make this unsatisfactory school an easier place in which to work and which change the teacher's view of the benefits to be gained by transferring elsewhere. Under the appropriate circumstances, a person's entire career may be spent in one such school.

During this initial stay changes take place in the teacher's skills and attitudes which ease the discomfort of teaching at the "slum" school. First, she learns new teaching and disciplinary techniques which enable her to deal adequately with "slum" children, although they are not suited for use with other social-class groups:

Technically, you're not supposed to lay a hand on a kid. Well, they don't, technically. But there are a lot of ways of handling a kid so that it doesn't show—and then it's the teacher's word against the kid's, so the kid hasn't got a chance. Like dear Mrs. G——. She gets mad at a kid, she takes him out in the hall. She gets him stood up against the wall. Then she's got a way of chucking the kid under the chin, only hard, so that it knocks his head back against the wall. It doesn't leave a mark on him. But when he comes back in that room he can hardly see straight, he's so knocked out.

Further, the teacher learns to revise her expectations with regard to the amount of material she can teach and learns to be satisfied with a smaller accomplishment; a principal of a "slum" school described such an adjustment on the part of her teachers:

Our teachers are pretty well satisfied if the children can read and do simple number work when they leave here. . . . They're just trying to get these basic things over. So that if the children go to high school they'll be able to make some kind of showing and keep their heads above water.

She thus acquires a routine of work which is customary, congenial, and predictable to the point that any change would require a drastic change in deep-seated habits.

Finally, she finds for herself explanations for actions of the children which she has previously found revolting and immoral, and these explanations allow her to "understand" the behavior of the children as human, rather than as the activity of lunatics or animals:

I finally received my permanent assignment at E——. That's that big colored school. Frankly, I wasn't ready for anything like that. I thought I'd go crazy those first few months I was there. I wasn't used to that kind of restlessness and noise. The room was never really quiet at all. There was always a low undertone, a humming, of conversation, whispering, and shoving. . . . I didn't think I would ever be able to stand it. But as I came to understand them, then it seemed different. When I could understand the conditions they were brought up in, the kind of family life and home background that they had, it seemed more natural that they should act that way. And I really kind of got used to it after awhile.

At the same time that these changes are taking place in the teacher's perspectives, she is also gradually being integrated into the network of social relations that make up the school in such a way as to ease the problems associated with the "slum" school. In the first place, the teacher, during a long stay in a school, comes to be accepted by the other teachers as a trustworthy equal and acquires positions of influence and prestige in the informal colleague structure. These changes make it easier for her to maintain her position of authority vis-à-vis children and principal. Any move from the school would mean a loss of such position and its advantages and the need to win colleague acceptance elsewhere.

Second, the problem of discipline is eased when the teacher's reputation for firmness begins to do the work of maintaining order for her: "I have no trouble with the children. Once you establish a reputation and they know what to expect, they respect you and you have no trouble. Of course, that's different for a new teacher, but when you're established that's no problem at all."

Finally, problems of maintaining one's authority in relation to parents lessen as one comes to be a "fixture" in the community and builds up stable and enduring relationships with its families: "But, as I say, when you've been in that neighborhood as long as I have everyone knows you, and you've been into half their homes, and there's never any trouble at all."

The "slum" school is thus, if not ideal, at least bearable and predictable for the teacher who has adjusted to it. She has taken the worst the situation has to offer and has learned to get along with it. She is tied to the school by the routine she has developed to suit its requirements and by the relationships she has built up with others in the school organization. These very adjustments cause her, at the same time, to fear a move to any new school, which would necessitate a rebuilding of these relationships and a complete reorganization of her work techniques and routine. The move to a school in a "better" neighborhood is particularly feared, desirable as it seems in the abstract, because the teacher used to the relative freedom of the "slum" school is not sure whether the advantages to be gained in such a move would not be outweighed by the constraint imposed by "interfering" parents and "spoiled" children and by the difficulties to be encountered in integrating into a new school structure. This complete adjustment to a particular work situation thus acts as a brake on further mobility through the system.

III

Either of these career patterns results, finally, in the teacher's achieving a position in which she is more or less settled in a work environment which she regards as predictable and satisfactory. Once this occurs, her position and career are subject to dangers occasioned by ecological and administrative events which cause radical changes in the incumbents of important positions in the school structure.

Ecological invasion of a neighborhood produces changes in the social-class group from which pupils and parents of a given school are recruited. This, in turn, changes the nature and intensity of the teacher's work problems and upsets the teacher who has been accustomed to working with a higher status group than the one to which she thus falls heir. The total effect is the destruction of what was once a satisfying place in which to work, a position from which no move was intended:

> I've been at this school for about twenty years. It was a lovely school when I first went there. . . . Of course, the neighborhood has changed quite a bit since I've been there. It's not what it used to be.
>
> The neighborhood used to be ninety, ninety-five per cent Jewish. Now I don't think there are over forty per cent Jews. The rest are Greek, Italian, a few Irish, it's pretty mixed now. And the children aren't as nice as they used to be.

Ecological and demographic processes may likewise create a change in the age structure of a population which causes a decrease in the number of teachers needed in a particular school and a consequent loss of the position in that school for the person last added to the staff. The effect of neighborhood invasion may be to turn the career in the direction of adjustment to the new group, while the change in local age structure may turn the career back to the earlier phase, in which transfer to a "nicer" school was sought.

A satisfactory position may also be changed for the worse by a change in principal through transfer or retirement. The departure of a principal may produce changes of such dimension in the school atmosphere as to force teachers to transfer elsewhere. Where the principal has been a major force upholding the teachers' authority in the face of attacks by children and parents, a change can produce a disastrous increase in the problems of discipline and parental interference:

I'm tempted to blame most of it on our new principal. . . . [The old principal] kept excellent order. Now the children don't seem to have the same feeling about this man. They're not afraid of him, they don't respect him. And the discipline in the school has suffered tremendously. The whole school is less orderly now.

This problem is considered most serious when the change takes place in a "slum" school in which the discipline problem has been kept under control primarily through the efforts of a strict principal. Reactions to such an event, and consequent career development, vary in schools in different social-class areas. Such a change in a "slum" school usually produces an immediate and tremendous increase in teacher turnover. A teacher who had been through such an experience estimated that faculty turnover through transfer rose from almost nothing to 60 per cent or more during the year following the change. Where the change takes place in a "nicer," upper-middle-class school, teachers are reluctant to move and give up their hard-won positions, preferring to take a chance on the qualities of the new incumbent. Only if he is particularly unsatisfying are they likely to transfer.

Another fear is that a change in principals will destroy the existing allocation of privilege and influence among the teachers, the new principal failing to act in terms of the informal understandings of the teachers with regard to these matters. The following quotations describe two new principals who acted in this fashion:

He knows what he wants and he does it. Several of the older teachers have tried to explain a few things to him, but he won't have any part of it. Not that they did it in a domineering way or anything, but he just doesn't like that.

He's a goodhearted man, he really means well, but he simply doesn't know anything about running a school. He gets things all mixed up, listens to people he shouldn't pay any attention to. . . . Some people assert themselves and tell him what to do, and he listens to them when he shouldn't.

These statements are the reaction of more strongly intrenched, "older" teachers who depend greatly for their power on their influence with the principal. Their dissatisfaction with a new principal seldom affects their careers to the point of causing them to move to another school. On the other hand, the coming of a new principal may be to the great advantage of and ardently desired by younger, less influential teachers. The effect of such an event on the career of a younger teacher is illustrated in this quotation:

I was ready to transfer because of the old principal. I just couldn't stand it. But when this new man came in and turned out to be so good, I went downtown and took my name off the transfer list. I want to stay there now. . . . Some of those teachers have been there as long as thirty years, you see, and they feel like they really own the place. They want everything done their way. They always had things their way and they were pretty mad when this new principal didn't take to all their ideas.

Any of these events may affect the career, then, in any of several ways, depending on the state of the career development at the time the event occurs. The effect of any event must be seen in the context of the type of adjustment made by the individual to the institutional organization in which she works.

IV

This paper has demonstrated the existence, among Chicago schoolteachers, of what has been called a "horizontal" plane of career strivings and movements and has traced the kind of career patterns which occur, at this level, in a public bureaucracy where movement is achieved through manipulation of formal procedures. It suggests that studies of other occupations, in which greater emphasis on vertical movement may obscure the presence and effects of such horizontal mobility, might well direct their attention to such phenomena.

Further research might also explore in detail the relations between the horizontal mobility discussed here and the vertical mobility more prominent in many occupations. Studies in a number of occupations might give us answers to questions like this: To what extent, and under what circumstances, will a person forego actions which might provide him with a better working situation at one level of an occupational hierarchy in the hope of receiving greater rewards through vertical mobility? Hall notes that those doctors who become members of the influential "inner fraternity" undergo a "rigorous system of selection, and a system of prolonged apprenticeship. The participants in the system must be prepared to expect long delays before being rewarded for their loyalty to such a system." [8] We see that the rewards of eventual acceptance into this important group are attractive enough to keep the fledgling doctor who is apprenticed to it from attempting other ways of bettering his position. Turning the problem around, we may ask to what extent a person will give up possible vertical mobility which might interfere with the successful adjustment he has made in terms of horizontal career movement. A suggestion as to the kinds of relationships and processes to be found here comes from the following statement made by a high-school teacher with regard to mobility within the school system:

> That's one reason why a lot of people aren't interested in taking principal's exams. Supposing they pass and their first assignment is to some school like M—— or T——. And it's likely to be at some low-class colored school like that, because people are always dying to get out of schools like that. . . . Those schools are nearly always vacant, so that you have a very good chance of being assigned there when you start in. A lot of people I know will say, "Why should I leave a nice neighborhood like Morgan Park or South Shore or Hyde Park to go down to a school like that?" . . . These guys figure, "I should get mixed up with something like that? I like it better where I am."

Finally, we have explored the phenomenon of adjustment to a particular work situation in terms of changes in the individual's perspectives and social relationships and have noted the way in which such adjustment acted to tie the individual to the particular situation and to make it difficult for him to consider movement to another. We may speculate as to the importance and effects of such a process in the vertical mobility prominent in many occupations. One further research problem might be suggested: What are the social mechanisms which function, in occupations where such adjustment is not allowed to remain undisturbed, to bridge the transition between work situations, to break the ties binding the individual to one situation, and to effect a new adjustment elsewhere?

[8] Hall, "The Stages of a Medical Career," p. 334.

WHAT IS THE EVIDENCE CONCERNING READING?[1]

William S. Gray

DISCUSSION AND ANALYSIS

Few controversies have stirred so much passionate partisanship than has that over the teaching of reading in today's public schools. If you have been reading the papers, the book review columns, the letters to the editor, the women's magazines, you no doubt have run into several versions of the controversy already: phonics vs. sight-word reading; reading readiness vs. "teach 'em now."

It is not just elementary-school personnel who have been drawn into the argument. The problem of reading reaches up through high school; there are some very fine remedial reading programs at the college level also. In prior centuries when all man had was the written word, do you think there was all this hue and cry about reading? What current social factors do you think focus public attention on reading?

As you read this article you might try to recall how you learned to read. We would wager that you can't remember. It is a subtle and extraordinary process—when the child first *sees* that d-o-g is *dog*. It is one of those insights that psychologists can't quite explain. The teacher who guides the student toward this insight—which makes man civilized instead of primitive—is truly in the position of tremendous importance. Perhaps, instead of recalling how you learned to read, you might consider other milestones in your educational progress in which your later attitudes toward reading were formed. How did you come to like or dislike reading some kinds of books? What kinds of reading did the school ask you to do? How has this affected your present attitudes?

One important item to remember as you read this article by Gray is that there is a tremendous body of research on the question of reading. True, there is much we do not know. But teachers would do well to become familiar with the research before saying yes or no to any particular point of view on reading.

In the current attack on schools, the efficiency of instruction in reading has been challenged repeatedly. It seems appropriate at this time to examine the validity of a number of the criticisms offered, and to review briefly certain facts and principles underlying sound procedure in teaching reading.

VALIDITY OF CURRENT CRITICISMS

Because of the number and variety of the criticisms that have been made it will

[1] From *Progressive Education*, January, 1952, pp. 105–110. Reprinted by permission.

not be possible to examine all of them within the scope of this article. The plan has been adopted rather of centering attention on three that have been made repeatedly and with great vigor. They are introduced here in question form.

Has Reading Been Neglected?

Of major importance is the validity of the charge that the teaching of reading has been grossly neglected during recent years. This question can certainly be answered in the negative for the profession as a whole. There never has been a period in the history of education when problems relating to reading have been considered more extensively and reforms made more widely than during recent years. Since 1925 one reform has followed another in rapid succession: emphasis on a clear grasp of meaning and on breadth and depth of interpretation has increased steadily; the activities of the reading period have been vitalized and enriched; wide provision for purposeful reading, adjusted to the varying achievements and needs of pupils, has been made in all curriculum areas; the value of guidance in reading different kinds of material and for various purposes has been widely recognized; library facilities have been greatly extended; and methods of diagnosing and providing for the needs of the poor readers have developed rapidly. These and other significant reforms indicate the character and scope of the changes that have been proposed.

The notable improvements made have been the product of research, classroom experience and the pooling of judgments on the part of thousands of teachers and school officers. At least 2500 classroom and laboratory experiments [2] have been carried on which provide the factual basis for many of the changes made. Scores of committees have been appointed to study current reading problems and to make such recommendations as changing personal and social needs and experimental evidence justify. Innumerable conferences have been held in which reading needs have been discussed at length, experiences shared and judgments pooled in reaching conclusions. Workshops have been conducted in thousands of school systems for the purpose of evaluating current practices and deciding on needed improvements. A veritable wealth of professional literature relating to reading has been published, which has no parallel in previous decades. Furthermore, the development of improved instructional materials in reading has occurred in this country during the last decade at a rate which excites the admiration and envy of representatives of other nations. These and many similar developments supply convincing evidence that the improvement of reading has been and still is a matter of vital concern to teachers and school officers throughout the nation.

Unfortunately, the public has not kept pace with these developments. Parents, as well as adults in general, tend to evaluate methods of teaching reading in terms of the practices which prevailed when they went to school. They were drilled daily, for example, in the art of reading aloud to others, participated in endless drills on word recognition, and studied prefixes, suffixes, and roots of words at length in the effort to acquire an expanded meaning vocabulary.

As they observe modern procedures in teaching reading, they fail to identify the traditional earmarks of reading instruction. They do not recognize many of the improved techniques adopted for developing some of the reading skills they tried to acquire through more formal procedures. As a result, they often reach the unwarranted conclusion that reading is being neglected today. What is even more un-

[2] "Reading," *Encyclopedia of Educational Research*, New York, The Macmillan Co., 1950, pp. 965–1005.

fortunate, they are often unaware of the broader aims sought through an improved reading program, and, as a result, fail to recognize the praiseworthy efforts made by the schools in those directions.

The implications of the foregoing facts are quite clear. It is of major importance, first of all, that each school should have a clearly defined, carefully coordinated reading program which stimulates and directs cooperative effort among staff members. Second, the teachers and officers of each school, or school system, should carry on a series of conferences with parents and the public in general which aim to familiarize all concerned with the nature and scope of the reading program followed and with the methods of teaching used. The reasons which justify recent changes in the scope and organization of reading programs, and in the teaching techniques used, should also be discussed at length. Third, parents and others should be encouraged to ask questions about and point out possible limitations in current provisions made for reading. Finally, if such conferences reveal evidence of significant weaknesses, or questionable procedures, steps should be taken to overcome or correct them.

Do Pupils Read Less Well Today Than Formerly?

Critics of the schools often proclaim boldly that the pupils of previous generations read much better than do pupils today. Comparative studies of the reading achievement of pupils "yesterday" and "today" reveal three pertinent facts. They show, first, that the average reading achievement of pupils today is equal to, if not greater than, the achievement of pupils of previous generations. For example, Tiegs [3] compared the reading scores of approximately 230,000 elementary school pupils in seven states on the Stanford and the Progressive achievement tests given before and after 1945. The results show that "the achievement of public school pupils is not failing; in fact, the data show a slight, although probably not statistically significant, gain in achievement." These results have been achieved during a period when an increasing proportion of pupils who formerly failed and dropped out of school have remained in school. At the same time, there has also been a slight decrease in many school systems in the average chronological age of pupils per grade, due to changes in promotion policy.

A second fact revealed by comparative studies is that the progress made often varies widely for different aspects of reading. This is shown clearly by the results of a recent study.[4] In 1916 the investigator gave the Gray Oral and Silent Reading Tests to hundreds of pupils in Grand Rapids, Michigan. In 1949 he again made use of the same tests in a survey of the schools of that city. A comparison of the scores made in 1916 and 1949 shows that the pupils had made notable progress in the comprehension of what is read. They did less well, on the other hand, in both oral reading and speed of silent reading. The low scores in speed of reading were due to poor advice concerning the best procedure to adopt when encountering a difficulty in silent reading. Other recent studies show that pupils in general read much more rapidly today than formerly. It is also true that achievement in the rate and accuracy of oral reading is often not as high as formerly. This is unfortunate, because parents often judge the child's total efficiency in reading in terms of his oral-reading performance.

[3] Ernest W. Tiegs, "A Comparison of Pupil Achievement in the Basic Skills before and after 1945," *Growing Points in Educational Research*, Official Report, American Educational Research Association, 1949, pp. 50–57.

[4] William S. Gray, "Comparative Study of Achievement in Reading in 1916 and 1949," *Grand Rapids Survey*, Grand Rapids, Michigan, Board of Education, 1949, pp. 273–279.

A third fact revealed by available data is that individual schools and school systems vary significantly in their comparative standing today and formerly. Some schools are achieving far better results than they did a decade or more ago. For example, Finch and Gillenwater [5] compared the achievement of sixth grade pupils in Springfield, Missouri, on the Thorndike-McCall Silent Reading Test given in 1931 and 1948. The study led to the conclusion that "the teaching of reading in Springfield is now more successful in producing the outcomes we have measured than it was seventeen years ago." Other schools are doing far less well than they did formerly, due to a variety of factors and conditions such as radical changes in the character of the school population, inability to secure adequately prepared teachers or inadequate supervisory assistance. Unfortunately, decreases in efficiency have been due, at times, to the adoption of unsound policies, such as relying largely on free or unguided reading in developing increased power of interpretation.

The situation is such today that no school should fail to make frequent appraisals of the progress of its pupils in reading. Each school staff should be prepared to defend itself against unjust criticisms through the use of actual records of achievement. If the results of given tests are unsatisfactory, vigorous steps should be taken to eliminate retarding influences, if possible, and to overcome deficiencies. Furthermore, frequent conferences should be held with parents and reports made to the public in general concerning the current achievements of pupils and the efforts being made to secure improved results.

Are Present Standards High Enough?

A third criticism is that current standards of achievement in reading are not adequate to meet contemporary needs. Those who maintain that traditional standards of achievement in reading are inadequate do so on the assumption that the demands made on readers are far greater today than formerly. We are all aware that recent curriculum changes call for a larger amount of reading, greater breadth and depth of interpretation, and the use of reading for more varied purposes. As a result, the schools of this nation face the challenging task of raising the general level of reading competence of children and young people and of preparing them to read with increased independence, discrimination and penetration in all school activities.

The need of greater competence in reading is also felt keenly at the adult level. After receiving all the evidence available, a committee on reading of the National Society for the Study of Education [6] concluded that increased levels of competence in reading are imperative "if the future citizens of a democracy are to react intelligently to conflicting arguments, to choose wisely between alternatives" and "to contribute to rational solutions of the challenging personal, social and political issues faced today." The fact was also emphasized that the development of greater depth and breadth of interpretation and of increased capacity to read critically and to make intelligent use of the ideas acquired was a challenging responsibility of all schools and colleges.

What have been the trends in reading interests and tastes of children and young people? Records of free reading show that the schools have made notable progress during the recent decades in developing almost universal interest in personal read-

[5] F. H. Finch and V. W. Gillenwater, "Reading Achievement Then and Now," *Elementary School Journal* (Apr., 1949), Vol. 49, pp. 446–454.

[6] *Reading in the High School and College*, Forty-Seventh Yearbook of the National Society for the Study of Education, Part II, Chicago, University of Chicago Press, 1948, pp. 1–3.

ing among pupils. Surveys of reading preferences, however, show clearly that the quality of what is read is far from satisfactory. The problems faced have been intensified by the publication of a tremendous amount of material of a questionable character; for example, many types of comic books, cheap lurid romance, and tales of horror. Studies of the influence of movies, radio, and television indicate that in some cases it has been positive and in other cases negative. On the basis of all the facts available we may safely say that schools never faced as many challenging problems in promoting desirable reading interests and tastes as they do today.

At least three steps should be considered in an effort to meet the current situation. It is imperative, first of all, that the need for greater competence in reading and for improved reading interests and tastes be clearly recognized and that definite provisions be made in all areas of instruction to secure needed improvements as rapidly and as effectively as possible. In the second place, the goals sought by schools, the provisions made for achieving them, and the problems and difficulties faced should be presented and discussed frankly with patrons and the public. Finally, possible ways in which the home, and the public in general, can cooperate with the school in promoting greater reading competence and improved reading interests and tastes, should be discussed frankly with individual parents and at regular meetings of parent-teacher associations. As was pointed out earlier, an informed and cooperating public forms our first line of defense against unjust criticism.

PRINCIPLES UNDERLYING SOUND TEACHING PROCEDURES

In addition to the broader types of criticisms referred to thus far, the teaching of reading has been criticized repeatedly on the ground that many of the methods used are inefficient or inappropriate. Accordingly, an effort will be made in the remainder of this paper to direct attention to various facts and principles that underlie sound instructional programs in reading.

1. *Growth in reading is a continuous process throughout the school life of the child.* Many of the criticisms made concerning the teaching of reading assume that by the end of the elementary-school period pupils should have acquired a relatively high level of achievement in reading. This point of view is reflected in the traditional statement that boys and girls learn to read in the grades and thereafter read to learn. Recent investigations made by Olson [7] and others show, however, that growth in reading parallels closely the total development of the child. Accordingly, the scope of a sound reading program and the specific goals sought should expand from grade to grade throughout the elementary and secondary school period, in harmony with the changing interests, achievements, and developmental needs of children and youth.[8]

Recent expansions of the reading program make possible the development of far higher levels of competence in reading on the part of all pupils than was possible formerly. Parents and citizens in general should be made aware of the nature of these changes and their implications for the development of greater independence, self-reliance and discrimination in reading. The argument will carry conviction, however, only to the extent that each school system can provide concrete evidence that such a program is in operation.

2. *Pupils vary widely in the rate at which they mature and in the amount and*

[7] Willard C. Olson, "Reading as a Function of the Total Growth of the Child," *Reading and Pupil Development*, Supplementary Educational Monographs, No. 51, Chicago, University of Chicago Press, 1940, chap. 18.

[8] *Reading in High School and College*, chaps. 2 and 4.

character of the training needed in reading. The fact that individuals differ widely in their capacity to learn, and in their rate of progress is so widely recognized that little or no supporting evidence is necessary here. Unfortunately, however, individual teachers and schools are often severely criticized because they make different provisions for pupils within a classroom in harmony with observed or objectively determined differences in capacity, interests and needs. One such practice is to delay the introduction of reading on the part of children who are not ready when they enter the first grade to learn to read with reasonable ease and rapidity. Not infrequently, reading is postponed in such cases for one, two, or indeed, several months. Many parents object strenuously to having their children thus "held back" while their neighbors' children are given daily instruction in reading. They are either unaware that repeated experiments have supplied clear evidence of the wisdom of preliminary experience and training before reading is introduced or they are blinded by false pride to the fact that the findings apply to their own children.

A second form of differentiation is to classify pupils in each of the primary grades into groups at different levels of advancement for purposes of basic reading instruction. This practice is based upon the results of observations and experiments which show that progress is much more rapid on the part of all pupils when instruction is adjusted to their respective levels of advancement. Nevertheless, parents often object strenuously to any kind of differentiation that fails to place their children in the most rapidly advancing group. When questioned pointedly they admit that their own children differ widely in many significant respects, do not mature at the same rate, and require different kinds of treatment in the home. Nevertheless, they often fail to admit the validity of the same policy as applied to school practice. It is of major importance that teachers make clear to parents the nature and extent of individual differences among children that affect progress in reading. They should present one example after another showing how the needs of all pupils are best served by adjusting basic instruction in reading to their respective levels of achievement and needs.

3. *Both systematic instruction in reading and less formal guidance in reading contribute to maximum growth in reading.* In earlier decades practically all instruction in reading was given in reading classes. Because the training provided was often very formal in character, it was open to vigorous criticism. In order to overcome some of its limitations, reforms were attempted in two directions. Those who believed that some systematic instruction in reading is desirable tried to vitalize and enrich the activities of the reading period. Others sought to provide needed guidance in learning to read as an integral part of various school activities in which reading was an essential aid to learning.

In the course of time questions began to arise concerning the relative merits of the two procedures. As early as 1926, Gates and others [9] compared the relative merits of a systematically organized program of teaching reading with a very informal one. During recent years a score or more of related studies have been reported. They have been reviewed briefly by Wrightstone [10] who reached the conclusion that

[9] Arthur I. Gates, Mildred I. Balchelder, and Jean Betzner, "A Modern Systematic Method Versus an Opportunistic Method of Teaching," *Teachers College Record* (Apr., 1926), Vol. 27, pp. 679–700.

[10] J. Wayne Wrightstone, "Research Related to Experience Records and Basal Readers," *The Reading Teacher*, Bulletin of the International Council for the Improvement of Reading Instruction (Nov. 5, 1951), Vol. 5, pp. 5–7.

"the real issue is not which of the two procedures is better but rather what is the role of each in contributing to more effective pupil development in reading." In harmony with such findings the trend recently has been for reading programs to incorporate the advantages of both systematic training in reading and guidance in reading in all other school activities.

In a well-conceived program of the type just described, the daily reading period does not stand out as conspicuously as it did formerly. As a result, parents who visit schools may gain the impression that only limited attention is given to reading. They need help in recognizing the various types of guidance in reading which their children are receiving and the distinctive values that attach to each.

4. *No one method of teaching insures progress in all essential aspects of reading.* During the last three decades scores of investigators have sought to find out which of various methods of teaching reading is the most effective; for example, a sentence, story or experience method, a look and say method, a phonic method, and so on indefinitely. A procedure which has been used widely in efforts to answer this question is to compare the achievements of pupils in two groups of schools using different methods. When the results of all such studies are compared, two conclusions stand out impressively. The first is that no one method secures uniformly high or poor results. In fact, schools using a given method vary all the way in reading achievement from very high to very low. The second conclusion is that there are many factors other than the specific methods used which influence achievement, such as the insight, interest and skill of the teacher.

Further illuminating information was secured by Buswell [11] who followed for a year the various kinds of progress made by two groups of pupils, one taught by an elaborate phonetic method which stressed word recognition, and the other taught by a method which emphasized a thoughtful reading attitude and meaningful experience. A careful study of the reading scores and eye-movement records of the pupils and of other evidence secured through observation, showed that the first group excelled in ability to follow the lines and to pronounce all the words but was not vitally interested in the content. The second group acquired vital concern for the content but was less competent in word recognition and in ability to follow the lines. Buswell concluded that each method made distinct contributions to growth in reading. He rightly pointed out the fact that pupils must ultimately become proficient in all aspects of reading. To this end teachers should vary the emphasis and teaching techniques used from day to day to insure adequate growth in all aspects of reading.

Still another conclusion of large importance has been emphasized by Bond [12] as a result of experiments with children who differed significantly in their ability to see and hear. The data secured showed that pupils who have hearing deficiencies do not profit greatly from the use of methods that stress the sounds of words. Similarly, pupils who have visual deficiencies do not do well when methods are used which rely largely on visual discrimination. Other studies show, also, that best results are secured when the methods of teaching used are adjusted to pupils of varying levels of intelligence.

The foregoing discussion indicates that there is no one best method of teaching

[11] Guy T. Buswell, *Fundamental Reading Habits: A Study of Their Development*, Supplementary Educational Monographs, No. 21, Chicago, University of Chicago Press, 1922, pp. 63–64.

[12] G. L. Bond, *The Auditory and Speech Characteristics of Poor Readers*, Columbia University Contributions to Education, No. 657, 1935.

reading. Whereas some methods contribute most to growth in word recognition, others are most valuable in cultivating a thoughtful reading attitude and a clear grasp of meaning, and still others in increasing speed of reading, in improving oral reading and in stimulating interest in personal reading. A sound reading program makes use of the various procedures and techniques needed in promoting growth in all aspects of reading. An efficient teacher makes continuous studies of the progress of her pupils and varies the emphasis from day to day in harmony with their respective achievements and needs.

5. *Specific attention to growth in important aspects of reading is essential in securing rapid progress.* Much evidence has accumulated which shows clearly that specific efforts are essential in promoting growth in various aspects of reading. The excellent results secured through remedial instruction are due largely to the application of this principle. Its importance in developmental training has also been demonstrated repeatedly. Gray and Holmes,[13] for example, carried on a controlled experiment to determine the relative merits of specific versus incidental attention to growth in meaning vocabulary. The results showed that the use of the former procedure not only produced superior results in grasp of the meanings of the specific words taught but also in general vocabulary development, comprehension in silent reading, quality of oral reading, and effectiveness in oral and written expression. The conclusions justified by many similar studies are that teachers should be alert to the needs of pupils in all aspects of reading and should provide training and guidance to insure growth in each.

[13] William S. Gray and Eleanor Holmes, *The Development of Meaning Vocabularies in Reading: An Experimental Study*, Publication of the Laboratory Schools of the University of Chicago, No. 6, 1938.

CONCLUDING COMMENTS

The foregoing discussion does little more than provide an introduction to the topic assigned. It indicates clearly that reading has not escaped the storm of criticisms that is being directed against schools today. The point of view adopted throughout this article is that we face at least three challenging responsibilities. The first is to develop carefully planned reading programs that are supported by the results of both experience and experiments. The second is to make continuous studies of the progress of children and to correct any deficiencies that may be found. The third is to engage in a program of public relations which acquaints parents with the nature and scope of the reading instruction given, the evidence and arguments that support it, and the results secured. When these conditions are met satisfactorily, the patrons of a school usually become its heartiest supporters and defenders.

SCHOOLCHILDREN[1]

W. H. Auden

Here are all the captivities; the cells are as real:
But these are unlike the prisoners we know
Who are outraged or pining or wittily resigned
Or just wish all away.
For they dissent so little, so nearly content
With the dumb play of the dog, the licking and rushing;

[1] From *The Collected Poetry of W. H. Auden*. Reprinted by permission of Random House, Inc. Copyright 1945 by W. H. Auden.

The bars of love are so strong, their conspiracies
Weak like the vows of drunkards.
Indeed their strangeness is difficult to watch:
The condemned see only the fallacious angels of a vision;
So little effort lies behind their smiling,
The beast of vocation is afraid.

But watch them, O, set against our size and timing
The almost neuter, the slightly awkward perfection;
For the sex is there, the broken bootlace is broken,
The professor's dream is not true.

Yet the tyranny is so easy. The improper word
Scribbled upon the fountain, is that all the rebellion?
The storm of tears shed in the corner, are these
The seeds of the new life?

RECORD BOOK [1]

Alfred Kazin

DISCUSSION AND ANALYSIS

"Record Book" is a grimly realistic account of life in a public school in a big city. In many of the other narratives of school life in this volume, such as the selections from Mark Twain and Edward Eggleston, the harshness of conditions is alleviated by touches of humor. In "Record Book" the predominant tone is one of savagery, sex, and cement. The students live in constant fear of their teachers—a fear so great that it keeps them in the daily race for grades and "satisfactory marks of character." Success in school can be attained only by making a good impression, grinding work, and displaying "an ecstatic submissiveness in all things." Behind the struggle of the students there is also the struggle of the parents for socio-economic status. How do you imagine these parents? Are they native-born Americans or recent arrivals from Europe? What difference does this make in the structure of the educational system? Does this piece cast an optimistic or a pessimistic light on the ideals set forth in W. H. Burton's "Education and Social Class in the United States"? Does it make any kind of ironic comment on Henry Steele Commager's "Our Schools Have Kept Us Free"?

The second section of the Kazin selection is largely concerned with sex, or, rather, the impact of sexual knowledge upon students. Is Kazin's portrait of the school accurate in this respect? Or do you feel it may be slightly overwritten? How would you tie in this section with Frazier and Lisonbee's "Adolescent Concerns with Physique"?

[1] From *A Walker in the City*, pp. 17–20, 28–30, copyright, 1951, by Alfred Kazin. Reprinted by permission of Harcourt, Brace and Company, Inc.

All my early life lies open to my eye within five city blocks. When I passed the school, I went sick with all my old fear of it. With its standard New York public-school brown brick courtyard shut in on three sides of the square and the pretentious battlements overlooking that cockpit in which I can still smell the fiery sheen of the rubber ball, it looks like a factory over which has been imposed the façade of a castle. It gave me the shivers to stand up in that courtyard again; I felt as if I had been mustered back into the service of those Friday morning "tests" that were the terror of my childhood.

It was never learning I associated with that school: only the necessity to succeed, to get ahead of the others in the daily struggle to "make a good impression" on our teachers, who grimly, wearily, and often with ill-concealed distaste watched against our relapsing into the natural savagery they expected of Brownsville boys. The white, cool, thinly ruled record book sat over us from their desks all day long, and had remorselessly entered into it each day—in blue ink if we had passed, in red ink if we had not—our attendance, our conduct, our "effort," our merits and demerits; and to the last possible decimal point in calculation, our standing in an unending series of "tests"—surprise tests, daily tests, weekly tests, formal midterm tests, final tests. They never stopped trying to dig out of us whatever small morsel of fact we had managed to get down the night before. We had to prove that we were really alert, ready for anything, always in the race. That white thinly ruled record book figured in my mind as the judgment seat; the very thinness and remote blue lightness of its lines instantly showed its cold authority over me; so much space had been left on each page, columns and columns in which to note down everything about us, implacably and forever. As it lay there on a teacher's desk, I stared at it all day long with such fear and anxious propriety that I had no trouble believing that God, too, did nothing but keep such record books, and that on the final day He would face me with an account in Hebrew letters whose phonetic dots and dashes looked strangely like decimal points counting up my every sinful thought on earth.

All teachers were to be respected like gods, and God Himself was the greatest of all school superintendents. Long after I had ceased to believe that our teachers could see with the back of their heads, it was still understood, by me, that they knew everything. They were the delegates of all visible and invisible power on earth—of the mothers who waited on the stoops every day after three for us to bring home tales of our daily triumphs; of the glacially remote Anglo-Saxon principal, whose very name was King; of the incalculably important Superintendent of Schools who would someday rubberstamp his name to the bottom of our diplomas in grim acknowledgment that we had, at last, given satisfaction to him, to the Board of Superintendents, and to our benefactor the City of New York—and so up and up, to the government of the United States and to the great Lord Jehovah Himself. My belief in teachers' unlimited wisdom and power rested not so much on what I saw in them—how impatient most of them looked, how wary—but on our abysmal humility, at least in those of us who were "good" boys, who proved by our ready compliance and "manners" that we wanted to get on. The road to a professional future would be shown us only as we pleased them. *Make a good impression the first day of the term, and they'll help you out. Make a bad impression, and you might as well cut your throat.* This was the first article of school folklore, whispered around the classroom the opening day of each term. You made the "good impression" by sitting firmly at your wooden desk, hands clasped; by silence for the greatest part of the live-long day; by standing up obsequiously when it was so expected of you; by sitting down noiselessly when you had answered a question; by "speaking nicely," which meant reproducing their painfully exact enunciation; by "showing manners," or an ecstatic submissiveness in all things; by outrageous flattery; by bringing little gifts at Christmas, on their birthdays, and at the end of the term—the well-known significance of these gifts being that they came not from us, but from our parents, whose eagerness in this matter showed a high level of social consideration, and thus raised our standing in turn.

It was not just our quickness and memory that were always being tested. Above all, in that word I could never hear without automatically seeing it raised before me in gold-plated letters, it was our *character*. I always felt anxious when I heard the word pronounced. Satisfactory as my "character" was, on the whole, except when I stayed too long in the playground reading; outrageously satisfactory, as I can see now, the very sound of the word as our teachers coldly gave it out from the end of their teeth, with a solemn weight on each dark syllable, immediately struck my heart cold with fear—they could not believe I really had it. Character was never something you had; it had to be trained in you, like a technique. I was never very clear about it. On our side *character* meant demonstrative obedience; but teachers already had it—how else could they have become teachers? They had it; the aloof Anglo-Saxon principal whom we remotely saw only on ceremonial occasions in the assembly was positively encased in it; it glittered off his bald head in spokes of triumphant light; the President of the United States had the greatest conceivable amount of it. Character belonged to great adults. Yet we were constantly being driven onto it; it was the great threshold we had to cross. *Alfred Kazin, having shown proficiency in his course of studies and having displayed satisfactory marks of character* . . . Thus someday the hallowed diploma, passport to my further advancement in high school. But there—I could already feel it in my bones—they would put me through even more doubting tests of character; and after that, if I should be good enough and bright enough, there would be still more. *Character* was a bitter thing, racked with my endless striving to please. The school—from every last stone in the courtyard to the battlements frowning down at me from the walls—was only the stage for a trial. I felt that the very atmosphere of learning that surrounded us was fake—that every lesson, every book, every approving smile was only a pretext for the constant probing and watching of me, that there was not a secret in me that would not be decimally measured into that white record book. All week long I lived for the blessed sound of the dismissal gong at three o'clock on Friday afternoon.

Down we go, down the school corridors of the past smelling of chalk, lysol out of the open toilets, and girl sweat. The staircases were a gray stone I saw nowhere else in the school, and they were shut in on both sides by some thick unreflecting glass on which were pasted travel posters inviting us to spend the summer in the Black Forest. Those staircases created a spell in me that I had found my way to some distant, cool, neutral passageway deep in the body of the school. There, enclosed within the thick, green boughs of a classic summer in Germany, I could still smell the tense probing chalk smells from every classroom, the tickling high surgical odor of lysol from the open toilets, could still hear that continuous babble, babble of water dripping into the bowls. Sex was instantly connected in my mind with the cruel openness of those toilets, and in the never-ending sound of the bowls being flushed I could detect, as I did in the maddeningly elusive fragrance of cologne brought into the classroom by Mrs. B., the imminence of something severe, frightening, obscene. Sex, as they said in the "Coney Island" dives outside the school, was like going to the toilet; there was a great contempt in this that made me think of the wet rings left by our sneakers as we ran down the gray stone steps after school.

Outside the women teachers' washroom on the third floor, the tough guys would wait for the possible appearance of Mrs. B., whose large goiterous eyes seemed to bulge wearily with mischief, who always looked tired and cynical, and who wore thin chiffon dresses that affected us much more than she seemed to realize. Mrs. B. often went about the corridors in the company of a trim little teacher of mathematics who was a head shorter than she and had a mustache. Her chiffon dresses billowed around him like a sail; she seemed to have him in tow. It was understood by us as a matter of course that she wore those dresses to inflame us; that she *was* tired and cynical, from much practice in obscene lovemaking; that she was a "bad one" like the young Polish blondes from East New York I occasionally saw in the "Coney Island" dives sitting on someone's lap and smoking a cigarette. How wonderful and unbelievable it was to find this in a teacher; to realize that the two of them, after we had left the school, probably met to rub up against each other in the faculty toilet. Sex was a grim test where sooner or later you would have to prove yourself doing things to women. In the smell of chalk and sweat and the unending smirky babble of the water as it came to me on the staircase through my summer's dream of old Germany, I could feel myself being called to still another duty—to conquer Mrs. B., to rise to the challenge she had whispered to us in her slyness. I had seen pictures of it on the block—they were always passing them around between handball games—the man's face furious, ecstatic with lewdness as he proudly looked down at himself; the woman sniggering as she teased him with droplets from the contraceptive someone had just shown me in the gutter—its crushed, filmy slyness the very sign of the forbidden.

They had never said anything about this at home, and I thought I knew why. Sex was the opposite of books, of pictures, of music, of the open air, even of kindness. They would not let you have both. Something always lingered to the sound of those toilets to test you. In and out of the classroom they were always testing you. *Come on, Army! Come on, Navy!* As I stood up in that school courtyard and smelled again the familiar sweat, heard again the unending babble from the open toilets, I suddenly remembered how sure I had always been that even my failures in there would be entered in a white, thinly ruled, official record book.

THE SECONDARY SCHOOL

ONE WITH SHAKESPEARE[1]
Martha Foley

DISCUSSION AND ANALYSIS

In this subtle and sensitive rendering of adolescence, we are presented more with a mood than a story. Yet, although there is no marked development of plot, the piece maintains an unmistakable aura of significance. By the time we have finished, we realize that we have been privileged to look upon an important stage in the development of a girl. The close of the selection is aesthetically satisfying; nevertheless, we realize that what we have witnessed is only a stage, only one step in the march toward maturity. Since this selection is so concerned with youthful emotions, it can be read to advantage in conjunction with Lawrence K. Frank's "Needs and Problems of Adolescents in the Area of Emotional Health," in this same chapter. The student will also find it an enlightening exercise to compare the narrator in this selection with the narrator in Beatrice Griffith's "One-World Kids." Are there any ways in which the different socio-economic status of the characters accounts for different attitudes toward school and teachers?

In "One With Shakespeare" there are several brief sketches of teachers. How do you feel about these teachers? What about Miss Foster who made her pupils count words in *Poor Richard's Almanac*? Miss Cox, of course, is a much more effective teacher, and yet one may well wonder if she is altogether mature herself. How, for example, did you respond to her remark that Elizabeth had "a spark of divine fire"?

When Elizabeth arrives home she is in a state of high-pitched, almost lyric emotionalism. When she tells her mother of the compliment she received at school, her mother answers: "Isn't that nice? Did you remember not to wipe your pen on your petticoat today?" This mundane

[1] Copyright 1930. Reprinted from Story, Inc.

reply seems to prick the bubble of Elizabeth's enthusiasm. Indeed, on first reading it may even appear callous. On second reading the student may become aware that in certain ways the mother understands Elizabeth very well. Elizabeth's sigh should also be understood in the light of her earlier expressed desire to suffer.

What is the significance of the final sentence: "Moon of Shelley and Keats and Shakespeare and my moon, said Elizabeth, and went in to dinner"?

Yes, Miss Cox was there, sitting at her desk in the almost empty classroom. Elizabeth took in the theme she had written to make up for a class missed because of illness.

A description of people under changing circumstances was the assignment.

Elizabeth had chosen immigrants arriving at a Boston dock. She had got quite excited as she wrote about the black-eyed women and their red and blue dresses, the swarthy men and their earrings and the brightness of a faraway Mediterranean land slipping off a rocking boat to be lost in the grayness of Boston streets.

Elizabeth had liked writing this theme better than anything she had done since the description of a sunset. Amethyst and rose with a silver ribbon of river. Elizabeth shivered. A silver ribbon—that was lovely. And so was scarlet kerchief in the night of her hair in this theme. Words were so beautiful.

Miss Cox read the new theme, a red pencil poised in her authoritative fingers. Miss Cox was so strong. She was strongest of all the teachers in the school. Stronger even than the two men teachers, Mr. Carpenter of physics and Mr. Cattell of math. A beautiful strongness. Thought of Miss Cox made Elizabeth feel as she did when two bright shiny words suddenly sprang together to make a beautiful, a perfect phrase.

Elizabeth was glad she had Miss Cox as an English teacher and not Miss Foster any more. Miss Foster had made the class last year count the number of times certain words occurred in Poor Richard's Almanac to be sure they read the book right through word for word. And the words were all so ugly. Like the picture of Benjamin Franklin. But Miss Cox made you feel the words. As when she read from the "Tale of Two Cities" in her deep singing voice, "this is a better thing than I have ever done." Poor Sydney Carton.

Miss Cox had finished the second page of the theme. She was looking up at Elizabeth, her small dark blue eyes lighting up her glasses.

"Let me give you a pointer, my dear."

Elizabeth automatically looked toward the blackboard ledge at the chalky pointer until the words "my dear" bit into her mind. My dear! Miss Cox had called her "my dear."

"You have a spark of the divine fire," Miss Cox said. "You should make writing your vocation."

Elizabeth flamed. Miss Cox, "my dear," themes about immigrants, blackboards and desks whirled and fused in the divine fire.

Miss Cox marked A in the red pencil at the top of the theme and Elizabeth said thank you and went away.

Elizabeth went back to her desk in the III A classroom which was in charge of Miss Perry. Miss Perry was her Greek teacher as well as her room teacher. Somehow Miss Perry made Elizabeth hate Greek. Elizabeth liked to think of Greece. White and gold in a blue Ægean. I, Sappho. Wailing Trojan women. Aristotle and

Plato and Socrates. Grace and brains said her father of the men. But that was outside of Greek class. To Miss Perry Greece was the aorist of tithemi and Xenophon's march in the Anabasis. Elizabeth always said to herself as she came into the III A room: "I hate Miss Perry, the aorist and Xenophon. Oh, how I hate them!"

But this morning Elizabeth only pitied Miss Perry. She had no spark of the divine fire, poor thing.

Greek was the first class this morning. Elizabeth didn't care. She should make writing her vocation. That was something Miss Perry could never do. If she were called on for the list of irregular verbs this morning she would like to tell Miss Perry that. It would explain why she hadn't studied her Greek homelesson. Why should she be bothered with conjugations when she had to describe blue and red men arriving on an alien shore?

"Now, Miss Morris, will you please give me the principal parts of the verb to give."

That was didomi. But what was the perfect tense? Divine fire, divine fire.

"If you don't know, you may sit down. But I warn you that unless you do your homelessons better you are not going to pass this month."

Divine fire, divine fire.

The second hour was study class. Under Miss Pratt with the ugly bulb of a nose, splotchy face and eternal smile. Miss Pratt taught something or another to the younger girls down in the sixth class. She always smiled at Elizabeth but Elizabeth seldom smiled back. Her smile never means anything, thought Elizabeth.

Elizabeth dumped her books down on her desk in Miss Pratt's room. She opened Vergil to the part she liked. Where Æneas told Dido the story of his wandering while the stars waned and drooped in the sky. It was not her lesson. She had had that months ago. But she liked going back over it just as she liked the beginning of the first book. Great bearded Æneas rang out in *arma virumque cano*. That was strong. She would write strong some day. Strong like Vergil and fine like Swinburne. I will go back to the great sweet mother, mother and lover of men, the sea. Swinburne had divine fire. Keats. Shelley, hail to thee, blithe spirit. And Masefield whose autograph she had bought for five shillings, not to help the British but to have a bit of the man who wrote *The Widow in the Bye Street*.

Elizabeth looked out into the school courtyard. Fine green shoots. Yellow on the laburnum. Spring was here. Divine fire, divine fire.

"Miss Morris, haven't you any work to do?"

Miss Pratt smiling. Nasty, nasty smiling. Didn't she know whom she was talking to like that? A great writer. A girl who would be famous. Let her ask Miss Cox. Why I have a spark of the divine fire. I am one with Shakespeare and Keats, Thackeray and Brontë and all the other great writers.

Elizabeth plumped her head in her hands and stared at the Latin page. Opposite was an illustration of an old statue, supposed to be Dido. Further on was a pen and ink sketch of Dido mounting the funeral pyre. Further on was a sketch of Æneas nearing Rome. Further on was the vocabulary. Then the end of the book. Elizabeth turned, page by page. She could not study and if she looked out the window at Spring again Miss Pratt would be nasty.

"Please, Miss Pratt, may I go to the library?"

"Must you go to the library? What for?"

"I have a reference in my history lesson to look up in the encyclopædia."

"Very well."

The library was large and quiet. A whole floor above Miss Pratt and the study class. It was divided off into alcoves. History in one. Encyclopædias in another. Languages, sciences. Fiction and poetry were in the farthest end which opened out toward the Fenway. The Fenway with its river and wide sky where Elizabeth liked to walk alone.

Elizabeth had read all the fiction and all the poetry. All of Jane Austen and "The Sorrows of Werther" and lots of other books which had nothing to do with her classes. She was always afraid one of her teachers would come in some day during study class and ask her what she was reading that book for. But that had never happened. And the librarian never paid any attention to her.

Now she went into the fiction and poetry alcove and sat on a small shelf ladder. She looked out the window at the long line of poplars rimming the fens. What would she call them if she were writing about them? Black sentinels against the sky. Oh, beautiful, oh, beautiful! That was the divine fire.

There was ancient history with Miss Tudor who had had the smallpox and it showed all over her face, and geometry with Mr. Cattell who had a gray beard and gray eyes and gray clothes and gray manner. Elizabeth liked that, gray manner. That was what the Advanced English Composition called penetrating analysis of character. She would do lots of penetrating analysis when she wrote in earnest.

She would write novels, the greatest, most moving novels ever written, like "Jean Christophe," Elizabeth was deciding when the bell rang for the end of the history lesson. And in between the novels she would write fine medallions of short stories like Tchekov's, Elizabeth told herself when the bell rang for the end of the geometry lesson. And she would always write lovely poems in between the novels and the short stories, she was thinking when the bell rang for the end of the school day.

Elizabeth walked past Miss Cox's room on her way out of the building. She slowed down her steps as she came to the door. Miss Cox was putting away her things in the drawer of her desk. Elizabeth would dedicate her first book to Miss Cox. To Miss Eleanor G. Cox this book is gratefully dedicated by the author.

Eileen and Ruth were waiting for Elizabeth at the entrance. Eileen was the cousin of a famous poet and her mother was an anarchist. Elizabeth liked the thought of any one being an anarchist. It sounded so much more beautiful than being a Democrat or a Republican. And Ruth, who was a class ahead, had already had her poems printed in the *Transcript*. Four times. And one of the poems had been reprinted by William Stanley Braithwaite in his anthology. Oh, they were going to be great and famous, all three.

"Let's walk home and save our fares for fudge sundaes," said Eileen.

"All right, only I am going to have pineapple," said Ruth.

"I'll go with you but I won't have any sundae," Elizabeth said. "I'm going to save my fares this week to buy Miss Cox flowers."

"You have a crush on Miss Cox."

"Perhaps I have and perhaps I haven't. Anyway she said something wonderful to me this morning.

"She said I had a spark of the divine fire and should make writing my vocation."

"Oh, that is wonderful. She never told me that, not even after Mr. Braithwaite took one of my poems for his anthology."

"This is the happiest day of my life. Even when I have written many books and proved Miss Cox's faith in me, I shall always look back to this day. I never expected to be so wonderfully happy."

The three girls, arm in arm, walked through the Fenway.

"I tell you, let's not get sundaes. Since Elizabeth's saving her money, it isn't fair to go in and eat them right before her. Let's you, Ruth, and I buy some of those big frosted doughnuts and some bananas and eat them on the Charles River esplanade. Then Elizabeth can have some too."

"All right, and we can watch the sun set."

"Oh, but that's what isn't fair. To save my money and then eat up what you buy."

"Next time you can give us something."

Elizabeth loved the Charles River. It always hurt her to think that it was on a Charles River bridge that Longfellow should have made up "I stood on the bridge at midnight." Perhaps that wasn't so bad, but so many parodies of the poem had ridiculed the river. Once Elizabeth had written a "Letter to a River." Elizabeth pretended she was away off somewhere, like in New York, and was writing to the river to tell how much she missed its beauty. She had put so many lovely phrases in it, she thought, and she couldn't understand why the editor of the *Atlantic Monthly* had sent it back to her. But great writers always had many rejections first. That Scottish writer in whose eyes Ruth said she saw his soul, had said in his lecture that to write greatly, one must first suffer greatly.

How she had suffered, thought Elizabeth. Her math and Greek teachers were so cruel to her. She who had a spark of divine fire to be treated as they treated her. Tears came to her eyes. And now, when she was tired, she was walking home instead of riding so she could buy Miss Cox flowers. Pink sweetheart roses. Little tight knots of flowers. That was suffering and sacrifice. But it was for love as well as for literature.

"I felt the rhythm of the universe last night," Ruth was saying. "I was sitting on the roof in the dark and I felt the night all around me."

"That makes me think of swiftly walk over the western wave, spirit of night. But it always bothers me that the wave is to the east in Boston," said Eileen. "Otherwise I like that poem very much."

"The rhythm of the universe? What do you mean?"

"Oh, you know. The way some one said the stars swing round in their courses. And that's why I never, never want to study astronomy. I want only to imagine the stars. That's so much more beautiful than any facts about them can ever be."

"I don't agree with you at all. Why, when you think that the light of the nearest star started coming to you three years ago and what you were doing then and how this minute some star is starting to send you light, that may not get to you until far away and old and—"

"Stop! Don't give me facts about the stars! You can have those facts about your stars, if you want. But leave me my stars to love as I please."

"Oh, very well. There, now the sky is coloring. See that lovely clear green high up. Pretty soon the deep colors will come. My, these frosted doughnuts are good. Much better than any near where we live."

"There's the first light on the other bank. Over near the Tech building."

That was what it was to have a spark of divine fire. Elizabeth's thoughts flowed on with the darkening river. She could put all this, the river and the sky colors and the lights into writing. People would feel the loveliness of the world as they had never felt it before. People would no longer walk with their heads bent to the street when there was a sunset to be seen. What have you done to her, masters of men, that her head should be bowed down thus, thus in the deepening twilight and golden angelus? Her father said Noyes wrote maudlin singsong. It was jingly sometimes but she did like it. And too many heads were bowed down, you masters of men.

"Mother'll scold me if I stay any later," said Eileen.

"And my mother said she wouldn't get me a new dress for the class party if I came home late again."

"Yes, we must all be going. But isn't it nice to think when you wake up at home in bed at night that the river is out here, creeping on and on under the stars?"

"No wonder Miss Cox said you had divine fire. Let's put our banana peels in here. This is Spring Clean Up Week, you know."

"Good night."

"Good night."

"Good night."

Holding the thought of her own greatness close to her, Elizabeth went home. A sliver of moon curled in the sky. That is the moon Shelley, Shakespeare, Spenser and yes, way back, Chaucer looked at. And now I am looking at it.

"Mother, Miss Cox says I have a spark of divine fire. I am to be a great writer some day."

"Isn't that nice? Did you remember not to wipe your pen point on your petticoat to-day?"

"Oh, mother, you know that's not a question of remembering. I never do it when I'm thinking about it. But you didn't half listen to what Miss Cox said about me."

"Indeed I did. She said you had a divine spark of fire. That means you'll get another A in English this month on your report card."

"It means more than any old report card. It means my whole life. I'm to be a writer, a great writer."

"But first you must finish school and college. And that means you have to do your mathematics better. Remember how angry your father was about that E in geometry last month."

Elizabeth sighed. She went out on the back porch which looked across the city. Lights pricked the blackness. Like a necklace which had spilled over velvet. Oh, words were lovely.

The moon was still there, a more emphatic sliver now. Moon of Shelley and Keats and Shakespeare and my moon, said Elizabeth, and went in to dinner.

THE PURPOSES OF THE JUNIOR HIGH SCHOOL—AFTER FORTY YEARS[1]

William T. Gruhn

The greatest development in the junior high school came during the period from 1910 to 1930. This was due in part to the fact that the philosophy and program of the junior high school offered splendid educational opportunities for children in early adolescence. Another reason for the tremendous growth of the junior high school after 1910 was the rapidly increasing enrollment nation wide in both the elementary and secondary schools. In many communities, the building of junior high schools relieved the pressure of a growing pupil population in both the elementary and secondary schools.

We are again in a period of tremendous growth in enrollments. The large group of children, born in 1942, is already in the fourth grade. In 1954, these children will be in the seventh grade. According to estimates of the Commission on Teacher Education and Professional Standards of the National Education Association, the seventh grade in 1954 will be 25 per cent

[1] From the *California Journal of Secondary Education*, (Mar., 1952), Vol. 27, No. 3, pp. 127–132. Reprinted by permission.

larger than the one of 1947.[2] Furthermore, the birth rate increased so much following World War II that the number of pupils entering the seventh grade in 1960 will be almost 75 per cent more than that in 1947. Already communities in all sections of the United States are engaged in building-programs to provide for these children. As in the 1920's, the junior high school is an important part of those building-programs.

As we enter this period of expansion in the junior high school, it is appropriate that we reflect seriously on the basic philosophy and purposes underlying its program. Questions such as these need to be considered: What were the original purposes for which the junior high school was established? How have the original purposes been modified? How well were those purposes implemented in the schools? What direction should future developments take if the purposes of the junior high school are to be achieved?

EARLY PURPOSES AND FUNCTIONS

The purposes of no other educational institution in America were as widely discussed and as specifically set forth as those of the junior high school. Beginning with the Report of the Committee of Ten on Secondary School Studies, which was presented to the National Education Association in 1893, the need for a more effective program of education for early adolescence was discussed in the report of one committee or commission after another for three decades. It is in the reports of these committees and commissions that the purposes of the junior high school, as expressed early in its history, may be found.

[2] National Education Association, Commission on Teacher Education and Professional Standards, "*Probable Demand for Teachers in the United States for the Decade 1949–50*," Washington, D. C., National Education Association, 1948. Mimeographed. 28 pages.

It is not the intention to summarize here the early purposes and functions of the junior high school. That has already been done elsewhere on a number of occasions.[3] For the present, it is desirable to refer to the early statements of functions primarily to see how they have been modified with forty years' experience in junior-high-school education.

Frequently, attention is directed toward the administrative aspects of the junior high school. For instance, it is suggested that grades 7 and 8 rightfully belong in the secondary rather than the elementary school; that the work in grades 7 and 8 should be departmentalized; that promotion by subject rather than by grade should begin earlier than the ninth grade; and that homogeneous grouping is appropriate for grades 7, 8, and 9. These matters have never been nor are they now of basic importance to the development of the junior high school. Interest in the reorganization of elementary and secondary education centered at first not in administrative practices but in the needs of children. The early reports pointed out again and again that the schools apparently were failing to meet the needs of children in grades 7, 8, and 9. This failure was emphasized particularly by studies, made in the decade after 1900 which showed that pupils withdrew from school in tremendous numbers in those grades.

Even before the publication of these studies, however, there was an awareness that the educational program in the upper-elementary and lower-high-school grades was not appropriate for early adolescence. The following shortcomings were mentioned most frequently:

1. That elementary school methods were continued too long.

[3] For instance, see William T. Gruhn and Harl R. Douglass, *The Modern Junior High School*, New York, The Ronald Press Company, 1947, chaps. 1–3.

2. That pupils in grades 7 and 8 needed subject matter which would be more challenging than that being taught, since it was largely a continuation of the work in the intermediate elementary grades.
3. That there were few, if any, activities outside the classes which were appropriate for early adolescence.
4. That pupils were unable to make a satisfactory adjustment upon entering high school because of the great gap in the program between grades 8 and 9.
5. That there was little guidance to help pupils with the peculiar emotional, social, and psychological problems that they encounter during early adolescence.

In other words, the various committees and commissions which issued reports beginning in 1893 were concerned with children—their needs, interests, and abilities. They were concerned because the educational program did not meet the needs of children during early adolescent years. And they urged the reorganization of the educational program to better meet those needs. This, then, may be stated as the over-all purpose for the program of junior-high-school education early in the reorganization movement: *To provide an educational program which was particularly designed to meet the needs, interests, and abilities of children during early adolescent years.* This, in 1951, is still the purpose which should dominate the development of the educational program in the junior high school.

The committees and commissions on the reorganization of elementary and secondary education did not content themselves, however, with suggesting the over-all purpose of education in the reorganized school system. They set forth in some detail the direction which that program should take. In the years after the first junior high schools were established, the task of defining the basic philosophy and purposes of the junior high school was continued by such leaders in secondary education as Leonard V. Koos, Thomas H. Briggs, James M. Glass, William A. Smith, Calvin O. Davis, and others. These men set forth the purposes of the junior high school in terms of functions which that institution should implement and achieve. For instance, they urged that in order to meet the needs of early adolescence, the educational program of the junior high school should (1) provide for the integration of learning outcomes, (2) offer exploratory experiences for pupils, (3) provide guidance for pupils to meet problems and make decisions and adjustments, (4) meet the different needs, interests, and abilities of individual pupils, (5) provide opportunities for socialization, and (6) bring about better articulation in all phases of the educational program.[4] By achieving functions such as these, it was believed by early junior-high-school educators, an educational program would be appropriate for children in early adolescence.

The basic philosophy and purposes which were proposed by educators early in the history of the junior high school are, with little modification, recognized and accepted as appropriate today. The changes which one finds are in emphasis and interpretation rather than in basic point of view. It is with these changes that we shall concern ourselves here.

INCREASED EMPHASIS ON INTEGRATION

Integration of learning outcomes, as a function of the junior high school, has been given increased emphasis in the last two decades. In fact, little was said about integration of learning outcomes in the reports of the various committees and commissions on the reorganization of elementary and secondary education. Thomas H. Briggs, in his statement of functions pub-

[4] *Ibid.*, chap. 3.

lished in 1920, proposed as the first of five functions for the junior high school that it provided a "common integration education." [5] Other statements of functions after 1920 tended to include the integration of learning outcomes as one of the essential purposes of the junior high school.

The implementation of the concept of integration has been extremely slow. In the 1920's some beginnings were made in that direction through emphasis on the planning and teaching of large blocks of work, developed around a major theme or objective. This approach to teaching, called the unit approach, has done much to bring about a better integration of learning outcomes in so far as that may be done through methods of planning and teaching. Today, the unit approach to teaching is generally accepted as the basis for planning and carrying on learning activities in the junior-high-school classroom.

There is little doubt but that departmentalization as practiced in the early junior high schools was inconsistent with the point of view that the program of education should contribute to the integration of learning outcomes. It was not until the 1930's, however, that some schools, particularly in California, initiated programs of curriculum organization that were more in harmony with the concept of integration. In these schools, certain subjects were combined and taught under one teacher, with the subject matter integrated or fused in so far as that seemed desirable. The language arts and the social studies were most often taught in this manner, although science and mathematics occasionally were also brought into the integrated program. This approach to curriculum organization, commonly referred to as the core curriculum, at first developed slowly. But in the past several years it has been introduced more and more in schools in all parts of the country. Like the emphasis on unit teaching twenty years ago, the reorganization of the curriculum according to the core approach is the most significant recent development in the junior high school that bears on the integrative function.

[5] Thomas H. Briggs, *The Junior High School*, Boston, Houghton Mifflin Company, 1920, chap. 6.

BROADENED CONCEPT OF EXPLORATION

Our concept of exploration as a function of the junior high school has broadened considerably since the first junior high schools were established. Originally, exploration was thought of largely in terms of opportunities for pupils to try out vocational interests and abilities as a basis for making vocational decisions. As more and more pupils continued in school beyond the ninth grade, it became obvious that vocational decisions might well be delayed, and that in the junior high school, pupils should explore their talents as a basis for educational decisions. Consequently, by the 1920's attention was being given to educational as well as to vocational exploration.

In the last two decades, however, exploration has been broadened to include far more than educational and vocational activities. Today, we believe that one of the major purposes of the junior high school is to help the child find himself not only in educational and vocational affairs, but in social, avocational, and cultural matters as well. He should, therefore, have exploratory experiences in every area of interest —in vocational activities, in opportunities for continuing his education, in sports, music and literature, in social activities—in short, in every area of human activity that is of interest to children during early adolescent years.

As our concept of exploration has broadened, so have the ways and means of providing exploratory experiences. A generation ago, certain courses in the junior-high-school program were designated as try-out or exploratory. At first, these courses emphasized experiences in vocational areas, such as industrial arts, homemaking, and business. Later, courses for educational exploration were added, such as general language and general science. There were also "sampling" courses, in which the pupil was exposed to several different subjects in a year—six weeks of Spanish, six weeks of typing, another six weeks of industrial arts, and so on. Today, we recognize that the exploration of pupil interests and talents, broadly interpreted, cannot be confined to specific courses or periods in the daily schedule. Rather, pupils should engage in exploratory activities throughout the entire school day—in the club, assembly, and social activities; in the language-arts and social-studies classes; in the band, orchestra, and glee clubs; in every class, every activity, and every subject.

Furthermore, it is believed today that exploratory opportunities are provided not so much by subject content as by methods of teaching. There should be sufficient flexibility in every learning situation to permit pupils to engage in some activities of their own choosing, to participate in planning the learning activities, and to decide how they may contribute towards carrying those activities to completion. For instance, regimented reading in the language-arts class has given way to much pupil selection of literature; in the industrial-arts classes, prescribed projects have been replaced by individual projects chosen by the pupils; and the formal art class limited to prescribed work in painting and drawing has become arts and crafts with pupils choosing their areas of interest.

EXTENSION OF GUIDANCE ACTIVITIES

Guidance, like exploration, has been greatly broadened in its scope and purpose. In the early literature on the junior high school, exploration and guidance were usually referred to as being part and parcel of the same process. And indeed they were, since both were at first confined to vocational activities, with pupils exploring vocational interests and abilities as a basis for vocational guidance. Soon guidance, like exploration, came to be applied to educational as well as vocational activities. That is, much attention was given to helping pupils meet educational problems, such as adjusting to a new school situation, succeeding in school, choosing curricula and courses, and deciding upon educational goals.

Today, guidance like exploration encompasses the total life of the child. The counselor is still interested in the educational and vocational problems of the child, but his concern with the child goes far beyond those areas. The counselor is of service to the boy or girl in any problem that arises, —vocational, educational, social, emotional, moral, and avocational. Furthermore, the intelligent counselor today makes no attempt to classify guidance problems into categories like those above. He realizes that each of these problems tends to be highly complex, and that it may concern many aspects of the child's growth and development. Our concept of guidance in the junior high school today is so broad that it concerns the total life, interests, and experiences of the child.

INDIVIDUALIZATION MODIFIED LITTLE

Our point of view with respect to individualizing the instructional program, as a function of the junior high school, has not been modified materially. We have changed our thinking considerably, however, concerning the manner in which that function can be most effectively implemented. The introduction of elective curricula and courses, patterned after the traditional high-school program, was the characteristic approach to an individualized educational program in the early junior high schools. Later, homogeneous grouping was introduced as a means of simplifying for teachers the task of meeting individual needs, interests, and abilities.

Although elective offerings and homogeneous groupings are still widely employed in the junior high school, educators are less certain that these practices are appropriate and sufficient to individualize the instructional program. They believe that, with flexible teaching methods, much individualization can be provided for pupils in the same courses and in heterogeneous groups. The unit approach, pupil participation in planning, and experience-centered activities contribute much to the individualization of the instructional program. Consequently, there is at present a tendency to limit rather than expand the offering of elective courses, while homogeneous grouping is being applied increasingly to those pupils needing special attention rather than universally to all pupils in school.

MORE OPPORTUNITIES FOR SOCIALIZATION

The concept of socialization, like individualized instruction, has not been modified greatly in recent years. As in the early junior high schools, it is concerned primarily with giving children in early adolescence experiences that will help them develop satisfactory social relationships. In the early schools this was accomplished largely through such extraclass activities as clubs, assemblies, and social functions—still a desirable practice today. We have come to realize, however, that socializing experiences can be provided with great effectiveness in the class as well as in the extraclass program. That is true particularly in the experience-centered classroom, where pupils assume much responsibility for planning and carrying on learning activities, and where group rather than individual activities predominate. The implementation, rather than the interpretation, of the socialization function has therefore been expanded.

ARTICULATION A MAJOR FUNCTION

Articulation continues to be a major function of junior-high-school education. In the committee and commission reports on reorganization, articulation as a specific function of the junior high school was mentioned more frequently than any other. There was great concern by the investigating committees over the gap between elementary and secondary education. It was the hope that this gap might be bridged through reorganization of the school system. Our point of view concerning the nature and importance of articulation in the educational program has remained consistently the same during the history of the junior high school.

Unfortunately, we have done little to implement this function. We believed that with the development of the junior high school better articulation would somehow take care of itself. Consequently, junior-high-school faculties have kept to themselves and developed programs for their schools without reference to the educational activities in other school units. It is rare, indeed, that the educational program for a school system is planned in its entirety with elementary, junior-high-school, and senior-high-school teachers participating. Educators are urging today, as they did before the advent of the junior high school, that there be satisfactory articulation as pupils go from one unit to another through the American school system. The junior high school is in a unique position to provide leadership in this respect. Articulation remains, therefore, a major function and a major problem of the junior high school.

CONCLUSION

The basic purpose of the junior high school in 1952 is, therefore, essentially the same as it has been since the beginning of the reorganization movement: namely, *to provide an educational program which is particularly designed to meet the needs, interests, and abilities of children during early adolescent years.* With respect to the specific functions of the junior high school, there has been increased attention to the integration of learning outcomes, while our concepts of exploration and guidance have been greatly expanded. There continues to be emphasis on the individualization of the educational program, provision for socializing experiences, and the articulation of educational activities from one unit to another in the school system; but our point of view has changed concerning the methods of implementation rather than the nature and interpretation of these functions.

As we develop junior-high-school programs, we should emphasize again that our chief concern is with children—their needs, their interests, their abilities. The implementation of the basic functions of the junior high school should be directed toward that end. The effectiveness of our junior high schools in the years ahead will be measured by the success we have in meeting the needs of boys and girls in early adolescence.

LANGUAGES IN THE AMERICAN SCHOOL[1]

Van Cleve Morris

DISCUSSION AND ANALYSIS

One of the most stimulating features of education to many of us is the fact that, while we have many unsolved problems, there is ample room for innovation, for discussion, for experimentation. There is nothing static about the American public schools. Many hallowed traditions guide policies, and at the same time new findings in child growth and development may bring in a whole new method of classroom control. Whatever happens, however, whether we abide by tradition or try new ways, there is plenty of room for discussion and argument. The high school today is the object of a great many such arguments. What do you feel are some controversial areas in the education of secondary-school students? What things would you like to see changed? What opposition would you expect to find to your proposals?

As we have said, there are many many areas of controversy here. We might have picked on family life, for instance. Or the grading system. Or core programs. We finally selected this article on the teaching of foreign languages in the schools for several reasons. First, it is certainly an area of controversy. There are opponents and proponents of every shade and kind when the question comes up. As professional educators, you probably

[1] From *The Educational Forum*, January, 1954, pp. 155–163. Reprinted by permission. *The Educational Forum* is the official publication of Kappa Delta Pi, national honor society in education.

will be involved sooner or later either in a discussion about this topic or in actual policy making in regard to such teaching. What you would decide could influence the total school program, as Van Cleve Morris points out.

The second reason this seemed like a valuable article is that the author has sought to look at *research evidence* to make his case, and carefully reasoned logic. Perhaps there are other reasons for teaching languages that Morris has not suggested. What would they be? Do you agree with his conclusions? Why or why not? Recently there has been considerable interest in programs to teach a foreign language to young children in the early elementary grades when learning to speak a second language seems to come with more facility. Do you think such a program would be acceptable to Morris if it meant omitting other elements in the curriculum?

This article has been included not because it necessarily reflects the opinions of the editors but because it sets one *thinking about real problems* facing the public schools, and because we are given a fair and judicious appraisal of the evidence at hand.

I

There are few topics of curricular concern which have received as much attention in recent years as the role of foreign languages in the educational programs of modern schools. Indeed the rapid disappearance of foreign language studies from school curricula in the last half century not only stands as a vivid reminder of the rapidly changing character of the school program but also constitutes a cause for concern and alarm at the apparent preoccupation of our schools with practical and immediately useful studies. The charge is made that American education has become obsessed with the phenomenon of social change, and in an effort to keep pace has summarily dumped by the wayside some of those studies which represent the most precious elements of our cultural heritage.

The literature of professional education is full to overflowing with harangues, impassioned pleas,[2] and, in some cases, tight logical briefs [3] for the resurrection of the study of foreign languages as a universal constituent element of the education of boys and girls in our democratic society. The literature is also full of equally impassioned and equally logical statements in rebuttal.[4]

What is so conspicuously absent in most of this verbiage is any recourse to scientific fact with which to support whatever position is advanced. The appeal is made to "common sense," on the assumption that common sense is the most reliable avenue to truth. If the scientific tradition has taught us anything, it has taught us to accept common sense notions only after they have been substantiated by objective proof.

[2] For instance, A. M. Withers, "On Teaching and Justifying the Foreign Languages," *Hispania* (Nov., 1946), Vol. 29, pp. 516–518; "Some Remarks on American, English, and Foreign Language," *Classical Journal* (Jan., 1947), Vol. 42, pp. 221–222; "To Safeguard American English," *School and Society* (Nov. 11, 1939), Vol. 50, pp. 628–630.

[3] Harvard Committee, *General Education in a Free Society*, Cambridge, Harvard University Press, 1948, pp. 119–127.

[4] For instance, F. T. Spaulding, "The Generalist's Case Against Modern Foreign Languages," *French Review* (Dec., 1933), Vol. 7, pp. 125–137.

There is no need, therefore, to ask the reader to undergo another such appeal, whether it be partisan or ostensibly objective and clarifying in purpose, so long as empirical evidence is left out. What is needed is an attempt to review and incorporate into our thinking the evidence that has been gathered to date with respect to the value of foreign language study in the educational life of the American youngster.

II

There are several principal reasons customarily advanced to justify the teaching of foreign languages in our schools:

1. The study of a foreign language aids in the learning of English, principally its grammar.
2. The study of a foreign language aids in the enlargement and enrichment of one's vocabulary.
3. The study of a foreign language is indispensable in coming to appreciate the expressive power and beauty of our own tongue.
4. The study of a foreign language aids in an individual's cultural development.
5. The study of foreign languages helps to develop international understanding, something that the world is greatly in need of today.
6. The study of a foreign language is an indispensable tool to an intelligent and scholarly understanding of the cultural group who speaks it.
7. The study of a foreign language is necessary preparation for intercourse with people who speak the language, either in travel, in the diplomatic service, or in international commerce.
8. The study of a foreign language is necessary to acquire mastery of the language for purposes of research in the literature of that language.

There are no doubt others,[5] but these shall furnish us with sufficient focus for discussion. They provide us with pedagogical hypotheses which, like all other hypotheses uttered in a scientific age, somehow mutely insist upon either support or denial within the context of empirical fact. What can we say about the evidence as regards these?

To work from the bottom up, we can say that Number Eight is self-evidently valid. Certainly no one could do research in, say, German literature unless he could read German. Nor, in the case of Seven, could anyone deal successfully with Frenchmen unless he knew French. Number Six also appears acceptable since so much of the cultural fabric of a people is carried in their own language and is frequently lost in translation; the scholar of Chinese civilization, for instance, would find it difficult to understand these people without the aid of the Chinese language. Six, Seven, and Eight, it should be noted, apply to the researcher, the traveller, the overseas merchant, the diplomat, and are educationally valid principally in a specialist or vocational sense. It is true, of course, that with the coming of rapid means of communication and travel there has been a parallel increase in inter-cultural traffic and social intercourse. It is also probable that this trend will continue and that a growing proportion of our population will in the years ahead have the opportunity to study and travel abroad or deal on an inter-lingual basis in their business or social pursuits. In all likelihood, however, these inter-cultural experiences will be limited for many years to a relatively small number of our people. Unlike Europeans and a few of our own people in border areas such as the Southwest, the vast majority of Americans simply

[5] It is assumed (somewhat gratuitously perhaps) that modern psychological science has laid to rest the nineteenth-century view that the mind is made up of faculties which can be developed through mental discipline. Therefore, it has not been considered necessary to treat an earlier belief that stemmed from this conception of the mind, i.e., that the study of a foreign language aids in the development of the faculty of reason.

do not have a truly *functional* need for facility in languages other than their own.

If not for functional use with foreign peoples, then for what? An examination of Number Five will reveal that it is closely related to Six except that it refers to cultural understanding not alone by the scholar, businessman, and governmental official but by the average citizen. This reason has considerable logical appeal and it has been developed with clarity and vigor by Earl J. McGrath, former U. S. Commissioner of Education.[6] We come, however, inevitably upon the blunt fact that there is little if any empirical evidence to support it. On the contrary, there is much in history that would tend to disprove it. One might cite the case of European peoples, who over centuries have understood each other's languages and cultures perhaps more than anywhere else on earth. Yet, they have been the participants in countless international, inter-cultural wars. Japan and China, sharing similar languages and cultures for centuries, and presumably understanding each other's problems, have traditionally been hostile toward one another. Other examples could be given. Indeed, it might even be possible for the military historian to show that international friction has most frequently arisen between people who were relatively well acquainted with one another!

III

Hypothesis Four represents the justification for foreign language study which, of all those presented, is perhaps the most popular in the lay mind. Certainly anything leading to culture should be thought well of. The investigator's immediate reaction, however, is to ask the question, "What is culture?" It is not sufficient to rejoin that everyone knows what it is. If educators are charged with effecting a certain behavior change in individuals, they must know clearly what the nature of this change is and how most effectively to bring it about. If by "culture" is meant the ability to insert into one's conversation or writing an occasional alien phrase or to understand the occasional alien phrase in the expressions of others (or other special abilities akin to these), then it would appear only logical to call for the direct study of these phrases as such and the peculiar way in which they embellish the thing being said.

If, in a second meaning, the quest for culture is essentially the reincarnation of the values of an earlier and presumably more glorious era, then the process by which this may be done becomes of primary importance. The term "culture" in this context has a rather vague, undefinable and, at the same time, tantalizing quality. Toynbee has graphically described the lengths to which societies will go in pursuit of it, and he points out that a favorite technique is the attempted resurrection of the language of this earlier period. His conclusion that most such attempts end up in failure is particularly significant for educators.[7]

If, in the third place, culture can be described as the general broadening of intellectual horizons and the intensification of human sensitivity to the world in which we live, our present state of knowledge does not seem to yield clear-cut evidence that foreign language study is the most direct road to this objective. In this case, the hypothesis becomes not so much meaningless as untestable, and we are left to rely on subjective determinants as to whether

[6] "Language Study and World Affairs," An address delivered at the 35th Annual Meeting of the Central States Modern Language Teachers Association, May 3, 1952, St. Louis, Mo.

[7] Arnold J. Toynbee, *A Study of History*, Abridgement of Volumes I-VI by D. C. Somervell, London, Oxford University Press, 1947, pp. 508–513.

we are moving closer to or further from the end in mind. This is certainly not to say that foreign language study does not contribute to the enrichment of a personal life. Many of these subjective judgments would seem to indicate that, for certain individuals, it does. The question the American educator must answer, however, is whether this "road to culture" is the most effective and the most direct route for the great majority of our boys and girls to take. As the social scientist continues to reduce cultural values to experimental units of study, it is likely that future research will shed more and more light on this point.

If by "culture" is meant something embodied in Number Three we may at least be inclined toward the view that only through the "discovery" of one's native tongue from the external vantage point of another can the learner really sense the semantic nuances—the overtones and undertones—which English, with its tremendous range and quality of meanings, makes possible. In this sense, language becomes not a tool but a discipline in the humanities. As it has been so well put by the Harvard Committee,

> To learn that other languages have words with meanings which no English word carries, that they sort meanings in other ways and link them up in other patterns, can be a Copernican step, one of the most liberating, the most exciting, and the most sobering opportunities for reflection that the humanities can offer.[8]

In the absence of objective data to support it, we at least can say that this claim deserves investigation and study. Certainly we can agree with the Harvard Committee that such disciplinary effects of language are likely to be manifest only in the more gifted pupils.

[8] *General Education in a Free Society*, Cambridge, Harvard University Press, 1948, p. 120.

IV

By far the most frequently offered reasons in support of foreign language teaching are embodied in Hypotheses One and Two. Fortunately it is in connection with these that the availability of scientific evidence reaches adequate proportions. These two hypotheses deal in educationally negotiable terms, i.e., in terms of learnings which are pedagogically measurable (as measurement is now conceived) and for which measuring instruments are already in existence. It would seem appropriate, therefore, to appeal to scientific fact in the validation of these two hypotheses.

Several studies, in attempting to test one or both of these hypotheses, yield rather unconvincing data because significant variables are left uncontrolled. For instance, Starch,[9] in a study more than thirty-five years ago, attempted to measure the "effect" of studying Latin on the size of one's English vocabulary and on knowledge of English grammar and proficiency in English usage. His experimental design called for the testing in these abilities of approximately 200 high school and college students, some of whom had had foreign language instruction and some of whom had not. He found that the foreign language students had larger vocabularies, a greater knowledge of grammar, and were more proficient in English usage, but the differences in all three measures were in most cases statistically insignificant.

However, these early findings are worthless since there was no effort to control the factors which led the foreign language group into such study and which led the non-foreign language group away from it. Since it is likely that boys and girls who are at home in English grammar and vocabulary would be more likely to take up

[9] Daniel Starch, "Some Experimental Data on the Value of Studying Foreign Language," *School Review* (Dec., 1915), Vol. 23, pp. 697–703.

the study of foreign languages than would those who have difficulty with English,[10] one cannot depend upon the validity of such studies.

One might surmise that the experimental naïveté of 1915 might have been dispelled by 1940, but such is not the case. Dean and Wall[11] in a study of 900 high school students made the same mistake of leaving uncontrolled the factors governing selection or rejection of foreign language as a study in school, and they quite expectedly emerged with findings in favor of foreign language. "The school grades of tenth-graders who take foreign language are higher than those who do not; therefore, the study of foreign languages improves one's school work"—a classic *non sequitur* into which dozens of investigators have fallen!

In a somewhat more specialized way, Thorndike and Ruger[12] got more tangible results. After administering to Latin and non-Latin students in forty-one schools an English vocabulary test at both the beginning and end of the control period, they concluded that significantly greater improvement was made by Latin students over non-Latin students on words of Latin derivation. There was no significant difference between the two groups in improvement on non-Latin derivatives.

A contrary judgment was returned in 1940 by Carroll[13] who, after much study of the smallest meaningful phonetic units of language (Morphemes), was forced to the conclusion that the study of derivations in Latin does not necessarily aid in enlarging the English vocabulary.

In 1935 Douglass and Kittelson[14] concluded that the transfer of training in high school Latin to English grammar, spelling, and vocabulary was so small that it was doubtful if any relationship between the two existed.

Pond[15] in 1938, after careful matching of subjects, found little if any difference in vocabulary knowledge on the part of Latin and non-Latin pupils.

V

Probably the most thorough and systematic of studies of this kind is that of Werner[16] in 1930. Entitling his work "The Influence of the Study of Modern Foreign Languages on the Development of Desirable Abilities in English," Werner postulated that "desirable abilities in English" could be classified as follows:

1. The ability to read with speed and comprehension.
2. The ability to appreciate the qualities of good literature.
3. The ability to express one's ideas correctly and effectively in both spoken and written English.

To measure these abilities he used five

[10] For a related study, see Robert P. Fischer, "Students Electing Foreign Languages," *Journal of Higher Education* (Feb., 1945), Vol. 16, pp. 97–98.

[11] Mildred Dean and Bernice Wall, "The Value of Foreign-Language Study for Tenth-Grade Pupils," *School and Society* (June 1, 1940), Vol. 51, pp. 717–720.

[12] E. L. Thorndike and G. J. Ruger, "The Effect of First-Year Latin Upon Knowledge of English Words of Latin Derivation," *School and Society* (Sept. 1, 1923), Vol. 18, pp. 260–270.

[13] J. B. Carroll, "Knowledge of English Roots and Affixes as Related to Vocabulary and Latin Study," *Journal of Educational Research* (Oct., 1940), Vol. 34, pp. 102–111.

[14] H. R. Douglass and C. Kittelson, "The Transfer of Training in High School Latin to English Grammar, Spelling, and Vocabulary," *Journal of Experimental Education* (Sept., 1935), Vol. 4, pp. 26–33.

[15] Frederick L. Pond, "Influence of the Study of Latin on Word Knowledge," *School Review* (Oct., 1938), Vol. 46, pp. 611–618.

[16] Oscar H. Werner, "The Influence of the Study of Modern Foreign Languages on the Development of Desirable Abilities in English," *Studies in Modern Language Teaching*, Vol. 17, (Chapter II), New York, The Macmillan Co., 1930, pp. 99–145.

tests (a punctuation test, a sentence structure test, a reading test, a language and grammar test, and a vocabulary test) and an exercise in composition, administering them at the beginning and at the end of the school year.

The two groups tested—the foreign language and non-foreign language groups—were equated for I.Q. and advancement in school. Moreover, I.Q.'s in each group were further extracted and sub-divided into Low (85–89), Medium (95–104) and High (110–114) ranges. The results of the tests are of interest:

1. *Reading—Speed:* Gain in reading speed was greater in the foreign language groups except in the Low I.Q. range where the gain was greater in the non-foreign language group.
2. *Reading — Comprehension:* Gain in comprehension was greater for the foreign language group.
3. *Punctuation:* The non-foreign language group showed slightly greater improvement in punctuation.
4. *Sentence Structure:* The non-foreign language group showed slightly greater improvement in constructing sentences. (It was noted that high mentality seems actually to interfere with normal improvement in the development of ability to recognize faulty sentence structure.)
5. *Language:* There was little or no difference between the two groups in improvement in the ability to discover language errors and correct them.
6. *Grammar:* The foreign-language pupil with low I.Q. showed an actual loss in his ability in grammar, while his classmates in the same group with high I.Q. realized a significant gain.
7. *Vocabulary:* The non-foreign language group at the secondary level showed relatively greater improvement in vocabulary. At the college level the foreign language group held the edge.

The net conclusions of the study were:

1. It is difficult to defend the general statement that the study of a modern foreign language will always aid in the development of desirable abilities in English.
2. The evidence indicates that the study of modern foreign languages materially aids in the development of speed and comprehension in reading, especially with high school pupils.
3. The evidence is favorable to the conclusion that modern foreign languages aid in the development of ability in grammar in high school but not in college.
4. The evidence indicates clearly that the study of a modern foreign language interferes with the development of ability to punctuate correctly and to discover faulty sentence structure.
5. The evidence indicates that it is doubtful if the study of a modern foreign language, in general, aids or hinders the development of ability in language and in vocabulary.
6. It is clearly evident that the lower the I.Q. of a pupil, the greater is the chance that the study of a modern foreign language will interfere with his attempt to develop desirable abilities in English, and vice-versa.
7. If a foreign language pupil is expected to develop desirable abilities in English, his mental ability should be above the average.

Some rather startling conclusions resulted from a study reported by Woody [17] in 1930. In an effort to determine the effect of the study of Latin and French on learning English words of French derivation, the investigator discovered that pupils with no experience in foreign language showed the greatest gain during the school year. Beginning students in Latin showed

[17] Clifford Woody, "The Influence of the Teaching of First-Year French on the Acquisition of English Vocabulary," *Studies in Modern Language Teaching*, Vol. 17 (Chapter III), New York, The Macmillan Co., 1930, pp. 149–184.

moderate gain, and beginning students in French showed the *least* gain! The same results were found in the learning of non-French derivatives. All of which would lead to the conclusion that if you want a youngster to develop his vocabulary, keep him away from foreign languages.

In summing all of this up, there is a temptation to agree with Palfrey [18] who in 1941, after surveying thirty years of studies on this problem (some referred to above), summarized by stating that the evidence thus far gathered was inconclusive due to faulty experimental design, size of experimental groups, and time intervals employed. No doubt, this is true of a great many of the studies that have been conducted over the past half century. But from many of the investigations described above, one gets the feeling that he may say with confidence that our Hypotheses One and Two are not confirmed. The confirming data gathered, as in the study by Thorndike and Ruger, are somewhat inconsequential in that they are concerned with the development of a very specialized language skill. Some of the evidence, as Palfrey says, is inconclusive. But a substantial share of the findings are definitely negative.

While we may therefore set aside Hypotheses One and Two as having been found somewhat untenable, additional pedagogical questions force themselves into our view in anticipation of possible conflicting evidence to be gathered in future studies. If, for the sake of argument, it should later be found that foreign language study *does* lead to the improved understanding of English, the question would still remain unanswered as to whether this time and energy spent in the study of the alien tongue could not have been more profitably spent in the direct study of English. The hypothesis restated would then become: That a given amount of time in the study of a foreign language will yield greater results in the learning of English (grammar and vocabulary) than a camparable amount of time in the study of English (grammar and vocabulary). If this hypothesis were tested today, a negative result would seem to be indicated, assuming of course that we are accomplishing something in our English classes in our schools. It is a generally accepted fact that transfer from one activity to another is never as great as that which results from a direct attack upon the activity itself.[19] On the basis of what is now known, one is inevitably led to the conclusion that if the aim is to learn English then the thing to study is English and not something else!

Having dealt with all eight hypotheses, we may now take inventory. Serious doubt has been cast upon One and Two, and a rejection of a restatement of these (discussed above) has been implied. Hypothesis Three commands some attention but no evidence concerning it is available. Hypothesis Four is ambiguous; certain interpretations of it may be valid but studies in areas other than foreign language suggest themselves as more appropriate means to the desired end. Number Five is in the doubtful class with little evidence available. Six, Seven, and Eight are valid primarily for post-secondary education.

VI

What adjustments in our thinking do these findings suggest to us? Certainly the comfortable and traditionally doctrinaire point of view that any kind of discipline in a foreign language is educative and therefore good is no longer tenable. And almost

[18] Thomas R. Palfrey, "The Contributions of Foreign Language Study to Mastery of the Vernacular," *Modern Language Journal* (Apr., 1941), Vol. 25, pp. 550–557.

[19] For results of investigations into the phenomenon of transfer, see P. T. Orata, "Recent Research Studies on Transfer of Training With Implications for Curriculum, Guidance, and Personnel Work," *Harvard Educational Review* (May, 1941), Vol. 11, pp. 359–378.

the same thing can be said of the companion notion that foreign language study is educative in certain special ways, i.e., in the learning of English. Moreover, it appears that whatever cultural or linguistic effects language study may have are largely limited to intellectually gifted individuals. Certainly foreign language study should be available to these youngsters. It has also been indicated that foreign language study is indispensable in the preparation of young people for special occupations, and since this special preparation normally begins at the college or university level, it would appear appropriate to concentrate foreign language study at that point.

In summary, it appears that the kind of things foreign language study *can* do are largely limited to gifted youngsters at all levels and to a special vocational group at the collegiate level. While there will continue to be increasing opportunities for the use of foreign language skill in a world which is rapidly shrinking and simultaneously becoming more and more dependent upon verbal communication, it is doubtful whether the American school should begin in any large-scale sense to turn its energies to the instruction of large numbers of boys and girls in the languages of the world.

It is to be hoped, of course, with the equalization of educational opportunity throughout the country, that eventually most of our schools will be able to provide this curricular element in their programs. For the foreseeable future, however, and in terms of educational reality, it would seem that there are other studies and activities which may justifiably be classified as more important for the primary attention of educators in America.

ONE-WORLD KIDS[1]

Beatrice Griffith

DISCUSSION AND ANALYSIS

It is rare that an author can catch the idiom, the sound and feel, of the spoken language of a distinctive group without making the reader feel awkwark and impeded. Beatrice Griffith has amazingly given us the tone, the nuance, the phrase, the feel of Mexican-American teen-agers. As you read this excerpt the young people truly come alive.

The book from which this selection was taken, *American Me*, was rather interestingly put together. The author spent considerable time in the Mexican American area in and around Los Angeles. She was able to gather a great deal of statistical and other data. In her book she gives us the factual background, then follows it with a story such as "One-World Kids" which takes one into the subjective world that facts cannot describe.

Children who must live in two cultures are to be found in schools in

[1] From *American Me*, pp. 144–152, by Beatrice Griffith. Reprinted by permission of and arrangement with Houghton Mifflin Company, the authorized publishers. Grateful acknowledgment is also made to *Common Ground*, in which "One-World Kids" first appeared.

every part of our country. Parents feel security in patterns of living that they knew in another country, perhaps, or another region of the United States, or in a particular socio-economic level. The children, going to American public schools, are expected to behave in terms of the dominant American middle-class culture. In what way is this demonstrated in the story of these one-world kids? Can you justify the way the teachers felt and acted? We hear only one side of the story here; what do you think the teachers would say about these young people? In what way are these youngsters caught between two cultures?

As you read this story, you may ask yourself what you might do, if you were the teacher, to reach and help these young people.

That afternoon we went drunk to school I was feeling fine. Feeling fine cause I was just sixteen, had a dime, and gave a penny to the Salvation Army. I hadn't felt so fine for a long time, not since I thought one day at junior high I would be somebody. So I gave myself with respect and dressed like a Square at school, and gave everybody good manners. But nobody would believe that I wanted to make something of myself and they only laughed. And that light-skinned cholo teacher who talked real dainty Spanish, she gave me the reputation of a gangster in that school. She used to ask me, "Wild woman, what alley did you come from?" But when she saw me dressed like a Square and giving myself with respect, she couldn't believe it and laughed too. So it was no go. But I sure felt good for a while.

Well, this noon we both walked past the vocational school where the schools send their bad kids. Singing all the way, Jitterbug and me. Only we couldn't walk very good. The girls yelled at us from behind the board fence, so we started back. When we got to the school door I threw my cigarette away and walked down the hall real fine. But one thing we forgot, we forgot to stop singing. So the principal came out and Jitterbug ran into one of the classrooms and sat down at a desk. But me—I walked straight into her office, I'm that dumb, and started talking. I told that principal I was going to be somebody big, real famous. But she wouldn't listen. She was only crying and was calling me honey and asking me, "How could you do this to me, honey. You were my sweetheart girl, look at the appreciation you gave me."

But one thing she didn't know, it wasn't to her, it was to me and my mother I was doing it, being drunk.

I saw Jitterbug coming from the room across the hall, and the teacher talking rough to her, pushing her along the hall, telling her, "We don't allow drunkards in this school." She yelled loud enough for another school to hear. Jitterbug never drank before today, and now already they think she is a Lost Weekend. So I tried to stop talking, cause I remembered how fakey they are at this school. You give them the trust and they don't keep the truth, so everything is dirty.

The principal was telling me that I was a dear sweet girl, and all that jive. And next door Jitterbug was crying and crying, asking them for the favor not to tell her mother. Jitterbug never asked any favors of anybody, only one. Just to play "Beat Bad Boogie" and "Ave Maria" when she died. That's all. But those teachers would promise not to tell her mother, and then would do her dirty and tell everything to the cops and her mother sure.

The principal was talking a lot of talk. "You aren't happy are you, honey? Why do you smoke the marihuana, honey? Tell me where you got the whiskey, honey."

So I told her the truth that a drunk man bought it for us, but she believed it for a lie. Then she looked at me with those missionary eyes and gave me that long-distance embarrassment, and promised her word not to tell my mother.

That day after school, while we was waiting for the old streetcar to take us home (all but Jitterbug, and the cops from Juvenile took her home), we tried to buy some ice-cream cones at the drugstore. But sometimes they wouldn't sell you any. Today was one of those days. We all crowded in there. I wanted to get some aspirin and went back in the store. When I heard them calling the girls, "You dirty Pachucas, get out of this store," I came up front.

"I bought some aspirin, mister. How about a glass of water?" I asked him.

But he yelled at me, "There's a gas station across the street, if you want water. We don't want you Pachucas in here. Now get out."

So I told him, "Maldita sea tu madre, and your grandmother, and your great-grandmother's mother's mother, and all their cows and goats. You don't stop to know if we are Pachucas or not, just because we dress this way."

The girls were sore. Everybody was mad, waiting outside that drugstore. Largo wrote her name real big on the Coca-Cola sign by the brick wall. "Remember, Cuata, when they used to make you scrub all the names off the basement walls at school just cause Negra put them there and they thought it was you?"

"Sure, man, just cause I was dark they thought those names were mine. Some were, but not all. I worked a lot for that chick cause my skin is dark—but then it took my mother a lot of months to get it just that color I guess."

I was getting tired hanging around and waiting for that streetcar, and none of the guys showed up yet.

Mostly when the girls wait for the streetcar they talk about that school and the teachers. All the troubles come out on that corner, cause we have to wait sometimes a long time. If the conductor sees a big bunch of us he won't stop, so we hang around.

Fushia was sore cause she got expelled from school today. "Just cause there was a big commotion when Yoyo and Chonto drove by the school, they thought it was me. Always those teachers give the blame someplace else. How come they aren't ever fair? They sit me in a room with a pencil and tell me, 'Now honey, write down on that paper why you're bad.' So when I drew a picture of Joan Crawford with a big overlip, old lady Wiggins got real real mad. Then they gave me a summons, nice and polite from the office. 'Well dearie, that's the last. We've tried our best with you. We're simply fed up. We just can't go on. We can no longer help you,' and all that jive, she told me. But it was dirty not to hear my story."

Some of the guys drove by then and there was a lot of commotion. Simon, Wapa, and Gege all got in the car and drove away downtown. Lola scratched her name on a brick that didn't have none. "Sure those teachers should know how to help girls with their problems, not shut them out because they're hard. Remember Miss Stevanson and those teachers at Lockwood, that other special school? They'd give you chances and chances. That's why we went in there real rugged and came out all squarey, with no overlip, no short skirts, or pompadours or zombie shoes. They didn't try to control our clothes, and no teacher's-pet stuff."

Caldonia lit a cigarette and sat down on the curb. "And they didn't yell at you. They were honest and equal. It's not the strictness that counts. I've sat in a lot of principals' offices for hours, with them trying to get me to take down my pompadour. But strictness and nothing else doesn't get control. Some teachers can keep you after school for hours, but couldn't make me mind ever." She passed me a cigarette then, cause another streetcar had just banged on up the street without stopping.

"Heck yes, if they expect a courteous answer they should set the example for someone to follow, and not yell like you are deaf. Remember that old teacher in junior high who used to yell at us, 'You stupid B-7's,' she'd yell. 'You blockheads.' But that day she called my mother a Mexican dumbbell was too bad for her. She was so surprised when I slapped her she just stared pop-eyed, while I walked down the stairs to the principal's office. That began all my trouble."

Changa bought some gum across at the grocery store and passed it around. "Sure, I remember her. Deeply deeply in my heart, to the last inch of my heart, to the deepest part of my heart, I shall always remember that s.o.b. How could I forget her?"

"Yeah, and Miss Stevanson never threw it to you that you were a Mexican, and would explain all the big long words, cause she came out strong for work. Remember, Changa, it took me two weeks to learn to say 'vulgar profanity'? But if you tried hard she didn't fail you. She was with respect and was fair, and those beautiful hair and eyes! Things would be different here if she was our teacher. She'd have control."

Huera let out a yell at the streetcar that almost stopped, then it banged the bell and went on. "Cholo cabrón, why doesn't he stop. I gotta get home."

I told the girls to pipe down, cause that old store guy would call the police if he heard so much noise, but it was no use. Everybody was talking at once.

"Why even if Stevanson wasn't for Roosevelt, she never let a Gabacho girl say something bad about him. I bet if Roosevelt was alive this school would be different. Remember the CCC's he gave us and all those things? And remember when Roosevelt talked on the radio? Man, it was real keen—made you all warm inside, like Lena Horne singing. Let's put his name here by ours, real big!" Cuata and Vicki started in making a big Roosevelt name on the Coca-Cola sign, standing high on the wall. We watched to see if the drugstore boss came out.

"Sure the school would be different. Cause Roosevelt knew our language even if he didn't speak Spanish, cause he knew the language the poor people talk. He knew the languages of all the people who don't speak American, and the poor people who speak American but not with rich money. We could write him and tell him about what we want in this school, and he'd do something I bet," I told him, "cause my aunt wrote him when her house was going to be sold, and it wasn't."

"Yeah, but it's different now. With Roosevelt alive you felt safe, like inside the house when it's raining outside. Or you've just had a long drag of tea and everything is comfortable and smooth. Cause he would protect you, there was nothing to fear like being hungry. He knew about being hungry I guess, cause he gave us the NYA and hospitals and WPA and lots of other things people need when they haven't money and can't speak." Beaver picked up a piece of dirt and threw it smack in the face of the cute little blonde chick in that Coca-Cola sign. "Make that name Roosevelt bigger—so everybody can see it."

I remembered what my mother said, "The only thing Roosevelt did to hurt his people was to die. If Americans could give their lives to save him you'd have to stand in line." But I think my mother isn't so sad that my brother is dead in Germany now, cause Roosevelt is with him and all the dead soldiers and sailors. She says she feels more comfortable, and I guess she does.

Just then a bunch of high-school chicks came by and gave us those looks of theirs. They're so stuck up they probably say they're Spanish and not Mexican. But we did them nothing, not since that day they called us dirty Pachucas and we beat them up.

I sat down on the fireplug. "Come on, let's write a letter to Roosevelt like if he was still alive, and tell him what we want for a school."

Larga gave me her notebook. "Sure man, that's it. *Jíjola,* let's begin."

I began to write.

Dear President Roosevelt,

The next time one of those old dames asks what will make our school better we're going to tell them what we're telling you. But you'll probably get this better before they ask us. So here goes!

We want to know out of that school the things you are supposed to know in life. How to fill out papers for work. How to put money in the bank. To know about the world we're living in. Not to know nothing about nothing. To know about the stars and moon, about shorthand and penmanship and power machines, so we can sew for our kids when we have them. And how to give them the understanding.

We want lots of clubs for all of us, not only honor clubs where you have wings like angels. To know what we're reading about, how to talk with people when they say, "Did you see this and that about Europe or Russia?" And how to say back, "Oh yes. I know. And did you know this and that, about some current events?" And if we could have one period to study health about ourselves, how our organs are made, and what to do if we get sick, that would be good.

And we would like, President Roosevelt, a course in beauty—combing hair, how to fix your make-up, what style and all that. Not this professional grooming course they give us, that means cutting paper dolls out of newspapers.

In grammar school we studied about things that were so fine, all about life in other countries, like you knew about. You know, that one-world business. We live in one world too—the Mexican world. But we want to go places and do things everywhere. To get out of these little grapes-of-wrath houses we live in.

But mostly, President Roosevelt, we want to know about the living of life real real good.

Your friends,
THE ONE-WORLD KIDS

Well, when we got the letter finished, after all the chicks had their say, we didn't know what to do with it. So I said I'd take it home, until we decided what to do I'd keep it.

About then a streetcar stopped cause there weren't so many of us left. Some had started walking home by now. When we piled on scrambling for seats, Cuata and Caldonia ran to the last window. "There's Roosevelt's name, real big, *qué suave!*"

The streetcar clanged and started up with a jerk. I saw Cuca waiting for the bus and yelled her, "Hyah Mexican! Get off the street, you Mexican."

The motorman turned around and yelled, "Sit down and shut up, you Pachucas, or get off."

"Okay, mister, okay," I told him.

Then I told the chicks not to sass him back cause they'd have to wait longer for a streetcar next time.

At home I slipped in real quiet, but it was okay. My sister was over at the settlement house and my mother was out. I took the letter to Roosevelt and put it in the wooden treasure box my brother made in manual training. Everything was in that box, our baptism certificates; my brother's Purple Heart and Silver Star medals, and a letter from his officer when he died; a report card from my school when I got good marks; and the old white maquerna ribbon from my mother's wedding.

I folded the things and put the rosary and paper rose back on top the box, then stuck it on the shelf under the Virgin's picture. Roosevelt's letter would be okay there for a while.

I went in the kitchen and started making tortillas, so to be busy when my mother came in full of mad, if she did, if they told her from school about me. And soon she did come in. She had been crying. I knew from her face she knew. When that old dame called me in before class was over and told me I was as free as the air to get a job, and that they didn't want drunks and tea smokers there, I knew if they expelled me they'd tell my mother. And sure enough—they snitched. But I knew one thing. She wouldn't let them have the satisfaction of seeing her cry. So for them she would have the smile that took her tears away. But she came home real sad with her sadness.

But for me there was just hell. My mother and dad got too many old-fashioned ideas. She's from another country. I'm from America, and I'm not like her. With Mexican girls they want you to sit in the house like moscas muertas, dead flies, like that. If you tell them what the teachers say, they say the teachers don't know, and what they tell us will only get us in trouble. They think they know what is good, not the American teachers. And even if we take our parents to school to explain them—our parents don't hear. They only know from Mexico.

I remember when me and my sister told my mother we wanted to dress neat and American they beat us and said no, to dress like they wanted us to, in old Mexico. So after a while it's no use. You can't have any fun, so you get your fun where you find it. Like little Cutdown said to the teacher when she asked her why she drank, "It's the only fun I have, Miss," she told her, and it's true.

My dad hadn't come home yet, so I knew I was going to get the preaching first. I'd rather they beat me silly than give me that preaching. She brings up everything since the day I was born. Gee what a memory. She tells me I don't appreciate the facts too. But I think she doesn't know the facts for understanding. Most Mexican parents don't. Cause it's sure that the strictest homes have the most trouble.

But I hate my mother to be unhappy, man. She was so cute when I bought that little bank and put in some money to start for a washing machine for her. I could kill that teacher. She did real dirty telling my mother all the record about me, piling it up for one time. My mother's old and sick and when she gets mad she gets all red and out of breath and I'm afraid for her. If anything would happen to her I'd die.

She yelled at me, "Why do you drink, why do you smoke those marihuana cigarettes?" And all that.

I'm asking myself the same question sometimes. And I can't tell her I drink cause I'm scared. I'm afraid I'm going to die—that my boy friend's mother is a bruja, and he says she'll put a curse on me since I broke with him, cause if he can't win me by the good he'll win me by the bad. I want to hide some fear inside me, like I want to hide my face when I'm drunk. But I can't tell her that cause my mother doesn't have the understanding.

So I tell her while I make the last little tortilla, "I smoke to have some fun. You probably did worse when you were a girl in Mexico." Real dirty I was, but real mad too. It's that way, they hurt your feelings and you get mean.

But in my heart I am crying for my mother. I really don't know what's the matter. If I did anything to my mother I'd kill myself. All Mexican mothers got is a flock of family and too much work, that's why they're old young.

I knew my dad would beat me, so I decided to get away to Changa's house or someplace before he come home. I remember how he beat me silly when he saw me on the street talking to a boy, a real decent boy. And it'd be worse now, with him calling me a dirty puta, and street lady. I couldn't stand it and wait for him to chase me out.

So when my mother went in crying to pray to the Virgin, I got my hands washed and took my coat from the closet. Some girls can't go to a friend's house if their mother knows you've got a bad reputation, no matter if you're not really bad, but just do some wrong things. So, if I couldn't stay at Changa's then someplace else, or stay the night at the bus station. And tomorrow I could get work at a malt shop, or a sewing factory or walnut place maybe.

I slipped out the back door quiet, and walked in a hurry down the alley towards town. Cause with me, it is to live life. You never live long, so the thing is to take life while you can make it.

NEEDS AND PROBLEMS OF ADOLESCENTS IN THE AREA OF EMOTIONAL HEALTH[1]

Lawrence K. Frank

Adolescents, as we are increasingly realizing, face many problems in growing up, as they are confronted by the life tasks of our culture and our social order. Since these life tasks involve their relationships with others, especially with parents, teachers and other adults who often do not understand them or frequently frustrate their efforts to grow up, adolescents are subject to a variety of emotional disturbances that they find difficult to manage.

The difficulty is increased by their lack of understanding of these emotional disturbances and by the frequent statements that emotions are bad, must be ignored or repressed so that the individual will live wholly rationally and intellectually. It is usually forgotten by those who condemn emotions that love and affection, loyalty, friendship and many other much prized human relationships and fulfillments are not rational or intellectual, but emotional. Also it is often ignored that spontaneous feelings are essential to living as a whole person.

There is much confusion over the terms emotion and emotional, emotional conflicts, problems, development, maturity and similar expressions, and no one has yet revealed the full processes involved in emotional reactions or in the less intense but often coercive chronic feelings or effects.

It will be helpful to adults who are parents, teachers, counselors, coaches, leaders of youth, or in similar positions, if they will recognize (and try to help adolescents to understand) that the second decade of life—the teen ages—are necessarily difficult and problematic because the child is being transformed into the adult, physically, intellectually, culturally and socially. In that process the boy and girl must relinquish much of their previously learned patterns of action, speech, belief and feelings and learn new patterns as they struggle to master their life tasks.

In these years of transition, the adolescent is subject to at least two kinds of

[1] From *The High School Journal* (Dec., 1951), Vol. 35, pp. 66–74. Reprinted by permission.

emotional disturbances that should be more clearly recognized.

First, and less clearly recognized, are the persistent feelings or chronic emotions, sometimes called affective reactions, that were established in childhood and have been carried over as "unfinished business" into adolescence. These, after being more or less quiescent during school years, almost suddenly are revived by the experience of growing up. We will return to these in a moment after noting the second and more obvious emotional disturbances of adolescence.

Second, there are the acute, sometimes almost overwhelming emotional reactions aroused by current experiences, especially interpersonal relations, and by the often disturbing process of physical growth and sexual maturation, with physiological instability, and increased awareness and sensitivity to stimulation and provocations of all kinds. New and heavy demands and requirements are imposed upon adolescents by adults and also by their own age group, calling for alteration in their conduct, relationships, ideas and beliefs and for achievement of academic and other tasks that frequently are not simple or easy.

These current problems of growing up, of undergoing these successive transformations, physically and as a personality, may be complicated and intensified by the persistent feelings or chronic emotions from earlier years. The adolescent boy or girl may be unaware of how much they are being disturbed by these "carry overs" from early childhood.

Thus from studies of personality difficulties in adolescents, it appears that boys and girls often become resentful and openly hostile to parents, not only because of parental restrictions upon their desire to follow their peer culture but because these conflicts with parents revive their earlier feelings of rebellion against authority and of antagonism toward parents.

It is as if the adolescent, in his new consciousness of his developing body, also becomes more aware of his resentment against his family. Their rules, requirements and prohibitions, their demands, and even long standing expectations and customary behavior of his younger brothers and sisters may suddenly provoke conflict and rebellion, openly expressed.

Sometimes adolescents display a resentful or critical, even aggressive, attitude to adults outside the home, to teachers or counselors or administrators. He carries over his feelings against parents into questioning of authority and shifting allegiances, feeling "picked on" or criticized or "bossed around."

Likewise feelings of anxiety and guilt begun in early childhood, but more or less quiescent during later childhood days, may become active again as the adolescent has new and strange impulses and becomes involved in the varied activities of his or her age group that are condemned or forbidden by adults.

All the feelings of childhood years may be revived to complicate his already difficult relationships. Volumes have been written upon the problems of adolescents, especially the acute and often serious cases that require specialized diagnosis and treatment. But it should be emphasized that *all* adolescents are confronted with the same problems, because they are all growing up in our culture, facing the same life tasks that every adolescent must meet.[2]

Those adolescents who are unable to cope with these, become the problem cases while others may be more competent or fortunate. But all are exposed during these years to greater or less perplexity, stresses and strains, and acute anxieties.

[2] Robert J. Havighurst, *Developmental Tasks and Education*, Chicago, University of Chicago Press, 1948. Caroline B. Zachry, *Emotion and Conduct in Adolescence*, New York, D. Appleton Century Co., 1940.

The clinical records indicate that some of the serious cases are often those who are unable to exhibit emotional reactions, who have become too rigid from denying or repressing their feelings, or those who have developed no capacity for managing their emotions. Many students of adolescent boys and girls have expressed their concern over the apparent lack of spontaneous expression of feelings which is normal and desirable in this period, almost essential to their maturation as healthy personalities.

Since adolescent boys and girls must free themselves from their childish dependence upon parental authority and learn to become self directing adults, they need the help and guidance of friendly, understanding adults to provide what they can no longer find or accept at home. Teachers, counselors, coaches, administrators and all the varied personnel in contact with youth must provide this needed help, not by playing amateur psychiatrists, but by understanding the struggles youth makes to grow up, to meet his or her life tasks, to attain to his or her own aspirations.

A great deal of the time, energy and abilities of youth are spent on often futile efforts to escape or to ignore or to resolve by arbitrary, often impulsive action, what they must learn to manage as the only way to grow up in our culture. They need, not preaching and moralizing, or scolding and punishment, but recognition of what they are striving to do and become, and helpful guidance toward those goals or reformulated goals.

We have tended to emphasize the intellectual aspects of life and academic tasks and have assumed that the schools could ignore or at least neglect these personal difficulties, leaving youth to blunder ahead with little or no insightful guidance. The recent recognition of how much youth needs help of the kind he wants and seeks, gives promise of large significance, because we can and should be able to reduce the present waste of human lives in anti-social or self-defeating activities, born of the blind struggles to grow up.

Adults in contact with youth should at the outset be aware of the life tasks confronting young people, which adults have forgotten in their own lives, often because they were such painful, unhappy years. But adults cannot help young people unless they do recognize and understand what adolescents are trying to do, what they are striving for and why they are so often emotionally unstable and disturbed.

Thus it is important to remember that the boy and girl must accept their own bodily transformations and maturing functions, revise their image of the self as no longer a child but an emerging young man or woman. This maturation brings not only the beginning of sexual functioning at puberty, but also all the new impulses, enlarged awareness, acute sensitivities, the constant feeling of being caught in a struggle between what is occurring inside and what is happening outside, especially the continual sexual provocation from other persons, from advertising, movies, pulps, picture magazines and now TV.

Adolescents are never free from this constant internal and external stimulation which they are expected to resist and manage rationally according to the prescribed code of conduct. It is probable that for a number of years the major focus of their reveries and day dreams, their conversation with their peers, their reading, entertainment and adjustment is on these sexual interests and their symbolic, if not actual, expressions. Being ready physiologically for sexual experience long before they are personally and socially prepared for adult mating, or permitted to do so, they are in a perpetual state of frustration and emotional disturbance.

As Bruno Bettelheim has pointed out, it is helpful to adolescents to be able to talk about these difficulties, to put their frustrations and aspirations into words, spoken or written, since they can thereby achieve some symbolic resolution of their problems and release vicariously some of their acute feelings.[3]

We have as a cultural ideal, to transform sex into a personal love relationship, which has great appeal to youth when just beginning to feel capable of concern for others, capable of thinking altruistically. But many adolescents come to this period burdened with strong feelings of guilt derived from their childhood teachings about sex as bad and dirty, and their early genital explorations as wicked.

Thus the boy and girl are often torn by the conflict between their eager hopeful expectations of love, so strongly emphasized in all our traditions and current literature and movies, and their fear of sex as something both fascinating and destructive.

How to help youth to reach some resolution of these conflicts, to express their strong feelings and emotional disturbances so they won't go on into adult years burdened with these unresolved problems is a major responsibility for high schools and colleges that wish to foster healthy personalities.

We can now say that many adults are unable to live as adults because during adolescence they did not resolve their adolescent perplexities. Much of our educational program encourages them to ignore or evade their adolescent life tasks for various academic goals, seeking escapes in various intellectual interests or extracurricular activities.

Adolescents, as indicated earlier, have to learn to make decisions, to accept personal responsibility, become independent individuals capable of self direction and of living with their age mates. This usually is a painful struggle because they have to escape from their parents, who are often reluctant to let them grow up and achieve independence. It is also infuriating to boys and girls because they are continually exhorted to be grown up, to exhibit judgment, to accept responsibility, but at the next moment are told they are too young and must be obedient children. Schools like homes treat adolescents as children, and by doing so must fail to foster their maturation.

The boy and girl must free themselves at whatever cost from dependence upon their parents and from parental control, and they must also make a place for themselves with their age group. It seems clear that the more parents resist or oppose the adolescent's desire to grow up, and deny his or her emerging individuality, the more the boy and girl will be responsive to their age group, conforming to all the changing fads and enthusiasms, following the patterns of the least responsible members of their group.

This is quite understandable since only in the age group or peer culture can the adolescent find the support and encouragement to break away from the family, to rebel against and often to defy their prohibitions and commands, in order to become an individual.

But conforming to the requirements of their age group is not easy and simple, and may involve many painful, unhappy experiences in the effort "to make the grade," to belong, to be accepted. It is especially important to be accepted by members of the other sex, whose approval is essential for adolescents in clarifying their masculine and feminine roles, to assure them that they are capable of being young males or young females.

All the clinical evidence emphasizes the worry of adolescents over their normality, their fear that they are not fully equipped or competent to become men and women.

[3] Bruno Bettelheim, "The Social Studies Teacher and Emotional Needs of Adolescents," *School Review*, December, 1948.

Not a little of the adolescent sexual experimentation expresses, not so much sexual impulses or "passion," or immoral tendencies (as so often asserted), as their urgent need to find reassurance of their sexual normality. Obviously with these continual worries and preoccupations adolescents are under considerable strain and emotionally very touchy—liable to explode at any slight provocation that touches off their accumulated feelings, especially since they are usually psychologically unstable while growing rapidly.

If our secondary schools are to help young people to grow up to become responsible adults, capable of managing their personal lives, they cannot ignore this striving of youth to achieve independence from continued parental control, which at present is expressed largely in sheer rebelliousness, often petulant, impulsive rejection of all adults, at a time when they need understanding and support from adults.

Adolescents want help in clarifying their perplexities, understanding their own impulses and feelings and finding more constructive ways of growing up. They have so many conflicting feelings: guilt over their criticisms and rejection of the family, while resentful at their parents' lack of understanding and frequent obstruction to their growing up. These feelings are legitimate in view of their experiences, but are not constructive nor conducive to learning. Such feelings need to be expressed in group discussions of novels, plays, movies, in role playing, in spontaneous dramatizations, including puppet plays, so that they won't go on festering inside the boy and girl, becoming chronic and so acting as handicaps in their adult lives, especially their marriage and parenthood. They need adults—especially guidance personnel, who genuinely like young people and who, without criticizing, scolding or lecturing, can listen understandingly and let boys and girls talk about their feelings, their aims and aspirations, without imposing their ideas on youth.

Providing opportunities to clarify and release these strong feelings is not a diversion or evasion of the tasks of adolescent education but rather a crucial element in helping adolescents to cope with these problems and to be more ready and capable of achieving their various academic tasks. So long as they are preoccupied with these personal difficulties and distracted by these unrelieved feelings, adolescents can and will give only part of their interest and attention and capacities to school work, in which they should find help in meeting another life task, of proving their competence in achievement.

Every one growing up in our culture feels the strong compulsion to achieve, and in adolescence is expected to show that he or she is capable of meeting the requirements of school and work of some kind. For long we have had a fixed rigid curriculum based upon the expectation that everyone should meet the same requirements, usually of learning material and mastering skills that may or may not have any interest for and relevance to the individual. We reacted against this "lock step" program by establishing very flexible programs, designed to meet the interest and individual capacities of children and youth, but now are finding that these programs are often too unstructured, putting too much of a burden of choice, decision and responsibility upon the young adolescent boy and girl at the very time they are least capable of carrying such burdens.

Adolescents are often irritated, resentful and feeling guilty because they are expected to do school work that has little or no meaning for them, in which they cannot find much that offers satisfaction. They are also often bewildered and made anxious by lack of definite tasks in the extremely "progressive" schools, which fail to give them something they can accept as goals to be achieved.

We are still waiting for secondary school programs that will provide meaningful experiences and achievable tasks for adolescents, avoiding the rigid, set academic curriculum and also the unduly flexible and unstructured curriculum. There should be opportunity for each boy and girl with their individual interests, capacities and their needs, to achieve something that will be meaningful and reassuring to them and accepted by the school and other students as appropriate performance, as evidence of their individual competence. The present situation gives rise to so much unnecessary defeat and humiliation with often lifelong resentment against schools that comes out later in adult antagonisms toward all education.

These are some of the now well recognized occasions for emotional disturbances and conflicts, each indicative of a need for various kinds of help that high schools can and should provide as essential to adolescents' education.

So long as we lived in a more or less stable social order and in an intact culture which provided the guiding beliefs and expectations for living, schools could concentrate upon the tasks of teaching content and skills, relying upon the homes and churches to provide the non-academic aspects of education. But today with the accelerating changes necessary to the development of an industrial civilization, and the breakdown of our traditional patterns, schools, especially high schools, should recognize these urgent problems of youth as their major responsibility.

If teachers and administrators are often perplexed and baffled by these new requirements to recognize the personality of boys and girls, to accept their emotional problems and needs as legitimate responsibilities of education, they should remember that physicians are likewise being expected to enlarge their knowledge and concern, to recognize the personality and emotions of patients as significant features of their illness and their treatment. Indeed every profession and occupation today is being asked to recognize that in all their contacts with people, in all their professional and other work, including business and industrial management, they must be more aware of the human personalities involved.

Indeed the growing concern for human relations is a realization that we all are "feeling our way through life" and that our present day concern is to find ways of managing our emotions and feelings so that we can live more spontaneously and productively, with less of the chronic disturbances, with less of the frequent burdens of anxiety and hostility that so often are crystallized in adolescence into lifelong feelings that block and defeat adult human relations.

Finally it should be remembered that adolescents, being troubled by their often strong feelings and acute emotions, of which they are fearful, especially when taught that emotions are bad, are liable to become rigid and gradually lose their capacity for spontaneous feelings. In the opinion of many psychiatrists this inability to feel and to react emotionally may be the greatest obstacle to their maturation as adults capable of developing the relationships in and through which they can find fulfillment of their sexual and personality needs.

Healthy personalities mean persons who can live and find fulfillment of their needs and aspirations as organism-personalities. The education of the emotions as resources for living more richly and fulfillingly is the great unfinished business of secondary education today.

TO BREAK THE WALL[1]
Evan Hunter

This selection from Evan Hunter's *The Blackboard Jungle* is, in its grim savagery, reminiscent of Alfred Kazin's "Record Book." In both instances, the schools are located in New York and attended by the children of underprivileged parents. The central conflict of "To Break the Wall" is, however, most like that in Edward Eggleston's "A Struggle for the Mastery." In comparing the two selections, the student should note not only the ways in which the plots are alike but also the similarities in character of the two teachers. Which of the two teachers acted more wisely? Why?

More than one critic has been shocked by the roughness of the boys in Evan Hunter's novel. The school, in fact, has often been viewed as a "daytime hangout for juvenile delinquents." A number of educators have felt that this picture may be somewhat exaggerated. What is your opinion? Can you document it with concrete data?

The question of violence, which is at the heart of the Hunter story, is seldom mentioned in textbooks. Is this because violence is so rare in the schools or because writers of texts are generally too idealistic? In this instance, was the violence entirely the fault of the students or did Mr. Dadier bring it, to a degree, upon himself? How would you avoid or handle such a situation?

The door to Room 206 was locked when Richard Dadier reached it for his fifth period English class. He tried the knob several times, peered in through the glass panel, and motioned for Serubi to open the door. Serubi, sitting in the seat closest the door, shrugged his shoulders innocently and grinned. Richard felt again the mixed revulsion and fear he felt before every class.

Easy, he told himself. Easy does it.

He reached into his pocket and slipped the large key into the keyhole. Swinging the door open, he slapped it fast against the prongs that jutted out from the wall, and then walked briskly to his desk.

A falsetto voice somewhere in the back of the room rapidly squeaked, "Daddy-oh!" Richard busied himself with his Delaney book, not looking up at the class. He still remembered that first day, when he had told them his name.

"Mr. Dadier," he had said, and he'd pronounced it carefully. One of the boys had yelled, "Daddy-oh," and the class had roared approval. The name had stuck since then.

Quickly, he glanced around the room, flipping cards over as he took the attendance. Half were absent as usual. He was secretly glad. They were easier to handle in small groups.

He turned over the last card, and waited for them to quiet down. They never would, he knew, never.

Reaching down, he pulled a heavy book

[1] Reprinted with permission of Scott Meredith Literary Agency, Inc.

from his briefcase and rested it on the palm of his hand. Without warning, he slammed it onto the desk.

"Shut up!" he bellowed.

The class groaned into silence, startled by the outburst.

Now, he thought. Now, I'll press it home. Surprise plus advantage plus seize your advantage. Just like waging war. All day long I wage war. Some fun.

"Assignment for tomorrow," Richard said flatly.

A moan escaped from the group. Gregory Miller, a large boy of seventeen, dark-haired, with a lazy sneer and hard, bright eyes said, "You work too hard, Mr. Daddy-oh."

The name twisted deep inside Richard, and he felt the tiny needles of apprehension start at the base of his spine.

"Quiet, Mueller," Richard said, feeling pleasure at mispronouncing the boy's name. "Assignment for tomorrow. In *New Horizons* . . ."

"In what?" Ganigan asked.

I should have known better, Richard reminded himself. We've only been using the book two months now. I can't expect them to remember the title. No.

"In *New Horizons*," he repeated impatiently, "the blue book, the one we've been using all term." He paused, gaining control of himself. "In the blue book," he continued softly, "read the first ten pages of *Army Ants in the Jungle*."

"Here in class?" Hennesy asked.

"No. At home."

"Christ," Hennesy mumbled.

"It's on page two seventy-five," Richard said.

"What page?" Antoro called out.

"Two seventy-five."

"What page?" Levy asked.

"Two seventy-five," Richard said. "My God, what's the matter with you?" He turned rapidly and wrote the figures on the board in a large hand, repeating the numerals slowly. "Two, seven-ty, five." He heard a chuckle spread maliciously behind him, and he whirled quickly. Every boy in the class wore a deadpan.

"There will be a short test on the homework tomorrow," he announced grimly.

"Another one?" Miller asked lazily.

"Yes, Mailler," Richard said, "another one." He glared at the boy heatedly, but Miller only grinned in return.

"And now," Richard said, "the test I promised you yesterday."

A hush fell over the class.

Quick, Richard thought. Press the advantage. Strike again and again. Don't wait for them. Keep one step ahead always. Move fast and they won't know what's going on. Keep them too busy to get into mischief.

Richard began chalking the test on the board. He turned his head and barked over his shoulder, "All books away. Finley, hand out the paper."

This is the way to do it, he realized. I've figured it out. The way to control these monsters is to give them a test every day of the week. Write their fingers off.

"Begin immediately," Richard said in a businesslike voice. "Don't forget your heading."

"What's that, that heading?" Busco asked.

"Name, official class, subject class, subject teacher," Richard said wearily.

Seventy-two, he thought. I've said it seventy-two times since I started teaching here two months ago. Seventy-two times.

"Who's our subject teacher?" Busco asked. His face expressed complete bewilderment.

"Mr. Daddy-oh," Vota said quite plainly. Vota was big and rawboned, a muscular, rangy, seventeen-year-old. Stringy blond hair hung over his pimply forehead. There was something mannishly sinister about his eyes, something boyishly innocent about his smile. And he was

Miller's friend. Richard never forgot that for a moment.

"Mr. Dadier is the subject teacher," Richard said to Busco. "And incidentally, Vito," he glared at Vota, "anyone misspelling my name in the heading will lose ten points."

"What!" Vota complained, outraged.

"You heard me, Vota," Richard snapped.

"Well, how do you spell Daddy-oh?" Vota asked, the innocent smile curling his lips again.

"You figure it out, Vota. I don't need the ten points."

Richard bitterly pressed the chalk into the board. It snapped in two, and he picked up another piece from the runner. With the chalk squeaking wildly, he wrote out the rest of the test.

"No talking," he ordered. He sat down behind the desk and eyed the class suspiciously.

A puzzled frown crossed Miller's face. "I don't understand the first question, teach'," he called out.

Richard leaned back in his chair and looked at the board. "It's very simple, Miltzer," he said. "There are ten words on the board. Some are spelled correctly, and some are wrong. If they're wrong, you correct them. If they're right, spell them just the way they're written."

"Mmmmm," Miller said thoughtfully, his eyes glowing. "How do you spell the second word?"

Richard leaned back again, looked at the second word and began, "D-I-S . . ." He caught himself and faced Miller squarely. "Just the way you want to. You're taking this test, not me."

Miller grinned widely. "Oh. I didn't know that, teach'."

"You'll know when you see your mark, Miller."

Richard cursed himself for having pronounced the boy's name correctly. He made himself comfortable at the desk and looked out over the class.

Di Pasco will cheat, he thought. He will cheat and I won't catch him. He's uncanny that way. God, how I wish I could catch him. How does he? On his cuff? Where? He probably has it stuffed in his ear. Should I search him? No, what's the use? He'd cheat his own mother. An inborn crook. A louse.

Louse, Richard mused. Even I call them that now. All louses. I must tell Helen that I've succumbed. Or should I wait until after the baby is born? Perhaps it would be best not to disillusion her yet. Perhaps I should let her think I'm still trying to reach them, still trying. What was it Solly Klein had said?

"This is the garbage can of the educational system."

He had stood in the teachers' lunchroom, near the bulletin board, pointing his stubby forefinger at Richard.

"And it's our job to sit on the lid and make sure none of this garbage spills over into the street."

Richard had smiled then. He was new, and he still thought he could teach them something, still felt he could mold the clay.

Lou Savoldi, an electrical wiring teacher, had smiled too and said, "Solly's a great philosopher."

"Yeah, yeah, philosopher." Solly smiled. "All I know is I've been teaching machine shop here for twelve years now, and only once did I find anything valuable in the garbage." He had nodded his head emphatically then. "Nobody knowingly throws anything valuable in with the garbage."

Then why should I bother? Richard wondered now. Why should I teach? Why should I get ulcers?

"Keep your eyes on your own paper, Busco," he cautioned.

Everyone is a cheat, a potential thief. Solly was right. We have to keep them off the streets. They should really hire a policeman. It would be funny, he thought, if it weren't so damned serious. How long can you handle garbage without beginning to stink yourself? Already, I stink.

"All right, Busco, bring your paper up. I'm substracting five points from it," Richard suddenly said.

"Why? What the hell did I do?"

"Bring me your paper."

Busco reluctantly slouched to the front of the room and tossed his paper onto the desk. He stood with his thumbs looped in the tops of his dungarees as Richard marked a large —5 on the paper in bright red.

"What's that for?" Busco asked.

"For having loose eyes."

Busco snatched the paper from the desk and examined it with disgust. He wrinkled his face into a grimace and slowly started back to his seat.

As he passed Miller, Miller looked to the front of the room. His eyes met Richard's, and he sneered, "Chicken!"

"What?" Richard asked.

Miller looked surprised. "You talking to me, teach'?"

"Yes, Miller. What did you just say?"

"I didn't say nothing, teach'." Miller smiled.

"Bring me your paper, Miller."

"What for?"

"Bring it up!"

"What for, I said."

"I heard what you said, Miller. And *I* said bring me your paper. Now. Right this minute."

"I don't see why," Miller persisted, the smile beginning to vanish from his face.

"Because I say so, that's why."

Miller's answer came slowly, pointedly. "And supposing I don't feel like?" A frown was twisting his forehead.

The other boys in the room were suddenly interested. Heads that were bent over papers snapped upright. Richard felt every eye in the class focus on him.

They were rooting for Miller, of course. They wanted Miller to win. They wanted Miller to defy him. He couldn't let that happen..

He walked crisply up the aisle and stood beside Miller. The boy looked up provokingly.

"Get up," Richard said, trying to control the modulation of his voice.

My voice is shaking, he told himself. I can feel it shaking. He knows it, too. He's mocking me with those little, hard eyes of his. I must control my voice. This is really funny. My voice is shaking.

"Get up, Miller."

"I don't see, Mr. Daddy-oh, just why I should," Miller answered. He pronounced the name with great care.

"Get up, Miller. Get up and say my name correctly."

"Don't you know your own name, Mr. Daddy-oh?"

Richard's hand snapped out and grasped Miller by the collar of his shirt. He pulled him to his feet, almost tearing the collar. Miller stood a scant two inches shorter than Richard, squirming to release himself.

Richard's hand crushed tighter on the collar. He heard the slight rasp of material ripping. He peered into the hateful eyes and spoke quietly. "Pronounce my name correctly, Miller."

The class had grown terribly quiet. There was no sound in the room now. Richard heard only the grate of his own shallow breathing.

I should let him loose, he thought. What can come of this? How far can I go? *Let him loose!*

"You want me to pronounce your name, sir?" Miller asked.

"You heard me."

"Go to hell, Mr. Daddy . . ."

Richard's fist lashed out, catching the boy squarely across the mouth. He felt his knuckles scrape against hard teeth, saw the blood leap across the upper lip in a thin crimson slash, saw the eyes widen with surprise and then narrow immediately with deep, dark hatred.

And then the knife snapped into view, sudden and terrifying. Long and shining, it caught the pale sunlight that slanted through the long schoolroom windows. Richard backed away involuntarily, eying the sharp blade with respect.

Now what, he thought? Now the garbage can turns into a coffin. Now the garbage overflows. Now I lie dead and bleeding on a schoolroom floor while a moron slashes me to ribbons. Now.

"What do you intend doing with that, Miller?"

My voice is exceptionally calm, he mused. I think I'm frightened, but my voice is calm. Exceptionally.

"Just come a little closer and you'll see," Miller snarled, the blood in his mouth staining his teeth.

"Give me that knife, Miller."

I'm kidding, a voice persisted in Richard's mind. I must be kidding. This is all a big, hilarious joke. I'll die laughing in the morning. I'll die . . .

"Come and get it, Daddy-oh!"

Richard took a step closer to Miller and watched his arm swing back and forth in a threatening arc. Miller's eyes were hard and unforgiving.

And suddenly, Richard caught a flash of color out of the corner of his eye. Someone was behind him! He whirled instinctively, his fist smashing into a boy's stomach. As the boy fell to the floor Richard realized it was Miller's friend Vota. Vota cramped into a tight little ball that writhed and moaned on the floor, and Richard knew that any danger he might have presented was past. He turned quickly to Miller, a satisfied smile clinging to his lips.

"Give me that knife, Miller, and give it to me now."

He stared into the boy's eyes. Miller looked big and dangerous. Perspiration stood out on his forehead. His breath was coming in hurried gasps.

"Give it to me now, Miller, or I'm going to take it from you and beat you black and blue."

He was advancing slowly on the boy.

"Give it to me, Miller. Hand it over," his voice rolled on hypnotically, charged with an undercurrent of threat.

The class seemed to catch its breath together. No one moved to help Vota who lay in a heap on the floor, his arms hugging his waist. He moaned occasionally, squirming violently. But no one moved to help him.

I've got to keep one eye on Vota, Richard figured. He may be playing possum. I have to be careful.

"Hand it over, Miller. Hand it over."

Miller stopped retreating, realizing that he was the one who held the weapon. He stuck the spring-action knife out in front of him, probing the air with it. His back curved into a large C as he crouched over, head low, the knife always moving in front of him as he advanced. Richard held his ground and waited. Miller advanced cautiously, his eyes fastened on Richard's throat, the knife hand moving constantly, murderously, in a swinging arc. He grinned terribly, a red-stained, white smile on his face.

The chair, Richard suddenly remembered. There's a chair. I'll take the chair and swing. Under the chin. No. Across the chest. Fast though. It'll have to be fast, one movement. Wait. Not yet, wait. Come on, Miller. Come on. *Come on!*

Miller paused and searched Richard's face. He grinned again and began speaking softly as he advanced, almost in a whisper, almost as if he were thinking aloud.

"See the knife, Mr. Daddy-oh? See the pretty knife? I'm gonna slash you up real good, Mr. Daddy-oh. I'm gonna slash you, and then I'm gonna slash you some more. I'm gonna cut you up real fine. I'm gonna cut you up so nobody'll know you anymore, Mr. Daddy-oh."

All the while moving closer, closer, swinging the knife.

"Ever get cut, Mr. Daddy-oh? Ever get sliced with a sharp knife? This one is sharp, Mr. Daddy-oh, and you're gonna get cut with it. I'm gonna cut you now, and you're never gonna bother us no more. No more."

Richard backed away down the aisle.

Thoughts tumbled into his mind with blinding rapidity. I'll make him think I'm retreating. I'll give him confidence. The empty seat in the third row. Next to Ganigan. I'll lead him there. I hope it's empty. Empty when I checked the roll. I can't look, I'll tip my hand. Keep a poker face. Come on, Miller, follow me. Follow me so I can crack your ugly skull in two. Come on, you louse. One of us goes, Miller. And it's not going to be me.

"Nossir, Mr. Daddy-oh, we ain't gonna bother with you no more. No more tests, and no more of your noise. Just your face, Mr. Daddy-oh. Just gonna fix your face so nobody'll wanna look at you no more."

One more row, Richard calculated. Back up one more row. Reach. Swing. One. More. Row.

The class followed the two figures with fascination. Miller stalked Richard down the long aisle, stepping forward on the balls of his feet, pace by pace, waiting for Richard to back into the blackboard. Vota rolled over on the floor and groaned again.

And Richard counted the steps. A few more. A . . . few . . . more . . .

"Shouldn't have hit me, Mr. Daddy-oh," Miller mocked. "Ain't nice for teachers to hit students like that, Mr. Daddy-oh. Nossir, it ain't nice at . . ."

The chair crashed into Miller's chest, knocking the breath out of him. It came quickly and forcefully, with the impact of a striking snake. Richard had turned, as if to run, and then the chair was gripped in his hands tightly. It sliced the air in a clean, powerful arc, and Miller covered his face instinctively. The chair crashed into his chest, knocking him backwards. He screamed in surprise and pain as Richard leaped over the chair to land heavily on his chest. Richard pinned Miller's shoulders to the floor with his knees and slapped him ruthlessly across the face.

"Here, Miller, here, here, here," he squeezed through clenched teeth. Miller twisted his head from side to side, trying to escape the cascade of blows that fell in rapid onslaught on his cheeks.

The knife, Richard suddenly remembered! Where's the knife? What did he do with the . . .

Sunlight caught the cold glint of metal, and Richard glanced up instantly. Vota stood over him, the knife clenched tightly in his fist. He grinned boyishly, his rotten teeth flashing across his blotchy, thin face. He spat vehemently at Richard, and then there was a blur of color: blue steel, and the yellow of Vota's hair, and the blood on Miller's lip, and the brown wooden floor, and the gray tweed of Richard's suit. A shout came up from the class, and a hiss seemed to escape Miller's lips.

Richard kicked at Vota, feeling the heavy leather of his shoes crack against the boy's shins. Miller was up and fumbling for Richard's arms. A sudden slice of pain started at Richard's shoulder, careened down the length of his arm. Cloth gave way with a rasping scratch, and blood flashed bright against the gray tweed.

From the floor, Richard saw the knife flash back again, poised in Vota's hand ready to strike. He saw Miller's fists, doubled and hard, saw the animal look on Vota's face, and again the knife, threatening and sharp, drenched now with blood, dripping on the brown, cold, wooden floor.

The noise grew louder and Richard

grasped in his mind for a picture of the Roman arena, tried to rise, felt pain sear through his right arm as he put pressure on it.

He's cut me, he thought with panic. Vota has cut me.

And the screaming reached a wild crescendo, hands moved with terrible swiftness, eyes gleamed with molten fury, bodies squirmed, and hate smothered everything in a sweaty, confused, embarrassed embrace.

This is it, Richard thought, this is it.

"Leave him alone, you crazy jerk," Serubi was shouting.

Leave who alone, Richard wondered. Who? I wasn't . . .

"Lousy sneak," Levy shouted. "Lousy, dirty sneak."

Please, Richard thought. Please, quickly. Please.

Levy seized Miller firmly and pushed him backward against a desk. Richard watched him dazedly, his right arm burning with pain. He saw Busco through a maze of moving, struggling bodies, Busco who was caught cheating, saw Busco smash a book against Vota's knife hand. The knife clattered to the floor with a curious sound. Vota's hand reached out and Di Pasco stepped on it with the heel of his foot. The knife disappeared in a shuffle of hands, but Vota no longer had it. Richard stared at the bare, brown spot on the floor where the knife had been.

Whose chance is it now, he wondered? Whose turn to slice the teacher?

Miller tried to struggle off the desk where Levy had him pinned. Brown, a colored boy, brought his fist down heavily on Miller's nose. He wrenched the larger boy's head back with one hand, and again brought his fist down fiercely.

A slow recognition trickled into Richard's confused thoughts. Through dazzled eyes, he watched.

Vota scrambled to his feet and lunged at him. A solid wall seemed to rise before him as Serubi and Gomez flung themselves against the onrushing form and threw it back. They tumbled onto Vota, holding his arms, lashing out with excited fists.

They're fighting for me! No, Richard reasoned, no. But yes, *they're fighting for me!* Against Miller. Against Vota. For me. For me, oh my God, for me.

His eyes blinked nervously as he struggled to his feet.

"Let's . . . let's take them down to the principal," he said, his voice low.

Antoro moved closer to him, his eyes widening as they took in the livid slash that ran the length of Richard's arm.

"Man, that's some cut," he said.

Richard touched his arm lightly with his left hand. It was soggy and wet, the shirt and jacket stained a dull brownish-red.

"My brother got cut like that once," Ganigan offered.

The boys were still holding Miller and Vota, but they no longer seemed terribly interested in the troublemakers.

For an instant, Richard felt a twinge of panic. For that brief, terrible instant he imagined that the boys hadn't really come to his aid at all, that they had simply seen an opportunity for a good fight and had seized upon it. He shoved the thought aside, began fumbling for words.

"I . . . I think I'd better take them down to Mr. Stemplar," he said. He stared at the boys, trying to read their faces, searching for something in their eyes that would tell him he had at last reached them, had at last broken through the wall. He could tell nothing. Their faces were blank, their eyes emotionless.

He wondered if he should thank them. If only he knew. If he could only hit upon the right thing to say, the thing to cement it all.

"I'll . . . I'll take them down. Suppose

. . . you . . . you all go to lunch now."

"That sure is a mean cut," Julian said.

"Yeah," Ganigan agreed.

"You can all go to lunch," Richard said. "I want to take Miller and Vota . . ."

The boys didn't move. They stood there with serious faces, solemnly watching Richard.

". . . to . . . the . . . principal," Richard finished.

"A hell of a mean cut," Gomez said.

Busco chose his words carefully, and he spoke slowly. "Maybe we better just forget about the principal, huh? Maybe we oughta just go to lunch?"

Richard saw the smile appear on Miller's face, and a new weary sadness lumped into his throat.

He did not pretend to understand. He knew only that they had fought for him and that now, through some unfathomable code of their own, had turned on him again. But he knew what had to be done, and he could only hope that eventually they would understand why he had to do it.

"All right," he said firmly, "let's break it up. I'm taking these two downstairs."

He shoved Miller and Vota ahead of him, fully expecting to meet the resistance of another wall, a wall of unyielding bodies. Instead, the boys parted to let him through, and Richard walked past them with his head high. A few minutes ago, he would have taken this as a sign that the wall had broken. That was a few minutes ago.

Now, he was not at all surprised to hear a high falsetto pipe up behind him, "Oh Daddy-oh! You're a *hee-ro!*"

A REPORT ON HIGH SCHOOL SORORITIES[1]

Isabella Taves

DISCUSSION AND ANALYSIS

It is often remarked that no one feels as strongly about being a part of a group as does the high-school adolescent. He wants to be "in." What does Frank have to say about this emotional need of adolescents in his article in this chapter? How do you think the needs of adolescents contribute to the problem of sororities—and fraternities—as described here?

It is very probable that you will recall incidents from your own high-school career that echo situations mentioned in this article. As you look back on the problem of exclusive clubs, groups, or cliques, what good do you feel was derived? What harm? As a teacher, now, what position do you think you will take on the matter of sororities?

In some places, of course, such clubs are against the law. The teacher then must support the legal position of the school. What things do you think the school can do to prevent the formation of such illegal groups, or to provide such attractive competition that they collapse from sheer lack of followers? In this article Taves quotes a student as saying that the main reason they liked their sorority was because it was one place where

[1] From *McCall's*, April, 1953. Copyright 1953 by McCall Corporation. Reprinted by permission of the author and *McCall's*.

the youngsters felt they were entirely their own bosses. How can the school meet this challenge?

This article, like the one by Morris in this chapter, explores another of the many controversial areas in secondary education. It is perhaps a minor one from some viewpoints. And yet the secondary school is the real social center, the real social life of the majority of adolescents. Therefore decisions made by the school will inevitably affect the kind, the quality, the quantity of social activities. This article is a reminder, in a very dramatic fashion, that education is more than what goes on inside a classroom or is written between the covers of a text.

One fall morning Kendall Howard, principal of Manhasset High School in Long Island, had a telephone call from the mother of a freshman. "I think you should know Sharon won't be at school for a few days," she said. "She took half a bottle of sleeping pills last night because she didn't get a sorority bid. Luckily we found her before it was too late. Mr. Howard, can't you do anything about high-school sororities?"

Mr. Howard does not believe in high-school sororities. He has had them in his school for around ten years. At various times at the School Community Association he had urged that they be abolished. Once he had called a community meeting to discuss the subject in open forum, only to have it boycotted by the faction in favor of sororities and fraternities.

Like many other educators, Mr. Howard is caught in the middle of a baffling situation. A little less than half his student body of 680 belong to sororities and fraternities. Some mothers are against them, including the president of the School Community Association, whose daughter is a sorority girl. They feel that clubs which select their own membership and perpetuate themselves are all wrong in a public school, where students are required by law to attend. But Mr. Howard is having no luck convincing the sorority and fraternity members—and frequently their parents—to disband them. The groups have, however, made certain concessions. At the persuasion of the school board they selected a sorority and a fraternity adviser from the faculty. They abolished the blackball and now elect members by popular vote. Last year, for the first time, they agreed not to pledge any freshmen. Now the president of the Inter-Fraternity Council says: "We've made our concessions. It's time for the Board of Education to make some to us."

About the only comfort for officials at Manhasset High School is that they are not alone in their problem. Over the country today, it is one of the most troublesome issues facing the P.T.A.'s and the high schools. Practically all educators deplore secret groups for their antidemocratic aspects and for the heart-ache they cause the rejected students as well. They deplore too the tendency of members to start drinking and smoking before they would otherwise. But few places have had the authority or the courage to abolish secret societies completely. For one thing, the students themselves won't let them get away with it. Even those who aren't greatly interested in societies will rise and fight when they feel the authorities are pushing them around. Parents usually not only stand behind the youngsters but are often out in front screaming "Unfair" and "Bullies." At one school in Ohio, and another in suburban Chicago, the principal and superintendent got rid of fraternities and sororities, only to have the parents practically get rid of the principal and the superintendent.

Paul E. Elicker, executive secretary of the National Association of Secondary-School Principals, says it is impossible to give an accurate count of secret societies because in twenty-five states they are prohibited or restricted by law and the high schools won't admit they have the problem. But his guess is that about 500 to 600 schools over the country have them—a fairly formidable number when you figure that only 650 senior high schools throughout the country have an enrollment of more than 1,000. Most sororities and fraternities exist in large senior high schools near big cities or colleges.

Some schools make the societies call themselves social clubs and put them under faculty control. Others, like White Plains, New York, consider sororities and fraternities outside the function of the school and permit them to exist only as community clubs. Still others have tried to eliminate them by the slow-death method, as in Lansdowne, Pennsylvania, where the sororities and fraternities have been allowed to keep going as long as they don't pledge new members. (By this June, Lansdowne hopes to be rid of the problem.)

Sororities and fraternities create the worst difficulty in places where, forbidden by law, they have gone underground. I am told this situation exists in many large cities, especially in the Great Lakes region, although school officials there insisted blandly that they knew nothing about them. The undergrounds have no school supervision. Frequently they take in older people who, instead of acting as checks, encourage gambling and drinking. Their "shindigs" extend to mixed week-ends at camps and roadhouses. One teacher told me: "These are supposedly nice kids, from our best families. I don't know what the parents are thinking of—or if the kids pull so much wool over their eyes that they don't know anything about it. But everything goes on—everything."

On July 18, 1949, a newspaper article datelined Lavalette, New Jersey (secret societies are illegal in New Jersey), began: "Mayor Chandler said teen-age sorority and fraternity groups have been renting cottages and raising 'Holy Hell' completely without morals and without restraint."

And in a suburb of Detroit (secret societies are illegal also in Michigan) a mixed "shindig" at the home of one of the parents resulted in fraternities and sororities being thrown out of the schools. A sorority meeting was held at the home of one of the girls. Her parents, as usual, were told they had to go out. That night the mother and father went around the corner to a bridge party. Toward the middle of the evening they came home to pick up some extra glasses for their host. Numerous cars were parked in front of the house, and they quickly realized that a fraternity group had "crashed" the meeting—a common practice all over the country.

The girl's father went down to the recreation room to see how things were going. He found the lights out. When he switched them on, several of the boys and girls had to grab their clothes hastily. He and his wife called the mothers and fathers of every boy and girl there, and in the resultant scandal sororities and fraternities were swept out of the high school.

The principal of White Plains High School in New York told me: "It's a parents' problem. Most of them think sororities and fraternities are terrible—until their children join. Then they think they are fine."

It is true that modern-day parents are careful not to do anything that will conceivably harm their youngsters with the group. Over and over I heard the statement: "I don't like the idea of sororities, but as long as they have them I want our daughter to belong."

I found some parents unwilling to talk because they feared the disapproval of neighbors. If the son or daughter of a neighbor is a "big wheel" in a fraternity or sorority, they refuse to fight them, no matter what their personal feelings.

A Long Island father, a lawyer, has one standard answer when sororities are mentioned (his daughter belongs to one): "These are purely social clubs, and no high-school principal or teacher has any right to tell my girl or any other girl whether she can belong or not."

Another argument which I heard everywhere is: "I belong to a lot of clubs which don't admit everyone. So does my wife. Even our little boy is a member of a Boy Scout troop that uses the blackball. Of course sororities and fraternities are undemocratic. But so is life."

And still another—and this has been a potent influence among the Boards of Education: "All the best kids belong. If we kicked out everybody who is in a fraternity or sorority we wouldn't have a football or a basketball team."

When I asked one mother about the girls who took rejection so hard that they tried to kill themselves or run away, I got this sharp answer: "Are we to suffer for every girl so emotionally unstable that she tries to commit suicide over a little disappointment? What about the girls who come to the big city to be models and jump out windows when they don't make the grade? Do we abolish modeling to protect them?"

All these arguments are logical—so logical that you can't blame a high-school principal for shelving social clubs and turning to some other problem, of which high schools have plenty.

Some schools where societies have never existed have found it necessary to allow them. For example, Jordan High School in Long Beach, California, didn't have them for six years, although the two other high schools in town did. In 1933, when the school was founded, the students themselves voted against secret societies. But by 1939 Dr. John Wilson, the principal, found that the boys and girls were forming underground groups or joining groups in the other schools. He called the students together, and this time they voted to lift the ban. Now about 10 per cent of the student body belongs to eight sororities and one fraternity. The sororities and fraternities are open organizations, however, with their memberships on file with school authorities, and each organization is required to have both a faculty and a parent supervisor at all meetings.

In other communities minority groups of youngsters who find themselves rejected form their own clubs. In Mamaroneck High School, New York, the rejected girls of Italian extraction formed an Italian sorority. Some schools with large Negro enrollments have extremely exclusive Negro sororities and fraternities. In Manhasset, for example, a Negro football player was asked to join one of the white fraternities which went in for athletes. He was friendly with many of the white boys, but he refused them and joined the Gaylords, a Negro group.

Parents of left-out youngsters seldom fight the secret societies in any public way. They are afraid the term "sour grapes" will be hurled at them. Nor do they want to hurt their children further.

I talked to a mother in Flint, Michigan, who had faced much social disapproval of both herself and her daughter when she insisted that her daughter resign from the Lambdas, the "best" sorority in Central High School.

Her daughter, Judy, was rushed by the Lambdas when she entered senior high. But she was not bid, and Judy and her mother were both disappointed. The Lambdas explained she was too young—although they had taken younger girls. However, they pledged her the following semester. And then the trouble began.

Pledging at Central High lasts from October until late spring. During all those months the pledges are subjected to hazing by the "actives." They have no time for other school activities and little even for routine schoolwork. A teacher told me: "We make no effort, of course, to find out who joins and who doesn't. But we can spot immediately a girl or boy who is pledged, for their grades go down."

Judy and the other pledges were busy every minute of the day and night doing chores for the "actives." Meetings were held on school nights. Afterward they were crashed by fraternity members. No parents were allowed in the house if the Lambda Phis were using it for a meeting. One mother came home and found a beautiful dining-room table broken in half. But Judy's mother was more concerned about temptations for a young girl, because one of the fraternities in school boasted it was a "drinking and gambling" fraternity. However, she decided to wait until initiation before she went into that.

"All the pledges were so worn out they were in near-hysteria," Judy's mother told me. "Judy came down with a virus, she was so exhausted. I wouldn't let her go out right after her temperature was normal, so she told the rest of the pledges to come to our house to rehearse their stunt for next week's shindig. They were all down in the recreation room, and I was making cookies as a treat. Suddenly two active Lambdas stormed in our front door and rushed down to the recreation room. They called those pledges every name in the dictionary for daring to be at my house when the pledge meeting was supposed to be held someplace else. Maybe I shouldn't have, but I blew my top. I made Judy resign. Her best friend resigned with her. She was miserable all through high school. Now she's in college and has made the best sorority. I tell myself that she is getting a much bigger kick out of it than if the whole sorority idea had been spoiled by belonging to the Lambdas. But maybe I'm just rationalizing."

A mother of two high-school boys took me aside afterward. "I felt terribly sorry for Judy," she said. "After she resigned my boys paid no attention to her. When I scolded them they told me that fraternity boys don't take out nonsorority girls. Even at school dances they gave her the brush because they said they didn't have anything to talk to her about any more."

The young woman who is faculty director of social clubs in a Michigan high school told me: "I dread pledging time. Hysterical parents phone me constantly, begging me to do something. Their daughters have locked themselves in their rooms and won't eat. Or they have packed their bags and are threatening to run away. I can't do much. But occasionally I am able to talk to a sorority or fraternity and ask them to reconsider some girl or boy they have rejected without much thought. It means a lot to me to save even one youngster's heartache. But think of the ones I can't help."

In Mamaroneck a suicide and the hospitalization of five boys for injuries during pledging sparked an investigation which has resulted in sororities and fraternities there being given the slow-death treatment —no new pledges. About ten years ago at White Plains a girl killed herself allegedly because her sister did not make her high-school sorority. Dr. Darl Long, the principal, was not with the school at that time. He says, however, that he learned there were far deeper reasons for her suicide. But the unsavory publicity in the New York papers was a major factor in the high school's decision to rid the campus of social clubs.

Faculty advisers tell me that many more girls are taken out of public school for sorority reasons than the students ever know. One explained: "It is unfair to say that a teen-age girl is unstable because she tries to run away or cut her wrists when she isn't taken into a sorority and the rest of her friends are. We all get rejected as we go through life. But early teens are a crucial period, and sometimes a rejection at this period is more than a sensitive child can take. I've seen girls—and boys too—so deeply wounded that I doubt if they will ever forget it. To me, and to the mothers of these particular kids, no sorority, no matter how much good it does, should exist when it has the power to hurt so bitterly."

Other mothers feel almost as strongly on the other side. A Birmingham mother said: "My twin girls got enormous benefits from their social club. They had always gone around with each other, a clique of two. They didn't even have dates with boys. The club brought them out and made a wonderful difference. They began to operate as separate individuals."

Shy boys and girls often get so much from the sense of "belonging" to a special group that parents cannot help being delighted. Some mothers, too, find that strong-minded youngsters who reject advice from their parents often accept it gracefully and gratefully from their "sisters" and "brothers."

I know a Los Angeles mother who is now enthusiastic about societies, although she once hated them. She has three daughters. The oldest, Martha, was a studious girl who wasn't asked to join one of the social clubs. The mother was very bitter about the groups and blamed them for giving Martha an inferiority complex that made her decide not to go to college. Then the two younger daughters went to high school. Both of them were bid to social groups, and their mother has seen the other side of the question. She likes what she has seen.

She says: "In a high school the size of ours the girls must have a feeling of belonging to something besides a student body of 2,400." She also thinks that the older girls have done a wonderful job of filing down the rough edges of the young initiates, and she admires the police job a sorority does on its members. "They know what is going on," she explains, "which isn't always true of mothers, no matter how hard they try. And the girls disapprove of any actions which might hurt the reputation of the group as a whole. I know instances of pledges who have been called up before the chapter and threatened with expulsion if they didn't stop drinking or necking."

But once in a while parents, interested as they are in their children's happiness, can find high-school social groups too tough to take. A Flint mother, wife of an important executive, told me:

"We thought it was fine when Jean made a sorority. But pretty soon we found ourselves going crazy. The telephone rang all day and night. At midnight she would be sent way across town to deliver some silly package to an 'active.' I wouldn't dream of letting her go alone, so I would pile out of bed and drive her. My husband began asking who was the Lambda pledge, me or Jean. The phone simply drove him out of his mind. Once we counted—it rang thirty times in one evening, all Lambda calls. And that wasn't just a rare occasion. Jean's dad is indulgent in most ways, but this was more than he could take and still do *his* job. He yanked Jean out of school and sent her East."

Education wouldn't be human if they didn't resent groups that take so much of a student's time and divide his loyalty—with the school invariably coming off second best. Dr. L. S. Michael, superintendent of Evanston Township High School in

Illinois, told me about the "stickwiths" that the groups used to hold before sororities and fraternities were banned at Evanston.

"A sorority or maybe a group of fraternities and sororities would decide they didn't approve of some event. They would hold a stickwith. All the people in the groups had to stick with each other and boycott it. I remember once we had a school dance and hardly any of the committee turned up because they were all in the stickwith."

Sororities and fraternities can seem to be extremely helpful to the school. In Manhasset last year the sororities put a hospital fund drive over the top. In Birmingham High School, Michigan, fraternities and sororities stepped in with already rehearsed acts and saved a school play. In Evanston, when Dr. Michael was trying to convince sororities that they should disband, they offered to perform all kinds of useful and necessary services to the school. But Dr. Michael finally had to tell them: "The only real service you can do the school is to break up." This is the way almost all educators feel.

For, more than once, high-school principals confessed to me that they had been put in the embarrassing position of having to check with the interfraternity council before they scheduled a school event. The leaders in school are usually fraternity and sorority members, and if they don't get behind the event its chances of success are pretty slim.

School officials have adequate legal authority to deal with the secret-society problem, but few educators are willing to resort to law. It has been done, but the resentment of students and parents afterward tends to create an unhealthy school atmosphere. Legal action would give sororities and fraternities good excuse to go underground and often would cause schools and principals more headaches than before. Then, too, the authorities don't always win.

Flint, Michigan, is one case in point where the educators didn't win. The test occurred after the senior-high school president was thrown out of office by the school after he and some other fraternity boys drank beer during a school play in which they were members of the chorus. A new election was ordered, and the faculty said no fraternity boys could run—citing the Michigan law which says that secret societies composed chiefly of high-school students are illegal. One boy challenged the edict. He hired a lawyer. After examining the case the school's lawyer admitted that the hitch was in the word "chiefly." Flint sororities and fraternities take members from private and parochial schools as well as from Central High. The boy was permitted to enter the race. He didn't win; in fact, he ran a poor third in a group of three candidates, and a nonfraternity Negro boy was elected. However, the legality of sororities and fraternities is now established in Flint, despite the state law.

When the sorority and fraternity problem was being contested in Birmingham, Michigan, students planned to get around the law by having their parents sign the membership lists so that they would not be composed chiefly of high-school students. But the school persuaded the groups to "disband" and form themselves into social clubs which function like the old sororities but have different names, like Tiara, Tri-A, Emerald Key and Black & White. By changing them to club status, the high school managed to put them under control of a social-club director. Students must make a C average to be initiated, personnel must be listed with the director, all meetings and social events must be cleared with her office, no 9th or 10-B graders can be pledged, and the director has a right to visit a club meeting any time she wishes, or to call and check to be sure parents are there as chaperons. Youngsters who are not bid are encouraged to form groups of their own, and occasionally a new group, by choosing leaders, becomes as powerful as the established clubs.

There is no question that sororities are the crux of the secret-society problem. If the girls can be persuaded to give up their groups the fraternities will hardly put up a struggle. In Evanston the fraternities had willingly offered to disband, and the sororities knew it, but the girls fought to the last ditch before they gave up—and even afterward tried to form underground groups.

The president of the Manhasset interfraternity council—a girl, and a pretty one—explained it to me: "A girl has to be asked for dates. A boy, even if he isn't anything special, doesn't have to be a fraternity man to go out."

At Manhasset the boys wear blazers with their fraternity insignia almost a foot high on the backs. (The school has designed a Manhasset jacket with "Manhasset" on the back to compete with them.) The girls wear discreet pins and blazers without identifying Greek letters, because, as one explained to me, "we think ostentation is in bad taste."

In Manhasset I invited a group of girls to talk over sororities with me. They were not only willing but eager. They came in such numbers that the small office we had chosen became overcrowded. They were all vocal.

One of the first questions I was asked was: "Why don't you think sororities are a good thing?"

I had not said a word one way or the other, but the fact that I was introduced by the faculty immediately tagged me. I answered this question with one of my own: "What about the girls who don't get in?"

A pretty brunette frowned at me. "Adults have the warped idea that a girl who doesn't make a sorority is a social ruin. That's ridiculous. She can do lots of things."

"Such as?"

"Well, school things. Manhasset has plenty of activities. And nonsorority girls are welcome. This year three out of our fourteen cheerleaders are nonsorority."

"Aren't you sorry for the girls who don't belong?" I persisted.

One girl piped up: "You aren't going to get everything you want all your life. If you can't take it now, you never will be able to. It's just life."

I talked about this matter with girls in Flint and Birmingham, Michigan. I found out that little sympathy is wasted on the nonsorority girls—in fact, little thought. Occasionally a "strong" girl will be mentioned who either refused to join a group or was stimulated by rejection into proving herself. These girls are apt to be not only leaders but top leaders, with added maturity because they have not merged their identity with groups.

Charity work was mentioned at some length. Not all the sororities do charity or civic work, but it is a growing trend in Manhasset, as elsewhere. A cynical observer told me: "It's their attempt to justify themselves. I can often see the fine hand of their mothers in the projects, and every once in a while the mothers step in and finish what the kids leave undone. For you just can't expect girls of that age to have well-developed social conscience as well as follow-through ability. Sometimes they make funny boners. I remember one sorority held a big plushy dance at our biggest country club and announced it was for charity. They were going to send *a* Christmas basket to *a* poor family."

I asked the Manhasset girls if sororities and fraternities weren't undemocratic. An attractive girl answered: "I think sororities are a lot more democratic than cliques.

When I was in eighth grade we had a clique we called The Big 13. It was much worse than any sorority. We just didn't speak to the girls who didn't belong. In my high-school sorority there are about fifty girls. I'm not best friends with them all, of course. But I've gotten to know a lot more girls fairly well than I would have otherwise, some of the younger girls especially. It has done me a lot of good."

Just before the session ended a question arose that troubles educators everywhere. Do high-school sororities and fraternities fill a gap in the school's outside activities? Manhasset, members of the faculty feel, does not seem to have a gap that needs filling. "Don't we have enough social life at school?" The girls were asked: "What need is the school failing to satisfy that makes you girls feel the necessity for sororities?"

One quick girl fired back: "Nothing! Don't you people realize that we get sick of being told by our teachers and parents how to amuse ourselves. Once in a while we want to do something on our own."

This necessity to "do something on our own," without teacher or parent supervision, is general. But high-school initiations often belie the ability of youngsters to act grown-up. There is a tinge of sadism in most initiations. The theory of them is to deflate the ego of the pledge and see if he or she can "take it." But behind the theory is sometimes just a little human urge to try to inflict hurt on someone else, to make up for your own hurts.

Although paddling and physical tests are prohibited by the national Inter-Fraternity Congress (operating in high schools) and many schools have strict penalties, the attempts of authorities and idealistic alumni to convert "Hell Week" into "Help Week" (where pledges help some community project or paint a neighbor's barn) have not taken much hold. Paddling is still practiced fairly widely in high-school fraternity initiations. Where it does not exist there are usually physical tests which are equally uncomfortable, if not so dangerous.

It is common practice to blindfold pledges and drive them to faraway beaches or woods, where they are left to find their way home without money—sometimes without shoes. Recently in White Plains older boys (not high-school students) drove a high-school sophomore and a town boy to Bear Mountain, a long distance home by foot. After being paddled, the initiates were left alone. It was a cold night, so they broke into a cabin and burned furniture to keep warm until daybreak. Later it became a matter for the police. But in this case the high school was not responsible, for White Plains fraternities and sororities are now exclusively community organizations.

Sororities deplore the practice of paddling and the bad name that incidents of broken legs and hospitalized pledges give Greek letter groups. Harm is seldom premeditated, but occurs through lack of judgment or restraint. However, the resultant publicity often hurts all Greek letter clubs. Sororities sometimes indulge in a kidding kind of paddling. Some of the Birmingham clubs frighten the girl pledges by making them bring their own paddles—but almost never is anyone physically hurt. However, there are tests to see if future members can "take it."

"My sister was a wreck after initiation," one boy told me. "She came home in such hysterics my mother wanted to call the doctor. She screamed and begged Mom not to. She said the other girls would persecute her more if they found out. The girls had made all sorts of fun of her, said she was knock-kneed and boy-crazy and that I was a drip. They even made fun of Mom and Dad. Of course she was tired out from the rest of those silly pledging stunts, and this was the last straw. I think paddling is humane beside this sort of thing."

One trick that is used to stir up girls is to tell thirteen pledges that only twelve are to be initiated. The pledges are put into a room together and are interviewed one by one. Toward the end the remaining girls inevitably become frantic. Parents at whose houses the initiations are held often have to calm down really bad cases of hysteria. Many sororities also use some form of a "hash session" to make the incoming pledge cry. In one sorority each girl is brought separately into a darkened room and made to stand in the middle of the floor while her prospective "sisters" tell her every mean thing they can think of until the girl breaks down.

"Then the lights are turned up, and your sorority mother and everybody kisses you," a happy initiate told me. "It doesn't mean a thing, really. But at the time you think you are going to die. My best friend was the horridest."

The problem of high-school fraternities and sororities is not new. They have existed in Evanston since 1890 and in White Plains since 1893. The Evanston organization was called L.S.C.—Literary and Science Club—and the White Plains group was called Alpha Alpha Literary Society.

When Dr. Michael came to Evanston four years ago, L.S.C. was still the "best" fraternity in school. It attracted the most carefully brought up boys, because it forbade smoking and drinking and concentrated on standards and ideals. Said Dr. Michael: "If I had had a son coming into Evanston High School I would have wanted him to belong to L.S.C." But he did not want sororities and fraternities at Evanston. And when he brought the matter up before the students he was gratified but not surprised when L.S.C. was the first to offer to disband.

In Evanston, "Y" clubs for girls and boys have taken care of the joining urge. These, although they are under the supervision of the Y.M.C.A., are selective clubs which meet at the homes of their members. But they are not self-perpetuating. The clubs break up when the group of members is graduated. Any group of friends can form a club. "Y" clubs existed while Evanston had Greek letter societies, but now they have assumed new importance. Mothers who previously knew noththing about them work with the "Y" to improve club leadership. So far as Dr. Michael knows, no fraternity or sorority has succeeded in forming underground groups, and he gives the credit for this to the students themselves.

Wherever the sorority and fraternity problem has been successfully resolved I found the educators giving the bows to the pupils. At White Plains High School, now that sororities and fraternities exist openly in the town, students are conscientious about not holding meetings or wearing secret identification on the school grounds. At other places where the slow-death method of no new pledges was followed the cooperation of both fraternity members and new students was evident.

Florence Riddell, assistant principal of Central High School in Flint, told me she thinks the best way to combat sororities and fraternities is not through rules and restrictions but through a systematic and patient program of education in the grade and junior high schools.

One Los Angeles High School sophomore, member of Vogue, the "best" social club there, said that she entered high school with a "strong" group of about twenty girls who were considered leaders and were wanted by all the clubs. The twenty held long discussions about clubs and decided they would refuse as a group. Then one or two weakened and the whole group joined.

One problem in persuading girls in

grade school and junior high against sororities is that the arguments are always negative. Girls are being asked *not* to do something while the sororities offer them definite action. Youngsters who pledge feel very "hep" because to them secret societies seem very modern.

But that, strangely enough, is where they are wrong. Says Dr. Darl Long of White Plains High School: "These groups started back in the days when a high school meant a place of higher learning. Only the exceptional student went to college, and the high-school clubs had an intellectual and social purpose. Today over half of our 1,450 senior-high-school students go on to college. High-school fraternities and sororities no longer have a reason for being. They are archaic."

A California mother whose daughter belongs to a club at Los Angeles High School said to me: "I think the whole idea of high-school fraternities and sororities is thirty years behind the times. Beside college groups they're small-time. Beside all the other fascinating activities a modern high school offers its students they are a waste of time. I'm waiting until some of these modern girls find out for themselves."

I talked to one modern girl who has found out. She is a senior in the Shades Valley High School in Alabama. Her name is Barbara Brown. She was homecoming queen. She and Charles Kidd, a school athlete, have gone before the County Board of Education asking that high-school fraternities and sororities be banned in the school. Both are former members.

Says Barbara: "Sixty per cent of the freshman class and ninety per cent of the seniors are opposed to them. Student activity programs have completely taken their place. And they aren't in keeping with the times. I think in high school today we ought to know everybody and learn to get along with all kinds of people. Charles and I would like to see high-school sororities and fraternities banned everywhere. Since we can't do that, we want to take them out of this school."

14 HIGHER EDUCATION

UNIVERSITY DAYS[1]

James Thurber

DISCUSSION AND ANALYSIS

The student should be close enough to his own introduction to college life to appreciate fully Mr. Thurber's inimitable humor. Behind this humor lies a wealth of observation and sharp comment. If we can see that Mr. Thurber's bewilderment as a student was quite normal in view of the circumstances, then perhaps we can criticize the circumstances. What can we say of the curriculum? Was it adapted to the needs of the students, or was it the aim of the college to adapt students to the curriculum? Which course of action seems preferable to you? Study Ordway Tead's article in this same chapter. What comment might Dr. Tead make on the kinds of courses and activities Mr. Thurber had to undertake? Usually, when we encounter our own shortcomings, as Mr. Thurber did when he tried to see through the microscope, the situation strikes us as painful. How, then, does the author give it a comic air? Is a sense of humor helpful to students? To teachers? How?

I passed all the other courses that I took at my University, but I could never pass botany. This was because all botany students had to spend several hours a week in a laboratory looking through a microscope at plant cells, and I could never see through a microscope. I never once saw a cell through a microscope. This used to enrage my instructor. He would wander around the laboratory pleased with the progress all the students were making in drawing the involved and, so I am told, interesting structure of flower cells, until he came to me. I would just be standing there. "I can't see anything," I would say. He would begin patiently enough, explaining how anybody can see through a microscope, but he would always end up in a fury, claiming that I could *too* see through a microscope but just pretended that I couldn't. "It takes away from the beauty of flowers anyway," I used to tell him.

[1] Copyright 1933 James Thurber. Originally in *The New Yorker*. In *The Thurber Carnival*, Harper & Brothers, 1945.

"We are not concerned with beauty in this course," he would say. "We are concerned solely with what I may call the *mechanics* of flars." "Well," I'd say, "I can't see anything." "Try it just once again," he'd say, and I would put my eye to the microscope and see nothing at all, except now and again a nebulous milky substance—a phenomenon of maladjustment. You were supposed to see a vivid, restless clockwork of sharply defined plant cells. "I see what looks like a lot of milk," I would tell him. This, he claimed, was the result of my not having adjusted the microscope properly, so he would readjust it for me, or rather, for himself. And I would look again and see milk.

I finally took a deferred pass, as they called it, and waited a year and tried again. (You had to pass one of the biological sciences or you couldn't graduate.) The professor had come back from vacation brown as a berry, bright-eyed, and eager to explain cell-structure again to his classes. "Well," he said to me, cheerily, when we met in the first laboratory hour of the semester, "we're going to see cells this time, aren't we?" "Yes, sir," I said. Students to right of me and to left of me and in front of me were seeing cells, what's more, they were quietly drawing pictures of them in their notebooks. Of course, I didn't see anything.

"We'll try it," the professor said to me, grimly, "with every adjustment of the microscope known to man. As God is my witness, I'll arrange this glass so that you can see cells through it or I'll give up teaching. In twenty-two years of botany, I—" He cut off abruptly for he was beginning to quiver all over, like Lionel Barrymore, and he genuinely wished to hold onto his temper; his scenes with me had taken a great deal out of him.

So we tried it with every adjustment of the microscope known to man. With only one of them did I see anything but blackness or the familiar lacteal opacity, and that time I saw, to my pleasure and amazement, a variegated constellation of flecks, specks, and dots. These I hastily drew. The instructor, noting my activity, came back from an adjoining desk, a smile on his lips and his eyebrows high in hope. He looked at my cell drawing. "What's that?" he demanded, with a hint of a squeal in his voice. "That's what I saw," I said. "You didn't, you didn't, you *did*n't!" he screamed, losing control of his temper instantly, and he bent over and squinted into the microscope. His head snapped up. "That's your eye!" he shouted. "You've fixed the lens so that it reflects! You've drawn your eye!"

Another course that I didn't like, but somehow managed to pass, was economics. I went to that class straight from the botany class, which didn't help me any in understanding either subject. I used to get them mixed up. But not as mixed up as another student in my economics class who came there direct from a physics laboratory. He was a tackle on the football team, named Bolenciecwcz. At that time Ohio State University had one of the best football teams in the country, and Bolenciecwcz was one of its outstanding stars. In order to be eligible to play it was necessary for him to keep up in his studies, a very difficult matter, for while he was not dumber than an ox he was not any smarter. Most of his professors were lenient and helped him along. None gave him more hints, in answering questions, or asked him simpler ones than the economics professor, a thin, timid man named Bassum. One day when we were on the subject of transportation and distribution, it came Bolenciecwcz's turn to answer a question. "Name one means of transportation," the professor said to him. No light came into the big tackle's eyes. "Just any means of transportation," said the professor. Bolenciecwcz sat staring at him. "That is," pursued the professor, "any medium, agency, or method of going from one place to another." Bolenciecwcz had the look of a man who is being led into a trap. "You may choose among steam, horse-drawn, or electrically propelled vehicles," said the instructor. "I might suggest the one which we commonly take in making long journeys across land." There was a profound silence in which everybody stirred uneasily, including Bolenciecwcz and Mr. Bassum. Mr. Bassum abruptly broke this silence in an amazing manner. "Choo-choo-choo," he said, in a low voice, and turned instantly scarlet. He glanced appealingly around the room. All of us, of course, shared Mr. Bassum's desire that Bolenciecwcz should stay abreast of the class in economics, for the Illinois game, one of the hardest and most important of the season, was only a week off. "Toot, toot, too-tooooooot!" some student with a deep voice moaned, and we all looked encouragingly at Bolenciecwcz. Somebody else gave a fine imitation of a locomotive letting off steam. Mr. Bassum himself rounded off the little show. "Ding, dong, ding, dong," he said, hopefully. Bolenciecwcz was staring at the floor now, trying to think, his great brow furrowed, his huge hands rubbing together, his face red.

"How did you come to college this year, Mr. Bolenciecwcz?" asked the professor. "*Chuf*fa chuffa, *chuf*fa chuffa."

"M'father sent me," said the football player.

"What on?" asked Bassum.

"I git an 'lowance," said the tackle, in a low, husky voice, obviously embarrassed.

"No, no," said Bassum. "Name a means of transportation. What did you *ride* here on?"

"Train," said Bolenciecwcz.

"Quite right," said the professor. "Now, Mr. Nugent, will you tell us ——"

If I went through anguish in botany and economics—for different reasons—gymnasium work was even worse. I don't even like to think about it. They wouldn't let you play games or join in the exercises with your glasses on and I couldn't see with mine off. I bumped into professors, horizontal bars, agricultural students, and swinging iron rings. Not being able to see, I could take it but I couldn't dish it out. Also, in order to pass gymnasium (and you had to pass it to graduate) you had to learn to swim if you didn't know how. I didn't like the swimming pool, I didn't like swimming, and I didn't like the swimming instructor, and after all these years I still don't. I never swam but I passed my gym work anyway, by having another student give my gymnasium number (978) and swim across the pool in my place. He was a quiet, amiable blonde youth, number 473, and he would have seen through a microscope for me if we could have got away with it, but we couldn't get away with it. Another thing I didn't like about gymnasium work was that they made you strip the day you registered. It is impossible for me to be happy when I am stripped and being asked a lot of questions. Still, I did better than a lanky agricultural student who was cross-examined just before I was. They asked each student what college he was in—that is, whether Arts, Engineering, Commerce, or Agriculture. "What college are you in?" the instructor snapped at the youth in front of me. "Ohio State University," he said promptly.

It wasn't that agricultural student but it was another a whole lot like him who decided to take up journalism, possibly on the ground that when farming went to hell he could fall back on newspaper work. He didn't realize, of course, that that would be very much like falling back full-length on a kit of carpenter's tools. Haskins didn't seem cut out for journalism, being too embarrassed to talk to anybody and unable to use a typewriter, but the editor of the college paper assigned him to the cow barns, the sheep house, the horse pavilion, and the animal husbandry department generally. This was a genuinely big "beat," for it took up five times as much ground and got ten times as great a legislative appropriation as the College of Liberal Arts. The agricultural student knew animals, but nevertheless his stories were dull and colorlessly written. He took all afternoon on each of them, on account of having to hunt for each letter on the typewriter. Once in a while he had to ask somebody to help him hunt. "C" and "L," in particular, were hard letters for him to find. His editor finally got pretty much annoyed at the farmer-journalist because his pieces were so uninteresting. "See here, Haskins," he snapped at him one day, "why is it we never have anything hot from you on the horse pavilion? Here we have two hundred head of horses on this campus—more than any other university in the Western Conference except Purdue—and yet you never get any real low down on them. Now shoot over to the horse barns and dig up something lively." Haskins shambled out and came back in about an hour; he said he had something. "Well, start it off snappily," said the editor. "Something people will read." Haskins set to work and in a couple of hours brought a sheet of typewritten paper to the desk; it was a two-hundred word story about some disease that had broken out among the horses. Its opening sentence was simple but arresting. It read: "Who has noticed the sores on the tops of the horses in the animal husbandry building?"

Ohio State was a land grant university and therefore two years of military drill was compulsory. We drilled with old Springfield rifles and studied the tactics of the Civil War even though the World War was going on at the time. At 11 o'clock each morning thousands of freshmen and sophomores used to deploy over the campus, moodily creeping up on the old chemistry building. It was good training for the kind of warfare that was waged at Shiloh but it had no connection with what was going on in Europe. Some people used to think there was German money behind it, but they didn't dare say so or they would have been thrown in jail as German spies. It was a period of muddy thought and marked, I believe, the decline of higher education in the Middle West.

As a soldier I was never any good at all. Most of the cadets were glumly indifferent soldiers, but I was no good at all. Once General Littlefield, who was commandant of the cadet corps, popped up in front of me during regimental drill and snapped, "You are the main trouble with this university!" I think he meant that my type was the main trouble with the university but he may have meant me individually. I was mediocre at drill, certainly—that is, until my senior year. By that time I had drilled longer than anybody else in the Western Conference, having failed at military at the end of each preceding year so that I had to do it all over again. I was the only senior still in uniform. The uniform which, when new, had made me look like an interurban railway conductor, now that it had become faded and too tight made me look like Bert Williams in his bellboy act. This had a definitely bad effect on my morale. Even so, I had become by sheer practice little short of wonderful at squad manoeuvres.

One day General Littlefield picked our company out of the whole regiment and tried to get it mixed up by putting it through one movement after another as fast as we could execute them: squads right, squads left, squads on right into line, squads right about, squads left front into line etc. In about three minutes one hundred and nine men were marching in one direction and I was marching away from them at an angle of forty degrees, all alone.

"Company, halt!" shouted General Littlefield, "That man is the only man who has it right!" I was made a corporal for my achievement.

The next day General Littlefield summoned me to his office. He was swatting flies when I went in. I was silent and he was silent too, for a long time. I don't think he remembered me or why he had sent for me, but he didn't want to admit it. He swatted some more flies, keeping his eyes on them narrowly before he let go with the swatter. "Button up your coat!" he snapped. Looking back on it now I can see that he meant me although he was looking at a fly, but I just stood there. Another fly came to rest on a paper in front of the general and began rubbing its hind legs together. The general lifted the swatter cautiously. I moved restlessly and the fly flew away. "You startled him!" barked General Littlefield, looking at me severely. I said I was sorry. "That won't help the situation!" snapped the General, with cold military logic. I didn't see what I could do except offer to chase some more flies toward his desk, but I didn't say anything. He stared out the window at the faraway figures of co-eds crossing the campus toward the library. Finally, he told me I could go. So I went. He either didn't know which cadet I was or else he forgot what he wanted to see me about. It may have been that he wished to apologize for having called me the main trouble with the university; or maybe he had decided to compliment me on my brilliant drilling of the day before and then at the last minute decided not to. I don't know. I don't think about it much any more.

THE SPECIES PROFESSOR AMERICANUS AND SOME NATURAL ENEMIES[1]

Marten ten Hoor

I

Some years ago, when I was planning to spend some time in Europe, I was, as is usually the case, offered a tremendous lot of advice by those of my colleagues who had already made one or more trips to the old country. There was much in this advice which filled my simple and untraveled soul with wonder. But there was nothing which astonished me quite so much as the following urgent suggestion made by an old and trusted friend: "Listen, my boy," said he, "whatever preparations you make or don't make, *I beg of you*, have a lot of calling cards engraved with 'Professor Doctor' in front of your name. Then when you want to get into a library—or out of a jam—you'll find that you have a supply of Aladdin's lamps right in your pocket. I tell you, old fellow, nothing so impresses and intimidates the European aborigines as the title 'Professor Doctor.' "

Needless to say, I followed my colleague's advice. And I found that he was gloriously right. That card was an "open sesame" to persons as well as to places. If an attendant in a library at first sight looked on me with suspicion, the sight of my card transformed him at once into an obsequious servant. If a certain exhibit was closed, for one or the other of the mysterious reasons which always conspire to keep some part of a European museum out of circulation, the presentation of my card magically effected a personally conducted tour through the quarantined area. And these special privileges were granted with

[1] From Michigan Alumnus *Quarterly Review* (Apr. 27, 1940), Vol. 46, No. 19, pp. 225–234. Reprinted by permission.

a demonstration of respect which warmed the soul. Indeed, my friends, it was a pleasure to discover how truly civilized the European peoples were.

However, it is now several years since that visit to Europe, and the memory of that pleasure has become somewhat dulled. And in its stead there has gradually been developing in my mind a scholar's passion to inquire into the why and the wherefore of the striking difference between the European and the American attitude toward the college professor. Why is it, I have been asking myself, that in Europe an ordinary mortal, when he sees a professor, tips his hat, whereas in these United States he taps his forehead? Why is it that in Europe the professor is the jewel of the salon while in the United States he is the skeleton at the feast? Why is it that in Europe a professor is a lion who is diligently hunted by the arbiters of society, while in the United States he is as a lone ass braying in the desert? Such startling differences, my friends, cannot be due to accident or caprice, and therefore they cannot be safely ignored. In the name of scholarship, and for the sake of the future of the American professor, they must be examined and, if possible, explained.

II

If we are intelligibly to show how, when and why the American species came to deviate from the European, it will be necessary to take a moment or two to draw a hasty picture of the Old World variety. And to this end we shall, by way of introduction, first indicate how the European species arose and how it developed.

The first mention of anything akin to the contemporary professor in the annals of European history occurs in Greek literature. I have reference, of course, to the teacher-philosopher, Socrates. This remarkable Athenian showed great promise of becoming a genuine professor, and he would doubtless have developed into one, but for his untimely end. From young manhood on, he made it his lifework to ask people to define terms which they and everybody else used, but which nobody understood. And the young Athenian aristocrats thought this habit of his so eccentric and so amusing that they persistently sought him out and even invited him to their dinners. Thus Socrates may be said to have been the progenitor of the modern professor, at least with respect to two essential characteristics: he enjoyed exposing ignorance and he enjoyed going out to dinner.

Unfortunately, his fondness for asking people to define their terms became such a consuming passion that he lost all sense of the proprieties. One day he met a member of the Athenian senate, an eloquent and persuasive politician, whom he addressed as follows: "My friend, I have these many days been seeking a definition of justice. How fortunate is our encounter, therefore; for you who are a member of the assembly which makes the laws by which we Athenians are governed certainly must know what justice is. I pray you, therefore, share your knowledge with me."

When, as anyone but a professor would have expected, he received no satisfactory answer to his question, he approached another senator, and another, and still another, in each case with the same result. Nevertheless, he persisted and continued his search, until finally the indignant members of the senate, all of whom were very busy making laws and devising taxes for the people, had no recourse but to charge him with impiety and condemn him to death. Thus ended the career of the first professor, a career the early and unfortunate termination of which was the result of an inquisitiveness and simplicity of mind which ultimately became innate characteristics of the species.

However, Socrates had created a demand for professors; and fortunately a group of his contemporaries, the Sophists, were able to provide the supply. But though these Sophists carried on the professional tradition of giving instruction, their technique showed that they had learned much from the unhappy fate of Socrates. The latter had conceived it to be the duty of a professor to teach people how to think, and that was why he had sought to induce every person with whom he talked to develop clear definitions, each for himself. The Sophists, however, noticed that the Athenian people, like all democratic peoples, accepted its definitions from the politicians ready made. And they also noticed that, where rival definitions were offered by contending political parties, those of the most eloquent and persuasive speakers rather than those of the clearest thinkers were accepted. It therefore seemed to them that the proper function of the professor was to teach oratory rather than philosophy. And thus it came about that this new generation of professors devoted itself to the teaching of the arts of persuasion, namely, rhetoric, oratory, argumentation, and judicial pleading, rather than to the art of thinking.

Now, whereas Socrates had made himself a good deal of a nuisance with his persistent attempts to make people think, the Sophists made themselves extremely popular. Did they not teach one how to induce other people to accept one's opinions as their own? Moreover, then as now, oratory seemed so much more attractive an art than thinking. It is "done" before an audience, it wins applause and acclaim, and brings fame and fortune. But thinking, on the contrary, is done in private; it is disturbing, difficult, and useless; and, though one devote a lifetime to it, it leaves one unknown and obscure. Politicians as well as the common people, therefore, at once appreciated the *practical* usefulness of the kind of instruction which the Sophists had to offer, and the youth of Athens besieged the new professors and begged for instruction.

Nor were the Sophists slow to take advantage of this. Whereas Socrates, being fully aware of the fact that the art of thinking is not practically useful, and feeling, besides, that teaching people to think is merely a friendly service, had never even entertained the notion of asking pay for his instruction, the Sophists were quick to realize the market value of their teaching and promptly began charging substantial fees for their lessons. And this change in professional policy had two very important results: first of all, since to work for money was, in the opinion of the Athenian aristocrats, the occupation of slaves, menials, and artisans, the teaching profession immediately lost social standing and the best people no longer invited the professors to dinner. From this social reverse the teaching profession has not to this day recovered. Secondly, since the profession had allowed commercialism to creep in and could therefore no longer lay claim to teaching for the love of truth or for the love of teaching, the professor promptly lost his amateur standing.

III

Though it is unfortunately true that the professor has never regained his amateur status, it is equally true that he has never become a really successful professional. For society, agreeing with the Greeks that it is a mistake to pay professors for their teaching, has ever since the classical period diligently seen to it that the mistake did not become more serious. Thus we find that in the next great period of history, the Middle Ages, the educational authorities of that day refused to pay their professors anything at all. The reasons for this were so original, and so characteristic of the medival period, that we must take a moment to consider them.

It must be remembered that during the

Middle Ages education was entirely in the hands of the Church. The "professors" of that time were members of the clergy, that is, priests and monks. Now, there seemed no point to paying these medieval teachers, first, because they needed no money, and, secondly, because they were sure to receive their reward in heaven—an interesting contrast incidentally, with the condition and prospect of the contemporary professor, who badly needs money, and concerning whom there is a growing doubt as to whether or not he will be rewarded in heaven.

IV

When we turn to the consideration of the New World variety and undertake an inquiry into the nature, habits, and natural enemies of the species *Professor Americanus*, we encounter at the very outset a very serious problem, namely, the exact denotation or extent of reference of the term "professor" as employed in the United States. In the European countries the term has but one meaning, that of a scholar who lectures in a university. But in the United States the term may have any one of a number of meanings.

A professor in our country may first of all be a teacher in a college or university, that is, the exact counterpart of the European "Professor Doctor." Even in this subspecies there is a wide range of meaning, for in an American college or university you will find professors lecturing on subjects ranging from classical language and philosophy to hog-raising, dishwashing, and cheerleading. Hospitality to such a great variety of subjects is the expression of our typically democratic philosophy of curriculum making, which may be summarized in these two slogans, addressed to the student: "If you don't see what you want, ask for it!" and "If we haven't got it, we'll order it for you."

However, in our country a professor may be many other things besides a member of a university faculty. He may be a high-school teacher or the principal of a rural grammar school, a teacher in a business college, in a beauticians' institute, or in a school for barbers or undertakers, an itinerant music teacher, a purveyor of "psychological" misinformation to the public, the leader of the village choir, a juggler, a palmist, a fake hypnotist, a barker in a circus, an orchestra leader in a vaudeville show, or a piano player in a house of ill fame.

Before we can undertake an intelligent definition of the nature of the species *Professor Americanus*, therefore, we must sharply delimit the reference of our term: henceforth in this essay we shall use the term "professor" only as referring to an individual, of either sex, who is a teacher or lecturer in an American college or university.

What now are the generic characteristics of the typical American college and university professor? Obviously, this depends somewhat upon the point of view of him who undertakes to furnish the definition, whether he be himself a professor or only an objective observer, whether he be simply a college student in course or an alumnus whose memories of his professors have been dimmed by time or have been overcast with sentimental recollections of his college days. If he is a member of the general public, his principal sources of information will be the vaudeville theater, the movie, and the funny paper. And if you asked such a person to name the most universal and distinctive characteristic of the species professor, he would promptly answer, "Absentmindedness."

So general is the impression that a professor is *par excellence* absentminded that we must take this opportunity to show how fallacious this notion is. What, to begin with, is absentmindedness? Psychologically considered, it is merely the habit or power of intense concentration on some primary idea or purpose, a concentration so complete as to make the subject inattentive to some secondary action which he is concomitantly performing. As an example, we may cite a recent illustration from the newspaper comics: A professor, who has been sent out on a domestic errand, during his return journey becomes so absorbed in thinking about some problem that, on entering his home, he puts his shoes in the refrigerator and the steak in his bedroom closet. Now this misadventure is clearly a comic by-product of the professor's power of concentration. The comic character of the incident is not really due to the erratic disposition of shoes and steak but to the extreme contrast between the triviality of the professor's actions and the dignity and importance of his personality. The incident would not be half so funny if the hero of it were a plumber. It is therefore not true that the professor is generally more absentminded than other men with equally great powers of concentration; it is merely that the unexpected consequences of his absentmindedness are usually so trivial as compared with his dignity.

This will at once become clear if we examine a few cases of absentmindedness in other professions. A banker, for example, may concentrate so intensely on the business of investing the money which has been deposited in his bank that he forgets to whom it belongs and is as careless with it as if it were his own. The criminal lawyer becomes so intensely absorbed in the business of defending his gangster client that he forgets that he, the lawyer, is an officer of the court, and of justice, and acts as if he were engaged in saving an early Christian martyr from the stake. A preacher may become so absorbed in defending a theological dogma that he will forget all about the salvation of his parishioners' souls, and sometimes even of his own. These illustrations, and many others which could be adduced, clearly indicate that the professor is not more absentminded than members of other professions but merely more entertainingly so.

V

Helpful as it may be to prove this and other popular notions of the essential characteristics of the professor wrong, our real problem is to define the species affirmatively. An interesting self-definition, affirmative in nature, and offered by a particularly cynical member of the species is this one: A professor is a man who casts artificial pearls before natural swine. But this definition is both too poetic and too passionate to be scientifically acceptable. With considerable trepidation, we suggest instead one of our own, which is free at least from the aforementioned errors: A professor is a person who cannot be disillusioned with respect to the educability of his fellowman.

It will be clear to the reader that this definition implies that there are agents or objects which are persistently trying to disillusion the professor on this subject. These agents are the natural enemies of the species *Professor* and they are the student, the parent, the administrator, and society at large. Since it is in his struggle against these enemies that the professor most completely reveals his nature, we shall continue our study of the species by defining these enemies and by surveying their efforts to compel, cajole, and tempt him to give up, or to relax, his efforts in behalf of the improvement of his fellowman.

VI

This concluding purpose of our study will possibly best be realized if we submit to careful analysis and evaluation the relations of the professor to these enemies, the relations, namely, of professor to student, professor to parent, professor to administrator, and professor to society at large.

All human relations are of two kinds, fortunate or ill-starred. As outstanding examples of the fortunate relationships we have the relationship of parent and child, the relationship of friend to friend, and the relationship of lovers. All of these, *because* they are so fortunate, have since the dawn of history been celebrated in story and song. And justly so.

But has anyone ever seen a poem, or has any archaeologist ever discovered even a fragment of a poem, celebrating the relation of a husband to his mother-in-law, or of a professor to a member of his board of administrators? So well known is the answer that to ask the question is nothing more than a rhetorical affectation. No, dear reader, no one ever has and no one ever will, because these two relations belong in the class of the ill-starred, to which class, it grieves us to say, we must also assign the relation of professor to student, professor to parent, and professor to society at large.

The fact that the undergraduate is and must be the student and the professor is and must be the teacher establishes *a priori* the certainty that any hope of making their relationship more fortunate is unjustified. They are naturally allergic to one another. The undergraduate is congenitally convinced that what the professor has to teach is not what he, the student, wants; and the professor is congenitally convinced that what the student wants he should not want, or at any rate that he is not going to get it.

The trouble with the professor, according to the student, is that he is too academic; and the trouble with the student, according to the professor, is that he is a philistine. The professor has his eye on a remote, intangible, only partially definable something which he calls culture; the student has his eye on the proximate, tangible, clearly recognizable fleshpots of Egypt. The attitude of the student toward this thing called culture is expressed with characteristic undergraduate emphasis and brutality in the following quatrain from a popular college song:

> To hell with Latin, Math, and Greek!
> My mom she no can English speak.
> And as for all this culture slop,
> "No catch 'em," says my selfmade pop!

Neither dares even for a moment take his eye off his goal, for to do so means to lose social and professional standing. If the professor of philosophy, for example, were to attempt to demonstrate to his students that the study of philosophy is practical, even if he did so only for strategical pedagogical reasons, the professor would at once lose caste with his fellow professors. As for the reaction of the student, he would promptly see through it and would be indignant at this attempt of the leopard to change his spots. And if the student were to reveal, or pretend to reveal, some symptoms of a hunger and thirst for culture, the professor would take the next opportunity to point out to his class that culture is not something which can be deliberately acquired, that the consciousness of the need of culture *ipso facto* proves the absence of it, and that, therefore the conscious manifestation of interest in culture on the part of a student can be nothing more than a symptom of a vulgar interest in grades. Thus an attempt on the part of either the student or the professor to manifest a more sympathetic attitude toward the other is looked upon by colleagues as a bit of unsportsmanlike leg-pulling.

Absorbing as this theme of the professor-student relation is, we cannot overlook the relation of professor and parent. The difficulties inherent in this relationship are due to the fact that the parent and the professor take such hopelessly divergent views of an innocent third party, the child. For the professor, the child is a biological consequence; for the parent, the child is a work of art. The parent is excited by potentialities; the professor is embarrassed by actualities.

Over and over again, in every corner of the land the drama unfolds itself. On a bright sunny day in September, the parent presents the pupil to the professor: "This is my little sow's ear, Johnny," says the parent (usually female). "I'll call for the silk purse later." But before many days are gone the parent receives from the professor a letter, the tenor of which is as follows: "Dear Sir and/or Madame: We regret to inform you that your product is inferior." And the consequent misunderstanding is as inevitable as it is unfortunate. As well expect producer and consumer to agree on the value of an article as expect parent and professor to discover the same explanation of Johnny's failure. To speak of blame here is really absurd, because, in the last analysis, we are face to face here with the fateful workings of the educational process, on the one hand, and with the mysterious consequences of the laws of phylogenesis, on the other.

The relationship of professor to administrator can be considered only with a certain degree of trepidation, not only because of its complex character but also because of what might be called its combustibility. There are, of course, two types of administrators, internal officers, such as deans and presidents, and external officers, such as regents, that is, members of boards of administration. The explosive potentialities of the relation of professor to dean or to president are suggested by the following definition of these officers, offered by a particularly incendiary professor: A dean is a man who has too little sense to be a professor and too much to be a president.

Although this definition is, no doubt, a product of extreme provocation, or of extreme irritability, or of both, it gives us a slight clue to the respective positions of the professor and the internal administrator. A dean, as a matter of fact, occupies, in the academic class struggle, the front line trenches. Or, to use another figure, he is the official shock absorber of the educational machine. He receives his most frequent and irritating shocks from a species of youthful professor who is still full of illusions concerning the perfectibility of the educational process. So firm is the faith of this type of professor in the educational machinery that he does not hesitate to test it as often as possible by throwing a monkey wrench into it. He is full of ambition and courage, of enthusiasm and romance. Some administrators have discovered that such professors, if they are not too strenuously radical, can be very quickly transformed into conservatives by making them third or fourth assistant deans. Other administrators prefer to let nature take its course.

The proper attitude of the professor to the external administrator, that is, to a member of a board of administrators, is a fluctuating one, the gap being sometimes so wide that there seems to be hardly any relation at all. However, a cat may look at a king, and in such cases, even if professor and board member never meet, each has a decided opinion about the other. What an external administrator thinks about a professor is likely to be determined by the administrator's knowledge of education. If he knows little or nothing about it, he will be inclined to look upon a professor as some species of hired help; if he knows a great deal about education he will look upon him as a partner in an educational enterprise.

What a professor thinks about a member of a board of administrators will, in turn, be determined by the professor's conception of financial administration. Most professors look upon a board member as a big butter and egg man whose business it is to raise funds for the institution; and such professors are usually content to cross their fingers and to wish him luck. Others, however, wish to reserve for themselves the privilege of making this business of raising money as difficult and exciting as possible; and thus they insist upon attempting to reform potential contributors or even on calling public attention to their sins, preferably at the time when they are being solicited. Whereupon the administrators shake their heads and remark to one another that evidently some professors have not yet learned that in this world one cannot both eat one's cake and keep it. In the light of these considerations and of others which we cannot here recount, we may therefore justifiably conclude that the relation between professor and external administrator is so unstable because it never seems to have been settled between them who shall pay the fiddler and who shall call the tune.

When the philosophic observer of the educational scene finally turns his attention to the question of the professor and society at large, he quickly discerns that this relation is a product of the gigantic struggle between two educational forces; the struggle, namely, between school and environment, between the educational institution and the civilization which gave it birth. This contest reduces itself, in the last analysis, to a struggle between precept and practice. The professor teaches by precept, society teaches by practice. And unfortunately, precept and practice are almost never in agreement.

Society insists, for example, that our professors of political science shall expound to the student the truly just state and that they shall inculcate in him the highest ideals of public service. But when the student looks about him and examines concrete political practice, he sees little relation between this and what he has been taught. And he very naturally concludes that his professors are impractical idealists. If the student survives the educational process with his respect for ideals intact, a year or two of practical political experience prove to him that *whatever* he may have been taught, it was not how to be successful in *this* world.

Nor is it only in the realm of politics that this discrepancy between precept and practice exists. It exists in the case of all social interests, for it is nothing less than the eternal conflict between the inertia and the momentum of a civilization which seeks to improve at the same time that it strives to maintain itself. And the professor is an earnest of society's desire to reform itself. He is the spokesman of the New Adam, of civilization in its chastened, its repentant, its "morning after" moods. He is the symbol of society's perpetually violated but perpetually renewed vows. He is thus at the same time the savior and the scapegoat of the society in which he lives and has his being. And that is why, in a very real sense, society is his most implacable enemy.

And now our tale is told, at least as far as we have dared to tell it. We have presented for your sympathetic understanding a study of the species *Professor Americanus*. We have traced his origins, analyzed his nature, and described his natural enemies. And we cannot but conclude with the expression of the conviction that he will be in the future exactly what he has been in the past, and what he is in the present; namely, a prophet without authority, a preacher without unction, an orator without sex appeal, a martyr without a crown. But, my friends, *how he did, and does, and will continue to enjoy it.*

ON THE INAUGURATION OF WILLIAM ROBERT ROSS AS PRESIDENT OF COLORADO STATE COLLEGE OF EDUCATION, JUNE 23, 1948[1]

George Willard Frasier

MR. PRESIDENT:

We charge you to provide better teachers for a better world!

This should be your main object in the years ahead.

Those who have gone before you have failed to provide the American schools with a sufficient number of teachers.

Many of those who have been provided lack in education, culture, and skills.

Teachers should be better paid.

You must exert every effort to raise the present level of pay.

We charge you to remember that education is a state function.

The State must be induced to take over a larger part of the cost of education.

The National Government must also help equalize the cost of education.

We view with alarm a nation that has "billions for defense" and "not one cent for education."

[1] Reprinted with the permission of George Willard Frasier. This is the charge that the outgoing President delivered to the new President.

The task ahead of you is a colossal one.

You must attack it with imagination, courage, and skill.

Better teachers for a better world.

That is your task.

We charge you with this great responsibility.

You must attract more and better students to the field of teaching.

You must see that they get the best possible education.

You cannot do this job alone.

You must surround yourself with great teachers.

You must provide them with the best possible working conditions.

You must fight for their academic freedom.

This college needs teachers with vision!

Teachers with a dynamic philosophy:

Teachers who dare the enemies of public education!

Teachers more interested in children than subjects:

Teachers who will share with you this great dream of better teachers for a better world.

COLLEGES NAMED STREETCAR DESIRED[1]

Terrel Spencer

Its tracks are laid from the river front through the congested business district, to the azalea studded estates of an exclusive residential area, on out to the small suburbs that always nest close to a large city. It stops at each point to pick up passengers—the ones who travel only a short distance, sometimes with transfer in hand, and those whose destination is the end of the line. Its friendly service and attractive accommodations invite all who envision new horizons. And what conveyance could be more suitable to new intellectual horizons than this urban service

[1] From *Junior College Journal*, December, 1952, pp. 204–207. Reprinted by permission.

institution of higher learning frequently called a "Streetcar College"?

To be worthy of the name, a service institution should be motivated by the philosophy that educational opportunity is for everyone. Not only must its leaders offer the customary liberal arts instruction, but they must keep their fingers constantly on the pulse of the community in order to anticipate and fulfill other educational needs, sometimes even before the community itself is aware that such needs exist. Becoming dedicated to this philosophy imposes a far greater burden of responsibility upon educators than does a philosophy which provides only for the intellectually elite. However, commensurate with the responsibility is an intense satisfaction known only to those who are operating Streetcar Colleges.

What is meant by the term, "educational opportunity for *everyone*"? To the University of Houston—a Streetcar College—it means some type of training for all above high school age who desire it.

In addition to thousands of high school graduates in and near Houston, there are thousands more who did not finish high school, but who "want to go to college." To these mature individuals the University offers college entrance examinations. Should the applicant successfully pass the examination, he may enroll and be placed in the same category as those who have finished high school. If he fails, but insists on pursuing a degree, he is enrolled for a one year trial period, and should he then fail to meet certain requirements, he is held ineligible for a degree but is still privileged to take courses.

In this way individuals are not excluded on the basis of tests or the Carnegie Unit. Instead, requirements for admission are maturity and a desire to learn. A basic principle governing the operation of an institution under this philosophy is that it must be democratic.

Many of the students who undertake training are more interested in improving their way of life than they are in college degrees. The University offers them a wide variety of technical and vocational courses such as aircraft and automobile mechanics, welding, machine shop, TV and radio repairing, diesel technology, air conditioning and refrigeration, and others. These programs often serve as buffers, particularly for engineering students who discover they do not have the ability to pursue some of the more theoretical engineering subjects.

It is quite natural that such sharp deviation from established educational practices should provoke some criticism and create some problems. The University of Houston answers criticism honestly and meets its problems squarely as they arise.

Invariably the standards of a Streetcar College are criticized—admission requirements, degree requirements, selection of instructors, and method of instruction—without full knowledge of how well the institution might be conforming to the criteria of accrediting agencies. Generally, the only standard that might actually be open to question is that of admissions. Certainly the policies followed by the University of Houston in this respect can be justified educationally.

There is no occasion for degree requirements in a service institution to be any less rigid than those in a traditional liberal arts college, and the instruction should be, and usually is, better in a service institution.

A vast amount of time and work is involved in arranging schedules, organizing teaching and library materials, and selecting instructors. Since many short-term courses need to be taught by authorities in the field, it may become necessary for a dean in a large institution to employ thirty to fifty instructors to teach for one semester only. This number represents in many instances more instructors than a dean would employ on a contract in a decade. Yet the qualifications of each instructor are carefully scrutinized, and only those meeting rigid requirements are employed.

STUDENT SATISFACTION

The very success of a service institution is based on the satisfaction of a student with the instruction he is buying. For many years curricula and methods of teaching on all levels have been continually evaluated and reorganized because of the important part played by motivation. In a service institution the average student who is attending of his own volition, who is paying his own way, who is holding a part-time job with small income, who is often attending school after a day's work is certainly well motivated, usually more so than the student who attends college at the insistence of parents, or because it is a socially acceptable practice.

Administrators of the service institution wisely meet the demand for good instructors, knowing that their institution can not long survive with an inferior teaching staff. Thus, the University of Houston's claim seems justifiable—that no instructional standard is lowered by the admission of mature individuals who are sometimes more interested in an education than in a degree.

One of the more serious problems in the operation of a Streetcar College involves the process of orientation and education of the faculty. As a rule, the vast majority of faculty members have been trained in a traditional type of university, and at first it is difficult for them to grasp the democratic concept of educational opportunity for everyone. Unfortunately, the Streetcar College and its staff members are frequently ostracized educationally. Apparently only time, patience, and evidence of success will surmount this ostracism.

There are also financial problems peculiar to a Streetcar College. Knowing that the psychology of the American people prompts them to have little respect for things that are free, directors of a service institution wisely require tuition for all courses. This policy, followed by the University of Houston, also serves as a selective device. A person only mildly interested might be inclined to take a course if it were free. He would be more likely to master its contents if he were intrinsically interested and had paid for the privilege of taking the course. However, again the basic democratic principle cannot be overlooked, even in the execution of this policy. There may be many who are possessed with a zeal to improve themselves but cannot afford college. For these the University provides job opportunities, loans, and for those who prove themselves capable, scholarships.

In trying to determine how much should be paid by the student, administrators of the University concluded that each individual course should be economically self-sustaining. This principle may be violated in the initial stages of developing a course program, but the estimated total cost is amortized.

Operation of a Streetcar College demands promotion, such as developing ideas, interpreting them to all individuals concerned, and contacting those in the community who might be interested. The promoter must have a wide acquaintance in the community, he must participate in community-wide projects, he must instill confidence in everyone in his institution, and he must be capable of entertaining proposed ideas which at first may seem unconventional.

Offsetting, and by far outweighing these unique problems are the contributions made to the community by the college and its students. The administrators of a successful service institution are intensely proud of these achievements. They see a bridge-playing housewife convert her energies to courses in government and parliamentary law, and then take an active part in civic organizations. They see engineers return for refresher courses that lead to quick and remunerative promotions. They see plumbers' helpers learn welding in order to lay the ribbons of pipeline that criss-cross our nation.

These are some of the achievements that cause the operators of a Streetcar College to welcome and encourage *all* passengers who are seeking the new horizons of learning and self-improvement—that cause them to believe sincerely that they offer an excellent mode of transportation to modern education.

THE JUNIOR COLLEGE IN AMERICAN EDUCATION[1]

Robert Gordon Sproul

The state of California now supports more than sixty public and private junior colleges which registered last year, even in this temporary period of general decline in college enrollment, some seventy thousand young men and women. Setting the number of junior colleges more definitely is difficult because new institutions frequently come into existence before school census figures can appear in print. While this situation may not be duplicated in states where population is growing in a more conservative and orderly fashion, it does exemplify in a forceful manner the vigor of the junior college movement and the importance of recognizing and solving the problems which are inevitably associated with its rapid expansion.

Among these problems, it seems to this writer, none is more fundamental or more urgently in need of attention than that created by public misconceptions of what a junior college is, and what it should be. Too often junior college administrators are criticized for holding educational objectives which unnecessarily overlap those of other types of institutions offering instruction beyond high school graduation, or for failing to hold educational objectives which would broaden and deepen the opportunities of youth for self-development in fields of interest and on levels of capacity not adequately served by previously existing types of institutions. This type of criticism results too often in well-intentioned but short-sighted public pressures being brought to bear upon junior college administrators. The solution of this problem would seem to lie in the education of the public concerning the fields in which junior colleges can do their best work, and the channeling of lay interest and activity into forward rather than backward moving currents.

Junior colleges owe their birth to the faith of the American people in the values of formal education beyond the twelfth grade and to a desire to offer these values to a larger percentage of each generation of young people. They were organized as two-year colleges rather than as four-year colleges primarily because of the realization that the majority of young people involved would need shorter and less academic curricula than those offered by the orthodox four-year colleges and universities. Their role as preparatory schools for the upper division of four-year colleges and universities was conceived, and should continue to be recognized as a secondary one, meeting the needs of a minority of those matriculating.

[1] From *Junior College Journal*, January, 1953, pp. 243–49. Reprinted by permission.

Other problems of the junior college have arisen because of a misunderstanding on the part of the general public as to the need for differentiating between these two purposes outlined, and a failure to recognize the dignity and importance of the two-year terminal curriculum. The people of the United States are ambitious and optimistic by tradition, and particularly so when planning the lives of their children. Commendably, they attach a premium to family advancement on the economic and social scale from generation to generation. They have associated this advancement with the accumulation of wealth on the one hand, and most pertinently for this discussion, with the traditional American four-year college training and college degrees on the other hand. Even though it might involve the performance of a miracle, they would like their local junior college to give to all young people either a course of training or a set of labels comparable to those earned at four-year colleges or universities by a selected few young people who have vocational or professional talents, aptitudes, and interests which require a course of four years or more for their development.

If young people of high merit but without desire or aptitude for academic instruction on the university level are to benefit as they should from junior colleges, then educators generally must join together in building the prestige and in making clear the usefulness of junior college curricula frankly designed to fit young people for immediate entry into jobs, marriage, and enlightened citizenship. There must be, also, a concerted effort to combat the tendency of occupational groups to build their prestige by setting higher than necessary educational requirements, and of employers of technicians to feel that they profit by recruiting personnel who have reached an educational level far above that required by the job to be performed.

Fortunately, the values of a junior college do not need to be sold to the people of California, but there is still need for demonstrations on how to use this most serviceable institution for highest benefit to the local community, the State and the Nation.

ADULT EDUCATION IN THE UNITED STATES[1]

Paul L. Essert

Adult education in the United States is a way of learning, voluntarily selected by an individual or group of people, usually 18 years of age or over, in which they carry on sustained inquiry, with the objective of directing and organizing their experiences in such a way that they are able to create new and meaningful experiences in the improvement of themselves or their environment.

[1] From *The Annals of The American Academy of Political and Social Science*, September, 1949, pp. 122–129. Reprinted by permission.

In most respects adult education does not differ from any other significant education; its chief difference lies in the degree of voluntary selectivity of the way of learning, and the ages of the participants. Most adult education is "tailor-made" to suit the particular needs of the participant. Because its participants are usually engaged in a vocation or are seriously seeking to find one, adult education deals with people who are no longer engaged in full-time formal schooling.

Like any other valuable education, however, good adult education is selected by the learner. It does not include chance or accidental experience, even though some of these may have educational values. The way of learning must be consciously planned, organized, and vigorously followed by both the learner and the leader in order to yield the return of increased control over environment or the opening of the way to new and meaningful experience.

Educating adults in such a way that the educational experience itself closes the door to new inquiry and fresh exploration is a violation of the principle of creative search, implied in the above definition. Acceptance of anything learned as final and absolute or permanent is not adult learning, because the spirit of inquiry is taken from the learning. Acceptance of the Communist Manifesto, the philosophy of Adam Smith or of Thomas Jefferson, or Newton's law, or the only way to run an assembly line or a trade union, as the final truth, no matter how accurately stated or frequently quoted it may be, is not adult education unless these ideas and learnings are used to search for new meanings.

Tentative acceptance and use of a partial truth may be a good start toward continued learning if such acceptance is accompanied by honest doubts and questions leading toward further search. Thus, the acquisition of simple skills of cooking, sewing, speaking, writing, the mastery of machines, a textbook or a "great" book can be a phase of adult education, but it is not adult education until it becomes a means to constant and continuous inquiry.

Adult education in the United States is a continuous and sustained inquiry, clearly distinguished from propaganda or creed. Because its success in this country depends upon the reality with which it has recognized the participants' personal concern, it has never taken on the appearance of a standardized mass movement, stemming from a highly centralized source of authority. The adult learner is always a partner in the control of process and content.

EXTENT OF ADULT EDUCATION

It is estimated that one person in every four over twenty-one years of age in the United States is engaged for a part of his time in continued learning activities in some adult education institution, agency, or association. National and state polls to determine adult interest in continued learning indicate that approximately 35,000,000 adults, or two in every five, would like to attend classes or take special courses in addition to carrying on their daily work or occupations. It is not impossible, therefore, that we may soon have in the United States more people studying in adult education groups than we have in formal schools and colleges for children and youth.

This prospect seems more likely when we consider several significant trends in our culture. These are: (1) the shift from a predominately juvenile population to one which will become largely adult; (2) the historical phenomena, demonstrated over the past quarter of a century, that the popular demand and supply of part-time adult learning goes on alike in depressions, times of war, and "prosperity booms"; (3) the fact that the more serious and complex our national problems and international crises become, and the more bewildered the citizen, the more he tends to recognize that he cannot learn during the first twenty years of his life all that a changing world demands that he know, or know how to do skillfully.

In brief, adult education as *continued learning* is apparently to become a reality and a necessity for most citizens of the United States, rather than a purely recreational part-time activity for a few who have nothing else to do, or a remedial or emergency activity for those who have lost out in their childhood and youth education.

Let us bring these facts into a more intimate focus. If the reader were to canvass 100 adults living in his neighborhood in almost any city or rural area and ask them if they were now undertaking or planning to undertake some form of continuous study outside their working hours, he might find, to his surprise, that 30 to 50 of them were in that category.

Probably the reader who undertook such a survey would also be surprised at the numerous ways and means of study that these 30 to 50 neighbors would employ.

MEANS OF ADULT EDUCATION

In rural areas, by far the larger number of adult learners would be studying through the Cooperative Extension Services of the United States Department of Agriculture—taking courses, attending lectures, planning or attending rural farm and home demonstration programs, carrying on experiments, reading bulletins, and hearing radio programs.

In the urban areas the largest number would report that they were following a regular study program of music, literature, public issues, book reviews, scientific or historical lectures, or dramatizations carried on by the commercial broadcasting companies or a neighboring college educational radio station. Some of these radio stations would be sending reading guides to the adult learner to accompany his studies, some would be sending course outlines and textbooks at reasonable costs, some would be providing a way to secure college credit through home radio study.

Some of the neighbors would be using the day or evening schools of the public schools, or the extension classes of a nearby college or university—attending one or two nights a week, studying almost anything they wanted to learn; and some would restrict their efforts largely to evening vocational classes, evening high school classes, or evening elementary school classes for adults.

Others would be carrying on their continued learning through the public library, where the library not only lent the adult participants books, records, and sometimes films, but had developed a readers' advisory service which helped them plan a sequential and continuous course of reading on almost any problem they chose, from "leisure-time hobbies" to "problems of world peace." They might also be attending regular forum meetings or book discussion groups in their local public library.

Some persons would be carrying on their adult learning in their churches; others in their women's clubs, their parent-teacher association study groups, the League of Women Voters, the civic planning study groups, the service clubs, or the American Legion.

Some of the 30 to 50 neighbors might be studying or planning to study labor history, collective bargaining processes, or shop stewardship in their trade unions, or in "workers' education" classes, where many union and non-union workers study common interests. In some of the better workers' education programs the worker would have the additional benefit of studying with his co-workers, of his own occupational status, in classes in music, arts and crafts, dramatics, public issues, literature, and history.

Many of the neighbors would show the investigator their textbooks and study outlines and lesson sheets from a private correspondence school or the university extension division which enabled them to study at home after the day's work. Some would tell him of their sons in the armed forces, who, with 250,000 others, study in an off-duty program courses that will give them college or high school credit when they are discharged and return to their civilian education, or courses which they choose simply because they are interested in the subject or problem.

Some would be making more or less frequent visits to the city museum, the symphony concerts, the town meeting or forum program; and some would be following up these visits with reading, collections, discussion groups, reading clubs, dramatic groups, choral societies, and travel clubs.

MOTIVES FOR CONTINUED LEARNING

It is difficult for most people to analyze accurately their true motive for continuing their learning; expert psychological help is usually necessary. But assuming that adult learners could do this, if the reader were to carry his survey one step farther and ask his neighbors why they were studying or wanted to, he would probably get the following range of answers in more or less the order named: (1) to improve occupational opportunities and gain advancements; (2) to meet problems encountered in managing a family; (3) to advance educational status for family or social reasons; (4) to cultivate a long cherished but undeveloped interest; (5) to take part in civic and economic leadership. The answers would, of course, vary from place to place and from time to time, but for the most part the motivations for adult study and the opportunities created to meet them would be very personal. They could be broadly summarized as adult education to help adults *adjust* to cultural changes.

Historically, adult education in the United States has always been a response to environmental and cultural change—an aid in adjusting to the accomplished fact in our culture. Seldom has it exerted a direct positive influence upon cultural change. There are some indications, however, that adult education may increasingly become an aid to adults in learning to control and direct their environmental changes. A brief look at its history will make this emerging function more clearly understood.

ADULT EDUCATION AS A CULTURAL INFLUENCE

The meandering stream of adult education in the United States from 1800 to 1940 was, for the most part, a *response* to the changing conditions of the culture. The New England town meeting of the seventeenth century and the town meetings of the American frontier communities were perhaps exceptions, since here the people of the community studied their common problems together, shaped their plans, and made decisions about activities for the future. These associations represent a co-operative search for a way of life, and almost all adults shared in the planning and decisions. Benét visualizes the relation of adult education to the practical problems of building the frontier community:

> To the people of the frontier, colonial governors and assemblies were far away, and the rule of England still farther. Engaged in a life—and death—struggle with the wilderness, they had to govern themselves, for nobody else would do it for them. The king of England could not make your clearing. The governor of Virginia could not plant your corn. You had to do these things yourself. And, as soon as other men moved into your neighborhood, you had to get along with them. You had to arrange for mutual protection—a log fort, for instance, where the scattered settlers could go in case of Indian attack. If you wanted a church to worship in, you had to build one. All of you. If you wanted a mayor for your log town, a leader for your community, a captain to fight the Indians, you had to get together and choose him. All of you. . . .[2]

Gradually, however, as the frontier be-

[2] Stephen Vincent Benét, *America*, New York, Farrar & Rinehart, 1944, p. 25.

came settled and more time was available foı learning, the educational and cultural activities became more personal and less community-centered. The first lyceum in Massachusctts was established in 1826. But the rapid growth of lyceums, chautauquas, and public libraries (these last stimulated by the gifts of Andrew Carnegie) represented a response to the challenge of cultural isolation and increased leisure time, rather than forces that anticipated changes and attempted to direct them. Americanization and literacy education was a response to the challenge of our vast immigration problem during the nineteenth century. Agricultural extension and public school vocational education for adults were responses to the increasing specialization of occupation. The evening high school, home correspondence courses, and university extension programs, taking root and growing rapidly in the late nineteenth and early twentieth centuries, were results of the specialization of occupations, the industrialization of a continent, and the increase of leisure time, rather than factors contributing to them.

The studies of the American Association for Adult Education, aided by liberal grants from the Carnegie Corporation of New York,[3] have revealed a vast array of agencies, institutions, and groups offering continued learning opportunities, largely centered around the objective of meeting the personal needs of adults who were seeking to adjust to changing conditions of the culture, rather than to shape or control them.

INFLUENCE OF STUDIES OF ADULT EDUCABILITY

Studies of Thorndike, Lorge, Strong, and others regarding the educability of the adult gave impetus and scientific basis to the surge of adults toward self-improvement. These studies revealed that the inhibitions that many adults had entertained about their power to grow and ability to learn throughout life were groundless. Adults could learn anything about as well as they could have learned it as children and youth,[4] and they had additional qualifications for effective learning, namely, intensity and clarity of interests. These interests in learning could be identified and reduced to a "stable core of intellectual interests."[5] While adults tend as they grow older to resist change as individuals,[6] they are never too old to "modify an attitude or habit, acquire a skill, render a service, keep up to date, create something beautiful, or say to a new idea: I'll try it; not *every* new idea is bad; nor *every* change a revolution."[7] Studies of mental health have added much to the significance of continuous learning as a personal experience essential to healthful living, particularly studies based on adult educational rehabilitation during the war.[8]

We know from these and other studies that most adult education, designed as it is to help adults find ways of directing their experience toward self-improvement, is sound and important to the welfare of the people. Adult education directed toward personal needs is one step toward the essential requirement for mental and social health, namely, that each person have a "task, a plan, and freedom to work it

[3] *Studies in the Social Significance of Adult Education*, a series of books, each dealing with an intimate examination of what a special field of adult education is and its significance to our culture, New York, American Association for Adult Education, 1937–41.

[4] Edward L. Thorndike, *Adult Learning*, New York, The Macmillan Co., 1928.

[5] Irving Lorge, "Never Too Late to Learn," *Journal of American University Women*, October, 1937, p. 32.

[6] E. K. Strong, *Changing Interest With Age*, Stanford, Stanford University Press, 1931.

[7] George Lawton, *Aging Successfully*, New York, Columbia University Press, 1946.

[8] Thomas A. C. Rennie and Luther E. Woodward, *Mental Health in Modern Society*, New York, The Commonwealth Fund, 1948.

out."[9] We also know that what adult education is to become in the future in the United States is closely bound up with what the education of children and youth is today.

During the past decade the growing interest of educators in developing the community-centered school and the society-centered school for children and youth[10] has had important implications for adult education in the future. The increasing stress on the importance of relating the interests of children and youth in schools and colleges to what the schools and colleges *can do to improve the community* is a recognition of the idea that education is potentially a creative force in management of environment, rather than merely a response to changes and an aid in adjusting to change.

A NEW CULTURAL INFLUENCE

Adult education in the United States is already feeling the effects of this change in concept of the role of education in society. During the war new impetus was given to community planning in the development of shoulder-to-shoulder planning of local citizens in civilian defense councils. Many communities learned that these councils possessed great educative value in developing citizenship in the participants, and since the war many efforts have been made to carry on the same type of co-operative study and planning in civilian groups.

Syracuse, Rochester, and Colgate universities have co-operatively provided leadership in New York State for continuing these activities of local citizen groups, with the result that the New York State Citizens Council has been formed and is operating under a grant from the Carnegie Corporation and voluntary subscriptions to make the citizens' participation more valuable and effective. These agencies emphasize the fact that American democratic citizenship involves definite skills, acquired only by continuous practice, and that the practice must be provided in "laboratories" formed by the citizens themselves, where they can work at solving real and important problems of their community.

Developing in quite a different way, but with a similar objective, is the Committee for Kentucky, existing largely to help local citizens to learn through practice how to improve their environment.

The Extension Division of the University of Virginia has just completed a five-year study of how education can help communities to help themselves.[11] The results of this study have major implications for adult education, with fairly objective evidence that adult education can become a positive factor in controlling and directing change if it is centered on meaningful community problems.

The recently published report of the South Chicago Area Project[12] sheds new light on the possibilities of focusing citizenship education in great metropolitan centers upon the participation of adults in practical problems of planning and changing the environment.

[9] William H. Burnham, *The Normal Mind: An Introduction to Mental Hygiene and the Hygiene of School Instruction*, New York, D. Appleton & Co., 1927, pp. 225–226.

[10] A few books dealing with this recent trend in the education of children and youth are: Metropolitan School Study Council, *What School Can Do*, New York, The Council, 525 West 120th Street, 1945, pp. 181–192; Edward G. Olsen, *School and Community*, New York, Prentice-Hall, 1945; Harold Rugg, *Foundations for American Education*, Yonkers, N. Y., World Book Co., 1947.

[11] Jean and Jess Ogden, *These Things We Tried*, University of Virginia Extension (Oct. 15, 1947), Vol. 25, No. 6.

[12] Southside Community Committee, *Bright Shadows in Bronzetown*, Chicago, The Committee, 3548 State Street, 1949.

Kansas State College, through experimental studies of the Institute of Citizenship, is finding that there is a close relationship of international and world interest of adults to the close-at-hand personal problems of the local community and the state.

Labor also, in its increasingly important educational program, is moving toward the idea that "the way to achieve labor's goals is to merge its interests with those of the community and go forward together." [13]

The practical education of adult citizens as vital and essential parts of community growth and improvement has been demonstrated in numerous ways in the Tennessee Valley Authority program. Its far-flung experimentation in the realm of adult citizenship education is being carried forward and made a significant part of adult education practices by the universities of North Carolina, Georgia, Alabama, and Florida, and many other co-operating agencies.

These creative experiments in control of environment through education suggest the possibility that during the next decade one of the major emphases of adult education may be to focus the development of personality on community problems. The experiments thus far have shown that such a shift of emphasis does not replace adult education for personal needs; on the contrary, it gives new meaning to individual enterprise and motivation. The adult citizen clarifies his *task*, and as the community environment changes, he finds more freedom to work out his plan. The worker or business man will not only be motivated by the desire to be competent in his skills and techniques of doing business; he will have the added motivation of making his neighborhood, his nation, and his intergroup and international environment more predictable, so that he can carry on his daily work in peace and with dignity.

Furthermore, the experiments in adult citizenship mentioned above, and many others, are showing the adult educator in the United States that there must always be personal meaning in order for the learner willingly to take an effective part in affairs of the community—be it neighborhood, nation, or world relationships. That there usually are personal relationships and that such relationships are keenly realized by the educator is not enough; the meaning and relationships of the community enterprise must be personalized by the learner himself. The newer trend in adult education is, therefore, not a substitute for education for meeting personal needs, but an extension of it.

FINANCING ADULT EDUCATION IN THE UNITED STATES

As the essential relationship of continued learning to good living becomes more apparent to our people, there is little question that the people will be willing to pay for it; the major question regarding the cost of adult education is whether the people will prefer to pay for it from public taxes or in fees and tuition, or a combination of both.

At the present time most of the cost of adult education in the United States is paid from private fees by the learner. No serious attempt has ever been made to secure data on over-all expenditures for all forms of adult education. Even complete data on public expenditures are lacking, because expenditures are made by a host of Federal, state, and local agencies that are not accounted for as "adult education," but which definitely implement the opportunities for continued learning of our adult citizens.[14] A most casual estimate of the

[13] A. H. Raskin, "Reuther Explains the Reuther Plan," *New York Times Magazine*, March 20, 1949, p. 17.

[14] A recent digest by the *New York Times*

relationship of public to private expenditures for adult education of all types would be about one-fourth for public adult education to three-fourths for private, in an estimated total of $500,000,000 per year. Even many of the adult education activities sponsored by public agencies are fully or partially supported by fees and tuitions paid by the consumer.

However, public support of adult education is increasing. Public school, college, and university activity seems to be moving in the direction of state and local support of a broad program of general adult education. State legislation favoring, encouraging, or making permissive adult education in local communities was enacted into statute in twenty-five states in 1939; today local programs are operating in every one of the forty-eight states, and in the territories of Hawaii and Puerto Rico.

Adult education, however, is increasingly regarded as essential to the welfare of the state, and, as such, should receive more of state and Federal support. It has been so considered in certain of its branches and specializations. The state has generally considered education for improving technical and industrial effectiveness essential to its welfare. Likewise, the education for naturalization of foreign-born adults; education of military personnel for national defense; education of adult farmers in improving agricultural resources and productivity; and education of adults in public health, safety, and thrift—these have been deemed essential to the public welfare.

of May 23, 1949, of the Task Force report of the Hoover Commission under the direction of Dr. Hollis P. Allen, notes that "two hundred separate educational programs are sponsored by more than a score of Federal departments and agencies" in which "the United States Office of Education has been completely by-passed." This pattern is duplicated on a smaller scale in state and local governments.

Is it too great a step for us to take to recognize that the education of adults for home and family improvement might contribute to the basic welfare of the state, or that the modern problems of society demand continuous training of all adults in citizenship responsibilities?

What is more important is that, as the findings of psychology and sociology reveal the emotional and intergroup and international tensions under which the ordinary adult citizen is living, and the importance to him of being a participating, creative, and active part of his community, it becomes an increasingly important function of public education to provide for a broad, general, diversified, and comprehensive adult education program.

Adult education in the United States has ceased to be only a privilege or a grant; it has become essential to the full life of all citizens.

HIGHER EDUCATION: FOR WHOM AND FOR WHAT?[1]

Ordway Tead

One of the purposes of any consideration of the role of the college is surely to hold the mirror up to going policy and practice, to confront sins of omission and commission, to clarify and refresh high purpose, and to arrive at new insights about desirable directions and methods.

We are not heard in higher education for our much speaking, even though some of us may speak much. We are profited by

[1] From *The Educational Forum*, January, 1955, pp. 133–149. Reprinted by permission of the author and publisher. *The Educational Forum* is the official publication of Kappa Delta Pi, national honor society in education.

having our complacency disturbed, by having questions asked which challenge accepted views and practices, and by the proffer of appealing ideas capable of some adaptation within our several institutions. Shared deliberation on education is not for corroboration of the current, but for the confrontation of the conceivable.

My premise here is that liberal education is practical education in the long-run view, and that this assumption throws light on the questions: for whom are colleges designed and what are they intended to do?

I affirm also as a premise my great faith in the indispensable mission of college education, both retrospectively, currently and prospectively considered. We may not do all we should or do it as well as we should. But if one asks—what would American life be like in all its multiform operational activities for which rational thought and effort, superior abilities, disciplined intelligence, scientific and engineering training, and informed, directive capacity are indispensable, if we had no college graduates to staff the many key positions—one quickly realizes the necessity of college and university education in our kind of large-scale technological culture. The questions posed by my title presumably take all this for granted and center attention on whether we have gone far enough as a society in assuring a college education to a sufficient fraction of those, both young men and young women, of from 17 to 23 or 24 years of age, who must presently staff these thousands of necessary posts. This implies also that they have the ability and willingness to occupy positions as responsible followers no less than as leaders in our employments and avocations. Hence my first topic—who should go to college?

WHO SHOULD GO TO COLLEGE?

A generation ago this problem did not present undue and confusing complexities, either to colleges or to the community. This is no longer true. And it is essential to see this question in perspective if any defensible answer is to be offered for the foreseeable future. For there is a clear national trend here which needs statement in its historic setting.

Our elementary schools were originally private and restricted. Today, they are universal, public, and attendance is required of virtually all children.

Our present high schools were originally private academies designed for the selected few to prepare them for the small number of colleges then extant. Today's high schools cover the country, are publicly supported and include around 80% of our population in this age group. And with the present rate of extension of high school facilities, it appears that well over 90% of those of high school age will at least be entering high school within the next few years.

A similar pattern is observable in the growth of the American college. It too started as exclusively private with attention centered primarily upon education of young men for the major professions, especially the ministry. Only many years later did we see the gradual extension of public state universities; then, after 1862, came land-grant colleges with specific aims in the direction of training for agricultural and mechanical pursuits. And finally beginning slowly in 1890, there has come the growth of two-year institutions beyond the high school, called junior colleges or, under public auspices, frequently now referred to as community colleges.

The increase of enrollments in this overall college and university picture has been little short of breath-taking. As of 1953–54, a little over 2¼ million students are participating in higher education; and careful forecasts as to the insistent and qualified demand for college entrance in the next ten years place this figure at anywhere from 3 million to 4 million in the 1960's.[2]

The increasing pressure for and expectation of the opportunity to go to college are due to the following important reasons: the larger number who now complete high school; the larger number who are stirred with the desire to go to college; the experience of tens of thousands of veterans under the G.I. Bill of Rights in securing a free college education which raised the sights of their families and friends as to the possible values of going to college; the unprecedented increase in the post-war birth rate to a point where in a few years the high school populations will inevitably provide much larger numbers ambitious and fully qualified for some college education; the progressively higher wage and salary levels making it practical for more and more families to entertain this expectancy as economically possible for their children.

As to why this heartening desire for more education should constitute a problem, I am here not giving consideration to such staggering difficulties as the inadequacy of plant facilities in existing colleges, nor to the insufficiency of the supply of qualified teachers, nor to the financial ways and means which will assure college enrollment for able students from the bottom income brackets. These are all fundamental and crucial issues.

[2] See among others, with their own added bibliographical references, *Who Should Go to College?* by Byron S. Hollinshead, New York, Columbia University Press, 1952; *Equalizing Educational Opportunities Beyond the Secondary School*, by Ordway Tead, Cambridge, Harvard University Press, 1947; Section II, *Higher Education for American Democracy*, for U.S. President's Commission on Higher Education, New York, Harper & Brothers, 1947; Report rendered by Dr. Ronald B. Thompson, Registrar, Ohio State University, Columbus, Ohio, prepared for the American Association of College Registrars and Admissions Officers, entitled "College Age Population Trends: 1940–1970," 1953.

The problem upon which I shall center attention is the *qualitative* one. In the first place, authoritative studies have indicated that at least 40% and perhaps nearly 50% of our young people have the requisite intellectual capacity—namely, an I.Q. of 105 or over, to profit from at least two years of college work. And presumably one third in this age group would qualify to complete four years. The percentage figure of present college enrollment of young people is around 26 per cent of the age group of 18 to 21 years.

Again, the testimony is conclusive that in recent years there have been as many young people of equal capacity with those enrolled, who are *not* in college for a combination of reasons.

A further disconcerting fact is that at present approximately one-half of the young people who enter high school never stay to graduate. And equally shocking is the fact that in the national average, only one-half of those who enter college remain to get their degrees.

This last situation is profoundly serious in ways that reflect far more upon the educational institutions than they do upon the students who leave school. My contention, supported by much evidence, is that one of the primary reasons for such large withdrawals is that students—both in high school and in college—fail to find that the subject matter offered for study is in their view and experience relevant or valuable as helping them to know themselves and to get assistance as to their effective place in the world outside. At both these levels, taking our country as a whole, educational programs are not believed by many young people to be significant for any kind of progress or "success" in life for them on any terms.

Other reasons for leaving should, of course, be noted. There are frequently economic motives of necessary family or personal support pressing students to withdraw. And there is the subtle but important fact that, especially in the low income brackets and in areas where high schools are inferior or geographically remote, there may be no tradition, potential expectation or stimulated family or individual desire (even for students of top ability) to aspire to a college education.

Further potential enrollments will mean an even greater unevenness than at present in respect to the content and quality of secondary school preparation viewed nationally, with which students will seek to enter college. There is the added fact that with widened expectancy or availability of socially justified college entrance, there will increasingly be on the campus not only young people with a relatively high capacity to verbalize and conceptualize, but also those with mechanical, scientific, engineering and artistic aptitudes, as well as those with vigorous extrovert characteristics manifested often in a predominant interest in various forms of human relations, including the extra-curricular programs all the way from athletics to class politics. There is the further factor of a widened spread in the cultural backgrounds of the homes from which students are coming. And the implication of all this already is, and will increasingly be, that the present *conventional* college curriculum as typically taught will surely *not* enlist the interest and the sense of need of more than a relatively small fraction of such a variegated student body.

There has also to be clearer recognition of the variety of motives and aspirations prompting the students of today and tomorrow to go to college. Along with the traditional motives of those wanting to get a fuller education for nurture and potential fulfillment, there are those motivated by ambition for economic advancement, for making the right social contacts, for assuring their entrance to professional schools for reasons partly selfish and partly social. In short, any imputed singleness of purpose for college attendance as we used to think of it, is unrealistic. An acute problem is therefore the adaptation of the college's curricular offerings to varied individual purposes, to varied intellectual levels, and most importantly to a wide spread of aptitudes, interests and potential vocational skills.

I should refer next to one point which has been raised by a number of critics but as to which I find myself not at all alarmed. I allude to the view of those who, drawing an analogy with the plight of the university graduates in Germany prior to World War II, are fearful that we may be in danger of educating too many too much. They doubt that there will be enough vocational opportunities at "high" levels with an accompanying possible higher standard of living for graduates; and they conclude that this disparity of expectation and actuality will create a body of educated but disaffected and frustrated persons having to work at callings using less than their full abilities.

I am reasonably sure that the answer to this fear is that the whole expanding, dynamic character of our technological economy is such that it is hard to conceive of too many people too well educated to staff the critical posts. Furthermore, it is a false view that the purpose of college education which students and society generally should primarily entertain is economic advancement, rather than the capacity to live a fuller and a more fruitful existence as individual, as parent, and as citizen. In other words, given the rightful equalitarian assumptions of a democratic society, plus the increasing birthrate, plus the need for trained intelligence in more and more occupations, plus the desirable, enriched cultural sensitivity of more and more people, this objection is a bogey. It is a feeble alibi for failing to face up to the total situation which realistically the colleges confront.

The central issue is not a misconceived equalitarian sentiment on the part of those of us who are said to be carried away by our democratic convictions. It is rather an academic lag which is slow to face the facts of the greater potential for more college education of many more selected students once their several kinds of ability are identified, are challenged, and are ministered to in a variety of educationally effective ways.

It is not practicable here to spell out a complete program for offsetting this combination of untoward conditions. But some of the outstanding features of corrective effort should be noted. The program has to start with certain secondary school changes. The arousing of improved motivation for study and increased desire to attend college is one which has to receive its primary attention at the secondary school level. This will involve a much more competent high school program than is now typical, of guidance and counsel for each individual student. It will require an improvement in the educational standards of the high schools in numerous states where they are now below par. It will require a program far more generous than any yet being pushed of liberal provisions for state scholarships on a basis of need for those secondary school students who qualify for and wish to, but cannot afford to go to college, and for Federal scholarships if individual state provisions cannot be made sufficient for the need. It should further mean that more and more high schools will be so organized as to satisfy the designation of being *comprehensive high schools* in which there is a reasonable balance between semi-vocational studies and general liberal studies in the subjects now characterized as the "academic" or college preparatory curriculum. This raises the whole question, also, as to whether the over-all intellectual and personality potentialities of the high school student are to constitute the basis for determining college eligibility. I am convinced that we are all at present far too much fouled up in the arithmetic of credits and not enough concerned about the total promise of college applicants.

A further approach, as to which I find myself in substantial agreement with former President Conant of Harvard, is the desirability both of increasing the number of two-year colleges and allowing them to be effectively terminal for some, while readily providing for others transfer into the third and fourth college years. However, as this approach gains the momentum which I am sure it inevitably will, there must be assurance that the programs of two-year colleges are including enough provocative and relevant general education making its contribution to citizenship, personality development, human relations and emotional maturity, so that the student leaving college at the end of his second year will be entering life with some genuine competence to handle himself as an individual and as a citizen who will make his best social contribution; and so that he will have been stirred with the desire to continue through the years with some broad program of adult education.

This corrective program has also to be confronted at the college level by invoking the following features: First, and of major importance, there has to be eager acceptance by all responsible for the conduct of our colleges of the democratic conviction that *all* the young people of some specified and agreed intellectual caliber not only should have the right to, but the readily available opportunity to go to college for at least two years. We should all agree—professionals, citizens generally, and parents—that the present situation is one of conspicuous and indefensible waste of the maximum talents and contributions of too many young people who are for the above stated reasons precluded today from going to college, or who are not remaining to complete their courses of instruction.

If in individual colleges we who are in responsible posts say in response to this democratic aspiration that our institutions are already as large as they should be or as we desire them to be, or that the danger of creating even larger mass education units especially in our state universities is great, or that we do not see where the financial resources will come from either to enlarge present institutions public and private, or to create needed new ones, the answer would seem to be that at this point we confront a problem beyond the competence of individual institutions to resolve. And our society therefore requires the shaping of policies through some disinterested and over-all national agency, perhaps a temporary ad hoc commission reporting to the President and the Congress, which will bring home to our citizenry the enormity of this problem on the national level, and point out that a solution may well be beyond the possible present responsibility and competence of trustee and alumni bodies of individual institutions to arrive at.[3]

What I have in mind here is the emphatic documentation of a situation of acute need in a way that would supply ammunition to the President, the Congress and state legislatures as to desirable legislation. It would, of course, be essential that any such legislation, presumably for grants for capital purposes, for scholarships and for other necessary assistance, would be planned and provided in such ways as to assure a complete absence of Federal interference with the processes of education itself.

A second important point is the need for a fresh scrutiny of college admission policies toward a lessening of stress on the arithmetic of secondary school credits.

[3] See in this connection the excellent pamphlet published by the American Council on Education (1954), *A Call for Action to Meet the Impending Increase in College and University Enrollment.*

Joined closely with this is the need from the outset of college entrance and throughout the two or four year period, of a more personalized, consecutive academic guidance program, which will help students to find their way into and through such courses of study as will be congenial to their capacities and interests, and helpful to them in ways which will assure their remaining for a graduation which they will find rewarding to their ultimate effectiveness as adults. This implies also, of course, a total student guidance program on *all* phases of individual adjustment and subsequent employment.

The fourth responsibility for the colleges is a fresh scrutiny of the methods of teaching, the quality of teachers, and the offerings of subjects available for study in the first two college years. I shall not here elaborate upon the point that there is too much indifferent and ineffectual teaching in the first two college years. We have by no means addressed ourselves adequately to the use of modern psychological findings as to how students may be brought to learn, and to want to learn, what true learning actually is, and how real learning can assuredly result.[4] All too often, with our failure to use the best teaching methods in the critical early college years, students are likely to find themselves being constantly lectured at rather than *actively involved* in some experimental sharing of subject matter, the relevance of which for them is being made clearly manifest.

An added requirement is that the teach-

[4] There is a growing literature on this important subject. In my own book, *College Teaching and College Learning*, New Haven, Yale University Press, 1949, I have not only discussed this subject but offered an extended bibliography of other relevant volumes. A new quarterly has recently been initiated at the Oregon State Teachers College, Corvallis, Oregon, entitled *Improving College and University Teaching*. Its several issues to date constitute a helpful resource.

ers assigned to the first two college years should be the best, the most mature, and most dynamic available in each department. Also with a fostering of cooperative professorial attitudes, the introductory work can gradually be brought to be regarded by them as equally if not more important than their senior seminars. But this assumes, of course, that those teachers who are eager to focus on good teaching, are rewarded for good teaching in salaries and rank and themselves regard this as the major commitment of a *dedicated* teacher. A most significant and practical program in this direction which has come to my attention is the annual award given to a conspicuously good teacher each year at Carnegie Institute of Technology along with which goes recognition in salaries and promotion to others selected because of unusually high teaching attainments.

As to the subjects and courses to be available in the first two years, we have made notable progress in a number of outstanding institutions in the provision of a general studies program,—in the natural sciences, social sciences and humanities,—in ways designed to quicken interest, pose significant problems and challenge the students to further study of those problems as the college work progresses. Many of the best programs in general education have already been well described in a growing body of published literature.[5]

Pedagogically, this new look at instructional programs is stressing the active participation of the student, the personalizing of the instruction through small sections, the introduction of some type of laboratory or field work or of alternated study-work programs in designated periods away from the campus. Not all the questions of method about general education programs have been answered; but experience is conclusive that this approach is proving much more evocative, self-propulsive and exciting to students in the first two college years than the older curricula ever did.

Nor can we ignore the problem of the adequate challenging of the intellectually superior student who should not be allowed to be satisfied with those lesser or different standards of attainment which may necessarily have to be held for the more average students. Honors courses, tutorial or preceptorial provisions, majors with rigorous standards of achievement, supervised reading periods and extended senior theses,—these are some of the ways in which we can more and more in all colleges assure that the best students will do their best.

At the other end of the intellectual scale, there is, I venture, a kind of unconscious snobbery on the part of all of us in education who claim some degree of superiority in verbalizing and conceptualizing talents. With us ability to use words and a good education come close to being synonymous. It is, of course, those with this approach who are largely responsible for the programs of present higher education. We all seem reluctant to recognize that there are other gifts, perhaps more directly possessed or apprehended or perceived, but good and useful gifts, which—and here is the key point of a fruitful new outlook—can be improved by education, if only the education can be freshly conceived as heightening perceptive powers of awareness and reality not necessarily reducible to verbal facility and not eventuating solely in conceptualizing skill. It is probable, for example, that the creative and performing arts supply a clue to a kind of education for immediacy of apprehension, which has equal and complementary value to education in verbal felicity and ability to reach reasoned conclusions. I wonder, quite seri-

[5] A splendid over-all view of this problem may be found in *Accent On Teaching: Experiment in Education*, edited by Sidney J. French, New York, Harper & Brothers, 1954, this being a symposium report by the Committee on General Education of the Association for Higher Education (NEA).

ously in this connection, whether any college teacher ever asked the athletic coach *how* he trains his less intellectually able but ranking student players. If something of this outlook of greater instructional flexibility is valid, I submit that as the colleges of tomorrow enroll more of the less intellectualistic individuals, their education will surely have to embrace efforts different from the purposes and methods with which we have had such long and loving familiarity.

One final general observation needs to be made. If colleges are *necessarily* and *rightfully* to broaden their instructional program in order that it may become vital for the less endowed, for those well endowed with other than conceptualizing aptitudes, and for the many who mature late mentally, it becomes essential that teachers increasingly strike the note that all college experience is in reality but a *beginning* of the student's needful education; and therefore the desire to *continue to learn* has to become central as one of the reiterated objectives with all students. And the further educational consequence will have to be a continuously strengthened program under various auspices of an adult education which ministers to the total needs of our society beyond the present offerings which seem too heavily slanted toward hobbies or refresher courses for vocational advancement.

COLLEGE EDUCATION FOR WHAT?

The question in the second part of my title was infrequently raised as a major problem up to the time when the total tensions of the second World War, including problems of the draft or of some form of universal military service, became a reality. The changing character and size of our college populations necessarily entail a searching re-examination of purpose, objective and direction.

I by no means always agree with former Chancellor Hutchins of the University of Chicago. But on one score it seems to me that he, among others, has reiterated a valid point, namely that the purpose of the American college is not completely clear in any widely accepted way, is confused, and is infrequently well-articulated. While the following paragraph from his most recent book, *University of Utopia,*[6] may seem exaggerated and oversimplified, it embodies an essential kernel of truth. He says:

Civilization is the deliberate pursuit of the common ideal. Education is the deliberate attempt to form men in terms of an ideal. It is the attempt of a society to produce the type of man that it wants. How does it determine the type of man that it wants? If it does not know the type of man that it wants, how does it judge the educational efforts it makes? It may be said that the type of man a society wants is the product of many historical and psychological factors and that whatever philosophy enters into the formation of its vision of man is simply a rationalization of this largely unconscious product. But, even if this were so, we know that in every society there is some vision of man, his nature and his destiny, elaborated by philosophers living and dead, which interacts with the traditional view of the type of man desired and which amounts to a criticism of the tradition and the practices of the educational system. Education without a philosophy of education, that is, a coherent statement of the aims and possibilities of education, is impossible.

Dr. Hutchins continues relevantly to our present condition and pressing budgetary needs, as follows:

The claim upon the financial resources of the country that a university can legitimately make rests on the same ground. Public bodies or private persons who have money to dispense must be asked to do so not on the promise that the university will

[6] University of Chicago Press, 1954, p. 52.

produce a lot of people in their image but on the assurance that the university will do its best to carry on the independent thought and criticism that the country requires and to turn out graduates who are capable of independent thought and criticism, graduates, that is, who are committed to the fullest development of their highest powers and who can do their part as responsible citizens of a democratic state. . . . A university that is not controversial is not a university. A civilization in which there is not a continuous controversy about important issues, speculative and practical, is on the way to totalitarianism and death.[7]

Those are brave words and they need to be courageously taken to heart. They do not, however, offer us more than a general view as to what the college is purposively about and how it should work to attain its goals.

I see no point in the recital of excerpts from the numerous and often splendidly formulated statements of individual college objectives which have in recent years poured forth from a goodly number of faculties in a mood of encouraging self-examination. Moreover, the more difficult problem lies in the translation of these objectives into operational terms which give promise of marked improvement in the quality of the graduates. It will perhaps be more helpful if we make several more generalized characterizations regarding ways of stating college purposes, indicating as they may both agreements and diversities, yet looking toward some common denominators from which improved programming may derive.

I regret to acknowledge, however, that I shall in the following statement about objectives not be able to discuss a number of vital points which merit inclusion, not to say important emphasis. I refer to such problems as effective citizenship education at the college level; consideration of instruction in political and cultural problems in a global view; the difficulties of scientific education for general students; and the necessary balancing of liberal and vocational claims in the individual college program.

All of these, I shall assume, do or should stem from a common base which says that the educational purpose must look at once at the growth of each individual student and at the claims, tensions and possibilities of our society. There has to be a realization of the virtually complete interdependence and interaction of individual and society in the forwarding of nurture, growth, and responsible freedom for the individual. I shall assume that what society should want from each individual can be reconciled and harmonized with what each individual at his best can be educated to want for himself.

There is, first, the familiar view that college education should be in considerable measure culture-centered. It is charged to conserve the American cultural heritage, to interpret it in its present setting, to stimulate students to accept, to criticize and to extend the realizing of this heritage—in other words to become committed to a responsible regard for the further potentialities of our culture.

Another familiar statement is that colleges are concerned to purvey knowledge, develop intellectual capacity, increase ability to exercise personal power in socially channeled ways, and to enable graduates to achieve amicable, cooperative relations with their fellow men. The singling out of intellectual capacity alone as the college purpose in the way that many utterances of Dr. Hutchins can be interpreted, seems to me erroneously oversimplified. It is impossible to separate intellectual development from concern about physical, moral and spiritual growth. One may heartily agree with Hutchins "that every man and every free citizen needs a liberal educa-

[7] *Idem*, pp. 88, 91.

tion" and yet not conceive it possible to narrow this to its purely rationalistic aspects.

A further interesting expression bearing on the philosophy of education is found in the following paragraph, even though its labored vocabulary invites translation. Professor Richard D. Mosier of the University of California concludes a recent article on "The Crisis in Education" as follows: [8]

> The conception of *reason as the logic of experience*, if it were allied with the conceptions of the aim of education as an *axiological* problem, the method of education as an *epistemological* problem, and the content of education as an *ontological* problem, would go a long way toward resolving the conflicts that form the underlying philosophic foundation of the current crisis in education.

My own rendition of the above would be that college education has to recognize and cultivate the capacity to reason, a process embracing at once its problem solving effort, the criticizing and evaluating of experience, and the ability of imaginative mental rehearsing of or over experimenting with the possible ways out of confronted difficulties. Along with this has to be stressed the purpose of clarifying standards as to what is valuable, together with identification of the valuable in different departments of living. Also included is some awareness by teacher and student of how we may come to know, of what we can know, and of that in human experience, beyond the tests of science, which involves commitment to certain great and enduring truths and beliefs, or faith. Finally, there is requisite some consideration of the realities as to our own being, the grounds or foundations of Being, and the enrichment of awareness of what we sense as the natural and beyond that the self-transcendent in experience, out from which the learner should be stirred to a heightened sense of responsible dedication. In short, higher education has to advance the qualities of rationality, of evaluative and appreciative capacity, of affection for one's fellow, and of willingness to assume responsibility for personally and socially creative conduct in a community upon which he is dependent and in which he has a real but limited freedom or independence.

There is, again, a point of view often referred to as the functional view with which, among others, the name of Dr. W. W. Charters is associated, especially in his advisory work with Stephens College in Missouri. In this approach, the typical life functions which each individual has to confront are those of being a citizen, a worker, a family member, a leisure-time person, and an individual soul in its inescapable aloneness. And the educational program is therefore to be shaped so that the student is enabled to function more effectively in each of these five areas in which life requires his participation. There is, moreover, no reason why this functional view cannot be in some measure interwoven with other concepts of college purposes. But in any case it is important that these functions be viewed educationally in an intellectually rigorous way that gets beyond purely practical methods, toward a probing in the direction of first principles and philosophic justifications.

One other approach to the problem of objectives which I shall briefly characterize is at once my own expression and the conviction also of a growing number of others who are now raising similar questions. What, in short, are we deeply *about* in carrying on colleges? Why do we make so little effort to confront explicitly in college the problems and issues which bedevil us in the numerous areas of life itself? Why do we not more fully face *head on* the tension and conflicts of the human spirit today and of the society and culture in which

[8] See *Educational Theory*, October 1953, p. 346.

we live? Why do our colleges not address themselves *more directly* to the central concerns of human bewilderment and aspiration? Why do we not ask ourselves more insistently what *are* the major life needs and possible enduring satisfactions [9] of our students, and how are they to be more assuredly ministered to? Why not acknowledge frankly that education of the mind can be dangerous unless the purpose of cultivating moral responsibility and individual commitment to truth-seeking, excellence and righteousness, is also kept ascendant?

Take as an illuminating approach to the kind of life issues which require direct confronting the six polarities or dichotomies to which Professor Huston Smith of Washington University, St. Louis, has called attention in an as yet unpublished report on curricular reorganization now being studied by his faculty colleagues.[10] He reminds us of the following areas of stress which plague us with uncertainties, both in the realm of thought and in practical affairs, personal and social. Indeed, as to these we are bound to ask ourselves to what extent our colleges even pretend to clarify some helpful outlook upon them. These opposed views concern:

absolutism versus relativism
objectivity versus commitment
authority versus freedom
egoism versus altruism
the state (and all other large corporate organizations) versus the individual
the secular versus the sacred

I believe that under these several conceptual frames subsume many of the basic confusions of our day,—confusions which glorify the relative, make a virtue of moral neutrality, minimize our vigilance as to the need for freedom, misconstrue the deeper meanings of selfhood and of solicitude for others, oppose the state to the welfare of the individual, and preoccupy us with secular and material values to the ignoring of the sacred.

It will be said, of course, that certain of these six polarities are likely to be considered in one or another course in political science or philosophy. It will also be said that in listing these six areas of tensions I depart from the usual course subjects and that we have to have something to study "about" beyond such broad concepts as these. My point about all this would be that *of course* we have to study some subject matter and that *of course* content has to be tough and rigorous. And, most important, that the only fruitful way of studying the most profound issues is by an interdisciplinary attack.

But the further and still unanswered point is that if the basic issues relevant to our living are not identified and confronted by every student in *some* college instruction with some illumination as to possible reconciliations of opposites or possible new integrations, when and where will the student ever confront reflectively those exigent and spiritually disturbing tensions? Also, if there is to come, as there has to, a more consistent and persistent effort at interdisciplinary courses in general education, it is problems of this kind which have inevitably to be introduced. Indeed, within the frame of the familiar water-tight compartments now too typical of college instruction, there can always properly be recognition by the teacher not only of primary but also of supplementary purposes and broad, humane insights which should enrich every course in every subject.

A final noble testimony to that liberality which is the over-arching college purpose is expressed by Karl Jaspers in these words: "We humans need education in critical thought and comprehension, we need the world of history and philosophy if we are

[9] See W. P. McEwen, *Enduring Satisfaction*, New York, Philosophical Library, 1949.

[10] This report was published in the spring of 1955 under the title *The Purposes of Higher Education*, Harper & Brothers.

to become competent to form independent judgments. The whole population must be raised to a higher level in a continually intensified educational process; it must be brought from half knowledge to whole knowledge, from the contingent thinking of the moment to methodical thinking, in which everyone can lift himself out of dogmatism into freedom. This is the hope for the evolution of the majority, that in its decisions and resolutions by vote it will consciously and deliberately choose that which is better." [11]

I have deliberately refrained from offering a simple answer to the question as to what colleges are for. Indeed, the present diversity of expressed college objectives is itself a stimulating and encouraging evidence of vitality. However, the general approaches and outlooks suggested by this discussion do perhaps require a concluding section as to the ways and means of implementing the probable outcomes of any reexamination of the purposes of a college.

IMPLEMENTATION

On this score I shall place first emphasis upon the central role of the college teacher. He is no longer to be only the dispenser of facts and knowledge. He is no longer merely *telling*. He has to be the guide, counselor and friend, pointing each student to the ways and means by which he can himself become a willing, eager, self-propulsive learner of what he is helped to discover to be needful for himself and deeply satisfying for his fulfillment and social creativity. Beyond being a walking bibliography, the teacher has to have phosphorescence, intellectual glamour, moral dedication and some insight into the things of the spirit. I realize full well that there are not enough good college teachers to go around. But I also realize and believe that American college leaders have to rise up in active affirmative and virtually missionary zeal to proclaim first, that we are not attracting the best minds and the warmest personalities into teaching; and, second, that even if we were, the usual process of attaining a Ph.D. is all too often in grave danger of killing the incipient spark of intellectual and spiritual spontaneity which is the teacher's priceless asset. There will be no ultimate improvement in the college teaching situation without a virtual revolution in the way in which young people are selected and prepared for the high vocation of being a college teacher. And in this process the importance first of an operational grasp of the fundamentals of the learning process and, second, of guided apprentice experience in teaching actual college classes has to be recognized as indispensable.

I venture, also, that in the colleges of the future the broad orientation of instruction is not to be "subject-centered" or "student-centered" in the limited sense in which those phrases are often used. It is no mere rhetoric to affirm that instruction has to be increasingly *life-centered* in the profound sense of confronting great living issues. It has to be life-centered with great enhancement both in the instructional appeal to students and in the gain in their capacity to attack life. And this they will achieve through the utilization of any one of a number of fresh and vigorously pursued methods of approach.

There is, for example, on this score of fresh approaches to subject matter, one avenue through the explication of a selection of great and influential concepts. I refer to study which would focus on constellations of ideas which surround the words democracy, leadership, justice, personal power, selfhood, the state, science and similar basic concepts. I have been interested to see that in a recent address Dr. Alvin

[11] See his *The Origin and Goal of History*, New Haven, Yale University Press, 1953, p. 168.

Eurich agrees with me about the probable fruitfulness of this approach.

There is the approach through the study of "persistent issues" as exemplified in contemporary society. This is already being utilized in a number of institutions.

There is, again, the approach through a sampling of carefully selected "representative and significant problems"—in history, the social sciences, philosophy, political science and the natural sciences.

I emphasize that such approaches to newly oriented, significant subject matter would for instructional effectiveness all have to be interdisciplinary in character, drawing upon insights and knowledge from a variety of fields.

Two further points merit highlighting in conclusion. I refer to the new importance having to be assumed by the humanities in the college of tomorrow; and some understanding of what is meant by a freshly conceived recognition of the relations of a purified religious outlook to higher education.

E. E. Cummings, in his recent Harvard lectures, quotes Rilke as follows: "Works of art are of an infinite loneliness and with nothing would be so little reached as with criticism. Only love can grasp and fairly judge them." And to this quotation, Cummings adds the following: "In my proud and humble opinion, these two sentences are worth all the *soi-disant* criticism of the arts which has ever existed or will ever exist." [12] This may be exaggeration, but it should remind us that the philological and linguistic approaches to the study of the literary humanities is horrendously deficient and bleak. One is reminded in this connection of the imprecations which Bernard Shaw called down upon any teacher who might subject his plays to analysis in the manner in which all too many teachers have analyzed and desiccated the sublimities of Shakespeare's plays. These comments are warnings against a continuation of unimaginative outlooks in too much present soulless and visionless teaching of the humanities.

It is important to make the vigorous affirmation that the humanities supply the eloquent open sesame for fulfilling the purposes of value affirmation which are central to the mission of the liberal college. The anguished, aspiring, prophetic voices of mankind have their articulation and their communicative power in the utterances of the great books and the other great art expressions as globally evoked throughout history. And I use the words "great books" in a more inclusive sense than that employed by the cult which centers attention on the study of a too restricted list of classic volumes. We have to reconceive radically the functions and the methods of the study of the humanities to assure that they speak vitally and on eternal issues to which today's students eagerly seek answers. It is in these studies that the visions of human greatness are suggested. For the essential contribution of the humanities is to illuminate and reaffirm the great human ideals of beauty, freedom, justice, mercy, loving kindness, truth-seeking and the centrality of the spiritual in the life of man. This contribution has also to interpret to students as nothing else can the meaning and the human impact of guilt, sin, suffering, tragedy, death, destructive hate and redemptive love. The humanities have to tell us, as Karl Jaspers [13] says, that "tragedy is not enough" in our philosophy of life. They have to tell us, as Paul Tillich [14] puts it, that the "courage to be" is, when once possessed, a releasing power of tremendous

[12] See J. Donald Adams, in *New York Times Book Review Section*, February 14, 1954.

[13] See his volume, *Tragedy Is Not Enough*, Boston, Beacon Press, 1952.

[14] See his volume, *The Courage to Be*, New Haven, Yale University Press, 1952.

force in its ultimate assertion of the human outreach toward the Source of our being.

There is, indeed, a sense in which a lively awareness of what the humanities have to say in their historic perspective comes close to being a disclosure of that aspect of human experience which we are entitled to identify as religious. And my concluding point is as to whether our growing sense of the reality of high religion, beyond dogmas, doctrines and denominations, may not lead us on to seeing that exclusion of a religious awareness from education is indefensible and prevents these two great areas of thought, insight and action from cross-fertilizing as fully and helpfully as they properly should. Why, quite simply, is not all education at once an intellectual, moral and *sacred* enterprise? Is not every effort to fulfill the individual and to make his society contributory to that fulfillment a sanctified or *sacred* as well as humane effort?

I am not ignoring obvious issues of the separation of church and state, of possible state support for church-related schools, nor the issue of what, if any, kind of instruction about religion is acceptable in colleges which are not church-related. It rather seems to me that beyond the legal phases, it is not only possible but essential to approach this concern more profoundly in relation to human needs as viewed in historic and universal context.

I find a possible approach here if we ask dispassionately what are the modes, moods, or component elements which the religious spirit embodies when the sacred is being realized and awareness of a transcendent relation of humanity to that beyond itself is striving to find human expression. I suggest (out of the thought of many beside myself) that we find a number of such widely agreed components. The following are needful as aspects or attributes of high religion:

1. participation in individual action, performance and *accomplishment*, in which *creativity* and growth are dominant purposes;
2. recognition that continuous *change* characterizes all life in a disturbing but inevitable flux and novelty;
3. acknowledgment of human *dependence* on powers beyond ourselves which are by no means completely identifiable or definable;
4. recognition of lawfulness, form and *order* to be somewhat apprehended through present knowledge and by persistent continuous study of the interrelations of man with the rest of the cosmos;
5. appreciation of the stirring and heartening *beauty* to be found in the cosmos and in works created by men;
6. recognition of the reciprocal interdependence of individual fulfillment and an awareness of membership and *belonging* in an ever widening *community* of love and fraternal regard;
7. recognition that the appraising of what is valuable, of what has Godlike *value*, is deep in our natures as a continuing imperative upon us;
8. recognition that in our individual *aloneness* we seek to transcend our little selves by meditation, contemplation and otherwise, in order to be at one with a larger whole which partakes of the *holy* —or, as the old phrase has it, the search "to be alone with the Alone." Finally, I propose,
9. recognition that there is for each individual a genuine if limited *freedom* of choice, together with an ever-present reality of *redemptive love* proffered freely, if inexplicably, to all who sense that in their freedom they have fallen short or fallen away from their own highest commitments.

I ask that you note the key words here. They are: creativity, change, dependence, rational order and lawfulness, knowledge, beauty, community membership, value, aloneness, meditation, freedom, redemptive love.

In appropriate, reasonable, loving and committed combinations expressed in concrete experiences, these components qualitatively pursued *characterize the religious way of life.* These several words identify natural and universal experiences. And an individual life that comprehends within itself experiences consciously possessed of these attributes at a devoted, high level of quality is *sharing religious experience.* Individual motives and actions may thus come to have a kind of sanctity. The individual when his conduct is possessed of such qualities is participating in experience which transcends the secular or the perfunctory. He shares an immanent naturalism combined, when the individual's awareness is most deeply felt, with an ecstatic upward transcendence of the human toward the divine or sacred. It is largely thus that there comes to pass the individual realization of the eternal and unutterable mystery of man in God and of God in man. And this insight of religion (always capable of being extended by education) can be for our day the advance intimation of a renewal of the human spirit in purpose and direction which promises to the committed an unrealized power for good.

I am suggesting, in short, that it becomes increasingly possible for college teachers to accept a modern, intellectual and spiritual outlook and devotion beyond positivism or scientific humanism. To the extent that teachers may already have religious affiliations, these will be enriched and deepened. And to the extent that they have no such affiliations, it becomes rationally defensible and desirable for them to become sensitive to the possible fusion of education with a high religious attitude and faith.

In summary, I have been affirming the necessity that a greatly enlarged fraction of qualified young people should have the benefit of a college education. I have said that as this occurs it will be necessary that there be appropriate modifications and diversifications in the content and methods of instruction supplied to students with differing aptitudes and interests.

I have reaffirmed the crucial value of the liberal arts to be transmitted through the approaches today characterized as general education; and with a reinterpretation of the humanities as central in assuring that they become the vehicle for imparting the vision of man's spiritual greatness and freedom.

I have also indicated that the college's purpose of forwarding individual growth for social responsibility and creativity requires changes in our methods of educating teachers; requires the far wider use by teachers of new psychological insights into the learning process. And it requires the dedicated and essentially moral and sanctified outlook on the part of more and more teachers which will enrich their scholarship and their personalities, and thus assure that pervading their instruction is a winsomeness of appeal and a spiritual relevance which students will find increasingly irresistible.

AUTHOR INDEX